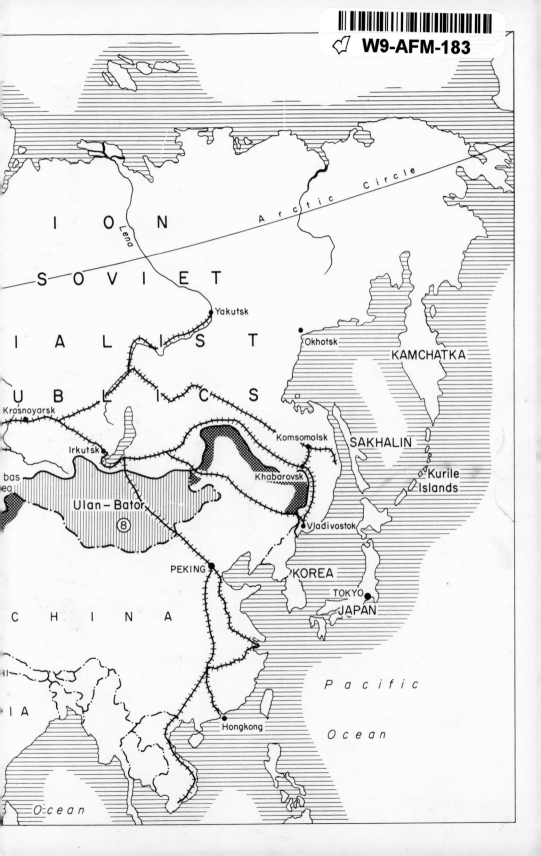

STALIN

Books by H. Montgomery Hyde

Henry James at Home
The Rise of Castlereagh
The Russian Journals of Martha and Catherine Wilmot
  (with the Marchioness of Londonderry)
More Letters from Martha Wilmot: Impressions of Vienna
  (with the Marchioness of Londonderry)
The Empress Catherine and Princess Dashkov
The Trials of Oscar Wilde
Mr and Mrs Beeton
Cases that Changed the Law
Carson
The Trial of Craig and Bentley
United in Crime
The Strange Death of Lord Castlereagh
The Trial of Sir Roger Casement
Sir Patrick Hastings: His Life and Cases
An International Case Book of Crime
Room 3603: The British Intelligence Center in New York
Oscar Wilde: The Aftermath
A History of Pornography
Norman Birkett
Cynthia
The Story of Lamb House
Lord Reading
Strong for Service: The Life of Lord Nathan of Churt
The Other Love
Their Good Names

H. Montgomery Hyde

STALIN

The History of a Dictator

New York
FARRAR, STRAUS AND GIROUX

Quotations from *Khrushchev Remembers* with an Introduction, Commentary and Notes by Edward Crankshaw, translated and edited by Strobe Talbott, copyright © 1970 by Little, Brown and Company (Inc.), are reprinted by permission of Little, Brown and Company (Inc.).

Quotations from the following books are reprinted by permission of the publisher, Houghton Mifflin Company: *Facing the Dictators* by Anthony Eden; *The Reckoning* by Anthony Eden; *The Second World War* by Winston Churchill; *Churchill: Taken from the Diaries of Lord Moran. The Struggle for Survival* 1940-1965 by Lord Moran.

Quotations from *The Winter War: Finland Against Russia* 1939-1940 by Vaino Tanner are reprinted by permission of Stanford University Press.

Quotations from *One Who Survives* by Alexander Barmine, copyright 1945 by Alexander Barmine, are reprinted by permission of G. P. Putnam's Sons.

Nero, too, was a product of his epoch. Yet after he perished his statues were smashed and his name was scraped off everything. The vengeance of history is more terrible than the vengeance of the most powerful General Secretary. I venture to think that this is consoling.

Leon Trotsky, 1940

We cannot keep silent for ever about the crimes of Stalin. For those were crimes committed against millions of human beings and they cry out to be exposed.

Alexander Solzhenitsyn, 1969

Contents

Illustrations

Maps

Acknowledgements

The basic research for this book was undertaken in the library and archives of the Hoover Institution on War, Institution and Peace, at Stanford University, unique as a clearing house for Russian studies. I wish to thank the Institution's staff for the generous help and facilities which they extended to me throughout my visit last year, notably Dr Richard F. Starr, Mr Alan H. Belmont, Dr Witold S. Sworakowski, Dr Franz G. Lassner, Mr Karol Michael and Mme Boris Nicolaevsky.

My thanks are similarly due to the library staffs of the Houghton Library at Harvard University, the Humanities Research Centre at the University of Texas, and, in London, the British Museum, the London Library, the Public Record Office, and the Royal Institute of International Affairs.

I have also had the benefit of the expert knowledge and advice of the following who have written biographies or studies of Stalin: Professor Sweryn Bialer of the Russian Institute at Columbia University, the late Mr Isaac Deutscher, Professor George F. Kennan of the Institute of Advanced Study at Princeton, Mr Isaac Don Levine, Mr Edward Ellis Smith, and Mr Bertram D. Wolfe, Senior Research Fellow at the Hoover Institution. I am grateful to them for talking to me at length and answering my questions with invariable patience and courtesy. In addition, Mr Smith and Mr Wolfe were good enough to allow me to see and use their private files and bibliographical collections, which have proved invaluable to me.

Field Marshal Viscount Montgomery of Alamein has kindly given me his personal recollections of Stalin and his views on Stalin's military strategy. Similar recollections of Stalin as a politician have been graciously imparted by Lord Strang, former Permanent Under-Secretary of State at the British Foreign Office. Dr D. M. Lang, Professor of Caucasian Studies at the School of Oriental and African Studies in the University of London, has rendered substantial help with Georgian language and other sources. Mr K. P. S. Menon, former Indian ambassador in Moscow and the last member of the foreign diplomatic corps to be received by Stalin before his fatal illness, kindly communicated his impressions of their remarkable interview when I met him near Moscow in 1957. Others who have assisted me in various ways are Mr W. E. D. Allen, Mr Constantine Brancovan, Professor John Erickson, Mr Martin Gilbert, Mr Michael Glenny, Mr Alexander Lieven, Mr Harrison E. Salisbury, Dr Harold Shukman, Mr Alan U. Schwartz and Miss Hilary Sternberg. My debt to them is considerable.

I am grateful to various Soviet authorities for allowing me to visit a number of places in the USSR particularly associated with Stalin. These include his birthplace and the Stalin museum in Gori, some of the scenes of his youth as an underground revolutionary in Tbilisi, the flat belonging to the Alliluyev family in Leningrad where he lived in 1917, his quarters in the Moscow Kremlin and his new grave in the railed off space between the Lenin Mausoleum and the Kremlin wall. No assistance was afforded me in my search for the grave of his second wife Nadhezda Alliluyeva on the ground that she was 'a person of no public interest whatsoever'. Nevertheless I was eventually able to locate her grave out of several thousands of others in the Novodevichy cemetery in Moscow and to take the photograph which is reproduced in this book. On the other hand, unexpected co-operation was forthcoming in Moscow from the Lenin Library, which possesses a rare periodical, of which I had failed to discover a copy in any British or American collection. At my request the periodical was lent to the British Museum where I was able to note and abstract its contents.

Mr Robert Conquest and Colonel C. H. Ellis have both been good enough to read the original text in typescript, as a result of which I have been able to make some useful revisions. Mr Conquest's expertise as a leading British Kremlinologist and authority on the Great Purge has been of the greatest help, although we do not always see eye to eye on the credibility of some of the sources I have used, for example, Khrushchev's recently published memoirs.

My thanks are due to the following publishers for permission to quote from works of which they control the copyright: Arthur Barker Ltd.: *Face of a Victim* by Elizabeth Lermolo. Houghton Mifflin Company:

Facing the Dictators and *The Reckoning* by the Earl of Avon; *The Second World War* by Sir Winston Churchill; and *Winston Churchill: The Struggle for Survival 1940–45* by Lord Moran. Little, Brown and Company: *Khrushchev Remembers.* Jarrolds (Publishers) Ltd.: *The Secret History of Stalin's Crimes* by Alexander Orlov. Oxford University Press: *Conversations with the Kremlin and Despatches from Russia* by Stanislaw Kot. G. P. Putnam's Sons: *One Who Survived* by Alexander Barmine. Stanford University Press: *The Winter War: Finland Against Russia 1939–1940* by Vaino Tanner. Souvenir Press Ltd.: *Stalin and his Generals: Soviet Military Memoirs of World War II* edited by Seweryn Bialer.

I am indebted for cartographic assistance to Mr W. H. Bromage. His maps which I have used have previously appeared in *An Atlas of World Affairs* by Andrew Boyd and *Russia at War 1941–1945* by Alexander Werth. Credits for use of copyright photographs appear underneath the relevant pictures. I apologise to any copyright owners I have failed to trace.

Last, but by no means least, I thank my wife for typing this book from my original draft, and for her help and understanding in innumerable ways.

H.M.H.

Westwell House,
Tenterden,
Kent.

May, 1971

STALIN

CHAPTER I

The Education of a Revolutionary

I

Joseph Vissarionovich Djugashvili, universally known by his party pseudonym as Stalin, was by birth Georgian. His ancestors were reputedly Ossetes from the mountains of the north Caucasus, and in later life he was accustomed to refer with pride to his Asiatic origin, although some of his party comrades were less flattering. The first person to call Stalin an Asiatic, according to Trotsky, was the Soviet diplomat and fellow Bolshevik revolutionary Leonid Krassin. 'In saying that,' remarked Trotsky, 'he had in mind no problematical racial attributes, but rather that blending of grit, shrewdness, craftiness and cruelty which has been considered characteristic of the statesmen of Asia.'[1]

For most of two thousand years, until its incorporation in imperial Russia at the beginning of the nineteenth century, Georgia had been an independent kingdom with its own peculiar language, literature and distinctive culture, comprising at various periods in its history the whole of Transcaucasia, and, besides pure Georgians, nearly a score of other peoples and tongues including the Ossetian, Imeretian, Circassian, Mingrelian, Chechen, Lesghian and Aserbaijanian. It was a country of pre-historic legend. The valley of the river Aras, the ancient Araxes, to the south bordering Armenia, was the traditional site of the Garden of Eden, while Noah's Ark was supposed to have come to rest on nearby Mount Ararat after the Flood. The principality of Mingrelia in western Georgia, known as Colchis to the ancients and extending to the Black Sea, was the mythical scene of the raid of Jason and the Argonauts in their quest for the Golden Fleece. Beyond the great mountain range to the north was the important town of Vladi-kavkaz, founded as a Russian fortress in the time of Catherine the Great to contain the Ossetes and renamed afterwards in honour of the Georgian Communist leader Ordzhonikidze. A hundred miles or so to the south and linked with Vladikavkaz by a military road lay the old city of Tiflis, or Tbilisi as the Georgians still call it, the country's capital since the sixth century and the cultural centre of the whole of Transcaucasia. Fifty miles along the railway to the north-west linking Batum on the Black Sea with Baku on the Caspian one reached Gori, a district town beside the river Kura and especially noted for its corn, which was reputed to be the best in Georgia. In a small one-storey wooden dwelling in this town Stalin's father Vissarion Ivanovich Djugashvili, familiarly known as Beso, plied his trade as shoe maker and cobbler.

An important factor in the historical development of the Georgian people had been their early conversion to Christianity by the Roman Emperor Constantine and their subsequent steadfast devotion to the Orthodox Church. Indeed it was their religious faith which led the Georgian rulers to call in aid the Christian Muscovites against the proselytising attempts of the country's Moslem neighbours, the Turks and the Persians, and which ultimately brought about the extinction of its political independence. Nevertheless, the Church continued to play a great part in the life of the community. There were church schools and a great theological seminary in Tiflis. After the Georgian peasantry became free to move about the country, following the abolition of serfdom in the 1860s, many peasants and small farmers liked to see at least one of their sons entering the priesthood.

At the time of Stalin's birth, in 1879, the Georgians were still largely a rural people, composed of an impoverished feudal aristocracy and a peasantry with some artisan tradition. There was no native middle class, and the local bourgeoisie was made up for the most part of Russian bureaucrats and Armenian traders and manufacturers. The Georgians were noted particularly for their courage and love of music and wine and also for the fine physique of their men and the dark beauty of their women. During the period of Moslem ascendancy they had supplied along with the Circassians the largest number of slaves for the Turkish harems and recruits for the Sultan's armies, more especially the *élite* corps of the famous Mamelukes. But they were also capable of great fierceness and cruelty. Georgian princes thought nothing of flogging their serfs for trifling offences, as indeed happened throughout the Russian Empire.

Stalin's father-in-law Sergei Alliluyev, whose father and grandfather were both serfs, used to recall how his grandfather would sometimes bare his back and show the deep scars from flogging which had not healed even in old age.[2] (Though nominally restricted by law, corporal punishment of serfs could in practice be applied to an unlimited extent.) The landlords also habitually beat their wives and children, a practice followed by the peasants and artisans, as Stalin was to know well.

The local landowner in the neighbourhood of Gori, Prince Simeon Amilakhavari, who used to bring his fine soft leather boots to Beso Djugashvili's workship to be mended, once had the Tsar Alexander III's military representative publicly flogged for having had the effrontery to order his Highness's bodyguard to move their stables, looking on while two of the bodyguard seized the unfortunate colonel and took down his breeches. The spectacle is said to have been witnessed by a considerable body of the Gori townsfolk, including the young Stalin. Tsar Alexander, who was the Prince's godfather, remonstrated with unusual mildness. 'Another time please do not thrash one of my officials but just write to me. If a man does not suit you, I will have him transferred.'[3]

However, although a Russian military officer or civil servant from St Petersburg might occasionally be assaulted by a petty Georgian chieftain, the policy of the Russification of Transcaucasia was relentlessly pursued by the central government – what the imperial viceroy of the Caucasus called 'the great work of installing Russian civics in the territory and instilling the principles of civilisation into it'. As for the agglomeration of small nationalities and local enmities with which the viceroy was faced, the example of the British Raj in India pointed the way. The Russian viceroy, Count Ilarion Vorontsov-Dashkov, could write with open satisfaction to his imperial master from the viceregal palace in Tiflis:

> I must point out that if there are no separatist tendencies on the part of the various nationalities, neither are there any separatist tendencies on an all-Caucasian scale because all the nationalities of the Caucasus are at loggerheads with one another and submit to cohabitation only under the influence of the Russian authorities, without which they would plunge into bloody rivalry at once.[4]

The political catalyst, the significance of which does not seem to have been fully appreciated by the Tsar's viceroy at this time, was the growing revolutionary movement. This movement assumed various forms, adopting the principles of Marxian socialism and ultimately manifesting itself in the Russian Social Democratic Labour Party, of the Bolshevik wing of which the future founder of the Soviet State Vladimir Ilyich Ulianov, generally known as Lenin, was eventually to become leader. As a young revolutionary Stalin was to play an adventurous and equivocal part in the party's fortunes in Transcaucasia.

At this point what is known of the young revolutionary's personal family background may be conveniently noticed. It does not amount to very much. Stalin was always extremely reticent on the subject, and apart from one brief reference to his parents in an interview which he gave the German writer Emil Ludwig in 1931 ('My parents were uneducated, but they did not treat me badly by any means.') and one other reference to his father having been a cobbler, he never made any public allusion to them. Nor is he ever known to have referred to his earlier forebears. Fortunately a little evidence has been provided by a number of his childhood contemporaries and from their accounts it has been possible to reconstruct something of his family story.

It is clear that on both his father's and his mother's side Stalin's ancestors were serfs, and that his father Vissarion was born into serfdom on a landlord's estate. The landlord was a certain Prince Machabeli, whose property included the small village of Didi-Lilo in the hill country between Tiflis and Gori. 'My husband was a cobbler,' Beso's wife Ekaterina recalled in her old age. 'His father and his father's father and as far back as we could remember, all his folks had been cobblers – peasant cobblers.' At one time the Djugashvilis are said to have been serfs on the great estate of Prince Eristavi at Annanur in the Aragva valley, about half way between Tiflis and Vladikavkaz. The Aragva Eristavis were the hereditary rulers of the whole region and with their troops recruited from the peasantry they guarded the northern borders of the Georgian kingdom against the raids of the Caucasian mountain tribes. According to one account, Stalin's paternal great-grandfather Zaza Djugashvili was involved in two peasant risings on the Eristavi estate, escaped while awaiting trial, and was recaptured, finally making good his escape after the second rising and becoming a nomadic shepherd. He is supposed eventually to have found his way to Didi-Lilo, where he worked again as a serf for the local landlord, presumably Prince Machabeli, who was probably glad of his services and asked no inconvenient questions. Zaza had a son Ivan (Vanos), who was also a peasant cobbler and also worked in the vineyards.

By this time the emancipation of the serfs had taken place, and

14

although they were given the opportunity of acquiring half the land they had previously cultivated for the landlords, their holdings had to be redeemed by payments to the State spread over forty-nine years. In many cases this placed such a heavy financial burden on them that many preferred to realise their few savings and move to the towns in search of other work. No doubt this explains why Vano's son Vissarion (Beso) decided to leave Didi-Lilo and seek employment in nearby Gori. He arrived there about the year 1870, eventually setting up for himself as a boot and shoe maker and cobbler.[6]

Gori is picturesquely situated on the bend of a river – the shallow and slow moving Kura which also flows through Tiflis – at the foot of a cone-shaped hill surmounted by the ruins of an ancient fortress. When Beso Djugashvili first set foot there, the town had some five thousand inhabitants and was still noted for its silks and cottons as well as its corn and wine. Refreshed by the mountain breezes, the local climate was delightful in summer, though in the winter time it could blow disagreeably hard. The nearby valley supplied an abundance of grapes, pears and peaches. In many ways it was a thriving little community. Yet Beso never found it easy to make a living. This may have been partly due to his fondness for vodka. 'Drunk as a cobbler' was a common expression in those parts, just as 'drunk as a lord' was in England. But even allowing for this, contemporary witnesses agree that Beso was inordinately fond of the bottle.

No photograph or other visual likeness of Beso has survived, so that we do not know exactly what he looked like. Joseph Iremashvili, a boyhood friend of his son's, has described him as a heavy-set man of imposing appearance, with thick black eyebrows and a black bristling moustache, who habitually wore the conventional Georgian *tchoka*, blue trousers thrust into knee-length boots, and a fur cap. Beso was practically illiterate, and it is unlikely that he ever learned to read or write, at least with any degree of fluency, or indeed to do much more than sign his name. Although Russian had for many years been the official language in Georgia, he made no attempt to master it, but always spoke Georgian, as did his wife Ekaterina (Keke), who was the daughter of a potter called George Galadze. She was a red-haired beauty, who married Beso in 1874, when she was eighteen and he was twenty-two, and she came from the nearby village of Gambareuli, east of Gori, where her people like Beso's had been peasant serfs. Her father is said to have been a gardener on the estate of the local landowners, the Gambarovs. 'Her mother Melanie Geladze became a widow early,' wrote one who knew the family from childhood. 'Keke learned to read and write at home, she dressed cleanly and was a charming child. She had chestnut-coloured hair and beautiful eyes.' She lived in Gambareuli until 1864, when she was nine years old and the family moved to Gori after the abolition of serfdom.

Beso Djugashvili rented a drab wooden dwelling for himself and his bride at No. 10 Sobornaya, a street leading to the town's main church. The rent he paid for the two rooms, a living room and a kitchen was one and a half roubles a month, about two shillings or twenty-five cents. The living room with its brick floor was about five square yards in size, and had one small window through which the daylight dimly filtered. The furniture consisted of a small table, a stool, a sofa and a plank bed covered with a straw mattress. It was in this sparsely furnished room that Vissarion Ivanovich and Ekaterina Georgievna Djugashvili lived and worked and slept, and it was here that she bore her husband four sons, three of whom died in infancy.[7]

Years later the place was to become a national shrine, with an inscription recording the fact that the 'great Stalin, leader of the workers of the world' had been born and lived there. The inscription was the work of Stalin's fellow Georgian and much feared police chief Lavrenti Beria, who also erected an ornate marble pavilion over the humble dwelling house. This pretentious superstructure was to remind Stalin's daughter Svetlana, when she saw it for the first and only time in 1951, of one of the lesser underground railway stations in Moscow. ('Under the marble canopy you can barely see the little hovel, which ought to have been left as it was and could perfectly well have told its story without the marble.') Stalin's mother was also brought to see it on one occasion and after taking one look at Beria's grandiose creation is said to have uttered a rude but expressive Georgian word and returned to her simple but comfortable home in Tiflis where she was then living. Today it is no longer a national shrine, and although it has been allowed to remain in deference to local opinion, it has taken on a sadly neglected air and the walls of the edifice are crumbling. However, the nearby Stalin Museum, after a period of temporary eclipse, is still open despite the fact that it contains little more than a few faded photographs of the dictator's family and of himself in his younger days. 'The people who come here,' its loyal director was recently reported as saying, 'do so because they love Stalin.'[8]

To return briefly to his parents. Beso died when his son was eleven years old. His widow Keke, who was to survive her husband by nearly half a century, worked mostly as a dressmaker while her son Joseph was growing up. She was a devoutly religious woman and hoped her only surviving son would become a priest. Eventually she moved to Tiflis, where after the Revolution she was accommodated in two modest rooms on the first floor of the old Viceroy's Palace when it became the headquarters of the Council of People's Commissars of the Transcaucasian Republic.

According to the Georgian Menshevik leader Gregory Uratadze, the local secret police suddenly received orders one night that more guards should be posted outside Keke's quarters in the palace. Next morning, when the commissars arrived for work, they found the building ringed with two rows of sentries. One of the commissars asked their chairman Budu Mdivani the reason.

'It's not my doing,' said Mdivani. 'The orders came on the direct wire from Moscow that Keke's bodyguard should be strengthened.'

'But why?'

'So she shall not give birth to another Stalin!'

The story of this witticism is said to have spread through Georgia and eventually reached the Kremlin where it made Stalin furious. At all events, shortly afterwards Stalin had the unfortunate Mdivani removed from his post and later shot following a specially staged show trial.

Keke's granddaughter Svetlana has recalled being taken as a child with her brothers Yakov and Vasily to see 'Granny Keke' when she was ill in Tiflis in 1934. Her bedroom was small and dark, with a low ceiling and little windows overlooking a courtyard.

> There was an iron cot and a screen in one corner. The room was full of old women wearing black, as old women do in Georgia, and a little old lady was perched on the iron cot. We were led up to her...she kissed us and spoke a few words in Georgian. Yakov was the only one who understood.
>
> I remember that she had light eyes and that her hands and her pale face were covered with freckles...She offered us hard candies on a plate. The tears were rolling down her cheeks... There were bunches of herbs in the window and the place smelled of them... Though I was only about eight at the time, I wondered why Grandmother seemed so poor. I'd never seen such an awful-looking black cot...

Four years before this, the American journalist H. R. Knickerbocker had interviewed her for the *New York Evening Post*, when she was already over seventy. To him she appeared grey-haired and slender, dressed in a grey woollen Georgian peasant costume and peering at him through silver-rimmed spectacles. 'I'm sorry I speak so little Russian,' she said through the Georgian interpreter whom the newspaperman had wisely brought with him.

They all three sat round a big table covered with a worn red cloth, and as the visitors' call was quite unexpected Ekaterina Georgievna also had to apologise for having no coffee or tea to offer them.

'Are you still religious?' she was asked.

'I'm afraid I'm not as religious as I used to be,' she replied. 'My son has told me so much.' Then pointing to a photograph on the wall of Stalin in a student's coarse, straight-collared jacket, she went on. 'See! That's how he looked in the theological seminary.'

There was another much more recent photograph of him, wearing a white *roubashtia*. It was inscribed 'To my mother'. On the opposite wall hung a large portrait of Lenin, and facing the windows was a reproduction of the Soviet artist Brodsky's well-known drawing of the shooting of the twenty-six Bolshevik commissars of Baku by Menshevik troops at Krasnovodsk in 1918, allegedly with British complicity. This bore an inscription from the artist, 'To Comrade Ekaterina Djugashvili'.

She felt that worrying over her son in his early days as an underground revolutionary had prematurely aged her. 'The worst of it was when I never knew where he was,' she said. 'Always in jail, in exile, in Siberia, at the last in the Arctic.' It seemed difficult for her to appreciate fully the change that had taken place in his status. 'I visited the Kremlin once,' she went on. 'Just once I've been in Moscow. I lived with my son there. I didn't like it. The trip is too far and it's not like Georgia.' (She spent an unhappy month in the Kremlin puzzled, so the story went, at her boy's prominence, because she could not discover what he 'did' to earn a living.) 'Oh, yes,' she went on, 'he often comes to Georgia. But he seldom gets farther than Sochi, over there on the coast. I think he is there now.' She added that he had been twice to see her, once in 1921 and once three years ago. 'Moscow is very far,' she murmured wistfully like a character in one of Chekhov's plays.

'See!' she exclaimed, getting up and going over to a corner table piled high with newspapers and periodicals, every one of them containing an article, speech or picture of her son. 'See how he works. All this he has done. He works too hard.' She referred to him as Soso – 'that's our Georgian pet name for Joseph.'

'And he has a family of his own, but he's much too busy for any family. There's my grandson Yasha, Soso's boy by his first wife. Yasha is twenty-four. His mother Ekaterina died of pneumonia before the revolution. And now I've two more grandchildren, Soso's boy Vasily ...and the little girl Svetlana...Both of them are by Soso's second wife Nadezdha Alliluyeva. She was a great Communist, a friend of Lenin's.'

The mention of Lenin reminded her of something important. 'You know, it was Lenin who gave him the name of Stalin. Lenin said he was like steel. It was a good name.' Although Lenin doubtless approved of the pseudonym, it is more likely that it originated with Stalin himself and was suggested by his real surname. In old Georgian Djugashvili meant literally 'son of iron', so that the change to the Russian 'man of steel' was quite logical.

Granny Keke refused to be photographed in her old clothes, but later she consented to pose in the park outside, after she had changed into the black dress which elderly Georgian women habitually wore on formal occasions, an outfit which included a touch of white lace and a tightly drawn black head cloth held in place in a velvet ring.

In the summer she used to go to Borzhom, a well known health resort in the mountains, where it was sometimes very warm. On one occasion, her friend Anna Alliluyeva, whose niece had married her son as his second wife, encountered her sitting on a bench in the local park, wearing her usual thick black clothes. Anna expressed surprise that she should be dressed as she was on what was an unbearably sultry day. 'I'm afraid I've no choice,' replied Stalin's mother. 'You see, everyone knows me here!'

As she grew older, Granny Keke became very religious again. She is said to have turned one of her rooms into a private chapel, hung about with ikons and lamps, where she used to spend hours in silent prayer. She would also regularly attend the services in the nearby church, go to confession and receive the Holy Sacrament. Her conduct contrasted so strongly with that of her godless dictator son in the Kremlin, and her appearances in church aroused such public interest that she was persuaded by the local authorities at her son's instigation to return to Gori. But she did not remain there for long. In May 1937, she contracted pneumonia, as had her first daughter-in-law and namesake, and since the hospital facilities in Gori were considered inadequate for the treatment of her case, she was brought back to Tiflis. There she died a few weeks later, on 7 June, without having been allowed to see a priest or to receive absolution.

She was buried secretly, at night, without any religious ceremony in the cemetery on St David's Hill in a suburb of Tiflis overlooking the town. Later her grave was marked by a simple granite slab with her name inscribed in Georgian characters – Ekaterina Georgievna Djugashvili. Stalin, who had not attended the funeral, refused to allow a cross to be placed by the headstone as she would have wished.[9]

2

The Djugashvilis' fourth child was born in the *domik* or 'little house' on Sobornaya Street in Gori on 9 December 1879 according to the Old Style calendar used in Russia until the Revolution. In the nineteenth century the Old Style was twelve days behind the New Style which was in vogue in most other countries, so that Stalin's birthday really fell on 21 December, and it was on this date that it was to be celebrated with increasing adulation in the days to come of his dictatorial power in the Soviet Union. In the interview with the American H. R. Knickerbocker, quoted above, Ekaterina Georgievna declared that he was born 'eight days after Christmas Old Style', which would mean 14 January 1880. ('I don't know what date it would be by this new way of reckoning. I never could learn it.') However, it is most likely that she confused his birthday with the date of his baptism or name day, a date which would have stuck in her mind as being much more important to her than his actual birthday. For it was on this date that he was given the name Joseph, after the saint and stepfather of Jesus, by the local parish priest, who duly recorded it in the church register. It was a proud day for the mother, who hoped that the infant should eventually become a priest himself, and possibly even rise to be a patriarch in the service of the holy Orthodox Georgian Church.[10]

In later years, when Stalin was world famous, the neighbouring village of Didi-Lilo used to claim the honour of being his birthplace. But Keke firmly denied this. 'They talk a lot about Soso's being born in Didi-Lilo, but that's entirely wrong,' she told Knickerbocker. 'Soso was born in Gori. I could show you the place. I know he was born there. I'm his mother and I ought to know.'

Although formally christened Joseph Vissarionovich, the boy was known in the family circle as Soso. Relatively little has been discovered about his childhood, apart from the fact that it was one of grinding poverty. According to his official biographer Emilian Yaroslavsky, in the eulogistic *Landmarks in the Life of Stalin*, his mother had to 'slave day and night to make ends meet in her poor household' and was obliged to go out to work as a washerwoman. ('Stalin was acquainted with poverty and want from his earliest childhood.') Keke also sewed, baked bread, and served as a 'daily' maid – in fact, anything to scrape a living and supplement her husband's meagre earnings from his trade which appears to have gone from bad to worse, a development probably due to his drinking habits. Then, in 1883, when Soso was four, his father left Gori and went to Tiflis where he got employment in a shoe factory owned by 'a fat Armenian' named Adelkhanov, and situated in the oriental quarter of the town near the well known sulphur Turkish baths belonging to Prince Orbeliani and much frequented by locals and visitors alike. Meanwhile Keke and her son remained in Gori, although they later left the house near the church for other lodgings in the town.

Beso Djugashvili appears to have contributed little if anything to the support of his wife and son during his absence. Yet Keke is said to have kept the child neat and clean and to have clothed him in a warm winter coat during the cold weather. She would often sing him Georgian folk songs and such fondness as he later showed for music and singing he derived from her. In spite of her struggles, they seldom went hungry, and indeed ate tolerably well on the staple Georgian diet of roast meat, red beans, boiled potatoes, greens, tomatoes, rice and fruit. Otherwise it is not possible to account for Soso's strong and healthy physique, to which his boyhood contemporaries all testify. It is related that he could swim by the time he was six, which he liked to do in the nearby Kura and Liakhva rivers, and showed early prowess as a wrestler. If he was a little boy, whose height was never to exceed five feet four inches, he made up for his short stature by surpassing most of his boyhood companions in games and sports.[11]

When Soso was seven, he became ill with smallpox, and the disease left his face scarred with pockmarks which remained visible all his life. Soon after this he contracted blood poisoning from an ulcer on his left hand, from which he nearly died. 'I don't know what saved me then, my strong constitution or the ointment from the village quack,' he later told his sister-in-law Anna Alliluyeva. When he recovered he could not easily bend his left arm at the elbow, a physical defect which was later to exempt him from compulsory military service.[12] He was afterwards to wear a warm glove on his left hand, alleging rheumatism as the reason. According to his sister-in-law, his left arm was always two or three inches shorter than the right; although in the days of his dictatorial power this physical defect was to be carefully concealed by official Soviet photographers, it does clearly appear in a picture which an American photographer took of Stalin with President Truman at Potsdam in 1945. It is possible that Soso suffered from a mild form of infantile paralysis as a boy, although his enemies assert on somewhat dubious authority that his condition was syphilitic in origin. An addition physical defect, as appears from subsequent police records of his revolutionary career, was that the second and third toes of his left foot were joined together.

From time to time his father would appear from Tiflis, get drunk, and according to some accounts would beat both the boy and his mother. 'Undeserved, frightful beatings eventually made the boy as grim and heartless as was his father,' writes his boyhood friend Iremashvili. One day, according to Stalin's daughter Svetlana, the boy threw a knife at his father in an attempt to defend his mother whom the father had struck. Beso rushed after his son screaming, and neighbours hid the boy until his father's anger had subsided.[13] Like many other boys of his age, he was up to all kinds of tricks, and for these his father would thrash him. Once he killed some chickens belonging to a neighbour in a stone-throwing contest with another boy; on another occasion he broke a neighbour's window, and one day he dropped a brick down another neighbour's chimney into the open hearth, frightening and scorching the inmates. A favourite game he played with other boys was called 'the war against Russia', in which young Soso usually took the part of a Georgian insurgent leader. It was one such hero, the guerrilla fighter Koba, whose name he was to adopt first as a nickname and then as a revolutionary pseudonym.

When he was eight, his mother sent him to the local church school where he began to learn Russian – hitherto he spoke only Georgian – in addition to ancient Greek, Hebrew, arithmetic, drawing, science and music. That she was able to do this was due to her getting a small grant for him from the school of three roubles a month, to which were added a monthly wage of ten roubles for her work as laundress, sewing-woman and part-time charwoman for the school. She was proud of him, and he loved and respected her unlike his father whom he feared and detested. 'Soso was always a good boy,' his mother afterwards recalled. 'I never had occasion to punish him. He studied hard, always reading or discussing, trying to understand everything...His father said he would make a good cobbler out of Soso...But I didn't want him to be a cobbler. I didn't want him to be anything but a priest. I did dream that one day Soso would finish his studies and become a priest.'[14] But Soso wanted to be neither a cobbler nor a priest.

One day, probably during the school holidays in 1889, Beso turned up from Tiflis and announced that he was taking Soso back with him to the Adelkhanov factory to learn his trade. 'You want my son to be a priest, a church official, don't you?' he said to Keke. 'You'll never live to see it happen! Yes, I'm a cobbler and my son must become a cobbler like me.' In spite of his wife's remonstrances, and apparently also the remonstrances of some of their friends and neighbours who 'explained at length to him the absurdity of such a decision', Beso insisted on dragging the boy back with him to Tiflis. However, Soso does not seem to have spent very long in the factory, perhaps not more than a few weeks in all, if that, since Keke followed him to the capital and, as she was later to recall, 'succeeded in putting him to school again'.

It was from this period, probably from this actual episode, that the story later gained credence, particularly among Stalin's political opponents, that as a boy in Tiflis he had been a *kinto* or ragamuffin who roamed the streets, part jester, part ribald rhymster, smart and cunning, with a small cap stuck on the back of his head, the typical Georgian street urchin who lived largely by his wits. There may be a slight element of truth in this, but from the evidence available it would seem to be a fanciful and far-fetched picture. If any member of the Djugashvili family was given to vagrant habits, it was Soso's father Beso, who is described in one of the police reports of the period as a tramp. Beso may well have been paid as a pieceworker in the shoe factory, and towards the end of his life his absences from the bench became more and more frequent as his drinking increased.

In later official biographies dictated by Stalin for Soviet reference books, his father's having been a worker in a shoe factory was stressed in order to indicate that Stalin wished the Russian people to think that this was his own proletarian origin. Yet Beso's object in taking the factory job was 'capitalist' rather than 'proletarian', as his son was later to point out in an article written for a local Georgian language newspaper. Stalin clearly had his father in mind when he referred to the time when 'the consciousness of men', still 'imbued with the sense of private property', was gradually becoming 'imbued with socialist ideas', although Beso did not realise it in his case.

Let us take a shoemaker who owned a tiny workshop, but who, unable to withstand the competition of the big manufacturers, closed his workshop and took a job, say at Adelkhanov's shoe factory in Tiflis. He went to work at Adelkhanov's factory not with a view to becoming a permanent wageworker, but with the object of saving up some money, of accumulating a little capital to enable him to reopen his workshop. As you see, the position of this shoemaker is *already* proletarian, but his consciousness is *still* non-proletarian, it is thoroughly petty bourgeois. In other words, this shoemaker has *already* lost his petty bourgeois position, it has gone, but his petty bourgeois consciousness has *not yet* gone; it has lagged behind his actual position...

This proletarianised shoemaker goes on working, but finds it is a very difficult matter to save money, because what he earns barely suffices to maintain an existence. Moreover, he realises that the opening of a private workshop is after all not so alluring: the rent he will have to pay for the premises, the caprices of the

23

customers, shortage of money, the competition of the big manufacturers and similar worries – such are the worries that torture
the mind of the private workshop owner...

Time passes and our shoemaker sees that he has not enough
money to satisfy his most essential needs, that what he needs very
badly is a rise in wages. At the same time, he hears his fellow
workers talking about unions and strikes. Here our shoemaker
realises that in order to improve his conditions he must fight the
masters and not open a workshop of his own. He joins the union,
enters the strike movement, and soon becomes imbued with
socialist ideas.[15]

This description exactly fits Beso Djugashvili, except that he never became a true 'proletarian' worker. Nor was he ever able to save enough
to enable him to start up again on his own account. He died in Tiflis
in 1890, at the age of thirty-eight, his end no doubt hastened by alcohol-
ism. His widow brought his remains back to Gori, where they were
interred in a pauper's grave.[16]

Meanwhile Soso was doing well at school and his mother was
pleased with his examination results, where his marks were uniformly
high; indeed he was considered the 'best student' in all subjects. 'He
was first in study and play, a leader in all games, a good friend and a
favourite among his school fellows,' Yaroslavsky wrote afterwards in
his official *Landmarks in the Life of Stalin.* 'He was fond of reading,
drawing and singing.' This description is only partly true. Quick with
his fists and the school's leading wrestler, Soso was intolerant of any of
his classmates who ventured to disagree with him; according to Iremashvili, who was one of them, he enjoyed frightening the other boys
and lacked compassion both for people and animals. To him friendship
meant the submission of others to his domineering will, unless of
course the friend was older and stronger than himself. In other words,
he was a typical school bully.

One school friend was Vano Ketskhoveli, who later related how they
used to go for long rambles together in the countryside on Sundays,
scaling the nearby mountains and exploring the fantastic cave dwell-
ings cut out of the rock at Uplis-Tsikhe in the time of Alexander the
Great. Together they began to read Georgian literature, particularly
the stirring poems of Ilya Chavchavadze denouncing serfdom and
landlordism, and also the stories by Kazbegi about Koba and the other
guerrilla fighters against the Russian overlords. 'Kazbegi's heroes
awakened in our youthful hearts a love for our country, and each of us,
on leaving school, was inspired with an eagerness to serve his country,'

wrote Vano afterwards. 'But none of us had a clear idea of what shape this service should take.'[17]

As a step towards the further Russification of the country, the authorities replaced the local schoolteachers who were Georgians by Russians, a change against which Soso is said to have incited some of his schoolfellows to demonstrate. In this way he may well have incurred the risk of expulsion, but possibly the new teachers were unwilling to expel a boy whose scholastic record was so consistently good.

Soso is also reported to have made up for this lapse by diligent attendance at church services. When he was twelve or thirteen, he sang several solo chants at a solemn mass in the Gori church to mark the anniversary of the Tsar Alexander III's accession or name day, and heard the prayers read for the welfare of the imperial family, including the Tsarevich, the future Nicholas II.[18] His mother was delighted. She was even more pleased when, at the end of the summer term of 1894, he passed out first in the school examinations with a certificate of merit. Shortly afterwards his mother accompanied him to Tiflis to sit for the entrance examination for the Theological Seminary. He passed brilliantly and was awarded a scholarship, which was to supply him free with half his board, tuition, books, clothing and other necessaries.

3

At this date the Georgian capital had a population of close on 150,000, comprising Russians, Germans, Persians, Armenians and Tartars, in addition to Georgians. Its handsome streets, gardens, bridges, opera house, hotels and other buildings illuminated by electricity were evidence of western civilisation. Separated by only a short distance from the main square at the end of Rustavili Avenue were the eastern bazaars with their narrow, steep streets, mysterious houses with shuttered windows, silversmiths, carpet dealers, arms merchants, perfume vendors and shoemakers. Tiflis was thus ideally situated for trade and other communication purposes between east and west, being the principal junction of the Transcaucasian Railway with lines going east to Baku, west to Batum and south to Kars. At the same time it was directly connected with Vladikavkaz and Russia proper to the north by the great Georgian military road across the Caucasus, which still afforded the quickest route to Europe.

The Tiflis Theological Seminary, reckoned the best institution of its kind outside European Russia, was an austere looking building in classical style facing Pushkin Square and the monument to the poet in the middle of the town. For some years past it had been the scene of repeated student troubles and was in fact a hotbed of Georgian nationalism. A previous rector had been violently assaulted by a student called Sylvester Dzhibladze, and later murdered by another. There were student strikes and boycotting of classes, one such demonstration having been led the year before Soso arrived by Vano Ketskhoveli's elder brother Lado, who was also destined to play a conspicuous part in the revolutionary underground movement in Transcaucasia. Noi Zhordania, afterwards President of the Georgian Republic, conceived *Messame Dasy*, the first 'Social Democratic' Marxist movement in Georgia, while he was a student at the seminary in the eighteen-eighties.* *Messame Dasy* later became in effect the Georgian section of the Russian Social Democratic Labour Party. Seditious literature was smuggled into the seminary in spite of frequent confiscations and soon Soso was eagerly absorbing it like most of his Georgian classmates.

The seminary was anything but a happy place, since its outwardly forbidding appearance was equalled by the atmosphere of suspicion and repression on the part of the indoor staff. 'Our instructors treated us like animals,' was how one of Soso's contemporaries put it. Breaches of discipline, such as reading newspapers and forbidden books or going to the theatre, were punished by long periods of solitary confinement in a monastic cell. The day started at seven o'clock in the morning with a service in chapel which sometimes lasted several hours; as the students were obliged to remain standing throughout, their legs and feet were often numb with cold. Sharp at five o'clock in the afternoon, the seminary gates would be shut fast and the student inmates locked in until next morning. 'We felt like prisoners,' said Iremashvili, 'guiltless of any crime, who were forced to spend a long term in jail'. Father Germogen, the rector, and Father Abashidze, the government inspector, were both 'fearful jesuitical inquisitors'. Another monk, Father Dmitry, who was to succeed Father Germogen as rector, often tried to catch Soso for bringing forbidden literature into the seminary, but he was usually outwitted, although frequent searches were made of the students' belongings. 'Even the few literary works that the lay authorities permitted us to read were forbidden by the Church authorities because we were future priests,' Iremashvili remarked. 'We could not read Dostoyevsky, Tolstoy, Turgenev and many other authors.'[19]

* Literally 'The Third Group' to distinguish it from *Meori Dasy* ('The Second Group'), a progressive liberal organisation composed of Georgian intellectuals in the eighties, and *Pirveli Dasy* ('The First Group'), an older body drawn from progressively minded members of the Georgian aristocracy, who had advocated the abolition of serfdom.

26

Years later, in the course of his celebrated interview with Emil Ludwig, Stalin described the prevailing atmosphere at the seminary and its direct effect upon himself. 'In protest against the outrageous regime and the jesuitical methods prevalent at the seminary, I was ready to become, and actually did become, a revolutionary, a believer in Marxism as a really revolutionary teaching.'

'But do you not admit that the Jesuits have good points?' asked the German writer.

'Yes, they are systematic and persevering to achieve their sordid ends,' Stalin replied. 'But their principal method is spying, prying, worming their way into people's souls and outraging their feelings. What good can there be in that? For instance, the spying in the hostel. At nine o'clock the bell rings for morning tea, we go to the dining room, and when we return to our rooms we find that meantime a search has been made and all our chests have been ransacked...What good can there be in that?'[20]

This is confirmed by accounts of Stalin's fellow students. According to one of them, he was caught with illicit literature when his locker was searched and on another occasion he was detected in possession of a notebook filled with seditious material for use in a handwritten magazine which circulated surreptitiously in the seminary. We know that Stalin first became acquainted with Karl Marx's *Das Kapital* from a manuscript Russian translation of this work which was similarly passed from hand to hand among the students. It is noteworthy that Stalin also told Emil Ludwig that he joined the revolutionary movement at the age of fifteen. This assertion, no doubt made for propaganda purposes, is contradicted by the known facts. For his first two years at least in the seminary, he was much too busy with his studies to devote any time to an outside movement; at the end of his first year he was placed eighth in the class list, moving up to fifth in the following year, when he is stated to have received the highest marks in civil law, history and literature. It was not until 1898, when he was eighteen, that he joined *Messame Dasy*, then a bourgeois nationalist organisation under Zhordania's leadership, which could hardly be regarded as Marxist and indeed was permitted to operate openly by the police at this time. It was later to be transformed into the Menshevik right wing of the Russian Social Democratic Labour Party. On the other hand, it appears that Joseph Djugashvili attended a number of secret students' meetings at which Marxist ideas were discussed, while at the same time he increased his reading in the field of forbidden literature. According to Vano Ketskhoveli, the seminary completely changed his character by turning him away from games,

27

though not from books, and making him pensive and reserved.

Early in his third year (November 1896), a conduct report signed by the rector records that he was caught with a copy of Victor Hugo's *Toilers of the Sea*, which he had obtained from the local lending library on Kirochnaya Street. The book was confiscated and, since he had already been warned when he was found with another of Hugo's novels, *Ninety-Three*, the recalcitrant student was ordered to be confined to the punishment cell 'for a prolonged period'. A few months later, he was discovered reading Letourneau's *Literary Evolution of the Nations* on the chapel steps. 'The library ticket was found in the book,' reported the Assistant Rector. 'This is the thirteenth time this student has been discovered reading the books from the lending library. I handed over the book to the Father Rector.' On this occasion the rector directed that he should be confined to the punishment cell 'for a prolonged period with a strict warning'.

On 29 September 1898, it was reported that at 9.0 p.m. 'a group of students gathered in the dining hall round Joseph Djugashvili, who read to them from books not sanctioned by the seminary authorities, in view of which the students were searched'. A little later, on 16 December, the following report appeared in the students' conduct book:

> In the course of a search of students of the fifth class made by members of the board of supervision, Joseph Djugashvili tried several times to enter into an argument with them, expressing dissatisfaction with the repeated searches of students and declaring that such searches were never made in other seminaries. Djugashvili is generally disrespectful and rude towards persons in authority and systematically refuses to bow to one of the teachers, as the latter has repeatedly complained to the board of supervision.

This time Joseph was reprimanded and confined to the punishment cell for five hours on the rector's orders.

Once, when the rector entered his room in the course of a search, Joseph went on reading as if he had not noticed him.

'Don't you see who is standing before you?' the rector asked.

The student got up from his chair and rubbed his eyes. 'I don't see anything,' he answered insolently, 'except a black spot in front of my eyes.'

Iremashvili gives a reason for his friend's increasing rebelliousness, which is quite credible. 'People who ruled over others because of their seniority or power reminded Soso of his father,' Iremashvili was to write. 'Soon he began to hate everyone who had any authority over him.' This was reflected in his growing atheism, as related by a student to whom he lent a copy of Ludwig Feuerbach's *Essence of Christianity*. 'The first thing we had to do, he would say, was to become atheists,' remarked the student in question whose name was Pavkadze. 'Many of us thus began to acquire a materialist outlook and to ignore theological subjects.'

Another student named Glurdjidze later recalled how he once spoke to Soso about the living God. Soso heard him out, and then after a moment or two of silence said: 'You know, they are fooling us. There is no God.'

'How can you say such things, Soso?' asked the other, astonished by such heresy.

'I'll lend you a book to read. It will show you that the world and all living things are quite different from what you imagine, and all this talk about God is sheer nonsense.'

'What book is that?'

'Darwin's *Descent of Man*. You must read it.'

If this story is true, it proves that Soso had begun to lead what was in a sense a double life, since he continued his theological studies with an outward show of religious conformity while in reality disbelieving in the existence of a divine being.

In an interview which he gave the Moscow correspondent of a Finnish journal thirty years later he recalled his early religious doubts.

If God exists, he must have ordained slavery, feudalism and capitalism; he must want humanity to suffer, as the monks were always telling me. Then there would be no hope for the toiling masses to free themselves from their oppressors. I knew that humanity could fight its way to freedom...

The monks said that it was not my place to worry about such questions, that I could trust God to arrange all for the best in the end...They were very lazy, the monks.[21]

Some of Soso's student contemporaries have related that not only was he given to reading poetry, in addition to works on economics, sociology and the like, but that he wrote verses himself. Five poems attributed to him appeared in *Iveria*, a newspaper edited by Prince Ilya Chachavadze in the second half of 1895, and a sixth in July, 1896, in *Kvali* (The Furrow), a political weekly published by Zhordania. One of these poems entitled 'To the Moon' contained the following:

29

Know well that those who once
Fell to the oppressors
Shall rise again and soar,
Winged with hope, above the sacred mountain.

The allusion to the mountain was to St David's Hill overlooking Tiflis, site of the fortress prison where many Georgian patriots were confined and of the cemetery where they were buried, the same which contains the remains of Stalin's mother. It is significant that when the poems were republished with some alterations many years afterwards, Stalin would neither confirm nor deny that he was their author. They were not signed with his name and neither Iremashvili nor any other of his student contemporaries refer to his supposed poetic talent. It may well be that the poems are the work of another hand, but that when they were disinterred at the time of Stalin's sixtieth birthday and claimed as his on account of their patriotic sentiments, it flattered his vanity to allow the claim to stand without contradicting it.

Stalin's official biographers such as Yaroslavsky and Beria have naturally tended to exaggerate their hero's role in the illegal workers' movement of the period. Indeed Beria makes the astonishing assertion that in 1898, while still a student in the seminary, Stalin 'conducted' more than eight workers' circles plus others at small workshops, printing plants and the like.[22] Soviet historians have likewise claimed that he played a leading part in the Tiflis railway workers' strike in December 1898, which was in reality led by Lado Ketskhoveli and was broken after the police had made forty-one arrests. Contemporary police reports do not mention Joseph Djugashvili, who seems to have done no more than look on and possibly encourage a few of the men to come out on strike. There is some evidence, however, that he may have been privy to the strikers' plans, since Iremashvili has recalled how one evening he and Soso stole out of the seminary and secretly made their way to a small shack owned by a railway worker on the side of St David's Hill. 'Other students who shared our views soon joined us,' noted Iremashvili. 'Here we met a Social Democratic organisation of railway workers.'

No doubt Soso first made the acquaintance of these workers and others earlier the same year when he joined *Messame Dasy*. This was in a house in Elisavetinskaya Street in Tiflis, where a group of them lived in two small rooms on the first floor, which were rented by a worker named Vano Sturua. This appears to have been the first of the workers' circles in which Stalin participated, but as a learner rather than a teacher. 'When replying to his questions,' one of the group named George Ninua later recalled, 'we would cite facts from our own lives as workers, recount what happened in the factories and how we were exploited by the management, the contractors and the foreman. Whenever such subjects were touched on, Comrade Stalin would show a particularly keen interest. He would put many questions to the workers and then draw conclusions...Comrade Stalin was our teacher, but he would often say that he himself learnt from the workers.'[23]

This account was to be confirmed by Stalin himself in a speech which he made to the workers of Tiflis in 1926, before Russian revolutionary history had been rewritten by the dictator's sycophants.

I have been and still am a pupil of the pioneer workmen of the Tiflis railway shops...I remember the year 1898 when for the first time the workers in the railway shops put me in charge of a circle. I remember how, at Comrade Sturua's rooms, in the presence of Sylvester Dzhibladze* – he was then one of my teachers – of Ninua and other advanced workers of Tiflis, I learned practical work. In comparison with these men I was then a tyro.

Perhaps I had a little more book learning than many of them. But in the practice of revolution I was certainly a beginner. Here, in the circle of these comrades, I received my first baptism of fire in revolution.[24]

On the subject of Stalin's conduct of this particular workers' circle, of which he is stated to have been in charge for over two years, Comrade Ninua wrote:

He had a splendid knowledge of the history of the working class movement in the West and of revolutionary Social Democratic theory, and his talks at once riveted the attention of the workers. Stalin would quote from fiction and scientific works; he was always citing examples. When addressing us, he had a notebook before him or just a sheet of paper covered with fine writing. It was obvious he carefully prepared for every talk. We usually met in the evenings, at dusk, and on Sundays would go into the country in groups of five to ten and would carry on our discussions without regard for time.

This account, which appeared with similar reminiscences on the occasion of Stalin's sixtieth birthday in 1939, is questionable, at least so far

* Dzhibladze had recently returned from Siberia, to which he had been exiled when a student for assaulting the rector of the theological seminary in Tiflis.

as Stalin's book knowledge is concerned. More credible is the version given by Noe Zhordania, then an exile living in Paris in the 1930s. Zhordania recalled an occasion at the end of 1898, when he was editing *Kvali* and a young man appeared at the editorial offices and introduced himself. 'I am Djugashvili, a student at the Theological Seminary,' he said. 'I am a faithful reader of your journal and your articles. All of them have made a great impression on me. I have decided to quit the seminary and spend my time amongst the workers. Give me your advice.'

Zhordania first of all proceeded to put some questions to the young man in order to test his knowledge of history, sociology and political economy. The editor was not very favourably impressed. Djugashvili's knowledge so far as it went appeared to be largely based on articles in *Kvali* and also the so-called Erfurt programme of Karl Kautsky, in which Marx's leading disciple and interpreter of his philosophy attacked 'revisionists' like Zhordania who believed that the Georgian people could be regenerated economically under a capitalist system, and in which Kautsky defended the necessity of revolution and of the overthrow of capitalism by a revolutionary struggle. This was also Lenin's view.

According to Zhordania, he explained to his caller that it would be difficult for him to function as a Social Democratic propagandist in the circumstances. 'Our workers are curious and want knowledge,' he said. 'When they see that a propagandist is ignorant, they will turn away and refuse to listen to him. I advise you to remain for another year at the seminary and undertake some self-education.'

Joseph Djugashvili looked disappointed. 'I'll think about it,' he said, and went away.[25]

Shortly afterwards, a classmate of Joseph's named Kapanadze went into Pushkin Square during the tea break one morning and found Joseph engaged in a heated argument about Zhordania's political views and quoting Lenin by way of contraverting them. 'The bell rang and we all hurried off to our classes,' Kapanadze noted at the time. 'I was astonished at Joseph's trenchant criticism of Zhordania's view and spoke to him about it. He told me that he had just read an article by Lenin which he liked very much. "I must meet him at all costs" he said.'[26]

Joseph Djugashvili left the Tiflis Theological Seminary for good on 29 May 1899. According to the seminary inspector's official report, he was expelled for having failed to take his end-of-term examinations 'for an unexplained reason'. Yaroslavsky states that he also neglected to pay his tuition fees, but adds that the real cause of his expulsion was his political activities as 'a person who harboured views dangerous to Tsarism', and that his failure to sit the examination merely served as a pretext for dismissing him. This received some confirmation from the student himself when he wrote many years later, in answer to a Communist party questionnaire, that he had been 'turned out of a theological seminary for propagating Marxism.'[27] According to his mother and his classmate Iremashvili, on the other hand, he left for reasons of health.

Iremashvili says that he became ill through reading revolutionary literature by candlelight, but is silent on the question of his expulsion. In her old age his mother denied that he had ever been expelled. 'I brought him home on account of his health,' she declared. 'When he entered the seminary he was as strong as a boy could be. But overwork up to the age of nineteen pulled him down, and the doctors told me that he might develop tuberculosis. So I took him away from the seminary. He did not want to leave.'

No doubt there is an element of truth in all these versions of why he left the seminary. It is quite likely that his health had suffered and that his mother did take him home to Gori before he was formally expelled, but that she did not care to admit later on that 'the great Stalin' had in fact suffered the ignominy of expulsion from the institution where she hoped that he would eventually have become a priest. No doubt, too, that the seminary authorities had for long suspected him of disloyalty to the prevailing political system and were glad of an excuse to get rid of him. By this time he himself must have been convinced of the futility of further prolonging his studies within the cold seminary walls.

One thing is certain, as his friend Iremashvili was to put it. 'He left the seminary, taking with him a vicious, ferocious enmity against the monastic administration, against the bourgeoisie, against everything that existed in the country and embodied Tsarism.' In fact, he hated all constituted authority with a bitter hatred.

4

At the end of 1899, a minor clerical post in the Tiflis Geophysical Observatory fell vacant and on Lado Ketskhoveli's advice Joseph applied for it. He got the job. But how he spent the previous six months, since the date of his departure from the theological seminary, has always been something of a mystery, by no means the only one in his career. For some of the time he may have been convalescing at home with his mother in Gori. It has been said that he did some private tutoring, his pupils coming from various middle class families in the Tiflis area, although they cannot have been many since most parents would have been unlikely to engage a spoiled priest as a tutor. It does appear, however, that he had at least one pupil. This was an Armenian named Semyon Ter-Petrosyan, who like himself came from Gori; his parents thought he should go into the army and engaged Joseph Djugashvili as a coach. Young Semyon, later known as Kamo, is stated to have been converted by Joseph to Marxism. At all events, he was to become one of the most courageous and dedicated of revolutionary terrorists in Georgia.

According to Essad-Bey, Stalin's somewhat gossipy biographer, the future Soviet leader wrote a letter to the rector of the theological seminary shortly after his departure, giving the names of a number of his former classmates who, he said, had like himself become 'politically unreliable'. He added what was quite untrue, namely that they had been in the habit of stealing out of the seminary at night to attend the workers' circle in Vano Sturua's rooms and elsewhere. Somehow the news that Djugashvili had turned informer leaked out and as a result he received a summons to attend an informal court of inquiry in Elisaventinskaya Street.

'Did you, comrade, denounce your fellow socialists and former classmates to the seminary authorities?' he was asked.

'I did,' was the reply.

'So you admit it!'

'Of course,' said the informer coolly. With that he jumped up, and bowing his head, a habit of his when speaking, he proceeded to explain himself. 'Comrades,' he said, 'our Party has too few members. The pupils of the seminary were all destined to be priests and monks, that is to say, servants of the Church. But I have saved them for the Revolution. Now in view of the decision of the authorities to expel them, all access to the ranks of the bourgeoisie has for ever been barred to them, and they have no alternative but to become and to remain our associates. By my denunciation I have added to the Party a dozen educated and trusted revolutionaries, the very men we most require!'[28]

Some years later, during his imprisonment in Baku jail, Joseph admitted to a fellow political prisoner Semyen Vereshchak that he had denounced several students in the seminary to the rector as related above. What he failed to add was that his malicious and unfounded statements prompted the police to spy on hitherto innocent individuals. He himself also became an object of police attention at this time. According to Yaroslavsky, whom there is no reason to doubt on this point, 'the police and *gendarmerie* began to keep a close watch on him, and a dossier was started in which all his movements were recorded'.[29] In the 1930s Lavrenti Beria, who began his career in the Soviet secret police in Georgia and later became Stalin's secret police chief, published a number of judiciously selected and in some instances carefully doctored Tsarist police records on Stalin's subversive activities as a young underground revolutionary. Although these reports, or the extracts from them as published, indicate that Joseph was under close surveillance from the time he joined the Tiflis Geophysical Observatory, they do not tell the whole story.

Russia had known some form of secret police since the days of the Tsar Ivan the Terrible in the sixteenth century, but it was not until the assassination of Alexander II by revolutionary terrorists in 1881 that the Russian security service, colloquially known as the Okhrana, was established. Under the general supervision of the Ministry of Internal Affairs in St Petersburg, the Okhrana was responsible for all security intelligence, espionage, counter-espionage and secret police operations generally throughout the Russian empire including Finland and Poland. It also had a foreign agency with headquarters in Paris, which directed operations in western Europe, the Balkans, the Near East and North America. This was considered necessary since many of the underground revolutionary organisations functioned from foreign territory. Its hosts of spies were trained to act as *agents provocateurs* and as such to penetrate every known and suspected subversive group at home and abroad. Some of them played a devious game under the guise of underground revolutionaries. The most notorious of these 'double agents' was Yevno Azev, an absconding butter salesman, who went over to the Okhrana and organised a number of important terrorist acts including the assassination of the hated Minister of the Interior V. K. Plehve, while at the same time supplying the secret police with much pertinent information about his revolutionary comrades. The Okhrana would sometimes deliberately cause an agent to be arrested and imprisoned or exiled to Siberia in order to allay possible suspicions on the part of the revolutionaries about whom the agent had been reporting.

Several other former seminary students worked and slept at the observatory. One of these was Vano Ketskhoveli who later recalled: 'We had to keep awake all night and make observations at stated intervals with the help of intricate instruments. The work demanded great nervous concentration.'[30] The inference that Joseph was one of these astronomical observers is not borne out by a contemporary police report which simply describes him as a bookkeeper. But whatever was the precise nature of his work, it gave him enough free time to be able to get away to secret workers' meetings and report back accordingly. According to another observatory employee, Vaso Berdzenishvili, whose room was next to his, Djugashvili used to procure copies of *Iskra*, which Lenin published from Germany, and other illegal literature which he would circulate, 'but where and from whom he got them none of us knew'. Nor would he tell his colleagues in the observatory how he spent his time off duty, although Ketskhoveli and Berdzenishvili must have known that he used to go to various workers' study circles in the evenings. Apparently he was also concerned with a worker named Mikho Bochoridze in setting up an underground printing press in a room in Lotinskaya Street for the production of revolutionary pamphlets. Unknown to Joseph, the money for this project may well have been provided by the secret police, which is not surprising seeing that the Okhrana had previously financed a journal for the earlier revolutionary People's Will group, *Narodnaya Volya*, which had been responsible for the Tsar Alexander II's murder.

Some years previously, May Day – 23 April Old Style in Russia – had been chosen by the International Socialist Congress (The Second International) in Paris as a day of public celebration for trade unions, Socialist parties and labour organisations generally. In Tiflis, in 1900, Joseph took a hand in the *mayevka*, as it was called, the first demonstration of its kind in the Caucasus: the occasion also gave him the opportunity of making his first public speech. About five hundred workers, mostly from the railway shops, some carrying red banners with portraits of Marx and Engels, made their way in small groups to the Salt Lake, about eight miles from the city, where they were also harangued by Vano Sturua, Mikho Bochoridze and others. Among those present were Sergei Alliluyev who has recalled in his memoirs how his future son-in-law and the other speakers spoke of the significance of May Day as a day of international workers' solidarity, about their difficult conditions of work, the humiliations and other ill-treatment meted out to them by their bosses. 'We must fight for our rights,' they proclaimed, 'we must protest, organise strikes, demand better working conditions.'

In his speech Joseph Djugashvili went further when he exhorted his hearers each to collect ten or more comrades for the following year's demonstration which he suggested should be staged within the city. 'Our red flag must be in the centre of Tiflis,' he said, 'so that tyranny shall feel our strength.'[31]

This pronouncement was greeted with loud cheers and shouts of 'Hurrah!', 'Long live the first of May!' and 'Down with autocracy!' The enthusiastic audience does not appear to have realised that a public demonstration in the streets of Tiflis would only be asking for trouble from the police and the military, notably the Cossacks, who would break it up brutally and arrest the ringleaders.

Returning home from the *mayevka*, Alliluyev and his comrades 'felt happy, filled with determination to struggle and conquer'. But this feeling of euphoria was quickly dissipated by the wave of strikes which occurred during the exceptionally hot summer of that year and on the wisdom of which *Messame Dasy* was sharply divided. The majority in the party group, led by Zhordania and Dzhibladze, was opposed to the strikers' demands, particularly for the abolition of overtime, which Alliluyev and the other strike leaders were convinced led to ill-health among the workers, increased unemployment and lower basic wage rates. The biggest strike, when four thousand workers downed tools, took place in August 1900, in the railway yards under the direction of a metal worker named Mikhail Kalinin, the future President of the Soviet Union. After Zhordania and the majority of the *Messame Dasy* had come out as strike breakers, a bitter struggle developed within the group, for which Joseph never forgave Zhordania. When he came to rewrite the history of these times, Beria attempted to show that Joseph had been the principal leader of these strikes.[32] This was not so – Alliluyev, Kalinin and others played a much more prominent part on the shop floor. On the other hand, Joseph was becoming increasingly involved in local industrial disputes at this time, and he did play some part with Kalinin in promoting the big railway workers' strike. A further impetus was given to the strike movement by the arrival in Tiflis of a chemical engineer named Victor Kurnatovsky, who had belonged to the banned *Narodnaya Volya* and had become a staunch Marxist and adherent of Lenin, whose acquaintance he had made when they were both serving terms of exile and whose emissary to the Georgian comrades in fact he now was. That Kurnatovsky met Joseph Djugashvili at this time is certain, although their relationship was not as intimate as Beria subsequently claimed.

During the following winter in Tiflis, when Joseph was sometimes 'on the run' from the *gendarmerie*, Ninua and others gave him food, and provided him with a special hideout in one of the houses in the town. According to the French Communist writer Henri Barbusse, to whom Stalin in his heyday emphasised his conspiratorial talents, the youthful political agitator would suddenly appear at workers' meetings and would sit down without a word and listen until the time came for him to speak. He was always accompanied by two or three comrades, one of whom would keep watch by the door. He never spoke for long, and if he had to make a railway journey he would 'take endless trouble' to see that he was not being followed. One secret meeting which he attended was held in a room beside the wings of a theatre, with the result that 'when the police surrounded the building, they had only to break down a door and mix with the audience with a look of absorbed attention on their faces'. On another occasion, so Barbusse tells us, Joseph walked into a large library in Tiflis, asked for a book by the Russian literary critic Belinsky, which he began to read attentively, all the time watching out of the corner of an eye the movements of one of the library assistants, to whom he handed two false passports, unseen and unrecognised by anyone else. 'They were to secure the escape of two comrades whom the police intended to arrest a little later – a little too late.'[33]

During the night of 21–22 March 1901, the police raided every suspect building in Tiflis in a concerted attempt to smoke out all known or suspected subversive elements. More than fifty individuals were arrested, including Zhordania, Dzhibladze and Kurnatovsky. The observatory and adjacent living quarters of the staff did not escape. On this occasion, Joseph Djugashvili was conveniently and unaccountably absent. However, they found his colleague Berdzenishvili, who later described how they ransacked his room and sealed up a quantity of Marxist literature which they discovered there. According to Berdzenishvili, the police then searched Joseph's room. 'They turned everything upside down, poked into every corner, shook out the bedding – but found nothing. Comrade Stalin would always return a book after reading it and never kept it at home. As to illegal pamphlets, we used to keep them concealed under a pile of rocks on the bank of the river Kura.' Berdzenishvili adds that Joseph was very cautious in this respect, 'as well he might be, since, when his friend Iremashvili had called on him about a year previously he had found his table piled high with seditious material'.[34]

Sometime after the police had gone, Joseph returned to the observatory and told Berdzenishvili that he had in fact come back earlier, but when he realised that a police raid was in progress he had walked the streets until the coast was clear and he judged it safe for him to return. According to Soviet historiographers, he immediately made up his mind that it would be unsafe for him to remain at the observatory. On the day after the search, according to a minute by the Tiflis police chief, in the Georgian Okhrana archives, it was decided to

prosecute the said Joseph Djugashvili and examine [him and the other] accused persons on the evidence of the investigation, conducted by me in pursuance of the State Security Regulations, into the degree of political unreliability of the members of the Social Democratic circle of intellectuals in the city of Tiflis.[35]

38

'This search, and the warrant which he learned had been issued by the secret police for his arrest, induced him to go into hiding,' so we read in his official biography. 'From that moment and right up to the revolution of February 1917, he lived the underground life, full of heroism and unflagging effort, of a professional revolutionary of the Lenin school.'[36]

For the next few weeks Joseph was lost to view and positive evidence of his precise movements is lacking. He certainly reappeared in the Georgian capital for that year's May Day demonstration. It has been stated that he found lodgings in the house of an elderly Georgian woman called Ekaterina Svanidze, who had a pretty, dark, eighteen-year-old niece of the same name living with her. From the first Joseph appears to have been strongly attracted by young Keke. She was to play a significant part in his private life.[37]

5

The action taken by the police in Tiflis on May Day 1901 seems to have been the second stage in a carefully planned operation against the enemies of the Tsarist establishment. The intellectuals had been dealt with as a result of the raids and arrests six weeks before. Now it was the turn of the militant workers, who were 'provoked' to demonstrate at this *mayevka*, which took place, not discreetly beyond the suburbs as in the previous year, but openly in the centre of the town, as Joseph had urged on the earlier occasion. His official biographers state that he organised and led the demonstration. This is not true, although it appears that he did play some part on the sidelines inciting the demonstrators to clash with the police and military. In fact, the demonstration, which had been planned some time in advance, was to have been led by Victor Kurnatovsky, but after his arrest on 21 March, it was arranged that his place at the head of the workers' march should be taken by Vano Sturua.

Sergei Alliluyev, who had recently been released from prison where he had spent some months for his part in the strikes of the previous summer, witnessed what happened in the Tiflis streets that Sunday morning and afterwards described it in his memoirs. The day was warm with a bright sun overhead. Alliluyev walked along the Golovinsky Prospect towards the Vera Park, where he noticed that many people were out like himself taking the air. Among them he recognised workers from the rail depot and Tiflis factories.

Some of the strollers appeared to be reasonably dressed in heavy overcoats and Caucasian sheepskin caps. Among them, dressed in similar fashion, was Vano Sturua.

'What's the matter? Are you sick?' I asked, in astonishment.

Vano lifted his cap and smiled.

'No, I'm fine.'

'Then what's the meaning of this get-up?'

'Soso's orders.'

'Whatever for?'

Vano came up and whispered in my ear.

'You see I'm supposed to head the demonstration with others...
Get it? We'll be the first to receive the blows from the Cossacks'
whips. The coat and cap should soften the blows. You follow?'

'Yes, I follow.'

'Smart, isn't it?'

Alliluyev agreed that it was a sensible plan, since he now saw that the
police were out in strength supported by the Cossacks and other military contingents. Sturua dashed off to lead the workers who were
beginning to march down the street, one worker holding a red banner
aloft. There were shouts from the crowd of 'Long live the first of
May!', 'Down with autocracy!' and 'Long live freedom!' Suddenly
the Cossacks appeared on their horses and broke up the march, 'shov-
ing, pushing and beating up the demonstrators and onlookers'. The
workers thereupon made for the Soldatsky Bazaar, where they had
arranged to meet after the demonstration was over. It was here that the
struggle with the forces of authority began in earnest.

> The police hurled themselves, with drawn sabres, on the man
> holding the banner. But the banner was passed from hand to
> hand. Whenever the police charged, the banner reappeared in a
> different part of the crowd. A bloody riot ensued. Cossack whips
> whistled through the air, sabres flashed: the workers replied
> with sticks and stones. It was a desperate encounter. Many work-
> men were wounded: the police also suffered casualties.[38]

Fourteen leading workers were seriously wounded and over fifty were
arrested that day. The victims did not include Joseph who contrived to
slip away undetected and physically unscathed. When he heard what
had happened, Lenin, who was somewhat out of touch with the reality
of the situation, wrote in *Iskra*: 'The event that took place on Sunday
in Tiflis is of historical importance for the entire Caucasus. That day
marks the beginning of an open revolutionary movement in the Cau-

casus.'[39] In fact, the workers had been worsted by the authorities, and with so many of their leaders in jail or hospital it would be some time before they would be ready to stage another demonstration in the streets of Tiflis.

The imprisoned Kurnatovsky's place as Lenin's personal representative in Georgia was taken by another Russian engineer, whose name was Leonid Borisovich Krassin and who like so many of Lenin's associates was to play a part in the later revolutionary events. It was through Krassin that Lenin appears to have learned of Joseph's organising role in the *mayevka*, giving him considerably more credit than he deserved. After the event Joseph withdrew again to the relative safety of the Gori area, where his old friend Iremashvili, then a schoolmaster, is said to have persuaded a cousin who had a small wine farm in the mountains to afford him temporary refuge. It was in this remote spot that Iremashvili is stated to have taken Krassin to meet Joseph and convey Lenin's congratulations to him. 'Lenin knows that it was you who directed the whole affair. You will meet him one day. But for the moment you must remain here in the Caucasus. You are more useful here than you would be abroad.'[40]

Iremashvili has also recalled that Joseph seemed obsessed with the recent *mayevka* and could talk of little else, apparently deriving some sense of exhilaration from the bloody events of that day. Iremashvili admitted that at first he was put at a loss to understand his friend's attitude. Then, as he put it, 'I realised that the blood that had flowed during the demonstration had intoxicated him.'[41]

By the autumn of that year, Joseph was back in Tiflis and reported to be co-operating with Lado Ketskhoveli in the clandestine production of the Georgian language journal called *Brdzola* (The Struggle), which took a similar political line to *Iskra*. The journal was printed in Baku on a press operated by Ketskhoveli. Soviet historiographers are noticeably silent on how the funds for this operation were provided – certainly the workers' meagre contributions would have been insufficient to defray the purchase of relatively costly plant and equipment. Here again the Okhrana may well have put up the money as part of their general tactics; they had secretly financed similar undertakings in the past and they were to do so in the future. '*Brdzola* insisted on the need for an open revolutionary struggle of the working class,' to quote Yaroslavsky. 'It stood for the hegemony of the proletariat in the coming bourgeois-democratic revolution, and it attacked the opportunist views [in support of collaboration between the workers and the capitalists] as expounded among others by Zhordania...The leading articles in this journal were written by Stalin and Lado Ketskhoveli.'[42]

The first article in which Joseph's hand is clearly recognisable, although it was not signed, appeared towards the end of the year 1901 in the second issue of *Brdzola* under the title, 'The Russian Social-Democratic Party and Its Immediate Tasks.' It amounted to a plea for the extension of what the writer called 'the new street movement,' but it contained some rather curious and sinister sentiments.

Street demonstrations give rise to street agitation, to the lure of which the backward and timid section of the society cannot help succumbing. A man has only to go out into the street during a demonstration to see courageous fighters, to understand what they are fighting for, to hear free voices calling upon everybody to join the struggle, and stirring songs denouncing the existing system and exposing our social evils. That is why the government fears street demonstrations more than anything else. That is why it threatens with dire punishment not only the demonstrators, but also the 'curious onlookers'.

In this curiosity of the people lurks the chief danger that threatens the government. The 'curious onlooker' of today will be a demonstrator tomorrow and rally new groups of 'curious onlookers' around him. And today there are tens of thousands of such 'curious onlookers' in every large town. Russians no longer run into hiding, as they did before, on hearing of disorders taking place somewhere or other. ('I'd better get out of the way in case I get into trouble', they used to say.) Today they flock to the scene of the disorders and evince 'curiosity': they are eager to know why these disorders are taking place, why so many people offer their backs to the lash of the Cossack's whips.

In these circumstances, the 'curious onlookers' cease to listen indifferently to the swish of whips and sabres. The 'curious on-lookers' see that the demonstrators have assembled in the streets to express their wishes and demands, and that the government retaliates by beatings and brutal suppression. The 'curious on-lookers' no longer run away on hearing the swish of whips; on the contrary, they draw nearer, and the whips can no longer distinguish between the 'curious onlookers' and the 'rioters'. Now, conforming to 'complete democratic equality' the whips play on the backs of all, irrespective of sex, age and even class. Thereby the whip lash is rendering us a great service, for it is hastening the revolutionisation of the 'curious onlookers'. It is being transformed from an instrument of taming into an instrument for rousing the people.

Hence, even if street demonstrations do not produce direct results for us, even if the demonstrators are too weak today to compel the government to yield to popular demands, the sacrifice we make in street demonstrations today will be repaid a hundredfold. Every militant who falls in the struggle, or who is torn out of our ranks, rouses hundreds of new fighters. For the time being we shall be beaten more than once in the street. The government will continue to emerge victorious from street fighting again and again. But these will be Pyrrhic victories. A few more victories like these, and the defeat of absolutism is inevitable. The victories it achieves today are preparing its defeat. And we, firmly convinced that that day will come, that that day is not far distant, risk the lash in order to sow the seeds of political agitation and socialism.[43]

Joseph's harping on the swish of whips and sabres, which characterises this article, is early evidence of the sadistic streak which was to reappear from time to time in his recorded sayings. His theory that the whip, so long an instrument of public and private repression, was now being transformed into a desirable instrument for rousing the masses to a sense of their wrongs was an unnecessarily cruel one, since its victims real and potential included the 'curious onlookers', who could be innocent women and children without any political consciousness. The bloodier street demonstrations became the better, according to Joseph's jesuitical line of reasoning which argued that the end justified the means, however cruel. That Joseph himself was on occasion a 'curious onlooker', fascinated by the use to which the Cossacks' whips were being put, is quite clear. It was a striking psychological revelation of the blood lust which was to persist throughout his life.

On 11 November 1901, twenty-five delegates from the various workers' circles met in a small one-storey house in the Tiflis working class suburb of Avlabar to elect the Tiflis Committee of the Russian Social Democratic Labour Party. According to a police report later unearthed by Beria and quite possibly doctored by him, Joseph Djugashvili was voted on to the committee, 'took part in two meetings of this committee and at the end of 1901 was sent to Batum for propaganda work'.[44] Soviet sources inspired by Stalin suggest that he 'headed' the new committee. But this was not so. Sylvester Dzhibladze was elected chairman, and it is extremely doubtful that Joseph was even a member. However, it is beyond dispute that he attended the initial meeting. A reliable early historian of the labour movement in Georgia named S. T.

Arkomed has stated that at this meeting Djugashvili, who had now begun to call himself Koba, spoke out strongly in favour of restricting members of the committee to socialist intellectuals and excluding manual workers on the ground of their lack of conspiratorial training and even their lack of class consciousness. 'Here they flatter the workers,' he is stated to have said, turning to the workers in the room. 'I ask you are there among you even one or two workers fit for the committee? Tell the truth, placing your hand on your heart.' His argument was apparently rejected with some acrimony, and the workers proceeded to choose several of their number to serve on the committee. It is worth noting that Trotsky, writing in exile many years afterwards, accepted Arkomed's account as being quite credible and indicated his appreciation of the young delegate's reasoning. 'Koba was protecting the *apparat* against pressure from below.'[45]

It is likely that Koba wished to run the committee himself and was disappointed when Dzhibladze – older, more experienced but more conservative than himself – was elected chairman. Relations quickly became strained between the two and it appears that Koba began to intrigue against the chairman and his supporters on the committee. 'That good for nothing,' Dzhibladze afterwards complained to Zhordania. 'We appointed him to conduct propaganda against the government and the capitalists, but as it turned out he was conducting propaganda against us.' According to the same source, he was warned to mend his ways but took no notice and was eventually 'brought before a party court of honour and found guilty of unjustly slandering Dzhibladze and was, by a unanimous vote, excluded from the Tiflis Social Democratic organisation'. This decision may not have amounted to expulsion in the formal sense, but it probably afforded a convenient pretext for the transfer of his activities to Batum. He certainly went to Batum with the knowledge of the Tiflis committee, but whether he was expressly sent by this committee 'to form a Social Democratic organisation there', as he was later to claim, is questionable.[46]

This account has been confirmed by the Georgian Social Democratic leader Gregory Uratadze in his recently published reminiscences.

From the beginning, in the workers' circles in which he participated, he intrigued against the party leader – S. Dzhibladze. When this was discovered, the party organisation had him up and reprimanded him with a caution. And when this produced no effect and he continued as before, the organisation brought him before a party court. This was the first party court established by the Georgian Social Democratic organisation to try a comrade in the party. The court was composed of regional representatives.

After questioning him, the court unanimously decided to exclude him from the Tiflis organisation for slander and unprincipled intriguing. When this sentence had been passed, they also excluded him from the running of the workers' circles with which he had been identified. Then he moved from Tiflis to Batum. In Batum they knew about the Tiflis decision.[47]

CHAPTER II

In the Bolshevik Underground

I

With a population of some 35,000, Batum was less than a quarter the size of the Georgian capital, but it was relatively more highly industrialised, with several large oil refineries, two tobacco factories, an iron foundry and a water bottling works, employing about 11,000 workers in all. The oil refineries were fed by a pipeline from Baku which had been laid down the previous year. The working day amounted to fourteen hours with compulsory overtime, which sometimes brought it up to a sixteen- or seventeen-hour day, while the daily wage varied between sixty kopecs and one rouble. Batum was consequently a fertile ground for a political agitator like Koba Djugashvili. He made the journey from Tiflis by rail, bringing with him a bulky printing press which surprisingly did not arouse the suspicions of the railway police.

There were two prominent members of *Messame Dasy* in Batum at this time, Nikolai Chkeidze and Isidor Ramishvili, who were friends of Zhordania and followed the 'legal' Marxist line in their conduct of the local workers' circles. They were opposed to street demonstrations and other forms of 'illegal revolutionary work', which they considered impolitic and unrealistic in the circumstances. The new arrival soon showed that he had little time for the local leaders and their committee. 'Your work is going very slowly,' he told them. 'It must proceed more swiftly.' He appealed to the factory workers to follow the example of their comrades in Tiflis who 'have awakened from their sleep and are preparing for the struggle with their enemies'. On 31 December 1901,

46

shortly after his twenty-second birthday, he established an inner circle of militants, the occasion being a party held in a room in the suburbs which he shared with a worker named Silibistro Lomdzhariya.[1]

Recalling Koba's activities in Batum at this time, Zhordania described him as a boring speaker, who appeared to be reciting a lesson learned by heart and who in order to attract the attention of his listeners often used coarse language. At the same time he admitted his organising ability, though he deplored the manner in which it was employed.

> Going behind the backs of the local leaders, N. Chkeidze and I. Ramishvili, he based himself in the workers' quarter and began to gather workers around himself. Detesting all the progressive comrades, he accused them of cowardice, lack of ability, and treason to the working class and appealed to the workers for demonstrations on the streets. He created inside the organisation a *personal* organisation loyal only to himself and which denied any responsibility to the committee.

Meanwhile Koba was busily turning out revolutionary pamphlets and manifestos on his printing press, which for greater safety as the work increased was moved to a house in the workers' settlement known as *Chaoba* (The Swamp) kept by two brothers named Darakhvelidze. The road to this settlement was so soft and muddy as to be almost impassable, and for this reason apparently the local police left its inhabitants alone. The house, which was a large one, was shared between the two brothers and several others, including an ardent revolutionary named Kotsia Kandelaki. The illegal press was installed in a room without a window, which had an inner and an outer door, the space between these two doors being hung with clothes, which gave it the appearance of a clothes cupboard. The house soon became the headquarters for the factory 'agitators', strike plans were concerted there, and after these meetings Koba would go down to the windowless room and turn out 'proclamations' and leaflets until dawn. In this he was helped by a young consumptive worker called George Teliya, with whom he became very friendly.

In February 1902, Koba helped to promote a strike in the Mantashev oil plant and another strike a few weeks later in the Rothschild plant after the management had dismissed nearly four hundred workers. Alarmed by these stoppages, the provincial military governor arrived from nearby Kutais. According to official Soviet accounts, 'the governor tried to intimidate the workers into calling off the strikes, but all to no purpose'. On the night of 7 March the police arrested thirty workers and put them in Batum jail. Koba led three hundred demonstrators in protest outside the prison, and the result was that all three hundred were arrested apart from Koba, who was left free to spread the word round all the other plants and factories in Batum; in doing so he called for a monster demonstration the following day outside the military barracks where the arrested workers were being held since the jail was already full. About two thousand workers duly assembled, waving red banners and chanting the *Marseillaise*. Koba's voice was heard above the din urging on the demonstrators. 'The soldiers won't shoot us,' he shouted. 'Don't be afraid of the officers. Just go on and hit them right on the head, and our comrades will be freed.' As the workers pressed on, the officer in command of the barracks gave the order to fire. Although many of the troops deliberately fired in the air or above the heads of the crowd, nevertheless in the result fifteen of the demonstrators were killed and fifty-four were wounded. At the same time the police made over five hundred arrests. One of the casualties was a worker named Gerontii Kalandadze, who was wounded in the arm and later taken home by Koba.

According to Yaroslavsky, Koba arranged a 'revolutionary funeral' for the dead workers three days later. He is also said to have written a memorial pamphlet 'filled with revolutionary fire and passion' and widely distributed in Batum and other cities. It certainly shows his characteristic obsession with bloodshed, expressed in a liturgical style reminiscent of the theological seminary.

> All honour to you who have laid down your lives for the truth! All honour to the breasts that suckled you! All honour to those whose brows are adorned with the crowns of martyrs, and who with pale and faltering lips breathed words of struggle in your hour of death! All honour to your shades that hover over us and whisper in our ears, 'Avenge our blood!'

For this bloodshed, which far exceeded the Tiflis *mayevka*, Zhordania put the entire blame on Koba's tactics. 'This cannot be called anything but a provocation,' he said when he heard what had happened.[2]

It now appeared that the police were on the track of the wounded worker Kalandadze and had traced him to the house in *Chaoba*. This prompted another move with the printing press to a neighbouring cemetery, where it was concealed in a barn behind the gravedigger's cottage, as a posse of mounted police and Cossacks galloped past in hot pursuit. Then, with the help of Comrade Lomdzhariya, who knew a reliable Moslem worker named Khashim Smyrba, Koba again moved the printing press, this time to Khashim's house in the Moslem quarter of the town, where we are told that the comrades who did the typesetting used to enter and leave the house disguised as Moslem women heavily veiled. Khashim also helped to distribute the leaflets which came off the press in his house. He would hide them at the bottom of a large basket which he filled with vegetables for sale, using the leaflets in which to wrap the purchases by 'reliable customers'. Khashim survived the Bolshevik Revolution, and in his old age he liked to recall how the neighbours got wind of the clandestine use of the printing press which they thought was for the purpose of making counterfeit money. According to Khashim, Koba told them that he wished to help the impoverished peasants but not with roubles. He explained that he was engaged in printing leaflets 'to hasten the overthrow of the Tsar, to return power to the people, who could then improve their lot by their own labour'. Khashim's Moslem neighbours were sympathetic. 'And now each of us will be a good helper to you,' said one of them. 'Until today only Khashim has protected you, for which we are thankful, but now all of us will protect you and your work.'

Nevertheless, Koba may have thought that the secret of the printing press was known to too many in the neighbourhood, and he suggested another move. But Khashim would not hear of it.

'You're a good man, Soso,' Khashim told Koba. 'I'm only sorry you are not a Moslem.'

'But what would happen were I to become a Moslem?'

'Then I would get you a wife, a beauty the likes of whom you have never seen. Now, do you want to be a Moslem?'

Koba smilingly agreed. 'That's a great idea,' he said, and they shook hands on it.[3]

The illegal printing operations at Khashim's only lasted a few weeks and were abruptly terminated as a result of Koba's unexpected arrest. On the evening of 5 April 1902, the Darakhvelidze brothers gave a small workers' party at their house, to which Koba came. After a while someone noticed that the place was surrounded with what appeared to be secret police in plain clothes and he alerted the others. 'It's nothing,' said Koba, puffing away at a cigarette, apparently unconcerned. A few minutes later, the sound of heavy feet was heard on the stairs, the police burst into the room and arrested everyone present. Thus for the first and by no means the last time in his revolutionary career, Koba found himself occupying a prison cell.[4]

'He was lucky to be arrested,' remarked Zhordania afterwards. 'This partly retrieved his prestige with the Batum workers and saved him from being condemned as an *agent provocateur*.' But many of the comrades in Batum never forgave him for the bloodshed for which, like Noi Zhordania, they regarded him as mainly responsible.[5]

2

Official reports on all those arrested in Batum in April 1902 were duly filed at police headquarters and signed by the local police chief Colonel Sergei Petrovich Shabelsky. Koba's was as follows:

> *Joseph Vissarionovich Djugashvili*
> Height: About 5 feet 4 inches.
> Body: Medium.
> Age: 23 [Actually 22]
> Special features: Second and third toes on the left foot joined.
> Appearance: Ordinary.
> Hair: Dark brown.
> Beard and moustache: Brown.
> Nose: Straight and long.
> Forehead: Straight and low.
> Face: Long, swarthy and pockmarked.

Of the prisoner's physical features, the most readily distinguishable were the signs of smallpox. Indeed the Batum police used to refer familiarly to him as *Riaboi* (the pockmarked one). What is particularly remarkable about the report is that it contains no reference to his shortened left arm, which would single Koba out more than his pockmarked face which was a much more common feature in those days than having one arm considerably shorter than the other.[6]

A few weeks after his arrest, it appears that Koba threw two notes through the bars of his cell window on to the courtyard where he hoped that they would be picked up by a friendly visitor to the prison. One was addressed to his boyhood friend Joseph Iremashvili, then a schoolteacher in Gori, asking him to tell his mother of his arrest and to impress upon her that, should she be asked by the police when he had left Gori, she was to say that he had been there throughout the previous summer and winter and had not left until the middle of March. The other note was addressed to G. I. Elisabedashvili, a Tiflis teacher and former classmate at the seminary, who had hitherto escaped arrest, urging him to persevere with his underground work in spite of what had happened at Batum.

The notes were picked up by prison guards and turned over to a police officer Captain George Davidovich Dzhakeli, who gave orders for Iremashvili's lodging to be searched and for Elisabedashvili to be arrested. In describing the incident in his book on Stalin, Trotsky expressed amazement at what he called the carelessness with which Koba had subjected two of his comrades to danger, considering it to be a typical act of 'revolutionary conspiracy' designed to deceive the gendarmes. Its net result was that it led to the arrest of Elisabedashvili and also to the interrogation of Iremashvili and Koba's mother. The two latter were able to provide a good 'cover' story for use in the trial of the Batum demonstrators to the effect that Koba was in Gori during the labour troubles in Batum. This may well explain why Koba was never brought to trial but like other comrades who were arrested at this time was dealt with by 'administrative action'.[7]

On this occasion Koba spent eighteen months in prison, which was the average period of confinement in those days for a political prisoner while his case was under investigation and, what usually followed if he escaped the gallows, banishment to Siberia or the Arctic Circle. Left-wing politicals in custody habitually refused to co-operate with the investigating officers, beyond admitting that they were dedicated members of the Russian Social Democratic Labour Party. During the long drawn out investigations, the accused were sometimes knocked about and beaten in an attempt to secure 'confessions', particularly in some of the provincial prisons, though on nothing like the scale that was to be resorted to thirty years later in Stalin's prisons and labour camps. It is significant that none of the depositions taken from him in the course of the investigation was ever published by the Soviet authorities when they opened the Tsarist archives after the Revolution, an omission which was later to form the subject of adverse comment by Trotsky. Having 'attempted to establish his alibi by a ruse for which others were obliged to suffer', Trotsky surmised, 'it may be supposed that on other occasions as well he relied more on his own cunning than on the standard behaviour obligatory to all. Consequently the entire series of police depositions present, we should think, not a very attractive – at any rate, not a "heroic" record. That is the only possible explanation why the records of Stalin's police examinations are still unpublished.'[8] On this point it remains only to add that Trotsky was writing from exile, and thirty yeas later the records have not appeared in print. Nor are they ever likely to be, having in all probability been long since destroyed by Beria acting on Stalin's orders.

Koba was exercising in the prison yard when Elisabedashvili was brought in under escort by Captain Dzhakeili. According to this prisoner, Koba whispered to him as they passed, 'You don't know me!' Thus, when the prisoner was later interrogated by Dzhakeli and asked if he knew Koba, if he had been in Batum and if he could identify any of the Marxists there, he loyally answered '*Nyet*' to every question. When his interrogator questioned him as to why such Marxists as Chkeidze and Ramishvili had been so quiet before Joseph Djugashvili's appearance on the scene, which was followed by the strikes and demonstrations, he answered that he did not know.[9]

After a year in Batum, Koba was transferred to the prison in Kutais, the principal town in western Georgia and capital of ancient Colchis. Tsarist prisons, particularly in the provinces, reflected a curious mixture of paternalism and barbarism in those days. At times relations between the prisoners and their jailers were friendly and familiar, but these were liable to be broken at any time by violent disturbances when the inmates would bang their boots against the doors of their cells, shout, whistle, and break up the furniture and feeding utensils. At least one demonstration which occurred at Kutais was inspired by Koba, notwithstanding that Gregory Uratadze, then a fellow prisoner, has described him at this time as insignificant looking. 'His face was pitted with smallpox which did not give him a particularly clean appearance,' wrote Uratadze, who considered his appearance then very different from his later well-known portraits executed when he was the Soviet dictator. 'In prison he had a beard, his long hair being brushed back. His gait was smooth – short steps. He never laughed with an open mouth, but only smiled. And the measure of his smile depended upon the measure of his emotion.' Uratadze added that during the six months they were together in Kutais prison, he never once saw Koba angry or shout or argue vehemently or in a word conduct himself other than in a completely calm and self-possessed manner. 'And his voice corresponded exactly with his frigid character.'[10]

During his imprisonment news reached Koba through the prison grapevine of two significant happenings in the outside world. They both occurred in August 1903, when he was in Kutais. The first was the shooting of Lado Ketskhoveli in the Metekh fortress prison in Tiflis. Sergei Alliluyev, who witnessed what happened, has described in his memoirs how Lado stood at his cell window and began calling to a group of Armenian shepherds who had appeared on the opposite bank of the river Kura. One of the prison guards, who spotted him, raised his rifle and took aim, apparently on the instructions of the superior officer. Sergei and several other prisoners shouted to Lado to get away from the window. But he took no notice and stayed where he was. Suddenly a shot rang out and the figure at the window fell back, killed with a bullet through his heart. 'Thus perished one of our best revolutionary comrades,' wrote Alliluyev, 'a glorious son of the Georgian people, one of Soso's closest friends and companions in arms.'[11] Many years afterwards Stalin described Lado Ketskhoveli as the finest, most gifted and energetic revolutionary he had ever known.[12]

The other incident, which occurred later the same month, was the split which took place at the Second Congress of the Russian Social Democratic Labour Party in London into two opposing factions, henceforward known as Bolsheviks and Mensheviks. The former took their name from the 'majority' which supported Lenin at the end of the Congress, after a number of delegates had left, although in fact Lenin only carried the day by a single vote. Lenin's object was avowedly militant, but the proletarian revolution he desired was to be controlled in practice by an intellectual *élite*. 'A dictatorship *over* the proletariat' was how Trotsky described it. On the other hand, the 'minority', the Mensheviks, who counted Trotsky among their adherents as well as Zhordania and Dzhibladze in Georgia, wanted a 'dictatorship *of* the proletariat', for which they were prepared to collaborate with the bourgeois Liberals within the framework of a democratic constitution. In fact they constituted the majority of the Party delegates, if the absentees are taken into account. Somewhat surprisingly the veteran Marxist George Plekhanov, so-called 'father of Russian Social Democracy', sided with the Bolsheviks, though afterwards he changed his mind and joined the Mensheviks, whose leader he quickly became. Many years later Stalin's official apologists were to assert that he was a Bolshevik from the beginning, while Trotsky has stated, following an inaccurate police report, that he was originally a Menshevik. Actually there is no convincing evidence to suggest that Koba was ever a Menshevik or that he declared himself a Bolshevik immediately after the split. It is more likely that he took some time to make up his mind which group to join, and that he did not come out into the open as a Bolshevik agitator until the following year.[13]

On 17 August 1903 – by a coincidence, the same day as Lado Ketskhovili was killed – the Minister of Justice in St Petersburg signed an administrative order directing the prisoner Joseph Djugashvili to be deported to eastern Siberia, there to remain for three years 'under open police surveillance'. Unlike a score of others who were tried for their part in the Batum strikes and demonstrations of the previous year, Koba was never publicly put on trial, no doubt for lack of evidence. He appears to have been brought back to Batum jail whence he set out sometime in October for a small settlement called Novaya Uda, three hundred miles north of Lake Baikal in Irkutsk province, and altogether some four thousand miles distant from Georgia.*

It is stated in official Soviet publications that Koba was transferred from Kutais back to Batum in the autumn of 1903 and was then de-

* Now in the Buriat Mongol Republic of the Soviet Union.

ported under escort to eastern Siberia, arriving at his destination on 27 November. It is further stated that he escaped from his place of exile on 5 January 1904, and a month later reappeared in Tiflis 'where he assumed the leadership of the Bolshevik organisations of Transcaucasia'.[15]

Doubts have been cast upon this account in view of the fact that the transport of exiles was usually accomplished 'by stages', that is with stops along the route to allow for the collection of more deportees and that this could take anything up to three months, particularly in the severe climatic conditions of the winter of 1903–1904 when the trains on the Trans-Siberian Railway were frequently unable to average more than fifteen miles an hour. If in fact he travelled at all, Koba would have proceeded northward from Batum by rail via Sochi, Rostov, Tsaritsyn (later to be renamed Stalingrad), to Samara, where he would have changed trains and have continued his journey along the Trans-Siberian line through Chelyabinsk, Omsk, Novo-Nikolaevsk (later Novo-Sibirsk) and Krassnoyarsk, to where Lenin had spent part of his Siberian exile, the small town of Nizhne Udinsk on the river Uda in the Irkutsk province. From there he would have gone on by sleigh to his ultimate destination, a wretched hamlet of some 150 souls some way to the north. It has been argued that if he was treated as an ordinary prisoner he could not possibly have accomplished the journey in the time and indeed could not even have reached Novaya Uda by the date on which he is officially stated to have escaped.[16]

But Koba was not an ordinary prisoner. He was a prisoner in a special category, and it is likely that he travelled not in the usual convoy, but with a special two-man police escort by the normal train service and with a minimum of stops. Assuming that he left Batum on 24 October, which he is stated to have done, there is no reason why he should not have completed the whole journey within five weeks.

Less plausible is Stalin's story, later widely publicised by him, that while at Novaya Uda he received a letter from Lenin, about whom he had written to 'a close friend of mine who was living as a political exile'. Over twenty years later, when in the course of an address at the memorial meeting of the Kremlin Military Academy shortly after Lenin's death, Stalin said:

When I was already in exile in Siberia – this was at the end of 1903 – I received an enthusiastic letter from my friend and a simple but profoundly expressive letter from Lenin to whom, it appeared, my friend had shown my letter. Lenin's note was comparatively short, but it contained a bold and fearless criticism of the practical work of our Party, and a remarkably clear and concise account of the entire plan of work of the Party in the immediate future...

This simple and bold letter strengthened my opinion that Lenin was the mountain eagle of our Party. I cannot forgive myself for having, from the habit of an old underground worker, consigned this letter, like many other letters, to the flames. My acquaintance with Lenin dates from that time.[17]

Lenin had been living in Switzerland since the dramatic split at the Second Party Congress and it seems hardly likely that he could have written such a letter, even if he had known that Koba had been exiled to Novaya Uda, since such particulars were never publicly announced by the authorities. Furthermore, all Lenin's correspondence was being regularly intercepted, read and copied by the Tsarist censorship, and there is no trace of any such letter in the Okhrana archives. Everything in this tale evokes perplexity, as Trotsky was to remark – everything except its purpose. It seems probable that in this context Stalin rewrote a piece of history to emphasise his early relationship with the Bolshevik leader. This piece of historical rewriting was supplemented in the heyday of Stalin's dictatorial power by the Soviet artist Mariasch, who painted a picture of a transfigured Koba sitting at a rough wooden table in his log cabin at Novoya Uda and reading Lenin's letter. But that is not to say that the story of his exile and escape from Siberia is also a fabrication. On the contrary, it has been confirmed by a police report that 'Djugashvili escaped from his place of settlement in the Balagansk district of Irkutsk province on 5 January 1904 and was on the wanted list'. Although the question of Koba's exile is beset with difficulty, there is some credible evidence that he did reach Novaya Uda and spent thirty-nine days there before making good his escape.[18]

The small population of Novaya Uda included fifteen other political deportees. The police surveillance under which they were supposed to reside consisted of a corporal of the *gendarmerie* (*ouriadnik*), and shortly after Koba's arrival we are told in an unconfirmed report that a police lieutenant arrived from the district headquarters at Balangansk and warned his subordinate that the 'pockmarked one' was to be closely watched and any suspicious actions on his part which pointed to an escape plan were to be immediately reported to Balagansk.[19] That Koba was able to make two such attempts, of which the second succeeded, was due to the *ouriadnik* becoming conveniently drunk. The first time, Koba was forced to retrace his steps owing to the intense cold – the temperature sometimes fell to fifty degrees below zero Fahrenheit in those parts – and to being attacked by wolves which he was able to drive off with the aid of a sporting gun which he had been lent by the local grocer. According to another account, he was caught in a blizzard and a kindly peasant gave him shelter in his hut where he thawed out and slept for eighteen consecutive hours. His ears were frost-bitten, but the experience, so he afterwards told Henri Barbusse, cured him of any lingering traces of tuberculosis in his system. ('Siberia is like that: if it doesn't kill consumptives, it cures them permanently.')[20]

On the second occasion, the exile succeeded in making his way by sleigh to Irkutsk where he had been given the name of a Party sympathiser named Kolotov who could help him. The obliging Kolotov supplied him with a passport made out in the name of Kaios Vissarion Nizheradze, a Georgian carpet dealer who had died two years before. Armed with these false papers, Koba boarded a westbound train at Irkutsk. A week later he was in Samara; another week brought him to Batum, where he is said to have found refuge in the house of a certain Natalia Kirtadze.

According to this lady's account, she was woken up one night after midnight by a knock on her door.

'Who's there?' she called out.

'It's me, let me in!'

'Who are you?'

'It's me, Soso.'

But Natalia refused to open up until her visitor had given her the local comrades' password: 'Long live a thousand times!' This he did and she let him in.

She then asked him how he came to be in Batum.

'I escaped,' he replied simply.

From Batum, Koba (as he was now generally known to his party comrades) went straight to Tiflis. 'That fact cannot help but evoke argument,' commented Trotsky when he came to deal with this episode in his unfinished biography of Stalin. 'Fugitives who were in the least conspicuous seldom returned to their native haunts, where they could be easily observed by the ever-vigilant police, especially when that place was not Petersburg or Moscow but a small provincial city like Tiflis...It is hardly possible that a fugitive from Siberia could have shown himself in workers' circles in Tiflis, where many knew him.' In fact, Koba did show himself there but not for long. He soon learned through the revolutionary underground that his name was on the police wanted list and that a warrant had been issued for his re-arrest, all security authorities throughout the Tsarist empire having been alerted to 'detain him and telegraph Police Headquarters in St Petersburg for further instructions'.[21]

МИНИСТЕРСТВО
ВНУТРЕННИХЪ ДѢЛЪ

ДЕПАРТАМЕНТЪ
ПОЛИЦIИ

По Особому Отдѣлу.

1 Маi 1904 г.
№ 5500.

Секретно.
Циркулярно.

**Господамъ Губернаторамъ, Градона-
чальникамъ, Оберъ-Полицiймейстерамъ,
Начальникамъ Жандармскихъ Губерн-
скихъ и желѣзнодорожныхъ Полицей-
скихъ Управленiй, Начальникамъ
Охранныхъ Отдѣленiй и на всѣ погранич-
ные пункты.**

Джугашвили, Iосифъ Виссарiоновъ, крестьянинъ села
Диди-Лило, Тифлисскаго уѣзда и губ., родился въ 1881 г.,
вѣроисповѣданiя православнаго, обучался въ Горiйскомъ
Духовномъ училищѣ и въ Тифлисской Духовной Семинарiй,
холостъ; отецъ Виссарiонъ, мѣстожительство не извѣстно,
Мать Екатерина проживаетъ въ г. Гори, Тифлисской губер-
нiи.

На основанiи ВЫСОЧАЙШАГО повелѣнiя, послѣдовав-
шаго въ 9 день Iюля 1903 г., за государственное преступленiе
высланъ въ Восточную Сибирь подъ гласный надзоръ полицiи на три года и былъ водворенъ въ Балаганскомъ уѣздѣ,
Иркутской губ., откуда скрылся 5 Января 1904 года.

Примѣты: роста 2 арш. 4½ верш., тѣлосложенiя посред-
ственнаго, производитъ впечатлѣнiе обыкновеннаго человѣка,
волосы на головѣ темнокаштановые, на усахъ и бородѣ каш-
тановые, видъ волосъ прямой, безъ пробора, глаза темно-
карiе, средней величины, складъ головы обыкновенный,
лобъ прямой, невысокiй, носъ прямой, длинный, лицо длин-
ное, смуглое, покрытое рябинками отъ оспы, на правой сто-
ронѣ нижней челюсти отсутствуетъ переднiй коренной зубъ,
ростъ умѣренный, подбородокъ острый, голосъ тихiй, уши
средней величины, походка обыкновенная, на лѣвомъ ухѣ
родинка, на лѣвой ногѣ 2-й и 3-й пальцы сросшiеся.

Задержать и телеграфировать Департаменту Полицiи для
полученiя дальнѣйшихъ указанiй.

'Detain and telegraph Police Department for further instructions'.
Secret police circular describing Joseph Vissarionovich Djugashvili and authorising his
arrest after his first escape from Siberia in 1904. Place of origin and year of birth are incorrectly given as Didi-Lilo, 1881. 'Distinguishing features. . .average build, gives the
impression of an ordinary man. . .dark-skinned, covered with pock-marks from smallpox. . .second and third toes of left foot joined together.'[22]

3

One worker whose apartment the fugitive is definitely known to have visited at this time was Mikho Bochoridze, with whom it will be remembered that he worked four years previously in the setting up of an underground printing press in Tiflis. Sergei Alliluyev has related how he came up from Baku to collect a similar press which had been hidden in Bocharidze's apartment, how he met Koba there, and how interested Koba appeared in their conversation. Koba asked Sergei what kind of press it was and how the parts had been packed. Sergei replied that they had packed the cylinder or drum in a soft wicker basket and covered it with provisions.

'A splendid idea,' said Koba. 'But how are you going to get it to Baku?'

Sergei told him that he and a friend were going to take it between them and would sit in the same carriage on the train.

'That won't do,' said Koba. 'One of you should take the drum, and the other the rest of the parts. Sit in separate carriages and don't contact each other.'

When this was agreed, Koba added: 'As for the type face, we'll send that along by the safe hand of another comrade a little later.'[23]

Since the previous summer the illegal printing of revolutionary pamphlets and other literature in Tiflis had been carried on from a secret cellar underneath a house in the Avlabar district on the outskirts of the city. Stalin's official apologists such as Yaroslavsky have claimed that the Avlabar press was set up expressly on his instructions and that 'its excellent organisation singled it out from all the known illegal printing presses'. In fact it was set up by Mikho Bochoridze in conjunction with Sergei Alliluyev and his assistant Gigi Lelashvili, who had also been concerned with the original venture in Lotinskaya Street. The Avlabar press was the best run and longest lived of all the illegal presses in Transcaucasia; and, although it seems unlikely that Koba had anything to do with its initiation, since he was in prison at the time, he soon became aware of its existence and after his release he was responsible for a number of leaflets which came off this remarkable underground press. These were for the most part appeals to the workers exhorting them to militant action and carried such titles as 'Workers of the Caucasus! It is Time for Revenge!', 'Brother Soldiers!', 'To the Reservists', and 'Down with the War!', all inspired by the hostilities which had broken out between Russia and Japan when the Japanese launched a surprise attack upon Russian warships at Port Arthur on the night of 8 February 1904.[24]

The personal and private life of an underground revolutionary in Russia was almost invariably kept in the shadows. It was usually identified with a common concept of revolution. On this aspect of revolutionary life Trotsky is a pertinent witness. According to his experience, the same struggle, the same danger, a common isolation from the rest of the world, all these welded strong bonds between the sexes. Couples came together in the underground, were parted by prison, and again sought each other out in exile. Such, too, was the experience of Koba and Keke Svanidze. They had first met about the time of the Tiflis *mayevka* three years before and had managed somehow to keep in touch while Koba was in jail. That Koba lost no time in seeing her on his return to Tiflis is certain, since they were married a few months later. It is possible that they began by living 'in sin', since the story goes that young Keke, who was a religious girl, complained to Koba's mother that her lover showed no inclination to take her to church and that it was the elder Keke who made her son go through with the religious ceremony. She liked the quiet, pretty girl of Koba's choice, and it was at her insistence that the ceremony was performed by a priest in the church at Gori on 22 June 1904. Besides Koba's mother, it was attended by various members of young Keke's family who came from the neighbouring village of Didi-Lilo as also had the bridegroom's cobbler father. According to Svetlana Alliluyeva, Stalin's daughter by his second marriage, Granny Keke was not the only one to 'arrange' her son's first marriage. It was also promoted by the bride's brother Alexander Svanidze, one of the few Georgian Bolsheviks at this period, since weddings, as well as other family festivities, were always taken advantage of by the political underground for its meetings. A few days after the wedding, Koba departed on a secret mission to the workers in the Baku oilfields leaving his young bride in Gori with his mother.[25]

Official Soviet publications are completely silent on the subject of this union, from which one son was to be born and ultimately disowned by his father. The most compelling evidence of the marriage is provided by Joseph Iremashvili, the Gori schoolmaster and friend of Koba's since childhood.

His marriage, according to his lights was a happy one, [wrote this witness, who had an opportunity of observing it at close quarters]. True, it was impossible to discover in his home the equality of the sexes which he himself advocated as the basic form of marriage in the new state. It was not in his character, however, for him to share equal rights with anyone. Because his wife could not measure up to him, regarding him as a demi-god, his marriage was happy. As a Georgian woman, brought up in the sacrosanct tradition which obliges the woman to serve, she looked after her husband's welfare with all her heart, spending her nights in fervent prayer while waiting for her Soso, who was busy at this meetings, praying that he might turn away from ideas that were displeasing to God and revert to a quiet home life of labour and contentment. So this restless man alone found love in his own impoverished home where only his wife, child and mother were free from the scorn he poured out upon everyone else.

Strictly speaking, the targets of Koba's scorn from this time onwards were the Mensheviks who were later to include Iremashvili in their ranks, a fact which was to lead to a permanent estrangement between the two men.[26]

The precise location of Koba's 'impoverished home' has not been established; but, since a police report refers to him as being based on the Tiflis area at this time, it seems safe to assume that it was in the neighbourhood of the Georgian capital, although he would appear to have moved about the country fairly often in connection with his work. Official Soviet publications confirm that in the month of his marriage he was in Baku where he formed a Bolshevik committee in opposition to the local Mensheviks. He was later to return to Baku, where Sergei Alliluyev visited him and noted that he and his wife were living in a small one-storey house.[27]

Later in the summer he visited other centres in Transcaucasia, engaging in debates with the Mensheviks and other groups; he also apparently formed a similar committee in Kutais. From the latter town he wrote in September to an unnamed party comrade:

> What we need here now is *Iskra*. Although it has no sparks, we need it: at all events it contains news, the devil take it and we must know the enemy thoroughly...We need everything new that's published, from simple declarations to large pamphlets, which in any way deal with the struggle now going on within the Party...
>
> There was a comrade here from your parts who took with him the resolutions of the Caucasian committees in favour of calling a special congress of the Party.
>
> You are wrong in thinking that the situation is hopeless. Only

the Kutais Committee wavered, but I succeeded in convincing them, and after that they began to swear by Bolshevism. It was not difficult to convince them: the two-faced policy of the Central Committee became obvious thanks to the Declaration, and after fresh news was received, there could be no further doubt about it. It [the Central Committee] will break its neck; the local and Russian comrades will see to that. It has got everybody's back up.[28]

By this time *Iskra* had fallen completely under Menshevik influence and Lenin was on the point of resigning from the editorial board in order to found another journal called *Vpered* (Forward), which was designed as a Bolshevik organ. In Georgia *Iskra* was taken over for the Mensheviks by Krassin, who applauded Lenin's resignation from the Party's Central Committee at this time, since he disliked his dictatorial methods. But Lenin quickly fought back. 'We have no party,' he wrote at this time, 'but we have a new party coming into being, and no subterfuges and delays, no senile malicious vituperation from *Iskra* can hold back the final and decisive victory of this party.'[29] The new party was to become the Bolshevik Party and the declaration referred to in Koba's letter was an appeal to the whole of the Social Democratic Party which went out from twenty-two Bolsheviks in Geneva, headed by Lenin, with the object of summoning another Party Congress. Afterwards Stalin's official apologists were to exaggerate the part he played during this period, but there seems no doubt that he did encourage the local committees to press for such a 'special congress' which would be predominantly Bolshevik in character. He also claimed to have participated in the editing of the illegal Georgian language newspaper *The Proletarian Struggle*, and he certainly contributed to the journal. In his first article entitled 'The Social Democratic View of the National Question' he pleaded for a united proletariat among the different nationalities in Transcaucasia and opposed what he described as 'bourgeois prattle about an independent Georgia' to be protected by a tariff wall and by means of 'patriotic' tricks of this sort to achieve a capitalist success. 'As we know, the goal of every struggle is victory,' he wrote in this article. 'But if the proletariat is to achieve victory, *all* the workers, *irrespective of nationality*, must be united. Clearly the demolition of national barriers and close unity between the Russian, Georgian, Armenian, Polish, Jewish and other proletarians is a necessary condition for the victory of the proletariat of all Russia.'[30]

At this time some of the Georgian Social Democratic Committees urged the peasants not to sow any corn for the landowners. Many peasants observed the boycott, but some disregarded it and sowed the fields by secret agreement with the landowners. In July 1904, rumours circulated to the effect that someone had come at night to the village of Nagomari in Guriya province near Batum and cut all the corn. There was a search for the culprit, but the local Party committee tried to hush up the affair and persuade the peasants who had sown the corn not to bring the matter to the notice of the authorities. A few days later the story went round that two strangers had arrived in the neighbourhood and were staying in the house of Feodor Kalandanze, possibly a relative of the Kalandanze who was wounded in the Batum demonstration and taken home by Koba. One of the strangers turned out in fact to be Koba, and when questioned by the local Party members as to whether he could throw any light on the corn-cutting incident, he answered quite candidly that he was responsible for it, and that he would do it again.

'You want to make a revolution on the cheap,' Koba went on. 'You encourage the masses to stage a coup without an armed rising. That is no use. We must force the authorities to impose repressive measures. The worse they are, the better for us! Your tactics are not revolutionary. You are preventing the real revolutionaries from making a revolution!'

A few weeks later, a Menshevik named Leontii Zhgenti happened to be sitting in the municipal park in Kutais with Chola Lomtatidze, later a Social Democratic deputy in the Russian Parliament (the Duma), and two other Party comrades, when a young man approached them, smiling through his black beard. 'Well, if it isn't Comrade Koba!' said Lomtatidze. They all adjourned to a restaurant in the town called 'The Bear', a safe place to talk in since the manager and staff were all Social Democratic sympathisers. Zhgenti later recalled how a waiter immediately brought two bottles of wine and a plate of *hors d'oeuvres* to the table without their asking for them. They had hardly begun when Koba began talking about how the revolutionary intelligentsia ought to lead the masses, who 'without the help of the intelligentsia would not be able to achieve liberation and the establishment of the rule of the proletariat'. He then pulled a copy of *Iskra* out of his pocket, which he appeared to have got from abroad. But no sooner had he done this than he folded it up again and replaced it in his pocket, a gesture which intrigued the others considerably. Koba then said that he was in a hurry and could not read them any quotations from the newspaper.

'Is that really the only difference between Bolshevism and Menshevism – the role of the intelligentsia in organising revolution?' asked

Shvelidze, another Menshevik who was present. 'After all if local cells are not set up in the villages, formed from the more class-conscious elements of the population, how is it possible to move the masses to revolution?'

Koba smiled. 'The peasants on their own are reactionary, or at best conservative, now they have gained a little material improvement in their lot,' he argued. 'Therefore we should not help them to consolidate their private property. As for the working classes, all they can do, through their trade union organisations, is to get wages increased. That is all. They are hardly capable of thinking in terms of revolution without the outside influence of the revolutionary intelligentsia, who alone are able to understand and grasp the idea of revolution and spread it through the written and spoken word.'

'Ah,' exclaimed Zhgenti, who had to admit that Koba put his case convincingly. 'That is why you cut down the corn in Nagomari!'

This remark caused a general laugh. Koba, who appeared to take it in good part, immediately got up from the table, grinning broadly. 'I'm in a hurry, comrades, goodbye!' he said. And with that he left them.[31]

A conference of local Bolsheviks was convened at Tiflis in November 1904, but Koba's name does not appear as a delegate. In the chair was the brilliant Caucasian Jew Lev Borisovich Kamenev, whose real surname was Rosenfeld and who was later to marry Trotsky's sister Olga. A Muscovite by birth, he had come as a youth to Tiflis where his father had a job on the railway. Later he had met Lenin abroad and had been dispatched by him to organise the Caucasian Bolsheviks; although he was four years younger than Koba, he seems to have played the major role in Georgia at this period. That Koba did not attend the conference, which was to pave the way for the Third Party Congress, may have been due to the fact, as Trotsky surmised, that he did not formally declare himself a Bolshevik until some weeks later. However, there was no doubt where he stood by the beginning of 1905 when he returned to Batum and met Razden Arsenidze, a member of the local committee, who described him as 'a completely definite, orthodox, devoted Leninist, repeating arguments and ideas of his teacher with the precision of a gramophone'. To Arsenidze, Koba appeared lean and bony, his face marked by a brownish pallor, pitted with smallpox, his eyes lively and crafty, and his whole manner exuding an air of self confidence. 'More than once I asked myself the question, what kind of a revolutionary is this?' wrote this witness afterwards. 'A revolutionary, whose entire soul is devoted to the affairs of the people, or a dry, heartless, soulless mechanism in the form of a man whose aim is simply to destroy something completely and put something else in its place?'[32]

What he hoped to destroy, it must be admitted, was hardly worth preserving, at any rate in its current form. It was well described by Cecil Spring-Rice, first secretary and *chargé d'affaires* at the British Embassy in St Petersburg at this time.

> It is a curious state of things. There is the Emperor, a religious madman almost – without a statesman, or even a council – surrounded by a legion of Grand Dukes – thirty-five of them and not one of them at the war at this moment, with a few priests and priestly women behind them. No middle class; and aristocracy ruined and absolutely without influence, an underpaid bureaucracy living, of necessity, on corruption. Beneath this, about a hundred million of people absolutely devoted to their Emperor, absolutely ignorant, kept ignorant for fear of the consequences of knowledge (by an elaborate conspiracy between Church and State), gradually becoming poorer and poorer as they bear all the burden of taxation, drafted into the army in thousands...
>
> This army, devoted, brave, enduring, religious, will do everything which their Tsar tells them, Poles keep Caucasians down, Caucasians garrison Poland; both fight side by side for Russia in the Far East or Central Asia for the glory of the Tsar...There never was, I am sure, since this world began such a tremendous engine in one man's hand; not in Napoleon's – because his army depended on his success, but the Russian army is faithful to the Tsar, successful or unsuccessful. And the Tsar's two objects are to suppress the heathen and to suppress the Liberal, and he is convinced that the Lord is with him. How long will it last? Of course, the system has the obvious objection that the peasants will ultimately find out how they are being treated – in one way, by actual starvation. But short of that nothing seems to affect them very much.
>
> It is certainly a wonderful country. It is the paradise of snobs and the Emperor is, I suppose, the snob's ideal. I don't think I should care to be his subject...[33]

The year 1905 in Russia was in effect a dress rehearsal for the grand revolutionary performance which was to sweep away the Tsarist monarchy a dozen years later. It opened with a workers' demonstration outside the Winter Palace in St Petersburg on 9 January – 'Bloody

Sunday' – led by the Orthodox priest Father Gapon, when hundreds of demonstrators carrying icons and pictures of the Tsar in orderly procession were fired on by the troops on refusing to disperse. Hundreds lay wounded or dead in the snow. ('A grim day!' the Tsar recorded in his diary.) The year ended with the grant of a constitutional government and the convocation of a legislative assembly, known as the Duma. The intervening months were marked by numerous strikes culminating in a general strike, mutinies in the armed forces, the seizure of landed estates by the peasants, armed uprisings and general unrest through the country. Koba's part in this widespread revolutionary movement appears to have been largely confined to agitation and propaganda, particularly in denouncing the Tiflis Mensheviks. He did this with considerable bitterness in a pamphlet published in May under the title 'Briefly about the Disagreements in the Party' which attracted the favourable attention of Lenin and his wife Krupskaya.

Two trends had appeared in the Social Democratic Party, he wrote, and were personified in the recent Party split – 'the trend of proletarian firmness', represented by the Bolshevik 'majority', and 'the trend of intellectual wavering' represented by the Menshevik 'minority'. Then, asked the 'tiresome Mensheviks', why were the workers on their side in some towns? Koba supplied a ready answer.

Yes, it is true in some towns the workers are on the side of the 'minority', but that proves nothing. Workers even follow the revisionists (the opportunists in Germany) in some towns, but that does not prove that their stand is a proletarian one. It does not prove that they are not opportunists. One day a crow found a rose, but that did not prove that the crow was a nightingale. It is not for nothing that the saying goes:

> When a crow picks up a rose
> 'I'm a nightingale,' it crows.

Another reason why Koba disliked the Mensheviks was on account of the preponderance of Jews in their ranks. 'Lenin is exasperated that God sent him such comrades as the Mensheviks!' he exclaimed in one anti-Semitic outburst. 'Really what kind of people are these! Martov, Dan, Axelrod – nothing but uncircumcised Jews! And that old bitch Vera Zasulich! All right! Go work with them. They won't fight and there is no rejoicing at their feastings, cowards and shopkeepers. Don't the workers of Georgia know that the Jewish people produce only

65

cowards who are useless in a fight?'[34]*

The Tsar's announcement of the grant of a constitution in October 1905 was hailed by the Tiflis Mensheviks as a victory. On the following day Koba addressed a meeting in Nakhalovka, a working-class suburb of the town. 'What do we really need in order to win?' he asked his audience. 'We need three things – understand that well and bear it in mind – the first is arms, the second is arms and the third is arms and arms again.'[35] The need was appreciated a few days later when a chance shot fired in a crowd outside the Viceroy's palace, whether by a *gendarme* or a worker is uncertain, resulted in a bloody clash between workers and police in which many lives were lost. Iremashvili, who was a witness to the scene, saw Koba haranguing the crowd from a lamp-post which he had climbed. It has also been stated, though not by Iremashvili, that the twenty-six year old agitator hurled several home-made bombs into the Cossack ranks, after which he made his escape to a neighbouring hotel with some comrades who barricaded themselves inside where they continued to fight, subsequently escaping through the hotel cellars as the Cossacks stormed the building.[36]

This story may well be apocryphal. Certaintly it does not accord with the testimony of Social Democrats generally in the Caucasus that Koba's principal contribution to the revolution was in the field of agitation and propaganda rather than physical action. Abel Yenukidze, a veteran Bolshevik and friend of Koba's, thus remembers him at this time. 'In addition to going to meetings and attending to a lot of business in the Party locals, he sat in his little cubby-hole filled with books and newspapers or in the similarly roomy editorial office of the Bolshevik newspaper,' presumably *The Proletarian Struggle*. The official Soviet edition of his *Works* reproduces twelve articles, leaflets and pamphlets attributed to his authorship in 1905. All were unsigned and originally appeared in the Georgian language except the last. This final article was a leader in the *Caucasian Workers' Newsheet*, the first legal daily Bolshevik newspaper in the Caucasus edited jointly by Koba and the Armenian Stepan Georgievich Shaamyan. It ran for only seventeen issues being suddenly terminated by Shaumyan's arrest.

> Led by Social Democracy [wrote Koba in the first issue dated Tiflis, 20 November 1905] the revolutionary urban proletariat and the revolutionary peasantry which is following it will, in spite of all the machinations of the liberals, staunchly continue

* Juli Martov (Tsederbaum), Fedor Dan, Pavel Axelrod and Vera Zasulich were all founder members of the RSDLP. They followed the right-wing Menshevik line and consequently broke with Lenin.

their struggle until they achieve the complete overthrow of the autocracy and erect a free democratic republic on its ruins.[37]

During this year of revolution, and indeed for some years afterwards, the authorities feared the Mensheviks in Georgia much more than the Bolsheviks – there were three thousand Mensheviks in Tiflis alone as against a few hundred Bolsheviks – and the Okhrana may well have encouraged Koba Djugashvili to denounce individual Menshevik comrades. A case in point was provided by Stepan Shaumyan. After he had been arrested Shaumyan told the Menshevik leader Noi Zhordania that he was certain Koba had given him away. 'Here is the proof,' he said. 'I had a secret hide-out where I sometimes spent the night. No one except Koba knew the address. When they arrested me the first thing the police asked about was the apartment...What could I tell them?'

After Shaumyan was released from prison, suspicion naturally fell on Koba, and there was some talk of summoning him to appear before a party court of honour. However, his own arrest and subsequent exile to Siberia for a second time saved him again, just as it had done in Batum, from what might well have been a most embarrassing investigation.[38]

'The Viceroy has had a nervous breakdown,' wrote the chief of police in the Caucasus to St Petersburg at the beginning of December 1905. The last straw for His Excellency was the railway strike which paralysed communications.[39] ('The insurgents have disarmed the *gendarmes*, made themselves masters of the western line of the railway and are themselves selling tickets and keeping order.') The strike also affected Lenin who had returned to Russia from Switzerland and hoped to convene the next Party Congress in Stockholm. The strike made this impossible. Instead Lenin summoned a Bolshevik party conference to meet at Tammerfors in Finland, which was then a Russian province.

For this occasion Koba was selected as a delegate, whether self-appointed or otherwise is not clear. According to official Soviet sources, he was appointed by the Caucasian Union of the Social Democratic Party in Tiflis as representing the district known as Borchalo; but this seems unlikely since the Union was almost entirely Menshevik and anyhow the majority of its members thoroughly detested Koba. No witnesses or documents have survived to confirm the selection, which is more likely to have been the work of one of the small local Bolshevik committees. At all events Koba was able to provide himself with a false passport in the name of Ivanovich and in due course arrived at the conference, having safely passed through nineteen police check points on the journey. He was accompanied by a pale and emaciated looking comrade from Kutais, his friend G. P. Teliya, who was now in the final stages of tuberculosis.[40]

4

The Tammerfors Bolshevik Conference, which lasted for five days from 12–17 December 1905, provided Koba with an opportunity to meet Lenin for the first time. Years afterwards he confessed to a keen sense of disappointment at his first sight of 'the mountain eagle of our Party'. In his imagination he had pictured Lenin as a giant, physically as well as politically. To his surprise, when the forty or so delegates assembled on the first day of the conference, Lenin appeared 'a most ordinary looking man, below average height, in no way – literally in no way – distinguishable from ordinary mortals'. What was more, instead of arriving when the other delegates were already in their places waiting with bated breath for the 'great man' to make his entrance, Lenin got there before most of the others and settled himself in a corner where he unassumingly carried on 'a most ordinary conversation with the most ordinary delegates at the Conference'. Such behaviour seemed to Koba 'to be rather a violation of certain essential rules'. Only later, he admitted, did he realise that 'this simplicity and modesty, this striving to remain unobserved, or, at least, not to make himself conspicuous and not to emphasise his high position – that this feature was one of Lenin's strongest points as the new leader of the new masses...'[41]

According to Lenin's wife Krupskaya, who was also there, it was a lively gathering in spite of the bitterly cold weather. 'The enthusiasm was tremendous. Every comrade was ready for the fight. In the intervals we learned to shoot. One evening we attended a Finnish mass torchlight meeting, and the solemnity of it fully harmonised with the delegates. I doubt whether anyone who was at that conference could ever forget it.' Unfortunately all the minutes of the proceedings were subsequently lost, and nothing is known of what took place apart from the fact that Lenin made two speeches, a number of 'local reports' were presented by delegates, and the conference concluded by passing a resolution calling for 'the immediate preparation and organisation of an armed uprising'. In the event this revolution proved superfluous, since, even as the delegates were discussing it, fighting broke out between workers and troops in Moscow – deliberately provoked by the Okhrana, like other sporadic risings elsewhere in the country, in order to give the authorities an excuse for their brutal suppression. The nation-wide strikes similarly petered out. Those in St Petersburg had been inspired by the formation of the first Soviet or Workers' Council under Trotsky's energetic chairmanship; but this had been broken up and the whole Soviet arrested, while Lenin and his Bolshevik comrades were secretly on their way to Tammerfors.[42]

Although the Caucasian delegate subsequently eulogised what he called the 'irresistible force of logic' in Lenin's speeches, he did not agree with their content at the time. In the first place, Lenin spoke in favour of joining up with the 'tiresome' Mensheviks, whom Koba had been castigating so vigorously in Georgia, and a resolution to this effect was adopted by the conference in order to draw the workers away from the Mensheviks and win them over to the side of the Bolsheviks.[43]* Secondly, Lenin thought that the Bolsheviks should participate in the forthcoming elections to the Duma, which Koba wished to boycott. A parliamentary democracy as such did not hold any attractions for Lenin, but he saw no reason why the cause of revolution should not be promoted from a parliamentary platform. It could be preached in a dungheap or a pigsty, he argued, so why not preach it in the pigsty of the Tsarist Duma?

But the feeling of the majority of the delegates including Koba was against him. To them it sounded like pure Menshevik opportunism. Indeed Lenin was shaken by the unexpected strength of the opposition to his proposal. Perhaps, he said, the practical workers were right after all; and he jovially announced that he was 'withdrawing from his position in good order'. Koba Ivanovich was elected, along with his future official biographer Yaroslavsky, to the commission that was to draft a resolution on the subject. 'This was his first success at a national party gathering. That he obtained it against Lenin could not but enhance his self-confidence.'[44]

On his return to Tiflis, which he reached early in January 1906, Koba wrote a pamphlet 'Two Clashes', in which he contrasted the initial St Petersburg demonstration with what had just happened in Moscow. 'This time you saw no church banners, no icons, no portraits of the Tsar,' he wrote. 'Instead, red flags fluttered and portraits of Marx and Engels were carried. This time you heard no singing of psalms or of "God Save the Tsar" – instead the strains of the *Marseillaise* and other revolutionary songs deafened the tyrants.' As for the proletariat, it had merely retreated in order after mustering its forces to

---

* Beria in his rewriting of history stated that subsequently 'under the leadership of Comrade Stalin the Bolsheviks of Transcaucasia settled the question of unity in a Leninist spirit'. L. P. Beria, *On the History of the Bolshevik Organisations in Transcaucasia* (1949), p. 150.

enter the final clash with the Tsarist government. 'The proletariat of Russia will not lower its bloodstained banner. It will yield the leadership of the insurrection to no one. It will be the only worthy leader of the Russian revolution.'[45]

This pamphlet was followed some weeks later by an article in *The Dawn*, a short-lived Georgian Menshevik newspaper published by the Tiflis committee, in which the editor gave the Bolshevik Koba a chance to reply to the Menshevik case for participation in the Duma elections.

The Duma will be a mongrel Parliament, [he declared]. Nominally it will enjoy powers to decide; but actually it will only have advisory powers because the [nominated] Upper Chamber and a Government armed to the teeth will stand over it in the capacity of censors...The Duma will not be a people's Parliament, it will be a Parliament of the enemies of the people, because voting in the election of the Duma will be neither universal, equal, direct nor secret.

Although all taxpayers and property owners were enfranchised, the elections were to be conducted through electoral colleges based on social status except in the five largest cities. Of the ninety-eight electors who were to choose the deputies for the Tiflis province, only two could be workers. 'The other ninety-six must belong to other classes – that is what the Manifesto says.' Similarly out of thirty-two electors for the Batum and Sukhum areas, only one could be a working class representative. Therefore, argued Koba, the best course to follow was to boycott these police-controlled elections, which must inevitably arouse false hopes among the masses. 'Boycott tactics – this is the direction in which the development of the revolution is now going. This is the direction in which Social Democracy should go.'[46]

There is some evidence that Koba was also engaged in terrorist activities in Tiflis at this time. It is known that by the time he got back to the Georgian capital from Finland there was a plot afoot to assassinate General Gryasnov, the hated military governor of the Caucasus, who was notorious for his floggings of demonstrators and for his bombardment of the Tiflis workers' suburb, and furthermore that Koba had a hand in the plans for his killing. The terrorists are said to have assembled with others including Koba at a small tavern in the outskirts of the town and there drawn lots as to who should do the deed. The terrorist thus chosen was a young worker named Arsenius Dzhordzhashvili. While the others were congratulating this youngster,

Koba is said to have suggested that he himself should make alternative arrangements as a precaution against anything going amiss with Dzhordzhashvili's efforts. 'The killing of General Gryasnov is far too important a matter to be left to one man,' he argued. 'If his hand shakes a little or he chucks his bombs too hastily the attempt may fail.' The others agreed and Koba departed in search of substitute volunteers.

The General was in the habit of taking the air in an open carriage, and thus was expected to provide an easy target. But when it was seen that he was accompanied by his young daughter, the operation was called off, since 'no Georgian gentleman would willingly harm a woman'. According to another comrade, Kote Tsintsadze, Koba sent for him and said: 'If Dzhordzhashvili does not get rid of Gryasnov inside the next week, the job is yours and you must organise it.' But this proved unnecessary as the General was alone next day and Dzhordzhashvili was able to throw his bombs with deadly effect. He was immediately seized by the General's Cossack guard, hurriedly tried and condemned to death by a drum-head court martial and publicly hanged in the town's main square at dawn next day. He met his end bravely, refusing under severe interrogation to reveal the names of any of his accomplices. One bystander, a worker, afterwards stated that he saw Koba standing near the terrorist at the moment the bombs were thrown and that Koba thereupon walked coolly off. 'What are you loafing about here for?' a policeman is said to have asked him, as he pushed him out of the way.[47]

Koba's role in this and other terrorist operations in Georgia was not to execute them but to direct those who did. He was always careful to avoid compromising himself in the event of failure. He preferred to act as an intermediary between the heads and the lower ranks of the revolutionary organisation. He did not on occasion lack physical courage himself, says the Menshevik Zhordania, but only when prison or exile rather than the firing squad were the penalties for detection. In short he felt that it was better to live for the revolution than to die for it. Prominent Mensheviks like Zhordania and Zhgenti, when they came to record their reminiscences of the revolutionary struggle in the Caucasus, tended to write off Koba as a coward. 'During this period Koba was considered a common coward in Georgia,' wrote Zhgenti, 'a man only capable of provocations and of encouraging his accomplices to blackmail and expropriations, hiding his identity and keeping out of danger'. As an example, Zhordania mentions a plot in which Koba was implicated to rob the municipal treasury in Gori by digging a tunnel under the building and goes on to state that when it was being constructed Koba refused to go down and inspect the tunnel in case it caved in on top of him. 'Maybe,' commented Zhordania, 'this physical fear was one of the features in his psychology of cruelty to his friends, as if their deaths would avenge his cowardice.' In the matter of 'expropriations', hold-ups, robberies and the like, Koba was frequently the intermediary between Lenin and the terrorists in the field, notably the Armenian Ter-Petrosyan, otherwise Kamo. In the words of David Shub, a renegade member of the Social Democratic Party, 'Kamo was the field commander of these operations [in the Caucasus;] Koba represented Lenin's supreme headquarters.' Between 1904 and 1908 over eleven hundred acts of terrorism took place in the Caucasus alone.[48]*

There now occurred one of the strangest incidents in the whole of Koba's underground revolutionary career. Mention has already been made of the secret printing press in the Avlabar district of Tiflis. Some time in March 1906, other illegal operations were added to printing at Avlabar, including a laboratory for the fabrication of false passports and also the manufacture of bombs and explosives. At the same time the Tiflis Okhrana received the first definite information about Avlabar, where operations were carried on in a skilfully concealed cellar. According to official police reports, the information came from 'agent sources' (*ot agenturnikh istochnikov*) received by Colonel Nikolai Zasypkin, Chief of the Tiflis Okhrana, on 29 March, but the agent was not specifically identified.† As a result the premises were put under strict police surveillance with a view to raiding them. The raid took

---

* A statistical table in the Okhrana Archives preserved in the Hoover Institution on War, Revolution and Peace at Stanford University, California, shows that in the period October 1907 to May 1910, revolutionary bands in imperial Russia carried out 23,044 terrorist acts, in which 4,322 officials and others were killed and 4,465 wounded: Index No. XXIV (i), folder 2.

† On 1 April 1906, Colonel Zasypkin reported to the Director of Police for the Caucasus: 'According to information received from an agent on 29 March the secret printing plant of the Caucasian Union of the Social Democratic Party, now known as the United Committee of the SDP, is located on the outskirts of the city near the railway tracks opposite the Petropavlovsk cemetery ... on a piece of land belonging to a former locksmith in the railway shops named Rostomashvili, who gave the land for the construction of a building suitable for a printing plant, which was erected in 1903 ... Underneath this building there are said to be vaulted underground quarters, with a specially concealed entrance, where the printing plant has been set up ... The plant is said to be large and well equipped, comprising hand presses, a Boston machine etc. ... In submitting the foregoing to your Excellency, I wish to report that I intend to check the above information by means of a search conducted after keeping the premises under a limited degree of observation.' Cited from the archives of the Marx-Engels-Lenin Institute of Georgia in *Istoricheskiy Mesta Tbilisi* (Tiflis, 1944), p. 119.

place at dawn on 15 April 1906. Trotsky states that Koba was arrested during the raid and released on the same date.[49] But this would not have been possible since he was then in Stockholm for the Fourth Democratic Party Congress. However, it is virtually certain that he was arrested a short time before the raid and was promptly released after supplying the police with particulars of the Avlabar operations. In other words, he was the agent source reported by Colonel Zaspykin. For obvious reasons the official Soviet biographies of Stalin are silent on his being taken into police custody on this occasion and it does not figure in the official Soviet chronicle of his arrests. But one Tiflis comrade is quite definite on the point. This was Razden Arsenidze who was a political prisoner in Metekh fortress at this time. 'The arrest of Soso actually took place,' Arsenidze afterwards declared, 'and I can categorically verify that Soso was released from the *gendarmerie* headquarters and did not appear with the other prisoners in Metekh fortress.' According to this witness, the arrest was carried out by Colonel Zaspykin, 'who proposed that he should become an agent of the Okhrana'.[50] The inference is that he agreed to do so. Arsenidze, who was to end his career on the Georgian language desk of Radio Free Europe in Munich, and was to live until 1965, revealed the source of his information in a letter to Isaac Don Levine, Koba's Russian-born expatriate biographer:

> The fact that Stalin was under arrest briefly in the spring of 1906 was confirmed to me by one of the old Social Democratic workers, Kakheladze, who at that time was a member of the Tiflis Committee of the Social Democratic Party. He remembered well the arrest and speedy release of Stalin, but was unable to fix the exact date of the arrest.[51]

At the same time, the police descended on the offices of *Elva* (Lightning), then the legal newspaper of the nominally unified Tiflis Social Democrats, to which Koba had recently contributed several articles under the signature 'J. Besoshvili'. Twenty-four people were arrested including Mikho Bochoridze, who had played a leading part in setting up the Avlabar press, and Philip Makharadze, a prominent party member and future historian of the revolutionary movement in the Caucasus. Arrests of other Bolshevik comrades were carried out in the city. These included Mikha Tskakaya and his mistress Nina Aladzhalova; the latter was employed as a 'technical' secretary of the local party and kept a 'safe house' or 'conspiratorial apartment' where Koba sometimes stayed in hiding. Here, too, revolutionaries were trained in the use of dynamite, but following an explosion on the premises the neighbours became suspicious and the detonators and other equipment were moved to the house in Avlabar.

Aladzhalova was arrested in her apartment, but the police failed to find any incriminating material, though they are said to have searched the place for three hours. After being kept in custody for a short time, she and Tskakaya were released, since in the words of the relevant police report 'there was insufficient proof of their activities for a formal charge to be brought'.* Much later, when Georgia came under Soviet rule, Aladzhalova was to hold several important official positions, being greatly favoured by Stalin whom she outlived, having survived all the purges of the Bolshevik Old Guard. She eventually retired to enjoy a comfortable government pension. It is worth noting that, apart from Koba, who had departed for Stockholm at the time of the arrests, Nina Aladzhalova and Mikho Tskakaya were the only Bolsheviks in the Avlabar affair to have been treated with relative lenience by the authorities. She never divulged her precise role in the affair, and, though she published a slight volume of reminiscences after Stalin's death, she still preserved the secret of her relations with Koba and the police.

Koba's own arrest and immediate release, which enabled him to reach Stockholm in time for the opening of the Fourth Party Congress, pose a number of pertinent questions. How was a man with no known regular means of livelihood able to support himself, a wife and baby son, and at the same time to move about the country and travel abroad? Is it not permissible to assume that the Tiflis Okhrana, which had ample funds at its disposal for making supplementary payments to secret agents, financed Koba's trip to the Swedish capital – to which he is known to have travelled on a passport made out in the name of 'Ivan Ivanovich Vissarionovich, journalist' – in return for services rendered? Confirmation of these services has been allegedly supplied by Colonel Alexander Mikhailovich Eremin of the Tiflis Okhrana, who would appear to have written to a colleague in 1913 that 'on his arrest in 1906 Joseph Vissarionovich Djugashvili Stalin provided the Chief of the Tiflis Provincial Gendarme Administration with valuable denunciatory information'.[52]

The publication of this letter with a photograph of the original by Isaac Don Levine in *Life* magazine in 1956 created an international

---

* Tskakaya was afterwards allowed to go to Switzerland, where he was to work closely with Lenin and to be one of the party which accompanied the Bolshevik leader in the famous sealed train through Germany to Russia after the outbreak of the February Revolution in 1917.

sensation and, needless to add, it was hotly denounced by the Soviet authorities as a fake emanating from emigré White Russian sources just as was the notorious Zinoviev letter which contributed substantially to the defeat of the British Labour Government in the General Election in 1924. So far as the Eremin document is concerned, there is no doubt in the present writer's mind that it was a deliberate fabrication designed to discredit Stalin's reputation further following the Soviet leader Nikita Khrushchev's revelations in his now famous 'secret' speech at the Twentieth Party Congress.* On the other hand, while the letter appears to be a plausible forgery concocted on genuine Okhrana writing paper with a typewriter of the make commonly used in Russia at the time, it does not necessarily follow that the information which it contains is false: it may well have been written by a former Okhrana officer who embodied in it particulars from Stalin's file which he remembered.

The evidence now available strongly points to the conclusion that Stalin was arrested on or about 29 March 1906, and immediately released in return for information which he gave the police – leading to the raid on the Avlabar printing press a fortnight or so later; furthermore, that he was recruited by the Tiflis Okhrana at this time as a secret agent or police spy, and that in respect of his trip to Stockholm, as also for a similar trip to London for the Fifth Party Congress in the following year, the Okhrana provided him with money and false papers. On arrival at Stockholm, he had to produce his passport to the city police, who recorded its details as above stated.†

---

* For further details of this extraordinary letter, the original of which is now preserved in the Tolstoy Foundation in New York, see Appendix, p. 612 below.
† The following appeared in the American magazine *Newsweek*, 7 November 1966: – *A Czarist Spy Named Stalin*
'George Kennan, former U.S. ambassador to Russia and an astute student of Russian affairs at Princeton's Institute for Advanced Studies, has long suspected that as a young Bolshevik Joseph Stalin was an agent of the Tsar's secret police. Now Kennan has the evidence. He recently learned that the passport Stalin used to attend a party congress at Stockholm in 1906 was issued by the secret police. Kennan's research also uncovered the fact that Stalin admitted during a party seminar in 1920 that he had been a Tsarist agent. The statement was published in a Soviet theoretical magazine that disappeared a few months ago from all Russian libraries. Kennan traced the activities of each member of the seminar group, together with the Georgian and Armenian Communists who were closely associated with Stalin between 1906 and 1912 – and found that all had been liquidated in the 1920s.'
When questioned by a news reporter about this account, Professor Kennan declined to elaborate beyond stating that it was 'not entirely accurate'. *New York Times*, 31 October 1966.

Koba was the only Bolshevik in a delegation of eleven from Georgia, the other ten being Mensheviks who would certainly not have contributed a single kopec to his travelling expenses, since they did not regard him as a properly accredited delegate at all. He claimed to have been chosen by the district of Borchalo south of Tiflis; but, as there was no Social Democratic organisation in that region, the credentials commission at the Congress at first refused to accept him. According to Gregory Uratadze, who was one of the Menshevik delegates, he was actually asked to leave. However, it appears that he was eventually allowed to remain with a consultative voice after some of the other Bolsheviks requested the Mensheviks not to object to his admittance on this basis. It is also worth noting that he was registered at the Congress in the name of Ivanovich, although, as has been seen, he appeared in his passport as Vissarionovich.[53]*

The Armenians also sent a delegation which included Stepan Shaumyan, who had been released from prison. In all there were sixty-six Mensheviks and forty-four Bolsheviks fully accredited, besides a number of observers from Poland and the Baltic provinces. There was more than one Okhrana agent present to furnish police headquarters in St Petersburg with detailed accounts of the proceedings. Most of the delegates including Koba travelled by sea from the Finnish port of Abo and they narrowly escaped disaster when their vessel, which was flying the Danish flag, struck a submerged rock off one of the many islands in the Gulf of Bothnia. The passengers had to be transferred to another steamer as the damaged vessel had shipped so much water that it appeared in danger of sinking, and their apparent unconcern throughout this operation astonished the crew, since they continued to debate the agrarian question in Russia as if nothing untoward was happening. 'Those Russian revolutionaries certainly are curious people!' commented one of the sailors.

The hosts to the congress were the Swedish socialists, in whose headquarters the participants met from 10–25 April, after being greeted by Hjalmar Branting, then the only Social Democrat in the Swedish Parliament and later the first Social Democratic Prime Minister of his country.

From time to time those present would break off their deliberations,

---

* In the usual form filled up by arriving travellers, Koba gave his address in Stockholm as the Hotel Bristol; but when the police came to check they found that no one answering to the description of Ivan Ivanovich Vissarionovich was 'entered there'. Information from the Stockhom City Police Archives communicated by Edward Ellis Smith.

when they would be served with free tea, milk and sandwiches by their Swedish comrades.

The news of the successful police raid on the Avlabar printing plant, which was generally reported in the Russian press, must have reached the delegates while they were still in session. Indeed the fact that such quantities of dynamite, arms, ammunition and materials for the manufactures of bombs had been seized may well have prompted the Congress to pass a resolution outlawing 'partisan warfare' and condemning all forms of raids except attacks upon arsenals. The delegates from the Caucasus who were in the know probably wondered how the police had managed to discover such a cleverly concealed underground establishment. In fact, the police nearly missed it, since the initial search of the house and yard yielded nothing. Just as the police were about to leave, one of their number noticed some pieces of waste paper near the well. He picked one up, put a match to it and threw the burning paper down the well. When the paper reached the bottom, he noticed that it was drawn to one side and the flames extinguished by what he rightly guessed was a draught from another opening. A fireman was then lowered down the well and found the secret entrance to the cellar with its considerable armoury.[54]

Comrade Ivanovich is reported to have intervened briefly on three occasions during the sittings of the Congress. He attacked the Mensheviks for their 'opportunist tactics' over the approaching Duma elections; he urged the proletariat to take 'an active part in the organisation of armed insurrection' with a view to the seizure of power; and he advocated the 'complete confiscation and division of land' among the peasants, in other words small holdings embodying a system of rural capitalism rather than full-scale nationalisation which Lenin supported but which Koba thought should at first only be applied to such features of the landscape as forests and lakes. 'The object of the agrarian revolution is primarily and mainly to emancipate the peasants,' he told the delegates. Although he did not state it openly at the time, he regarded this type of rural capitalism merely as an intermediate stage in the revolution, and a quarter of a century later when he had achieved dictatorial power he was to replace it by a ruthless policy of collectivisation.[55]

The Stockholm chief of police had allowed the meetings to be held in the capital provided they were conducted 'in a civilised and orderly manner'. Although he had no cause for complaint on this score, he may well have regretted his decision. When the Congress ended it was found that the delegates did not have enough money to defray their travelling expenses back to Russia, and the police chief had to advance a sufficient sum for this purpose, since this was the only way in which he could get rid of the embarrassing visitors.

Back in Tiflis, Koba resumed his party journalism. Apart from the bare record of the articles which he wrote and which were subsequently republished in his collected *Works*, practically nothing is known of his activities throughout the succeeding twelve months. In June 1906, in conjunction with G. P. Teliya and others he started a daily Bolshevik newspaper called *Akhali Tskhovreba* (New Life). This ran for twenty issues, and after a lapse of several months it was replaced by a trade union weekly *Akhali Vremya* (New Times) which, though a legal publication like the other, eventually fell foul of the authorities and was closed down by order of the Governor of Tiflis after a couple of months. Three other legal Bolshevik journals appeared during the first quarter of 1907, *Mnatobi* (The Torch), *Cheveni Tskhovreba* (Our Life), and *Dro* (Time), all of which are stated to have been 'directed' by Comrade Koba Ivanovich, who now began to sign his articles 'Koba' or simply 'Ko'.

From his considerable output of party polemics, one short article stands out as unusual revelation of human sympathy, occasioned by the death of G. P. Teliya, Koba's former assistant in his illegal printing operations in Batum. Koba was clearly fond of Teliya, a former domestic servant in Tiflis and later a carpenter in the railway workshops, who was entirely self-educated. Originally a Menshevik, Teliya seems to have been converted by Koba to the cause of Bolshevism. There is a suggestion, too, that he was in the pay of the Okhrana. At all events he was the perfect comrade in Koba's eyes, 'a man of irreproachable character and of inestimable value for the Party'. He kept up a stream of articles from his sick-bed, and a few days before he died, in March 1907, he told Koba that he was working on a pamphlet on the history of Social Democracy in the Caucasus. However, as Koba put it, 'cruel death prematurely tore the pen out of the hand of our tireless comrade'.[56]

5

Shortly after Teliya's death Koba left for the Fifth Party Congress, to which the biographical chronicle appended to the official Soviet edition of his *Works* states, quite wrongly, that he was elected a delegate by the Bolshevik workers in Tiflis. As at the Fourth Congress he purported to represent the Borchalo district, where there was no local party branch, and this was to cause his credentials to be called in question again. The Fifth Congress had been originally planned to take place in Copenhagen, and for this purpose most of the delegates travelled to Finland in order to catch a connecting steamer. However, when they arrived in Copenhagen, the Danish Government refused to allow the Congress to be held there, since this would have offended the King, whose sister was the Tsar's mother and widow of the late Tsar Alexander III. Lenin and Plekhanov, leader of the Mensheviks, thereupon tried for Oslo through the Norwegian comrades, but again met with a refusal. The Swedes in Malmo proved equally unco-operative, the local authorities no doubt having heard about the Stockholm police chief's experience at the end of the previous year's gathering. Eventually London was chosen as the venue, since England posed no immigration problems and its Liberal Government did not object to the presence of foreign party political representatives provided they did not conduct subversive activities on its shores. As Lenin's wife Krupskaya put it on the occasion of an earlier visit, 'from the conspiratorial point of view things could not have been better. No identification documents whatever were needed in London then...Another advantage was that to English people all foreigners look the same, and our landlady took us for Germans the whole time.'

There remained the question of funds. Russian congresses, unlike those of other nationalities, often lasted for weeks, and the housing and feeding of more than three hundred delegates, besides the additional travelling expenses incurred by transferring the Congress to London, called for further financial assistance if the delegates were going to reach their destination. It was decided to appeal to the German Social Democratic Party, and for this purpose some of the leading delegates including Lenin went to Berlin where they spent several days. Although it is not mentioned in the official chronology of Stalin's journeys, he told the French communist Henri Barbusse that he twice went to Berlin in 1907 to confer with Lenin. Since Lenin is definitely known to have been in the German capital between 24–28 April in that year, it is reasonable to suppose that Koba met him there or possibly even travelled with him from Copenhagen.[57]

What could Lenin have wished to talk over with Koba which could not just as well have been discussed in Copenhagen or London? The answer to this question would appear to have been the details of a big 'expropriation' which had been planned and was to be carried out by Bolshevik terrorists against the Tiflis branch of the Imperial Russian Bank. At this time Krassin used to come to Berlin in connection with his work as an electrical engineer, and no doubt his advice was also required as to how the proceeds of the proposed bank robbery could be most readily disposed of. Koba explained that the operation should produce at least three hundred thousand roubles to replenish the depleted Bolshevik exchequer, and that it would be in the hands of the Armenian Ter-Petrosyan, otherwise Kamo, the principal Bolshevik terrorist in the Caucasus. Lenin gave his approval, and it was agreed that the business should be carried out as soon as practicable after the London Congress had ended and Koba had returned to Georgia.

Koba and the others who were going on to the Congress, presumably travelled by train to the Hook of Holland, and thence to Harwich, where they were joined by the remaining delegates who had in the meastime gone from Copenhagen to Esbjerg, where they caught a steamer. The whole delegation eventually arrived in two large train loads at Liverpool Street station on 8–9 May New Style. The English press, which showed some curiosity in these novel arrivals, recorded that few of them had any luggage and some were dressed in their blue working blouses. They were met by a number of English Socialist comrades headed by George Lansbury and H. L. Brailsford, who took them off to Whitechapel in the East End of London. Most of them were accommodated in a disused military barracks where the Special Branch of the metropolitan police from Scotland Yard kept a discreet eye on their activities between the sessions of this extraordinary Congress. The women of the party, 'conspicuous for their unflinching courage and nerve', were reported as indulging in mock revolver practice in front of mirrors to improve their quickness at the draw. Outstanding among the women was Lenin's friend Angelica Balabanoff, who represented the organisation of Russian university students, and Rosa Luxemburg, the Polish-born German Social Democrat, considered by many to be the best speaker at the conference. Generally, the press reporters did not find the 'revolutionaries' at all forthcoming. 'We will neither be photographed nor interviewed,' one of them informed a representative of the *Daily Express* through an interpreter. 'It would not be safe.' Another delegate protested that the reproduction of photographs might mean death for the individuals caught by the camera. 'Most of us have to cross the frontier again.'[58]

The newspaper also gave the name of an officer of the Russian secret police, 'Mr Sevieff', who was said to be shadowing the delegates and a question was asked in the House of Commons as to whether the Tsar's police were really behaving in this reprehensible manner. In fact, they were going much further and had more than one agent reporting on the deliberations of the conference which was supposed to be taking place in secret. It is now known that before the delegates left Copenhagen, the head of the Paris office of the Okhrana informed his headquarters in St Petersburg that he had sent five hundred francs to an agent to enable him to travel to London, this sum being in addition to the thousand francs previously given him as travelling and subsistence expenses. There is nothing in the police archives to identify this particular agent with Koba. But the possibility cannot be dismissed altogether, since that agent did submit a most detailed report of the composition and voting strength and other details of this Congress to the Okhrana and afterwards Koba wrote an equally detailed account of the proceedings for a Bolshevik paper in Georgia, in particular pin-pointing Rosa Luxemburg's attacks on the Mensheviks as being of 'exceptional interest'.

Koba is said to have shared a room in Whitechapel with a young Jewish Bolshevik called Meier Moisevich Wallach, who had registered at the Congress under the name of Maxim Maximovich Litvinov, by which he was one day to become the Soviet Union's best known Commissar for Foreign Affairs. Litvinov, who was three years older than Koba, came from Bialystok, a predominantly Jewish town on the borders of Russia and Russian Poland. A cheerful tubby looking man, whose nickname was Papasha, he had been imprisoned in Kiev as a revolutionary and on his release had fled abroad where he had come to the notice of Lenin. He had later returned to Russia where he became a party organiser in Riga and was now engaged in various underground activities including the smuggling of arms into Russia. Many years afterwards he recalled his brief stay in Whitechapel with Koba.

I remember I got rather fed up with him because he wanted to see all the sights of London, and especially the docks at night. One of these excursions could easily have ended tragically for us. We got involved in a brawl with some drunken sailors who were fighting about girls. I remember Koba put up a good show, laying about two of the sailors with perfect knock-out blows, although he knew nothing about boxing. I came out of the affair with broken glasses and a torn jacket.

'Of course I remember,' said Koba when Litvinov reminded him of the incident. 'You defended me very gallantly, Papasha, although your skill in the use of your fists was nil.'[59]

The conference, which began in the evening of 13 May NS and lasted for nearly three weeks, was held in the Brotherhood Church in Southgate Road, Whitechapel. Maxim Gorky, who attended as an observer, recalled twenty years later the unattractive impression it made upon him at the time. 'I still see vividly before me those bare wooden walls unadorned to the point of absurdity,' he wrote in his memories of Lenin, 'the lancet windows looking down on a small, narrow hall which might have been a classroom in a poor school.' Five organised groups were represented – Bolsheviks, with ninety-two votes, Mensheviks with eight-five, and the remainder distributed between Poles, Letts and Jewish Bundists mostly from Poland and the Ukraine. They were all accommodated on long wooden benches, with the Bolsheviks on the right, the Mensheviks on the left and the other groups in between, the whole assembly being described by one London paper as a 'mock Duma'. The Caucasian delegates were especially conspicuous in their big sheepskin *shakos* and created quite a sensation whenever they appeared in the streets.

The proceedings began in an atmosphere of good will with a speech from Plekhanov, in which the Menshevik leader expressed satisfaction that the five groups had thus come together. However, his gospel of liberal socialism did not appeal to the Bolsheviks, and it is recorded that when he remarked that there were no 'revisionists' in the Russian Social Democratic Party, Lenin started to fidget, bent down, showing the bald spot on his head which grew red, and his shoulders shook in silent laughter. This was followed by the election of a praesidium of five members, one from each of the five groups. When Lenin was chosen for the Bolsheviks, there were vigorous protests from the Mensheviks who objected to his approval of terrorist activities and 'expropriations'. 'At the end of the meeting there was quite a row,' to quote from the report of a Russian secret police agent who was present in the guise of a delegate. 'Three or four Mensheviks protested at the election of Lenin, but the Bolsheviks shouted them down and the meeting was adjourned.'*

However, after a stormy debate, which was continued next day, the first of many during this momentous gathering, Lenin's election was confirmed while Dan was elected for the Mensheviks. The praesidium members took it individually by rotation to preside. When it was Lenin's turn in the chair, he proposed the adoption without discussion of a resolution of the credentials commission, which recommended the granting of 'deliberative participation', i.e. the right to speak but not to vote, to four delegates including Koba Ivanovich.

'I should like to know who is being given an advisory voice,' shouted

* Reports on the Congress were written by at least two secret police agents who had penetrated the Social Democratic Party. One was probably Dr J. A. Zhitomirsky, the Okhrana's principal intelligence operative in western Europe and a great friend of Lenin's – he was also in charge of the distribution of Bolshevik underground literature in Russia at this time from abroad. These reports, together with other material on the London Congress, are preserved in the Archive of the Imperial Russian Secret Police (Okhrana) in the Hoover Institution at Stanford University.

Martov from the Menshevik benches. 'Who are these people, and where do they come from?'

'I really don't know,' replied Lenin, 'but the Congress may reply on the unanimous opinion of the credentials commission.'

Trotsky, who was present as a voting delegate – each such delegate represented five hundred party members – has surmised that Martov possibly had 'some secret information about the specific nature of Ivanovich's record', and that it was for this reason that Lenin again stressed the unanimity of the credentials commission. At all events the non-voting status of the four comrades was approved though with a considerable number of delegates abstaining. Thus Koba was again documented in the name of Ivanovich.[60]

The official record of the Fifth Congress shows that during its long drawn out sessions Lenin and Martov spoke well over a hundred times, and Trotsky and Zhordania, who led the Caucasian Mensheviks, between fifty and sixty. A single speech of a twenty-five-year-old Bolshevik delegate named Gregory Zinoviev so impressed his fellow delegates that it gained him a place on the Central Committee along with Lenin, Krassin and two other named Bogdanov and Rykov. Yet Comrade Ivanovich did not intervene once in the discussions, while his signature appeared only on two short statements by the Caucasian Bolsheviks about their conflicts with the local Mensheviks, and then only in third place. Nor does he figure in any recollections of the Congress by other participants or observers, such as Trotsky, Angelica Balbanoff and Maxim Gorky, though mention is made of other relatively obscure Bolsheviks at that time like Litvinov, Voroshilov and Tomsky. Furthermore, the Bolshevik delegation held a number of separate sessions of its own and at the end of the Congress elected a secret Bolshevik Centre, composed of fifteen members, which included in addition to the Bolshevik delegates on the Central Committee already mentioned two figures later to be well known in the party, Lev Kamenev and Mikhail Pokrovsky, the latter as the leading Bolshevik historian as well as like Kamenev chairman of the Moscow Soviet. But Koba was not a member of this inner circle of Bolsheviks, although an authoritative representative from the Caucasus was badly needed.

Trotsky, who did not even notice Comrade Ivanovich at the Congress, was later to ask some questions about his role there. But he failed or was unwilling to provide answers to them.

In view of all this, why did Koba come at all to London? He could not raise his arm as a voting delegate. He proved unnecessary as a speaker. He obviously played no role whatever at closed sessions of the Bolshevik faction. It is inconceivable that he should have come out of mere curiosity – just to listen and to look around. He must have had other tasks. Just what were they?[61]

In his account of the Congress, Koba expressed his dislike of the Jewish element being so strong, quoting a jest made by G. A. Alexinsky, a Bolshevik member of the Duma, to the effect that 'the Mensheviks constituted a Jewish group while the Bolsheviks constituted a true Russian group and, therefore, it wouldn't be a bad idea for us Bolsheviks to organize a pogrom in the Party'. The Jewish Trotsky, whose real name was Bronstein, was at this time a Menshevik supporter, and Koba echoed Lenin's description of him as 'pretty but useless'.

Several days were devoted to discussing the report of the Duma group of the Party, in which Martov was the leading Menshevik and Bogdanov the leading Bolshevik. When it came to the various formal resolutions on the agenda, the Bolsheviks usually defeated their opponents, though one significant Menshevik resolution as at the Stockholm Congress was carried condemning the 'guerrilla actions', Koba's euphemism for terrorist activities. This resolution, according to Koba, the Bolsheviks let pass purely out of a desire to 'give the Menshevik comrades at least one opportunity to rejoice'. It was the first occasion on which Koba had seen Lenin in the role of victor, and he noted at the time that the Bolshevik leader was not the type to sit back and rest on his laurels. 'The first thing is not to be carried away by victory,' Koba later remembered him as saying. 'The second thing is to consolidate the victory. The third thing is, crush your opponent, because he is only defeated but far from being crushed yet.' These tactics were to be followed by Koba himself with decided effect after Lenin's death.[62]

The conference was interrupted from time to time, since the church where the delegates met was required for its proper purpose of religious services. Then, funds ran out and it looked as if the proceedings would come to an abrupt end leaving a lot of unfinished business. However, an English Liberal well-wisher of Polish origin named Joseph Fels, who was also a wealthy soap manufacturer, came to the rescue with a loan of seventeen hundred pounds, in exchange for which he accepted a promissory note which he insisted should be signed by all three hundred delegates, after he had listened to the delegates debating for several hours, although he did not understand a word of Russian. ('How young they all are!' he remarked.) Two days after the October Revolution of 1917, by which time Fels was dead, his heir presented the note for payment to Angelica Balabanoff, who had helped to negotiate the loan. She turned the note over to Lenin, and it was duly honoured by the Soviet government.* 'Revolution carries out its obligations,' noted Trotsky of the incident, 'although usually not without delay.'[63]

The lively and seemingly interminable discussions in the Brotherhood Church were held behind closed doors, but the English public had an opportunity of hearing some of the leading delegates in action at an open meeting and reception organised by the British Socialist Party in the Holborn Town Hall. The chair was taken by the veteran English Marxist H. M. Hyndman, who had founded and edited the socialist weekly *Justice*, which incidentally contains the fullest account in English of the congress. The other English members of the platform party included the picturesque hidalgo-like figure of R. B. Cunninghame-Grahame, traveller, poet, horseman, socialist and ex-MP who is said to have been the first member of the House of Commons to be suspended for using the word 'damn' in the chamber. Plekhanov, who should have been the principal visiting speaker, was kept away through illness. Nor does Lenin appear to have been present at what seems largely to have been a Menshevik affair. But Angelica Balbanoff and Trotsky both made rousing speeches, the former relating the part women had played in 'the great struggle for emancipation in Russia'; the latter attacked the British Foreign Secretary Sir Edward Grey for endeavouring to bring about an *entente* with the Tsarist Government, 'which would simply mean English gold going to strengthen the arm of the tyrant and murderer'. A choir in attendance sang the *Internationale*, the whole audience British and Russian joined in the chorus, and the meeting broke up with the chanting of the *Red Flag*. Afterwards the Russians were entertained to Munich beer and sandwiches and in the account of the evening given by *Justice* 'our guests appeared to thoroughly enjoy their reunion with their British comrades'. Hyndman chose this as a pretext for delivering another speech of welcome in which he congratulated the Russians on the number of young men in their ranks. Whether the youngsters in the hall included the twenty-eight-year-old Joseph Djugashvili, alias Koba Ivanovich, is not known, but very likely they did, since it was obviously an occasion on which an Okhrana agent would be expected to report to his superiors.[64]

The London Congress ended on 1 June. Three weeks later Koba was back in Tiflis, apparently putting the finishing touches to the prepara-

---

* 'When last I was in Moscow,' wrote the American historian Bertram Wolfe in 1948, 'it lay on velvet in a glass case, a curious memento of an infinitely remote and incomprehensible day when the Revolution was not a state power but an inspiration.' Bertram D. Wolfe, *Three Who Made A Revolution*, p. 385.

tion of what was to prove the most spectactular though hardly the most profitable of all the Bolshevik 'expropriations'. Planned and executed in the flagrant disregard of the London resolution condemning 'guerrilla actions', it was the most elaborate terrorist operation ever carried out in the Caucasus, involving as it did the co-operation of more than sixty conspirators. Unfortunately it also caused considerable injury and loss of life to more than fifty innocent bystanders, Cossacks and police.

6

Shortly after ten o'clock in the morning of 26 June 1907 – 13 June Old Style – two bank clerks signed for a bag of mail in the Tiflis main post office, entered a carriage with the bag which contained banknotes and other securities to the value of 300,000 roubles, and made their way under escort of a detachment of Cossacks to the local branch of the Imperial Russian Bank. As they approached Erevan Square, a bomb was thrown from the roof of a house belonging to Prince Zumbatov. Other bombs were hurled in rapid succession, one of which exploded between the horses' legs. Another conspirator was able to snatch the bag from the remains of the carriage and convey it to Mikho Bochoridze's house. The contents were then removed and taken to the Tiflis Observatory where they were sewn into the mattress of the director's bed. Afterwards this man used to relate that he never dreamed he was sleeping on a fortune. According to the same source, Koba collected the notes three weeks after the raid and sent them by an underground route to Krassin. 'Koba's complicity was unsuspected, indeed his presence was unknown. He continued to sit around the riverside taverns drinking freely, often with the police.'[65]

The extent of Koba's complicity in this celebrated bank robbery, which was widely reported and did the Bolshevik cause much harm, is difficult to determine precisely. He is stated to have been drinking with some of the conspirators in the cellar bar of the Tilipuchuri tavern in Palace Street near the Theological Seminary shortly before the attack took place. Many years later, Gregory Bessedovsky, a Soviet diplomat who defected to the west, told Trotsky that Stalin used to boast that it was his hand that had thrown the first bomb from the roof of Prince Zumbatov's house.[66] On the other hand, when directly taxed with participation in the affair by Emil Ludwig when he interviewed him in 1931, he equivocated.

'In Europe you are described either as a bloody Tsar or as a Georgian bandit,' said Ludwig, who then went on to ask him about the Tiflis bank robbery.

According to Ludwig, the dictator began to laugh in his characteristic heavy way, blinked several times and stood up for the first time in their three-hour interview. He walked over to a writing table, where he picked up a small book and handed it to Ludwig. 'You will find all the necessary information here,' he remarked, laughing slyly to himself.

When he came to examine the book, which was an official biography, Ludwig realised that Stalin had 'put one over' on him, since the work contained no reference whatever to the robbery. Ludwig also noted that it was the only question of the many which he asked him in this interview which Stalin had declined to answer. 'His method of evasion gave me a new insight into his character,' was Ludwig's comment on the incident. 'He could have denied it; he could have confessed it; or he could have simply described the whole thing as a legend. But he acted instead as a perfect Asiatic.'[67]

The consequences of this tragic adventure, as Trotsky called it, were serious for the whole Social Democratic Party and in particular for its Bolshevik wing, embittering and poisoning comradely relations with each other and the outside world and causing Lenin considerable embarrassment. In the result the Bolshevik exchequer benefited little, since the securities were non-negotiable and most of the notes were in five-hundred-rouble denominations and their serial numbers were known. Thus attempts made by Maxim Wallach, alias Litvinov, the future Soviet Foreign Minister, and others to change them in various European capitals failed, and the would-be money changers including Litvinov were arrested and imprisoned by the respective national authorities. Lenin's wife Krupskaya, who was then living in Geneva with her husband, noted that 'the good Swiss burghers were frightened to death by this incident. The only thing we heard talked about were the Russian expropriators. They were discussed with horror around the dining table in the boarding house where Ilyich and I usually dined.' The Bolshevik leader, who had previously approved of such terrorist tactics, now set his face against them and supported a Menshevik resolution condemning the Tiflis affair as 'an inadmissible violation of Party discipline', though at the same time excusing the participants who had been 'guided solely by a faulty understanding of Party interests'.[68]

However, the Georgian Mensheviks, who formed the large majority of the Party, went further and appointed a special commission under Sylvester Dzhibladze to inquire into the circumstances of the Tiflis robbery in the light of the resolution of the London Congress expressly forbidding terrorist acts. The commission recommended that anyone proved to have had anything to do with the affair including Koba Djugashvili should be forthwith expelled from the Party. The precise outcome is unclear. It is quite likely that in Koba's case no formal act of expulsion took place, but that he was merely requested to leave Tiflis and take up other Party work, just as he had been six years previously when he went to Batum after his exposure for intriguing against Dzhibladze and other members of the Tiflis Committee. Anyway he was always to be very touchy on the subject. In 1918, when the Menshevik Martov wrote in an editorial in a Moscow newspaper that Stalin, then Soviet Commissar for Nationalities, had been expelled in his time from the Party organisation in the Caucasus 'for having had semoething to do with expropriation', Stalin indicted him for criminal libel. 'Never in my life was I placed on trial before my Party or expelled,' Stalin indignantly declared in court. 'This is a vicious libel...One has no right to come out with accusations like Martov's except with documents in one's hand. It is dishonest to throw mud on the basis of mere rumours.' Martov thereupon asked for an adjournment to collect further evidence and, on his request being granted, he was able to do this in the shape of affidavits from Dzhibladze, Ramishvili, Shaumyan and others which were procured for him by Boris Nicolaevsky, later Director of the Historical Archives of the Revolution. But when the court resumed, it was found that all this documentation and other records of the case had mysteriously 'disappeared', with the result that Martov was dismissed from the case with a reprimand for 'insulting and damaging the reputation of a member of the Government'.[69]

Since Tiflis was now closed to Koba, and also Batum, where his 'provocation' of the workers was still bitterly remembered, there was only one major city left in the Caucasus to which Koba might with advantage transfer his activities. This was Baku, the great oil-producing centre on the Caspian, which had a mixed population of 200,000, of which one-tenth was working class, divided between Tartars, Armenians, Persians and Russians, thus comprising the largest industrial proletariat in Georgia, and thanks mainly to the efforts of Leonid Krassin, the most impregnated with Marxist socialism in the Russian empire after St Petersburg and Moscow. That Koba was in the 'black city' by early July 1907 is evident from the fact that an editorial article by him appeared in the first number of *Bakinsky Proletary* (The Baku Proletarian), and illegal workers' newspaper which he helped to launch at this time; and also that he was living in a small one-storey house in Baku with his wife, since Sergei Alliluyev stated in his memoirs that 'on the advice of friends' he went to see Koba and Keke there towards the end of that month. While in Baku, Koba was known to the local authorities as Kaios Vissarion Nizheradze, the alias of a dead Georgian

88

carpet dealer which, it will be recalled, he had used in escaping from Siberia.[70]

The article, which was unsigned, was prompted by the Tsar's dissolution of the Second Duma, the arrest and imprisonment or exile of most of the Social Democratic deputies and the alteration of the electoral law by the Tsar's reactionary chief minister Peter Stolypin so as largely to nullify the workers' franchise and produce a more compliant legislature.

All the more clearly, therefore, is the proletariat faced with the task of overthrowing the Tsarist regime [wrote Koba]. Just think! There was the First Duma. There was the Second Duma. But neither the one nor the other 'solved' a single problem of the revolution, nor, indeed, could either of them 'solve' these problems. Just as before the peasants are without land, the workers are without the eight hour day, and all the citizens are without political freedom. Why? because the Tsarist regime is not yet dead; it still exists, dissolving the second Duma after it dissolved the First, organizing the counter-revolution, and trying to break up the revolutionary forces, to divorce the vast masses of the peasants from the [industrial] proletariat...

Clearly it will be impossible to satisfy the broad masses of the workers and peasants unless the Tsarist regime is overthrown and a Popular Constituent Assembly is convened. It is no less clear that the fundamental problems of the Revolution can be solved only in alliance with the peasantry against the Tsarist regime and against the Liberal bourgeoisie.

There is an unconfirmed report that Koba was employed at the Rothschild oil refinery in Baku at this period, and indeed he may well have acted as a kind of shop steward there. According to official Soviet sources, he organised a conference of all the Baku oil workers at the end of July with a view to a general strike, while winning over many Mensheviks to the Bolshevist line. In this he was aided by a young metal worker from the Don basin named Kliment Voroshilov, whom he had previously met at the Stockholm and London party congresses and who in spite of his youth was already an experienced strike organiser. Their association in Baku was to form the foundation of a firm and lasting friendship, one of the relatively few in Koba's tempestuous career to withstand every shock and threat. With Klim's help, Koba brought out another Bolshevik organ *Gudok* (The Whistle) expressly devoted to the interests of the oil workers; he represented the workers in direct negotiations with the management on pay and hours of work, and when these broke down he fomented a series of strikes in the oil fields. He was also instrumental in forming a vigilante committee among the workers as a means of defence against the assaults of the notorious Black Hundreds, the armed reactionary groups which promoted pogroms of Jews and revolutionaries. In the election campaign for the Third Duma, which took place in the autumn, he busied himself drumming up Bolshevik votes for the candidate for workers deputy and composed a 'mandate' to the Social Democratic group in the new legislature, which he declared 'must pursue its constant tasks of criticism and agitation and not pursue the object of direct legislation; and must explain to the people that such legislation is ephemeral and futile so long as real power remains entirely in the hands of the autocratic government'.[71]

> By working in the Third State Duma in this way, the Social Democratic group will facilitate the revolutionary struggle which the proletariat, and the peasantry along with it, are at present waging against the Tsarist autocracy outside the Duma.

His collected *Works* contain a note to the effect that Koba arrived in Tiflis at the end of November 1907, 'on Party business'. No doubt this was when he was on his way to Berlin for his second secret meeting that year with Lenin, which took place in December for the primary purpose of discussing future Bolshevik tactics in Georgia, but on which the official biographical record is curiously silent. It was on this occasion that the incident occurred, which Koba would afterwards recall with a chuckle, when the Berlin Social Democratic Executive arranged a definite day and hour for a workers' demonstration in the city to be attended by all members of suburban branches.

> A group of about two hundred from one of the suburbs arrived in the city punctually at the hour appointed, but failed to arrive at the demonstration, the reason being given that they had waited two hours on the station platform because the ticket collector at the exit had failed to make his appearance and there had been nobody to give their tickets to. It used to be said in jest that it took a Russian comrade to show the Germans a simple way out of their fix – to leave the platform without giving up their tickets!'

This was how Stalin was to describe the incident a quarter of a century later to Emil Ludwig, himself a German. It evidently made a strong impression on his mind since he was also to repeat it to President Roosevelt and Winston Chutchill during the Second World War as evidence of the fundamental German devotion to legality. 'He seemed to think that this mentality of discipline and obedience could not be changed,' commented Roosevelt's special adviser Harry Hopkins at the Teheran conference. Stalin repeated the story to Churchill at Potsdam, saying that 'the Germans have no minds of their own' and agreeing with the British Prime Minister that 'they were like sheep'.[72]

Official Soviet literature is also silent about another event in Koba's life at this time. This was the death of his beautiful young wife, apparently from pneumonia aggravated by tuberculosis. 'I promised Keke she should be buried in accordance with the Orthodox rites,' he said, 'and I shall keep my promise.' He did so, after which he handed over their three-year-old baby son Yakov (Yasha) to Keke's Svanidze relatives to be brought up.

According to Iremashvili, who attended the funeral, Koba was extremely upset by the loss of his 'faithful companion'. Although the two men were parted from each other politically – Joseph Iremashvili was a staunch Menshevik – Koba greeted him in a friendly manner as of old. At the cemetery gate, he pressed his old friend's hand and, pointing to the coffin, said: 'Soso, this creature softened my stony heart. She is dead and with her my last warm feelings for all human beings have died.' Then, placing his hand over his heart, he added: 'It is all so desolate here inside, so unspeakably desolate!'

Years later, when Trotsky first learned of this theatrical outburst, he was inclined to accept it as genuine, because, as he remarked, it reflected not only the heartfelt grief of a young man overwhelmed for the first time by a profound personal loss, but also a characteristic penchant for strained pathos, which Trotsky had noted on other occasions and now described as 'a trait not unusual among persons of harsh character'.

Iremashvili's comment is also worth recording:

From the day he buried his wife, he indeed lost the last vestiges of human feeling. His heart filled with the unalterably malicious hatred which his cruel father had begun to engender in him while he was still a child. Ruthless with himself, he became ruthless with everyone else.[73]

CHAPTER III

Prison and Exile

I

Looking back some years later on his time in Baku, Koba put this important period of his career in its proper perspective. 'Two years of revolutionary work among the oil workers of Baku hardened me as a practical fighter and as one of the local practical leaders,' he recalled in 1926. 'Association with such advanced workers in Baku as Vatsek... and others, on the one hand, and the storm of acute conflicts between the workers and the oil owners, on the other, first taught me what it means to lead large masses of workers. It was there, in Baku, that I thus received my second baptism in the revolutionary struggle. There I became a journeyman in the art of revolution.'[1] Official Soviet historians have made much of the fact that Koba was elected a member of the Baku Committee of the Social Democratic Party at this time and they have proclaimed how under his leadership Baku became 'a citadel of Bolshevism'. There was of course no question of winning over the committee to this way of political thinking, since the committee was in fact an exclusively Bolshevik one, and there was already a separate Menshevik committee in being from which the Baku Bolsheviks constituted in effect a breakaway organisation. It is however true to say that for the first time in Georgian Social Democracy, hitherto almost completely Menshevik dominated, the Bolsheviks gained the upper hand in an important industrial area. In this development Koba was only one of a number of leading Bolsheviks. Stepan Shaumyan, Prokofy Dzhaparidze and Suren Spandarayan were all more prominent; they were also better known. But Koba had his own particular followers like Sergo Ordzhonikidze, Klim Voroshilov and Sergei Alliluyev, and with their aid he fought the local Mensheviks as bitterly as he did the oil owners. And with their aid, too, he did much to foment the wave of strikes which virtually paralysed the Baku oil wells in the early months of 1908.[2]

In the Baku region at this time, 47,000 oil workers were on strike, by far the greatest proportion in any part of the Tsar's empire, a fact which caused Lenin a certain melancholy satisfaction. 'These are the last of the Mohicans of the political mass strike,' so Lenin called them. The strikers elected delegates to a general workers' council, a body which the management reluctantly recognised as a negotiating body on behalf of the whole industry, one of the earliest examples in Russia of the admission of the principle of collective bargaining. 'We must be ready to confront the oil owners fully armed at any moment,' Koba wrote in *Gudok* on 16 March 1908. 'For this we must immediately set out to draw up demands.'[3] Whatever demands the writer had in mind he had no time to formulate since he was arrested nine days later. Stepan Shaumyan had already been arrested, and as in Tiflis two years previously suspicion fell upon Koba for having given this comrade away to the police. Consequently it may well be that Koba's arrest, which took place on 26 March, was for his own protection. He was taken to Bailov prison, a rambling two-storey building situated on the promontory of Cape Bailov extending into the Caspian sea about a mile or so to the south-west of Baku harbour.

The prison had been built to accommodate four hundred inmates, but at this period it contained nearly three times that number, ordinary criminals being allowed to mix indiscriminately with political prisoners on an 'open' system – that is to say, the inmates were not locked in their cells except at night but were allowed to wander at will through the corridors and yards and outbuildings, arguing, debating, quarrelling and fighting. A permanent gallows had been set up in the main courtyard and midnight executions were a frequent feature of the prison routine. Apart from those condemned to death, the prison was used as a transit prison where prisoners from the whole of the Transcaucasus and Transcaspian regions were collected prior to being dispersed to exile in Russia or Siberia. The cells were quite full and many prisoners were obliged to sleep in the corridors and even on the stairs.

A prisonr named Semyen Vereshchak, a Social Revolutionary whose Party advocated self-determination for the Georgians and other non-Russian peoples and thus differed from both the Mensheviks and the Bolsheviks, had many opportunities of observing Koba in prison; in his old age Vereshchak was induced to set down his recollections which rank with those of Iremashvili, Uratadze and Arsenidze as the most vivid and at the same time most trustworthy memories of the young Stalin to have survived. What impressed Vereshchak about Koba was his revolutionary professionalism and his one-track mind. With Koba the welfare of 'the people' ceased to be an ideal and became merely an object of political experiments. His most pronounced quality was his cunning, but this tended to conceal his other qualities even from experienced and observant eyes. First impressions of him were always negative, since his physical appearance was unattractive. 'He knew this,' wrote Vereshchak, 'and so never appeared at large meetings...His presence in workers' districts was detectable only by increased activity among the workers.' According to Vereshchak, the prison was in effect a militant propagandist revolutionary school, and Koba played a leading part in organising discussion groups and indoctrinating the novices. On Marxism Vereshchak considered Koba unbeatable – 'nothing would cause him to alter his position once he had stated it'. Vereshchak never forgot one debate on the agrarian question, when Sergo Ordzhonikidze, who was defending a proposition of Koba's, got so heated that he seized his Social Revolutionary protagonist Ilya Kartsevadze by the throat. 'For that Koba himself was roughly beaten up afterwards by the Socialist Revolutionaries in the prison.'

Vereshchak remembered in particular how Koba arrived wearing a blue satin shirt with an open collar, having neither belt nor cap but wearing a *bashlyk* (hood) draped over his shoulders. He walked slowly like a cat, his small eyes peering out of his pointed pockmarked face. He always had a book in his hand. As a rule the political prisoners kept to themselves and did not mix with the criminals. But Koba went out of his way to associate with thieves, murderers, blackmailers, counterfeiters and the like. According to Vereshchak, he was always impressed by men who were 'in for something real', while he regarded politics as just 'a thing to be done and done thoroughly'. Once a week meat soup Caucasian style was served to the inmates from the prison kitchen, and somehow or other Koba always managed to get some meat in his bowl. 'I still recall the weekly scene,' noted Vereshchak, 'the cook with his ladle, and the "leader" supervising the fair distribution of the soup, and Koba's face as he looked longingly at the tureen and uttered the same words every week, "Please, chief, a bit more meat for me!" '⁴

Koba's seemingly iron nerves also impressed Vereshchak. No amount of needling or teasing or provocation by other prisoners did he allow to get under his skin. The nocturnal executions likewise left him unmoved, although earlier the same day he might have eaten and argued with the condemned men whose shrieks and moans on their way to the gallows and then as they were being strung up greatly upset the other prisoners. But Koba either slept through it all or else ostentatiously studied Esperanto which he believed would be the language of the Communist International. As a penalty for some real or supposed infraction of prison discipline, all the prisoners were made to run the gauntlet on Easter Sunday 1908, provided by soldiers of a local regiment who belaboured the prisoners with sticks and rifle butts. While most of the prisoners ran, in order to get the punishment over as quickly as possible, Koba walked slowly down the line, book in hand – as one might expect a book by Marx, according to the official Soviet apologists. On another occasion he knocked loudly on the door of his cell with a slop bucket, undeterred by the threats of the guard's bayonets.

What particularly impressed Vereshchak was Koba's cleverness at inciting others to cause trouble while himself remaining in the background. On at least two occasions he started rumours that a particular fellow prisoner was a *shpik* (spy), and on each occasion the unfortunate prisoner was violently assaulted, one being saved in the nick of time by the guards who carried him off to hospital and the other being knifed with fatal results. In this latter case Koba exhibited what Vereshchak described as a great capacity for murder by proxy. Vereshchak does not seem to have suspected that Koba was himself a police spy, although he noted that while Koba was often detained by the police in the course of his revolutionary career, he was never once convicted of any specific offence. 'His conspiratorial wit and cunning stood him in good stead, and he was always able to avoid being brought to trial.'[5]

On the whole Koba contrived to remain popular with the other prisoners and once he helped to organise an escape. The oil worker Ivan Vatsek, who was chairman of the Bailov Social Democratic Committee, lived on a hill opposite the prison. His wife usually sat sewing by a window which was visible from Koba's cell, and it was understood that if Koba was seen to wave a handkerchief from the cell window this would indicate a wish for a meeting. One day, in response to this signal, which was given during the daily visiting period, Mrs Vatsek hurried over and on her arrival Koba took her aside and engaged her in conversation, deliberately drawing the attention of the guards to them both. When the bell rang to mark the end of the visiting period, the visitors trooped out, and one of the prisoners succeeded in escaping in the guise of a departing visitor, while Koba was still talking to Mrs Vatsek. 'Good for Koba,' was the general comment

95

when the news of the escape got out. 'He certainly cooked up something clever!'[6]

After five months in Bailov prison, Koba was officially informed that he had been exiled to Vologda Province in the north of European Russia, on the whole an easier place of exile than eastern Siberia. He left Bailov on 29 September 1908, and should have arrived in a matter of weeks at Solvychegodsk, where he had been ordered to reside for two years 'under open police surveillance'. But he fell ill on the journey with typhus and in consequence was taken to hospital at Vyatka, with the result that he did not reach his final destination until the end of February 1909. Solvychegodsk was a small fur trading settlement near the Sukhona River, some seven hundred miles north-east of St Petersburg. Little is known of the short time, barely five months, that Koba spent there apart from a local police report in which he is described as 'coarse, insolent and disrespectful to his superiors'. According to the official Soviet accounts, he 'escaped' from Solvychegodsk on 24 June 1909, and there can be little if any doubt that this took place with the connivance of the Okhrana.[7]

Indeed Beria, in his desire to underline Koba's importance as a revolutionary, inadvertently admits as much when he quotes from a Tiflis police report dated 24 October 1909, to the effect that Koba had been issued with a passport No. 982 by the local police in the name of Oganess Vartanovich Totomyants, an Armenian resident of Tiflis, dated 12 May of the same year, that is about six weeks before his 'escape' from Solvychegodsk. The inference is obvious. The Okhrana needed him for further work in the Caucasus and so engineered his 'escape', which he made good by travelling via St Petersburg and Moscow and eventually reaching Baku about the end of July.[8]

Some of the Baku Mensheviks were in the habit of meeting in a dairy called Gabuniya near Bagirov Square, where they could get cheap yoghourt and the manager was sympathetic to their cause. Among those who foregathered there one Sunday in August 1909, were Leontii Zhgenti, Gregory Aiollo, and Andrey Vyshinsky, a young lawyer of Polish descent, three years Koba's junior, who was later to go over to the Bolsheviks and play a sinister role as Chief Public Prosecutor when they came to power. On this particular Sunday, the chief topic of conversation was a leaflet attacking the Mensheviks which had been printed in considerable numbers in the name of the 'Baku Social Democratic Party Committee', that is a breakaway Bolshevik organisation. What intrigued those present was the question of how the leaflets had come to be printed at all, since the local printers' trade union was exclusively Menshevik and none of its members would have printed leaflets of such an anti-Menshevik character. Suddenly Vyshinsky looked up and whispered, 'Koba!' The other followed Vyshinsky's gaze. Koba approached, smiling ironically and greeting the others by raising his hand. 'That's who the Baku Committee is,' said Vyshinsky laughing. 'That's whose hand is behind the leaflets!'

The others gathered round Koba and fired questions at him. When had he arrived in Baku? And where had he come from? But Koba refused to satisfy their curiosity. 'It's none of your business,' he said. Then he added, 'It is *we* Bolsheviks who are making the revolution, while *you* Mensheviks are just opportunists.' The others laughed. But Aiollo, who was perhaps a little shrewder than his companions, looked hard at Koba and said, 'You are nothing but a *provocateur* of the workers – admit it at least for the sake of your conscience!' But Koba did not appear in the least upset by this remark. 'We'll take all possible measures against you in due course,' he replied, 'you corrupt traitors!' And with that he turned on his heel and walked off without another word.

Zhgenti and the other Mensheviks were determined to find out where the leaflets had been printed, and they asked Arshak Kachiev, the president of the local trade union. ('It was pure curiosity on our part, no more and no less.') Kachiev undertook to inquire. A few days later he came back with the answer. The leaflets had been printed on a press belonging to the Baku Central Police Department.[9]

2

On 23 March 1910, Koba was again arrested by the Baku police, this time in the name of Zakhar Grigorian Melikiants. The discovery in the Okhrana archives of a report from the Baku *gendarmerie* to Colonel Eremin, the officer in charge at Tiflis, suggests that Koba had been making a nuisance of himself to the Baku authorities by alerting various local Bolsheviks to the fact that they were under police surveillance and actually identifying the police 'tails' for the information of these comrades. By so doing, says the inter-departmental report, he had 'evidently damaged the entire operation' of police surveillance of revolutionaries in Baku, and so the local authorities had no alternative but to lock him up. He was again lodged in Bailov prison where he met several old acquaintances including Semyen Vereshchak.[10]

On the day following Koba's arrest, Captain Fedor Ivanovich Galimbatovsky of the Baku *gendarmerie* submitted a report to St Petersburg in which he recommended that in view of the prisoner's 'persistent revolutionary activity and his escape on two occasions from the locality of his exile...recourse should be had to a more severe measure of punishment, namely exile to a remote district of Siberia for *five* years'.[11] However, a study of Koba's file in the St Petersburg headquarters of the Okhrana may have suggested that he could still be of use to the secret police, since Captain Galimbatovsky's recommendation was turned down and an order was issued directing that Koba Djugashvili should merely be sent back to Solvychegodsk to serve out the remainder of his term of exile there. At the same time he was banned by viceregal decree from living in the Caucasus for a period of five years.[12]

Koba reached Solvychegodsk for the second time in October 1910, and remained there until the expiry of his term of exile in the following June. There seems to have been little for him to do there apart from attempting to organise a local Social Democratic Party group, and debating with other exiles. He was consequently restless and bored. He lived in the house of a certain Maria Kuzakova, who subsequently complained that his mail was carefully scrutinised by the local police and that his movements and those of the other exiles were restricted – for instance, they were not allowed to go into the country outside Solvychegodsk to pick mushrooms or berries. Two letters which he wrote at this time were intercepted and copied by the secret police. In both of these he offered his services as a party organiser in Russia since he was prevented by the residence ban from returning to Georgia. And in both he indicated plainly that if he was needed before the expiry of his term of exile, there would be no difficulty in his escaping.

The first letter was addressed to a Bolshevik named Isaak Shvarts, known as 'Comrade Semyen', whom Koba had met in the Caucasus and who was then on a visit to Paris where he was helping Lenin with the arrangements for the next party conference which was being planned to take place in Prague. In fact this letter was primarily intended for Lenin's eyes and deliberately flattered him for his prescience in reaching an understanding with the Menshevik leader Plekhanov, who had recently broken away from the majority of his party faction on the question of 'liquidationism' and with a small group of followers was once more working with Lenin. 'Liquidationism' was the pejorative term used by the Bolsheviks to describe those Social Democrats, mostly Mensheviks, led by Martov, Trotsky and Bogdanov, who advocated wholehearted co-operation with the State Duma and other legal institutions and who wished to 'liquidate' the conspiratorial apparatus which was the principal feature of the Bolshevik underground.[13]

Solvychegodsk,
31 December 1910

Comrade Semyen!

Yesterday I received your letter from the comrades. First of all, hearty greetings to Lenin, Kamenev and the others. Next about your letter and in general about the 'damned questions'.

In my opinion the line of the Lenin–Plekhanov bloc is the only correct one. This line, and it alone, answers to the real interest of the work in Russia, which demands that all real Party elements should rally together...A fight for influence in the legal organisations is the burning question of the day, a necessary stage on the road towards the regeneration of the Party; and a bloc is the only means by which these organisations can be cleansed of the garbage of liquidationism.

The plan for a bloc reveals the hand of Lenin – he is a shrewd fellow and knows where the crayfish hide in the winter...

But that is not all, nor even the most important. The most important thing is to organise the work in Russia. The history of our Party shows that disagreements are ironed out not in debates, but mainly in the course of work, in the course of applying principles. Hence the task of the day is to organise work in Russia round a strictly defined principle...

In my opinion, our immediate task, the one that brooks no delay, is to organise a central group in Russia, to co-ordinate the illegal, semi-legal and legal work at first in the main centres (St Petersburg, Moscow, the Urals, the South). Call it what you like – the 'Russian section of the Central Committee' or auxiliary group of the central Committee – it makes no difference; but such a group is as essential as air, as bread. At the present time lack of information, loneliness and isolation reign among the Party workers in the regions and they are all becoming discouraged...

Now about myself. I have another six months to go here. When the term expires I shall be entirely at your service. If the need for Party workers is really acute, I could get away at once...

There is a decent crowd here in exile, and it would be a very good thing if they could be supplied with the illegal periodicals...

With comradely greetings,
K.S.

Don't send by registered mail. Write about how things are going on your side, I beg of you.

This letter, the first of Koba's to have survived, is an extraordinary production. In the first place, by using the ordinary mails, it violated the conspiratorial rule that such confidential communications as this should always be entrusted to a safe hand. When Koba dropped it into the mail box at Solvychegodsk, he must have known that it was certain to be picked out by the censors and passed over to the Okhrana, which in fact was what happened. The proposal for the establishment of a Bolshevik centre inside Russia, which conveyed an oblique hint that he should head it, may have been deliberately calculated to impress the secret police with his desire to attain a place in the upper ranks of the Bolshevik hierarchy, since the role that he envisaged for himself in the centre must surely carry with it membership of the Central Committee. While designed to convince Lenin that he could thereby considerably advance the Bolshevik cause, at the same time Koba hoped to secure the goodwill of the secret police for the project, since he knew that they still regarded the Mensheviks as by far the better organised and more dangerous opponents of the Tsarist government. In these circumstances the Okhrana might be expected to accept the proposed centre as a convenient instrument for playing off one wing of the Social Democratic Party against the other and so undermining the power of the Mensheviks.

The second letter, which was not intended for Lenin's eyes, was addressed to the Moscow Bolsheviks through a local woman teacher named Bobrovskaya. Dispatched barely three weeks after the first letter, on 24 January 1911, it showed the writer's cunning and duplicity, since Koba blatantly dismissed the secession of Plekhanov and his followers from the Menshevik camp as a 'tempest in a teapot' and compared the whole breed of expatriate Social Democrats with 'insects who crawl on the wall'. The reference could not have been more tactless or offensive.

> I am finishing here in July of this year. Ilyich [Lenin] and Co. are calling me to one or two centres, without waiting for the end of the term (there are more possibilities for a legal person)...But if there is a great need, then, of course, I'll fly the coop...We are stifling here without anything to do. I am literally choking.
>
> We have heard, of course, about the 'tempest in the teapot' abroad – the blocs of Lenin–Plekhanov on the one hand, and those of Trotsky–Martov–Bogdanov on the other. The workers' attitude towards the first bloc is, as far as I know, favourable. But in general the workers are beginning to look contemptuously on 'abroad' saying: 'Let them crawl on the wall to their heart's desire, but the way we feel about it is that he who has the interests

of the movement at heart should keep busy. As for the rest it will take care of itself.'

This, I think, is for the best.

Joseph

My address: Solvychegodsk, Vologda Province, political exile, Joseph Djugashvili.[14]

By some means or other Lenin heard of this letter as well as the other and not unnaturally was quite annoyed. Sergo Ordzhonikidze, who was with him at the time, participating in a school for revolutionaries which Lenin was running at Longjumeau near Paris, did his best to stick up for Koba as 'a good comrade'. Lenin was not easily mollified. 'You say that Koba is a good comrade,' he remarked with a scowl. 'But do you not close your eyes to his inconsistency? Nihilistic little jokes about "a tempest in a teapot" betray Koba's immaturity as a Marxist.'[15]

It took Lenin some time before he consented to forgive Koba for his 'immaturity'. Thus he was allowed to serve out his term at Solvychegodsk without receiving any request from Lenin and the other comrades to 'fly the coop'. He was released in June 1911, and since he was forbidden to live either in the Caucasus or any large industrial city, he chose Vologda, the provincial capital, as the most convenient centre from which to maintain contact with both St Petersburg and Moscow, being equally distant from the two cities. As a result of an understanding with the St Petersburg Okhrana, he was supplied with identity documents in the name of Peter Aleksandrovich Chizhikov, an employee of a Vologda fruit store, and under this alias he is known to have left Vologda by the afternoon train for the capital on 6 September 1911.[16]

It was a grey, drizzling morning when Koba arrived at the Nikolaevsky station in St Petersburg. He decided to reconnoitre the town in the hope of running into some party comrade or other acquaintance rather than to try to find a room immediately. After wandering about for several hours, he eventually returned to the Nevsky Prospect when the day shift workers were knocking off work. Suddenly he recognised a printing trade worker whom he knew named Sila Todria and accosted him after following him for a short time. 'Things are extremely dangerous,' explained Todria. 'The entire police force has been alerted, and all front doors and gates have to be closed by midnight.' The reason for these strict security precautions was the assassination of the Prime Minister Stolypin who had just been shot by a revolutionary at a gala performance in the Kiev Opera House in full view of the Tsar and the imperial family.

Koba suggested that they should find a small hotel and Todria accordingly took him off to one he knew, the Hotel Rossiya, in nearby Goncharnaya Street. The *concierge* eyed him suspiciously and scrutinised his identity papers before eventually allowing him to register, which he did in the name of Chizhikov. Todria arranged to call for him on the following morning. He kept the appointment and together they went off in search of Sergei Alliluyev in the Viborg district, then a working-class stronghold. They did not notice that they were being followed by two plain-clothes policemen.

The door was opened by Alliluyev's daughter Anna. 'Is your father at home?' asked Todria.

On being told that he was expected shortly, the two men were invited to come in. Anna Alliluyeva noticed that Todria's companion looked very thin and wore a black overcoat and soft felt hat. 'Meet our comrade, Soso,' said Todria simply. Anna then realised that this was the man whom she had often heard her father speak of, the revolutionary with whom he worked in Tiflis and Baku, the comrade who had been arrested and exiled several times but who had always managed to escape.

It was nearly supper time when Alliluyev returned from work. According to Anna, he greeted his guests with undisguised pleasure, shaking Koba's hand warmly. The three men then retired to the adjoining room, whence some snatches of conversation drifted into Anna. 'What the devil is the matter with you?' Koba was heard to say. 'Well, well...you seem to have them on the brain...Some comrades are turning into scared Philistines and yokels!'

'Take a look yourself through the window,' answered Alliluyev. 'I recognised them as soon as I approached the house.'

Then, opening the door into the next room, Alliluyev called out to Anna and her young brother Fedya. 'Hey, there, you children go down to the yard, one at a time, and see if there are a couple of men prowling round – you know – the ones in bowler hats...'

The children duly returned and reported that one was posted at the arch leading out of the yard and the other in the street facing the front window. 'We'll have to wait a while,' said Koba.

Later in the evening a fitter named Zabelin called and when he realised the circumstances offered to take Koba to his place for the night. It was quite late when they managed to slip out and by taking a number of devious back streets succeed in shaking off the two policemen, who were by this time feeling extremely tired and hungry. Koba spent the remainder of the night at Zabelin's place and, according to Anna Alliluyeva, 'made the necessary contacts with people during the following day and evening', before returning to the Hotel Rossiya, 'so as not to embarrass his friends'.

At dawn he was awakened by a loud knocking on the door of his room. 'Why don't you let me sleep?' he shouted. There was an answering shout from the corridor to him to open up as it was the police. There was nothing left for it but to obey, and a few minutes later he was on his way to the St Petersburg Detention Prison, where he was to spend the next three months kicking his heels when he was not being interrogated by the Okhrana.[17]

In the middle of December 1911, he was sent back to Vologda, there to begin a further three-year term of exile under open police surveillance. Although he did not know it at this moment, the fact that he was sent to Vologda rather than eastern Siberia was a great stroke of luck since it meant that he was to be comparatively easily accessible to the Bolshevik hierarchy at what was to prove the principal turning point in his career.[18]

The key to the sudden change in Koba's political status which took place at this time lay in the action taken by Lenin following the Sixth Social Democratic Party Congress, which Lenin had convened in Prague in January 1912. Although Lenin had impressed upon the Czech comrades that it must be a gathering conducted in conditions of secrecy, since most of the Russian delegates had crossed the frontier illegally without proper passports, no obstacles were put in its way by the Prague police authorities, no doubt at the instigation of the Okhrana who rightly guessed that it would be the means of making the division between the two wings of the Social Democratic Party final and irrevocable. A new and entirely Bolshevik Central Committee was elected, headed by Lenin and including Zinoviev, Ordzhonikidze, Spandarayan, and Roman Malinovsky, one of the Moscow delegates, to whom Lenin had taken a great fancy. Malinovsky, a Pole by origin, was a talented young man in his early thirties; he had a seemingly impeccable working-class record as a trade union organiser – as a former Menshevik he had helped to organise the St Petersburg metalworkers' union. He had previously been a tailor, and he was known to the Okhrana, for whom he also worked, by the cover name of *Portnoi* (the tailor). He seems to have been recruited by the Okhrana following a prison sentence for burglary and rape at the turn of the century. He was a plausible speaker and a heavy drinker, although he held his liquor well. Lenin was quite captivated by his charm and appointed him to take charge of the organisation in the shape of a

Bolshevik centre inside Russia which it will be remembered Koba had recommended should be set up. Fresh elections to the Duma had been announced for early in the New Year. When Malinovsky suggested that he (Malinovsky) should stand as a Bolshevik candidate for Moscow, Lenin welcomed the idea enthusiastically. So, it may be added, did the Okhrana, who by this time regarded Malinovsky as their most important agent inside Russia.[19]

Before the Sixth Party Congress broke up, the delegates empowered Lenin to co-opt further members to the Central Committee at his personal choice. Lenin immediately exercised this power by adding two members to the Committee. One of these was Koba, whom he had by now forgiven for his indiscreet 'tempest in a teapot' letter to the Moscow comrades. According to one Social Democratic Party source, the person directly responsible for persuading Lenin to take this action was Malinovsky.[20] Other sources have suggested that Ordzhonikidze won over Lenin. Both may have had a hand in the co-option, Ordzhonikidze out of pure comradely affection for Koba and Malinovsky because he knew it would suit the Okhrana's book. Ordzhonikidze made a special journey to Vologda to inform Koba, or Ivanovich as he was known to Lenin, that he was now a member of the Central Committee. 'I have seen Ivanovich and have a definite understanding with him,' wrote Ordzhonikidze to Lenin on 24 February 1912. 'He is most pleased with the turn of events and is greatly impressed.' Five days later, Koba-Ivanovich once more escaped from Vologda.[21]

This time his spell of liberty lasted for less than two months. But if the official Soviet chronology is to be believed, he was busily occupied during this brief period in writing leaflets and articles, defying the viceroy's ban by visiting Tiflis and Baku to explain to the workers the decisions of the Prague Congress and the role of the new Central Committee of which he was now a member, inaugurating the election campaign for the next Duma, and on his return to St Petersburg helping to plan and produce at Lenin's prompting a daily underground newspaper which was to become the chief organ of the Russian Communist Party. In the leaflet entitled *For the Party!* he summarised the Central Committee's role as he envisaged it and as indeed it was later to develop under the direction of an all-powerful General Secretary.[22]

An influential Central Committee connected by living roots with the local organisations, systematically keeping the latter informed and linking them up together; a Central Committee which constantly intervenes in all matters concerning general proletarian actions; a Central Committee which possesses an

illegal newspaper published in Russia for the purpose of conducting wide political agitation – such is the direction in which the
renovation and consolidation of the Party must proceed.

Preparations for the production of the newspaper, which was to be
called *Pravda* (Truth), were already well advanced when Koba returned to St Petersburg early in April 1912; the necessary finance was
apparently provided by the Okhrana through Malinovsky in order to
compete with the Menshevik daily *Luch* (Light). In the days of his
supreme power Stalin liked to claim a much more important part in
the foundation of *Pravda* than the known facts disclose, purporting to
be the editor-in-chief and the author of the original editorial setting out
the aims of the new journal ('to illuminate the paths of the Russian
labour movement with the light of international Social Democracy, to
spread the truth among the workers about the friends and enemies of
the working class, to guard the interests of labour's cause').[23] The
secretary of the editorial board was a twenty-two-year-old Bolshevik of
immense industry and stubborn pertinacity named Vyacheslav Mikhailovich Scriabin, whose uncle Alexander Scriabin was the well-
known musical composer. Young Vyacheslav was later to change his
surname to Molotov, and under this pseudonym meaning 'hammer'
his career was to be closely linked with that of Koba, when the latter
took the name Stalin, which he was shortly to do.

Koba was hiding out at this time in St Petersburg, in the house of
N. G. Poletayev, an experienced journalist and one of the Bolshevik
members of the Duma; this fact enabled him to be present at the meeting in Poletayev's house when the contents of the first issue of *Pravda*
were agreed and the make-up approved. The paper appeared for the
first time on 22 April 1912. Later the same day Koba was again
arrested, having unwisely left Poletayev's house which owing to its
owner's membership of the Duma was immune from police search.
This time he was dispatched considerably further afield than Vologda
– to the Narym territory of Tomsk province in central Siberia, about
sixteen hundred miles from St Petersburg. Yet within five months he
had managed once again to escape and to make his way back to the
capital.

Little is known of Koba's time in Narym apart from the fact that he
had as companions in exile several prominent Bolsheviks including the
outstanding party organiser and future head of state Jacob Sverdlov, as well as two future Red Army commanders Mikhail Lashevich
and Ivan Smirnov, as well as Semyen Vereshchak, his old prison associate in Baku. There was also a Social Revolutionary in Narym called

Semyen Surin, who had been with Koba at Vologda and is also known to have been a police spy. According to Vereshchak, Koba's arrival was marked by a great increase in activity among the exiles who planned a series of escapes. Sverdlov escaped but was recaptured, although he had a false passport fabricated by Vereshchak. Koba was more fortunate; he got away by boat and made his way up the river Irtysh through Tobolsk to Tomsk, continuing his journey by train on the Trans-Siberian line to St Petersburg. As usual he passed through the numerous police checkpoints without difficulty.[24]

3

When Koba reached the Alliluyevs' hospitable house on Sampsoniev-skaya Street, the campaign for the elections to the Fourth Duma were in full swing. Anna Alliluyeva later recalled how Koba used to appear at her father's electrical repair shop in the morning. He would sit on a sofa in the dining room, looking very tired. 'If you feel like taking a rest,' her mother Olga would say to him, 'go and lie down on the bed in the store room. It's not good trying to snatch a nap in this bedlam.' Another refuge was a small room behind the kitchen of their flat. He would come in after a sleepless night, usually accompanied by Sverdlov, who had by now returned from Siberia, since illegal workers' meetings during the campaign stretched well into the night. 'If they happened to pass a workmen's café they would drop in and sit over a cup of tea until two o'clock in the morning,' pretending to be slightly tipsy if they met a policeman on his beat.[25]

Koba's principal contribution to the election campaign was writing a mandate from the St Petersburg workers to the Bolshevik candidate, which was printed as a leaflet and widely distributed among the local factories. Lenin is said to have been greatly impressed by it when he received a copy, which he republished in his own emigré paper *Social Democrat*, giving instructions that the copy he had received from Koba should be carefully preserved.*

Under present conditions the floor of the Duma is one of the best means of enlightening and organising the broad masses of the proletariat [Koba wrote in this historic document]. It is precisely for this reason that we are sending our deputy to the Duma and instructing him and the entire Social Democratic group in the Fourth Duma to proclaim our demands...We want to hear the voices of the group ring out loudly from the Duma tribune, proclaiming the ultimate goal of the proletariat, proclaiming the

* The copy, with Lenin's instructions, is now in the Lenin Museum in Moscow.

full and uncurtailed demands of 1905, proclaiming the Russian working class as the leader of the popular movement, the peasantry as the most reliable ally of the working class and the liberal bourgeoisie as the betrayer of 'popular freedom'.[26]

Shortly after the elections, in which seven Mensheviks and six Bolsheviks were returned, including the police spy Malinovsky who became Bolshevik deputy for Moscow and Vice-Chairman of the Social Democratic Group in the Duma, Lenin summoned the Central Committee to a meeting in Cracow, then part of Austrian Poland. He also requested the attendance of a woman named Valentina Lobova, who had been acting as unofficial secretary to the Bolshevik faction in the Duma, and he instructed her to obtain a Finnish passport for Koba to enable him to make the journey. This she was asked to do through Alexander Shotman, a Bolshevik who was living in Helsinki and who had acquired such a facility for obtaining passports for pretended Finnish citizens that he was nicknamed the 'Bolshevik Minister of Foreign Affairs'. There were two possible routes for the illegal traveller, one by sea from Abo to a port on the Baltic coast, which entailed a certain amount of risk, and the other going north through Tornio to Harapanda and thence crossing the frontier into Sweden on foot, which was considerably longer but much safer. Lobova, who travelled with Koba to Helsinki, told Shotman that she had received a directive from Lenin that Koba had to be dispatched 'with maximum speed and absolute security'. Shotman replied that he could not guarantee this and asked to see Koba, to whom he explained the details of the two routes. Having weighed them up, Koba said he would go via Abo, and accordingly Shotman accompanied him and Lobova, who chose the same route, as far as the port of embarkation.

As they approached the steamer from the train, there was a check point where there were two policemen verifying passengers' travel documents. Shotman suddenly became apprehensive when Koba handed over his Finnish passport for scrutiny, since he did not in the least resemble a Finn. However, there was no hitch and he was passed safely on board. A few days later he and Valentina Lobova reached Cracow without mishap.[27]*

* Valentina Lobova was exiled to Siberia in 1913 and died of tuberculosis in 1924. Alexander Shotman, who was to play an important part as liaison between the Central Committee and Lenin, when the latter went into hiding during the period of the Provisional Government in 1917, was arrested during one of Stalin's final purges of the 'Old Bolsheviks' in 1939. Shotman's wife wrote to Kalinin, then President of the Soviet Union, asking for an interview with Stalin. 'I am certain that Stalin will see me,' she wrote. 'He surely remembers me from Finland, when

The purpose of the meeting of the Central Committee was to take stock of the situation in the light of the Duma elections. Lenin pressed hard for an open split between the Bolshevik and Menshevik deputies, but he failed to carry conviction with the group. The fact was that, in the face of a legislature largely dominated by the extreme Right, the thirteen Social Democratic deputies were unwilling to expose their differences and considered it better tactics to preserve an outward semblance of unity. On his return to St Petersburg Koba supported this line, particularly in *Pravda*, much to Lenin's annoyance. By early December Lenin was planning to counteract the influence of his latest recruit to the Central Committee in the running of the party newspaper, although he admitted that Koba had 'done the most important work' and was still 'needed'. To this end he called a further meeting of the Central Committee, including the six Bolshevik deputies, for the end of the month in Cracow.

For this second meeting, which began on 26 December, Koba travelled by train from St Petersburg without a passport, no doubt to save time. Afterwards he laughingly told Anna Alliluyeva how he had scared two fellow passengers in the same compartment who were also travelling to the frontier between Russian and Austrian Poland. They spent their time reading aloud from leaflets put out by the reactionary Black Hundreds until at last Koba could stand it no longer. 'Why do you read such rubbish?' he burst out. 'You should read other papers.' The two men immediately exchanged frightened glances and without another word got up and left the compartment.

Koba had been told to get out at the frontier station, Dabrowa Gornicza, and then find some means of smuggling himself across the border into Austrian territory. He deliberately chose to take a train that arrived at Dabrowa early in the morning, so as to avoid the *gendarmes* at the station. As soon as the train began to slow down, he jumped out of the last coach, and avoiding the station buildings ran through the darkness in a southerly direction which he had been told was the way to Austria and Cracow. After a while he came to a road which seemed to be going the right way and hurried along it, though still feeling uncertain. Then he saw a light in a peasant's hut at the roadside. He approached it cautiously and looking through the window he saw a man mending boots. He decided to take a chance and knocked.

'Who's there?' said the cobbler.

Without thinking twice, the traveller replied, 'A revolutionary.'

I helped to organise his trip abroad in 1912.' Stalin refused to see her and he signed Shotman's death warrant which was duly carried out. See A. Tolmachev, *Kalinin*, (Moscow, 1963), p. 226.

'And what do you want?' asked the cobbler.

Koba, who saw the cobbler's face by the light and felt more confident, asked him if he could show him the road to the frontier, as he had to get to Cracow and had no passport.

'I'll take you to the frontier if you're a revolutionary. I know the way.'

The cobbler, who turned out to be a Pole, invited Koba to come in and have something to eat, which he was glad to do. His host asked him if he had come far. 'Yes, quite a way,' answered Koba.

Then, glancing at the cobbler's last and the tools of his trade, Koba remarked, 'My father was a cobbler too, at home in Georgia.'

'So you're from Georgia,' said the Pole. 'You must be a Georgian then?'

Koba nodded.

'I'm told your country is very beautiful with mountains and vineyards,' the cobbler continued. 'And Tsarist policemen just like Poland.'

'Yes, just like Poland,' answered Koba. 'No schools in our own language, but plenty of policemen.'

They started off together, and for a while Koba thought that the cobbler was going to hand him over to the *gendarmes*. They walked for about an hour, until they reached a forest. By this time it was growing light. 'There,' said the cobbler, pointing to a forest path. 'That's the frontier. I won't go with you any farther. Follow that direction for a good hour, then go west till you see a railway station, named Trzebinia. Get into a train there going to Vienna and that will take you to Cracow.'

Koba tried to press some roubles into his guide's hand, but the man pushed him away. 'No, don't,' he said. 'I didn't do it for money. We are both sons of oppressed nations and should help each other.'

With that they shook hands. 'Best of luck on your journey,' said the Polish cobbler.

Koba followed the cobbler's direction and after a couple of hours arrived at Trzebinia. He immediately made for the station restaurant. What happened next is best described in the account which he gave many years later to Stanislav Kot, the Polish Ambassador to the Soviet Union during the Second World War, at a banquet in the Kremlin.

I was terribly hungry. I ordered some food and sat down at a table. The waiter carted a lot of food around, but he continually gave me a miss, and then I heard a bell. Some of the people got up and ran to a train going westward. I went up to the buffet and said sharply: 'This is scandalous. Everybody else has been served except me.'

The waiter filled a plate with soup and handed it to me. Then there was another bell, a train for Cracow arrived and everybody rushed to get in. In my fury I threw the plate on the floor, flung a rouble at the waiter and flew out.

In due course he reached Cracow and was greeted by Lenin. 'Give me something to eat at once, for I'm half dead,' he exclaimed. 'I've had nothing since yesterday evening.'

'Why didn't you eat at Trzebinia? There's a good restaurant there.'

'The Poles wouldn't give me anything to eat,' said Koba, and proceeded to relate what had happened.

'But what language did you order the food in?' queried Lenin.

'Why, in Russian of course,' replied Koba. 'I don't know any other.'

'What a fool you are!' said Lenin. 'Don't you know that the Poles think of Russian as the language of their persecutors?'

'But how could I order anything when I don't know Polish?'

'How?' repeated Lenin, laughing at the other's simplicity. 'Why, you should just have pointed at what you wanted and you'd have got it!'

After the Revolution, when he had become a commissar in the first Bolshevik Government, Stalin (as he then styled himself) related the story of the Polish cobbler and the illegal frontier crossing to Anna Alliluyeva. 'I should very much like to know where that man is now and what has happened to him,' he said. 'What a pity I have forgotten his name and cannot trace him!'[28]

Lenin's first step at the newly convened meeting in Cracow was to dispatch Jacob Sverdlov to reorganise the board of *Pravda*. 'Of course, *Pravda* is badly managed,' complained Lenin's wife Krupskaya. 'Every Tom, Dick and Harry is on the editorial staff, and most of them are not literaries.' Then so as to keep Koba otherwise occupied while Sverdlov was overhauling the paper, Lenin devised several new assignments for him. One of these was to write an article for Lenin's expatriate journal *Social Democrat* on the elections in St Petersburg, since Koba had been the Central Committee representative in the campaign. This Koba did, signing the article 'K. Stalin'. It was the first time that he had used the pseudonym which he now adopted in place of his various other aliases. Joseph Djugashvili had finally become Joseph Stalin.[29]

Koba-Stalin's principal assignment was the production of a detailed thesis on the nationalities question, which Lenin discussed at length with his colleagues on the Central Committee and which Stalin composed at Lenin's directive for another illegal Bolshevik journal called *Proveshcheniye* (Enlightenment). 'We've got a wonderful Georgian here who has settled down to write a big article for *Proveshcheniye* bringing together all the Austrian and other material,' wrote Lenin to Maxim Gorky at this time. 'We will really put our backs into this.'[30] Lenin maintained the right of self-determination up to and including separation, but at the same time he inculcated in all workers the duty of organisation for trade union, or political purposes in a single group in each country irrespective of nationality. This was the thesis he gave Stalin to develop and in order to collect the relevant material for it, Lenin suggested to him that he should pay a visit to Vienna, which as the capital of the ramshackle Hapsburg empire with its welter of different nationalities – Austrians, Hungarians, Italians, Serbs, Croats, Slovenes, Montenegrins – seemed the most suitable place for such a research project. It was arranged that Stalin should stay with Alexander Troyanovsky, future Soviet Ambassador to the United States, who was living with his wife Elena in Vienna at this period. Other Russian exiles whom Stalin was to meet in the course of his visit included Nikolai Bukharin, a brilliant Marxist theorist and future head of the Communist International, and Leon Trotsky, who was to become the outstanding Bolshevik War Commissar. The meeting with Trotsky took place in the apartment of a Menshevik named Skobelev who had just been elected a deputy to the Duma. Neither man spoke unless the guttural growl which Stalin gave on entering the room can be taken for a greeting. As Trotsky recalled the incident, he and Skobelev were talking when a stranger whom he did not recall having seen before, although they had both been at the London Congress, entered the room with an empty glass in his hand, went to the samovar, filled the glass with tea and silently withdrew. Skobelev then explained that this was the Caucasian Djugashvili, who had recently become a member of the Bolshevik Central Committee and seemed to be acquiring some importance in it. Trotsky retained a vivid memory of this first sight of his future adversary and of the disagreeable impression which Stalin made upon him. In particular, he noted Stalin's 'dim but not commonplace' appearance, the expression of 'morose concentration' on his face, and the 'glint of animosity' in his 'yellow eyes'.

Stalin had been in Vienna for about a week when he wrote to Roman Malinovsky, the Okhrana agent and leading Bolshevik deputy in the Duma. The fact that the text of this remarkable document dated 20 January 1913, should have survived is due to the fact that it was copied by the St Petersburg Okhrana and the copy marked 'Top

Secret' dispatched to the Chief of the Okhrana Foreign Agency in Paris, where it was preserved with the rest of the Okhrana archive now in the Hoover Institution of Stanford University in California. In writing it, Stalin addressed Malinovsky by the familiar second person singular, *ty*, which shows that he must already have been on intimate terms with him. Besides a request for news of Party matters in the Russian capital, Stalin particularly asked that an article on the nationalities question, which had been written by a *Pravda* contributor named M. A. Savelev, later one of the editors of Lenin's *Collected Works*, should be sent to him immediately instead of being published in *Pravda*. The letter was signed 'Vas', an abbreviation of Vassilev, Stalin's cover name at the time.[31]

> Greetings, friend. I am still sitting in Vienna and I am writing all sorts of rubbish. We shall see each other [soon].
>
> Please answer the following questions:
> 1. How are things with *Pravda*?
> 2. How are things with you in the faction?
> 3. How is the group?
> 4. How are A. [Jacob Sverdlov], Sh [N. P. Shagov a Bolshevik deputy in the Duma], and Bi [Valentina Lobova?]
> 5. How is Aleksi [Valentina's husband]?
>
> Ilyich Lenin doesn't know anything about all of this and he worries. If you have no time, let B. [Valentina Lobova] write without delay.
>
> Tell Vetrov [I. F. Savelev] not to publish the 'Nation question' but to send it here. Address: Vienna, Schönbrunner Schloss-strasse, No. 30, G. Troyanovsky. If possible send the article this very day.
>
> The letter from B-na [Valentina Lobova] to Vienna received. Galina [Elena Troyanovsky] sends regards to you and her. Galina says that she gave Ilyich the letter you left behind with her for delivery, but Ilyich evidently forgot to give it back. I will shortly be with Ilyich and I will try to take it from him and send it to you.
>
> Greetings to Stefania [Malinovsky's wife] and the kids.
>
> Yours,
>
> Vas

This letter with its conspiratorial overtones, the only letter known to have been written by Stalin from abroad, was clearly prompted by one which he had received from Valentina Lobova, who seems to have been looking forward to seeing him soon again in St Petersburg. It is conceivable that Valentina, who had accompanied Stalin on his first visit to Cracow in the previous November, may have been having a love affair with him at this time. At all events she would appear to have been on particularly close comradely terms with him, and she may well have known of his connection with the Okhrana, since her husband was an Okhrana agent and she worked for the chief agent Malinovsky in her capacity as secretary of the Bolshevik Duma faction. At the same time, Alexander Troyanovsky was beginning to have his suspicions about Malinovsky if not about Stalin. The letter which his wife Elena had left with Stalin, and which he had forgotten to return, may have referred to the activities of the Bolshevik underground in the Ukraine. As we shall see, Elena's involvement with these activities was to lead to her arrest when she visited Kiev at Lenin's wish a few weeks later.

So far as the purpose of Stalin's stay with the Troyanovsky's went, the 'rubbish' which he wrote, and which was subsequently 'edited' by Lenin, duly appeared in three instalments in the Party journal *Prosveshcheniye* under the signature 'K. Stalin'.[32] Following the end of the Second World War, when the nationality question again attracted attention, Stalin's thesis was republished as a book which sold millions of copies in the Soviet Union. At the same time, during the Allied occupation of Vienna, in 1948, a marble plaque with Stalin's profile in bronze bas-relief was erected on the outside wall of the Troyanovsky's house in Schönbrunner Schlosstrasse, apparently at the request of the Soviet element of the Control Commission, since the house was in the British zone. The plaque, which is still in place, in spite of having been smeared with red paint during the Hungarian rising in 1956, bears the following inscription: *J. V. Stalin resided in this house during January, 1913. He wrote his important work* Marxism and the National Question *here.*

Stalin's solution of the problem of nationalities in the Russian empire was not really clear-cut, depending as it did upon the somewhat vague application of 'the principle of international solidarity of the workers'. Although he was to become Commissar of Nationalities in the first Soviet Government, it was not until the days of his supreme power in the Soviet Union that he was able to introduce the ideal solution from his point of view of power statesmanship – wholesale deportation.

After clearing his essay with Lenin in Cracow, Stalin returned to St Petersburg in the middle of February, well pleased with himself and his contribution to Party theory, which he felt had enhanced his reputation. In giving rein to his ambitions at this time, he may even have nursed thoughts of displacing Malinovsky both as the local Bolshevik leader and as the chief Okhrana agent. If that is so, or even if he merely suspected it, Malinovsky took immediate steps to 'double cross' him. Stalin was hiding out in the apartments of various Bolshevik deputies in the Duma, and so long as he did so, Malinovsky knew that he was safe from arrest. Malinovsky's opportunity came on the occasion of a musical evening to mark the first anniversary of the founding of *Pravda*, which the police gave permission to be held in the hall of the Kalashnikov Grain Exchange near the harbour. Stalin was anxious to attend this gathering, since he knew that it should provide a useful opportunity to meet other Party workers and bring himself up to date on events during his absence abroad. Accordingly he asked Malinovsky whether it would be safe for him to attend, and he was assured that it would. Meanwhile Malinovsky alerted the police.

When he arrived at the hall, the organisers of the concert took Stalin to a dressing room so that he could change his clothes and disguise himself. But he had not been there more than a few minutes when several police agents burst into the room. One of them seized Stalin, shouting as he did so, 'Djugashvili, we've got you at last!'

'I'm not Djugashvili,' said Stalin. 'My name is Ivanov.'

'Tell those stories to your grandmother,' was the police rejoinder. He was then taken away under arrest, with Malinovsky protesting at the police action and indicating that he would take every measure to secure his release.[33]

There was now no question of the kind of lenient sentence Stalin had received in the past. This time the Okhrana directive was that he should spend the next four years as an exile under open police surveillance in the remote Turukhansk region of northern Siberia.[34]

4

'Why is there no news of Vasily?' wrote Lenin to Malinovsky in a letter containing secret writing easily read by the St Petersburg police. 'What is wrong with him. We are worried.' And again: 'Take good care of him, he is very sick.' (The expression 'very sick' in this context may well have been plain language code indicating that the subject was under intensive police observation.) When the news of Stalin's arrest eventually reached Lenin in Cracow, Stalin was on the way to his place of exile with other Bolshevik comrades who had also been arrested, including Jacob Sverdlov, also co-opted on to the Central Committee by Lenin at this time. Lenin learned the news from an anonymous correspondent connected with *Pravda*, apparently a woman, in another letter intercepted and copied by the police. 'Our dear soul the Georgian was caught the day before yesterday,' wrote this correspondent on 25 February. 'Some fool brought him to our soirée. It was simply folly to go there. I didn't even know about his being in St Petersburg, and was stunned to see him in a public place. "You won't get away with it," I said to him. He didn't. Now we are all left holding the baby, especially me...The Georgian's arrest has shaken me, I can tell you.'

From Krasnoyarsk, 2,500 miles from the capital on the Trans-Siberian Railway, Stalin was taken by boat down the river Yenisei, a further thirteen hundred miles, to the village of Monastyrskoye. Meanwhile Lenin, who was preparing to convene another conference of the Central Committee, appealed to Malinovsky to try to secure Stalin's release. But the only effect of this gesture was that Malinovsky again alerted the police, security restrictions were increased, and Stalin was moved further and further into the sub-polar tundra. He eventually arrived with Sverdlov at Kureika, a tiny village inside the Arctic Circle.

Elena Troyanovsky ('Galina'), Stalin's hostess in Vienna, had been arrested when she visited her father's house in Kiev on an underground mission for Lenin and was held in the local prison. It will be remembered that her husband suspected Malinovsky as being responsible. In the event the steps he took to secure his wife's release were more effective than those taken by Lenin on Stalin's behalf with the chief Okhrana spy. What Alexander Troyanovsky did was to write a letter to his father-in-law in Kiev to the effect that he had reason to believe that a man playing a double role had been the cause of his wife's arrest and imprisonment and he threatened to make an immense political scandal if she were not released. Like the intelligent revolutionary that he was, Troyanovsky knew that his letter was bound to be intercepted and copied by the Russian secret police. This is just what happened. Malinovsky was panic stricken when he heard about the letter, and Elena Troyanovsky was promptly freed.[35]

At this period the chief of the Special Section of the St Petersburg Okhrana, which was particularly concerned with the penetration of revolutionary organisations by double agents, was Colonel Alexander Eremin, who had been in charge of the Tiflis Special Section at the time of the police raid on the underground Avlabar printing press in 1906. Eremin was undoubtedly aware of Stalin's role as a police agent, and in the summer of 1913, before leaving the capital to take up a new post in Helsinki, he is stated to have written to the officer responsible for the Yenisei division of the Okhrana in the Turukhansk region of Siberia, informing him of Stalin's work for the secret police in the past, which he described as 'distinguished by accuracy but fragmentary', adding that after his 'election' to the Party Central Committee Stalin 'went over into open opposition to the Government and completely broke off his connection with the Okhrana'. Unfortunately, while the statements contained in this communication are substantially true, the letter itself is demonstrably a forgery, fabricated by a White Russian formerly in the Okhrana service and, as has already been shown, circulated with the object of further discrediting Stalin's reputation after Khrushchev's dramatic denunciation of him at the Party Congress in 1956.

On the other hand, some genuine confirmatory evidence hitherto unpublished, from an officer employed in the St Petersburg headquarters of the Okhrana at this time, has recently come to light. In 1911, Nikolai Vladimirovich Veselago joined the Okhrana as a *Gubernskii Sekretar*, equivalent in rank to a Second Lieutenant in the army, and for the following two years he served in the headquarters building, No. 14 Fontanka Quay. Though he was only a junior officer at this period, he had a retentive memory and his recollections of the structure and working of the St Petersburg Okhrana have been found to be quite accurate when checked against other sources. Therefore there would appear no reason to doubt his recollections of the following incident, which occurred during the preparation for the celebration of the three hundredth anniversary of the imperial rule of the Romanov dynasty in the spring of 1913.

The celebrations included a gala session of the Duma, and a number of foreign newspapers requested permission to send special correspondents to cover the occasion. A certain German journal asked for a pass for a man named Finkelstein, who was apparently a revolutionary agent as well as a journalist. The request was referred to the Director of the Okhrana, Colonel S. P. Beletsky, and as a result young Veselago was instructed to prepare a report. The Okhrana had a file on Finkelstein, but when Veselago inquired in the office registry the file could not be found. Veselago reported the loss to his immediate superior; he in turn informed the Vice-Director S. E. Vissarionov, who had been head of the Special Section before Eremin. Vissarionov told Beletsky, and the Director immediately sent for Veselago.

According to the latter's recollection, Beletsky was worried. If the missing file could not be found, he said, another one must be made up, and he entrusted to Veselago this task, by no means an easy one, since it entailed communicating with all the provincial Okhrana offices and agencies to obtain copies of the relevant reports about Finkelstein.

There was a pause, during which the Director appeared to be turning over something in his mind. Then he turned to his young subordinate and said: 'Nikolai Vladimirovich, if in these documents – which are to be obtained as soon as possible – you find one that refers to "Koba" bring it directly to me.'

'Yes, sir,' Veselago replied. 'But may I inquire who "Koba" is? Might he appear in a document under another name?'

'You are right,' said Beletsky. 'Koba may indeed be referred to as Djugashvili, which is his real name. *He is one of our agents.* That is all. Many thanks.'

Shortly afterwards, Veselago left for Moscow and other centres in order to collect copies of the missing documents. History does not recount any details of his mission or whether he found any documents on the subject of Koba. But he does recall how the Director sent for him again as he was on the point of leaving and asked him to give a special message to Colonel Martynov, then in charge of the Moscow Special Section, which had previously handled Malinovsky before this delicate operation was taken over by St Petersburg headquarters. 'When you arrive in Moscow, tell Colonel Martynov that he should not worry about Malinovsky,' said Beletsky. 'Everything is all right about Malinovsky. The Colonel will understand.' In view of Koba's recent arrest, the Director may have thought that Martynov might be apprehensive about the security of his former prize agent, and the message was sent to reassure him.[36]*

Some further evidence by way of corroboration has been provided by Alexander Orlov, a high ranking Soviet Secret police (NKVD) officer who defected to the west in 1938. According to this source, Vissarionov had a secret file which contained reports and letters in Stalin's handwriting addressed to the Vice-Director on his activities as an *agent provocateur*, 'who had worked assiduously for the tsarist secret police'. As will be related later, this file survived the Revolution and unexpectedly turned up during the purge trials in the late 1930s where it was to play a sinister part in the fate of Marshal Tukachevsky and other leading Soviet military commanders.[37]

5

There was little to do in such a forlorn spot as Kureika, and Stalin seems to have spent most of his daylight hours in trapping and fishing.

* Further particulars of the Eremin letter wil lbe found in the Appendix, p. 612. Veselago and Martynov, like many other Okhrana personnel, fought on the side of the Whites in the Civil War. Both subsequently succeeded in escaping to America, where they found new employment and were fortunately able to record their valuable recollections of the Okhrana for the Hoover Institution. Beletsky (later Assistant Minister of the Interior) and his deputy Vissarionov were arrested by the Bolsheviks and shot. Malinovsky's subsequent fate is described later in this book.

In later years he liked to recall some of his experiences in the Siberian Arctic. The local Ostyaks used to make holes in the ice and sit for hours there fishing. 'They called me Osip and taught me to fish,' he recounted afterwards. 'I began bringing in a catch larger than anyone else. Then I noticed that my hosts began whispering among themselves. One day they came up to me and said, "Osip, you know the magic word!" I was ready to burst out laughing. Magic word, indeed! The fact is they chose a place to fish and sat there whether the fish rose to the bait or not, whereas I waited for the fish to rise, and if not, I went to another place, and so on until I got a good catch. I explained all this to them. But I don't think they believed me. They thought I had kept the secret to myself.'

When he became a more practised angler, Stalin used to put lines down a number of ice-holes, placing a marker beside the holes. Once, when he went with several others to check the holes, several miles distant, he became separated from his companions, However, he found he had a good catch and strung the fish on his back, preparatory to returning to his hut in the village. Suddenly a blizzard blew up, accompanied by a biting wind and freezing fog. He struggled on with his load, which he was afraid to discard since food was so short. Eventually he heard voices, which he took to be those of his companions, whose shadows he could dimly make out.

'Hey, you, there!' he cried out. 'Wait for me.'

But the shadows quickly disappeared and the voices faded away in the fog. All Stalin could hear were the frozen fishes knocking against his back. He went on, knowing it was certain death to stop, although on the point of exhaustion. Just as he was about to give up, he heard the barking of dogs and realised he was back in the village at last. Feeling his way with his hands, he reached the door of a hut, burst in and collapsed on the nearest bench.

'Osip, is that you?' said the inhabitants, shaking with terror, as they pressed themselves against the wall.

'Of course it's me. Who did you think it was, a goblin?'

'We saw you outside and thought you were a water-sprite!' was the reply. 'So we became frightened and ran away.'

At that moment the crust of ice which had covered Stalin's face when he first appeared, fell to the floor. Then it dawned on him that with the icicles hanging from his head and body, he must indeed have looked like a water-sprite to the terrified Ostyaks. Again he could not help breaking into laughter.[38]

On another occasion, during the spring floods, about thirty men went down to the river to pull out timber which had been carried down stream after the break up of the winter ice. Towards evening they returned, but with one man missing. When asked about the missing man, the others replied that he had 'remained there'.

'What do you mean?' asked Stalin.

'Why ask?' was the reply. 'Drowned, of course.'

Thereupon one of the party hurried away, saying, 'I must go and water the mare.' When Stalin, according to his own account, reproached them for having more concern for animals than men, one of them remarked amid general approval. 'Why should we worry about men? We can always make men. But a mare! Just try and make a mare!'[39]

At one of his meetings with Churchill in the Kremlin during the Second World War, Stalin recounted to his guest how he had caught a sturgeon. 'With a rod and line?' asked Churchill. 'No,' said Stalin. 'I floated logs down the river with a hundred hooks on them, and with this contrivance I caught a big sturgeon – as long as from here to the end of the table.'

Churchill asked him what emotions it caused him; joy, elation? 'Oh, no, I was alarmed how in a small boat I could tow the big sturgeon in.' However, he succeeded.

Stalin also told Churchill on this occasion that the local chief of police said to him: 'We've had you in our power three times, and have never been able to find anything against you; but we shall, and then you will get twelve years.'[40]

Another account has been given by Vera Shveitser, who had been exiled with her husband Suren Spandaryan to Monastyrskoye. Although characterised by considerable hero worship, it is no doubt generally accurate. She described how she and her husband visited Stalin in the winter.

During that part of the year day and night merge into one endless Arctic night pierced with cruel frosts. We sped down the Yenisei by dog-sledge without a stop, across the bleak wilderness that lies between Monastyrskoe and Kureika, a dash of 125 miles, pursued by the continuous howling of wolves.

We arrived in Kureika and looked for the hut where Comrade Stalin lived. Of the fifteen huts in the village, his was the poorest: an outer room, a kitchen where the owner and his family lived, and Comrade Stalin's room – that was all.

Comrade Stalin was overjoyed at our unexpected arrival and did all he could to make the 'Arctic travellers' comfortable. The first thing he did was to run to the Yenisei, where his fishing lines were set in holes through the ice. A few minutes later he returned with a huge sturgeon flung across his shoulder. Under the guidance of this 'experienced fisherman' we quickly dressed the fish, extracted the caviar and prepared some fish soup. And while these culinary activities were in progress, we kept up an earnest discussion of Party affairs.[41]

Stalin shared his room with Jacob Sverdlov, an arrangement which seems to have got on the latter's nerves. 'He is a good chap,' wrote Sverdlov of his fellow exile, 'but too much of an individualist in everyday life, while I believe in at least a semblance of order.' Worse still, the owner's room was next to theirs and had no separate entrance, and they were constantly plagued by his children, not to mention people from the village who would drop in for a chat. This put an end to evening study, which had to be done by candles as their supply of kerosene had run out. But apparently they did not study very much as, according to Sverdlov, they had 'virtually no books', although Stalin is said to have attempted another essay on the nationalities question which was duly dispatched through the Alliluyevs to Lenin.[42]

6

The outbreak of the First World War in August 1914 found Russia and Austria ranged on opposing sides. Consequently Lenin, who was still living in Cracow, was suspected by the Austrian authorities of being a Russian spy and was expelled from the country. He and his wife thereupon returned to Switzerland, where he issued a manifesto in the name of the Russian Social Democratic Party, denouncing the imperialistic character of the war and the war guilt of all the great powers, who he alleged had long been preparing a sanguinary struggle for the purpose of extending their capitalist markets and destroying their rivals. In his manifesto Lenin called for the creation of a new International 'to undertake the task of organising the forces of the proletariat for the revolutionary attack on capitalist governments, for the civil war against the bourgeoisie of all countries, for the attainment of political power and the victory of Socialism'. Vera Shveitser has recorded that 'a particularly exciting moment in our life of exile' was the arrival of Lenin's manifesto which had been sent to her by Krupskaya through a secret address and which she duly passed on to Stalin, of whom she wrote lyrically. 'It is difficult to convey the joy, conviction and triumph with which Comrade Stalin read Lenin's theses, which confirmed his ideas and served as a pledge of victory for the revolution in Russia.'[43]

Only one letter to Lenin from Stalin during his exile – dated 27 February 1915 – has survived:

My greetings to you, dear Ilyich, warm, warm greetings. Greetings to Zinoviev, greetings to Nadezhda Konstantinovna [Krupskaya]. How are you, how is your health? I live, as before, chew my bread, completing half my term. It is rather dull, but it can't be helped. But how are things with you? It must be much livelier where you are.

Stalin went on to castigate, in somewhat crude language, some of their political opponents. He had been reading articles by the anarchist social philosopher Prince Kropotkin ('the old fool must be completely out of his mind') and the ex-Menshevik Plekhanov ('an incorrigible old gossip'), both of whom advocated an allied victory as a means of advancing socialism. As for the 'liquidators' as a whole, 'there's no one to beat them, the devil take me! Is it possible that they will get away with it and go unpunished? Make us happy and let us know that in the near future a newspaper will appear that will lash them across their mugs, and will do it regularly, and without getting tired.' Stalin signed the letter 'Your Koba', but so far as is known Lenin did not reply to it. This may have been because, curious as it may appear, Lenin had forgotten Stalin's real name, which of course he would have had to use in order to send a letter to the address which Stalin had given him in the letter. 'I have a great favour to ask,' wrote Lenin to a friend called V. A. Karpinsky later the same year. 'Find out the surname of "Koba" (Joseph Dj...??). We have forgotten it. Very important.' Karpinsky immediately replied: 'Joseph Djugashvili.'[44]

Shortly after the outbreak of the war, Roman Malinovsky resigned his place in the Duma, joined the Russian army and went off to the front. He was later captured in the fighting and held in a German prisoner-of-war camp, where Lenin sent him food parcels, steadfastly refusing to believe the rumours that he had been a top Okhrana agent. The remaining Bolshevik deputies were now arrested and charged with conducting various subversive activities, such as sabotaging the war effort. They were brought to trial early in 1915, found guilty, and sentenced to exile in Siberia. At the trial, Kamenev, who had taken Malinovsky's place as the leading Bolshevik deputy in the Duma, repudiated Lenin's defeatist views, a course of action which Stalin is stated in his official biographies to have stigmatised as 'cowardly and treacherous behaviour' when Kamenev arrived in Turukhansk in the summer of 1915, just as Lenin himself had publicly castigated Kamenev's conduct as 'unworthy of a revolutionary Social Democrat'.

There is no evidence that Stalin acted in this manner. It is true that Stalin was allowed to visit Monastyrskoe in the summer of 1915 for a meeting with the other exiled members of the Central Committee and the Bolshevik deputies, and that Kamenev was censured by Sverdlov and Spandaryan. However, the evidence is that Stalin did not commit himself, but sat silently smoking his pipe filled with cheap *makhorka* tobacco during the discussion, before hurrying back to Kureika where he was said to have acquired a mistress who bore him a son at this time. On the contrary, he remained on friendly terms with Kamenev throughout their exile and they were even photographed together. The photograph long ranked as a prominent exhibit in the pictorial history of the Bolshevik revolution, and it was not until Kamenev was 'purged' with other Trotskyites in the 1930s that his likeness was removed from the prints of the picture on exhibition in the various Museums of the Revolution throughout the country.

Stalin's most frequent correspondents appear to have been the Alliluyev family who regularly sent him parcels of clothing. A letter which he sent to Olga Alliluyeva, whose younger daughter he was later to marry, breathes an unusually tender air. Incidentally, apart from some trival notes to his daughter Svetlana and a few lines addressed to a dying comrade in hospital, it is the only purely private letter from Stalin, the text of which is extant.[45]

[Kureika,
Turukhansk District,
Yeniseisk Province]
25 November 1915

I am more than grateful to you, dear Olga Eugenievna, for your kind and good sentiments towards me. I shall never forget the concern which you have shown for me. I await the time when my period of banishment is over and I can come to Petersburg to thank you and Sergei personally for everything. I still have two years to complete in all.

I received the parcel. Thank you. I ask only one thing: do not spend money on me; you need money yourselves. I should be happy if you would send me, from time to time, postcards with views of nature and so forth. In this forsaken spot nature is reduced to stark ugliness – in summer, the river, and in winter, the snow, and that is all there is of nature here – and I am driven by a stupid longing for the sight of some landscape even if it is only on paper.

My greetings to the boys and girls. Wish them all the very best from me.

I live much as before. I feel quite fine. My health is good, as I have grown used to the conditions here. But nature is pretty fierce: three weeks ago we had up to forty-five degrees of frost.

Until the next letter.

Respectfully yours,

Joseph

Fortunately for Stalin, he had a robust constitution, and his health was impervious to the rigours of the Arctic climate. It was otherwise with Suren Spandaryan, who contracted tuberculosis and died in Siberia at this time. Some months before he became ill, Spandaryan and Stalin were separated. In fact, it was due to Sergei Alliluyev that Stalin heard of his companion's death. Alliluyev had sent Spandaryan some money and it was returned to him in the original envelope which had been marked, 'Undelivered due to the decease of the addressee'. Nor does Stalin appear to have made any attempt to escape, although there was a rumour that he was planning to do so and this led to an increase in the security precautions. In any event Russia was subject to martial law at this time and no doubt he concluded that such an attempt would not be worth the effort.

By the middle of 1916, the manpower shortage in the Russian army had become so critical that the authorities decided to call up the exiles for military service. They were directed to report to Krasnoyarsk, a thousand miles distant from the Arctic Circle, so that it took Stalin and the other exiles in Kureika nearly two months to reach the rail head on the Trans-Siberian line, which they eventually did in December 1916. According to the official Soviet histories, Stalin was rejected for political reasons, 'the Tsarist Government knowing how dangerous he would be'. However, the real reason, as he later told Sergei and Olga Alliluyev, was his shortened left arm, which made it impracticable for him to hold a rifle on its target.[46]

The authorities decided not to send Stalin back to Kureika, since his term of exile was due to end within a few months. He was told that he might spend the remainder of the term in Achinsk, a small district town about a hundred miles west of Krasnoyarsk on the Trans-Siberian line. Other Bolshevik exiles, also exempted from military service, included Kamenev whose wife Olga was a sister of Trotsky, and M. K. Muranov a former deputy in the Duma. Although he claimed to have engaged in revolutionary propaganda among the local garrison and troops bound for the front, Stalin found the place fairly dull. 'If Achinsk was not on the railway,' he said, 'it would be worse to live here than in Turukhansk.'

Another of the Bolshevik exiles, Anatole Baikaloff, who was later to defect to the west, has recorded his recollections of Stalin at Achinsk.

There was nothing striking or even remarkable either in Stalin's appearance or in his conversation. Thick-set, of medium height, with a swarthy face pitted by smallpox, a drooping moustache, thick hair, narrow forehead, and rather short legs...he produced the impression of a man of poor intellectual abilities. His small eyes, hidden under bushy eyebrows, were dull and deprived of that friendly humorous expression which forms such a prominent feature of his flattering post-revolutionary portraits. His Russian was very poor. He spoke haltingly, with a strong Georgian accent: his speech was dull and dry, and entirely devoid of any colour and witticism.

In this respect the contrast with Kamenev, a brilliant speaker and accomplished conversationalist, was striking. To chat with Kamenev was a real intellectual delight, and we spent hours at the customary Russian tea-table, drinking numberless glasses of tea from the boiling samovar, discussing international and Russian problems which had arisen during the Great War, or exchanging our revolutionary reminiscences.

Stalin usually remained taciturn and morose, placidly smoking his pipe filled with atrocious *makhorka*. I remember how the poisonous smoke irritated Olga Davidovna [Kamenev's wife]. She sneezed, coughed, groaned, implored Stalin to stop smoking, but he never paid any attention to her.

Stalin's rare contributions to the conversation Kamenev usually dismissed with brief, almost contemptuous remarks. It was evident that he thought Stalin's reasonings unworthy of any serious consideration...I should probably have forgotten ever having met him had he not attained the position of Autocrat of All the Russias.[47]

During the Tsar's absence at the front, a Siberian peasant by origin named Gregory Rasputin, claiming to be a mystic and clairvoyant, obtained a disastrous influence over the Tsarina, as a result of which he secured the dismissal of all the liberal ministers in the Government and virtually ruled Russia through ministers appointed on his advice. The Tsar received repeated warnings, even from foreign diplomatists, that if political concessions were not made revolution was inevitable. But, seemingly hypnotised by the Tsarina and Rasputin, he refused to listen. A conspiracy to remove Rasputin, organised by Prince Felix Youssoupoff, who was married to the Tsar's niece, resulted in Rasputin's assassination on the night of 17 December 1916, with the aid of the Grand Duke Dmitri and a leading right-wing member of the Duma named Purishkevich. But it was too late to save the monarchy. During the session of the Duma, which met in the middle of February 1917, disorders broke out in Petrograd as the capital had been renamed for patriotic reasons. On 26 February the Duma was prorogued, and on the same day the city garrison went over to the popular side. This was the signal for the outbreak of the revolution.

The establishment of a Provisional Goverment headed by the liberal Prince George Lvov was quickly followed by the abdication of the Tsar. The news reached Achinsk two days later and the local revolutionaries including Stalin immediately held a meeting welcoming the downfall of the Romanov dynasty. On 8 March Stalin and the other Bolsheviks boarded a westbound train stopping on the way at Perm to send a telegram to Lenin in Switzerland.

FRATERNAL GREETINGS. STARTING TODAY FOR PETROGRAD.
KAMENEV, MURANOV, STALIN.[48]

While the February Revolution found Lenin in Geneva, it found Trotsky in Canada. Thus, of 'the three who made a revolution', as Bertram Wolfe has called them, it was Stalin, the junior member of the trio, who was first on the scene in Petrograd.

CHAPTER IV

Revolution and Civil War

I

On reaching Petrograd Stalin immediately went to the Alliluyevs' flat in the Vyborg district only to be told by the neighbours that they had moved to a remote suburb so as to be near Sergei's job in the local power station. The family gave him a rapturous welcome, including the pretty fifteen-year-old Nadya when she got home from her music lesson. Her elder sister Anna thought that Joseph had changed: he had grown thinner and his cheeks were sunken, which he attributed to fatigue. He was wearing a dark buttoned-up blouse and felt boots, which she had not seen before. He had shaved off his beard and his moustache was trimmed short, but his eyes were the same. 'That mocking smile never leaves his lips – it is still there,' noted Anna.

They talked together for hours, long after the samovar had gone out. Stalin regaled them with stories of his experiences in the frozen tundra; at the same time he was avid for news of what had been happening in their world during his four years' absence. He threw them into fits of laughter with his imitations of the home-spun oratory with which he and his two companions were greeted on their journey from Achinsk at the stops along the Trans-Siberian line.

'What time are you getting up in the morning?' he asked. 'I have to be at the *Pravda* offices early.' At this time the offices were in the fashionable Moika, in the centre of the city, a few doors from Prince Youssoupoff's grand mission, where a few weeks previously the rascal Rasputin had been brutally done to death.

'We also have to be in town early,' said the girls, 'so we'll wake you up.'

A bed was made up for the guest in the dining room, where there was a divan on which Sergei slept. There the two men continued their conversation, snatches of which drifted in to the two girls in their room next door. Stalin asked his host about the workers' political sympathies in the power station and the local party committee.

'We have many Mensheviks and Social Revolutionaries on the executive committee,' replied Sergei, 'so one has to put up a pretty hard fight.'

'What's the workers' reaction to *Pravda*?' Stalin went on.

'It sells like hot cakes. We can't get enough copies.'

Next door the two girls were giggling in bed, which caused their father to knock on the wall and tell them it was time they went to sleep.

'Leave them alone, Sergei,' said Stalin. 'They're young. Let them laugh...'

Anna and Nadya did not have a chance to wake Stalin in the morning, since he was up before them. 'Hurry, hurry,' he chivvied them at breakfast. Then Stalin and the girls, along with their young brother Fedya, all climbed aboard the old steam train which slowly puffed its way into town.

Asked where they were off to, since it was a Sunday, the girls explained that they were going to look for a new flat and had heard of one much more conveniently located in Tenth Rozhdestvenskaya Street (now Sovietskaya) which might be suitable. It was just off the Nevsky Prospect and not far from the Tauride Palace, former seat of the Duma and at this time the headquarters of the Petrograd Soviet, the council of workers which had come into being immediately after the start of the February Revolution and at first consisted largely of Menshevik and Social Revolutionary delegates.

'That's splendid,' remarked Stalin at this news. 'But you must put aside a room for me. You really must.'

When they parted, Stalin mentioned the subject again. 'Now you won't forget, will you?' The girls promised they would bear it in mind.[1]

In the event, the tenancy of the flat was quickly secured from the resident landlady. A room was set aside for Stalin, carefully cleaned and furnished with a comfortable bed. But several months were to elapse before Stalin arrived to occupy it. In the meantime – or at any rate for much of it – he is known to have shared a flat in Shivokaya Street, in the old part of the city, with Molotov and Ivan Smilga, a friend of Lenin's and the leader of the workers' and peasants' deputies in Finland.[2]

On reaching the *Pravda* offices, Stalin found that the paper was being run by Molotov and two other Bolsheviks, Alexander Shlyapnikov and Peter Zalutsky, who were also members of the Central Committee's executive Bureau. The Bureau now unanimously elected Muranov to membership but merely expressed itself in favour of asking Stalin to attend in a consultative capacity 'in view of certain traits characteristic of him'. The Bureau also appointed Stalin, Kalinin and Lenin's sister Maria Ulyanov together with two others as constituting the editorial board of *Pravda*. But Stalin, using his position as senior Committee member, overruled the Bureau, purged the existing staff, and appointed Kamenev, Muranov and himself as joint editors. As Trotsky was to put it later, Stalin was in a hurry to show that he was boss. And in Lenin's absence he succeeded.

The Provisional Government under Prince Lvov included Professor Paul Miliukov as Minister of Foreign Affairs and the thirty-six-year-old lawyer Alexander Kerensky as Minister of Justice. (The latter was soon to supersede Lvov as head of the government.) Under Stalin's direction *Pravda*'s new editorial board took a moderate line, immediately declaring that the official Bolshevik organ would resolutely support the Provisional Government 'in so far as it is fighting reaction or counterrevolution'. (The paradox of this declaration, commented Trotsky later, was that the only important agent of counter-revolution was the Provisional Government itself.) When the issue containing this article reached the factories, 'the indignation in the outlying districts was stupendous', according to Shlyapnikov, and, 'when the proletarians found out that *Pravda* had been taken over by three of its former managing editors recently arrived from Siberia, they demanded their expulsion from the party'. The new *Pravda* line considerably upset Lenin, who considered that the Provisional Government was thoroughly untrustworthy. Stalin and Kamenev, on the other hand, favoured a deal with the Mensheviks; also, so long as the German army remained behind the Kaiser, the Russian soldier should 'staunchly stand at his post, answering bullet for bullet and salvo for salvo'. Indeed far from censuring the Provisional Government, Stalin wrote and published a signed article in *Pravda* in which he called for 'land for the peasants, security of labour for the workers and a democratic republic for all citizens of Russia'.

All this was anathema to Lenin and he plainly showed his displeasure when he arrived in Petrograd a few weeks later, travelling with his wife, Zinoviev and other Bolshevik exiles in the sealed railway train which the German had allowed to pass undisturbed. 'What have you people been writing in *Pravda*?' Lenin asked Kamenev who was one of the welcoming party. 'We saw several issues and were very angry with you.' Lenin, who thought that he might quite likely be arrested and sent to the dreaded Peter and Paul Fortress, where many earlier revolutionaries had been imprisoned in harsh conditions, was agreeably surprised by the friendly warmth of his reception. Instead of being taken to the fortress, he was driven in an armoured car; he stood up and shouted to the crowds, 'Long live the Socialist world revolution!' The cavalcade proceeded through the streets to the nearby Kshesinskaya Palace – the former home of the ballet dancer of that name and friend of the late Tsar – which had been requisitioned by the Bolshevik Central Committee as its headquarters. (Although called a palace, the building was rather an ugly looking villa.) Here Lenin delivered a rousing speech to his escorting followers, in which he rubbed in the point he had made to Kamenev on his arrival at the Finland station. 'We don't want a parliamentary republic, we don't want a bourgeois democracy, we don't want any government except the Soviet of Workers', Soldiers', and Peasants' Deputies!' At the same time he demanded that the Bolshevik wing of the Social Democratic Party should be renamed the Communist Party.[3]

Lenin expanded his views into what came to be known as the 'April Theses.' These were embodied in an article published in *Pravda* on 20 April. On the following day they were vigorously rebutted by Kamenev, who declared that they were 'unacceptable', that the Central Committee did not share them, and that *Pravda* was pursuing its current policy. Stalin tacitly supported this line, which indeed had the approval of most Bolsheviks in Petrograd at this time, the general feeling being that Lenin was out of touch with the realities of the situation. Ten days later, Stalin executed a complete *volte-face*; he afterwards admitted that he had been mistaken and that the line which he shared with other Party comrades at the time had been 'profoundly erroneous', since it 'hampered the revolutionary education of the masses'. 'I left them at the end of April,' he wrote, 'and adopted Lenin's theses.'

Stalin is said to have been won over as the result of a visit by Lenin to the *Pravda* offices, in which the Bolshevik leader praised Stalin as a man of action compared with other Party members who were no more than intellectual nincompoops. 'Come, we two shall form an alliance,' urged Lenin, clapping Stalin on the shoulder. 'The Provisional Government must be overthrown, and we shall overthrow it when the masses are with us. I guarantee they will be with us very soon, because we shall promise them everything they can demand for a glorious revolution. Will you join me?' Stalin replied with a warm handshake.[4]

According to his official biographers, Stalin went out with a delegation of workers to greet Lenin at Belo-Ostrov, the frontier station with Finland, where the train from Germany made a brief stop. 'It was with great joy that the two leaders of the revolution, the two leaders of Bolshevism, met after their long separation,' wrote Yaroslavsky, adding that 'during the journey to Petrograd Stalin informed Lenin of the state of affairs in the Party and the progress of the revolution.' In later years, Stalin was to commission a series of paintings showing Lenin stepping on to the station platform with Stalin at his side. All this is sheer invention, dating from the time that Stalin began to rewrite Soviet history books. Nor did he put in an appearance at the Petrograd terminus. Indeed Lenin asked Kamenev and Shlyapnikov for news of him. And, as might be expected, all the later histories are silent about the 'profoundly erroneous position', which Stalin at first adopted.[5]

This is how Stalin described his revolutionary role at this period in a speech which he made to the Tiflis railway workers in 1926.

> Finally, I recall the year 1917, when, by the will of the Party, after my wanderings from one prison and place of exile to another, I was transferred to Leningrad [then Petrograd]. There, in the society of Russian workers, and in direct contact with Comrade Lenin, the great teacher of the proletarians of all countries, in the storm of mighty clashes between the proletariat and the bourgeoisie, in the conditions of the imperialist war, I first learned what it means to be one of the leaders of the great Party of the working class. There, in the society of Russian workers – the liberators of oppressed peoples and the pioneers of the proletarian struggle of all countries and all peoples – I received my third baptism in the revolutionary struggle. There, in Russia, under Lenin's guidance, I became a master workman in the art of Revolution.[6]

During the next two months, while Lenin was working ceaselessly putting over his point of view with the masses, Stalin remained very much in the shadows. He carried out the tasks Lenin assigned to him, continued to edit and contribute to *Pravda* – 'the revolution is growing in breadth and depth', he wrote on 17 May – and attended the First All-Russian Congress of Soviets of Workers' and Soldiers' Deputies, which met in the Tauride Palace, being elected to the Executive Committee, which was largely composed of Mensheviks. He was also one of the candidates specially picked by Lenin for election to the new nine member Party Central Committee, and his election to this influential committee was his first as the result of a popular vote, his earlier election in 1912 having been by co-option. Besides Lenin himself, the other members included Zinoviev, Kamenev, Sverdlov, Smilga and the two emigré Bolsheviks, Vladimir Milyutin and Victor Nogin. At the Congress of the Soviets, Stalin encountered the Social Revolutionary Semyen Vereshchak, whom he had not seen since their exile in Narym. In his memoirs, Vereshchak has recorded how Stalin appeared convinced of the inevitable victory of the Bolsheviks. 'Semyen, go along with us,' Stalin urged him. 'Vote for us before it is too late, or tomorrow you'll be my bodyguard!' Vereshchak, who rejected this plea, was later to recall that, 'while Kamenev, Zinoviev, Nogin and Krylenko,* sat at the table of the congress praesidium,† and Lenin, Zinoviev and Kamenev were the main speakers, Sverdlov and Stalin silently directed the Bolshevik group. They were the tactical force. It was then for the first time that I realised the full significance of the man Stalin.'[7]

Early in July, Lenin and his followers made an abortive attempt to seize power in the city. It began on 4 July with Stalin, on Lenin's instructions, summoning the sailors from the naval base at Kronstadt to a 'peaceful demonstration'. There is a story that during the conversation which Stalin had with the sailors on the telephone in order to settle the arrangements for the demonstration, they asked him whether they should carry their rifles. 'Rifles? Comrades, it's up to you,' Stalin is said to have replied. 'We journalists always carry our weapons – our pencils – with us. As regards your weapons, you can judge for yourselves.'[8] The sailors duly sailed up the Neva, landed on the north bank and marched with their 'pencils' to the Kshesinskaya Palace where Lenin addressed them from the balcony in a short speech prophesying inevitable victory and appealing for 'firmness, steadfastness and vigilance'.

Kerensky, who was now Minister of War, had unwisely sanctioned all forms of political agitation in the armed forces, thus speedily undermining discipline. But as yet the average Russian soldier neither knew nor cared anything for the idea of a proletarian revolution as enunci-

* Nikolai Krylenko, a lawyer, had been an active Bolshevik during the revolution of 1905. He was Commissar for War in the first Bolshevik government and later Public Prosecutor and Commissar for Justice. He was arrested during the Great Purge in 1937 and died in prison.
† The praesidium was a small committee, composed of representatives of the various groups and political factions represented in the assembly. It arranged the order of business and its members could be called by the President to take the chair temporarily in his absence.

ated by Marx and preached by Lenin; so far as the soldier was concerned his country was at war and he had a duty to protect his country's sacred soil from the attacks of the German enemy. Thus when Kerensky called out troops on whose loyalty he could count and they found themselves faced with an armed mob of sailors, for that is what they had become, it was not long before shots were fired and a running battle took place at the corner of Sadovaya and the Nevsky Prospect. Afterwards the Bolsheviks claimed that there were four hundred casualties, dead and wounded, in the two days of sporadic fighting which followed, although the official figures were considerably less (twenty dead and 114 wounded).

The Provisional Government struck back by sending troops to occupy the Bolshevik headquarters at the Kshesinskaya Palace and also to accept the surrender of the sailors from Kronstadt who had taken possession of the Peter and Paul Fortress. When this was done, the Government troops raided the offices of *Pravda* and smashed the printing presses. Orders were then issued for the arrest of those who were considered to be the leading Bolsheviks, namely Lenin, Zinoviev and Kamenev, as well as several others including Trotsky, who had recently returned from Canada and had come out strongly on the side of the Bolsheviks – but not Stalin, apparently because he was not sufficiently known or thought to be dangerous enough. Anticipating the Government's latest step, Lenin and Zinoviev decided to go into hiding. They took refuge in the Alliluyevs' large apartment on Tenth Rozhdestvenskaya, possibly at Stalin's suggestion since he lost no time in visiting them there. Indeed Lenin was accommodated in the room which had been set aside for Stalin's use but which he had never occupied. Meanwhile, Kamenev and Trotsky were in favour of surrendering themselves to the authorities and standing trial, and Kamenev sent Lenin a message urging him to do likewise. But Stalin was vehemently opposed to this idea, pointing out that Lenin might quite well be murdered as an alleged German spy by a 'patriotic' soldier on his way to prison if he gave himself up. It would be folly, he argued, to trust the justice of the Provisional Government. However, he undertook to approach the Petrograd Soviet on Lenin's behalf and ask for a guarantee of his personal safety. When the Soviet's Executive Committee, which consisted for the most part of Mensheviks and Social Revolutionaries, refused to give such a guarantee, Lenin and Zinoviev agreed to leave the city for Razliv, a village on the northern coast of the Gulf of Finland, where a local factory worker named Nikolai Emilianov, whom Lenin knew and could trust, was willing to shelter the two refugees.[9]

132

'Wouldn't it be better if I shaved?' Lenin suggested to the Alliluyevs.

Everyone agreed, and Stalin offered to act as barber. A few minutes later Lenin's face was covered with soap and his beard and moustache shaved off, which made him quite unrecognisable. His disguise was complete when he borrowed Sergei Alliluyev's cap and coat, since this gave him the look of a Finnish peasant.

They all set out on foot for the railway station, where Emilianov was waiting for them with the tickets. There Lenin and Zinoviev, along with their host, boarded a train crammed with holiday makers and eventually arrived without mishap at their destination. Before they parted, Stalin promised to keep in touch and act as a liaison between Lenin and the Bolshevik Central Committee, or rather those members of it who were not under arrest.

'I should very much like to move in with you now,' Stalin told the Alliluyevs when he returned to their flat. At the same time he warned them that they would run a certain risk since the premises might be under police observation.

'Please don't worry about us, Joseph,' said Olga Alliluyeva. 'We are accustomed to such things.'

Stalin departed, saying he would think it over. When he dropped in a week later, Olga told him that no one seemed to be keeping watch on the house. 'You'd better come to live with us,' she added, 'rest and sleep properly, and generally lead a more normal life.' Stalin willingly agreed.[10]

The same day, Prince Lvov, disheartened by the events of the 'July days', resigned as Prime Minister of the Provisional Government. He was succeeded by Alexander Kerensky, who retained his portfolio of war.

2

Anna Alliluyeva's memoirs afford a glimpse of Stalin's private life, which he shared with the family for most of the next three months, although he would absent himself for days at a time. 'Now don't worry if I don't come here to sleep for a night or two,' he remarked at breakfast on the first morning. 'I shall be very, very busy. And besides,' he added in a characteristically conspiratorial air, 'there's no harm in taking precautions.' According to Anna, all his belongings were contained in a small wicker basket which he had brought with him from exile. In it he kept his few books, manuscripts and a few items of clothing. He wore his only suit, and it looked so shabby and the jacket was so often patched by Anna's mother that he was eventually persuaded to go and buy himself a new one. This he could now afford, since the Bolshevik Central Committee had just voted its members a monthly salary of 500 roubles. Olga Alliluyeva went round the shops and found a suit which fortunately fitted him exactly. He also asked for a chest protector, since he was having some trouble with his throat and he did not like wearing a collar and tie. Two black velvet chest protectors were specially made for him with a high neck, which he was able to wear. He would usually return to the flat at night dead tired and after reviving himself with tea would talk to the family for a short while and then go to his room where he would work, sometimes pacing up and down the room and puffing away at his pipe. Once he fell asleep with pipe still alight in his hand. He woke up to find the room filled with smoke and a smouldering hole in the blanket made by the pipe. 'That's not the first time it's happened to me,' he said. 'No matter how hard I try I suddenly drop off to sleep.'[11]

His arrival coincided with the opening of the Sixth Party Congress, which was held in conditions of semi-secrecy in Petrograd. Stalin, who took a hand in the proceedings, defended his absent leader against the Mensheviks who had published documents showing his connections with the German enemy. 'These were intended to provoke the anger of the soldiers against the Bolsheviks,' Stalin declared. 'Obviously they calculated on playing on the feelings of the soldiers who were influenced more than anything else by the news that Lenin was a German spy.' Stalin also gave the Congress an account of the happenings of the recent 'July days', showing how the Bolshevik sailors were no match for the superior Government forces which had surrounded them, while the wrecking of the *Pravda* offices made it impossible to acquaint the workers throughout the city with the true strength of Bolshevik support. 'Why didn't you flood Petrograd with leaflets?' he was asked. He answered sadly that, since the *Pravda* presses had been smashed, no other printing establishment in the city dared to accept an order from the Bolsheviks.[12]

The Congress proceeded to choose a fresh and enlarged Central Committee of twenty-four members. Besides Lenin, Zinoviev, Kamenev and Trotsky, who were elected *in absentia* – the first two were still in hiding and the others in prison – the Committee contained a number of other familiar names such as Sverdlov, Muralov, Shaumyan, Smilga, Nogin and Milyutin as well as Stalin. There were also several newcomers, who were to be associated in one way or another with Stalin, sometimes fatally for themselves. They included the sinister Pole Felix Dzerzhinsky, future chief of the Bolshevik secret police, and two Jews, Moses Uritsky and Gregory Brilliant alias Sokolnikov, besides Nikolai Bukharin, Aleksei Rykov, George Lomov, Andrei Bubnov, Nikolai Krestinsky and Alexandra Kollontai, all of whom were to carve niches for themselves in the Bolshevik hierarchy and to leave their mark in Russian revolutionary history. The forty-four-year-old Madame Kollontai, the only woman member of the Committee, was already known as an exponent of 'free love', which she put into practice in her own private life; according to her 'winged Eros' theory, individuals in a socialist society should be free to associate with different persons of the opposite sex for different purposes. Finally, since they had been turned out of the Kshesinskaya Palace, the Committee transferred the Bolshevik headquarters to the Smolny Institute, a former school founded by the Empress Catherine the Great for the daughters of the Russian aristocracy and housed in a handsome building beside the Neva.*

Next after Lenin in the line of Menshevik attack was Kamenev who was released from custody on the day the Congress ended. Kamenev, who was accused in the Menshevik press of having been an Okhrana agent, rebutted the attack indignantly and demanded a full inquiry by the Central Committee. With a fitting piece of irony, the Committee appointed Stalin to investigate the charge. This Stalin proceeded to do, coming to Kamenev's defence in the new party organ *Rabochy Put* (Workers' Road), which he edited after the destruction of *Pravda*. 'The reptilian hissing of the counter-revolution is again becoming louder,' he wrote with characteristic invective. 'The disgusting serpent of reaction thrusts its poisonous form round the corner. It will strike and slither back into its dark lair.'[13]

Did Stalin manage to penetrate the Okhrana headquarters in the course of his ostentatious exoneration of Kamenev, with a view to removing or destroying any compromising references to himself in the office files? One does not know. On the other hand, it has been established that a revolutionary mob broke into the building at this time and burnt many of the records.[14] But not all the files were destroyed in the holocaust. A sufficient number of documents survived to establish Roman Malinovsky's guilt as the Okhrana principal spy and to seal his doom when he returned to Russia after his release from a German

* Of the twenty-four members of the Central Committee elected in August, 1917, only seven died a natural death (Lenin, Stalin, Sverdlov, Nogin, Kollontai, Artem, Dzerzhinsky); eleven were shot by order of Stalin (Kamenev, Zinoviev, Rykov, Bukharin, Bubnov, Milyutin, Krestinsky, Muralov, Smilga, Berzin, Lomov), two died as the result of imprisonment (Sokolnikov, Stasov), one was assassinated by Stalin's order (Trotsky), one was killed by a Social Revolutionary terrorist (Uritsky), one was shot by the Mensheviks (Shaumyan), and one committed suicide (Yoffe).

prisoner-of-war camp. And Stalin was to insure that he paid the price of his treason, since the records clearly showed that it was Malinovsky who had caused Stalin's last arrest and longest spell of Siberian exile.

Kerensky's agents had shadowed the proceedings of the Congress, and apparently on the strength of their reports the Prime Minister feared another attempted Bolshevik coup. He thereupon appealed to General Kornilov, the commander-in-chief at the front, to dispatch some reliable units to the capital. Having surrendered Riga to the Germans, Kornilov ordered a detachment of troops to march on Petrograd with the apparent object, not merely of settling accounts with the Bolsheviks, but of suppressing the Soviets and ousting Kerensky himself and his whole Provisional Government from power. Kerensky's immediate reaction was to arrest Kornilov, whose projected counter-revolution thus failed miserably. Although the details of the 'Kornilov affair' remain obscure, there is no doubt that it weakened the Government and strengthened the Bolsheviks, particularly when Kerensky begged them as he now did to induce the Kronstadt sailors to 'protect the revolution'. As a result, the Bolsheviks, Mensheviks and Social Revolutionaries entered into an uneasy alliance.

Bolshevik tactics were dictated by Lenin from his hiding place, which had been transferred to Finland, and embodied in print by Stalin in *Rabochy Put*, still temporarily substituting for *Pravda*. ('We will fight Kornilov but will not support Kerensky,' said Lenin.) Soon Lenin was demanding that the Bolsheviks make another attempt to seize power. 'History will not forgive us if we do not do so now,' he declared on 12 September. But this proposed move was turned down in the Central Committee at the instigation of Kamenev and Zinoviev, mildly supported by Stalin. Lenin retorted by demanding the expulsion of Kamenev and Zinoviev from the Party, but again his request was not acted upon. 'Expulsion from the Party is not a cure,' remarked Stalin.[15] For the time being the matter was allowed to drop.

Although Stalin attended this meeting of the Central Committee and several others, there were many more from which he was absent. Again there is some mystery about his movements at this time. When he was not busy with his journalistic work, he appears to have spent much of his time in the Alliluyevs' flat. One attraction there was the pretty young Nadya, who had come back from a stay with friends in Moscow for the beginning of the school term. Her sister Anna tells a characteristic story of her on the morning after her return.

According to Anna, her young sister who liked housework got up early and started heaving the furniture around and cleaning up generally. Stalin, disturbed by the commotion, put his head out of his room and inquired 'What's going on here? What's all the noise?' Then, seeing Nadya in her apron and a brush in her hand, he remarked, 'Oh, it's you! A real housewife has settled down to work!'

'Is there anything wrong in that?' Nadya bridled.

'Go right ahead,' said Stalin approvingly. 'If the place is to be kept tidy, keep it tidy. Show 'em all how it should be done!'

Nadya was not only a keen young housewife but also a keen young Bolshevik, brushing aside the taunts of her schoolmates that the Bolsheviks 'want to destroy everything' and openly declaring her political allegiance. When Stalin was absent, she would pump Anna, who was now working at the Bolshevik headquarters in the Smolny. 'Who spoke today? What did you hear? What are our comrades saying?' Stalin told her that the Bolsheviks were going from strength to strength.

Once Stalin brought the terrorist Ter-Petrosyan, otherwise Kamo, to the flat. 'Do you know why they call him by this name?' he teased his old pupil in front of the Alliluyev girls. 'It's because he always says, "Kamo – Kamo".'* Stalin went on, 'You must ask him to tell you about his adventures.' Kamo obliged with a hair raising account of his prison experiences after the Tiflis bank robbery, in which he had feigned madness. He was planning to escape from Kharkov jail by pretending to be dead so that he could be taken to the mortuary when the February Revolution began and resulted in his release along with that of thousands of others throughout the Tsarist empire. Kamo was a dedicated Bolshevik, convinced that the party would eventually seize power, though not without 'a lot more fighting'. Stalin agreed.[16]

3

One morning in the first week of October, there was a ring at the door. Anna opened to see a smallish man wearing a black overcoat and a Finnish cap. He was clean shaven except for a small moustache. Anna did not immediately recognise him.

'Whom do you wish to see?' she asked cautiously.

'Is Stalin at home?' inquired the visitor.

Anna immediately knew it was Lenin from his voice. 'Good Lord! You look just like a real Finn, Vladimir Ilyich,' she said.

'Yes, it's quite a good disguise,' replied Lenin with a laugh. He also wore a wig, as well as spectacles.

Stalin, who had heard Lenin's voice, came out of his room. The ever hospitable Olga Alliluyeva invited them into the dining room for a

* Ter-Petrosyan was apparently in the habit of saying *Kamo* for 'To whom?' instead of *Komo*.

meal, but Lenin refused, and the two men then left the flat together.[17]

Unable to wait any longer and convinced that the hour to strike was at hand, Lenin had just arrived from Finland. The Central Committee must be summoned as soon as possible, he told Stalin, and it must meet in conditions of strict secrecy. For this purpose the Smolny was out of the question. It was accordingly arranged that the Committee should assemble in the flat of a journalist named Nikolai Sukhanov, whose wife Galina, an ardent disciple of Lenin, had conveniently arranged for him to stay the night in his office on the other side of the town because of transport difficulties. Twelve members out of twenty-four turned up for this historic meeting on the evening of 10 October. After a long discussion, which lasted until the small hours of next morning to the accompaniment of sausage sandwiches and innumerable glasses of tea provided by Galina Sukhanova, the question proposed by Lenin that an armed rising should take place in ten days time was put to the meeting. In the event the decision to embark on a course of action destined to shake the world was carried by ten votes to two. In favour were Lenin, Sverdlov, Stalin, Dzerzhinsky, Trotsky, Uritsky, Kollontai, Bubnov, Sokolnikov and Lomov. Against it were Zinoviev and Kamenev. Although he voted with the majority, Stalin did not contribute anything of consequence to the discussion, preferring to puff away at his pipe in silence.[18]

Before the meeting broke up, a small 'bureau' of Committee members 'for the political guidance of the insurrection' was formed on Dzerzhinsky's initiative consisting of Lenin, Zinoviev, Kamenev, Trotsky, Stalin, Sokolnikov and Bubnov. In fact, the bureau never functioned, since Lenin and Zinoviev were in hiding, and Zinoviev and Kamenev were opposed to the rising anyway, while Trotsky, who had resumed his old place as Chairman of the Petrograd Soviet, was kept busy running the Soviet's Military Revolutionary Committee, which planned the tactical details of the *coup* and was to put them into action. However, the bureau has some significance, since it must be regarded as the forerunner of the Political Bureau or Politburo, the Central Committee's powerful inner group of members entrusted with shaping party policy. Also, the fact that Stalin was a member of the original nominal body was to come in useful when he began to rewrite Russian history books with the object of showing that he was Lenin's most prominent coadjutor in the direction of the rising rather than the Bolshevik leader's relatively inconspicuous subordinate.

Next day (11 October), Zinoviev carried the struggle into the open by warning the public of the dangers of a rising in a letter published by Maxim Gorky in his paper *Novaya Zhizn* (New Life), a journal which was edited by Sukhanov and followed a line midway between Bolshevism and Menshevism. Lenin was furious and branded his two colleagues as 'traitors to the revolution', demanding their expulsion from the Party. Five days later, on 16 October, the Central Committee convened again with Lenin still heavily disguised in wig and spectacles. Stalin now spoke up for the first time, but he purposely did not castigate the two dissident comrades as his leader had done. 'Expediency must decide the date of the insurrection,' he said. 'What Kamenev and Zinoviev propose leads objectively to the opportunity for the forces of counter-revolution to organise themselves...There is need now for more faith...One policy is to steer towards the victory of the revolution and to look to Europe; the other policy has no faith in the revolution and hopes that the party will remain merely an opposition party.'[19] He concluded with the remark that the Petrograd Soviet had already embarked upon the road to insurrection. Thus he implied that, while the Central Committee was wasting time, the Soviet under Trotsky's guidance had passed over to action. The Committee reacted by delegating Stalin and four other members (Sverdlov, Bubnov, Dzerzhinsky and Uritsky) to represent the party on the Soviet's Military Revolutionary Committee.

Leonid Krassin, the able electrical engineer, who had been one of Lenin's early supporters but had later broken with the Bolsheviks, gives a vivid picture of life in the capital at this time.[20] In a letter to his wife dated 16 October, he wrote:

Petrograd makes a dismal impression at first by its dirt and many evidences of neglect; altogether a forlorn city, pitiably empty. The streets and pavements are coated with mud; the roadway, too, is badly in need of repair. Here and there railings are torn down, water pumps are dismantled, while windows remain unwashed and many of the bakers' and grocers' shops are closed. One would think that the city had been occupied by strangers who are so little interested in it that they cannot even be bothered to keep the place in order at all. The streets are deserted; it may be that the population has diminished, in spite of the statistics to the contrary, or simply that everyone prefers to stay at home. Certainly there is not much inducement to go out – no means of getting about except on foot. There seem to be fewer soldiers about, though still quite enough of them, and the idiots who call themselves revolutionaries still adorn the principal squares, talking in groups and spitting their sunflower seeds all over the place.

The popular mood is rather more sullen than it was in the summer. Some new form of anarchy is in the air – very likely it means more pogroms, and this is giving even the Bolsheviks something to think about...Possibly, if Kornilov had not been in such a hurry, his attack might well have succeeded. At present the cowed inhabitants are quite expecting the Bolsheviks to attempt a *coup d'état*, though the general opinion is that it will be a dismal failure.

Lenin and the rest of the Central Committee, apart from Zinoviev and Kamenev, still indulged in the hope that the rising would take place on 20 October, a date timed to coincide with the opening of the Second All-Russian Congress of Soviets due to meet on that date. This was too soon for Trotsky and his principal lieutenants, Antonov-Ovseenko and Podvoisky, to complete their preparations. Fortunately for them the opening of the Congress was postponed for five days, which enabled the Military Revolutionary Committee to arm all its 'Red Guards'. Afterwards Stalin admitted in a glowing tribute to the revolution's military genius:

All the work of practical organisation of the insurrection was conducted under the direct leadership of the Chairman of the Petrograd Soviet, Comrade Trotsky. It may be said with certainty that the swift passing of the garrison to the side of the Soviet, and the bold execution of the work of the Military Revolutionary Committee, the Party owes principally and above all to Comrade Trotsky. Comrades Antonov and Podvoisky were Comrade Trotsky's chief assistants.[21]*

Trotsky was later to remark, with some justification, that the greater the sweep of events at this time the smaller was Stalin's place in it. Throughout 24 October, when the Central Committee was in more or less continuous session at the Smolny Institute, Stalin was noticeably absent, although Dzerzhinsky and the others in liaison with the Soviet's Military Revolutionary Committee were on the spot and received their allotted tasks from Trotsky, such as maintaining contact with the telegraph and telephone operators and the railwaymen and

* Vladimir Antonov-Ovseenko and Nikolai Podvoisky were both 'Trotskyites', who helped Trotsky to organise the Red Army as high-ranking commissars. Antonov-Ovseenko, later demoted to be Soviet Ambassador in Prague, disappeared during the Great Purge, but Podvoisky managed to survive, though in a relatively obscure post in the Marx–Lenin Institute in Moscow. Both have since been 'rehabilitated'.

reporting on the activities of the Provisional Government at their headquarters in the old imperial Winter Palace. The latter task was assigned to Sverdlov, and he had plenty to report later that day when Kerensky belatedly struck back by sending a few soldiers to close down the Bolshevik paper which Stalin edited and calling in three regiments of Cossacks to put a stop to Trotsky and his committee from taking any further action. But it was too late. Although a seal had been placed on the door of the newspaper offices, the Cossacks refused to move, and Trotsky's Red Guards soon occupied the bridges, railway stations, post offices and other strategic points in the city. 'A piece of official sealing wax on the door of the Bolshevik editorial room as a military measure,' remarked Trotsky afterwards. 'That was not much – but what a superb signal for battle!'

What was Stalin doing on the eve of the revolution? No one knows for certain, as most of his movements on that fateful day are shrouded in mystery. Trotsky suggests that he was deliberately lying low so as to keep his options open and if something went wrong with the military committee's plans he could absolve himself from blame. This may likewise explain why he had been so 'soft' on Zinoviev and Kamenev in the Bolshevik Central Committee. The fact remains that he made surprisingly little impact on the eye-witnesses of the revolution who later described it in print. For instance, John Reed, the American-born and Harvard-educated Communist, who is buried beneath the Kremlin wall in Moscow, briefly mentions Stalin twice as a Bolshevik commissar in his dramatic *Ten Days that Shook the World*.[22] Nikolai Sukhanov, in whose flat the crucial meeting of the Central Committee had taken place on 10 October, described Stalin's role in the events of this time as bound to be perplexing by reason of his character and personality. 'The Bolshevik Party, in spite of the low level of its "officers' corps", had a whole series of most massive figures and able leaders amongst its "generals",' wrote this outspoken historian of the revolution. 'Stalin, however, during his modest activity in the Executive Committee of the Petrograd Soviet, produced – and not only on me – the impression of a grey blur, looming up now and then dimly and not leaving a trace. There is really nothing more to be said about him.'[23]

That Stalin undoubtedly knew what was going on may be seen from the fact that he 'came home' to the Alliluyevs' apartment on the evening of 24 October. Anna Alliluyeva later recalled how he took off his leather jacket and cap, which he always wore at the beginning of autumn, and went into the family living room. After taking tea and listening to what Sergei had to say, he remarked calmly: 'Yes, everything is ready. We take action tomorrow. All military forces are in our hands. We shall seize power...'[24]

Next morning – Wednesday, 25 October – was a typical autumn day in the capital, damp, cold and cloudy. Lenin slipped into the Smolny, still wearing his wig and also a bandage covering his face, to find that orders for the revolt had already been issued. During the ensuing hours, while he sat busily dictating orders and writing instructions, Trotsky's Red Guards speedily took control of the city with practically no bloodshed. The few troops, mostly women, on duty at the Winter Palace, put up a feeble show of resistance, there was some desultory shooting from the Peter and Paul Fortress, and the cruiser *Aurora*, which had sailed up the river to protect Kerensky and his ministers, fired some shells which turned out to be duds. Resistance crumbled quickly, Kerensky escaped ignominiously in an American motor car flying the Stars and Stripes, and the women's battalions departed to their quarters, complaining that some of their number had been raped.

Afterwards Stalin gave the Alliluyevs a highly coloured account of what happened when the sailors from the Baltic Fleet took over the telephone exchange building. 'They advanced like men of iron,' he said. 'Government troops were shooting down at them from the windows, and bullets mowed them down one by one, but they came forward without flinching. Splendid people! Splendid! Real Russian people!' The truth was that in the street fighting on that historic day, there were only six fatal casualties, five sailors and one soldier; and a score or so of people were wounded. The Bolshevik take-over was as simple as that.[25]

The Congress of Soviets duly opened the same evening in the Smolny. After Anna Alliluyeva had finished examining the delegates' passes and showing the workers and peasants to their seats, she ran home to fetch her sister Nadya. It had begun to snow as they walked through the silent and deserted streets. An old man and his dog passed them and asked, 'Where are you girls off to on a night like this? There's trouble in the town, fighting outside the Winter Palace, they say.' But there was cheering and a general air of excitement when they reached the Smolny assembly hall.

Suddenly they saw a familiar figure in the crowd. It was Stalin. He stopped and beckoned towards them. 'Oh, it's you! Delighted you're here. Have you heard the news? The Winter Palace has just fallen and our men are inside.'[26]

Next morning, as people went to work as usual, there was little outward evidence that the Provisional Government had been overthrown and that, in Lenin's words, 'the proletariat revolution had been accomplished'. The trams were running again, the shops and restaurants were open, and the theatres preparing for their performances. The Congress of Soviets continued its session, debating and approving the decrees of the Military Revolutionary Committee – the abolition of capital punishment in the army, the prohibition of pillage and looting under pain of death, the ending of private ownership of land, the arrest of Kerensky – all the other ministers were already in custody – and the confiscation of private stores of food. Lenin was wildly applauded when he made his appearance on the rostrum of the columned hall, dressed in a shabby suit of clothes, his trousers much too long for him. He had been busy forming his provisional Workers' and Peasants' Government to be called the Council (*Soviet*) of People's Commissars, a title suggested by Trotsky in reply to Lenin's objection to Ministers. ('That is a vile, hackneyed word.')[27]

It was after two o'clock in the morning, the atmosphere full of tobacco smoke and the smell of human sweat and unwashed bodies, that Kamenev, in his capacity as Chairman of the Congress Executive Committee, came forward and amid a tense hush read out the decree of the Constitution of Power, as drafted by Lenin. Governmental power was to be vested in the Council of People's Commissars, the commissars being the chairmen of commissions with which 'the administration of the different branches of state activity shall be entrusted' and 'whose composition shall be regulated to ensure the carrying out of the programme of the Congress'. It was also laid down that control over the activities of the commissars, 'and the right to replace them', should belong to 'the All Russian Congress of Soviets of Workers', Peasants' and Soldiers' Deputies, and its Central Executive Committee'. (This was a polite fiction, since it was Lenin's intention that real power should be vested in himself and the Bolshevik Party Central Committee.)

Kamenev went on to announce the names of the individual commissars with their respective departments under Lenin's chairmanship. Each announcement was greeted with cheering, the loudest being for Lenin and then Trotsky, who became the Commissar of Foreign Affairs. The others included Milyutin (Agriculture), Rykov (Interior), Shlyapnikov (Labour), Nogin (Trade and Industry), Lunacharsky (Education), and Lomov (Justice). The fifteenth and last name on the list was that of the Commissar of Nationalities – J. V. Djugashvili-Stalin.[28]

Lenin and Trotsky, looking haggard from lack of sleep, stood in the middle of a group of comrades including Stalin, receiving congratulations. Lenin turned to Trotsky. 'You know,' he said in halting words, 'to pass so quickly from an underground existence to power' – here he paused, searching for the right expression, and then suddenly finished in German – *'es schwindelt'* (makes one dizzy). Suiting his action to the words, he raised his hand and turned it round his head. They looked at each other and smiled. It was an unforgettable moment.[29]

4

The first meeting of the Council of People's Commissars, to become generally known in abbreviated Russian style as *Sovnarkom*, took place in a room in the Smolny which Lenin had hurriedly converted into an office. An unpainted wooden partition screened a cubby-hole which was shared by a typist and a telephone girl. Trotsky and Stalin were the first to arrive. From behind the partition they heard the thick basso voice of Paul Dybenko, a jolly young black-bearded sailor who had been appointed Joint Commissar for War and Marine along with Nikolai Krylenko and Vladimir Antonov-Ovseenko. Dybenko, who was known to be having a love affair with Madame Kollontai, was talking on the telephone in decidedly tender terms. Trotsky was surprised at the effect which this incident had on Stalin. The latter gestured with his shoulder towards the partition and remarked to Trotsky with a snigger, 'That's he with Kollontai, with Kollontai!'

Trotsky afterwards recalled the unpleasant impression Stalin's behaviour made upon him on this occasion.

> His gestures and laughter seemed to me out of place and unendurably vulgar, especially on that occasion and in that place. I don't remember whether I simply said nothing, turning my eyes away, or answered drily, 'That's their affair.' But Stalin sensed that he had made a mistake. His face changed, and in his yellow eyes appeared the same glint of animosity that I had noticed in Vienna. From that time on he never attempted to engage me in conversation on personal themes.[30]

The People's Commissars quickly got down to work, drafting and approving a wide range of decrees from the abolition of ranks and titles and the adoption of the western 'New Style' calendar, which was thirteen days ahead of the Russian 'Old Style', to the creation of special 'People's Courts' for trying counter-revolutionaries and other opponents of the new regime. Stalin, who had more time to spare from departmental duties than the rest of his colleagues, took a considerable hand in the preparation of these decrees, since a number of versions sent to the printers, though appearing to bear Lenin's signature, were in fact in

Stalin's handwriting. For instance, he would seem to have been responsible for a most far reaching decree, promulgated a few days after the formation of the new Government, conferring upon it plenary powers to make laws, though the Congress had not granted it these powers and never intended to do so. Lenin, who was surprised by this decree when it was first shown to him, eventually accepted it, since it was designed to achieve his personal dictatorship over the whole Russian people.

However, these legislative activities were only the beginning of 'the conquest of power', as Lenin described the Bolsheviks' principal task. Every move by the *Sovnarkom* and its individual members to take over the apparatus of government was vigorously resisted by the opposition parties and their adherents. Only the humbler grades of government employees, such as messengers and doorkeepers, showed any sympathy with the new rulers. The state officials as a whole were bitterly opposed to the Bolsheviks and many of them declared a protest strike when the commissars appeared to take possession of their new offices. When Trotsky turned up at the Ministry of Foreign Affairs, the staff refused to acknowledge him as their chief, locked themselves in their rooms, and when the doors were forced, resigned in a body. After a struggle to get the keys of the archives, in which he had to threaten to call in workmen to smash the locks, the commissar was handed the keys only to find that the former Assistant Foreign Minister had disappeared with the secret treaties. Shlyapnikov had a similar experience when he tried to take possession of the Ministry of Labour. It was bitterly cold and no one would light any fires, while not a single one of the hundreds of civil servants in the building would show him where the Minister's room was. When Madame Kollontai, who had been appointed Commissar of Public Welfare, was faced with the strikers, she was obliged to place many of them under arrest before they would hand over the keys of the office safe. When the safe was eventually opened, it was found that the late Minister had gone off with all the official funds.[31]

Since Stalin's commissariat had no ministerial counterpart in any of the previous administrations, he was not faced with situations of this kind. On the other hand, he had the problem of how to create a completely new government department. The problem was unexpectedly solved by an old Polish revolutionary named Stanislav Pestkovsky, who like Stalin had been exiled to Siberia and had returned to the capital in time to participate in the Bolshevik triumph; he was now looking for a job. Having knocked at several doors in the Smolny without success, he finally encountered Stalin.

'Comrade Stalin,' said Pestkovsky, 'are you the People's Commissar for Nationalities?'

'Yes,' replied the commissar.

'But have you a commissariat?'

'No.'

'Well, then, I will make you a commissariat.'

'All right, but what do you need for that?'

'For the present, merely a mandate.'

At this point, according to Pestkovsky, Stalin who 'hated to waste words', immediately went to the *Sovnarkom*'s executive office and a few minutes later returned with the necessary document. Armed with this, Pestkovsky scrounged a table and a couple of chairs, and when he had returned with them to Stalin's room proceeded to pin a sheet of paper on the wall with the following inscriptions: 'People's Commissariat for the Affairs of the Nationalities'.

Pestkovsky again addressed the commissar. 'Comrade Stalin, we haven't a kopec to our name.'

'Do you need much?' asked Stalin.

'A thousand roubles will do to begin with.'

'Come back in an hour.'

When Pestkovsky reappeared an hour later, Stalin said that he had arranged to borrow three thousand roubles from Trotsky. 'He has money. He found it in the former Ministry of Foreign Affairs.' He then told his new assistant to go and get the cash and give Trotsky a receipt. This was duly done. 'As far as I know,' Pestkovsky remarked some time afterwards, 'the Commissariat of Nationalities has not yet returned this money to Comrade Trotsky.'[32]

The most serious of the new government's teething troubles occurred ten days after its formation when five of the more moderate commissars, including Rykov, Nogin and Milyutin, resigned both from the Government and the Central Committee, since they wished to widen the basis of the administration with representatives of the other socialist parties; to this the sole alternative was, in their own words, 'the preservation of a purely Bolshevik Government by means of political terror', an idea which they repudiated. At the same time Kamenev and Zinoviev withdrew from the Central Committee; Kamenev also relinquished his office as chairman of the All-Russian Congress Executive, equivalent to President of the Republic, being succeeded by Sverdlov, while Zinoviev resigned as chairman of the Petrograd Soviet. Lenin retaliated by denouncing Kamenev and Zinoviev as deserters and pointing out that some of the Social Revolutionaries had been offered places in the Government and had declined, and also that the constitution of the Government had been unanimously ratified by the Congress. Lenin's uncompromising attitude thus put an end to all further efforts to reach any accommodation with the moderate socialists.[33]

The next problem for the Government was posed by the need to conclude a speedy peace with Germany and Austria. On 8 November, Trotsky addressed the Allied ambassadors with an offer of 'an immediate armistice on all fronts and the immediate initiation of peace negotiations'.[34] At the same time, he transmitted an order by radio to General Nikolai Dukhonin, the commander-in-chief, at general staff headquarters in Mogilev, to open direct negotiations with the enemy in the field. The Allied Governments immediately protested, and their representatives in Russia tried to enlist the general's support against the Council of Commissars. Their efforts were to prove fruitless.

Impatient to learn Dukhonin's reply to Trotsky's order, Lenin summoned Stalin and Krylenko, one of the defence commissars, to the Petrograd telegraph office shortly after midnight and for two hours they argued on the direct wire with the commander-in-chief, who categorically refused to open peace negotiations on behalf of the Council of Commissars. 'Only a central government supported by the army and the people can have sufficient weight and significance in the eyes of the enemy to lend these negotiations the authority necessary for their success,' said Dukhonin.[35]

The reply, as preserved on the telegraphic tape, was as follows:

In the name of the Government of the Russian Republic, and on the orders of the Council of People's Commissars, you are dismissed from your post for non-compliance with government instructions and for behaviour which threatens unprecedented calamity to the toiling masses in all countries, and particularly to the armed forces.

You are hereby ordered, on pain of responsibility under wartime laws, to remain at your post of duty pending the arrival of the new commander-in-chief, or of his authorised representative, who will take over from you. Ensign Krylenko has been appointed commander-in-chief.

LENIN
STALIN
KRYLENKO

Meanwhile the revolution was sweeping across the whole of Russia. There were a few days of intense street fighting in Moscow, where

147

Commissar Lomov had been dispatched to co-ordinate matters, and there was some sporadic resistance elsewhere. In the cities and towns the victory was won under the red flag of class warfare and the slogan 'All Power to the Workers' Soviets', while elsewhere the watchwords 'land', 'bread' and 'peace' insured the support of the soldiers and peasants. The right to self-determination was promised to the various 'nationalities' with Russia. One of Stalin's first public speeches was made at the party meeting of the Finnish comrades in Helsinki on 16 November.

> Complete freedom for the Finnish people, and for the other peoples of Russia, to arrange their own life! A voluntary and honest alliance of the Finnish people with the Russian people. No tutelage, no supervision from above over the Finnish people! These are the guiding principles of the policy of the Council of People's Commissars.
>
> Only as the result of such a policy can mutual confidence among the people of Russia be created. Only on the basis of such confidence can the peoples of Russia be united in one army. Only by thus uniting the peoples can the gains of the October Revolution be consolidated and the cause of the international socialist revolution be advanced.
>
> That is why we smile when we are told that Russia will inevitably fall to pieces if the idea of the right of nations to self-determination is put into practice.[36]

By the end of the month the Soviets held power throughout the country. Kerensky, who had hoped to make a come-back with the army's help, quickly gave up the struggle and disappeared into obscurity, subsequently managing to escape from the country when he heard that the Bolsheviks had put a price on his head. General Dukhonin was not so fortunate. He could easily have got away by road on the morning of Krylenko's arrival in Mogilev, but he unwisely chose to remain after the town had been occupied without resistance by his successor, whose immediate promotion from petty-officer to commander-in-chief must be unprecedented in military history. He was taken prisoner and brought before Krylenko in the coach which Krylenko had established as his temporary headquarters at the railway station. There Krylenko left him to the mercies of a drunken crowd of sailors, soldiers and peasants who dragged him from the train and beat him to death.[37] Dukhonin's fate marked the end of the old Russian army and the emergence of a new 'democratised' Red Army with no epaulettes and badges of rank. The Allied military missions had left Mogilev before the town fell to the Bolsheviks, who shortly thereafter concluded a truce with the Germans, pending the opening of peace negotiations by Trotsky at Brest-Litovsk.

While these events were taking place, Stalin was kept busy churning out decrees for Lenin and the rest of the *Sovnarkom* in Petrograd. One particularly flamboyant example, expressed in Stalin's characteristic liturgical prose, was addressed to the Moslem world, particularly the Mohammedan Indians, 'crushed and tortured by a foreign yoke': they were exhorted to 'throw off these robbers and enslavers of your countries'.

> Great events are taking place in Russia. The end of the sanguinary war, which began for the sake of dividing up other people's countries, is approaching. The rule of the robbers, who have enslaved the peoples of the world, is falling. Under the blows of the Russian Revolution, the old edifice of servitude and slavery is shaking. The world of arbitrariness and oppression is living through its last days. A new world is being born, a world of workers and freed people...The working people of Russia burn with the sole desire to get a just peace and to help the oppressed peoples of the world to conquer freedom for themselves.

This decree, which was headed, 'Appeal to the working Moslems of Russia and the East', and signed by Stalin and Lenin, is one of the very few in which Stalin's name as Commissar of Nationalities appears before Lenin's and no doubt it gave him particular satisfaction. A million copies were supposed to be printed in the various Moslem languages, but it is doubtful whether they had much if any effect outside Russia. But it considerably annoyed the British Ambassador, Sir George Buchanan, who complained in a press statement that 'the attitude of the Soviet leaders is more calculated to estrange than to attract the sympathies of the British working classes.'[38]

Another decree, destined to have a more immediate and far-reaching effect, followed a few days later. It created an 'All-Russian Commission for combating Counter-Revolution and Espionage' (*Chrezvychainya Kommissia*), usually known from its Russian initials as the Cheka, the dreaded secret police organisation, later called the GPU and the NKVD. From the beginning it was headed by Felix Dzerzhinsky and was eventually to become a byword in terror and espionage. Dzerzhinsky, who was two years older than Stalin and belonged to the

Polish nobility by birth, had been a keen Bolshevik since his youth and had served several terms of imprisonment and exile in Siberia on account of his political activities in the Baltic provinces. Like Stalin he was freed by the February Revolution and, as has been seen, was elected a member of the Bolshevik Central Committee. At first, Dzerzhinsky operated with a small staff and limited resources, and the few death sentences which the Cheka passed in the early days of its existence were on bandits and ordinary criminals. Later it began to deal with alleged counter-revolutionaries and 'enemies of the people'. The Cheka was also made responsible for security arrangements in the Smolny and for the personal protection of the People's Commissars. After Dzerzhinsky himself, the two best known members of the eight-man *Kommissia* were a Lett named Jacob Peters and Stalin's fellow Caucasian Sergo Ordzhonikidze. From the beginning the Cheka made its Moscow headquarters at No. 11 Lubyanka Street, a former insurance office building near the Kremlin. Soon 'the Lubyanka' was to attain a disagreeable notoriety in the eyes of the Russian citizens, who would hurry fearfully past the building and look in the other direction.[39]

With Trotsky away for much of the time at Brest-Litovsk, Lenin came more and more to lean on Stalin and to consult him on most matters of importance before coming to a decision. 'Lenin could not get along without Stalin even for a single day,' wrote Pestkovsky. 'In the course of the day he would call Stalin out an endless number of times, or would appear in our office and lead him away. Most of the day Stalin spent with Lenin in his office. What they did there, I don't know, but on one occasion, upon entering Lenin's office, I came upon an interesting picture. On the wall hung a large map of Russia. Before it stood chairs. And on them stood Ilyich [Lenin] and Stalin, moving their fingers over the northern part, I think across Finland.' This account was later endorsed by Trotsky when he revealed Lenin's replies to some of his communications from Brest-Litovsk. For example, 'As soon as Stalin returns I will show your letter to him,' and again, 'I should like to consult with Stalin before replying to your question,' and 'Stalin has just arrived – I shall consider with him and we shall give you our joint answer.'[40]

Meanwhile the Congress of Soviets had undertaken to arrange for the election and convocation of a new Constituent Assembly. On this subject Krassin's forecast was more accurate than his previous one about the Bolshevik *coup*. 'If the Constituent Assembly turns out to be an anti-Bolshevik body, which means it will have no power behind it,' he wrote on 3 January 1918, 'then it will simply be a debating society, or more likely it will be destroyed by the Bolsheviks. In that case the country will be literally in a state of civil war.'[41]

The elections were duly held, but the Bolsheviks, who secured a majority of votes in Petrograd, only collected some nine million votes as against sixteen and a half million votes cast for the Social Revolutionaries in the country as a whole. The Assembly held its first and sole meeting in the Tauride Palace on 18 January 1918, electing a Social Revolutionary as President. After passing a land law on Soviet lines and sanctioning the armistice and the peace negotiations, which it proposed to carry on itself, the Assembly adjourned. The building was already ringed with Red soldiers. Next day the Bolsheviks formally dissolved the Assembly on the ground that it was serving 'only as a cover for the struggle of bourgeois counter-revolution for the overthrow of the Soviets'.[42]

The Congress of Soviets broke up about the same time. 'Our schoolwork is hardly going on at all,' wrote young Nadya Alliluyeva to a friend. 'We've spent the whole week at the All-Russian Congress of Workers', Soldiers' and Peasants' Deputies. It's pretty interesting, especially when Trotsky or Lenin is speaking, but the others are very dull and don't say anything. Tomorrow, 17 January, is the last day and we'll just have to go.' A week or so later she was complaining about the scarcity of food. 'There's a real hunger in Petrograd. They hand out only an eighth of a pound of bread every day, and one day they gave us none at all. I've even cursed the Bolsheviks...I've lost twenty pounds and had to alter all my skirts and underclothes. They were all falling off me. I've lost so much weight people are even suspecting me of being in love!' Very soon afterwards this suspicion would have been justified when she did fall in love with the People's Commissar of Nationalities.[43]

The peace negotiations, which were resumed by the Bolsheviks at Brest-Litovsk, caused an acute crisis in the Central Committee. The German demands were such that Trotsky, who anticipated a rapid proletarian rising in Germany, refused to sign what he called 'a peace of annexation'. A Left-wing group in the Committee, headed by Bukharin and including Dzerzhinsky, went further and were for fighting on even at the risk of extinction, as in their view to do otherwise would be a betrayal of the revolution. Lenin, on the other hand, was for making peace in spite of the severity of the German terms, since it would afford a much needed 'breathing space'. Although at first in a minority, he was supported by Stalin, who took the realistic view that the international aims and ideals of the October Revolution had as yet made little if any headway in the west. Eventually, after the most protracted in-fighting among the members, during which Lenin threatened to resign, the Committee came round to his view. On 3 March 1918, Sokolnikov, who had replaced Trotsky as leader of the Soviet peace delegation at Brest-Litovsk, signed the treaty, under which Russia gave up large territories in the west, including the Baltic provinces and the Ukraine, and undertook to demobilise what remained of the imperial armies."

At the same time, again not without some opposition, particularly on the part of Zinoviev, who had resumed his old place as chairman of the Petrograd Soviet, the decision was taken by the Central Committee to transfer the Bolshevik government to Moscow. For one thing, Moscow had been the capital before Peter the Great built the city named after him on the banks of the Neva; also it was much more secure than Petrograd, which was a standing temptation both to the Germans and the anti-Bolshevik Allies to attack and occupy so long as the Council of People's Commissars and their staffs remained there. The move, which was welcomed by Stalin, took place on 12 March 1918. It included Nadya Alliluyeva, who had learned to use a typewriter and had consequently got a job working in Lenin's secretariat.

5

The Council of People's Commissars immediately established itself in the old domed Senate building, which had served the Tsarist government as the seat of the Supreme Court in the Kremlin. Few if any of the commissars had ever set foot inside this city within a city, and to Stalin, like Trotsky, the Kremlin with its medieval walls and battlements must have seemed, at least at first sight, an utter paradox as a fortress of revolutionary dictatorship. All the commissars were allotted offices in the former Senate building or in the nearby Kavalersky building which also housed the Kremlin commandant and his guard troops. Trotsky, in particular, did not find the atmosphere conducive to work. 'The aroma of the idle life of the master class emanated from every chair,' he later recalled. However, steps were soon taken to change the surroundings. The ornate furnishings were removed to a museum and replaced by simple office tables and chairs and beds. The musical clock on the top of the Spassky Gate leading on to the Red Square was rebuilt, and the old bells, instead of chiming 'God Save the Tsar', rang out the *Internationale* at quarter-hour intervals. Stalin and the other commissars usually ate together in a makeshift canteen, where the food was far from good. Trotsky complained that there was no fresh meat, only corned beef, and that the flour and barley had sand in them. Only red caviar was plentiful, since its export had ceased; as Trotsky put it, 'this inevitable caviar coloured the first years of the revolution, and not for me alone'.[45]

Stalin and the other departmental heads had their private offices in the Kremlin, where the Council of People's Commissars continued to meet from time to time under Lenin's chairmanship. Under the terms of the constitution, each commissariat consisted in turn of a chairman and a collegium or board of half a dozen or more members. According to Pestkovsky, Stalin was frequently at odds with the collegium and would sometimes find himself in a minority of one. On these occasions he used to excuse himself for 'just a moment' and disappear, as he had done in the Smolny, to ponder on how the conflict could best be resolved. 'He decided to educate us and worked at it persistently,' said Pestkovsky. 'In this he displayed a lot of gumption and wisdom.' As often as not, Lenin would send for him. 'Find him at once,' he would tell Pestkovsky. Stalin's long suffering chief of staff would then begin a search of the Kremlin's multifarious buildings and would eventually come upon his master in the most unexpected places. Twice he ran him to earth in the quarters of Comrade Vorontsov, the deputy commandant, lying on a divan in the kitchen and smoking. It was in Vorontsov's apartment that Stalin first made the acquaintance of Henry Yagoda, a young Jewish chemist from Nizhni-Novgorod, who had the job of making up medical prescriptions and ordering pharmaceutical supplies for the Kremlin policlinic. Yagoda had a particular knowledge of poisons, a fact which was not lost upon Stalin.[46]

The commissariat staffs were necessarily accommodated outside the Kremlin and this led to some sordid squabbles between the various departmental heads. Stalin's own commissariat was distributed among five separate private houses. 'It is quite impossible to keep an eye on you all,' the commissar complained. 'We ought to find one large building and get everyone together there.' It was not long before he discovered a former hotel, the Grand Siberian, which seemed ideal for his purpose. Unfortunately it had already been earmarked by the Supreme Council of National Economy. When he heard of this, Stalin determined to get it first. 'I shall not give way,' he said. He told Pestkovsky to tell Nadya Alliluyeva, who had been borrowed from Lenin's office, to type out several notices on pieces of paper with the following legend: THESE OFFICES ARE OCCUPIED BY THE PEOPLE'S COMMISSARIAT OF NATIONALITIES.

When they reached the building, there was already a notice on the front door proclaiming the fact that it belonged to the Supreme Council of National Economy. Stalin tore it off and substituted one of his own notices. 'Now we must get inside and stick up the others,' he

153

said to his assistant, 'otherwise we have no authority.' What happened next is best described by Pestkovsky.

It was no easy task. With great difficulty we found the service entrance. The electric light was not working. I struck a match and we went up to the second floor, where we came into a long corridor with a number of doors on which we placed the notices indiscriminately. We had to return by the way we came, but I had no more matches left. Going down in the pitch darkness we reached the basement, where Comrade Stalin tripped and nearly broke his neck. Fortunately he got off with a few scratches on the right cheek.

Next day, when Lenin saw him at a *Sovnarkom* meeting, he asked Stalin what had happened to his cheek. He replied jocularly: 'It's the result of the beginning of the civil war between the People's Commissariats!'[47]*

By this time the 'Reds' and the anti-Bolshevik 'Whites' were fighting a much bigger civil war on a number of extended fronts, particularly on the east and the south. The two contending forces were almost identical in social composition: on both sides most of the officers were former professionals who had previously served in the imperial army with a sprinkling of intelligentsia, while most of the rank and file were peasants as in pre-revolution days, with the addition of some workers the majority of whom naturally supported the Reds. Since most of the Red Army officers, like the Whites, had previously served the Tsar, special political commissars were attached to each unit to ensure the officers' reliability and loyalty to the Bolshevik cause. This was Trotsky's idea and it was to prove most effective in practice.

Politically the Whites were composed of the majority of Social Revolutionaries, right-wing Social Democrats and other parties of the right, all lumped together by their opponents as 'counter-revolutionaries'. The most notable figure on the side of the Reds was Trotsky, who was put in overall charge of military operations as Commissar of War and Chairman of the Revolutionary Military Council of the Republic. (Trotsky's post as Commissar of Foreign Affairs was taken by Yury Chicherin, a professional diplomat from Tsarist times, who had been imprisoned in London on suspicion of being a German agent and was later exchanged for Sir George Buchanan, the British Ambassador in Petrograd.) There was no similarly unifying figure among the Whites, although unsuccessful attempts in this direction were made by

* Stalin's manoeuvre failed, since the Supreme Council was considered relatively more important than the Commissariat of Nationalities.

154

General Anton Denikin, who took command of the anti-Bolshevik forces in south Russia on Kornilov's death in March 1918, and Admiral Alexander Kolchak, a Tartar from the Crimea, who led the struggle against the Bolsheviks in Siberia. The Whites received considerable support from the Czechoslovak Legion, consisting of deserters from the Austrian forces, which had been formed to fight against the Austrians alongside the Russians. After the collapse of the imperial armies, the Czechoslovaks, fearing internment by the Bolsheviks, had headed for Vladivostok, seizing large sections of the Trans-Siberian Railway and disarming the local Red Army garrisons on their way. During 1918 the Whites were further encouraged by the decision of the Allies to intervene and by the subsequent landing of British, French, Japanese and American contingents at different points in north and south Russia, Transcaucasia and Siberia.

Before the end of May 1918, the Whites had begun a concerted drive on Moscow, which was in danger of starvation through the cutting of communications with the grain supplies in the northern Caucasus. On 23 May, Sergo Ordzhonikidze, then chief political commissar attached to the Tenth Army at Tsaritsyn, which was commanded by Klim Voroshilov, wired to Lenin: 'The situation here is bad. We need resolute measures. The local comrades are too flabby. Every desire to help is regarded as interference in local affairs.' Things were equally bad in the Don and the Kuban regions where the Cossacks had joined the Whites. Every top ranking Bolshevik in Moscow who could be spared was now dispatched to some vital sector of the front. After Shlyapnikov had been ordered to the Kuban, Alexander Tsuryupa, the commissar in charge of supplies in Moscow, urged Lenin to send Stalin to Tsaritsyn. Possibly Stalin chose his assignment himself, since he knew he could work with old friends like Ordzhonikidze and Voroshilov. 'Do send him,' said Tsuryupa. 'He knows local conditions and Shlyapnikov will find it useful to have him around.' Thus the decision was taken to appoint Stalin 'Director-General of Food Supplies for the south of Russia invested with extraordinary powers'.[48] All local and provincial Soviet authorities were directed to 'obey the orders of Comrade Stalin'. It was essentially a civilian appointment and expected to last a few weeks at the most. Owing to unexpected circumstances it was to be prolonged by more than four months.

Stalin left Moscow on 4 June, with 'a detachment of workers' according to his official biography. The detachment included two armoured trains full of Red Guards. Two days later he arrived in Tsaritsyn on the Volga. 'There is chaos and profiteering,' he immediately reported to Lenin. 'Having secured the introduction of rationing and fixed prices in Tsaritsyn, the same must be done in Astrakhan and Saratov, otherwise all grain will flow away through these profiteering channels.' Rail transport had been completely dislocated 'owing to the multiplicity of collegiums and revolutionary committees' and he had been obliged to appoint 'special commissars' who had already discovered quantities of locomotives in places where their existence had not been suspected. River transport had also been held up, 'presumably because of the Czechoslovaks'. He went on to announce that the chief Soviet agent in charge of trade was being arrested for speculation in government-owned commodities and for other black-market activities, and he asked Lenin to tell the Commissar of Agriculture in Moscow 'not to send any more scoundrels'. However, Stalin was confident that 'despite the confusion in every sphere of economic life, order can be established'. Here indeed was the voice of the energetic administrator speaking in clear, crisp language, markedly different from the usual turgid and pedantic prose of Stalin's public utterances.[49]

A month later Stalin was still setting matters to rights in Tsaritsyn. At the same time, in the Kremlin, Lenin had to deal with an attempted *coup* by the Left Social Revolutionaries, the only non-Bolshevik political group which had originally supported his government. Now they advanced a number of demands, including the abolition of the Cheka and the declaration of guerrilla warfare against Germany. On Lenin's flatly rejecting their demands, they proceeded to stake an armed uprising coupled with terrorist acts against Germany's diplomatic representatives. The revolt broke out on 6 July with the assassination of Count Mirbach, the German Ambassador, by a Left Socialist Revolutionary named Blumkin, who turned out to be employed by the Cheka. The insurgents also arrested Dzerzhinsky and seized several public buildings, including the Moscow telegraph office. Lenin reacted quickly, mobilising the Communist workers who secured the Cheka chief's release unharmed, and shooting a number of Social Revolutionaries who were being held as hostages. 'We shall liquidate the revolt this very night ruthlessly and tell the people the truth,' he wired Stalin the same day. 'These wretched hysterical adventurers, who have become a tool of the counter-revolutionaries, must be ruthlessly suppressed everywhere …Therefore show no mercy to the Left Social Revolutionaries, and keep us regularly informed.'[50]

Stalin replied next day with a general progress report.

Tsaritsyn, 7 July 1918

To Comrade Lenin.

I am hurrying to the front, and writing only on business.

1. The railway south of Tsaritsyn has not yet been restored. I am firing or telling off all who deserve it, and I hope we shall have it restored soon. You may rest assured that we shall spare nobody, neither ourselves or others, and shall deliver the grain in spite of everything. If our military 'specialists' (bunglers!) had not been asleep or loafing about, the line would not have been cut, and if the line is restored it will not be thanks to, but in spite of, the military.

2. Large quantities of grain have accumulated on the rail south of Tsaritsyn. As soon as the line is cleared we shall be sending you grain by through trains.

3. Have received your communication. Everything will be done to forestall possible surprises. As regards the hysterical ones, you may rest assured our hand will not falter. We shall treat our enemies as enemies should be treated.

4. I have sent a letter by messenger to [the Council of People's Commissars in] Baku.

5. Things in Turkestan are bad; Britain is operating through Afghanistan. Give somebody (or me) special authority (military) to take urgent measures in South Russia before it is too late.

Because of the bad communications between the border regions and the centre someone with broad powers is needed here on the spot so that urgent measures can be taken promptly. If you appoint someone (whoever it is), let us know by direct wire, and send his credentials also by direct wire, otherwise we risk having another Murmansk.*

I send you a telegraphic tape on Turkestan.

That is all for the present.

Yours,
STALIN[51]

He followed this up three days later with his first direct attack on Trotsky's behaviour as Commissar of War. 'If Trotsky is going to hand out credentials right and left without thinking,' he telegraphed on 10 July, 'it may be safely said that within a month everything here and in the North Caucasus will go to pieces, and we shall lose this region altogether...Knock it into his head that he must make no appointments without the knowledge of the local people, otherwise the result will be to discredit the Soviet power.' He went on to ask for the dispatch of aircraft, pilots, armoured cars and six-inch guns, 'otherwise

* In March 1918, British marines landed in Murmansk at the request of the local Soviet to forestall a possible German landing. This was the origin of the subsequent Allied anti-Bolshevik front in North Russia.

the Tsaritsyn front cannot hold out and the railway will be lost for a long time'. Finally, he informed Lenin that he proposed to assume military powers himself.

> There is plenty of grain in the south, but to get it we need a smoothly working machine which does not meet with obstacles from troop trains, army commanders and so on. More, the military must assist the food agents. The food question is naturally bound up with the military question.
>
> For the good of the work, I need military powers. I have already written about this, but have had no reply. Very well, in that case I shall myself, without any formalities, dismiss army commanders and commissars who are ruining the work. The interests of the work dictate this, and of course not having a paper from Trotsky is not going to deter me.[52]

What Stalin did not tell Lenin, although Lenin probably inferred it, was that he also had in mind to make new military appointments. On the same day, he publicly announced that Voroshilov was to be 'in active command of the armies of the Tsaritsyn front' with effect from 10 July. Ordzhonikidze's authority as political commissar was similarly enlarged. Other members of the so-called Tsaritsyn group, which was to prove a sharp thorn in Trotsky's flesh, were Sergei Minin, the Bolshevik Mayor of Tsaritsyn, and Moisei Rukhimovich, an engineer from the Don basin. Rukhimovich had been a commissar there in the early days of the revolution and had given Voroshilov, who possessed no military experience whatever, a mandate to raise the guerrilla force originally called the Fifth Ukrainian Army and subsequently known as the Tenth Army. 'Placed in charge of supplies, the provincial minded Rukhimovich could conceive of no needs except those of the Tenth Army,' Trotsky was to complain. 'No other army swallowed as many rifles and bullets and at first refusal he yelled about the treason of the specialists in Moscow.' But the man who most detested the military 'specialists', according to Trotsky, was Voroshilov, whom the War Commissar described as 'a hearty impudent fellow, not overly intellectual but shrewd and unscrupulous. He never could make head or tail of military theory, but he was a gifted browbeater and had no compunction about utilising the ideas of brighter subordinates and no false modesty about taking full credit for them.'[53]

6

Following Lenin's directive Stalin enlisted the help of the local Cheka to deal with suspected counter-revolutionaries. This amounted in practice to the institution of a reign of terror. A large black barge was moored in the middle of the Volga. Here, on Stalin's orders, dozens of prisoners were shot each night, their bodies then being thrown into the river to float downstream. Every day new plots were discovered and soon the prisons were crammed full. An engineer named Alexeyev and his two sons were arrested for conspiracy. According to a local observer, Stalin's decision was brief: 'Shoot!' The engineer and his sons and several officers with them, believed to belong to a counter-revolutionary organisation, were seized by the Cheka and immediately shot without trial.[54] Soon the terror spread outside the Volga town to the whole of the country under Bolshevik rule.

By the middle of July 1918, units of the White and Czechoslovak forces were converging on Ekaterinburg, the centre of the Ural mining district, to which the ex-Tsar Nicholas and his family had ultimately been transferred after their arrest. They were lodged in the house of a merchant named Ipatiev, and there it was decided to put them to death to prevent their falling into the hands of the Whites and so becoming a symbol of the counter-revolution. After the British Consul in Ekaterinburg had vainly tried to persuade the local Soviet to spare their lives, they were taken into the basement of the Ipatiev house on the night of 16 July and shot. Their bodies were then thrown down a neighbouring mine shaft after being set alight with petrol.[55] However, the responsibility for the executions lay not with the Ekaterinburg commissars, as was widely supposed outside Russia at the time, but with Lenin and Sverdlov in the Kremlin. According to Gregory Bessedovsky, a Soviet diplomat who later defected to the west, Stalin had the major share in the decision, telling Sverdlov (after whom Ekaterinburg was subsequently renamed Sverdlovsk) that 'under no circumstances must the Tsar be surrendered to the White Guards'.[56] No doubt this was Stalin's view at the time, but it is not true to say, as Bessedovsky suggests, that Lenin was in favour of keeping Nicholas and the family in Ekaterinburg and was persuaded otherwise by Stalin. 'We decided it here,' Sverdlov told Trotsky afterwards. 'Ilyich [Lenin] believed that we shouldn't leave the Whites a live banner to rally around, especially under the present difficult circumstances.' Trotsky who was away from Moscow at the time and had advocated a public trial for the Tsar, subsequently endorsed the decision as 'not only expedient but necessary'.*

* 'The severity of this summary justice showed the world that we would continue to fight on mercilessly, stopping at nothing. The execution of the Tsar's family was needed not only in order to frighten, horrify, and dishearten the enemy, but also in order to shake up our own ranks, to show them that there was no turning

A fortnight later the Red terror received a fresh impetus as the result of two other much publicised incidents – the assassination, by a student, of Uritsky the chief of the Petrograd Cheka, and an attempt on the life of Lenin, who was shot and severely wounded by a Social Revolutionary called Fanny Kaplan, as he was leaving a labour rally in Moscow. As a reprisal, about eight hundred people were executed in the two cities, most of them arrested at random on mere suspicion of belonging to Social Revolutionary groups, while in the provinces there was a wave of mass arrests and shootings. That Stalin's hand did not falter may be gathered from a telegram which he and Voroshilov dispatched to Sverdlov, as soon as the news about Lenin reached them.

Tsaritsyn, 31 August 1918
Having learned of the villainous attempt of the hirelings of the bourgeoisie on the life of Comrade Lenin, the world's greatest revolutionary and the tried and tested leader and teacher of the proletariat, the Military Council of the North Caucasian Military Area is answering this vile attempt at assassination by instituting open and systematic mass terror against the bourgeoisie and its agents.

STALIN
VOROSHILOV

A week later Stalin was able to report that the offensive mounted by Voroshilov against the Whites had met with considerable success. 'The enemy has been utterly routed and hurled back across the Don,' he telegraphed to Lenin on 6 September. 'Tsaritsyn is secure. The offensive continues.' He thereupon paid a flying visit to Moscow to render a personal account, and together with Lenin he concocted a telegram of congratulations to Voroshilov and the 'heroic flotilla crews and all the revolutionary troops on the Tsaritsyn front who are selflessly fighting to establish firmly the power of the workers and peasants'.

Hold high your Red banners, carry them forward fearlessly, mercilessly root out the counter-revolution of the landlords,

---

back, that ahead lay either complete victory or complete ruin. In the intellectual circles of the Party there probably were misgivings and shaking of heads. But the masses of workers and soldiers had not a minute's doubt. They would not have understood and would not have accepted any other decision. *This* Lenin sensed well. The ability to think and feel for and with the masses was characteristic of him to the highest degree, especially at the great political turning points ...' *Trotsky's Diary in Exile, 1935*, (1959), pp. 80–81.

generals and *kulaks*,* and show the whole world that Socialist Russia is invincible.

Trotsky persistently complained that his orders, and those of the commander-in-chief General Joachim Vatsetis, were being deliberately flouted. He had just cause for complaint, since Stalin and Voroshilov would often write across the telegraphed orders the words: 'To be ignored.' One such order urging the call-up of surveyors for work on the projected Volga–Don Canal, was inscribed 'We'll build the canal after we have drowned the liberals in the Volga and the Don.'[57] Their confidence in the security of Tsaritsyn was also misplaced, since the town was soon surrounded again by the Whites. After Trotsky had issued an order from General Paul Sytin's headquarters at Kozlov (a district town on the railway between Moscow and Tsaritsyn) likewise ignored, unifying the southern command under Sytin and requiring reports of all military operations in the Tsaritsyn area to be sent regularly to Kozlov, the War Commissar finally lost patience. On 5 October, he cabled Lenin:

> I insist categorically on Stalin's recall. Things are going badly on the Tsaritsyn front in spite of superabundant forces. Voroshilov is capable of commanding a regiment, not an army of 50,000. However, I shall leave him in command of the Tenth Army at Tsaritsyn, provided he reports to Sytin.
>
> Thus far Tsaritsyn has not even sent reports of operations to Kozlov. I have required reports of reconnaissances and operations to be sent twice daily. If that is not done by tomorrow, I shall remand Voroshilov and Minin to court martial and shall publish the fact in an Army Order. According to the statutes of the Revolutionary Military Council of the Soviet Republic, Stalin and Minin, as long as they remain in Tsaritsyn, are nothing more than members of the Revolutionary Military Council of the Tenth Army.

Needless to add, Trotsky's protest was warmly endorsed by Sytin ('Stalin's last military order must be cancelled') and by Vatzetis ('Stalin's activities undermine all my plans').[58]

Stalin apparently got wind of this ultimatum, since he hurried off again in Moscow, where he hoped to persuade Lenin to replace Trotsky. However, Lenin and Sverdlov, whose patience on this occasion was exemplary, concerned themselves in an effort to compose the differences between the two commissars.

---

* Prosperous peasants, who were disfranchised and subject to heavy taxation.

'Stalin would very much like to work on the Southern Front,' Sverdlov telegraphed Trotsky on 23 October. 'He expresses great apprehension that people whose knowledge of this front is poor may commit errors, of which he cites numerous examples. Stalin hopes that in the course of his work he will manage to convince people of the correctness of his approach.' Sverdlov went on to ask Trotsky if he would agree to talk matters over personally with Stalin, 'for which purpose he is ready to visit you', adding that it was his own belief that 'it is essential to make every effort towards arranging to work together with Stalin'.[59]

Trotsky agreed to see Stalin, and a few days later Stalin and Sverdlov left Moscow by special train to meet Trotsky at a pre-arranged spot *en route*.

As a sop to Stalin's pride he was also appointed a member of the Revolutionary Military Council of the Republic, which he wanted. The three men foregathered in the War Commissar's coach. Stalin chose the occasion to put in a word for the Tsaritsyn group.

'Do you really want to dismiss all of them?' he asked Trotsky with an air of exaggerated subservience. 'They're fine boys!'

'Those fine boys will ruin the Revolution,' replied Trotsky. 'All I want is to draw Tsaritsyn back into Soviet Russia.'

However, Trotsky remained adamant on the subject of Stalin's recall, and to this Sverdlov now agreed. Stalin accordingly returned to Moscow, while Trotsky continued his journey to Tsaritsyn. There Voroshilov was likewise obliged to submit after receiving a severe dressing down from Trotsky, who was not a man to trifle with – he had recently had a commander shot for disobedience.

Thus was Stalin, in Trotsky's words, 'recalled from Tsaritsyn, with deep anger and a thirst for vengeance in his heart'. Shortly afterwards Voroshilov was relieved of his command and transferred to the Ukraine. ('It is impossible to let Voroshilov remain after he has nullified all attempts at compromise.') Minin, who was also 'carrying on an extremely harmful policy', was given a job elsewhere as well.[60]

Stalin always regarded the defence of Tsaritsyn as his crowning achievement in the Civil War. He was determined to perpetuate its memory and after Lenin's death he succeeded when he had the town renamed Stalingrad. Alas for the vanity of human wishes. Since 1961 it has been officially known as Volgagrad.

7
While Stalin and Voroshilov were busy fending off the Whites in Tsaritsyn, German and Turkish forces landed at the eastern Black Sea

ports and advanced into Transcaucasia, their main objective being Georgian manganese and Baku oil. Meanwhile Georgia, Armenia and Azerbaijan had already declared their independence. In Baku the local Soviet consisted of a coalition of Menshevik Social Revolutionaries and Bolsheviks, the latter led by Stepan Shaumyan and Prokofy Djaparadze. When the Turks came within sight of the city, the Bolsheviks, who were for coming to terms with the enemy, resigned in a body. Their partners in the Soviet thereupon imprisoned them and proceeded to defend Baku with the aid of a small British force under the legendary General L. C. ('Stalky') Dunsterville. But they only succeeded in holding out for a few weeks. In the confusion of the imminent fall of the city, the imprisoned Bolsheviks, twenty-six in all, managed to escape and embark on a vessel bound for Astrakhan, then in Bolshevik hands, where they knew they would be safe. However, the crew changed course during the voyage, fearing that they themselves would be arrested if they went on to Astrakhan, and they brought the vessel into Krasnovodsk, where the Mensheviks and their allies were still in control. The unfortunate commissars were again arrested, and the Krasnovodsk Mensheviks referred to their official government headquarters at Ashkhabad for instructions as to what should be done with them. At this time there was a British mission at Meshed under Major-General William Malleson, whom the Ashkhabad Government had informed of the arrival of the commissars in Krasnovodsk. On being asked for his views, Malleson urged that they should be handed over to the British authorities in India, as sureties for the safety of British prisoners in Bolshevik hands. While seemingly agreeing to this course, the Ashkhabad Government sent word to Krasnovodsk that the commissars should be shot for having 'betrayed Baku to the Turks'. Shaumyan, Djaparadze and the rest were accordingly taken into the nearby desert and the instructions were carried out.[61]

Some time afterwards, a Social Revolutionary journalist named Vadim Chaikin, anxious to ingratiate himself with the Bolsheviks, published an article, later elaborated into a book, in which he claimed that the British were responsible for the shooting of the commissars, which he stated was carried out by Captain Teague-Jones, the Malleson mission's liaison officer with the Mensheviks, while taking the prisoners in convoy from Krasnovodsk to Ashkhabad. There was no truth whatever in this allegation. Teague-Jones was in Ashkhabad at the time of the shooting and no British officers were present at the execution, although the scene as depicted by the Soviet artist Brodsky shows two of them looking on. Unfortunately Chaikin's version was widely accepted in Soviet Russia (and still is) and it further embittered Anglo-Soviet relations, already deeply disturbed by the Allied intervention.

Stalin was not alone in publicly denouncing what he called 'the savage murder of responsible officials of Soviet power by the British imperialists'. He wrote in the official government newspaper *Izvestia*:

> In the 'civilised' countries it is customary to talk about Bolshevik terror and Bolshevik atrocities, and the Anglo-French imperialists are usually depicted as foes of terror and shooting. But is it now clear that the Soviet Government has never dealt with its opponents so foully and basely as the 'civilised' and 'humane' British, and that only imperialist cannibals who are corrupt to the core and devoid of all moral integrity need to resort to murder by night, to criminal attacks on unarmed political leaders of the opposition camp?[62]

While Stalin was in Moscow at this time, another event which had considerable interest for him likewise terminated before the firing squad. On the final collapse of the German armies and the imminence of the Armistice in November 1918, the former police spy and Bolshevik deputy in the Duma, Roman Malinovsky, got out of the prisoner-of-war camp where he had been held since his capture on the front, crossed the Russian border and turned up in Petrograd. His double-dealing had already become known through the opening of the Okhrana files; he now went to the headquarters of the Petrograd Soviet, which were still in the Smolny Institute, and demanded either to be arrested or taken to see Lenin. Eventually he was seen by Zinoviev who ordered his arrest and dispatch to Moscow for trial.

The consequent proceedings were swift and secret. The prosecutor was Krylenko, who was to participate in many more state trials until he eventually disappeared in the purges. In his defence the prisoner pleaded that he had been forced to become an *agent provocateur* because he was already completely in the hands of the police; and, while admitting the gravity of his crimes, he called the ex-Okhrana chief Beletsky to testify that his activities had benefited the Bolsheviks and the Revolution more than the police. Apparently Malinovsky thought that Lenin, who had previously refused to listen to any ill about him, would again come to his rescue. But Lenin did not testify, although he was in court throughout the trial, as in all probability were Stalin and other members of the Central Committee. Lenin sat with his head bowed making notes, and only once did he raise his head.

That was when defence counsel, in his closing speech in mitigation, stated that if Malinovsky had had friends to guide him properly, he would never have become a spy. Lenin looked up at Malinovsky and emphatically nodded.

The trial ended with the only possible verdict – guilty – followed by the passing of the death sentence. Lenin refused to interfere with the sentence and Malinovsky was shot the same night in the Kremlin. Afterwards Lenin confessed to Maxim Gorky how he had been taken in. 'I never saw through that scoundrel Malinovsky,' he said adding after a momentary pause, 'that was a mysterious affair, Malinovsky!'[63] Had Stalin possibly anything to do with the speed with which the sentence was carried out? One cannot tell. But knowing what his relations with Malinovsky had once been, he must have had some anxious moments as to how Malinovsky would behave in court. But Malinovsky kept silent and took Stalin's great secret with him to the grave.

The war between the Allies and the Central Powers was now virtually over, and when German soldiers raised the red flag in Kiel, Lenin's government saluted the event. But the Allies, through their intervention and reinforcement of the White armies, had still to be reckoned with. By the end of the year there were close on a hundred thousand Allied troops in the country, two-thirds Japanese, mostly occupying strategic positions in north Russia and Siberia. Reports of considerable demoralisation among Red Army units and desertions to the Whites kept coming into the Kremlin, including the Third Army under Lashevich's command on the Eastern Front. 'There are several Party reports from around Perm about the catastrophic condition of the Army and about drunkenness,' Lenin wired Trotsky on 31 December 1918. 'They ask that you come there. I thought of sending Stalin. I am afraid Smilga [the principal political commissar attached to the Third Army] will be too soft with Lashevich, who it is said drinks himself and is unable to restore order. Telegraph your opinion.' Trotsky replied that he agreed to Stalin's journey with special powers for 'restoring order, purging the staff of commissars, and severely punishing the guilty'. However, by the time Stalin, accompanied by the Cheka chief Dzerzhinsky, reached the front, Perm had fallen to Kolchak's forces. Consequently the two commissars established themselves at Vyatka which was still held by the Third Army and where they were able to report to Lenin on 5 January 1919, that their 'investigation' had begun. ('We shall keep you regularly informed of its progress.')[64]

Having 'acted swiftly and drastically', in the words of his official biography, Stalin returned to the Kremlin at the end of the month. Much of the trouble was due to what he called 'the unreliability of reinforcements sent from the rear due to old methods of recruitment', otherwise ex-Tsarist officers, for which he blamed Trotsky. Eager for further military work, he asked Lenin if he could be sent to the Ukraine sector of the Southern Front, to which Voroshilov had been transferred. Trotsky immediately scented more trouble, since he realised that Stalin, by virtue of his position as a member both of the Revolutionary Military Council and the Party Central Committee must necessarily be a dominant figure in every sector of every front that he visited. 'I must state categorically that the Tsaritsyn policy, which has led to the complete disintegration of the Tsaritsyn [Tenth] Army, cannot be tolerated in the Ukraine,' Trotsky protested to Sverdlov. 'Okulov [Voroshilov's successor as the Tenth Army Commander] is leaving for Moscow. I recommend that you and Comrade Lenin give the utmost attention to his report. The line taken by Stalin, Voroshilov and Rukhimovich means the ruin of everything we are doing.'

Next day Trotsky followed this up on the direct wire in his usual forthright language:

> Compromise is of course necessary, but not a rotten one. The fact of the matter is that all the Tsaritsynites are now congregated at Kharkov. You can see what the Tsaritsynites are from Okulov's report, which throughout consists solely of factual material, and the reports of commissars. I consider Stalin's patronage of the Tsaritsyn tendency a most dangerous ulcer, worse than any treason or betrayal by military specialists... Rukhimovich is only another name for Voroshilov...
>
> Once again I urge a careful reading of Okulov's report on the Tsaritsyn Army and how Voroshilov demoralised it with Stalin's co-operation.

In due course Stalin appeared in Kharkov, and this led to further friction with Trotsky, particularly when Stalin refused to countersign an operational order by General Yegorov, the commander-in-chief of the Southern Front, although it bore the signature of a subordinate political commissar. The matter was eventually referred to Lenin, who is said to have remarked with an embarrassed air, 'What can we do about it? Stalin again caught in the act!'[65]

Nevertheless, Lenin consistently sustained Stalin. At the Eighth Party Congress, which met in Moscow in March 1919, he procured his additional appointment as Commissar for State Control, in charge of what was commonly known as the Workers' and Peasants' Inspectorate.

The object of this new commissariat, which in a sense was Stalin's own brainchild, was to control every branch of the creaky governmental machine by eliminating inefficiency and corruption carried over from Tsarist times and training an *élite* civil service. When Stalin was at Vyatka with Dzerzhinsky, he had found that 'unreliable people' sat in the local Soviets and that the peasants' committees were controlled by *kulaks*, while the personnel of the local administration was largely the same as it was before the Revolution. ('Consider the significance, for example, of the fact that of the 4,766 officials and employees of Soviet institutions in Vyatka, 4,467 occupied the same posts as in Tsarist times.')[66] Admittedly the idea of this commissariat, which had Lenin's enthusiastic support, was a good one. But inevitably, through traditional administrative inertia, it was to turn the Workers' and Peasants' Inspectorate into a further source of muddle, corruption and bureaucratic intrigue, eventually becoming a kind of civil service police force.

It was also during the Eighth Party Congress that two important sub-committees of the Central Committee came into being. The first was the Politburo, which had never functioned since its creation in October 1918, and was now effectively reconstituted to deal with matters of high policy where urgent decisions were required. So as to allay the anxiety of the other Central Committee members, it was agreed that they could attend Politburo meetings without the right to vote and further that the Politburo should report regularly to the whole Committee. (In fact, the Central Committee only sat in plenary session at fairly long intervals and it could do no more than endorse the decisions of the increasingly powerful sub-committee.) The following were elected to serve on the new Politburo: Lenin, Kamenev, Trotsky, Stalin and Krestinsky, with the addition of Zinoviev and Bukharin as alternate or 'candidate' members. Sverdlov's name was absent, as he had died of influenza in that same month, being succeeded as President of the Republic by Kalinin and as secretary of the Central Committee by Krestinsky. The presence of Kamenev and Zinoviev in the Politburo was due to their power as the respective party bosses of Moscow and Petrograd, while Bukharin was included since he ran the monopoly press and official propaganda. The other sub-committee, lower in status than the Politburo, was the Organisation Bureau (Orgburo) in charge of party personnel; it was entrusted with the allocation of jobs in the army and government service according to the demands of the civil war. It is significant that from the beginning Stalin was the sole liaison between the two sub-committees, co-ordinating their work where necessary with the help of a common secretariat.[67]

8

On 24 March 1919, the day after the Congress ended, Stalin took a noteworthy step designed to regularise an important relationship in his private life. This concerned young Nadezhda (Nadya) Alliluyeva, the younger daughter of his friends Sergei and Olga. Nadya now worked in Lenin's private office as confidential code and cypher clerk and she shared a room in the Kremlin with an older woman named Natalia Trushina, who had been living with the Alliluyevs in Petrograd and had been asked by them to chaperone Nadya when the government move to Moscow took place. Besides employing her in the code room, Lenin would occasionally use her as a courier, and in this capacity he had sent her to Tsaritsyn with confidential dispatches for the military commander.

> I went with her to Tsaritsyn [Natalia later recalled]. At that time Stalin ran the show there. One evening, when he was somewhat tipsy, he made advances to Nadya. And when he returned from Tsaritsyn to the Kremlin, he started courting her. I decided to tell her family what was happening, but they at first attached no importance to it. Later when Kalinin, an old friend of the Alliluyevs, warned them of the budding romance, they became alarmed. But by then Stalin had succeeded in turning Nadya's head.
>
> At that time, a conflict was developing within the Kremlin between two opposing groups of Bolshevik leaders – one led by Trotsky, the other by Stalin. Nadya was fascinated by Stalin's political manoeuvrings. Stalin, in turn, was flattered by her interest in him, flattered not only because she was young and beautiful but also because of the key position she held in the administrative apparatus of the Kremlin. Nadya frequently helped him out by apprising him in advance of the contents of messages which she decoded for Lenin. Consequently, it was often possible for him to anticipate and block the moves planned against him by his adversaries.
>
> There could, of course, be no question of true love between them, [Natalia continued]. There was a disparity in their ages. He was twice as old as she, and most unattractive – pockmarked, swarthy, coarse looking. And he was of a different nationality. Nadya, on the other hand, had developed into a striking beauty. I can still see her as she looked then – graceful, gentle, rosy cheeked, her complexion like the sky at sunrise. Nadya was a dream.

And then what Natalia Trushina feared came to pass. One day, a Georgian friend of Stalin's named Lominadze arrived in Moscow with several bottles of a rare Georgian wine called Kakhetinsk. He decided to give a party, and for this purpose another Georgian friend Abel Yenukidze, who was secretary of the Congress Central Executive Committee, obligingly put his apartment at Lominadze's disposal. Just a few people were asked, including Stalin and Nadya, but not any of the other party dignitaries.

At this party Lominadze sang a song about a blossoming apple tree and the hurricane – how the hurricane fell ardently in love with the delicate apple tree, finally crushing the apple tree in its passionate embrace. The song made a strong impression on Nadya who by then had had one or two drinks too many. The party went on for hours. Nadya did not return home till morning, having (we are told) 'surrendered her innocence to Stalin'.

In due course Nadya confessed to her friend that she was pregnant. The news got round and eventually reached the ears of the Alliluyevs in Petrograd. 'As a true Communist Nadya's father had always upheld the principle of free love in a free socialist society,' remarked Natalia Trushina afterwards. 'But in this case he reacted as any bourgeois father would.' In other words Sergei Alliluyev demanded that Stalin should marry his daughter.

Stalin was agreeable and the ceremony took place on a March day in 1919 quietly in a Moscow registry office. None of the party high-ups attended; in fact, there were only two witnesses, Stanislav Redens, a Latvian Communist who worked in the Cheka and had married Nadya's sister Anna, and Abel Yenukidze. The commissar and his sixteen-year-old bride moved into a small house in the Kremlin, near the Spassky Gate, which had been used as servants' quarters under the Tsars and consisted of a large room and a kitchen on the ground floor and two rooms upstairs. The military commandant of the Kremlin found a few rather dilapidated pieces of furniture for them.[68]

Life under the Bolsheviks at this time was well described by Leonid Krassin who had joined the Government as Commissar of Trade and Industry.

> The conditions here are so absurd that, while the commissars are eating in the banquet hall at the Kremlin, their own families may be unable to procure a loaf of bread. In the big towns it is like living in a besieged fortress. In the villages, on the other hand, bread and other provisions are plentiful enough and the

moujiks have tons of paper to buy other necessaries. They very often refuse to sell what they have, except at an enormous profit, even higher than that which is made by the speculators. We are learning how to deal with them, however; sometimes goodwill does the trick, other times compulsion has to be applied. But distribution is very difficult with the railways in such a state of disorder. Passenger trains are practically suspended now, as the trains are wanted to supply the military with artillery and food – all this after four years of a great Eurpean war and two of revolution.

It is the civil war, of course, and our being cut off from the rest of the world which is responsible for this complete disorganisation of our economic life. Everything has to be taken for the army, metals, leather, cloth, etc. Any number of factories are idle, the Volga fleet is paralysed for lack of fuel...It is difficult for anyone to realise the extent of the calamity to which we are reduced.[69]

The spring and summer of 1919 were the most critical for Bolshevik chances of survival. In the south, Kharkov and Tsaritsyn fell to the Whites and Denikin's troops reached Orel, less than a hundred and fifty miles from Moscow. In the north-west, Yudenich's forces penetrated to within a few miles of Petrograd, while Kolchak, whose unwieldy and inefficient administration at Omsk was recognised by the Allied representatives at the Versailles Peace Conference as the *de facto* government of the whole country, advanced on a wide front from the Urals and for a time it looked as if the Admiral must eventually arrive at the Kremlin. The Whites were encouraged by the armed intervention of the Allies and allied sympathies generally, which openly condemned the regime which had butchered the Tsar, shot hostages, repudiated the national debt, deserted their allies and even, so it was said, nationalised women. In the British House of Commons Winston Churchill denounced what he called 'the foul baboonery of Bolshevism', and from a glance at the map, showing the distribution of the anti-Bolshevik forces, it seemed virtually certain that the Whites must eventually emerge as the victors in the struggle.[70]

This highly dangerous situation for the Bolshevik regime made Lenin anxious to bring the intervention with its accompanying economic blockade to an end. He made a spectacular effort to do this when the Americans sent a twenty-eight-year-old State Department official, named William Christian Bullitt, to Moscow on a special mission. Bullitt, who came from an old and wealthy Philadelphia family, had been included in the United States delegation to the peace conference in Paris at the instance of President Wilson's confidential adviser Colonel Edward House. Bullitt's instructions, which he subsequently told the Senate Foreign Relations Committee in Washington he received from House, were 'to attempt to obtain from the Soviet Government an exact statement of the terms on which they were ready to stop fighting'. The idea of this mission seems to have been suggested to House by Lincoln Steffens, a well-known American journalist, who in the event accompanied Bullitt to Moscow. Both men were well received by the Bolshevik authorities and a palace with a plentiful supply of caviar was put at their disposal.

On 14 March 1919, after three days of negotiations with Chicherin and his assistant Litvinov followed by a long talk with Lenin, the following terms for an armistice were agreed subject to ratification by the Whites and their interventionist allies. They were expressed according to the formula devised by Philip Kerr, Lloyd George's private secretary, and given to Bullitt before he left Paris.

All existing *de facto* governments which have been set up on the territory of the former Russian Empire and Finland to remain in full control of the territories which they occupy at the moment when the armistice becomes effective.

These lands, which Lenin was prepared to sign away in return for a cease-fire, the withdrawal of all foreign troops and the ending of the blockade, amounted in all to about three-quarters of the former Tsarist dominions. In addition to Poland and Finland, they comprised the Murmansk–Archangel area, the Baltic states, the western part of Byelorussia, more than half the Ukraine including the Crimea, the whole of the northern Caucasus and Transcaucasia, the Urals and all Siberia. Bullitt was informed that the terms must be ratified by 10 April, otherwise the deal was off.

One of the most tantalising historical riddles is what would have happened had Lenin's astonishing offer been accepted by the western Allies. Fortunately for the future of the Soviet state it was rejected or rather allowed to go by default. Indeed there is some doubt whether President Wilson was aware that the Bullitt mission was anything more than a purely fact finding one and whether the eager young diplomat had the President's authority to negotiate at all. Bullitt was understandably bitter when he was disowned by both Wilson and Lloyd George, and he promptly resigned from the State Department. He was to reappear on the Moscow diplomatic scene fourteen years later as the first United States Ambassador to the Soviet Union after the establishment of full diplomatic relations between the two countries.

Meanwhile the Civil War continued to be fought with renewed ferocity on both sides. By the autumn of 1919 the White forces had been hurled back on every front, and the brilliant twenty-six-year old commander of the Red Fifth Army, Mikhail Tukachevsky, had pushed into Siberia occupying Omsk and driving Kolchak further east to Irkutsk where the French were eventually to hand him over to the Bolsheviks who executed the ill-fated 'Supreme Ruler'. Stalin was sent to various fronts, where he was active in the type of purge in which he had excelled at Tsaritsyn and Vyatka. It is to his credit that he promoted the formation of mounted detachments which had been advocated by Voroshilov and were now grouped together to form the First Cavalry Corps under the comand of a swashbuckling trooper named Semyen Budenny. With Voroshilov as his political commissar, Budenny drove Denikin's army back to the Don, while outside Petrograd, where Stalin had also been busy as well as Trotsky, Yudenich was flung back into Estonia. Lenin and his colleagues in the Kremlin could now breathe more easily.

In the early days of the Red Army, successful commanders in the field were usually rewarded with wrist watches, since all military decorations which dated from Tsarist times had been abolished during the Revolution. A little later a Soviet decoration was introduced, the Order of the Red Banner, its first recipient being Vasily Blyukher, the future Marshal. The decoration was primarily intended for bravery and outstanding leadership under fire.[71] However, it was proposed in the Politburo that it should be given to the civilian Trotsky for his successful defence of Petrograd against Yudenich. The War Commissar felt that he should accept it, as to do otherwise would be to disparage a mark of distinction which he had so often bestowed upon others. At the close of the meeting, Kamenev, looking slightly embarrassed, proposed that the decoration should also be given to Stalin. 'What for?' asked President Kalinin, who was at the meeting. 'I can't understand why it should be given to Stalin.' However, the objection was overruled and Kamenev's proposal accepted.

As the meeting dispersed, Kalinin was buttonholed by Bukharin, 'Can't you understand? This is Lenin's idea,' said Bukharin. 'Stalin can't live unless he has got what someone else has got. He will never forgive it.'

A general award of decorations was publicly made at a mass meeting in the Grand Opera House, now the Bolshoi Theatre, after the War Commissar had made a progress report on the current military situation.

Towards the end of the proceedings the chairman read out Stalin's name. Trotsky immediately began to applaud. 'Two or three hesitant handclaps followed mine,' he afterwards recalled. 'A sort of cold bewilderment crept through the auditorium; it was especially noticeable after the ovations that had gone before. Stalin himself was wisely absent.'[72]

CHAPTER V

Struggle for Power

I

By the end of 1919 the Bolsheviks had virtually won the Civil War.
With the capture and execution of Kolchak in February 1920, the
allied intervention was brought to an end, although fighting continued
on a reduced scale in Siberia and also in the Crimea, where the White
commander Baron Wrangel made a gallant attempt to rebuild Denikin's shattered forces. At this time, while Stalin was engaged in what is
known in military parlance as mopping-up operations against the remnants of the White forces on the south-western front, he received a
telegram from Lenin asking him to expedite reinforcements to the
Caucasus. Stalin's somewhat brash reply to this request produced a
well deserved rebuke. The exchange was as follows:

From Stalin to Lenin, 20 February 1920
    It is not clear to me why the concern about the Caucasian
Front is imposed first of all upon me. In the order of things the
responsibilty for strengthening the Caucasian Front rests entirely
with the revolutionary Council of War of the Republic, whose
members, according to my information, are in excellent health,
and not with Stalin, who is overloaded with work anyway.

From Lenin to Stalin
    The concern for expediting the shipment of reinforcements
from the south-western Front to the Caucasian Front has been

imposed upon you. Generally one must try to help in every way possible and not quibble about departmental jurisdictions.[1]

The Bolsheviks were confronted by a new danger in the shape of Poland. The Allies had decided that Poland should be reconstituted as an independent state, and this was formally recognised by the Treaty of Versailles. However, Poland's eastern frontier was not clearly defined. The *de facto* frontier followed the river Bug, the so-called Curzon Line, but this did not satisfy the Poles, who wished to recover territory in western Russia and the Ukraine which had once been Polish. Encouraged by France and the United States, which provided them with supplies of war material and food, the Poles demanded all the territory between the Bug and the frontier as it was at the time of the First Partition of Poland in 1772, as well as a large cash indemnity and the occupation of the Russian town of Smolensk as a guarantee. Although in no mood for war, Lenin's Government rejected the Polish demands, hoping that in the event of hostilities the Polish peasants and workers would rise and welcome the Red Army as their saviour. The Poles immediately reacted by advancing eastwards through the Ukraine to Kiev, which they captured early in May 1920.

The Bolsheviks were thus obliged to strike back. Tukachevsky, who had recently smashed Denikin's army in the Crimea, was switched to command the main sector of the Russian western front. He decided to make a strong feint through the Ukraine into southern Poland, while reserving his main blow for central Poland north of the Pripet Marshes. His strategy was most effectively carried out. Kiev was quickly retaken by Budenny's First Cavalry Army, which dashed on through 660 miles of enemy territory, eventually reaching the Polish town of Rowne (Rodno). Meanwhile Tukachevsky's main troops advanced from Smolensk through Minsk and Vilna to Brest-Litovsk on the river Bug, eventually cutting the Warsaw–Danzig railway. They met with little opposition, the Polish retreat became a rout, and by the middle of August Tukachevsky was within thirteen miles of Warsaw.

In answer to an appeal from Marshal Pilsudski, Poland's Head of State, France dispatched General Weygand and a military mission of experts to Warsaw. Weygand lost no time in organising a swift attack on Tukachevsky's exposed left flank in the direction of Brest-Litovsk. Tukachevsky naturally looked to Budenny and his cavalry to reinforce him, and orders were transmitted to this effect to Budenny's headquarters. But Tukachevsky had reckoned without Stalin, who with Voroshilov's backing in the south-western command used his position as the chief political figure in the Military Council to tell Budenny to go for

Lvov, which he was anxious to enter at the same time as Tukachevsky took Warsaw. As Trotsky put it, 'Stalin was waging his own war.'[2]

Alexander Barmine, a Soviet diplomat who defected to the west, was an infantry officer during this ill-fated campaign. He summed it up in these words:

> It is not difficult to understand Stalin's psychology at this time. Overshadowed by more brilliant men, he wanted to gain a place in the limelight. He had long been resenting the secondary role he was playing in military affairs. He resented the leadership of Trotsky and of newcomers like Tukachevsky. For these reasons he attempted to manoeuvre without reference to the main army and win a little victory of his own. The result was two defeats and the loss of the war.
>
> The Polish attack on our left flank began on 16 August. Few of the Red troops were in a position to offer resistance. Even after this fact and the strategy of the enemy were clear to all, Stalin instructed Budenny to continue his attempt to capture Lvov. Thus while in the south Budenny's army was futilely kicking away at the Lvov defences, the Poles sliced their way through to Brest-Litovsk and Bialystok. Meanwhile a second attack reinforced by French artillery was developing against our front.[3]

It was only after several days had elapsed that Tukachevsky's frantic messages, reinforced by threats from the War Commissar himself, took effect, and Budenny along with Stalin and Voroshilov at last changed direction. But it was too late. Tukachevsky's main force was already in headlong flight. Two Red Armies were annihilated with the capture of 70,000 prisoners by the Poles. An armistice was hurriedly concluded in October 1920, and in the resulting peace settlement Poland was able to regain most of the territory west of the 1792 frontier together with a portion of the Ukraine.

At the Tenth Party Congress, which approved the settlement in March 1921, Stalin attempted to defend his role, blaming Smilga, the Military Council member and political commissar with Tukachevsky's main force, who he alleged had 'deceived the Central Committee' by 'promising' that Warsaw would be taken by a definite date and failing to make good his 'promise'. According to Trotsky, who was present, Stalin was listened to in silence, and he was not supported by a single vote after Trotsky had delivered a strong protest, pointing out that all Smilga's 'promise' amounted to was that it was *hoped* to take Warsaw, 'but that hope did not eliminate the element of the unexpected, which is peculiar to all wars, and under no circumstances did it

176

give anybody the right to act on the basis of an *a priori* calculation instead of a realistic development of operations'. Lenin, who was said to have been 'terribly upset' by this incident, tried to pacify his conflicting lieutenants by expressing himself to the effect that 'we did not want to blame anybody personally'.⁴ The matter was then allowed to drop. But Stalin did not forget nor forgive Trotsky or Smilga or Tukachevsky, all of whom had openly pointed out his responsibility for the defeat of the Red Armies outside Warsaw. All three were eventually to perish at Stalin's order.

Towards the end of 1920, Stalin became ill. His doctor diagnosed appendicitis and he went in to the military hospital in Moscow for the appendectomy. Lenin was very worried, particularly when he was informed that a wide incision had to be made round the appendix and that the patient's recovery could not be guaranteed. Lenin invariably called twice a day, morning and evening, insisting on a thoroughgoing report. 'If anything should happen,' he told the doctor, 'telephone me at once – any time night or day.' After four or five days, when it appeared that the operation had been successful and Stalin was out of danger, Lenin was greatly relieved. 'Thank you ever so much,' he said on hearing the news. 'But I am going to go on pestering you with my phone calls all the same.'

One day, after Stalin had come out of hospital and was convalescing in his quarters in the Kremlin, the doctor happened to meet Lenin there when he was making his rounds. In answer to Lenin's questions about the patient's condition, the doctor replied that he ought to go away somewhere if he was to make a reasonably quick recovery.

'That's what I told him,' said Lenin. 'But he won't listen to me! However, I'll take care of that. But not in one of the sanatoriums. I am told they are good now, but I haven't seen anything good about them yet.'

'Why doesn't he go straight to his native hills?' the doctor suggested.

'You're right,' said Lenin. 'There he'll be further away from everything and no one will bother him. We'll have to see to that!'⁵

But Stalin again demurred. The reason was not immediately apparent. In fact, he ardently desired Georgia's newly won independence under a native Menshevik Government which was headed by Noe Zhordania to be brought to an end. This he had in mind to achieve through the invasion of the country by the Red Army. However, Georgia's political independence had been recognised both by the western Allies and the Bolsheviks, and the latter had concluded a treaty to this effect with Georgia in May 1920. Stalin's attitude to this agreement was later summarised by his old boyhood friend Joseph Iremashvili.

Stalin was opposed to the treaty. He did not want to let his native land remain outside the Russian State and live under the free rule of the Mensheviks he detested. His ambition pushed him toward rulership over Georgia, where the peaceable, sensible, population resisted his destructive propaganda with icy stubbornness...Revenge against the Menshevik leaders, who had persistently refused to countenance his utopian plans and expelled him from their ranks, would not let him rest.

This feeling was reflected in the chilly reception given to the Georgian plenipotentiary when he came to Moscow to negotiate the treaty and called on the Commissar of Nationalities in his private office. The plenipotentiary was the veteran Menshevik Gregory Uratadze, who had been imprisoned with Stalin in Kutais jail in 1903. 'Do you think he was pleased to see me?' Uratadze later recalled. 'He greeted me, it is true, with a smile, but he still smiled out of the side of his mouth as I used to remember. He did not ask what sort of a trip I had had to Moscow, how things were going in his "motherland", and how his old comrades and acquaintances in Georgia were getting on.'

While the Georgian plenipotentiary was sitting in Stalin's office, Kamenev came in. As soon as he saw Uratadze the two men embraced warmly. 'Oh, you Georgian blackguards!' said Kamenev, poking Uratadze good-humouredly in the ribs. 'You want to get away from us and eat *shashlik* and drink Kakhetian wine by yourselves. That's naughty of you, brother, and it won't be so easy! Indeed we won't let you go so easily! Isn't that right, eh, Comrade Stalin?'

Stalin smiled faintly but said nothing.

Kamenev then went on to question Uratadze about people and happenings in Georgia, showing particular interest in the plenipotentiary's own doings, where he was staying in Moscow and so on. After Uratadze had told him about his mission, which was then more or less secret, Kamenev remarked after a pause, still in a tone of banter: 'This is a difficult business, but for the nice, kind Georgians it will be possible!'

Afterwards Uratadze pondered on how Kamenev, whom he had not known nearly as well as Stalin, had greeted him, and had shown such interest in Georgia, compared with the aloof Commissar of Nationalities, who never once inquired about his 'motherland'.

Did Stalin, in the words of the poet, remember 'where he was born, where he grew up, where the graves of his ancestors were'? I do not think so. Or, to be more accurate, perhaps he did remember but never experienced any tender feelings for these places.

I knew him for many years. We worked together in the Social Democratic Party for many years, we were together in jail when we were both young – and we all know that one's youth is never forgotten – and I do not recall that there was anything the slightest bit 'human' about him. His spiritual 'misanthropy' could be clearly seen on the surface, almost too clearly...And yet this gloomy, unsociable man, who never perhaps in his whole life laughed or smiled except out of the side of his mouth, who did not possess any outstanding intellectual qualities, was to reign for more than a score of years over one sixth of the globe.

Perhaps it was about such a one that the poet wrote:

> The giant suffers at the hand of the pygmy,
> The ruler dies at the hand of the slave,
> And often an infamous scoundrel,
> Is crowned with laurels by fate.[6]

On 11 February 1921, the Red Second Army crossed the Georgian frontier on Stalin's orders, the movement being unknown at the time either to the Commander-in-Chief or to Trotsky, who was away in the Urals. Three days later Stalin confronted the Politburo with the *fait accompli* and secured the approval of the other members on the pretext that the Red troops had gone to the aid of the local Bolsheviks who had staged a rising in Georgia, which had the support of the majority of the population. Lenin agreed somewhat reluctantly, since he believed that the sovietisation of Georgia and indeed the whole of Transcaucasia should proceed more slowly and gently than by brute force which was the impression given by this sudden invasion. Stalin's decision to dispatch Ordzhonikidze to Tiflis as political commissar with plenary powers was also approved. (Ordzhonikidze was already a member of the Revolutionary War Council of the Caucasian Front and head of a special committee which had been created for the establishment of Soviet authority in the Caucasus.) 'The Central Committee was inclined to permit the Second Army to support actively the uprising in Georgia and the occupation of Tiflis, while maintaining the international norms,' wrote Lenin at the time in an instruction to the army commander, 'and on condition that all the members of the Second Revolutionary War Council, after seriously considering all the evidence, are certain of success.'[7]

As Commissar of Nationalities, Stalin had assured the Politburo that the Mensheviks had been virtually overthrown by the Georgian

179

masses, and that it only needed the appearance of a few Red Army soldiers to consolidate a victory that had in effect been won. Both Lenin and Trotsky were shocked when they heard that heavy fighting was taking place and that Tiflis, which it took Ordzhonikidze and his men a fortnight to reach, had been given over to the most frightful pillage, rape and murder. The Red Army's mopping-up operations were followed by the arrival of the Cheka and the arrest of hundreds of Mensheviks who crammed the old Metekh fortress in the Georgian capital. To smash 'the hydra of nationalism', so Stalin urged the Georgian Bolsheviks, the Party must purge its ranks of local patriots and get rid of everyone who would not subordinate Georgia's interests to those of the whole of Soviet Russia. In return for renouncing their local independence, Stalin promised the Georgians unlimited free oil from Baku and a loan of several million roubles from Moscow.[8]

In July 1921, Stalin arrived in Tiflis and attended a mass meeting in the Opera House on Rustaveli Avenue, as the Golovinsky Prospekt had been renamed. His reception was anything but friendly. As soon as he appeared on the platform surrounded by Cheka agents and Red guards, the audience began to hiss. Old women, some of whom had fed and sheltered him in the old pre-Revolution days, hurled abuse at him. Surrounded by the angry faces of old comrades, he could only stammer out a few words of attempted self-justification, after which he hurriedly left the building cowering behind his bodyguard. 'Never before and never after,' noted Iremashvili who was present, 'did Stalin have to listen to such open courageous indignation.'[9] Next day, he stormed into the local Bolshevik headquarters and violently abused Philip Makharadze, who had made the arrangements for the meeting and whom he consequently held responsible for his humiliation. Indeed the incident made Stalin quite ill. At all events he had to receive medical attention, a fact which was brought to Lenin's attention. 'Send name and address of doctor attending Stalin,' Lenin telegraphed Ordzhonikidze on 25 July, 'also how many days Stalin kept from work.' Shortly afterwards, when Stalin returned to Moscow, Lenin asked the commandant of the Kremlin 'to transfer Stalin to more comfortable quarters, as the noise from the adjoining kitchen prevented him from sleeping at an early hour in the morning'. This was to be done at once.[10] Accordingly he and Nadya moved into a suite of rooms in the Poteshny Palace.

The excesses committed by the Cheka and the Red Army of occupation in Georgia led to the formation of a well-organised resistance movement with resultant guerrilla warfare and the capture and execution of its Menshevik leaders, thus further inflaming local patriotic feeling. At the same time, of all the foreign powers which had recognised the independence of Georgia a short time before, not a single one came to her assistance. Great Britain's excuse, expressed through the mouth of Mr Lloyd George, the Prime Minister, was that a trade agreement had recently been concluded with Moscow, under which the British Government undertook among other things to refrain from anti-Soviet activity in all territories which had formed part of the old Tsarist empire. Stalin's behaviour over Georgia, with the active assistance on the spot of Ordzhonikidze and Dzerzhinsky, the Cheka chief, was eventually to disgust Lenin, when the Bolshevik leader came to realise what had happened. Then he blamed himself 'for not having intervened vigorously and drastically enough in this notorious affair', and he blamed Stalin as well for having let his personal vindictiveness run away with him and shown that he was 'not merely a genuine social chauvinist, but a coarse brutish bully acting on behalf of a Great Power'.[11]

Stalin was also concerned with several important developments on the domestic front at this time. In March 1921, a serious mutiny broke out at Kronstadt, where the sailors demanded an end to the dictatorship of the Bolshevik party and the establishment of the type of government by Soviets which the Bolsheviks had originally promised. The rising was suppressed with considerable bloodshed by Red Army troops who raced across the frozen waters of the Gulf of Finland and stormed the fortress, shooting hundreds of sailors in the process.

The Tenth Party Congress, which met a few days later, banned all opposition groups within the ruling party. One such group was the Workers' Opposition led by Shlyapnikov and Alexandra Kollontai, who desired the transfer of all economic power to the trade unions. Trotsky and Bukharin, on the other hand, wanted the trade unions to be completely absorbed by the State. Lenin, with Stalin's open support, advocated a middle way, arguing that the Soviets were strictly speaking not a workers' state but represented two classes, the workers and the peasants, and that so far as the workers were concerned they should be free to join trade unions or not as they pleased and that the unions should enjoy some form of independence, at any rate for the time being. That the Communist experiment had been proceeding too rapidly was the lesson that Lenin learned from the Kronstadt rising, and this led him to put the economic machine into reverse gear. The result was his New Economic Policy (commonly called NEP), which allowed a return to private enterprise in trade and small and medium-sized industry.[12]

According to his official biographer Yaroslavsky, Stalin was one of the strongest supporters and defenders of this novel policy, and he later gave a 'classical definition' of its meaning. It may also be considered as an example of the kind of Communist double talk, which sometimes marked his public utterances.

> NEP is a special policy of the proletarian state designed to tolerate capitalism but retain the key positions in the hands of the proletarian state; it is designed for the struggle between the capitalist and socialist elements, for the growth of the importance of the socialist elements at the cost of the capitalist elements, for the abolition of classes and the laying of the foundation of a socialist economic system.[13]

This measure of economic freedom was offset by a tightening up of political control, since the ban on opposition groups meant that Soviet Russia was in effect transformed into a one-Party state.

Of particular significance in this context was the creation of the Central Control Commission by the Tenth Congress. The duty of the commission was to supervise Party morals, and to carry out 'purges' in the various party echelons throughout the country with the help of similarly constituted local commissions, removing Communists who had acquired a taste for bourgeois life or who were considered otherwise deficient in Party loyalty. At first, the penalties were relatively mild, usually a reprimand or in more serious cases expulsion from the Party. The Central Committee secretaries acted as the link between the Committee and the Control Commission, and the two bodies regularly held joint sessions.[14]

These developments were reflected in current changes of personnel. In March 1921, Zinoviev was elected a full member of the Politburo in place of Krestinsky, who was suspected of favouring the Workers' Opposition, while in the Party secretariat Krestinsky and his two liberal-minded colleagues, Serebriakov and Preobrazhensky were replaced by two of Stalin's friends, Molotov and Yaroslavsky, who were considered politically more 'reliable'. At the same time Molotov and Kalinin joined the Politburo for the first time as candidate members. A year later, following the Eleventh Party Congress, Rykov and Tomsky were added to the Politburo as full members, and Valerian Kuibyshev became a candidate.* In Lenin's words, 'the key of the situation lay in the choice of men'.[15]

---

* During the Revolution, Kuibyshev had organised the Bolshevik seizure of power in Samara, a town which was subsequently renamed after him; he was one of the bright young men like Molotov whom Stalin brought on in the Party at this time.

By this date, the Central Committee's secretariat staff had risen to more than six hundred, who dealt with over four thousand reports reaching the secretariat every month from local Party organisations. There were nine different departments in the secretariat, and this had led to overlapping with outside organisations as well as with each other.[16] It was consequently decided by the Congress to create a new post of General Secretary to be filled by a senior Party member who would co-ordinate the various branches, including the Orgburo, and the Central Control Commission, a task which had got beyond the powers of Molotov and Yaroslavsky. Zinoviev proposed Stalin for the job. At first Lenin expressed misgivings. 'This cook can only serve peppery dishes,' he told Trotsky.[17] Lenin was also privately critical of Stalin's handling of the Workers' and Peasants' Inspectorate. However, he eventually came round, and when the former joint secretary Preobrazhensky complained that Stalin already headed two commissariats, Lenin dismissed the complaint as 'frivolous'. 'We must have a man of authority in charge,' he said, 'otherwise we shall be submerged in petty intrigue.'[18] Preobrazhensky, who was to die in prison during the Great Purge, also foresaw what Lenin was only to realise later, that too much bureaucratic power was being concentrated in the hands of one individual. For instance, the skill with which the members of the Central Control Commission were chosen at this Congress revealed the mastery over the party apparatus which was gradually but surely passing into Stalin's control.* The General Secretaryship, for which Stalin's candidature was formally moved in plenary session, was the climax in this process. 'Thus, unofficially Stalin became the chief conductor of the purges.'[19]

On 3 April 1922, the day the Eleventh Congress ended, it was announced that J. V. Stalin had been appointed General Secretary of the Central Committee of the All-Russian Communist Party. Molotov and Kuibyshev were appointed as his assistants. The news was briefly reported in the Russian press as a minor Party event, to which no particular political significance was attached.[20] None of the other Central Committee and Politburo members, even Trotsky, seems to have envied Stalin what was generally assumed to be the drudgery of his new assignment. After all, Lenin was the leader, while Stalin was no

* 'Only one of the members elected in 1921 was re-elected in 1922, but of the seven elected in 1922, four were to remain in their posts for many years to come. Thus was begun the transformation of the control commissions into a second highly centralised hierarchy, parallelling the hierarchy of party secretaries. From their original conception as a check on the party bureaucracy, they now became an integral part of this bureaucracy, and a powerful instrument in the hands of the party leaders.' L. Schapiro, *The Communist Party of the Soviet Union*, p. 257.

more than Lenin's assistant and the servant of the Party. What nobody could foresee was that the reins of power were about to slip from the leader's hands.

2

Shortly after breakfast on 26 May 1922, a small blood vessel burst in Lenin's brain. He had not been feeling well during the preceding weeks and his doctors had advised him to take a holiday. He had considered going to some watering-place in the Caucasus like Borzhom and had been corresponding with Ordzhonikidze about the possible trip. Now there was no question of his being able to undertake such a long journey, since his right hand and leg were paralysed and his speech seriously impaired. Instead he was taken by his doctors from the Kremlin to his country house at Gorki near Moscow, where he had recuperated after the attempt on his life in 1918. This time his convalescence lasted four months. 'I could not even speak or write and I had to learn everything over again,' he told Trotsky later.

Stalin was allowed to see the sick man for a few minutes some days after the stroke when Lenin was still practically speechless. Thereafter the General Secretary appears to have gone out to Gorki at fairly regular intervals. During a visit he made about the middle of July, Stalin noted that Lenin looked better but still showed signs of fatigue and overwork. 'I am not allowed to read newspapers and I must not talk politics,' Lenin ruefully told his visitor. 'I carefully avoid every scrap of paper lying on the table, lest it turn out to be a newspaper and lead to a breach of discipline.' Stalin laughed heartily and praised the patient warmly for his obedience to discipline, as he afterwards recalled. 'We then proceeded to make merry over the doctors, who cannot understand that when professional politicians get together they cannot help talking politics.' Stalin gave the patient the latest news about all the topics on which he 'thirsted for information', such as the internal economy, the prospects for the harvest, the pending trial of the social Revolutionaries and the international conferences at Genoa and the Hague where the new Soviet state's relations with the western powers were under discussion.

A fortnight later, Lenin was well enough to discuss the forthcoming Twelfth Party Congress, for which purpose Stalin was summoned to Gorki along with Trotsky, Zinoviev and Kamenev. By the middle of August, Stalin found the leader surrounded by a pile of books and newspapers, having been given permission to 'read and talk politics to his heart's content'. On this occasion a marked improvement was noted. Lenin looked rested and no longer exhibited a nervous craving for work, having recovered his customary calm and self-assurance, so Stalin was able to inform the readers of *Pravda*. ('This was our dear old Lenin, screwing up his eyes and gazing shrewdly at his interlocutor.') They were photographed seated together on a garden bench, Stalin having thoughtfully brought along a photographer whose camera produced a picture which was later to be broadcast in millions of copies.

According to Stalin, the leader showed particular interest in the differences which had occurred between France and her two wartime allies Great Britain and America over the treatment of Germany in the matter of reparations. 'They are greedy and they hate one another profoundly,' Lenin observed. 'They will be at loggerheads yet. As for us, we need be in no hurry. Ours is a sure road: we are for peace and freely negotiated international agreements. But we must keep a firm hand on the wheel and steer our own course without yielding either to flattery or intimidation.' Lenin also made a characteristic comment on a rumour of his death which had appeared in the White Russian press abroad. 'Let them lie if it is any consolation to them,' he remarked with a smile. 'One should not rob the dying of their last consolation.'[21]

The account of his meetings with Lenin during the latter's illness which Stalin published in *Pravda* at this time did not mention any matters on which they disagreed. Most of *Pravda*'s readers were consequently unaware of two fundamental political differences. The first of these concerned the state monopoly of foreign trade which Lenin wished to preserve intact against the wishes of a considerable section of the Central Committee, led by Bukharin and Sokolnikov, and eventually supported by Stalin with the full weight of the General Secretariat of the Party, that foreign traders should be able to deal with individual businessmen inside the new Russian state in the spirit of Lenin's New Economic Policy which permitted internal private trading. Lenin argued that, if the monopoly were relaxed or abolished, then 'the foreigners will buy up and take home with them everything of any value'. On the other hand, foreign traders were holding off in the hopes of being able to deal direct with individuals rather than the Soviet government of which they had little experience in the matter of trade negotiations. 'At this stage I am not opposed to the strict prohibition of measures that would lead to the weakening of the monopoly of foreign trade,' Stalin had written to Lenin just before his illness. 'I think however that such a weakening is becoming inevitable.' Stalin's forecast was right. There was such a sharp falling off in Soviet foreign trade during the next few months and consequent loss of badly needed foreign currency that a plenary meeting of the Central Committee on 6

October ratified Sokolnikov's proposals for considerable reductions in the monopoly. Lenin, who had returned to his Kremlin office a few days previously but had not attended the meeting, regarded the decision as a personal blow in which he thought he detected the covert hand of Stalin.[22]

The second point of difference between the Soviet leader and the General Secretary was a highly important constitutional matter particularly affecting the Commissariat of Nationalities of which Stalin was in charge. Because of his interest in Soviet nationalities, particularly in the three Caucasian Republics of Georgia, Armenia and Azerbaijan, as well as Byelorussia and the Ukraine, a commission headed by Stalin had been charged by the Politburo through the Orgburo with the task of preparing a scheme of political and economic union with Russia proper, then known as the Russian Federation (RSFSR). The other members of the commission included Ordzhonikidze, Kuibyshev, Sokolnikov and Molotov. In the event Stalin's plan provided for 'the formal adhesion of these Republics to the RSFSR', specifically merging the individual republics' hitherto separate services of foreign affairs, defence, foreign trade, communications and posts and telegraphs with those of the central government in Moscow and stipulating that other branches of local government such as finance, food, labour and economy generally should be 'strictly subject to the directives of the corresponding commissariats of the RSFSR', while the Moscow headquarters of the Cheka (GPU) should likewise be free to impose its directives locally in the matter of 'the counter-revolutionary struggle'. Only a few departments such as justice, education, agriculture and health and social insurance were to be 'regarded as independent'. Thus, while the five republics were described as 'autonomous', the degree of their autonomy were severely limited and in many important respects they were to be subject to Moscow's control. When the local Party Central Committee were consulted, only Armenia and Azerbaijan wholeheartedly accepted the scheme; Georgia was strongly opposed to it, while the other two republics had reservations.[23]

Lenin, who wished the republics to have a much greater measure of independence including the right to secede from the Union if they so desired, was considerably upset when he received Stalin's draft. On 15 September 1922 Stalin went out to Gorki and discussed the draft with his leader, agreeing to one significant change. He also agreed to defer the presentation of the draft to the Politburo for approval until Lenin's return to Moscow a fortnight later. On the same day as Stalin's visit, Lenin addressed a letter containing some critical comments to Kamenev for circulation to all the members of the Politburo.

186

In my opinion the matter is of the utmost importance. Stalin tends to be somewhat hasty. You must think about it seriously – you once intended to deal with it and even had a bit to do with it – Zinoviev too.

Stalin has already agreed to make one concession, that of replacing the term 'adhesion' to the RSFSR in paragraph 1 by 'formal unification with the RSFSR within the framework of a Union of the Soviet Republics of Europe and Asia'. I hope the purport of this concession is clear. We recognise that we are equals in law with the SSR of the Ukraine, etc. and join it on an equal footing in a new Union of Soviet Republics.[24]

Stalin, who received a copy of this letter as a Politburo member, responded with a brash attack upon the leader for his interference and 'national liberalism'. At a meeting of the Politburo where the letter was brought up Kamenev passed over a note to Stalin which read: 'Ilyich is going to war to defend independence.' To this Stalin immediately replied: 'We must be firm with Lenin.'[25] However, on reflection and no doubt discussion with his colleagues, he changed his attitude, and decided as a matter of tactics to give way to Lenin, who (as he told Kamenev) had 'declared war to the death' on what he called 'dominant nation chauvinism'. As a result, the draft which he brought before the Central Committee on 6 October incorporated all Lenin's suggested admendments including the right of secession by the outlying republics and other concessions to their 'independence', since Stalin was convinced that through the apparatus of the general secretariat the central government must eventually achieve the supreme power, whatever concessions might be made on paper to the other republics. At Lenin's insistence, he also agreed to bring up again the question of the foreign trade monopoly for reconsideration by the committee after the ratification of Sokolnikov's proposals for its reduction on the same date.

On his return to the Kremlin at the beginning of October 1922, Lenin quickly became absorbed in office work. He was supposed to limit himself to a five hour working day, 11 a.m. to 2.0 p.m. and 5.0 to 7.0 p.m., with Wednesday and Sunday as rest days. But this regimen was not adhered to very strictly. For the next two months, until he again showed signs of a breakdown and was ordered back to the country for a short rest, he wrote or dictated 224 official letters, received 171 callers, presided at 32 meetings and conferences and delivered several public speeches – according to his devoted principal private secretary Lydia Fotieva.

But to those who had known him of old, he was a pale shadow of his former self. On 13 November he made a speech in German to the delegates of the Fourth Congress of the International, when he practically broke down and was unable to finish. It was to be his last public appearance.[26] After 16 December he was never able to return to work in his Kremlin office.

That Stalin was kept informed of the details of all Lenin's engagements, conversations and other activities during this period was due to the fact that his wife, Nadya Alliluyeva, was a member of the private secretariat under Fotieva and dutifully reported everything that happened to her husband. The recent publication by the Marx–Lenin Institute in Moscow of the office diary kept by Lenin's duty secretaries at this time enables us to follow his daily routine with minute precision.[27] The following entries are some of those made by Stalin's wife.

21 November, morning In the morning Vladimir Ilyich [Lenin] received Gorbunov [Assistant Secretary of the Council of People's Commissars]. After 11.30 Kamenev. Meeting at 6 o'clock of the Council of People's Commissars at which Lenin presided].

Lydia Alexandrovna [Fotieva] has a voting paper [to enable Lenin to vote *in absentia* in the Politburo] which Vladimir Ilyich asked to be reminded of [during his visit to the office] from 5 to 6 p.m. in order to have a talk with Stalin. But Lydia Alexandrovna kept it and said that the explanations he wished to receive from Stalin she would give him [Lenin] herself, so there was no need to remind him. But Lydia Alexandrovna would remind him. Kamenev 10.15 to 10.45.

23 November, evening At 11 in the morning Vladimir Ilyich attended a meeting of the Politburo which lasted till 2.30. So far he has given no instructions.

25 November, morning Vladimir Ilyich is unwell, he stayed only five minutes in his office, dictated three letters over the phone, to which he wanted inquiries made later for answers.

Maria Ilyinchina [Lenin's sister] said that he should not be bothered in any way – if he asked about the answers himself, then inquiries should be made in the proper quarters.

No appointments, no instructions so far. There are two packets from Stalin and Zinoviev, but these are to be kept under our hats until special instructions and permission are given.

27 November, morning Vladimir Ilyich came into the office

around 12, asked for no one and went away shortly afterwards. Through Nadezhda Konstantinova [Krupskaya] he requested all the material on foreign trade. This was sent to his flat. No instructions, no callers and no letters.

29 November, morning Vladimir Ilyich was in his office at 12.20, sent for Stalin, who sat till 13.40

1 December, morning Vladimir Ilyich phoned Lydia Alexandrovna at 11.20, asked to see Molotov at 12.

Molotov and Syrtsov [from the Central Committee Secretariat] called, were together from 12 till 1.30...

2 December, morning The doctor was with Vladimir Ilyich in the morning and told him that once or even twice every two months Vladimir Ilyich had to go away for several days for a rest. On Tuesday he did not allow him to preside [at the Politburo meeting], but would allow him to do so on Thursday, but not for long – and after Thursday he was positively to go away for several days.

Gorbunov phoned and asked that Vladimir Ilyich be told at the first opportunity that Rykov had left Tiflis on 1 December by express train. Vladimir Ilyich has to be told this as he is very interested in it.

Vladimir Ilyich asked for Kamenev to see him at 8 p.m. (he phoned at 14.05)

4 December, morning When Rykov arrives (if Vladimir Ilyich is in the country by that time – he is leaving on Thursday), he is to be put through on the telephone to Vladimir Ilyich.*

6 December, morning Vladimir Ilyich came to his office a little after 11. He asked Lydia Alexandrovna to write several letters on his behalf (to Yakovleva, Kamenev, Tsuryupa). Asked to be put through to Stalin, made arrangements to see him. At 12.40 Stalin came, sat with him till 2.20. Asked for Dovgalevsky to come at 6, Bogdanov at 7, Eiduk at 7.30. After Stalin he wanted to talk with Meshcheryakov.†

At 2.25 Vladimir Ilyich went home, Kamenev phoned, said he

* In the 'action column' of the diary, Alliluyeva wrote, 'Watch this', underlining the words three times.
† V. N. Yakovleva and N. L. Meshcheryakov were board members of the Commissariat for Education. V. S. Dovgalevsky was Commissar for Posts and Telegraphs. Alexander Bogdanov, whose real surname was Malinovsky, was an old member of the party, well known as a sociologist, economist and surgeon. He founded the first institute in Russa devoted to the study of blood transfusion, dying in 1928 as the result of an experiment on himself. A. V. Eiduk was chairman of the Commission on Agricultural and Industrial Immigration.

was sending a packet addressed to Comrade Lenin, which has to be handed to him personally.

9 December, morning Maria Ilyinchina phoned, saying that Vladimir Ilyich was going to dictate something [over the telephone from Gorki] at 5.45 and at 6 he was to talk with Rykov, who has arrived and is waiting at home for the call.

12 December, morning Vladimir Ilyich arrived in Moscow at 11, came to his office at 11.15, stayed there a short time and went home before 12. At 12 he was to see Rykov, Kamenev and Tsuryupa. (He saw them.)

Vladimir Ilyich left his office at 2 o'clock. Rykov, Kamenev and Tsuryupa sat with him till 2.

These prosaic and business like entries tell their own story. They show that Stalin's wife had a shrewd eye for essentials, that she had access to all the confidential files in Lenin's private office, that she was fully aware of all his movements, knew exactly whom he saw on business and when, and overheard all his telephone conversations. She particularly noted his steadily deteriorating health. He had hoped to address a plenary meeting of the Central Committee on 18 December, but on the morning of that day Nadya noted in the diary that he was ill and could not attend. In fact, he had suffered a second stroke.

Although Lenin soon recovered sufficiently to continue working from his flat in the Kremlin where he carried on gamely until a third stroke permanently incapacitated him ten weeks later, the 18 December entry was the last to appear in Nadya's handwriting in the diary. Shortly afterwards, apparently within a few days, she gave up her job in the secretariat. The fact that Lenin was no longer able to come to the office may well have served as a convenient pretext for easing her out. Furthermore, Lenin had at last come to realise that the state of his health obliged him to wind up his affairs and retire from public life. Before doing so he had one supremely important piece of work to complete. This was the preparation of what came to be known as his political testament, a highly confidential document which was to prove of intimate concern to the General Secretary of the Party, among others. Since the ailing leader was naturally anxious that not a word of it should leak out in advance of the plans he had for its eventual release, he doubtless felt happier that Nadezhda Alliluyeva should no longer be working among the confidential files in his private office.

3

Throughout most of the year 1922, in spite of his illness and his political differences with Stalin on the questions of the state monopoly of foreign trade and the proposed new Soviet constitution, Lenin had consistently sustained the General Secretary in the face of the attacks of his opponents. Trotsky, for example, continued to needle Lenin about the affairs of the Workers' and Peasants' Inspectorate, although Stalin had ceased to be head of this commissariat on his appointment as General Secretary. There were also the Georgian Party members headed by Budu Mdivani, who protested at the high handed methods of Ordzhonikidze which they rightly suspected were employed on Stalin's initiative. On 10 October, Lenin sent the Georgians a telegram sharply reproving them and 'insisting' that their quarrel with Ordzhonikidze should be conducted 'in a more seemly and loyal tone'. Nevertheless, complaints continued to pour into Moscow from Tiflis so that Lenin referred the matter to the Party Secretariat. At Stalin's suggestion, a three-man commission headed by Dzerzhinsky was dispatched to Georgia to try to reconcile the differences, but as might be expected this only had the effect of whitewashing Ordzhonikidze. Gradually it dawned on Lenin that he might have been mistaken in his judgment of the Georgian comrades. He thereupon asked Rykov, a member of the Politburo, who was apparently going on leave to Georgia towards the end of November, to look into the 'conflict' and let him have an independent report. This explains Lenin's being so anxious to talk to Rykov on his return to Moscow, as is reflected in the diary kept by Lenin's duty secretaries.[28]

No record is available of what Rykov reported to Lenin by telephone on 9 December and presumably repeated at their meeting in the Kremlin three days later. No doubt Rykov told Lenin of a disgraceful scuffle which had occurred at Ordzhonikidze's house in Tiflis when Ordzhonikidze beat up one of the Georgian Party members present named Kabakhidze. Dzerzhinsky, who was summoned to Lenin's office later the same day, was unable to deny the incident, which according to Fotieva 'upset' Lenin 'deeply' when he heard about it, as Lenin himself later confirmed.[29] Indeed his worrying about the Georgian trouble may well have contributed to the second stroke which afflicted him four days later.

Lenin had hoped to speak at the plenary meeting of the Central Committee on 18 December when the question of the foreign trade monopoly was due to come up again. The second stroke was less serious than the first he had suffered seven months previously and he made a quick recovery. Nevertheless, Krupskaya insisted that he should stay in bed. He was greatly heartened when he learned that the Committee, with strong support from Trotsky, had reversed its earlier decision and restored the monopoly. He thereupon dictated a short note to Krupskaya congratulating Trotsky. 'It seems we have captured the position without firing a shot by mere manoeuvring,' he said. 'I propose that we should not stop but continue the attack.'[30] At the same meeting, the Committee resolved that the General Secretary should ensure that the Doctor's orders were carried out and Stalin was consequently instructed to keep himself informed of everything that happened at Lenin's bedside. Normally the patient would have been moved to the country, but there had been a heavy fall of snow during the past week which made the roads impassable for motor traffic, and the doctors felt that the only alternative means of transportation, an open sleigh, would be too much for him to withstand. Consequently he was confined to his room in the Kremlin, a fact which was to assume considerable importance during the succeeding three months of his illness when he was struggling desperately to put his affairs in order and at the same time to keep himself posted on current news of interest.

By some means, possibly through his wife who was still working in the private office, Stalin got wind of the note to Trotsky. He immediately telephoned Lenin's flat and asked to be put through to Krupskaya. As soon as she came on the line, he began to berate her in foul language for letting Lenin give her any dictation in disobedience to medical orders. He even threatened to have her prosecuted by the Party Central Control Commission for dereliction of duty. In this, of course, Stalin was wrong, since the patient had been expressly allowed by the doctor in attendance to give Krupskaya the note.

As might be expected, Krupskaya was greatly put out by Stalin's behaviour. She did not tell her husband, at any rate not immediately, no doubt wishing to spare him further worry. Instead she addressed a strongly worded letter of complaint to Kamenev, then acting chairman of the Politburo.

> Moscow,
> 23 December 1922
>
> Lev Borisovich!
> Yesterday Stalin subjected me to a storm of the coarsest abuse over a brief note that Vladimir Ilyich dictated to me with the permission of the doctors. I didn't join the Party yesterday. In the whole of these last thirty years I have never heard a single coarse word from a comrade. The interests of the Party and of Ilyich are

Gori about 1880.

Stalin was born here, 21 December 1879.

Above Stalin's birthplace as a museum.

Right Ekaterina Georgievna Djugashvili, Stalin's mother.

Above The Tiflis theological seminary from which Stalin was (according to himself) expelled for 'propagating Marxism'.

Left The theological seminarist, aged 15.

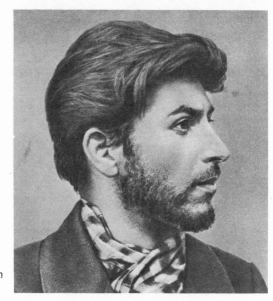

Right The young
revolutionary, 1900.

Below The Tiflis Observatory
where Stalin worked between
1899 and 1901.

Left The cell in Batum jail where Stalin was confined on his arrest in April 1902, and where he spent a year of his first prison term as an underground revolutionary.

Below The house in the Avlabar district of Tiflis with the cellar containing the illegal printing press which was raided by the police on 15 April 1906. Stalin was suspected of having given the police advance information which enabled the raid and accompanying arrests to be carried out.

Right Stalin's first wife
Ekaterina Svanidze. She
died of pneumonia about 1907.
'This creature softened my
stony heart. She is dead and
with her my last warm
feelings for all human beings
have died.'

Below Stalin in 1906, at the
time he is believed to have
become a police informer.

Lenin

Trotsky

Kalinin

Zhordania

Shaumyan

Ketskhoveli

Some of Stalin's
revolutionary
contemporaries.

Voroshilov

Some of Stalin's
revolutionary
contemporaries.

Teliya

Kamo

Sverdlov

Malinovsky

Krassin

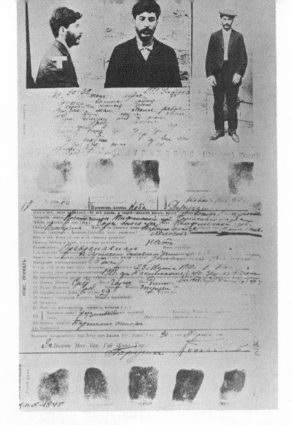

Police records of Stalin in
1910 (*left*) and 1913 (*below*).
The shorter left arm
is apparent in both
photographs.

With Suren
Spandaryan in
exile in
Siberia in
1915.

The house in Kureika in the
remote Turukhansk district
of Siberia where Stalin lived
with Sverdlov from 1913 to
1916.

Above Olga and Sergei Alliluyev, parents of Stalin's second wife Nadezhda.

Below The room in the Alliluyevs' flat in St Petersburg where Stalin lived during the revolution in 1917.

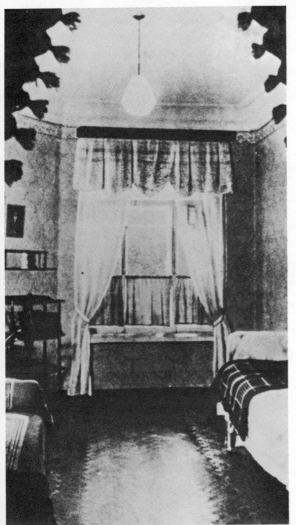

Top Street fighting in the
Nevsky Prospect, Petrograd,
July 1917.

Bottom Bolsheviks guarding
their Headquarters at the
Smolny Institute in Petrograd,
1917. *Both Radio Times Hulton
Picture Library.*

A Postcard widely
circulated on the first
anniversary of the Bolshevik
coup, entitled "The Leaders
of the Proletarian
Revolution," showing
(1) Lenin, (2) Trotsky,
(3) Zinoviev, (4) Lunach-
arsky, (5) Kamenev,
(6) Sverdlov.

Stalin, Rykov, Kamenev and Zinoviev, on
their way to attend a meeting at the Bolshevik
revolutionary headquarters at the Smolny
Institute in Petrograd in the autumn of 1917.

Lenin speaking in Sverdlov Square in Moscow,
May 1920. Trotsky is standing immediately
below the platform on the right with Kamenev
(partly hidden) behind him.

Above Lenin and
Stalin. This much
publicised photograph
was taken in the
grounds of Lenin's
country house at Gorki
during the summer of
1922 when Lenin was
recovering from his
first stroke.

Below Lenin's wife
Krupskaya. 'Stalin
subjected me to a
storm of the coarsest
abuse . . .' *Radio Times
Hulton Picture Library*

The Kremlin in Stalin's time. The Grand Palace is on the extreme left.

no less dear to me than Stalin. At the moment I need all the self-control I can muster. I know better than all the doctors what can and what cannot be said to Ilyich, for I know what disturbs him and what does not, and in any case I know this better than Stalin.

I am turning to you and to Gregory [Zinoviev] as much closer comrades of Vladimir Ilyich, and I beg you to protect me from gross interference with my private life and from vile abuse and threats.

I have no doubt as to the unanimous decision of the Control Commission with which Stalin takes it upon himself to threaten me. However I have neither the time nor the energy to waste on such a stupid farce. I too am human and my nerves are at breaking point.

N. KRUPSKAYA[31]

It is possible that Kamenev, who was on good terms with Stalin at this time, showed him Krupskaya's letter when the Politburo met next day. At all events, it is known that Lenin's illness was discussed at the meeting and as a result stringent sick room rules were imposed. Apart from the doctors, Lenin was only allowed to see his wife and sister and two or three of his secretaries. His dictation was restricted to from five to ten minutes daily and he was not to expect replies to any notes he might dictate. Visits from outsiders were strictly forbidden and his entourage were enjoined to withhold all information on current political affairs 'in order not to give him any cause for reflection or concern'. Thus Lenin found himself in effect the prisoner of Stalin and the Politburo. Nevertheless, he was determined to complete his 'testament', and for this purpose he succeeded in memorising the document piecemeal which he would dictate each day within the time allowed to one of his female secretaries. The lady chosen for this duty was Maria Volodicheva and she was instructed to treat it with the utmost confidence and keep all her notes in a safe place, afterwards burning them and any rough copies. Five fair copies were to be typed, three for Krupskaya, one for the secret file in his private office and one for himself. All the copies were to be placed in sealed envelopes with directions that they should only be opened by him or in the event of his death by his wife. Volodicheva carried out these instructions faithfully. Apparently Lenin intended that the document should be read out at the next Party congress and acted upon by the congress: indeed he called it 'Letter to the Congress'.

The big question troubling Lenin's mind was the succession to the leadership, since he felt that this might eventually lead to a split in the Politburo on the point of the rival merits of Trotsky and Stalin, 'the two most able leaders of the present Central Committee'. Of the two Lenin regarded Trotsky as the abler, but in his view Trotsky's admitted abilities were offset by 'too far reaching a self-confidence and a disposition to be too much attracted by the purely administrative side of affairs'. On the other hand, *'Comrade Stalin, having become General Secretary, has concentrated an enormous power in his hands; and I am not sure that he always knows how to use that power with sufficient caution.'** Kamenev and Zinoviev were ruled out on account of their opposition to the Revolution at the time of its outbreak in 1917, although Lenin did not wish this to be held against them any more than the fact that Trotsky had once been a Menshevik should be held against him. Of the younger Party members in their thirties Nikolai Bukharin ('the favourite of the whole Party') and Gregory Pyatakov ('very able') received honourable mention; but Lenin did not consider them yet ripe for the highest political responsibility.[32]

Lenin's initial observations in his testament were cautiously drawn and inconclusive. Of the two protagonists for the reversion of the leadership, it appeared that Stalin if anything had a slight edge over Trotsky. But the more Lenin pondered over Stalin's role in the creation of the Soviet Union as a 'federation of soviet republics', especially in the light of the trouble in Georgia, the more he turned against the General Secretary. On 26 December 1922, before more than 2,200 delegates to the Tenth All-Russian Congress of Soviets, Stalin moved the adoption of the new constitution which was adopted unanimously. Four days later he delivered a victory speech before the same assembly now transformed into the First Congress of Soviets of the USSR. No doubt Lenin was apprised of the content of the General Secretary's speeches and it can hardly have escaped his attention that he was not once mentioned in either, although Lenin was by common consent regarded as the chief architect of the Soviet State.

> What is the Soviet power now? [asked Stalin] A great state of the working people which evokes among our enemies not derision but the gnashing of teeth. Such are the results of the development of the Soviet power during the five years of its existence.
>
> But, comrades, today is not only a day for summing up; it is at the same time the day of triumph of the new Russia over the old

* Present author's italics.

Russia, the Russia that was the *gendarme* of Europe, the Russia that was the hangman of Asia. Today is the day of triumph of the new Russia, which has smashed the chains of national oppression, organised victory over capital, created the dictatorship of the proletariat, awakened the peoples of the East, inspired the workers of the West, transformed the Red Flag from a Party banner into a State banner, and rallied round that banner the peoples of the Soviet republics in order to unite them into a single state, the Union of Soviet Socialist Republics, the prototype of the future World Soviet Socialist Republic.[33]

Thus the General Secretary harangued the delegates. On the same day, 30 December, Lenin began to dictate a memorandum on the 'Nationalities Question'. He began by blaming himself 'before the workers of Russia' for not having intervened before 'with sufficient energy and incisiveness', giving his illness as the excuse, and he went on to express grave misgivings about the newly approved constitution. The 'single apparatus' designed to emerge from the founding of the Soviet Union, he felt, was nothing more than a 'Tsarist-bourgeois mixture', which had been 'borrowed from Tsarism' and was 'only barely anointed with the Soviet chrism'. The right of secession, 'with which we justify ourselves', he prophesied would prove to be 'nothing but a scrap of paper, in reality incapable of defending the minorities in Russia from the inroads of that hundred per cent Russian chauvinist – the scoundrel and violator, which the typical Russian bureaucrat is'. For all this he blamed Stalin's 'hastiness and administrative impulsiveness and also his spitefulness', remarking that 'spitefulness plays the worst possible role in politics'. Ordzhonikidze should be punished by expulsion from the Party for two years for having assaulted a Georgian comrade, and he censured Dzerzhinsky for having taken such a lighthearted view of the incident. 'Of course,' Lenin added, 'Stalin and Dzerzhinsky must be held politically responsible for this truly Great Russian nationalistic campaign.' Lenin's general conclusion was that the Party should think again about the embryo Soviet Union and that the central government's jurisdiction should be confined to the military and diplomatic spheres, leaving the individual republics completely independent in all other respects.[34] Needless to say, this suggestion was not to be followed.

By this time Lenin had also come to a conclusion about the future of the General Secretary of the Party Central Committee. On 24 January 1923, he added the following celebrated postcript to his testament, which he dictated to Fotieva.[35]

Stalin is too rude, and this fault, though tolerable enough in dealings among us Communists, becomes quite intolerable in the office of the General Secretary. Therefore I propose to the comrades to find a way to remove Stalin from that position and appoint to it another man who in all respects differs from Stalin in superior qualities – namely more patient, more loyal, more polite, and more attentive to other comrades, less capricious, etc. This circumstance may seem an insignificant trifle, but I think that from the point of view of preventing a split and from the point of view of the relations between Stalin and Trotsky, which I have discussed above, it is not a trifle, or else it is such a trifle as may acquire a decisive significance.

Lenin's reference to Stalin's characteristic rudeness suggests that Krupskaya may now have given her husband at least a hint of her distressing telephone conversation a fortnight previously. At all events Lenin had come down decisively in favour of Trotsky as his political successor, a decision which Stalin was soon to suspect he had made.

4

Having completed his 'testament', Lenin turned his attention to a number of other subjects on which he wished his views to be placed on record for the benefit of the Party. It must have been painfully difficult work for him, since he was still only allowed to dictate for ten minutes each evening, although he was gradually able to extend this period. During the next three weeks he dictated two versions of an article ultimately entitled *How We Should Reorganise the Workers' and Peasants' Inspectorate*. Although he did not mention its late head by name, it was clear from the context that Lenin blamed Stalin for the present condition of this bureaucratic commissariat with its twelve thousand *apparatchiki,* which he described as the worst organised of all the commissariats and 'utterly devoid of authority'. The article was duly sent off to *Pravda*, where its publication – it appeared on 25 January 1923 – was arranged by Lenin's sister Maria, who was on the *Pravda* editorial board. Incidentally, it is perhaps worth noting that this criticism of the corruption of the Party apparatus, its bureaucratic indifference to the needs of the governed, and its general inefficiency, had already been made by the Workers' Opposition and sternly silenced by the Tenth Congress in 1921 with vigorous support from both Lenin and Stalin.[36]

Lenin continued to worry about the situation in Georgia where opposition to incorporation in the Soviet Union had flared up. He asked Fotieva to obtain all the relevant data on the special commission's findings from Dzerzhinsky or Stalin. Dzerzhinsky, on his return from a second visit to Tiflis, informed Fotieva that Stalin had all the material. Fotieva then tried to reach Stalin, but it appeared he had gone to the country for the weekend. On his return two days later Stalin telephoned to say that he could not hand over the material without the permission of the Politburo. He also pointedly asked Fotieva whether she had not been telling Lenin 'things he was not to be told'. How was it he was so well posted about current affairs, as instanced by his recent article in *Pravda*? Fotieva replied that she had 'told Vladimir Ilyich nothing and had no reason to believe that he was fully informed on current affairs'. According to Fotieva, when she reported this to Lenin later that day, he declared that 'he would fight to get the material'.[37]

The matter was considered by the Politburo on 1 February. 'Since Vladimir Ilyich insists,' said Kamenev who was presiding, 'I think it would be even worse to refuse.'

'I don't know,' Stalin remarked in a surly tone. 'Let him do as he likes.'

Stalin went on to ask to be relieved of his responsibility for Lenin's medical supervision. According to Fotieva, this request was not granted. However, the Politburo agreed to let Lenin have all the data collected by the commission on the Georgian question, although it was not clear to the Politburo members what he intended to do with it. In fact, Lenin wished to check the facts himself, and to this end he asked Gorbunov, Fotieva and another of his secretaries Maria Glyasser to examine all the papers and submit an independent report of their findings to him.[38]

Two days later, Lenin sent for Fotieva and asked how they were getting on with their work. She replied that the papers which had been received were 'less than we had expected', which suggests that Stalin or Dzerzhinsky may have abstracted the more compromising contents of the dossier. Nevertheless, Lenin was told, there were enough to keep them busy for the next three weeks or so. During this period, while Lenin's health held out, he kept plying his research assistants with questions. For instance, did Stalin know of the beating up incident? If so, why didn't he do something about it?

Meanwhile Lenin continued to dictate more articles, including a further long one on the need for reorganising the Workers' and Peasants' Inspectorate which he entitled 'Better Fewer, But Better'.*

* Although the articles which clearly blamed Stalin, was completed on 10 February, its publication in *Pravda* was held up by the Politburo on account of its strongly

But it was clear that the strain was telling on him. Once he completely lost the thread of his argument and apologised to the secretary taking his dictation. He complained of increasing headaches, and by the middle of February his speech was noticeably more slurred.

Stalin continued to look in at the sick room, though his visits can hardly have been welcome. Towards the end of the month, he reported an extraordinary request to an informal meeting of the Politburo consisting of Trotsky, Kamenev, Zinoviev and himself. Lenin, he said, had suddenly sent for him and after the duty secretary had left the room he had demanded poison.

The others were flabbergasted by this news. According to Trotsky, Stalin's face wore a sickly smile as on a mask, and although his colleagues were accustomed to the difference between his facial expression and his speech, 'this time it was utterly insufferable'. Their horror was enhanced by Stalin's failure to express any opinion about Lenin's request, as if he were waiting to see what the others would say. 'Did he want to catch the overtones of our reaction to it, without committing himself?' Trotsky asked himself afterwards. 'Or did he have some hidden thoughts of his own?' Meanwhile, Kamenev, who 'sincerely loved Lenin' sat pale and silent, while Zinoviev looked bewildered 'as he always did at difficult moments'. It was Trotsky who at last broke the silence.

'Naturally we cannot even consider carrying out such a request!' he exclaimed. 'The doctor has not lost hope. Lenin can still recover.'

'I told him all that,' said Stalin obviously annoyed. 'But he wouldn't listen to reason. The "Old Man" is suffering. He says he wants to have the poison at hand...He'll use it only when he is convinced that his condition is hopeless.'

'But it's out of the question,' Trotsky insisted. 'He might succumb to a passing mood and take the irrevocable step.' Zinoviev murmured assent.

'The "Old Man" is suffering,' Stalin repeated, staring vaguely past the others, as Trotsky later recalled, and adding nothing in the way of a personal opinion. To Trotsky, Stalin's behaviour on this occasion, his whole manner, was baffling and sinister. What does the man want? Trotsky asked himself. And why doesn't he take that insidious smile off his mask?

---

critical tone. At first the Politburo opposed publication, and Kuibyshev even suggested printing a special copy of the paper with the article for Lenin to see. But Trotsky argued strongly that it should appear in the normal way, and his motion was finally carried. The article eventually came out in the issue of 4 March 1923. See Lenin, *Collected Works*, XXXIII, pp. 487–502.

No vote was taken on the matter, since it was not a formal meeting of the Politburo. However, Trotsky was positive that the four men parted with the implicit understanding that they could not even consider sending poison to Lenin.

Afterwards Trotsky posed the question – how and why did Lenin, who was extremely suspicious of Stalin at this time, turn to him with such a request which on the face of it presupposed the highest degree of personal confidence? 'Obviously Lenin must have thought that Stalin was the only one of the leading revolutionists who would not refuse to give him poison,' argued Trotsky later. 'He knew Stalin, his schemes and plans, his treatment of Krupskaya. He knew that all Stalin's actions were based on the assumption that he would not recover.' Trotsky's answer to the question he posed was consequently quite simple.

Lenin saw in Stalin the only man who would grant his tragic request, since he was directly interested in doing so. With his faultless instinct, the sick man guessed what was going on in the Kremlin and outside its walls and how Stalin really felt about him. Lenin did not even have to review the list of his closest comrades in order to say to himself that no one except Stalin would do him this 'favour'. At the same time, it is possible that he wanted to test Stalin : just how eager would the chef of the peppery dishes be to take advantage of this opportunity? In those days Lenin thought not only of death but of the fate of the Party. Lenin's revolutionary nerve was undoubtedly the last of his nerves to surrender to death.

As Trotsky reflected in the diary which he kept in exile, it was possible that Lenin's request, besides its main purpose, was designed to test both Stalin and the forced optimism of the doctors. 'Anyhow, Stalin did not comply with the request, but reported it to the Politburo. Everybody protested; the doctors still maintained there were grounds for hope; Stalin kept his own counsel...'[39]

On 3 March, Gorbunov and the other two secretaries, who had completed their analysis of the Georgian dossier, presented their secret report to Lenin.[40] The contents of this document are unknown, since it has never been published and presumably still reposes in the archives of the Marx–Lenin Institute in Moscow. But whatever it contained, it gave Lenin great cause for concern in what were to be the last few days of his intellectually active life. Having read it through, it seems that he wanted further information on some specific point and he asked his wife to get it from Stalin. However, the latter was in the country and a telephone message was left for him there to call back. By this time, according to the Soviet diplomat S. Dimitrievsky, who knew all the gossip going round the Central Committee secretariat, Stalin had become 'thoroughly sick' of Krupskaya 'because of her constant annoyances'. When he eventually telephoned, he again upbraided her 'in the most outrageous language' as on the previous occasion, so she told Kamenev and Zinoviev. But this time she also went to her husband in tears. Naturally Lenin was furious. 'He is devoid of the most elementary honesty,' he said, 'the most simple human honesty...'[41]

About noon on 5 March, Lenin sent for Volodicheva and asked her to take down two letters, one to Trotsky and the other to Stalin. The one to Trotsky he asked should be telephoned to him personally with an urgent request that Trotsky should reply as soon as possible.[42] The secret report together with Lenin's notes on the national question was to be delivered to him by safe hand. Trotsky was also asked to see the matter through the forthcoming Twelfth Party Congress in April.

Private and strictly confidential

Esteemed Comrade Trotsky,

I earnestly ask you to undertake the defence of the Georgian affair in the Party Central Committee. It is now being 'prosecuted' by Stalin and Dzerzhinsky, so that I cannot rely on their impartiality. Indeed, quite the contrary! Should you agree to undertake its defence, I would rest easy. If for some reason you do not agree, please return the papers. I shall consider that a sign of your disagreement.

With the very best comradely greetings,

LENIN[43]

Trotsky replied immediately by telephone in the affirmative, and his reply was taken down by Volodicheva in shorthand and repeated to Lenin.

The dictation of the letter to Stalin was put off after Lenin had confessed to his secretary that 'he wasn't feeling too good'. Apparently he was able to dictate it later in the day with instructions that the letter was to be given to Stalin personally and the answer received 'from his own hands'. But it was not brought to Lenin for his signature until the following morning.

Top secret. Personal.

To Comrade Stalin (Copies to Comrades Kamenev and Zinoviev)
Dear Comrade Stalin,

You allowed yourself to be so ill-mannered as to call my wife on the telephone and to abuse her. She has agreed to forget what was said. Nevertheless, she has told Zinoviev and Kamenev about it. I have no intention of forgetting what has been done against me, and it goes without saying that what was done against my wife I also consider as having been directed against myself. I ask you, therefore, whether you are agreeable to withdrawing your words and apologising or whether you prefer to break off relations between us.

Yours sincerely,
LENIN[44]

At this time Trotsky was confined to his quarters in the Kremlin with an acute attack of lumbago. When Lenin's secretaries Fotieva and Glyasser visited him on the morning of 6 March, they told him that, as Kamenev was leaving next day to attend a Party congress in Georgia, he could entrust him with any business he had there. Trotsky, according to his own account, then suggested that Lenin's letter to himself might be shown to Kamenev so that he might initiate on the spot whatever measures he considered necessary in the circumstances.

'I don't know,' replied Fotieva. 'Vladimir Ilyich did not instruct me to transmit a copy of the letter to Comrade Kamenev, but I can ask him.'

Fotieva left the room and returned after a few minutes. 'Absolutely not,' she said. 'Vladimir Ilyich says that Kamenev would show the letter to Stalin, who would make a rotten compromise, in order to double-cross us.'

'In other words,' remarked Trotsky, 'the matter has gone so far that Ilyich does not consider it possible to compromise with Stalin even along correct lines?'

'Yes,' she confirmed. 'Ilyich does not trust Stalin. He wants to come out openly against him before the whole Party. He is preparing a bombshell.'

About half an hour later Fotieva was back again with another message from Lenin. He had changed his mind, she told Trotsky, and had decided to act immediately. She also had with her a copy of a note which Lenin had just addressed to Mdivani, Makharadze and other Georgian comrades, which she handed Trotsky, telling him that another copy was to go to Kamenev. 'I am with you in this matter with all my heart,' Lenin had written to the Georgians. 'I am outraged by the arrogance of Ordzhonikidze and the connivance of Stalin and Dzerzhinsky. On your behalf I am now preparing notes and a speech.'[45]

Trotsky was naturally interested to learn the reason for Lenin's changed attitude towards Kamenev. Fotieva explained that it was due to his rapidly deteriorating state of health. 'His condition is getting worse every hour,' she said. 'You must not believe the reassuring statements of the doctors. He can speak now only with difficulty. The Georgian question is a terrible worry to him. He is afraid he will break down altogether before he can achieve anything. When he handed me this note for the Georgian comrades, he said: "Before it is too late...I must now come out into the open before the proper time!" '

'This means I can talk to Kamenev?' Trotsky broke in.

'Obviously.'

'Then ask him to come and see me.'

Kamenev arrived at Trotsky's flat about an hour later, having come straight from Krupskaya. In spite of Lenin's warning about a compromise, Trotsky was in a magnanimous and forgiving mood. 'I am against removing Stalin and against expelling Ordzhonikidze and displacing Dzerzhinsky,' he told Kamenev. 'But I do agree with Lenin in substance.'[46]

It now appeared that Lenin had read over and signed the letter to Stalin earlier that morning, but it had not yet been dispatched. 'You know Vladimir Ilyich,' Krupskaya had remarked to Kamenev. 'He would never have considered breaking off personal relations if he had not thought it necessary to crush Stalin politically.' At the same time, she seems to have been doubtful of the tactical wisdom in sending a letter which might have unpleasant repercussions on herself.

Exactly what happened next remained for long unclear. In fact, it was not until thirty-three years later, shortly after Nikita Khrushchev's famous 'secret' speech attacking Stalin's memory at the Twentieth Party Congress, that Volodicheva, who was still alive, was called in by the editors of Lenin's collected works in the Marx-Lenin Institute to decipher the last few sentences in the final entry in the duty secretaries' diary, which she had hurriedly appended at the time in shorthand.[47]

Nadezhda Konstantinova [Krupskaya] asked that this letter to Stalin should not be sent, and it was held up throughout the 6th. On the 7th I said I had to carry out Vladimir Ilyich's instructions. She spoke to Kamenev, and the letter was handed to Stalin and Kamenev, and afterwards to Zinoviev when he got back from Petrograd. Stalin's answer was received immediately on receipt of Vladimir Ilyich's letter. (The letter was handed to Stalin personally by me and his answer to Vladimir Ilyich dictated to me.) The letter has not yet been handed to Vladimir Ilyich, as he has fallen ill.

'Vladimir Ilyich was unable to read Stalin's reply because he had a bad attack of his illness the day it arrived,' Fotieva also noted. 'That day marked a sharp change for the worse in Vladimir Ilyich's condition generally.'[48] The same night, 7–8 March 1923, Lenin suffered his third and most serious stroke, which altogether deprived him of the power of speech, leaving his left side partly paralysed and his right side completely so. He never recovered his speech and, though the husk of his body was to survive for another ten months, his brain was permanently impaired and his political life was over. Nor did he ever see, or at any rate comprehend, Stalin's reply to his last letter, which we know from Lenin's sister was couched in apologetic terms, although its text has not been revealed.[49]

According to Stalin's biographer Boris Souvarine, a French Communist of Trotskyite sympathies, who was a frequent visitor to the Kremlin at this time and knew Lenin, Stalin at Trotsky's suggestion also wrote a letter of apology to Krupskaya, which likewise arrived too late for Lenin to read.[50]

If the final stroke of apoplexy had been delayed for a few months or weeks, or even days, Lenin might have succeeded, even without Trotsky's help, in ousting Stalin from his place of power, such was the immense following Lenin could command in the Party and the country. But it was not to be.

5

Although Stalin was unaware of the existence of Lenin's 'testament' with its devastating postcript, nevertheless he suspected that there was some move afoot between Trotsky and the Party leader to undermine his position as General Secretary. His suspicions were confirmed on 16 April 1923, the eve of the opening of the Twelfth Party Congress, when he learned from Kamenev that Trotsky had promised Lenin to take up the case of the Georgian 'deviationists' and in so doing to acquaint the delegates with the leader's views on Stalin's behaviour. It appears that Fotieva felt that it was her duty to inform Kamenev as acting chairman of the Politburo that Lenin's memorandum and notes on the nationalities question, which he had dictated at the end of the preceding December, had been given to Trotsky, 'to whom', as she told Kamenev, 'Vladimir Ilyich entrusted the defence of his position on this question at the Party Congress because they have both held identical views on this matter.' Kamenev promptly turned over Fotieva's letter with this information to the Central Committee Secretariat, 'because', he said, 'it contains nothing which pertains to me personally'. At the same time, Fotieva sent Stalin a copy of the memorandum on the nationalities in his capacity as General Secretary of the Central Committee, with a note to the effect that Lenin, who had hoped to make use of the material in a speech to the Congress, did not consider it to be 'in its final form and ready for the printer'.[51]

Stalin immediately seized on this point as a pretext for suppressing the memorandum. His action was approved in advance at a hastily summoned meeting of the Politburo that same evening, when it was decided that the material should not be published in the press but could be communicated in strict confidence to a few selected delegates. At the same time Stalin circularised the Central Committee with a statement giving as the reason for non-publication that the material 'had not been reviewed by Comrade Lenin'. He also censured Trotsky for having kept the material secret for over a month 'without making its contents known to the Political Bureau or the Central Committee plenum until one day before the opening of the Twelfth Congress of the Party'. Stalin further suggested that Trotsky had deliberately 'leaked' the contents to his friends among the delegates. In his reply to Stalin's statement, also transmitted to the Central Committee, Trotsky defended himself by saying that 'notwithstanding my expressed intention to acquaint the members of the Politburo with the memorandum, Comrade Lenin categorically expressed himself against this through Comrade Fotieva'.* Otherwise Trotsky remained silent throughout the Congress, except for a brief contribution on industrialisation, thereby letting slip a unique opportunity to attack Stalin with the full authority of Lenin. It was the Party Secretary's first tactical success in this phase of his struggle with the Commissar of War.[52]

Stalin's animosity against his brilliant but erratic colleague went back to the days of the fighting on the Tsaritsyn front in 1918, and it had recently become exacerbated by Trotsky's criticisms of Stalin's administration of the Workers' and Peasants' Inspectorate, with which he knew that Lenin agreed. By now Stalin had guessed that Lenin desired Trotsky to be his successor, and it was primarily to counteract any ambitions which Trotsky may have formed in this direction that

* In his authoritative work *The Communist Party of the Soviet Union* (1960), p. 269, Leonard Schapiro states that Fotieva's action in handing over the material to the Politburo 'cannot on the evidence be explained' and 'is all the more difficult to understand, unless she was subjected to pressure, because she had previously informed Trotsky that Lenin was anxious that his notes should not become known to Stalin before the Congress'. Although the possibility that Fotieva was subjected to pressure by Stalin cannot be excluded, the simplest explanation of her action seems to be that she considered herself bound to communicate with Stalin in their official capacities before the Congress opened but delayed doing so until the latest possible moment.

Stalin now began to make common cause in the Politburo with Kamenev and Zinoviev. Thus there came into being the triumvirate or *troika*, as it was called, whose members pledged themselves to work together to minimise Trotsky's influence and isolate him in the Party. Although he was related to Trotsky by marriage, Kamenev went along with the others largely because he believed that the principle of collective leadership should be applied during Lenin's illness; also, while he deputised for Lenin in the Politburo, Kamenev unlike Zinoviev had no ambitions to succeed him. Of the remaining full members of the Politburo, Tomsky had never forgiven Trotsky for his attack in 1920 on the trade union movement which was led by Tomsky; this had resulted in the latter's temporary banishment to Turkestan. Only Bukharin, the outstanding young Party theorist, sided with Trotsky. The two alternate members, Rykov and Kalinin, were moderates who were unhappy about what they felt to be Trotsky's hostility to the peasants as well as his militant support of international communism, and they could be relied upon to keep a watchful eye on Trotsky's movements, notwithstanding the fact that Kalinin was on friendly terms with him and indeed owed his position as nominal Head of State to Trotsky's sponsorship after Sverdlov had died.

Stalin, Kamenev and Zinoviev thus contributed to form a powerful combination which virtually controlled the Party and the Government. The *troika*'s existence was first publicly admitted by Stalin at the Twelfth Congress in answer to a criticism levelled at Zinoviev by V. V. Ossinsky, a delegate who had joined the Bolsheviks although he belonged to the nobility – he had formerly been Prince Obolensky.

Comrades, I cannot ignore the thrust that Comrade Ossinsky made at Comrade Zinoviev [declared Stalin]. He praised Comrade Stalin, he praised Comrade Kamenev, but he attacked Comrade Zinoviev, calculating that it will be enough to get rid of one of us for the time being, and the turn of the others will come later. He has set out to break up the core that has been formed within the Central Committee in the course of years of work...If Comrade Ossinsky seriously thinks of pursuing that aim, if he seriously thinks of launching such attacks against individual members of the core of our Central Committee, I must warn him that he will collide with a wall against which, I am afraid, he will break his head.*

* In the version of his speech published in Stalin's *Collected Works* during his lifetime, the word 'Comrade' is omitted before the names of Ossinsky, Zinoviev and Kamenev. This was because the three latter had been shot as 'enemies of the people' during the Great Purge.

He also rebuked another delegate named Lutovinov, who later committed suicide, for complaining that there was no longer any freedom of speech within the Party.

> Now that we are in power, now that we have four hundred thousand members and no fewer than twenty thousand Party units in the country, I do not know what sort of thing that would lead to. The Party would be transformed into a debating society that would be eternally talking and would decide nothing. Above all our Party must be a party of action...[53]

Finally, he took the Georgian comrades, notably Mdivani and Makharadze, to task for continuing their opposition to the idea of federation within the Soviet Union, now that 'every republic retains the right to secede from the Union at its own discretion'. Just before Lenin lapsed into semi-consciousness, the General Secretary had agreed to redraft the resolutions he was preparing for the Congress, so that he now came forward in an apparent display of magnanimity to condemn 'Great Russian chauvinism' and to assure the minorities that their rights would be respected. What the Georgians in particular feared most, in Stalin's view, was that federation would deprive Georgia of her privileged geographical position by virtue of which she could regulate the supply of goods from the west to Armenia and Azerbaijan.

> Why should the three principal nations which inhabit Transcaucasia, which fought among themselves so long, massacred each other and warred against each other, why should these nations, now that Soviet power has united them by bonds of fraternal union in the form of a federation, now that this federation has produced positive results, why should they now break these federal ties? What is the point, comrades?[54]

In Lenin's regrettable absence both Trotsky and Stalin refused to deliver the principal speech, and the honour was eagerly assumed by the ambitious chairman of the Petrograd Soviet, Gregory Zinoviev. The Congress concluded by enlarging the Central Committee to forty members, and the new Committee again elected Stalin as its General Secretary. Trotsky, procrastinating in the hope that Lenin would eventually recover, made no attempt to oppose Stalin's reappointment, although he must have known that Lenin would never have tolerated it had he been able to attend the meetings. The Politburo was also re-established as before, while the business of the Orgburo under Stalin's direction was put in the charge of Molotov and Dzerzhinsky. Another of Stalin's henchmen, Kuibyshev, was made head of the Central Control Commission responsible for Party discipline. Thus through the patronage which he was able increasingly to exercise at local party level, Stalin gradually and imperceptibly became the master of the Party; in future only his nominees were to have any chance of being elected delegates to the Party Congresses, since they could be relied upon dutifully to endorse all the policy proposals of the Central Committee and its General Secretary. So with considerable dexterity did Stalin manipulate the levers of power to his own advantage.

As far as getting rid of real or potential rivals went, he was content to bide his time. The method he liked best to employ was one which he described in an unusual moment of candour when talking to Dzerzhinsky and Kamenev one summer evening of that year. 'To choose one's victim, to prepare one's plans minutely, to slake an implacable vengeance, and then to go to bed...There is nothing sweeter in the world.'[55]

His first victim was the Tartar Communist Mirza Sultan-Galiyev, whose protector Stalin had been when Sultan-Galiyev worked as a senior official in the Commissariat of Nationalities. Later Sultan-Galiyev was sent by Stalin to the Tartar Republic of the Crimea to observe the effects of Soviet rule on the Moslem population. While there he built up a considerable personal following, in effect running the local Council of People's Commissars. In the result he seemed to have come to fancy himself as the leader of an independent Tartar Republic, since proof of this was provided through the interception of his correspondence. Evidently he was in touch with the Basmichis and other movements of resistance to Soviet rule in the various Moslem territories, and even, so it was alleged, with Kemal-Ataturk in Ankara. 'There is a limit to everything,' said Stalin at a special conference of representatives of minorities in Moscow which discussed Sultan-Galiyev's treasonable activities. 'And the limit in this case was reached when Sultan-Galiyev crossed over from the communist camp to the camp of the Basmichis. From that time on he ceased to exist for the Party. That is why he found the Turkish Ambassador more congenial than the Central Committee of our Party.'

Sultan-Galiyev was arrested on Stalin's orders, with the agreement of the other two members of the *troika*. Further incriminating documents were found in his possession at the time of his arrest, but some of his followers in the Tartar Republic protested to the Central Committee that these documents were not genuine. Under interrogation the unfortunate Sultan-Galiyev told a different story. 'What did the investigation reveal?' Stalin asked the conference delegates, and went on to supply the answer. 'It revealed that all the documents were genuine. Their genuineness was admitted by Sultan-Galiyev himself, who in fact gave more information about his sins than is contained in the documents, who fully confessed his guilt, and, after confessing, repented.'[56]

However, Sultan-Galiyev's repentance did not save him from expulsion from the Party. 'This was the first arrest of a prominent Party member made upon Stalin's initiative,' Kamenev was afterwards to recall when his own Party political position was under fire. 'Unfortunately Zinoviev and I gave our consent to it. That was Stalin's first taste of blood.' It was also the first 'confession' of its kind and it was to set the pattern for countless others in the following decade. For the time being, Sultan-Galiyev suffered no further punishment, since Kamenev and Zinoviev would not agree to his being shot as Stalin wished. Some years later, after Kamenev and Zinoviev had themselves been expelled from the Party, Sultan-Galiyev was again arrested, this time to vanish permanently into the cellars of the Lubyanka prison.[57]

During the succeeding months, the conflict between Trotsky and the *troika* mounted in intensity. Trotsky's aim was a genuine workers' democracy headed by himself, a position which he knew that his popularity with the masses could ensure. Stalin, on the other hand, was willing to let Trotsky have any nominal office in the government hierarchy that Trotsky wished provided that the General Secretary could retain his hold over the political machine. In his personal dealings with the War Commissar, Stalin appeared more conciliatory than either of the other members of the *troika*, although his concessions were often relatively minor in character. For instance, at a meeting of the Politburo in June 1923, when a revised reply to the British Foreign Secretary Lord Curzon's 'ultimatum' note threatening to terminate the existing Anglo-Soviet trade agreement unless the Soviet Government acceded to certain demands by Great Britain was under discussion, the draft having been previously amended by Trotsky, the latter protested that his amendments had not been properly incorporated in the reply owing to the incompetence of the two Politburo secretaries who were the General Secretary's nominees. Stalin immediately agreed to their dismissal. They were replaced by Boris Bazhanov, who was to flee to the west some years later.

In his recollections of official life in the Kremlin at this time, Bazhanov gives a vivid picture of the behaviour of the principal characters at the first session of the Politburo which he attended. Trotsky was the first to arrive. ('The others were late, they were still plotting.') Zinoviev entered next. He passed Trotsky, and both behaved as if they had not seen each other. Kamenev, who followed, gave Trotsky a slight nod. Finally Stalin came in. He approached the table where Trotsky was sitting, greeted him in a most friendly manner and vigorously shook hands with him across the table.[58]

That summer, Stalin and Molotov stayed in Moscow perfecting the political machine, while Trotsky and the other Party leaders went on holiday to the Caucasus. At Kislovodsk, a watering-place where Trotsky was staying, an informal meeting was summoned to discuss future policy, apparently on Zinoviev's initiative; it met secretly in a nearby cave so as not to attract local attention. Stalin was invited to attend, but he declined in a rude telegram stating that he had no time for 'idlers'. At the meeting, Zinoviev proposed that the Politburo should be abolished and that in future policy making should be determined by a new triumvirate consisting of Trotsky, Zinoviev and Stalin. But Voroshilov and Ordzhonikidze, who were evidently holding a watching brief for the General Secretary, declared that they could come to no understanding without Stalin, and the meeting ended inconclusively. Stalin's old companion in exile Lashevich subsequently complained that all he got out of it, from having to sit on damp rock, was an attack of sciatica.[59]

At the next Politburo meeting after the 'troglodytes' had returned to Moscow, Zinoviev proposed that Stalin should become a kind of controller at the War Commissariat, which was still headed by Trotsky. The latter, who was visibly annoyed, said he would resign his office and asked to be allowed to go to Germany, which seemed to be on the verge of revolution, to aid the Communists there. This prompted Zinoviev to make a similar request for himself, since he was President of the Communist International. Stalin then intervened to put an end to the matter by declaring tongue in cheek that 'the Party could not possibly dispense with the services of two such important and beloved leaders'.[60]

Trotsky, with what he intended to be a dramatic gesture, thereupon rose and made for the door. The meeting took place in the old throne room of the Great Kremlin Palace, where the Tsars used to receive the nobility. The chamber had a massive door which Trotsky had some difficulty in opening, and still more in closing, as he tried unsuccessfully to bang it behind him in his fury. 'Thus, instead of witnessing a dramatic gesture, indicating a historic break,' so the secretary Bazhanov described the scene, 'we watched a sorry and helpless figure struggling with a door.'[61]

Most unfortunately for Trotsky, who needed all his strength in his struggle with the *troika*, he went down with a bad attack of malaria at this time, the result of a weekend duck shooting trip in the marshy country outside Moscow. This kept him indoors for many weeks. During his illness, the Politburo met in his Kremlin flat. His wife, who could hear the speeches from the adjoining bedroom, afterwards recalled how vehemently Trotsky spoke and how his arguments were met with 'cold and indifferent answers'. In particular he attacked the requirement introduced by Stalin and Dzerzhinsky for Party members to denounce to the Cheka, or the GPU, at it was now known, any of their colleagues or friends who were suspected of forming opposition groups against the official Party line. Trotsky also inveighed strongly against what he called 'the bureaucratisation of the Party machine'. This, he said, had developed into hitherto unheard of proportions through Stalin's innovation of appointing the secretaries of the provincial committees from Moscow.

> Consequently there has been created a very broad stratum of Party workers, entering into the administrative apparatus of the Party, who completely renounce their Party opinion, at least the open expression of it, as if assuming that the secretarial hierarchy is the apparatus which creates Party opinion and Party decisions. Beneath this stratum, abstaining from opinion, there lies the broad mass of the Party, before whom every decision stands in the form of a summons or a command.[62]

But Trotsky was powerless to stay this process of stratification in the Party *apparat*, now firmly under the General Secretary's iron control. So were forty-six of his supporters, who petitioned the Central Committee in the sense of Totsky's speech quoted above: they included such well known Party names as Pyatakov, Preobrazhensky and Antonov-Ovseenko. Indeed, Antonov-Ovseenko, the hero of the October rising in Petrograd and now chief political commissar of the Red Army, went so far as to declare that the armed forces would stand up 'like one man' for Trotsky, 'the leader, organiser, and inspirer of the Revolution's victories'. To this outburst, the *troika* reacted by removing Antonov-Ovseenko from his post. Other critics were similarly disciplined.

The subject of Trotsky's behaviour was brought up at the next Party conference which opened in Moscow in the middle of January 1924, when the *troika* denounced him and his forty-six adherents as guilty of 'petty bourgeois deviation from Leninism'. So skilfully did Stalin manipulate the delegates that only three votes were cast against the motion condemning Trotsky. But the War Commissar did not wait to hear the result of the vote. He left Moscow for the south on medical advice, having been granted extended sick leave by the Politburo.[63]

Shortly after seven o'clock in the evening of 21 January 1924, the telephone rang in Stalin's office. It was Henry Yagoda calling from Gorki to say that Lenin had just died. The General Secretary immediately ordered a strict censorship of all outgoing news, so that this item did not reach the general public for nearly twenty-four hours. Trotsky heard it when his train stopped at Tiflis station and a telegram from Stalin was handed to him. Ill as he was, he went to the direct wire to the Kremlin and told Stalin that he considered it necessary to return to Moscow for the funeral. Stalin replied that the funeral had been fixed for the next day but one, which was Saturday the 26th. 'You will not be able to get here in time,' he added. 'The Politburo thinks that because of the state of your health you must proceed to Sukhum.' In fact, the funeral did not take place until the following Sunday and there would have been plenty of time for Trotsky to make his appearance among the pall bearers.[64]

Stalin, who had planned to play the leading role himself at the dead leader's obsequies, did not relish the prospect of Trotsky's participation and the popular acclaim he felt Trotsky would be bound to attract. So Trotsky continued his journey to Sukhum, the Black Sea health resort where the Kremlin doctors had arranged for him to convalesce.

6

Some weeks after his third stroke, when the weather had improved and he was able to travel, Lenin had been moved on a stretcher from the Kremlin to Gorki. During the summer and autumn he was allowed to receive visitors. According to Lenin's cook Gavril Volkov, Stalin came out to Gorki 'a few times', although unlike the previous year his official biographical chronicle makes no mention of any such visits. At the end of 1923, Krupskaya had to go to Moscow for a couple of days, and during her absence Lenin's condition, which had earlier shown considerable improvement, grew noticeably worse. But he rallied again and as late as two days before his death he followed a hunting expedition by sledge in the nearby forest. But he suffered a relapse which required an injection from his doctor on the morning of 21 January. At the same time, Volkov brought him a meal, and according to the cook Lenin slipped him a note. This allegedly read: 'Gavrilushka, I've been poisoned...go fetch Nadya [Krupskaya] at once...tell Trotsky... tell everyone you can.' Volkov later stated that he took no action on the note and did not show it to anyone.[65]

It is difficult to credit this account on the face of it. The autopsy carried out the following day indicated that Lenin was suffering from advanced multiple arterio-sclerosis so that it would have been difficult, if not physically impossible, for him to have scribbled down even a few words. Naturally nothing was said in the Kremlin physicians' report of any traces of poison being found in Lenin's remains. However, the story that Lenin's end was hastened by poison – at Stalin's direct instigation – has long persisted, encouraged by Trotsky's writings in exile.

> The medical prognosis at the time [of Lenin's third stroke] was cautiously unfavourable. Feeling more sure of himself, Stalin began to act as if Lenin were already dead. But the sick man fooled him. His powerful organism, supported by his inflexible will, reasserted itself. Toward winter Lenin began to improve slowly, to move around more freely; listened to reading and read himself; his faculty of speech began to come back to him. The findings of the physicians became increasingly more hopeful...
>
> For Stalin himself it was not a question of the general course of development, but rather of his own fate: either he could manage at once, this very day, to become the boss of the political machine and hence of the Party and of the country, or he would be relegated to a third-rate role for the rest of his life. Stalin was after power, all of it, come what may. He already had a firm grip on it. His goal was near, but the danger emanating from Lenin was even nearer. At this time Stalin must have made up his mind that it was imperative to act without delay. Everywhere he had accomplices whose fate was completely bound to his. At his side was the pharmacist Yagoda. Whether Stalin sent the poison to Lenin with the hint that the physicians had left no hope for his recovery I do not know. But I am firmly convinced that Stalin could not have waited passively when his fate hung by a thread and the decision depended on a small, very small motion of his hand.[66]

Trotsky's surmise has received some corroboration from Russian emigré sources, which must however be received with caution. According to Yves Delbars (real name Nikolai Kossiakov), who states that he got the story from a former member of Stalin's secretariat who later left the country (probably Bazhanov), Stalin sent Yagoda with one of the Kremlin doctors to Gorki on the evening of 20 January. 'There will soon be another attack,' Stalin is said to have told

Yagoda. 'He has written a few lines to thank you for sending him a means of deliverance. He is terribly distressed by the thought of a fresh attack...' Several small bottles, empty, are also said to have been seen on Lenin's bedside table when Yagoda telephoned the Kremlin with the news of Lenin's death.[67]

On the other hand, as Delbars speculates, the fact of furnishing Lenin with 'the means of eventual euthanasia' might well appear in his case as 'a gesture of humanity'. At all events, the case against Stalin that he gave Lenin poison largely rests on conjecture: while it cannot be dismissed as a fabrication, it remains not proven, particularly when it is remembered that Trotsky never accused Stalin of acting in this way until long after he had been expelled from Russia.

Stalin personally took charge of all the arrangements for Lenin's burial, including the autopsy, embalming, transportation of the remains to Moscow, lying in state in the great hall of the House of the Trade Unions – at which he himself stood conspicuously beside the bier – and finally the interment in a makeshift mausoleum in the Red Square to the cacophonous accompaniment of bells, factory sirens, drums and other orchestral instruments. The whole proceedings were entirely out of keeping with Lenin's simple unaffected personal style, for he was known to dislike pomp and ceremonial of all kinds. Krupskaya too was opposed to such elaborate obsequies, as she also was later on to the grandiose red marble mausoleum which Stalin caused to be constructed in the place of the original temporary edifice enclosing the dead leader's mummified corpse. But Stalin justified his conduct in a speech which he delivered at a memorial meeting on the eve of the funeral. 'You have seen during the past few days the pilgrimage of scores and hundreds of thousands of working people to Comrade Lenin's bier,' he said. 'Before long you will see the pilgrimage of representatives of millions of working people to Comrade Lenin's tomb. You need not doubt that the representatives of millions will be followed by the representatives of scores and hundreds of millions from all parts of the earth, who will come to testify that Lenin was the leader not only of the Russian proletariat, not only of the European workers, not only of the colonial east, but of all the working people of the globe.'[68]

The mausoleum was a necessary part of the cult of Leninism to be assiduously propagated by the Soviet Communist Party's General Secretary, and designed to keep the dead leader's memory fresh in the minds of the masses, as also was the former capital of Petrograd which was now renamed Leningrad in his honour. As Isaac Deutscher has aptly put it, 'to myriads of peasants, whose religious instincts were repressed under the revolution, the Mausoleum soon became a place of pilgrimage, the queer Mecca of an atheistic creed, which needed a prophet and saints, a holy sepulchre and icons'.[69]

At the same time, there are grounds for believing that the process of Lenin's near deification was accompanied by so much physical decomposition, due to the failure of the initial embalming process and successive attempts at 'repair work', that a waxwork figure was eventually substituted, having been fitted with lifelike skin and Lenin's own red beard and hair. If this is so, the effigy has served its purpose equally well with the millions of Communist faithful.*

At the memorial meeting on 26 January 1924, Stalin swore faithfully to maintain Lenin's guiding principles, particularly 'to guard the unity of our Party as the apple of our eye' and 'to guard and strengthen the dictatorship of the proletariat'.[70] Having made this public vow, Stalin then turned to consider in private along with the rest of the Politburo what was to be done about Lenin's embarrassing testament, of which one of the sealed copies had been received from Krupskaya. After some discussion, it was agreed by all the members except Trotsky, who was still absent on sick leave, that no action should be taken, and the document was filed away in the secretariat registry.

A little later, Pyatakov, who had been praised in the testament, heard that it had been shelved and told Krupskaya. She immediately stormed into Stalin's office.

'I gave you an envelope sealed by Ilyich with instructions to open it after his death,' she told the General Secretary. 'What have you done with the envelope?'

'The Politburo has no information to give you, Nadezhda Konstantinova,' replied Stalin coldly.

'It's a matter of Vladimir Ilyich's last testament of his last wishes,' went on Krupskaya in mounting anger. 'The Party must be told of them. I warn you that if you don't read the testament when the Central Committee meets, I shall publish it myself. I am the testamentary legatee, and I have to fulfil his wishes.'

Krupskaya got her way, and the compromising document was duly read out at a plenary session of the Central Committee held in secret, when the Committee was asked to decide whether it should be made public at the next Party Congress, the Thirteenth, which was due to be held in the last week of May. According to Bazhanov, the reading is said to have caused considerable embarrassment. 'Stalin sitting on the steps of the rostrum, looked small and miserable...In spite of his self-

* The evidence on this point has been collected by Stefan T. Possony in his *Lenin: The Compulsive Revolutionary* (1964), pp. 372–375.

control and show of calm, it was clearly evident that his fate was at stake.'

Stalin was saved by Zinoviev who made an eloquent plea in his defence.

Comrades, every word of Ilyich is law to us...We have sworn to fulfil anything the dying Ilyich ordered us to do. You know perfectly well we shall keep our vow. But we are happy to say that in one point Lenin's fears have proved baseless. I have in mind the point about our General Secretary. You have all witnessed our harmonious co-operation in the last few months; and, like myself, you will be happy to say that Lenin's fears have proved baseless.

Zinoviev was followed by Kamenev, after Stalin had nonchalantly offered to resign as General Secretary in conformity with Lenin's wishes. Kamenev now appealed for him to be allowed to continue in office and this was agreed to. In spite of Krupskaya's protest against the suppression of her husband's testament, Zinoviev moved that it should not be published, but only confidentially communicated to the delegates at the forthcoming Party Congress. Trotsky did not raise his voice; if Delbars is to be believed, his silence was ensured by a threat from Stalin that, if he brought up the question of the testament, Stalin would publish a letter written by Trotsky in his Menshevik days in which he described Lenin as 'that professional exploiter of the ignorance of the members of his party' and 'the whole edifice of Leninism' as 'based on lying and falsification'. In the result, Zinoviev's motion was carried by forty votes to ten. Stalin could again breathe easily. He was back in the saddle, firmly and for good.[71]

At the Thirteenth Congress, everything went according to the General Secretary's plan. The delegates had been carefully handpicked, and there were no troublemakers, since all the senior party leaders who might have made trouble had been appointed to various posts, many in Soviet diplomatic and commercial embassies abroad.

Rykov, who had been deputising for Lenin as chairman of the Council of People's Commissars, now formally succeeded him in this office as nominal Prime Minister. But the real power lay with Stalin. All the existing members of the Politburo were re-elected, with the addition of Bukharin who took Lenin's place. New candidate members included Mikhail Frunze, an opponent of Trotsky's, whom Stalin had recently promoted to be Vice-Commissar of War. The size of the Central Committee was raised from forty to fifty-three members, and the candidates from seventeen to thirty-four, the newcomers being mainly provincial party members who had proved their loyalty to Stalin. The most spectacular rise was that of thirty-one-year-old Lazar Kaganovich, a Jew who began his career as a leather worker. He was elected a full member of the Central Committee with a place in both the Secretariat and the Orgburo, thus becoming with Molotov and Kuibyshev one of Stalin's chief assistants in the running of the powerful party political machine. Kaganovich was an exceptionally able administrator, but of all Stalin's lieutenants he was probably the most ruthless. Completely without pity, he took the extreme view that the interests of the Party justified any excess, and he was to be involved in some of the worst aspects of the subsequent terror. At the same time, he was a coward and a bully, evidenced by the fact that after his implication in the 'anti-Party plot' in 1957, he telephoned the victorious Khrushchev, begging not to be shot. Luckily for him in the easier circumstances of those later times, instead of facing the executioner he was sent to manage an asbestos plant in the Urals.[72]

The conflict between Trotsky and the *troika* now continued with increasing bitterness. In the autumn it was transferred to the literary field when Trotsky published a short book, *The Lessons of October*, on the theme of how to put over a revolution successfully in the light of an effective leadership. In this work he attacked Zinoviev and Kamenev for their opposition to the 1917 rising, quoting Lenin's description of them as the strike breakers of the Revolution. The two triumvirs reacted by trying to play down Trotsky's role in Petrograd, and in this they were helped by Stalin who replied to Trotsky in an essay of his own called *On the Road to October* and also in the columns of *Pravda*. 'I must say that Trotsky did not play any special role in the October rising,' Stalin declared, 'nor could he do so – being chairman of the Petrograd Soviet, he merely carried out the will of the appropriate Party bodies, which directed every step that Trotsky took.' Admittedly Trotsky 'fought well in the period of October', but merely as the agent of the Central Committee. Actually 'the organisational leadership of the uprising', Stalin went on, belonged to the 'practical centre' which was elected at the secret meeting of the Central Committee on 16 October 1917, to represent the Bolshevik Party on the Soviet's Military Revolutionary Committee. 'Strange to relate,' concluded Stalin, 'the "inspirer", the "chief figure", the "sole leader" of the uprising, Trotsky was not elected to the practical centre, which was called up on to direct the uprising' and which consisted of Stalin and four other party comrades.[73] The reason, of course, was that it was unnecessary to appoint Trotsky as a party representative on a body over which he already presided. In fact, as has already been noted the 'practical centre' never existed as a separate body and it played no part whatever in the leadership of the October Revolution. This was Stalin's first contribution to the rewriting of Soviet history, and his version of events sounded eminently plausible in the face of Trotsky's criticism of the party leaders (except Lenin) for their alleged inertia during the October days. But it must have come as a shock to those 'Old Bolsheviks' who remembered the actual course of the rising.

These polemic exchanges were temporarily interrupted by an extraordinary episode in England which suddenly propelled one of the Politburo members into the international limelight. Two days before the voters went to the polls in the General Election of October 1924, the British Foreign Office published the text of a letter, dated 15 September 1924 from Moscow and allegedly addressed by Zinoviev as Chairman of the Third International to the Central Committee of the British Communist Party, stating that it was essential to bring into the movement 'the army of the unemployed', to create Communist cells among the soldiers, sailors and munition workers of Britain, and to organise risings in Ireland and the colonies. The Soviet Embassy in London promptly denied the authenticity of the letter, which it stigmatised as a 'clumsy forgery', a description echoed by Zinoviev himself, who also pointed out that on 15 September he was not in Moscow but on holiday in Kislovodsk. But few of the British voters believed these disclaimers. Ramsay MacDonald's government, which had recently concluded a treaty with the Soviet Union, was turned out of office as the result of the 'Red Scare', and the electors voted the Conservatives back to power with an overwhelming majority. The new government took no action to have the treaty ratified by Parliament, while the Foreign Secretary, Austen Chamberlain, sent a stuffy note to the Soviet *chargé d'affaires* informing him that the information at the Government's disposal 'leaves no doubt whatever in their mind of the authenticity of M. Zinoviev's letter'. Needless to add, Stalin and the rest of the Politburo shared Zinoviev's astonishment that such a reputable institution as the British Foreign Office should have been taken in by a document which on the face of it was such a palpable fraud.*

On 17 January 1925, Stalin addressed a joint plenary meeting of the Central Committee and the Control Commission convened for the

* The official Foreign Office view still is that the Zinoviev letter was genuine, although it has been convincingly demonstrated that the document, for which the Conservative Party paid five thousand pounds, was fabricated by Russian emigrés in Berlin under the patronage of the Polish intelligence service. See Lewis Chester, Stephen Fay and Hugo Young, *The Zinoviev Letter* (1967).

purpose of passing judgement on Trotsky for 'attempting to bring about a radical change in the Party leadership'; in other words, to substitute Trotskyism in place of Leninism. It was an opportunity for its General Secretary to define the new role of the Party.[74]

Obviously Trotsky does not understand, and I doubt whether he will ever understand, that the Party demands from its former and present leaders not diplomatic evasions, but an honest admission of mistakes. Trotsky evidently lacks the courage frankly to admit his mistakes. He does not understand that the Party's sense of power and dignity has grown, that the Party feels that it is the master and demands that we should bow our heads when circumstances demand. That is what Trotsky does not understand.

Some members like Kamenev urged that Trotsky should be dismissed from the Politburo, others were in favour of his expulsion from the Party, while Zinoviev went so far as to demand his arrest as well. But Stalin played it cool. Trotsky still enjoyed considerable popularity with the rank and file as the founder of the Red Army which saved the country from the Whites and foreign capitalist interventionists, and the time was not yet ripe to remove him altogether from the domestic political scene. Faced with the prospect of being forced out of the War Commissariat, however, Trotsky agreed to resign and take up a new post in charge of an electricity undertaking. 'We obtained a majority on the Central Committee and restricted ourselves to removing Trotsky from the post of People's Commissar of Military and Naval Affairs,' Stalin recalled at the next Party Congress. 'We disagreed with Zinoviev and Kamenev because we knew that the policy of amputation, the method of blood-letting – and they demanded blood – was dangerous, infectious: today you amputate one limb, tomorrow another, the day after tomorrow a third – what will we have left in the Party?'[75]

None of the audience at the Fourteenth Congress could have foreseen the unprecedented amount of blood-letting which the General Secretary was himself to instigate in the next decade. Otherwise they might not have applauded him with such enthusiasm as they did on this occasion.

7
Stalin's next step towards achieving the complete political isolation of Trotsky was to break up the *troika* or rather to convert it into a quartet. First, he invited all the members of the Politburo except Trotsky to a private meeting in his Kremlin apartment. 'We thought it as well to

keep Trotsky in the Politburo in order to avoid an open conflict in the country and in the Party,' he explained. 'But we must be united so that Trotsky cannot profit by our occasional differences. For this reason I propose that we always meet here in private before each official meeting of the Politburo, in order to agree beforehand on our decisions.' Everyone present signified his assent and Stalin recorded the fact in a secret minute which each member signed.

'It was a real conspiracy,' so Trotsky described it. 'All questions were decided in advance at that secret centre, where the members were bound by mutual vows.'[76]

At the same time Stalin began to cultivate the right-wing members Rykov and Tomsky; also Bukharin, who had previously supported Trotsky but now joined Rykov and Tomsky in advocating Stalin's assertion of the self-sufficiency of the Russian revolution or 'socialism in one country' as against Trotsky's aim of 'permanent revolution', a thesis with which Zinoviev and Kamenev agreed in spite of their personal dislike of Trotsky for his attacks upon them. Thus Stalin was usually able, with the support of his three right-wing colleagues, to outvote Zinoviev and Kamenev and so present a united front at the formal Politburo meetings in which Trotsky participated. Stalin also profited from the fact that Zinoviev and Kamenev hesitated for a considerable time before swallowing their pride and joining forces with Trotsky. When they eventually did so and broke with Stalin, in the spring of 1926, it was already too late, since the political doom of all three of Stalin's opponents was now a foregone conclusion. 'Stalin will deceive and Zinoviev will sneak away,' Trotsky was warned by a friend.[77] By this time, the Politburo had been reinforced with three Stalinists, Voroshilov, Kalinin and Molotov. In addition, Voroshilov had succeeded Frunze as War Commissar on the latter's sudden death, after holding the office for only seven months.

Mikhail Vasilyevich Frunze was barely forty when he died. The son of a Moldavian settler in Turkestan, he had had an unblemished revolutionary record and had been an outstanding and popular military commander in the Red Army, having defeated both Kolchak and Wrangel in the Civil War. He was a man of spirit and independent character. 'I propose to run my Commissariat as I think best,' he told the Politburo on his appointment. 'I am responsible to the Party and I shall give reasons for my actions. But I won't put up with being pushed around by unnecessary instructions.'

On one occasion, having come to the Secretariat to see Stalin, he was kept waiting for nearly a quarter of an hour by Tovstukha, one of Stalin's private secretaries. 'I have no time to waste,' said the new War

Commissar. 'I must see Comrade Stalin immediately.'

'You know, Comrade Frunze,' Tovstukha replied, 'it is we who give the orders here.'

'What?' exclaimed Frunze, suddenly furious and, clapping his hand to the revolver at his belt. '*This* is what gives orders!' He thereupon opened the door of Stalin's office and went in.[78]

The manner of Frunze's death gave rise to some speculation and rumours involving the General Secretary. Frunze suffered from stomach ulcers but shrank from an operation, because his personal physicians feared that his heart might be unable to withstand the effects of chloroform.

But the Kremlin doctors whose advice Stalin sought took the contrary view, and the Politburo settled the matter by ordering Frunze to submit to the surgical knife. The result was that the operation was successful but the patient died – not on the operating table, as has been frequently but incorrectly stated, but afterwards in the Moscow Military Hospital. According to Trotsky and others, Frunze had displayed too much independence in protecting the Army from the supervision of the GPU, he had dismissed considerable numbers of provincial military commanders replacing them with his own nominees, and he had also sided with Zinoviev and Kamenev against the General Secretary, all of which led the latter to remark that 'Comrade Frunze will have to be called to order'. Hence the rumours that spread through the Party that Frunze's death took place 'because it was necessary to Stalin'. However, as even Trotsky admits, it is difficult to establish the facts.[79] Certainly the affectionate note which Stalin left at the hospital when he and his Armenian friend, Anastas Mikoyan,* called but were not allowed by Doctor Rozanov to see Frunze, is hardly what one would expect in the circumstances of Trotsky's hints that Stalin had deliberately engineered Frunze's end.

29 October 1925

Dear friend,

Today at 5 p.m. I went to see Comrade Rozanov (Mikoyan and I). We wanted to drop in on you, but the pest would not let us. We had to submit to authority.

Cheer up, *golubchik*.† We'll come again, we'll come again.

KOBA.[80]‡

---

* Mikoyan, then barely thirty, headed the party organisation in the North Caucasus.
† Literally 'little dove'.
‡ This letter was omitted from the official Soviet edition of Stalin's *Collected Works*, which Stalin himself revised. 'There are plausible reasons enough why

What is likewise certain and most significant, as Deutscher observes, is that the Politburo could arrogate to itself the right to take decisions on so personal a matter as a surgical operation. 'The individual Bolshevik, whether he was the commander-in-chief or the secretary of a provincial committee, belonged in his entirety to the party. He had no existence and no will beyond it. Even the most intimate side of his private life was open to inspection by his superiors. It goes without saying that where a Frunze submitted, the average member could hardly dare to assert himself. As a body, the party lay supine under the knife of its implacable surgeon, the General Secretary.' Well might Stalin, in his speech at Frunze's funeral, eulogise the departed commissar as 'one of the Party's most faithful and disciplined leaders'.[81]

Stalin was not in the least worried when he heard that Zinoviev and Kamenev had made common cause with Trotsky. 'Ah,' he remarked sarcastically, 'they have granted themselves a mutual amnesty!' When they met for their first private discussion for years, as might be expected, the main topic was the General Secretary, whose slyness, perversity and cruelty were particularly emphasised. 'As soon as we broke with him,' Kamenev told Trotsky, 'we composed something in the nature of a testament, in which we gave a warning that in the event of our "accidental" death Stalin was to be held responsible for it. This document is kept in a safe place. I advise you to do the same. You can expect anything from that Asiatic.'

Zinoviev added that Stalin could have put an end to Trotsky in 1924, but he had been afraid that some zealous young Trotskyite might have put an end to Stalin by way of retaliation.

That is why Stalin decided to begin by demolishing the Opposition groups and has postponed killing you until he is certain that he can do it with impunity. His hatred of us, especially Kamenev, is motivated chiefly by the fact that we know too much about him. However, he isn't ready yet to kill us either.[82]

Trotsky does not appear to have taken these revelations very seriously at the time; it was not until he was in exile ten years later and the Great Purge was in full swing that he recalled the conversation and realised that there was considerable truth in it. But in 1926, he was enjoying a breathing space in the struggle with Stalin and he was willing to work quietly in the minor electricity job which had been as-

---

Stalin chose to forget this letter, but one wishes that one could know what considerations were crucial in supressing it.' Robert H. McNeal. 'Caveat Lector. A Preface to Stalin's *Sochineniia*', *Survey* (London), October 1963, p. 145.

signed to him. In his anxiety to reach some sort of accommodation with the General Secretary, he further weakened his position with an almost incredible pronouncement on the subject of Lenin's last testament in which he went so far as to describe the story of its suppression as an invention, thereby gravely offending his friends and supporters abroad. One of these was Max Eastman, contemptuously dismissed by Stalin as 'a former American Communist who was later expelled from the Party'. In his book *Since Lenin Died*, which appeared in 1925, Eastman gave an account of the struggle over the succession to Lenin and summarised the contents of the 'suppressed' document, which he had learned from Trotsky with whom he had become friendly while working as a newspaper correspondent in Moscow.

The Politburo demanded that Trotsky should deny Eastman's account, and this Trotsky meekly consented to do in the interests of Party harmony. Accordingly, on 1 September 1925, there appeared in the Party journal *Bolshevik* a statement over Trotsky's signature which had been dictated by the Politburo and contained the following:

> Vladimir Ilyich did not leave any 'testament', and the very character of his attitude towards the Party, as well as the character of the Party itself, precluded the possibility of such a 'testament'. What is usually referred to as a 'testament' in the emigré and foreign bourgeois and Menshevik press (in a manner garbled beyond recognition) is one of Vladimir Ilyich's letters containing advice on organisational matters. The Thirteenth Congress of the Party paid the closest attention to that letter, as well as to all of the conditions and circumstances of the time. *All talk about concealing or violating a 'testament' is a malicious invention and is entirely directed against Vladimir Ilyich's real wishes*, and against the interests of the Party he created. [Stalin's italics]

About a year after this denial had been widely reproduced in the foreign press, Eastman reacted to Trotsky's disavowal of his book by publishing an English translation of the whole of the controversial document in the *New York Times* (19 October 1926).

By that date, the anti-Stalin opposition was reeling under the General Secretary's well directed blows. For one thing, it had been unwise enough to carry the struggle into the armed forces, where General Lashevich, who had succeeded Voroshilov as Vice-Commissar of War, showed some sympathy with the rebels. In July 1926, Lashevich's misdoings had been exposed by Stalin before the Central Committee, with the result that the Vice-Commissar was dismissed from his post and also expelled from the Central Committee. At the same time, Zinoviev who had been his protector lost his seat in the Politburo. In October, Trotsky and Kamenev were likewise deposed from the supreme policy-making body, notwithstanding that only a week or two previously they had signed a statement along with Zinoviev, Piatakov, Sokolnikor and others, in which they admitted that 'they were guilty of offences against the statutes of the party and pledged themselves to disband their party within the party'. Zinoviev was also relieved of the presidency of the Communist International, while in the Leningrad Soviet his opposition tactics were in effect hamstrung by the energetic Sergei Kirov, now a candidate member of the Politburo, whom Stalin had dispatched to make the Leningraders toe the Party line.

The first half of 1927 witnessed a lull in the struggle, as Trotsky applied himself to his minor administrative tasks and Stalin and the Politburo were wrestling with various difficulties on the domestic front. The peasants were resisting the policy of farm collectivisation which was reported to be proceeding 'at a tortoise's pace'. Andrei Andreyev, who came of peasant stock and had recently joined the Politburo as a candidate member, was detailed to get things moving in the agricultural sphere. Then there was a sudden war scare as the result of a police raid on the premises of the Soviet trade delegation in London known as ARCOS, thought by Scotland Yard with some justification to be the base of Soviet espionage operations in Britain. This was followed by the rupture of diplomatic relations between the two countries. A few weeks later, the Soviet envoy in Warsaw was murdered by a Russian emigré. About the same time, General Chiang Kai-shek, who had been supported by Stalin and the Chinese Communists, broke away from this alliance, much to Stalin's embarrassment. These various set-backs eventually induced a considerable body of opposition, eighty-three in all, to set their names to a public statement criticising Stalin and Bukharin for inefficiency and lack of foresight. This was followed up by Trotsky who declared that 'in an emergency he would strive to effect a change of government'[83]

Stalin defended himself before the Central Committee at a joint meeting with the Central Control Commission on 23 October 1927.

You have heard here how assiduously the oppositionists hurl abuse at Stalin, abuse him with all their might. That does not surprise me, comrades. The reason why the main attacks have been directed against Stalin is because Stalin knows all the opposition's tricks better perhaps than some of our comrades do, and it is not so easy, I dare say, to fool him. So they strike their blows primarily at Stalin. Well, let them hurl abuse to their hearts' content.

With characteristic mock modesty, the General Secretary went on to describe himself as 'only a minor figure' compared with the great Lenin against whom his Menshevik opponents headed by Trotsky after the split had 'waged an even more scurrilous campaign of slander'. After quoting Trostky's description of Lenin in 1913 as 'that professional exploiter of all that is backward in the Russian labour movement', he went on to speak about Lenin's 'testament', reminding his listeners of Trotsky's abject denial that it had been 'concealed' or 'suppressed'. He even quoted from the postscript about himself.

> It is said that in that 'testament' Comrade Lenin suggested to the Congress that in view of Stalin's 'rudeness' it should consider the question of putting another comrade in Stalin's place as General Secretary. That is quite true. Yes, comrades, I am rude to those who grossly and perfidiously wreck and split the Party. I have never concealed this and do not conceal it now. Perhaps some mildness is needed in the treatment of splitters, but I am a bad hand at that. At the very first meeting of the plenum of the Central Committee after the Thirteenth Congress I asked the plenum of the Central Committee to release me from my duties as General Secretary. The Congress itself discussed this question. It was discussed by each delegation separately, and all the delegations including Comrade Trotsky, Comrade Kamenev and Comrade Zinoviev, unanimously *obliged* Stalin to remain at his post.
>
> What could I do? Leave my post? That is not in my nature. I have never left my post, and I have no right to do so, for that would be desertion. As I have said before, I am not a free agent, and when the Party imposes an obligation upon me, I must obey...
>
> It is characteristic that [unlike Trotsky, Kamenev, and Zinoviev] there is not a word, not a hint in the 'testament' about Stalin having made mistakes. It refers only to Stalin's rudeness. But rudeness is not and cannot be counted as a defect in Stalin's *political* line or position.[84]

In the name of the General Secretariat Stalin refused to allow the publication of the memoranda which Trotsky and Zinoviev had prepared for the next Party Congress, the Fifteenth, due to convene in December, and the two opposition leaders responded by printing them unofficially. For this they were expelled from the Central Committee. This was followed by their expulsion from the Party itself after they had led their followers in street demonstrations in Moscow and Leningrad during the tenth anniversary celebrations of the Revolution.

A few days later, Adolf Yoffe, an old Bolshevik who had joined the Opposition, committed suicide by shooting himself in the Kremlin. He left a letter to Trotsky in which he besought him 'to fight the usurper Stalin with all the means habitually employed by revolutionaries to strike down the enemies of the people'. Yoffe's funeral was attended by a large gathering of the Opposition. 'The struggle goes on,' said Trotsky in a graveside speech. But it was to be Trotsky's last public appearance and also the Opposition's last public demonstration.[85]

Kamenev's turn came next after he had been shouted down at the Fifteenth Congress. 'Enough, comrades, an end must be put to this game,' said Stalin when the uproar had subsided. 'Kamenev's speech was the most lying, hypocritical, fraudulent and scoundrelly of all the opposition speeches delivered here from this rostrum.'[86] Kamenev and several others including Ivan Smilga were thereupon expelled from the Central Committee. Incidentally, the Committee's membership was increased with alternates to 121, an arrangement calculated to benefit the General Secretary.

Shortly afterwards, V. R. Menzhinsky, who had become head of the dreaded GPU on Dzerzhinsky's death in 1926, was instructed by Stalin to interrogate all those who had been expelled from the Central Committee. Although like Dzerzhinsky he belonged by origin to the Polish nobility, Menzhinsky was unlike his predecessor in almost every other respect, He was an admirer of the works of Oscar Wilde as well as an accomplished pianist; condemned prisoners, who had to cross the inner courtyard of the Lubyanka on the way to the execution cellar, often heard excerpts from Chopin or Greig being played by the GPU chief who had installed a grand piano behind a screen in his office. But he did not particularly relish his secret police work, much of which he left to his principal assistant Henry Yagoda. Nor had he any strong feelings against the Opposition, with whose leaders he was friendly; indeed during the Civil War he had warned Trotsky that Stalin and Voroshilov were intriguing against him. However, he had to carry out the orders of the General Secretariat, and so he summoned Trotsky, Kamenev, Zinoviev and Radek to his office in the Lubyanka, and informed them that he would be obliged to arrest them if they resumed any form of clandestine anti-Party activity.

'Many of our comrades have been arrested already,' said Trotsky. 'They are militants of no great importance, but they have been compelled to sign lying declarations about their activities.'

'Who forced them to sign these declarations?' queried Menzhinsky.
'Yagoda.'

Menzhinsky told Trotsky he would look into the matter and asked
his visitors to return on the following day.

'Well, Comrade Menzhinsky,' said Trotsky next day, 'have you
checked up on what I told you yesterday about those declarations?'

'Yes, it may be quite true...'

'What? May be? Show me the declarations and I'll undertake to
prove they are false.'

'That's impossible, Lev Davidovich.'

Here Kamenev broke in. 'Do you understand, Comrade Menzhinsky,
what these tactics are leading up to? You'll end by shooting the lot of
us in your cellar.'

Instead of replying, Menzhinsky got up and went behind the screen.
There he sat down at his piano and began to play the opening bars of
Solveig's Song from Greig's *Peer Gynt*.

'Stop playing! Stop!' Kamenev shouted. 'I insist you tell me as an
old Bolshevik if you believe that Stalin after shooting us could by himself ensure the final victory of our Party in its struggle for world
power.'

Menzhinsky ceased playing and returned to his desk. 'Why did you
ever allow him to obtain the immense power which he is wielding
already?' he asked, looking Kamenev straight in the eye. 'Now it's too
late. All the secretaries of the local Party Committees are on his side. If
you continue to struggle against him, you will break up the whole
Party just to get the better of this one man. Do you understand? Do
you want to dig the grave of our Party dictatorship and allow the
kulaks and the Nepmen to take over? I too am an old Bolshevik, I
belong to Lenin's brigade, and I shall do everything I can to prevent
the break up of the Party. But I shall obey the orders of the Politburo
and of Comrade Stalin, the General Secretary elected by the Central
Committee. I advise you to do the same.'[87]

Trotsky, however, refused to recant and was consequently banished
with his family to Alma-Ata in Kazhakstan. But Zinoviev, Kamenev,
Pyatakov, Krestinsky, Anton-Ovseenko, and more than 3,300 adherents
of the Opposition, issued statements of repentance, renouncing their
heretical views and promising to mend their ways. However, the
Congress left the question of their readmission to the Party and the
Central Committee to the discretion of the General Secretariat. With
Trotsky at a safe distance, Stalin had all the other trouble-makers
completely in his unrelenting grip.

The Fifteenth Congress was immediately followed by a country wide purge and reign of terror. According to Stalin's henchman Yaroslavsky, who was in a position to know, out of 5,755 Party members accused of 'deviations', 3,258 were expelled. Many of these were also deported or imprisoned. 'If Lenin were alive now,' said Krupskaya, 'he would probably be in one of Stalin's jails.'[88]

8

Although they feared him, Stalin's adversaries still tended to underrate the figure whom Trotsky had recently called 'the outstanding mediocrity in the Party'. Now that the Left opposition had been routed, many thought that power would pass into the hands of the Right wing personified by Bukharin, Rykov and Tomsky, when it became clear that their partnership with Stalin was being broken up, very much as that of the *troika* had been dissolved after Trotsky's forced resignation from the War Commissariat in 1925. In the new Politburo elected after the Fifteenth Congress, Kuibyshev became a full member, besides Yan Rudzutak, a Latvian supporter of Stalin, who had replaced Zinoviev after his expulsion. Bukharin and the other two right wingers knew that Stalin was certain of four votes – those of Molotov, Kuibyshev and Rudzutak besides his own – but they had reason to believe that they might count on Voroshilov and Kalinin, which would give them a majority. However, when it came to the crunch, both Voroshilov and Kalinin sided with Stalin. ('Stalin has some special hold over them that I do not know the reason of', Bukharin later told Kamenev.) The alternate or deputy members, who included Kaganovich, Kirov, Mikoyan, Andreyev and several others, were with one exception – N. A. Uglanov, Kamenev's successor as head of the Moscow Soviet – ranked among Stalin's followers. For the time being, Stalin did not come out in the open against the right-wing leaders, but contented himself through the General Secretariat with removing as many of Bukharin's followers from administrative positions as he could.

In spite of Andreyev's efforts, the peasants persistently held back their grain on account of the low prices offered by the Government, and by the beginning of 1928 there was a deficiency of two million tons in the amount needed to feed the population in the cities and towns. In other words, urban Russia faced a famine. The Politburo ordered 'emergency measures' designed to deal drastically with the well-to-do peasants (*kulaks*) and other suspected profiteers. During the next two years the collectivisation of peasant holdings, by conversion into State farms (*sovkhoz*) and collective farms (*kolkhoz*), was pushed through with appalling cruelty; even Stalin was obliged to denounce the 'administrative arbitrariness, violations of revolutionary law, raids on peasant houses, illegal searches' which took place on an extensive scale, the result in the main of his exhorting the Party to 'strike hard at the *kulaks*'. It was in vain for Bukharin, Rykov and Tomsky to attempt to stay the course of this fresh purge.

Bukharin now sought support from Kamenev, just as Kamenev and Zinoviev had previously turned to Trotsky. A secret meeting between the two men, who had formerly been such bitter political opponents, was arranged by Sokolnikov, who had joined the Left Opposition after losing his job as Commissar of Finance. Afterwards Kamenev made notes of what Bukharin told him and dispatched them to Zinoviev, then doing penance at Voronezh. It is an interesting record, coming from a man who had recently been so close politically to Stalin, and after Trotsky's evidence perhaps the most significant contribution to Stalin's biography at this period.

'We consider Stalin's line fatal to the Revolution,' Bukharin began. 'This line is leading us to the abyss. Our disagreements with Stalin are far more serious than those we have with you.' After expressing regret that Kamenev and Zinoviev were no longer in the Politburo, Bukharin continued: 'For several weeks I have refused to speak to Stalin. *He is an unprincipled intriguer who subordinates everything to his appetite for power.* At any given moment he will change his theories in order to get rid of someone...He manoeuvres so that *we* appear as splitters.' Bukharin added that, when he had recently read a declaration to the Politburo, he had to take great care not to let the paper leave his hands, 'because you cannot trust *him* with the smallest document'.

According to Stalin's view, described by Bukharin as 'idiotic illiteracy', the more socialism grew, the stronger grew popular resistance to it and as a result 'firm leadership is necessary', in other words 'a police regime'. And in foreign affairs, Stalin's policy was further to the Right than the Right itself. 'He has succeeded in expelling the Communist International from the Kremlin.'

Bukharin went on to compare Stalin with Genghis Khan and observed that whether the Right intervened or not, the Opposition would be 'suffocated' in any event, since Stalin, who was leading the country 'to famine and ruin', would accuse the Right of defending the *kulaks* and speculators. 'The *kulaks* can be hunted down at will, but we must conciliate the middle peasants.'

The Party and the State have become one: this is the misfortune...Stalin is only interested in power. While giving way, he has kept hold of the leadership, and later he will strangle us...Stalin knows only vengeance – the dagger in your back. We must remember his theory of sweet revenge.

Before a recent Politburo meeting, Bukharin (so he said) asked Stalin if a certain resolution on the Central Committee agenda could first be discussed by the Politburo. Stalin demurred, and when Bukharin insisted, Stalin tried to flatter him, saying: 'You and I are the Himalayas, the rest are unimportant.' Afterwards in the Politburo, there was a bitter exchange, when Bukharin reminded the General Secretary of the metaphor of the Himalayas and Stalin shouted back: 'You lie! You invented that in order to rouse the members of the Politburo against me.' After this any decisions which were adopted favouring what Stalin called 'the anti-Leninist Right' simply remained on paper. Bukharin's conclusion was that Stalin's policies of industrialisation and land collectivisation would lead to civil war. *'He will be forced to drown the rebellions in blood.'*[89]

Bukharin concluded by enumerating various organisations and individuals, on whose support he considered the Opposition could rely. At the same time he besought Kamenev to keep their conversation absolutely secret, since he was certain that their movements were being closely watched by the GPU. Unfortunately for the two some of the details leaked out several months later and came to Stalin's knowledge.

At the same time, Bukharin and Kamenev, representing anti-Stalinist elements from the Right and the Left respectively, entered into what was in effect a conspiracy to unseat Stalin. In this they had the aid of friends in the provinces as well as in Moscow, where they were in touch with Uglanov, also trade unionists and even some officials of the GPU. Bukharin unwisely embodied the details in a document which he placed in his locker in the Politburo offices. Furthermore, Kamenev sought to enlist Trotsky's support through a mutual friend in Alma-Ata named Maltchikov. The latter replied by telegram with the single word, 'Agree'. Naturally this was reported to Stalin, who had already got a set of duplicate keys of the Politburo members' lockers, where a surreptitious search revealed the compromising contents of the Bukharin document.

After Stalin had taken steps through Molotov to verify the loyalty of key Party workers, he summoned an extraordinary meeting of the Politburo at which he openly charged Bukharin with anti-Party and anti-Leninist acts.

'It's a lie,' protested Bukharin.

Stalin took a piece of paper out of his pocket. 'Do you recognise this, Nicholas Ivanovich?' he asked as he handed Bukharin a photocopy of the document embodying Bukharin's understanding with Kamenev and the other oppositionists. 'What have you to say?'

Bukharin, greatly taken aback, replied somewhat lamely that he and his friends were only defending their political platform.

'Well, then,' said Stalin, 'tell us what your political platform is. I shall convoke a plenary session of the Central Committee so that you will have an opportunity of defending it.'[90]

The session duly took place on 19 November 1928, when the Opposition case was put by one of Bukharin's lieutenants, the Finance Commissar M. I. Frumkin, who argued that the country's agriculture was on the verge of ruin, that 'the line taken lately has led to the main mass of the peasants being without hope, without prospects', and that the state farms should not be 'expanded by shock tactics or super-shock tactics'. The General Secretary brushed aside these criticisms, and they received practically no support from those present, as the provincial members on whose support Bukharin relied deemed it prudent to remain silent. Much of his reply was devoted to pin-pointing the various elements of the Opposition and exposing their errors.

> These deviators, both Rights and Lefts, are recruited from the most diverse elements of the non-proletarian strata, elements which reflect the pressure of the petty-bourgeois elemental forces in the Party. Former members of other parties; people in the Party with Trotskyist trends; remnants of former groups in the Party; Party members in the state, economic cooperative and trade union apparatuses who are becoming (or have become) bureaucratised and are linking themselves with the outright bourgeois elements in these apparatuses; well-to-do Party members in our rural organisations who are merging with the *kulaks*, and so on – such is the nutritive medium for deviations from the Leninist line. It is obvious that these elements are incapable of absorbing anything genuinely Left and Leninist...That is why a fight on two fronts is the only correct policy for the Party.

The Central Committee now proposed to expel Bukharin and also to discipline Rykov and Tomsky. But the General Secretary thought it best to hold up this proposal, since he preferred to preface his overthrow of the three Rightists in the Politburo by first defeating them on ideological grounds. 'It is one thing to arrest Trotskyist cadres and to expel them from the Party,' he said. 'It is another thing to put an end to the Trotskyist ideology. That will be more difficult.'[91] On the other hand, he was very conscious that his most dangerous opponent was still Trotsky himself, and so on 18 January 1929, he proposed in the Politburo that Trotsky should be deported. This proposal was carried in the face of Bukharin's indignant protests – Bukharin is said to have screamed and sobbed. A week later Trotsky and his family were on their way to Turkey, the only country which would receive them. In view of his popularity and the respect which he enjoyed from friend and foe alike throughout the country, Stalin was reluctant to imprison his principal rival. A few years later he would not have hesitated to have had him shot.

Before the year was out, Stalin had effectively silenced the Right-wing leaders. Rykov was dismissed from the chairmanship of the Council of Commissars, thus ceasing to be titular Premier. Tomsky was removed from his position as head of the trade unions, having been denounced by Stalin as 'a malicious fellow and not always clean in his methods'.[92] (He was accused of using his influence to turn the unions agains industrialisation.) Bukharin was demoted from the presidency of the Communist International, where he had replaced Zinoviev, the pretext being a review of a German book which he had written in *Pravda*, which he edited, criticising Stalin's policies. At the same time he had to vacate the editorial chair. He was also charged with forming a bloc with former Trotskyists, and for this he was deprived of his seat in the Politburo. Uglanov likewise lost his place as a candidate member and was also dismissed from his leadership of the Moscow Soviet. The four leading 'deviators' subsequently signed declarations repudiating their 'erroneous views' in the most grovelling terms; but their recantations were only to provide them with a temporary reprieve. Meanwhile Uglanov, Rykov and Tomsky were succeeded in their respective posts by three thoroughly reliable Stalinists, Kaganovich, Molotov and Nikolai Shvernik, of whom the last named was a political lightweight.[93]

Stalin's victory over his opponents was thus complete. All his rivals had been eliminated or had capitulated unconditionally and his ascendancy in the Politburo and the Party was for the time being un-challengeable. Towards the end of December 1929, his fiftieth birthday was marked by an astonishing spate of adulation in the press and the country at large. His virtues – he had no vices – were lauded to the skies. 'His modesty, his courage and his devotion to the cause were only equalled by his wisdom and foresight. It was he who had organised the Bolshevik Party, led the October Revolution, commanded the Red Army, and been victor of the Civil War and the wars outside Russia. Added to this, he was the leader of the world proletariat. His practical ability was on a level with his theoretical gifts: no one had ever seen him make a mistake.'[94] Huge portraits, statues and busts of the General Secretary of the Party decorated public buildings and squares everywhere; in addition to Stalingrad (the former Tsaritsyn), Stalinabad, Stalino, Stalinogorsk and many other towns and villages, his name was bestowed upon innumerable factories, power stations, schools, barracks and agricultural collectives. The Party slogan writ large on thousands of red banners throughout the land, was 'Stalin is the Lenin of today'.

> Stalin was always with Lenin, never lagging behind him, never betraying him [wrote his friend Abel Yenukidze]. After Lenin's death Stalin proved to the whole Party his loyalty to Lenin and Leninism. Stalin, together with the Party and its Central Committee, maintained the unity and firmness of the Bolshevik Party. The Party overthrew Trotskyism and the opposition; it declared a determined war against the Right deviation and opportunism within its ranks; and here too it has been plainly victorious... Stalin is interwoven with the whole thirty years' history of the Leninist Party. He is a true Bolshevik, a true Leninist. Working for many years yet, and, together with our Leninist Central Committee, leading our Party and our country ever forward to Socialism, Stalin will remain the same to the end of his life.[95]

For days the country was drenched with eulogies of the Georgian born Joseph Djugashvili, who had now become the universally acknowledged *Vozhd* or leader of the Russian people, just as the *Fuehrer* Adolf Hitler was of the German people and the *Duce* Benito Mussolini of the Italians – virtual dictators all. Perhaps the most uninhibited praise of all came from a Kazakh minstrel named Djambul whose words were quoted approvingly by *Pravda*: 'Stalin is deeper than the ocean, higher than the Himalayas, brighter than the sun, he is the teacher of the universe.' Yet in Stalin's case there was little real affection in these servile and flattering panegyrics. Although his features were familiar enough from myriads of official portraits, comparatively few of his millions of subjects had ever seen him in the flesh or had heard his voice, since he had never broadcast over the radio. He preferred to remain a mysterious and remote 'father' figure, as indeed the Tsarist rulers had been before him, his popular image benign but awesome and at the same time slightly unreal.

Then on his actual birthday, Stalin graciously acknowledged the flood of congratulations and greetings in words which had a faintly

Biblical flavour, perhaps unconsciously reflecting his education in the Tiflis Theological Seminary. *Pravda* and every other journal throughout the Soviet Union splashed them in large letters on their front pages.

Your congratulations and greetings I place to the credit of the great Party of the working class which bore me and reared me in its own image and likeness. And just because I place them to the credit of our glorious Leninist Party, I make bold to tender you my Bolshevik thanks.

You need have no doubt, comrades, that I am prepared in the future, too, to devote to the cause of the working class, to the cause or the proletarian revolution and world communism, all my strength, all my ability, and, if need be, all my blood, drop by drop.

With profound respect,
J. STALIN[96]

This widely publicised message produced a quip which was soon going the rounds in Moscow. 'Why all this modesty about shedding it drop by drop? Can't he give all his blood at once?'[97]

STALIN AS LENIN'S DISCIPLE
Remember, love and study Lenin, our teacher and leader.
Fight and vanquish the enemies, internal and foreign, as Lenin taught us.
Build the new life, the new existence, the new culture, as Lenin taught us.
Never refuse to do the little things, for from little things are built the big things — this is one of Lenin's most important behests.
J. STALIN

CHAPTER VI

A Domestic Tragedy

I

Having achieved absolute power, Stalin now had to consolidate and maintain his dictatorial rule. This was far from easy for him, certainly during the next few years when he was overwhelmed with domestic anxieties, public and private, and his personal popularity fell sharply in the Party and the country. Indeed it needed all his characteristic self-possession and steady nerves to overcome his troubles. Fortunately he had in the Politburo a hard core of adherents upon whose support he could normally rely. Here his principal lieutenant was the tough and unyielding Vyascheslav Molotov, whom Lenin had once called the best filing clerk in Russia. For his part Molotov was absolutely devoted to the General Secretary of the Party, and this ensured that the office of Chairman of the Council of Commissars, which he had taken over on Rykov's dismissal, would be carried on to his leader's liking. The British ambassador Lord Chilston described him as being perhaps the closest to Stalin of all the Kremlin circle.

> In person he is undistinguished and suffers from a painful stammer which does not prevent him from making long and tedious speeches. His official position is supposed to correspond to that of Prime Minister, but he is little more than Stalin's mouthpiece.[1]

Stalin's other henchmen in the Politburo were Klim Voroshilov, Lazar

234

Kaganovich and Mikhail Kalinin, although the latter sometimes swerved in his allegiance. Indeed all four men, with the exception of President Kalinin, who died in 1946, were to remain full members of the Politburo for the remainder of Stalin's life. Later on, a few others such as Mikoyan, Khrushchev, Beria, Malenkov and Bulganin, were to enjoy continuous membership of this *élite* body from the dates of their original election to the time of Stalin's death; they were likewise thoroughly proved and reliable Stalinists, but with the exception of Mikoyan and Khrushchev their terms were relatively short, a few years at the most. Of the dozen or so more, to be elected from time to time and subsequently dropped, almost all were to perish at Stalin's orders with the assent express or implied of the four long-term survivors.

The Politburo continued to meet in the old Senate building as in Lenin's time, as also did the Council of People's Commissars under Molotov's chairmanship. Stalin rarely presided at the Politburo meetings, leaving it to one of the other members, usually Kalinin, but sometimes Voroshilov or Molotov, to occupy the chair in which Lenin habitually sat. The fiction of voting was retained, but the vote rarely failed to adopt Stalin's 'suggestions', after which the collective decision would be signed by all ten members with Stalin's signature among the rest.

Alexander Barmine gives a typical example of the Politburo in action when he was working as a senior executive in Stanko-Import, a machine tool trust which imported this species of factory equipment from abroad. One of the trust's foreign customers was the German house of Stock, which supplied Stanko-Import with machine tools and spare parts, which would duly be passed on to Soviet factories which required them. The director of one such factory complained about the quality of the tools and also about the relevant accounts which he said were confused. Failing to obtain any satisfaction, the factory director then addressed his complaint to Stalin, whom he had met before and who apparently remembered him. The result was that a hearing of the complaint was ordered, and the head of Stanko-Import was instructed to appear with Barmine to answer the charges. The Commissar for Foreign Trade, Arcady Rosengoltz, also received a summons to attend, since he was regarded as being in a measure responsible for the quality of the goods supplied under the contract between Stanko-Import and the German manufacturers as well as for the details of the contract itself. Rosengoltz, a Jew with an impeccable revolutionary record, was an able administrator, but he had previously indulged in a brief flirtation with the Trotskyite opposition, and this had given him a black mark in Stalin's eyes, which was to be remembered to his cost when the final reckoning with the Trotskyites came in the Great Purge a few years later.

Barmine and the others arrived in the Kremlin at three o'clock on the afternoon of the hearing, and they all kicked their heels for several hours in the waiting room along with others who were waiting for their 'cases' to be called. They passed the time in munching ham and cheese sandwiches, drinking tea, smoking innumerable *papirossi* and exchanging gossip. They were eventually called in about seven o'clock. Kalinin sat at the end of a long table at which the other members of the Politburo were ranged, with the exception of Stalin who was pacing up and down opposite the window, his pipe in his mouth and his hands clasped behind his back. When they entered, Stalin looked round and nodded with a smile at the complaining factory director. 'This sign of favour was immediately reflected in the general attitude,' Barmine recalled afterwards. 'The rest of us already felt guilty.'

The director spoke for a long time, accusing our company of every crime on the Soviet calendar, from signing 'sucker' contracts with the capitalists to outright sabotage. Now and then Stalin, without waiting to be recognised by Kalinin, who was presiding, interjected a comment or an attempted witticism.

'So Stanko-Import was taken in by the Germans!' he said.

The entire hall roared with laughter at the surpassing humour of the Boss. I looked over at poor Rosengoltz. Even he attempted a weak smile.

A couple of hours passed while accusers and accused wrangled and perspired to the accompaniment of inept questions from the members of the Politburo. The issue was technical, relating to the specifications of machine tools. It was clear that neither Stalin nor the other members of the Politburo were following the discussion. Occasionally they asked a question. But in order to understand the problem, it would have been necessary, even for a competent specialist, to sit down with the documents, contracts and catalogues and study them for days.

Finally, Stalin, who had taken a seat near Molotov, rose.

'All right,' he said. 'That's enough. It's easy to see that Stanko-Import made a very poor contract. I propose that Comrade Rosengoltz be admonished, that Stanko-Import send a director to Germany to straighten matters out, that the president of Stanko-Import be severely reprimanded...'

Kalinin, scarcely bothering to look up, said: 'You have heard the proposal. If there are no objections, it is so ordered.'

There were no objections, and we were dismissed, to give way to the next victims.

As Barmine heard the other members of the Politburo mumble their approval of Stalin's 'proposal', he asked himself a question. What would happen if someone got up and said: 'I disagree with Comrade Stalin'? Then he dismissed the idea as fantastic on the ground that Stalin had devised techniques for ferreting out in advance any possible opposition. 'Any potential strong man is weeded out before he can try out his power – as was done in the case of Sergei Kirov,' noted Barmine. 'Stalin not only is generally called "the Boss" by the whole bureaucracy, but *is* the one and only boss.'

> For this reason among others, the Soviet bureaucracy is a cumbersome and frequently unworkable machine [wrote Barmine after he had fled to the west some years later]. Initiative on the part of subordinate bureaucrats is stifled. Everyone seeks to avoid responsibility. Everyone looks to the top for a covering order. And since thousands of relatively unimportant, was well as all-important, problems must pass through Stalin's hands for final decision, the top is always jammed. Weeks are spent in waiting: commissars wait in Stalin's office; presidents of companies wait in the offices of the commissars; and so on down the line. I often spent hours waiting for Rosengoltz to get a decision from Stalin, while subordinates waited for me to get one from Rosengoltz. When Stalin got bored or tired he would go off to one of his villas, giving orders that he was not to be disturbed; the top machinery would practically cease to function, and the whole thing was in a bottleneck.
>
> Why did Stalin insist on the direct control over every single phase of Soviet life, which imposed such a vast burden on him? The answer is that only in this way could a man like him continue as dictator. A genial and brilliant, and less suspicious man, having the confidence of large numbers of self-reliant and intelligent lieutenants, could manage to hold power without personally supervising every petty decision.[2]

The trouble over Kirov developed during the summer of 1932 when a group of Right-wing dissidents led by a minor Party member M. N. Ryutin produced a lengthy document advocating economic self-determination for the peasants who, he urged, should have the right to leave the collectives. Ryutin also proposed the immediate re-admission to the Party of Trotsky and others recently expelled. In particular, the Ruytin document contained a strong criticism of Stalin's policies, some fifty pages being devoted to his personal characteristics and a condemnation of his role in the Party. These views were expressed with considerable vigour and soon the document was going the rounds of various Party circles. At Nicolaevsky put it, 'Stalin was depicted as the evil genius of the Russian Revolution, who, motivated by vindictiveness and lust for power, had brought the Revolution to the verge of ruin.'

When he first read the document, Stalin was furious, regarding it in effect as a call for his own removal and 'liquidation'. He seems to have hoped that the GPU would shoot Ryutin and his fellow Rightists out of hand. But the GPU preferrred to 'pass the buck' by turning the matter over to the Central Control Commission, the organ responsible for party discipline and then under the direction of a former Politburo member, Yan Rudzutak. However, Rudzutak felt that the Ryutin affair was a political issue which went beyond the bounds of Party discipline, and he in turn referred it to the Politburo, where it was discussed at some length. Stalin demanded Ryutin's execution, arguing that the authors of propaganda plainly designed to inspire terroristic acts should be punished with the same maximum severity as the authors of the acts themselves According to Nicolaevsky, who was in a position to know what went on in the Politburo at this time, 'Kirov spoke with particular force against recourse to the death penalty', and 'moreover he succeeded in winning over the Politburo to this view'. In fact, it appears that only Kaganovich was wholeheartedly on Stalin's side. The result was that the Politburo's rejection of Stalin's demand was confirmed by the whole Control Committee and that Ryutin's life was spared, although he was expelled from the Party and sentenced to a long term in an 'isolator'.*

Some months later, another 'anti-Party' group, led by a distinguished Old Bolshevik and former member of the Orgburo, A. P. Smirnov, was similarly exposed. However its adherents, thanks again to Kirov's intervention, got off with their lives – much to Stalin's annoyance. The question which now began to take shape in Stalin's mind was : how best to get rid of Kirov? Those who had been most conspicuous in supporting Kirov could be dealt with later; they included Kuibyshev, Ordzhonikidze, Rudzutak and Stanislav Kossior, a Ukrainian from the Donbas who had been elected a full member of the Politburo after the Sixteenth Party Congress in 1930. The instrument which Stalin

* Isolators were special prisons administered by the GPU for important political prisoners, who were usually kept incommunicado until they died.

devised for the realisation of his prime objective lay in a sinister branch of his personal secretariat known as the 'Special Secret Political Section of State Security' or 'Special Section' for short. Little is known of the functioning of this highly secret unit, since there has never been any mention of it in Soviet printed sources. What we do know has been gathered from a few reliable refugees like Boris Nicolaevsky.[3]

In addition to the Secretariat of the Party Central Committee, which he headed as General Secretary, Stalin had for some years been building up a personal secretariat. Originating in his private office, this body of high-powered technical experts came to be known as 'Comrade Stalin's Secretariat' and was quite separate from the Secretariat of the Central Committee. Composed for the most part of unobtrusive young men, little known to the Party and country at large, these 'back room boys' would draft proposals and resolutions on their master's instructions for the official approval of the higher Party branches, the Central Committee Secretariat, the Politburo and the Orgburo. Where a serious difference of opinion arose, the matter in dispute would be referred to an *ad hoc* committee of the branch or department concerned. If this committee came up with any solution which did not suit Stalin, he would sabotage it in his personal secretariat and tell the committee to try again, this time with the secretariat's help. 'Everything depends on personnel,' Stalin used to say. And so his personal secretariat became a 'laboratory for filtering personnel'. The fate of every Party member from a local provincial secretary to a People's Commissar in the central government came to depend in effect upon the recommendation of the relevant section of 'Comrade Stalin's Secretariat' and its endorsement by 'the Boss'. At times several hundreds of individuals were employed there.[4]

They included a number of women, most of whom worked as typists and telephonists. One of them, Liza Semionova, later imprisoned, disclosed to her cell mate that she had been engaged on a particularly secret operation in what she called 'the chamber of monitoring private conversations'.

It was a 'most fascinating' job, according to Semionova. She would eavesdrop on private telephone conversations and report them to Stalin. It was also the function of the chamber to install hidden microphones in the homes of key government officials, to enable Stalin to keep a close check on his associates. Most of the information gathered by wire-tapping or hidden microphones was cleared through Semionova and was relayed by her to the Leader or to his personal secretary, Poskrebyshev.[5]

Among other documents kept in the personal secretariat were special secret files on the more important Party members. They recorded information on the past histories of these individuals, their sins and errors, which had been collected by the vigilant GPU. On occasion Stalin did not scruple to confront the errant comrade with the embarrassing details about himself. On one occasion, for instance, Gregory Petrovsky, a Bolshevik veteran who was President of the Ukrainian Soviet Republic, was sent for by Stalin and reprimanded for some alleged failing in his bailiwick. To rub home the point, Stalin suddenly produced the file on Petrovsky and proceeded to read from it. 'We know everything about you,' he told him. 'In 1905 you caroused with the chief of police in Pavlograd... Look out, it might prove unpleasant!'[6]

Stalin's chief assistant in the formation and running of his personal secretariat was Ivan Pavlovich Tovstukha, a Ukrainian from the Dnieperian Cossack district of Chernigov which is particularly associated with the famous Cossack hetman Mazeppa. Ten years younger than his master, Tovstukha had got to know him when serving as a senior official in the Commissariat of Nationalities, to which he had been appointed by Lenin whom he had met as an exile in Paris before the Revolution. He was a man of some literary ability, evidenced by his appointment as Deputy Director of the Marx–Lenin Institute where he was largely responsible for the preparation of the first and second editions of Lenin's *Collected Works*. He was later appointed to Stalin's private office, serving as principal private secretary along with Boris Bazhanov, and taking over the complete running of the personal secretariat after Bazhanov's defection to the west. He also wrote the first published life of Stalin, in 1927, a brief potted biography in *Who's Who* style. Tall and thin with a tactiturn manner, Tovstukha would laugh immoderately at his master's jokes, which freqently contained sly references to his name which in the Ukrainian language means 'fat woman'. On one occasion, Bazhanov recalled, the great man came into their office with a serious air and the two secretaries waited for what they imagined would be an important pronouncement. After gazing at the bespectacled Tovstukha for a few moments, Stalin remarked: 'My mother had a billy-goat who looked very much like you, Comrade Tovstukha, if I'm not mistaken. Only he didn't wear glasses!' Having delivered himself of this ponderous witticism, the General Secretary retired to his inner office followed by obsequious laughter from the 'fat woman'.[7]

Besides Tovstukha, the back-room boys in the personal secretariat included Alexander Poskrebyshev, Nikolai Yezhov, Peter Pospelov and

George Malenkov. Each was given an official title as a cover for his secret activities. Tovstukha, for example, ranked in the official hierarchy as Assistant Secretary of the Central Committee. Under him Poskrebyshev was in charge of the 'Special Secret Political Section of State Security', with Malenkov as his deputy, for which duties Poskrebyshev was given military rank. Pospelov and Yezhov were made responsible for propaganda and personnel respectively, work which in the latter's case involved close co-operation with the Special Section.

Without doubt the most devoted and trusted member of the secretariat was Poskrebyshev, who was to assume complete control on Tovstuka's death in 1935. Like Stalin, he had had smallpox and his face was heavily pitted with marks of the infection. He was accustomed to use the coarsest language and he gave the impression of being completely uneducated. However, despite these drawbacks Poskrebyshev had a card-index memory and he was also an excellent organiser, just the man for 'the Boss' whose junior he was by a dozen years. 'He was totally self-effacing and put himself entirely at Stalin's service,' wrote Boris Nicolaevsky from personal experience. 'On orders from Stalin he would carry out the most distasteful, dirtiest and bloodiest deeds. He became Stalin's *alter ego*. If Stalin ever trusted anyone, it was Poskrebyshev, to whom he even gave a rubber stamp with his signature to affix to documents of a certain kind.' The Special Section, which Poskrebyshev was mainly instrumental in creating and which he ran with deadly efficiency, had the duty of supervising the GPU, whose leading figures, Menzhinsky and Yagoda, no longer fully enjoyed Stalin's confidence. This secret branch of the secretariat consequently came to embody the machinery for carrying out the purges when the reduction in powers of the Central Control Commission took place after the Seventeenth Party Congress in 1934. While Malenkov compiled lists of victims, Poskrebyshev took them to Stalin who marked the names of those who for one reason or another he wished to be disposed of quietly without public accusation and trial.[8]

By such means the Special Section created vacancies in responsible posts which were immediately filled by the Personnel Section, first under Yezhov and then under Malenkov. It is therefore hardly surprising that the People's Commissars quailed before Tovstukha and Poskrebyshev, while members of the Central Committee licked the boots of Yezhov and Malenkov, in spite of the fact that the persons who wielded such authority and their colleagues were listed merely as 'technical employees' of the Central Committee. 'In a period of reconstruction technology decides everything,' said Stalin on one occasion. His own use of technology in operating the Central Committee through the Poskrebyshevs and Malenkovs in Moscow definitely decided the fate of the Party. Such then was the situation in the Party when Stalin moved into final battle for Lenin's heritage. What counted was not the elected Party members but the secretaries of *oblast* [provincial] and district committees and of Party central committees of the local national republics, all of whom had been appointed by the Personnel Section, and the iron will and desire for sole power of the chief 'constructor' of the conspiracy.[9]

The faithful Poskrebyshev was twice to be awarded the Order of Lenin, the highest Soviet decoration, and he was also to be made a Lieutenant-General in the Red Army. In his famous 'secret' speech to the Twentieth Party Congress in 1956, Khrushchev referred to him somewhat contemptuously as 'Stalin's loyal shield bearer.' Loyal Poskrebyshev most certainly was, but he was considerably more important and significant than a mere shield bearer. Nicolaevsky was much nearer the mark when he described him and the secretariat which he headed as 'the eyes, ears and hands of Stalin'. He was to remain close to his master almost until the day Stalin died.*

The only other member of Stalin's entourage who seems to have enjoyed his confidence to an equal degree was his principal bodyguard, K. V. Pauker, a Hungarian who also served as his master's valet and barber. As Stalin grew increasingly suspicious of those around him, Pauker was the only man he would trust near him with a razor. Pauker had begun his career as a hairdresser in Budapest, where he used to shave the actors in the local operetta; he was also something of a clown and a clever mimic, talents which he owed to his time with the Budapest operetta where he also used to be given walking-on parts. His antics amused Stalin, who found his company congenial and often drank with him. Pauker had been previously employed in the Moscow GPU, where he had risen to be chief of the Operations Division, in which capacity he was responsible for carrying out arrests of political

* The 'loathsome' General Poskrebyshev disappeared immediately after Stalin's death, and for some years it was thought he had been 'liquidated' for his part in the purges. However, he seems to have been occupied in retirement writing his memoirs, since he turned up at a conference of writers in Moscow in 1962. (The memoirs have not so far been published – no doubt they would make interesting reading.) The Soviet writer Galina Serebryakova, who met him there and later in a Moscow hospital, is stated to have found him 'completely callous about Stalin's crimes, even taking a grim humour in the plight of his victims'. He died in 1966. See Harrison Salisbury. *The Siege of Leningrad* (1969), p. 215.

suspects in the city. He was also charged with the security arrangements in the Kremlin including the protection of Stalin and the other members of the Politburo. This enabled him to become a purveyor of scarce consumer goods to the Soviet *élite*, whom he would supply with gastronomic delicacies, fine wines, pedigree dogs, perfumes, dresses, radio sets and similar goods of foreign origin which he contrived to import. For Stalin he was able to secure a particular kind of German herring and the fact that this went well with vodka led to Pauker becoming Stalin's drinking companion. Pauker further won his master's favour by having boots with specially high heels made for him so that he appeared at least two inches taller than his real height, which was only five feet four inches.

Alexander Orlov, a GPU man who later defected, described Pauker's role from personal observation.

> Everything that concerned Stalin and his family passed through Pauker's hands. Without his knowledge not a single crumb of food could pass to Stalin's dinner table, and without Pauker's supervision not a single person would be admitted to Stalin's apartment or his country estate. Pauker would not leave Stalin for a moment, and only after he had brought him at noon to his office in the Kremlin, would Pauker hurry off to the Operations Division of the NKVD to make a report to Menzhinsky and Yagoda for the past twenty-four hours and tell his cronies the latest news and gossip of the Kremlin.[10]

Poskrebyshev and Pauker made the most formidable combination of all the men around Stalin. But of these two particularly intimate aides only Poskrebyshev in the long term was to remain indispensable.

2

In his later years the legend grew up that from the time he achieved dictatorial power Stalin did all his work in the Kremlin which he never left except to drive to his country villa or to the railway station to take a train for his annual holiday in the south. This was not so. Although he kept a small private office in the old Senate building which was convenient for the bi-weekly meetings of the Politburo, most of his work was carried on outside the Kremlin in the offices of the Party Central Committee at No. 4 Old Square (*Staraya Ploschad*), at least until the later 1930s. This was quite logical seeing that he was the Committee's General Secretary. The Party headquarters were within easy walking distance of the Kremlin, and though as a rule he preferred to travel by car, Stalin would occasionally stroll over to Party Headquarters accompanied only by one or two guards, crossing the Red Square by Lenin's tomb and going the length of Ilyinka Street. There a few blocks brought him past several government departments, including the Commissariat of Internal Affairs (NKVD), to *Staraya Ploschad*, where the Central Committee building was situated on the right-hand side of the square. Stalin's somewhat drab office was on the third floor with a view over Lubyanka Street and the GPU headquarters which had not yet been incorporated with the NKVD. It was in this plainly furnished room with a long table and chairs, several telephones, one or two book cases and portraits of Marx and Lenin gazing down from the dull walls that the General Secretary transacted all the Party business. Special telephones provided him with direct connections to the Kremlin and nearby offices of the GPU and the Central Control Commission. Here too he used to receive visitors, including on occasion distinguished foreigners and very occasionally foreign press correspondents. But heads of foreign diplomatic missions and other VIPs on the rare occasions that he received them were usually summoned in the evening to the Kremlin. Afterwards he would often continue to work until the early hours of the morning, sometimes indeed throughout most of the night, a habit carried over from his days as an underground revolutionary.

Although he impressed different foreign visitors in different ways – native callers wisely kept their impressions to themselves – most people who have preserved their impressions are agreed about his initial shyness and friendliness when he received them and also his rather ordinary appearance. The English writer, H. G. Wells, for instance, who called on him in 1934, had this to say:

> My first impression was of a rather commonplace-looking man dressed in an embroidered white shirt, dark trousers and boots, staring out of the window of a large, generally empty room. He turned rather shyly and shook his hands in a friendly manner. His face was also commonplace, friendly and commonplace, not very well modelled, not in any way 'fine'. He looked past me rather than at me but not evasively; it was simply that he had none of the abundant curiosity which had kept Lenin watching me from behind the hand he held over his defective eye, all the time he talked to me.[11]

'I have come to ask you what you are doing to change the world,' Wells began.

'Not so very much,' replied Stalin.

By degrees the two men warmed to each other in spite of the slightly constricting presence of Stalin's interpreter whose alternate translating of Wells's remarks into Russian and Stalin's into English necessarily slowed down the exchanges. (The interpreter was one of Stalin's former back-room boys Constantine Oumansky, then working under Litvinov in the Foreign Affairs Commissariat.) After about forty minutes, Wells suggested breaking off the interview, but Stalin declared his firm intention of going on for three hours. And so they did, covering a wide field of international political, economic and social questions.

Although Wells had written an immensely popular *Outline of History*, he appeared to know less about certain aspects of English history than his host.

'Don't you think,' Stalin asked him, 'that the Chartist movement played a great role in the reforms of England in the nineteenth century?'

'The Chartists did little and disappeared without leaving a trace,' Wells answered.

'I do not agree with you,' said Stalin. 'The Chartists, and the strike movement which they organised, played a great role. They compelled the ruling classes to make a number of concessions in regard to abolishing the so-called "rotten boroughs" and in regard to some of the points in the "Charter".' The purpose of these concessions, as Stalin put it, was 'to avert great shocks'.

Stalin went on to express admiration for England's ruling classes. 'Generally speaking, it must be said that of all the ruling classes, the ruling class of England, both the aristocracy and the bourgeoisie, have proved to be the cleverest and most flexible from the point of view of their own class interests, from the point of view of maintaining their power,' he remarked. 'Take an example from modern history – the general strike in England in 1926. The first thing any other bourgeoisie would have done in the face of such an event, when the TUC called for a strike, would have been to arrest the trade union leaders. The British bourgeoisie did not do that, and it acted cleverly from the point of view of its own interests. I cannot conceive of such a flexible strategy being employed by the bourgeoisie of the United States, Germany or France. In order to maintain their rule, the ruling classes of Great Britain have never foresworn small concessions, reforms. But it would be a mistake to think that these reforms were revolutionary.'

Again Wells dissented. 'You have a higher opinion of the ruling classes of my country than I have,' he said. 'But is there a great difference between a small revolution and a great reform? Isn't a reform a small revolution?'

Stalin's reply underlined the fundamental cleavage between their respective conceptions of socialism, and he argued as a good Marxist should.

> Owing to pressure from below, the pressure of the masses, the bourgeoisie may sometimes concede certain partial reforms while remaining on the basis of the existing social-economic system. Acting in this way, it calculates that these concessions are necessary in order to preserve its class rule. This is the essence of reform. Revolution, however, means the transference of power from one class to another. That is why it is impossible to describe any reform as revolution. That is why we cannot count on the change of social systems taking place as an imperceptible transition from one system to another by means of reforms, by the ruling class making concessions.[12]

On this occasion none of Wells's remarks caused the interpreter any embarrassment when he came to translate them. It was otherwise when Stalin received Lady Astor, the American-born Member of the British House of Commons, along with her husband, her son David and her friends George Bernard Shaw and Lord Lothian, better known as Philip Kerr. The meeting took place in 1931, at ten o'clock at night in the Kremlin. Her Ladyship bluntly asked the Soviet dictator why he had slaughtered so many of his fellow countrymen. 'And how long are you going on killing people?'

The interpreter was afraid to translate the question and plainly showed his embarrassment. But Stalin demanded to know. When he heard the translation which was most reluctantly given, he took it unexpectedly quietly. 'As long as it is necessary,' he replied, adding that some slaughter was inevitable 'when the constitution of a country is fundamentally disrupted' and that 'the violent death of a large number of people was necessary before the Communist State could be firmly established'.[13]

Lady Astor told Stalin that they did not know how to treat children properly in the Soviet state. Stalin, visibly annoyed, made a gesture like the slash of a whip, as he exclaimed with real feeling, 'But in England you *beat* children.'

The ebullient Nancy Astor retorted that Stalin did not know what he was talking about, while she did. Indeed, had she not financed a child welfare experiment in the London dock area of Deptford? What she went on to say was repeated afterwards by Bernard Shaw.

Those prettily dressed little girls in their dainty nursery at the collective farm, with their unbroken new toys: why were they not out of doors? The nurse had said that it had rained that morning. Rubbish! A child should not know or care whether it was rain or shine. And the spotless dresses and the clean faces and hands! A child should be grubby, dirty, clayey, except at meals. It should not have a dress from the wardrobe of the Russian ballet: it should have a tough linen frock that could be washed in half an hour. 'Send a good sensible woman to me in London,' she ordered, 'and I will take care of her and show her how children of five should be handled.'

Stalin's reaction to this outburst was to take an envelope out of his pocket and ask Lady Astor to write down her address. This she did, but she got more than she bargained for when she returned to London. Instead of one woman, a dozen turned up at her house, and she had to entertain and instruct them and take them to Deptford. 'It was a comfort to know that her eloquence had not been wasted,' commented Shaw afterwards; 'but she must have felt that Uncle Joe had got a bit of his own back.'

Shaw's impressions of his host are also worth quoting.

Unlike the other dictators, Stalin has an irrepressible sense of humour. There is an odd mixture of the Pope and the Field-Marshal in him: you might guess him to be the illegitimate soldier-son of a cardinal. I should call his manners perfect if only he had been able to conceal the fact that we amused him enormously. First of all he let us talk ourselves empty. Then he asked if he might say a few words. We couldn't understand a syllable he uttered: the only word I caught was 'Wrangel', the name of one of the generals England had backed against the Bolsheviks. He was soon brimming with amusement; but as the utterly incompetent interpreter's teeth were chattering with fright, the point of his pleasantries escaped us. But for Litvinov, who was present, we should have left without a translation.

Wrangel's name cropped up when Lord Lothian, who had once been Lloyd George's secretary, suggested that his former master, now the elder statesman of the Liberal Party in England, should be officially invited to visit the country. According to Shaw, Stalin explained 'with more humour than was quite reassuring' that the part taken by Mr Lloyd George in the civil war as lately as ten years ago, when Baron

Wrangel was leading the Whites against the Reds, made an official invitation impossible. However, if Mr Lloyd George would come as a private tourist, he would be shown everything and have nothing to complain of.

Shaw interposed for the first time to ask whether Mr Winston Churchill would be equally welcome. Stalin replied enigmatically that he 'would be delighted to see Mr Churchill in Moscow, as they had every reason to be grateful to him'. Afterwards Shaw spelled out for the benefit of his friend and biographer Hesketh Pearson what Stalin had meant. 'Churchill equipped the Red Army with boots, uniforms and guns. When he was Secretary for War he handed over a hundred millions, which Parliament had voted for the war against Germany, to help the royalist counter-revolution in Russia. The Bolsheviks won and managed to clothe and arm themselves with the material so generously provided by Great Britain.'

Lord Astor, himself a prominent English Liberal, on whose account the interview had really been arranged, did his best to let Stalin know that in spite of the violent anti-Soviet feelings in certain sections of the British press – though not in the *Observer*, which Astor owned – there was in England plenty of friendly feeling towards Russia, and interest in her great social experiment. Indeed he went to such lengths in a characteristic desire to undo mischief and improve the atmosphere that Shaw, whose own sense of humour was of the Puckish variety, again intervened with an equally characteristic question. He asked Stalin whether he had ever heard of a person named Oliver Cromwell.

Stalin said a few words in Russian to Litvinov, who then turned to Shaw. 'What is the point of your question?' he inquired.

'Only this,' replied Shaw. 'In an old ballad well known in Ireland, Cromwell's word to his soldiers is to "Put your trust in God, my boys, and keep your powder dry!" All that Lord Astor has told you about your having friends in England is true. But keep your powder dry!'

Stalin was quick to get the message. Shaw noted that he said nothing about putting his trust in God, but intimated that Russia would keep its powder very dry.

Finally Stalin asked about the politicians in England. To this Lady Astor replied, 'Chamberlain is the coming man.'

'What about Churchill?' queried Stalin.

'Oh he's finished!'

'If your country is ever in trouble,' Stalin retorted, looking hard at Lady Astor, 'he will come back.'[14]

3

Several American visitors at this period questioned Stalin about the mechanics of Soviet government. One of these was Eugene Lyons, Moscow correspondent of the United Press news agency, who was fortunate enough to obtain an exclusive interview on 23 November 1930, and brought off a world-wide 'scoop' in consequence.

'Comrade Stalin,' Lyons tactfully addressed the Russian Communist Party's General Secretary, 'the press of the world is by this time in the habit of calling you a dictator. Are you a dictator?'

Voroshilov was also present on this occasion, and Lyons could see that the War Commissar waited with interest for the answer.

Stalin smiled his usual enigmatic smile. 'No, I am no dictator,' he said. 'Those who use the word do not understand the Soviet system of government and the methods of the Communist Party. No one man or group of men can dictate. Decisions are made by the Party and acted upon by its chosen organs, the Central Committee and the Politburo.'[15]

No doubt, as Lyons afterwards reflected, Stalin in his own fashion meant what he said, since he had identified himself with the Party so completely that he heard the Party's voice issuing from his own mouth. To other Americans Stalin admitted that it was the Party which ultimately exercised control over the government – he called it 'leadership'. The Party 'endeavours', so he put it, to have Communists appointed to all high government posts, and in 'a great majority of cases it succeeds'. Furthermore, the Party 'examines' the work of administrative departments, the work of government bodies, 'correcting their mistakes and deficiencies, which are inevitable...'

This was how he expressed the Party's role in Soviet life to the German writer Emil Ludwig.

> In our leading body, the Central Committee of our Party, which directs all our Soviet and Party organisations, there are about seventy members. Among these seventy members of the Central Committee are our best industrial leaders, our best co-operative leaders, our best managers of supplies, our best military men, our best propagandists and agitators, our best experts on state farms, on collective farms, on individual peasant farms, our best experts on the nations constituting the Soviet Union and on national policy.
>
> In this Areopagus is concentrated the wisdom of our Party. Each has an opportunity of correcting anyone's individual

opinion or proposal. Each has an opportunity of contributing his experience. If this were not the case, if decisions were taken by individual persons, there would be very serious mistakes in our work. But since each has an opportunity of correcting the mistakes of individuals persons, we arrive at decisions that are more or less correct.[16]

Thus Stalin allowed for a certain margin of error in the Party's collective wisdom. The margin was to increase with peculiarly horrible results. Within a few years most of the 'best experts' so glowingly described by Stalin were to be removed from the Central Committee as 'anti-Party traitors and Trotskyites' and 'enemies of the people', to disappear into remote labour camps or execution cellars.

A particular question which was apt to annoy Stalin when it was put to him, which happened more than once, was whether he believed in 'luck' or 'fate'. When Walter Duranty, the *New York Times* Moscow correspondent, asked him this, he banged the desk in front of him with his fist and exclaimed: 'What do you think I am, an old Georgian granny to believe in gods and devils? I'm a Bolshevik and believe in none of that nonsense.'

When Duranty hastened to explain that he meant nothing personal, but was thinking of Napoleon who 'believed in his star' and Cromwell who always said – 'and it happened so' – that his greatest successes occurred on his birthday, Stalin accepted his explanation with a frigid smile and said: 'I see what you mean, but the answer is still no. I believe in one thing only, the power of the human will.' He went on to quote Lenin as an example. 'Lenin differed from the rest of us in his clear Marxist brain and his unfaltering will…Lenin from the onset favoured a hard-boiled policy and picked men who could stick it out and endure.' It was clear, at least to Duranty, that Stalin felt that these characteristics applied to himself equally well.[17]

In his dialogue with Emil Ludwig, Stalin developed this point further.

'You have often incurred risks and dangers,' said Ludwig. 'You have been persecuted. You have taken part in battles. A number of your close friends have perished. You have survived. How do you explain that? And do you believe in fate?'

'No,' Stalin replied. 'I do not. Bolsheviks, Marxists, do not believe in fate. The very concept of fate, of *Shicksal*, is a prejudice, an absurdity, a relic of mythology, like the mythology of the ancient Greeks, for whom a goddess of fate controlled the destinies of men.'

'That is to say that the fact that you did not perish is an accident?'

'There are internal and external causes, the combined effect of which was that I did not perish. But entirely independent of that, somebody else could have been in my place, for somebody *had* to occupy it. Fate is something not governed by natural law, something mystical. I do not believe in mysticism. Of course, there were reasons why danger left me unscathed. But there could have been a number of other fortuitous circumstances, of other causes, which could have led to a directly opposite result. So-called fate has nothing to do with it.'[18]

The only occasion on which Stalin is on record as having discussed the question of sex relations, a subject of continuing interest in the west, was with a Finnish journalist in 1928. He made it clear that as a Bolshevik he was not hostile to indulgence in sex. In his view sex was a natural function like eating and drinking, men and women needed sex to stay healthy, and of course the procreation of children was necessary for the continuance of the human race. As for the idea of monastic abstinence in the Christian ethic and also feelings of guilt associated with sex, these were obsolete superstitions. But he thought that people who spent a great deal of time on sex were like gluttons who gorged themselves with rich food – they were neglecting their duty to the community. 'A man must work and fight, not enjoy himself loving, and women should model themselves on men in these respects.' During the current period of the Five Year Plan for the rapid industrialisation of the country, he thought people should cut down on sex, as on food, until the 'emergency' was over. For him there was nothing romantic about sex, and he rejected the popular western idea that mutual 'love' was the highest emotional and physical experience in human life. 'A man's real emotional bond,' he said, 'should not be with his mate but with his class and nation'. He disliked, or at least said he disliked, kissing scenes in films, certainly if they were in any way prolonged. Similarly he condemned promiscuity and liked to quote Lenin's quip to Alexandra Kollontai, the leading exponent of 'free love', when she told him that she regarded sex like a glass of water, from which she drank when she felt thirsty: 'But who wants to drink a glass of dirty water?'[19] When the more bizarre forms of sexual gratification were drawn to his attention, he professed to be astonished, as when he is said to have found a work on the history of morals by a German sexual psychologist in Radek's apartment. Turning the pages, his eyes lit on one of the more fantastic illustrations with which the book was embellished. 'Tell me, Radek,' he asked, 'do people really do this sort of thing?'[20]

In the general interests of the community, particularly of family life, he believed that marriages should be as enduring as possible. He consequently made divorces difficult and expensive to obtain, unlike the early days of the Revolution. Also prostitution was abolished in theory and drastically curtailed in practice, contraceptives had the lowest priority rating among consumer goods, and abortions were only allowed on the most pressing medical grounds. On the other hand, Stalin encouraged large families and had awards made for achievements in maternity. A mother of ten, for example, got the Medal of Heroic Soviet Motherhood and was styled Soviet Heroine. No doubt she deserved it.

Of all the interviews to foreign visitors granted by Stalin at this period, that with Emil Ludwig was the most revealing, perhaps because, as he told Stalin, he had been studying the lives and deeds of outstanding historical personages for over twenty years; he was also a very experienced interviewer. It received the fullest publicity inside the country, although the account as published in the Soviet press was considerably censored. Also Ludwig was considered of sufficient importance to be received in the Kremlin instead of Stalin's dingy office in Party headquarters. Earlier in the day, Ludwig had been shown some relics of the Tsar Peter the Great and this prompted his first question.

'Do you think a parallel can be drawn between yourself and Peter the Great? Do you consider yourself a continuer of the work of Peter the Great?'

'In no way whatever,' replied Stalin without the slightest hesitation. 'Historical parallels are always risky. There is no sense in this one.'

'But after all,' Ludwig broke in, 'Peter the Great did a great deal to develop his country, to bring western culture to Russia.'

'Yes, of course, Peter the Great did much to elevate the landlord class and develop the nascent merchant class. He did very much indeed to create and consolidate the national state of the landlords and merchants. It must be said also that the elevation of the landlord class, the assistance of the nascent merchant class and the consolidation of these classes took place at the cost of the peasant serfs, who were bled white...The task to which I have devoted my life is the elevation of a different class – the working class. That task is not the consolidation of some "national" state, but of a socialist state...So you see your parallel does not fit.'

The German author moved on to another point which had been exercising his mind. 'It seems to me that a considerable part of the population of the Soviet Union stands in fear and trepidation of the Soviet power, and that the stability of the latter rests to a certain extent on that sense of fear. I should like to know what state of mind is produced in you personally by the realisation that it is necessary to inspire fear in the interests of strengthening the regime. After all, when you associate with your comrades, your friends, you adopt quite different methods from those inspiring fear. Yet the population is being inspired with fear.'

'You are mistaken,' said Stalin. 'Incidentally, your mistake is that of many people. Do you really believe that we could have retained power and have had the backing of the vast masses for fourteen years by methods of intimidation and terrorisation? No, that is impossible. The Tsarist government excelled all others in knowing how to intimidate. It had long and vast experience in that sphere. The European bourgeoisie, particularly the French, gave Tsarism every assistance in this matter and taught it to terrorise the people. Yet, in spite of that experience and in spite of the help of the European bourgeoisie, the policy of the intimidation led to the downfall of Tsarism.'

'But the Romanovs held on for three hundred years,' Ludwig remarked.

'Yes, but how many revolts and risings were there in those three hundred years?' countered Stalin. 'As regards the people, the workers, the peasants of the USSR, they are not all so tame, so submissive and intimidated as you imagine...when in a brief period of time they made three revolutions, smashed Tsarism and the bourgeoisie, and are now triumphantly building socialism.'

However, Stalin did admit that Ludwig was right in regard to a few of the people. 'There is, of course, a certain small section of the population that does stand in fear of the Soviet power,' he said. 'I have in mind the remnants of the moribund classes, which are being eliminated, and primarily the insignificant part of the peasantry, the *kulaks*. But here it is not a matter merely of a policy of intimidating these groups, a policy that really does exist. Everybody knows that in this case we Bolsheviks do not confine ourselves to intimidation but go further, aiming at the elimination of this bourgeois stratum.'

Stalin's conclusion was that ninety per cent of the population were 'in favour of Soviet power' and that 'the vast majority of them' actively supported the Soviet regime. 'They support the Soviet system because that system serves the fundamental interests of the workers and the peasants. That, and not a policy of so-called intimidation, is the basis of the Soviet Government's stability.'

Ludwig for his part concluded, as he had begun, with a historical comparison, which Stalin again rejected.

'Is the October Revolution in any sense the continuation and culmination of the great French Revolution?' Ludwig asked.

'The October Revolution is neither the continuation nor the culmination of the great French Revolution,' answered Stalin. 'The purpose of the French Revolution was to abolish feudalism in order to establish

253

capitalism. The purpose of the October Revolution, however, is to abolish capitalism in order to establish socialism.'[21]

4

During his interview with Stalin and Voroshilov in 1930, the United Press correspondent Eugene Lyons requested permission to put some personal questions to the Soviet leader. 'Not that I myself care to pry into your private life,' he explained with a slight air of embarrassment, 'but the American press happens to be interested.'

'All right,' agreed Stalin, astonished at such bourgeois curiosity.

Voroshilov could not restrain his amusement. 'Sure,' he said. 'That's what the world wants to know.'

Stalin, who was in an equally good humour on this occasion, graciously consented to be cross-examined about some of the facts of his family life. Eventually Lyons came to his two sons Yakov and Vasily and his five-year-old daughter Svetlana. Stalin explained that Svetlana was at nursery school.

'And as yet,' Voroshilov broke in with a chuckle, 'she has no well defined political programme!'[22]

Yakov, known familiarly as Yasha, was now twenty-four and thus only four years younger than his stepmother Nadya. He had been brought up in Georgia by his aunt and uncle Alexander Svanidze and did not rejoin his father in Moscow until he was in his teens. The experiment was not a success. There was no spare bedroom in the Stalin's modest Kremlin flat and Yasha had to sleep on a sofa in the dining room. Nadya treated him kindly, but he did not get on at all well with his father who bullied him. He was sent to a technical institute to study electrical engineering, where he seems neither to have displayed any particular ability nor to have worked at all hard. Indeed, according to one report, he spent most of his time playing billiards with a fellow student, who was a son of Menzhinsky, the head of the GPU, with the result that he failed his examinations. Driven to desperation by his father's attitude, Yakov tried to do away with himself with a pistol in the Kremlin kitchens. But he only succeeded in wounding himself, which gave his father a further excuse for indulging in some biting sarcasm at his expense. 'Ha!' said Stalin. 'He couldn't even shoot straight!' After Yasha's attempted suicide, his stepmother sent him to stay with her parents in Leningrad. About this time he got married, a baby daughter of the union died, and Yasha quarrelled with his wife and they separated. Eventually his father shipped him back to the Caucasus where Stalin arranged that he should be apprenticed to an electrical engineer in the railway shops. 'If you don't want to be an engineer, be a shoemaker like your grand-father!' was Stalin's parting shot.[23]

With Vasily, his son by Nadya Alliluyeva, Stalin was more indul-gent, although Vasily did not turn out much better at his studies than Yasha. Stalin's impatience with his second son began when the latter was in his cradle, according to a foreign woman visitor who came to the Kremlin and is the authority for a record of the following bizarre incident.

One day, Stalin, his wife and the lady in question were sitting in a room with the five-months-old baby in the cradle beside them. Presently Stalin's wife found she had something to do in the kitchen, and begged her husband to keep an eye on the baby. Stalin, whose pipe is never out of his mouth, nodded silently. But as soon as its mother's back was turned, the child began to scream. Stalin went up to the cradle, groped helplessly about and, evi-dently with the idea of calming the child, puffed the smoke from his pipe once or twice into its face. Naturally it protested and howled lustily. Obviously ill at ease, Stalin lifted his offspring carefully out of the cradle and as a proof of paternal affection, stuck his pipe into its mouth. The child then began to yell as though it was being roasted alive. At last, Stalin, too, lost his temper. 'There's a blackguard for you!' he roared, flinging the baby none too tenderly back into the cradle. 'He's not a good Bolshevik!' The whole evening had been ruined for him, and until he went to bed, he pottered about, whining peevishly and finding fault with everything.[24]

It was Svetlana, his youngest child and only daughter, who was Stalin's favourite. 'Setanka', 'my little sparrow', 'little housekeeper', or 'little mistress' he used to call her. Certainly when she was young he liked to indulge her. 'Why are you only asking?' he would inquire when she wanted something in particular. 'Give an order, and I'll see to it right away.' As his 'little housekeeper', he wanted her to take an active part in the running of his household like her mother. With Vasily, or Vasya as he called him, he was less indulgent. 'I'm sending you pomegranates, tangerines, and some candied fruit,' he once wrote to his daughter. 'Eat and enjoy them, my little housekeeper! I'm not sending any to Vasya because he's still doing badly at school and feeds me nothing but promises. Tell him I don't believe in promises made in words and that I'll believe Vasya only when he really starts to study, even if his marks are only "good".'

Looking back many years later, Svetlana noted the contrast in her parents' attitudes towards their children. 'My father was demanding and strict with Vasily, but lenient towards me,' she recalled. 'He spoiled me and loved playing games with me. I was his rest and relaxation. My mother was more lenient with Vasily, since he already had enough discipline from my father, but was strict with me to offset my father's affection. Yet she was the one I loved more.'

Much of their time was spent at a small country estate about twenty miles due west of the centre of Moscow in the region of Usovo near the Moskva river. The property had once belonged to an oil millionaire from Baku named Zubalovo, who built himself a gabled villa there of German design which he surrounded with a massive brick wall. Voroshilov, Mikoyan and several other Old Bolsheviks and their families from the Caucasus also had *dachas* or villas on the Zubalovo estate, which had been sequestrated from its capitalist owner after the Revolution. Stalin took over his in 1919 at the time of his second marriage, clearing the woods surrounding the *dacha* and cutting down many of the trees, keeping bees and sowing the open spaces which he had cleared with buckwheat. As she grew up, Svetlana came to realise that her father's interest in the place was a practical one and at bottom profoundly a peasant interest. ('He was unable merely to contemplate nature; he had to work it and be forever transforming it.') He had made a large kitchen garden with strawberry, raspberry and black and red currant beds, and nearby there was a run enclosed with wire netting for chicken, turkeys and guinea fowl, with an adjacent pond for ducks.

Stalin's wife was less interested in these arrangements. According to Svetlana, her main interest was to see that the lilac bloomed properly every spring. But she did give Svetlana her own patch of garden where her nurse taught her how to dig and plant nasturtiums and marigolds. 'What a playground we had in the woods at Zubalovo!' Svetlana later recalled. 'We had a seesaw and swings and a wooden tree house, suspended between three pines, which you could only reach by a rope ladder!' The house was often full of visitors and there was much gaiety. Budenny would play the accordion, while Voroshilov and Stalin himself would join in the general sing-song and Nadya would dance the graceful Georgian *lezghinka*. The Ordzhonikidzes were often there, and also Bukharin before he fell out of favour, accompanied by a veritable zoo of hedgehogs and other animals and birds including a tame fox and a crippled hawk which glared from a cage. Years later, long after Bukharin was dead, his fox still raced round the Kremlin and made its lair in the empty and desolate gardens.

The only one of her husband's friends whom Nadya actively disliked was the Georgian GPU chief Lavrenti Beria. 'That man must not be allowed to set foot in our house,' she said.

'What's wrong with him?' asked Stalin. 'Give me facts. I'm not convinced, I see no facts.'

'What facts do you need? I just see he's a scoundrel. I won't have him here!'

'Oh, go to hell!' was Stalin's reply. 'He's my friend. He's a good Chekist. He helped us forestall the Mingrelian rising in Georgia. I trust him. Facts, facts are what I need!'[25]

At Zubalovo the children had their own nurse and governess, and when Vasily grew older his father engaged a tutor for him. There was also a resident housekeeper who looked after the *dacha* and saw to the meals. Another woman, a Latvian of German origin, was in charge of the Kremlin flat in the Poteshny Palace. At first meals used to be sent in from the Kremlin canteen, but later on with the arrival of Nadya's two children they had their own kitchen. Like most Georgians, Stalin liked to drink wine at dinner, but a good vintage Kakhetian was the only sign of luxury at table. The decoration of the flat was tasteless and the furniture ugly, the windows being draped with white canvas curtains. When he relaxed with a pipe in the living room which also served as a dining room, Stalin did not like to be disturbed even on government business. Once when Molotov rang up and Nadya answered the telephone, Stalin told his wife to tell Molotov that he was sleeping. 'Comrade Molotov,' Nadya dutifully relayed the message, 'he cannot be disturbed. He is asleep.'[26] Nor was even Molotov, although he was Chairman of the Council of Commissars and Stalin's most intimate colleague in the government, allowed to enter Stalin's presence armed. On one occasion, when he endeavoured to do so, Molotov was thrown to the ground by the Kremlin guards and none too gently relieved of his weapon.

In the summer, the family would usually move south to Sochi on the Black Sea for a holiday, though sometimes the children would be left behind at Zubalovo. At first they stayed at a small *dacha* at Matsesta, a spa near Sochi, where Stalin took warm baths as a cure for his rheumatism. He did not care for sea bathing, and in fact never went into the sea, as he had never learned to swim. Nor did he like to sit in the sun, preferring instead to walk in the woods or stretch out in a deck chair or hammock in the shade with a book or a newspaper. He would sit for hours at the dinner table arguing and discussing Caucasian style with any guests who might have been invited to the meal, usually Yenukidze, Mikoyan, Voroshilov and Molotov. Several more villas

257

were specially built for him at this time by the sycophantic Beria as 'gifts from the Georgian people'. Of these his favourite was at Sochi on a site which his wife helped him to choose. He also acquired three more properties in the neighbourhood of Moscow, of which one was at Kuntsevo not far from Zubalovo and where he was eventually to spend most of his time.

Built, altered and rebuilt many times to suit his whims of the moment, the Kuntsevo house was on an estate which had belonged for centuries to one of the oldest and best known families in Russia, the Naryshkins, one of whom was the mother of Peter the Great. The other estates, which boasted fine country houses and parks were Lipki and Semyonovskoye. But Stalin seldom visited either of them, according to his daughter Svetlana, sometimes not for a year at a time, although 'the staff always expected him at any moment and was in a perpetual state of readiness. And if a motorcade actually did take off from Kuntsevo in the direction of Lipki, pandemonium would break loose there and everyone from the cook to the guard at the gate, from the waitresses to the commandant, would be seized with panic. They all awaited these visitations like Judgment Day...'

During the first few years of their marriage, young Nadya Alliluyeva was deeply in love with her husband in spite of the difference of some twenty-three years in their ages. She was an intelligent and sensitive girl besides possessing considerable physical beauty; but there were limits to what her devotion could stand, and there was increasing bickering and quarrelling due to Stalin's selfish and overbearing ways. According to a high-ranking GPU officer, who later defected, it was soon no secret in the department that Stalin and his wife were on bad terms, and that she used to resent his coarse and obscene jokes, particularly in the presence of guests and at drinking parties when she felt purposely humiliated. Things came to a head about six months after Svetlana's birth when Nadya took the baby, two-year-old Vasily and their nurse off to her parents in Leningrad. Shortly aferwards a contrite Stalin telephoned from Moscow, asking if he could come to Leningrad and make things up and take them home. 'I'll come back by myself,' replied Nadya with a note of sarcasm in her voice. 'It'll cost the state too much for you to come here!' And so she brought the children home again. But she was far from happy. Indeed she told her sister Anna that she was seriously thinking of leaving Stalin and would like to get a job possibly in Kharkov where Anna and her husband Stanislav Redens were living and Redens was in charge of the local security organisation.[27]

Nadya felt herself to be virtually a prisoner in the Kremlin and she determined to make an attempt to break out. Her chance came in 1929 when there was a great drive on the part of Russian Communist youth to speed the industrialisation of the country through the first of the three Five Year Plans. She asked her husband whether she could enter a technical institute and become qualified in some branch of industrial production. At first Stalin would not hear of it, but eventually he listened to the arguments of Yenukidze and Ordzhonikidze, whose aid she had enlisted, and gave his consent. So she was enrolled in the Industrial Academy in Moscow and began to study the manufacturing processes of synthetic fibres, particularly viscose. Extraordinary precautions were taken not to let anyone in the Academy except the director know that the new student was the wife of the General Secretary of the Party. Pauker, who as chief of the Operations Department of the GPU was responsible for the Stalin family's personal security, detailed two young secret police employees on his master's instructions to attend the academy in the guise of students and submit daily reports about Nadya, whom she talked to and on what topics. Every morning she was brought to the academy by car, but the vehicle would deposit her round the corner in a side street so as not to attract undue attention. Later on, when Nadya was given a Soviet Ford car, she used to drive herself, followed by guards in another car. There was nothing unusual about this, since there were several hundreds of Soviet officials in Moscow at this time who owned these cars.

Nadya was careful to keep her identity secret. At the same time she talked freely with her fellow students and was appalled to learn from them the horrible truth about the mass deportations and shootings in the countryside in the course of the forced collectivisation of the peasants. She was horrified by what she heard about the famine in the Ukraine, particularly about a case of cannibalism related to her by two students who had first-hand knowledge of a terrible case where a dead body had actually been dissected and offered for sale. At first Stalin merely reproached her for 'collecting Trotskyite rumours', but later on, when he heard about the case of cannibalism, he stormed at his wife in the most abusive language, told her she could not go to the Academy any more and instructed Pauker to get the names of her two informants and have them arrested. A purge of colleges and similar institutions followed, particularly of students who had been mobilised into the villages to help with the collectivisation. Meanwhile Nadya was not allowed to return to the Academy, but eventually after two months Yenukidze interceded for her with Stalin and she was allowed to resume her studies provided she kept her mouth shut in future.

They had another quarrel on the eve of their annual summer holiday in 1931 as they were preparing to leave for the Caucasus. The day before they were due to leave, Stalin got angry with her for some reason and they had a violent row. Next day, after dinner, Stalin got up from the table and gave the guards his suitcase and brief-case to carry down to his car which was waiting outside. The heavy luggage had already gone on to the special train which was to take them to Sochi. Then Nadya picked up her hatbox and indicated to the guards two suitcases of her own which she had packed. Stalin looked at her sharply. 'You're not going with me,' he said. 'You're staying here.'

And with that he went out with Pauker to the car, got in and drove away to the station, leaving the stunned Nadya standing there with the hatbox in her hand.[28]

5

For some time there had been rumours in Kremlin circles of Stalin's infidelities, passing affairs with government secretaries and the like, whom he met at drinking parties organised by his boon companion Abel Yenukidze. As early as 1927, Nadya was said to have created a stormy scene and threatened to commit suicide if her husband did not discontinue his liaison with a certain Georgian singer, a Party member who was later got out of the way by being given a job in the Soviet consulate in Kandahar. Another of Stalin's mistresses is said to have been a girl called Yolka Andreyevna, rumoured to have borne Stalin a son whom he later adopted as his own child. It is impossible to state with any certainty what substance there is in these uncorroborated stories. However, it has been established that after the birth of their second child Svetlana, Stalin ceased to share his wife's bed and moved into a small bedroom beside the dining room of the Kremlin apartment. It has also been stated that, after the Georgian singer's departure for Afghanistan, the woman who was the chief cause of their difference was another dark-eyed beauty, the brunette Rosa Kaganovich, sister of the commissar Lazar, with whom Molotov had previously had an affair. At all events, by 1931 Nadya was thoroughly disillusioned with her husband and most unhappy.

According to the notes supposedly made by Litvinov for his diary at this time, a further cause of trouble between husband and wife was provided by a friend of Nadya's named Zoia Mossina, who worked in the confidential code and cipher department of the Commissariat of Foreign Affairs.* If not the actual head of the department, Mossina

* Maxim Litvinov. *Notes for a Journal* (1955). It is questionable how much of this work is by Litvinov and internal evidence suggests that certain passages are spurious. On the other hand, although the authorship may be disputed, it does

was certainly the most important member of it by reason of the fact that she was also the secretary of the Party group or 'cell' within the commissariat. Early in 1931, she fell under suspicion when the GPU representative in London reported evidence of someone in Mossina's department having passed secret information to an agent of the Polish military attaché in Moscow who in turn passed it to the British. As a result, so the story went, the British were able to break the departmental codes and cyphers and for the past few years had been reading all the confidential telegrams which passed between the Foreign Affairs Commissariat and Soviet embassies and consulates abroad. Litvinov considered that it was much more likely that the code had been broken by some old Russian cryptographic expert, since the codes and cyphers apparently had been little changed since Tsarist times, when they had been devised by a government official named Vinogradov who survived the Revolution and who might conceivably have supplied the Poles with the relevant information through his mother who lived in Warsaw and with whom he was known to correspond. However, when asked by Molotov as Chairman of the Council of Commissars whether he could guarantee that Mossina 'did not conceal from the Party' the treachery of one of her staff, Litvinov replied that, although he had no reason to suspect Mossina of such professional disloyalty, he could not give any formal guarantee.

'Therefore you can't vouch for her,' said Molotov. 'I thought as much.' Litvinov repeated that he did not think a guarantee was necessary, since Mossina had been a cell secretary and it was up to the Party's district committee to vouch for her. Molotov insisted that Litvinov should put it in writing that he could not vouch for Mossina and this the Foreign Affairs Commissar somewhat reluctantly agreed to do.

A few days later, Litvinov received an unexpected call in his office from Nadya Alliluyeva. She told him that Mossina had been banished to the Urals and reproached him for his action, adding that she had talked it over with her husband who had said, 'Comrade Litvinov, her immediate superior, has refused to vouch for her, and in these circumstances I cannot interfere.' When Nadya left Litvinov's office she was in tears. 'I had never seen her in such a state,' noted Litvinov. 'She said

<hr />

not necessarily follow that all or any of the statements contained in it are fictitious. Some of them at least are capable of corroboration from other sources. It is possible that the 'journal' is largely if not entirely the work of Gregory Bessedovsky, a Soviet diplomat who defected to the west in 1929, while serving in the Soviet embassy in Paris. See Bertram D. Wolfe. *Strange Communists I Have Known* (1966), pp. 207–222 and B. Souvarine in *Le Contrat Social* (Dec. 1968), p. 265 ff.

that if anything happened to Mossina she wouldn't survive it.'

Shortly afterwards, Nadya told her husband that she was going to the Urals to see Mossina who was living with friends in Perm. Stalin asked her not to go, but Nadya insisted and there was another angry scene. When she arrived in Perm, Nadya found that Mossina was no longer there, having been sent to a strict 'isolator' at Kotlas known as Camp No. 7 which was under Yagoda's personal supervision, since various members of the Opposition were confined there, and to which the GPU head in Perm had no authority to allow her to travel.* Nadya also learned that her friend's life was in danger, as Mossina was likely to be tried on a charge of participating in a conspiracy organised by Kamenev's nephew Rosenfeld, who had been charged with attempting to persuade the Commandant of the Kremlin to arrest the Politburo, including Stalin.

On her return to their villa near Moscow, Nadya began to plead with her husband to intervene on Mossina's behalf. He is stated to have refused categorically, 'declaring that he never interfered in Yagoda's work and that anyway Mossina was a Trotskyite and a traitor'. There was no reason, he said, to use kid gloves with such 'characters'. After a further angry scene, Nadya went out into the woods. When night fell she had not returned and Stalin sent the guards to look for her. She was eventually discovered lying on a rug in some bushes and carried back to the *dacha*. Later the same night she became hysterical and her husband summoned two of the top physicians, Guetier and Pletnev, to her bedside. She refused to submit to any treatment and again said she was going to commit suicide. Stalin thereupon threatened to put her in a clinic for nervous disorders, after which she calmed down when he promised to have Mossina transferred from Camp No. 7 at Kotlas to Camp No. 2 near Sverdlovsk, where the inmates were treated more leniently and had the right to correspond with friends outside. But Nadya did not trust Yagoda and she insisted that Mossina should be allowed to write to her confirming that she had actually been transferred.

In August 1932, Nadya heard from her friend to this effect. It was a brief letter in which Mossina thanked her for her help and added that she was 'pleased with everything' but begged her not to write as she did not want to cause Nadya 'embarrassment and trouble'. A few weeks later, Nadya received a much fuller letter, which had been

* Kotlas was situated a few miles from Solvychegodsk in Vologda Province, to which Stalin had been exiled in 1909. Between Kotlas and the Vorkuta coalmines to the north lay the largest single concentration of forced labour in the Soviet Union, amounting to more than a million prisoners.

smuggled out of the camp through one of the camp guards who was a secret Trotskyite and reached her by the safe hand of a Komsomol youth. Mossina wrote that the first letter had been in substance dictated by the local GPU boss and she was now able to write much more freely about the camp and various mutual friends there. In this second letter Mossina particularly asked Nadya to do everything in her power to save the lives of some forty Komsomols who were accused of conspiracy in Sverdlovsk and were shortly to be tried by a three-man judicial tribunal or *troika* in Moscow.

Nadya did as she was asked, and as a result more and more stormy scenes followed between her and her husband. At the same time she continued to keep up her clandestine correspondence with Mossina. Realising that someone must have been informing his wife of what was going on in the Urals, Stalin ordered an investigation with the object of discovering 'those guilty of revealing important state secrets'. Yagoda acted swiftly and the culprits were speedily identified, including the Trotskyite camp guard and the Komsomol youth. The latter, who had come to Stalin's *dacha* several times with Mossina's letters, returning to Sverdlovsk, with Nadya's replies, is said to have confessed after several interrogations in which he was probably tortured that he intended to kill Stalin if his comrades in the Urals were executed. As a result the *troika* to which the case was referred lost no time in dealing with it. Towards the end of October, death sentences were passed on Mossina, as 'leader of the group', and the Komsomol courier and his comrades as being accomplices. All were immediately shot. Nadya is said to have heard of the executions a few days later from a woman friend, who was a doctor in the Central Committee.

Meanwhile relations between Nadya and her husband rapidly approached breaking point. Stalin told her that she had lost all her old revolutionary ardour, that she had become transformed into a conventional housewife, and that as far as the Revolution was concerned she was just so much 'excess baggage'. What he now needed, he said, was 'someone to rekindle his spirit' and 'revive his will to leadership'.

'Rosa I suppose revives you!' Nadya retorted sarcastically and went on to taunt him with his own revolutionary record. 'I know the kind of leader you are. More than anyone else, I know the kind of revolutionist you are!' She then accused him of usurping the leadership of the Party dishonestly and of involving her in his 'shady schemes'. She was ashamed to look her comrades in the eye, she said, because of his 'blood purges and liquidations', and his brutal behaviour had been repeated in their home.

'You are a tormentor, that's what you are!' she shouted hysterically.

'You torment your own son...you torment your wife...you torment the whole Russian people!'

'Shut up, damn you!' roared Stalin, seizing her by the throat and shaking her vigorously.[29]

6

The fifteenth anniversary of the Bolshevik Revolution was celebrated on 7 November 1932, the date in the western calendar which had been adopted in the Soviet Union. The occasion was marked by a dinner given by Voroshilov at his *dacha* and attended by the leading members of the Government and the Party, including Stalin and his wife. This time they bickered in public. The pretext was trivial enough, but it had a terrible sequel. The glasses had been charged as usual with vodka and wine. After a while Stalin noticed that Nadya was not drinking. This was not surprising, since alcohol disagreed with her and she consequently disliked it: also as will be remembered it had directly led to her original seduction by Stalin, and this psychological factor may have further contributed to her feelings about strong drink. At all events, when Stalin said across the table, 'Hey you, have a drink!' she screamed back at him, 'Don't you dare "hey" me!' With that she got up from her chair and dashed out of the dining room in full view of the other guests.

Stalin made no move to follow her, and apparently the others attached little if any significance to Nadya's outburst except Molotov's wife Polina Zemchuzhina, who was one of Nadya's few intimate friends outside her parents' family. So that Nadya should not be alone, Zemchuzhina immediately left the gathering as well, and went back to the Kremlin with her. Together they walked about inside the Kremlin, until Nadya had calmed down. For a while they talked about the Academy, where Nadya was due to get her diploma in a few weeks' time, and the prospects of finding some rewarding job on the basis of her technical training and qualifications. Then they parted and went their own ways. Nadya returned to her own apartment in the Poteshny Palace and shut herself in her bedroom.

Next morning, according to the story Svetlana afterwards heard from her nurse, the housekeeper rose early as usual and went to call her mistress. What she saw on opening the bedroom door horrified her. She immediately ran to fetch the nurse and together they returned to the bedroom where the scene which met their eyes was to remain indelibly printed on the nurse's memory until she died. Nadya was lying beside her bed in a pool of blood. In her lifeless hand there was a little Walther pistol which her brother Paul had brought her from Berlin.

264

She had evidently shot herself through the head, but the sound of the pistol going off had not been loud enough to wake the rest of the household. The two women then laid Nadya's body on the bed and 'did what they could to make it look better', at the same time cleaning up generally and removing the traces of blood. They then telephoned 'the people who had precedence in their eyes' such as Abel Yenukidze, Zemchuzhina Molotov and the commandant of the Kremlin guard.

According to the story as related to Svetlana by the nurse, Stalin had returned late from the dinner at Voroshilov's and had gone straight to his own room where he fell into a sound sleep. Her account continues:

> Everyone came running. Meantime my father slept on in his little room to the left of the dining room. Molotov and Voroshilov came. They were all in a state of shock. No one could believe it.
>
> Finally my father woke up and came into the dining room. 'Joseph,' they said. 'Nadya is no longer with us.'

Many years later Polina Molotov spoke to Svetlana about the tragedy. 'Your father was rough with her and she had a hard life with him,' said Zemchuzhina. 'Everyone knew that. But they'd spent a good many years together. They had a family, children, a home, and everyone loved Nadya. Who could have thought she'd ever do such a thing? It wasn't a perfect marriage, of course, but then what marriage is?'[30]

The nurse's version, while in the main accurate as far as it goes, does not tell the whole story. For this we must turn to other sources such as Natalia Trushina, who it will be recalled had accompanied Nadya to Moscow as a kind of chaperone when she was working in Lenin's secretariat. After Nadya's marriage, Trushina joined the Stalin household first as domestic help, later becoming governess to the two children and in effect running the household after Nadya had enrolled in the Industrial Academy and was away from home for much of the time. On the night of the tragedy, according to Trushina, there was a ring at the door of the apartment about one o'clock. It turned out to be Nadya and Voroshilov who had apparently found her in the Kremlin grounds and escorted her home. Hastily thanking Voroshilov, and bidding him goodnight, she rushed off to her room, followed by Trushina who found her sitting on the bed, staring blankly into space. 'It's the end, Natalia Konstantinova,' said Nadya, breaking into tears. 'I've reached the limit of my endurance. Until now I've been a sort of wife to him, but not any more. I'm nothing. The only prospect is death. I shall be poisoned or killed in some pre-arranged "accident". Where can I go? What can I do?'

After she had recovered herself a little, she got up and went into the bathroom where she began to undress. Then, for no apparent reason, according to Trushina who was with her, she suddenly fainted. Thoroughly alarmed, Trushina did the first thing that came into her head. She went to the telephone and called Voroshilov's villa and asked that Stalin should return home at once. He arrived about twenty minutes later, flustered and impatient. According to another version, Nadya also telephoned and spoke to her husband at some length, crying, cursing and saying that she had decided to die, 'as she couldn't bear the shame of being responsible for all that was happening near him, with him'. She also told Stalin that Mossina's death had been 'a terrible blow to her, that he knew of it and shouldn't have allowed it to happen'. He tried at first to quieten her and begged her to come out to Zubalovo. Then he said he would come to Moscow himself at once 'to prove to her that there was no other way'. She replied that she could not trust him and that she thought him capable of anything, even of ordering her execution. Then she suddenly exclaimed, 'That's enough, I'm picking up the pistol...I know you are capable of ordering Leon* to send his men here to seize me.'

Precisely what happened next is not clear, since there is a gap in Trushina's story, as afterwards related by her to a fellow prisoner named Elizabeth Lermolo when they were in a 'political isolator' together. But it appears that when Trushina returned to the bathroom, she found Nadya lying on the floor with a large wound in her temple and a blood-stained revolver beside her. She then carried her into her bedroom and bandaged her wound, although Nadya showed no signs of life. Next she went to the telephone and was about to call one of the Kremlin doctors, when Poskrebyshev suddenly appeared and forbade her to use the phone. 'We don't need any doctors,' he told her. 'We'll do without them.'

A few minutes later Voroshilov arrived, followed a little later by a dishevelled looking Molotov and finally by Yenukidze, who appeared drunk and was 'hardly aware of what was going on'. They all repaired to Stalin's room, where at their request Trushina brought them liquor, valerian drops and soda water. Trushina then returned to Nadya's

* L. V. Mekhlis, an important Party functionary and one of Stalin's most trusted lieutenants, having originally belonged to his personal secretariat in which capacity Mekhlis was responsible for the monitoring of telephone conversations in the Kremlin. It was due to an alleged leak in Kremlin security that the details of Nadya's last telephone conversation with her husband are supposed to have become known through the 'tapping' of the line. Mekhlis later became Chief Political Commissar of the Red Army. He died a victim of Stalin's last purge in 1953.

room where she kept vigil by the corpse for the remainder of the night.

Towards dawn Trushina was interrupted by Yenukidze who by this time had sobered up. 'You, it seems, were the only witness to the tragedy. The children didn't hear anything?'

Trushina shook her head.

'Good,' said Yenukidze. 'It is necessary, Natasha, that no one should know about this. Let Vasya and Svetlana think that their mother died naturally.' He then asked her to help him with the body.

Together they set to work with water, scissors, comb, cold cream and face powder, making up Nadya's face, rearranging her hair to conceal the wound, and trying to make her appearance look as natural as possible. When they had finished, Yenukidze suggested that she go to her room and rest.

A couple of hours later, he came to her again, having no doubt received instructions from Stalin in the meantime. He again stressed the importance of secrecy and suggested a change of scene – 'a few days rest in some quiet spot'. And she had better go before the children were up. 'Be ready in five minutes,' he told her, 'and I'll bring the car round. Take things to last you for two or three days and later I'll bring you anything you need.'

Natalia did as she was told and a few minutes later she was on her way, never again to return to the Kremlin. After a short stay in a monastery cell, she was taken to an 'isolator'.[31]

Meanwhile Nadya's remains were placed in an open coffin, which was taken to the Hall of Columns in Trade Union House where Lenin's body had lain in state and where the traditional ceremony of 'leave taking' was now observed. This was when Nadya's friends and relations filed past and paid their last respects to the dead woman. Young Svetlana was led up to the coffin by Odzhonikidze and told to 'say goodbye'. But the child drew back with a frightened cry and was removed to an adjoining room where Yenukidze took her on his knee and gave her some fruit to eat. (She did not go to the funeral, but her brother apparently went.) Later she learned that her father had reacted angrily when he approached the open coffin. Apparently the reason was that Nadya had left him a letter which she had written the night she died.

Needless to say, I've never seen it, [Sevetlana afterwards recalled.] Very likely it was destroyed right away, but people who saw it have told me of its existence. It was a terrible letter, full of reproaches and accusations. It wasn't purely personal; it was partly political as well. After reading it, it would have been impossible for my father to think that my mother had been on his side only outwardly, but that in her heart she had been on the side of those who were in political opposition to him.

He was shocked and incensed. After the civil leave taking ceremony he went up to the coffin for a moment. Suddenly he pushed it away from him, turned on his heel and left.[32]

According to one witness who was present when Stalin arrived in the Hall of Columns with Voroshilov and Molotov, Stalin leaned over the bier and kissed his dead wife on the face. The coffin lid was then said to have been nailed down so that he remains were not seen by any members of the general public when they were admitted. No reason for her death was given in the Soviet press apart from a brief statement that she had died 'suddenly and prematurely.'

The statement about the letter was confirmed by others at the time. Those to whom Stalin showed it are said to have included Kirov, in addition to Voroshilov and Molotov. Stalin was also reported to be seen reading it again and again in his office in the Central Committee headquarters in Old Square and always to keep it in his pocket. Although Svetlana says nothing about it in her memoirs, there is an unconfirmed story that her mother also left a letter for her. The letter, in which 'Alliluyeva is said to have told her daughter that she hated her father' and 'that he was guilty of exterminating the best resolutionaries in the USSR', is supposed to have been stolen by someone during the confusion in the apartment after Nadya's body had been found. At the same time one of the Kremlin physicians called in to certify her death, although pledged to secrecy, is said to have talked. Both he and the man who stole the letter were supposedly detected and shot without more ado, as also was the GPU official who had listened in to Nadya's telephone conversation and had subsequently talked with the result that the details of what he had heard leaked out.

Nadya had also written without reserve to her friend Zoia Mossina, when the latter was in the labour camp in the Urals. Stalin accordingly dispatched Yagoda to the Urals to collect her letters, and when Yagoda returned to Moscow and handed them over Stalin was said to have been very much surprised at their contents, which included references to drunkenness and the 'moral distintegration of the higher Party hierarchy'. Particularly singled out for censure was Yan Rudzatak, the Chairman of the Central Control Commission and until recently a member of the Politburo. He was said to have indulged in disgusting orgies with girls at one of the Government villas which had been 'the talk of all Moscow'. The erring Rudzatak was no longer invited to attend meetings of the Politburo which apparently he had been *ex officio* in the habit of doing; at the same time a special bureau, attached to the Central Control Commission, was set up 'to receive and examine complaints against high officials of the Party'.

It was announced that Nadehzda Stalina would be buried in the Novedevichy cemetery, an ancient burial place belonging to a disused convent in a suburb of Moscow, where many of the old Russian nobility were buried including the first wife of Peter the Great, as well as various well-known musicians and writers such as Scriabin, Rimsky-Korsakov, Pisemsky and Chekhov. This announcemnt caused considerable surprise since there was a long established tradition that Party members were cremated in Moscow, and as a good Communist it was expected that the remains of the General Secretary's wife would be disposed of in this manner and that the urn containing her ashes would be placed alongside those of other prominent Bolsheviks in the Kremlin wall. When it also became known that she was to be interred beside the graves of Yoffe and Lutovinov, who had both committed suicide, this was taken to be an admission on Stalin's part that his wife had also taken her own life. However, it seems that the request of Nadya to be buried in the Novodevichy cemetery without being previously cremated was made by her parents when they arrived from Leningrad for the funeral. Yenukidze is said to have made the request on behalf of the Alliluyevs to Stalin who hesitated for a few moments and then nodded his assent.[33]

The security arrangements for the funeral were difficult, since Stalin said he would follow the bier on foot from the Kremlin to the cemetery, a distance of about four-and-a-half miles. Yagoda, who had virtually superseded Menzhinsky as head of the GPU, did his best to dissuade Stalin from his purpose, pointing out what an easy target he would make for an assassin with a rifle concealed in a front room in any of the houses along the route. But Stalin insisted, partly no doubt from motives of remorse for having driven his wife to commit suicide and partly to emphasise his devotion to her memory and hopefully to counteract any rumours – and there were rumours – that he had actually killed her with his own hand. As a result extraordinary precautions were taken. Besides lining the route with security police stationed every few yards, the front rooms of all the houses in the narrow streets through which the procession was to pass were cleared by GPU men and the tenants ordered into the back rooms where they were kept until the procession had gone by.[34]

At 2.35 in the afternoon of 11 November 1932, to the strains of a funeral march, the coffin was carried into the Red Square by Yenu-kidze, Molotov, Kaganovich and others, followed by Stalin and various members of the Alliluyev family. It had begun to snow as the procession moved off. But Stalin did not stay for long. After about ten minutes, he and Pauker, his chief bodyguard, got into a waiting car and drove by a circuitous road to the cemetery, where they waited for the procession to arrive. There was no religious service and the coffin was quickly lowered into the open grave. Brief speeches were delivered by Kaganovich on behalf of the Russian Communist Party and Professor Kalashnikov on behalf of the staff and students of the Industrial Academy, in which the unfortunate Nadezhda Sergeievna was characterised as 'the daughter of a worker revolutionary, a most devoted party member and a splendid responsive comrade'.[35]

Next day, the government newspaper *Izvestia* published a memorial tribute in verse by the poet Damyan Bedny, somewhat surprisingly in view of the fact that Bedny had recently been rebuked by Stalin for 'slandering' and 'discrediting' the Soviet people in a skit on 'short-comings in the manner and conditions of life in the USSR'. Stalin, who had remained silent at the graveside, contented himself with inserting a laconic notice in *Pravda* conveying 'my sincere thanks to the organisations, institutions, comrades and friends who have expressed their condolences on the occasion of the passing away of my beloved friend and comrade, Nadezhda Sergeievna Alliluyeva-Stalina'.[36] Later he had a fine marble headstone erected over the grave, surmounted by a sculptured likeness of Nadya, her chin resting reflectively on her left hand. Besides recording the dates of her birth and death, less than two months after her thirtieth birthday, the inscription on the tomb simply described her by name as a 'member of the Bolshevik Party'.

There were widespread rumours at the time that Stalin had killed his wife. But even if it was her finger which pulled the trigger and fired the fatal shot – and there is virtually no doubt about this – it was her husband's inconsiderate and at times downright unkind and even brutal behaviour that had driven her to take this desperate step. Apparently he experienced prolonged fits of remorse and tried to persuade both himself and others in his intimate circle that the tragedy was not his fault. Not long before she died he had seen her reading the fashionable English novel *The Green Hat* by Michael Arlen, an Armenian whose real name was Dikran Kouyoumdjian, and he would denounce 'that vile book' which he felt had had 'an important effect on her'. He kept wondering 'who had put her up to it', and alternately blamed her close friend Zemchuzhina Molotov, her sister Anna Redens and her brother Paul Alliluyev who had given her the tiny pistol with which she had ended her life.[37] For many years, indeed until nearly the end of his own life, Stalin used to visit the grave in the Novodevichy cemetery and gaze at the sculptured head above, while surrounded by armed guards who would first subject the cemetery to an intensive search and turn out all the other visitors; if he came at night, which he sometimes did, the tomb would be specially flood-lit for him. But he continued to nurse a grudge against Nadya's family whom he considered really responsible for her death, as well as against Nadya's memory. It was only in his very last years that he spoke 'more gently' about her to his daughter Svetlana. ('He even seemed to pity her and no longer blamed her for what she had done.') But by then it was much too late.

Letter from Stalin to his "little sparrow" Svetlana, thanking her for sending him some fish and asking her not to send any more.
"If you like it so much in the Crimea, you may stay at Mukhalatka all summer.
Here's a big kiss for you.
Your Paposchka"
7/VII 38.

CHAPTER VII

The First Five Year Plan

I

The first of the Five Year Plans conceived by Stalin for the industrial-isation of Soviet Russia covered the years 1928–1932, during which period enormous sums of money were diverted to the construction of heavy industry, particularly iron and steel, and also to the production of agricultural machinery as part of the farm collectivisation policy. 'We are fifty or a hundred years behind the advanced countries,' said Stalin. 'We must make good this lag in ten years. Either we do it or we go under.'[1] Belts were tightened hard and labour ruthlessly conscripted as in the Civil War, and in this Stalin succeeded in firing the imagina-tion of the younger generation of Communists who cherished the dream of Russia becoming a kind of socialist America. They felt, or were made by propaganda to feel, that they were at action stations fighting to raise the country from a state of poverty and degradation to one of happiness and material wealth. Food rations which had been increased in the middle 1920s were now reduced to near starvation limits, while the Government exported grain and other commodities in order to pay for imported machinery and the services of foreign technical experts.

Efforts to meet the target were hampered by the general slump and collapse of world markets in 1929 which meant that Russian exports could not command previously anticipated prices. The most drastic steps were resorted to in order to obtain vital foreign currency or *valuta*. In this context Stalin suspected, with some justification, that gold and silver trinkets, jewellery and the like, the equivalent of *valuta*, were being hoarded in the towns and villages and countryside. He accordingly instructed the GPU to conduct nation-wide searches for this valuable commodity and to go to the utmost lengths including torture to obtain it. The favourite methods employed by the GPU for extracting *valuta* to be developed with subtle refinements during the subsequent Great Purge, were known as the '*parilka*' and the 'conveyor'.

The '*parilka*' or 'sweat room' was a heated room in which most of the ventilation had been shut off and into which a hundred or more '*valuta* suspects' might be squeezed regardless of their sex. There was no space in which to squat let alone lie down, and soon each wretched inmate would be gasping for breath and near to if not actually suffocating. The stench was indescribable, since there were no toilet facilities and as often as not the room was infested with lice and other vermin. From time to time suspects who were often kept for days on end in these foul conditions would be removed to undergo the ordeal of the 'conveyor'. The victims would be interrogated by relays of questioners in different rooms, being forced to go from one to the other at the double, beaten, kicked and cursed on their way until they fainted from exhaustion or until they disclosed the whereabouts of their hidden treasure. The interrogators would also find out whether the suspect had any relatives in America and in this event he or she would be forced to write an 'extortion letter' asking for dollars, which would of course be confiscated as soon as the gift arrived.

Eugene Lyons, the United Press Moscow correspondent, whose interview with Stalin has been quoted, could never drive out of his mind the gnawing awareness of the '*valuta* tortures' as long as he was in the Soviet Union. 'They remained in the background of my consciousness to cast their shadow on the industrial triumphs about which I wrote every day,' he admitted when he returned to America. 'The thought that only a few blocks away, on Lubyanka Square, men were gasping in the *parilka* or staggering on the conveyor was under the surface of my mind: the counterweight to all the boasts and promises and revolutionary pretensions that filled the press, the billboards, the speeches and the plans.'[2]

Nevertheless, very considerable amounts of gold and silver and other precious family mementoes were obtained in this way and turned into cash.

Stalin pushed through the First Five Year Plan at the expense of unbelievable human suffering. Thousands died in the streets or dropped dead at work from dysentery, typhus, under-nourishment and sheer starvation. In the country the mortality was even higher, since the *kulaks* fought a bitter struggle against collectivisation, sabotaging the agricultural machinery which had been sent to the collective farms and refusing to co-operate with the specialists who had been sent to instruct them in the new methods. The *kulaks* went so far as to slaughter their cattle and burn their grain rather than surrender them to the State. The result was that millions of acres went to waste with consequent famine in much of the country. Other peasants simply could not or would not use tractors. Years later, when they met in the Kremlin during the Second World War, Churchill questioned Stalin about his collective farm policy. Stalin admitted that it was 'fearful' and 'a terrible struggle'.

'It was absolutely necessary for Russia, if we were to avoid periodic famines, to plough the land with tractors,' said Stalin, stressing the necessity to mechanise Russian agriculture. 'When we gave tractors to the peasants they were all spoiled in a few months. Only collective farms with workshops could handle tractors. We took the greatest trouble to explain it to the peasants. It was no use arguing with them. After you have said all you can to a peasant he says he must go home and consult his wife.' He also had to consult his herdsman. 'After he has talked it over with them he always answers that he does not want the collective farm and he would rather do without the tractors.'

'These were what you call *kulaks*?' queried Churchill.

'Yes,' Stalin agreed. Then he added, after a pause, 'It was all very bad and difficult – but necessary.'

Pressed by Churchill for details, Stalin admitted that 'some of them agreed to come in with us'. On the other hand, many were forcibly deported to cultivate land in Siberia, 'in the province of Tomsk or the province of Irkutsk or further north'. Others, it may be added, were treated like common criminals, being set to work to build roads, railways and canals in forced labour conditions where the wastage of human life was terribly high. But 'the great bulk' – upwards of ten millions, according to Stalin – were 'very unpopular' and were consequently 'wiped out by their labourers'.[3]

By the spring of 1930 Stalin realised that the collectivisation drive in the countryside had gone too far as well as too quickly. In a much publicised article entitled 'Dizzy with Success', which appeared in *Pravda* over his signature, he put the blame for what had happened on over-zealous officials, who had upset the collective-farm peasants by 'socialising' their dwelling houses, dairy cattle, and small livestock and poultry, when the grain problem was still unsolved. With heavy sarcasm he castigated these 'revolutionaries' who were accustomed to begin their work of organising a local *kolkhoz* by removing the bells from the churches. 'Just imagine removing the church bells – how revolutionary!'[4]

In thus applying the brake to further collectivisation, Stalin acted entirely on his own account without apparently consulting either the Politburo or the Central Committee. His pose as the 'good' ruler misled by 'bad' advisers provoked a protest from the Central Committee, whereupon Stalin issued another statement claiming that this had been the Committee's decision all along. 'Everyone knows of the muddle which resulted in those areas less prepared for the *kolkhoz* movement, and which had to be straightened out by the interference of the Central Committee.'[5] Consequently, during the next three years, only ten per cent more of all farms in the country were collectivised, making an aggregate of three-fifths of the total holdings by the end of the First Five Year Plan. At the same time the essential character of the *kolkhoz* was changed, it being made clear that it was a co-operative venture rather than a commune, and its members were allowed to own small plots of land together with poultry and some cattle. As an old Ukrainian peasant put it to Isaac Deutscher: 'Things were very bad in our collective farm, but have been easier since Stalin got over his dizziness from success.' Thus the authorities were enabled to proceed more slowly and eventually under the Second Five Year Plan, which began in 1933, to collectivise virtually all the remaining two-fifths of the holdings without provoking more bitter resistance on the part of the peasants.[6]

In the new factories and construction projects the combination of ignorance and red tape resulted in many machines breaking down, a phenomenon sometimes mistaken for deliberate industrial sabotage. This was the opinion of an American construction engineer at a big new steel plant:

> No pride in work. No incentive. Takes six to ten men for one man's work. No mechanical aptitude. Mental apathy. Great planners but small accomplishment. No resourcefulness. Initiative? The Russian can think of more new ways of doing things wrong than I thought possible. He has wonderful, fanciful ideas, but nothing practical.

The Russian technical director of a copper mining and smelting works, who had been trained in Tsarist times, told another American engineer that he had to attend six to ten workers' meetings daily, which burdened him with administrative work as well as his technical job. 'It may be that a group of labourers wants to pool their wages for two weeks; or a woman has become pregnant and needs his signature on a permit to lay off for three months; or someone's boots need repairing; or a food card must be revised so that the holder can obtain more provisions.' This particular director had between four and five thousand workers under him. His wife, whom the American engineer met at a dinner at their home one evening, was a highly cultured woman from an old aristocratic family. When the American asked her whether she did not long for the old times, she replied that all she ever thought of was to hope and pray, when her husband left home in the morning, that he would return safely at night, 'for so many of the technicals had been disappearing'.[7]

Considerable numbers of technical experts were arrested at this time on seemingly fantastic charges of 'wrecking activities', tried in secret and executed, sometimes indeed shot without any trial. In 1930, for instance, a group of prominent bacteriologists were accused of having organised an epidemic among horses. Later the same year forty-eight food officials headed by a distinguished professor were shot without trial for allegedly sabotaging food supplies. Thirty-five prominent officials in the Commissariat of Agriculture, including the Deputy-Commissar whose name was Konar, were likewise executed for having 'allowed weeds to grow in the fields', as well as on charges of economic espionage. (In this case the allegation that Konar was employed by the Polish Intelligence service was true. His real name was Poleschuk and he was sent to Moscow from Warsaw with a communist party card belonging to a Red Army man killed in action, subsequently rising to the high post which he filled at the time of his accidental exposure by someone who knew the genuine Konar.)[8] At the same time there was a number of 'show trials' of alleged saboteurs and machine wreckers specially staged for propaganda purposes by order of Stalin and the Politburo.

The first of these dismal court room spectacles, which was to serve as the pattern for the big purge trials of the later 1930s, became known as the Shakhty affair. Fifty Russian and three German engineers from the coal mines at Shakhty in the northern Caucasus were tried on charges of sabotage and espionage in the imposing Hall of Columns of Trade Union House in Moscow, where the crowds had filed past the remains of Lenin as well as those of Stalin's wife. The affair was sparked off by the local GPU representative, Efim Evdokimov, a common criminal who had been freed from jail by the Revolution, joined the Communist Party and had ingratiated himself with Stalin during the Civil War; it is said they used to go on holidays together. Evdokimov produced some letters which he said were in code and implicated the engineers. The key to the code, Evdokimov added, was in the possession of the addressees. But Menzhinsky, to whom he reported the matter in the first instance, told him that he was not satisfied unless Evdokimov could produce a better case, since the proposal to liquidate a number of skilled engineers without cause was indeed tantamount to sabotaging the economy. Evdokimov then went to Stalin and asked him to apply pressure on Menzhinsky through Rykov, who was still Chairman of the Council of People's Commissars.

'Nonsense,' said Stalin, 'go back to the North Caucasus and immediately adopt whatever measures you consider necessary. From now on send all your information to me only, and we will take care of Comrade Menzhinsky ourselves.'

Evdokimov thereupon returned to Tostov, the capital of the district in which Shakhty was located. The engineers were accordingly thrown into jail and during the year they were kept there before being brought to trial Evdokimov and his team of interrogators led by his assistant D. I. Kursky worked hard by the well tried methods of the GPU to obtain a 'sincere confession' from the accused. This was the kind of evidence Stalin required to make the case of one of importance at state level.[9]

What it was hoped to prove was foreshadowed in a speech by the General Secretary to a joint plenary meeting of the Central Committee and the Central Control Commission shortly before the trial opened. The speech was subsequently printed in *Pravda* for the information of the Party and the country.

The facts show that the Shakhty affair was an economic counter-revolution, plotted by a section of the bourgeois experts, former coal owners. The facts show further that these experts were banded together in a secret group and were receiving money for sabotage purposes from former owners now living abroad and from counter-revolutionary anti-Soviet capitalist organisations in the West. The facts show lastly that this group of bourgeois experts operated and wrought destruction to our industry on orders from capitalist organisations in the West...

We have internal enemies. We have external enemies. This, comrades, must not be forgotten for a single moment...We have the Shakhty affair, which is already being liquidated and undoubtedly will be liquidated. The Shakhty affair marks another serious attack on the Soviet regime launched by international capital and its agents in our country. It is economic intervention in our internal affairs.[10]

Stalin and indeed the whole of the Politburo at this time were convinced that, just as the capitalist powers had combined to launch a military intervention during the post-Revolution period of civil war, so now they were continuing their anti-Soviet machinations by concerted plans to disrupt the economy through the promotion of industrial espionage and sabotage. The extent of this conspiracy, they felt, must be brought home to the outside world by the use of the criminal trial as a political weapon. Hence the 'liquidation' of the Shakhty affair in the interrogation rooms of the Lubyanka and the Hall of Columns in Trade Union House. It hardly turned out to be the success that Stalin hoped, certainly not in foreign countries where few believed in the story of 'far reaching international intrigue' put forward by the prosecution, although as an exercise *pour encourager les autres* on the domestic front it doubtless had the desired effect in some degree.

Vyshinsky was the presiding judge in the Shakhty trial and Krylenko prosecuted the fifty-three defendants. There were some bizarre incidents in the court room, where the handpicked audience of factory and farm workers was changed each day and foreign journalists jostled with the official censors to file their stories. There was no lack of action in court, grim as the implications were, mostly centering on the repeated admission and retraction of confessions. One of the accused, whose name was Nekrassov, went mad during the proceedings, his counsel explaining to the court next day that he was suffering from 'hallucinations' and had had to be confined in a padded cell where he screamed about rifles pointed at his heart. The prisoner Bibenko said he had been 'driven to distraction by threats' and had signed a confession, which was really 'a pack of lies', but a few minutes later, under the chief prosecutor's withering gaze, he denied that he had been either intimidated or threatened.

Skorutto, another of the accused, said he had written out a confession of guilt the previous night implicating himself and various co-defendants. Suddenly a woman's voice was heard from the back of the hall. 'Kolya, Kolya darling, don't lie! Don't! You know you're innocent!' The effect on the wretched Skorutto of his wife's outburst was such that he collapsed on the floor, weeping and writhing and beating his breast. The judge adjourned the session for ten minutes. When the court reconvened, Vyshinsky asked the prisoner why he had confessed. 'I hoped the court would be more lenient with me if I pleaded guilty and accused the others,' Skorutto blurted out.

The following morning Skorutto once more stepped into the limelight. He spoke in a monotone, like a dead man from the

278

grave. The confession was true, he now declared, and its retraction a lie. It was the agonised cry of his wife which yesterday had broken his determination to attest his guilt – and the guilt of those he had implicated.

One of the prisoners whose name was Kolodoob was denounced by his brother and also by his twelve-year-old son, whose astonishing repudiation was later published in *Pravda*. His father, said the boy, was 'a whole-hearted traitor and enemy of the working class'. Consequently young Kolodoob demanded that he should be shot. 'I reject him and the name he bears,' he added. 'Henceforth I shall no longer call myself Kolodoob but Shakhtin.'

It was a foregone conclusion that all the Russian prisoners would be convicted. Most of them cut a sorry spectacle in court, and many of them repeated their confessions of guilt in their 'last word', the traditional privilege of every accused to address the court by way of mitigation. Two dignified exceptions were elderly Jews named Imineetov and Rabinovich. 'One day another Zola will arise,' said Imineetov, 'and will write another *J'Accuse* to restore our names to honour.' Rabinovich, a leading coal mining engineer whose expertise had been acknowledged by Lenin, declared that he had a clear conscience and had nothing to fear, although Krylenko demanded the death penalty for him. (In fact he got six years.) Eleven of the prisoners were sentenced to death, but of these six were reprieved for their 'services in elucidating the facts', in other words for their confessions incriminating their co-defendants. Of the remainder, thirty-eight of the Russians received sentences varying from one to ten years. One of the Germans was acquitted and two got suspended sentences which amounted to the same thing. Five Russians were executed.[11]

The impression gained by at least one foreign news correspondent who covered the Shakhty trial, and the persecution of the technical intelligentsia which it initiated and symbolised, was that it was as much a blunder as a tragedy. Few people outside the Soviet Union believed the charges, particularly the picture of an international plot concerted by former Russian industrialists who had fled abroad. From the point of view of the stage managers of the degrading exhibition, the performance could hardly be called a success. For one thing, there were too many defendants, while the confusing multiplicity of confessions, their subsequent retractions and later confirmations did not enhance the credibility of the prosecution's case in the eyes of the outside world.

Stalin let it be known to those responsible for the conduct of the trial that they must do better next time.

2

The first of the new style political trials which marked Stalin's long reign was staged late in 1930, shortly after the Sixteenth Party Congress at which the General Secretary had issued a stern warning to Rykov, Tomsky, Uglanov and others of the Right opposition, who had recanted and been taken back into the Party fold but had recently shown signs of backsliding, that if they did not mend their ways and break once and for all with their past, they would have nobody but themselves to blame for the consequences.[12]

There were really three interconnected cases, of which only two were the subject of public trial. The first was the so-called Industrial Party case, in which the principal defendant was Professor Leonid Ramzin, the country's leading authority on thermodynamics and an Old Bolshevik who was supposed to have fallen into bad company and become a wrecker. His 'party' was alleged to have more than two thousand members, but only eight including the Professor appeared in the dock; they were mostly high officials in the State Planning Commission (Gosplan), which was headed by the Stalinist Kuibyshev. It was suggested that the ringleaders had taken advantage of their trips abroad on technical missions to make contact with a variety of capitalist enemies of the Soviet state, including Lawrence of Arabia, the oil magnate Sir Henry Deterding and President Poincaré of France and the French General Staff, to undermine Soviet industry and wreck the Five Year Plan. There was the usual hysterical press campaign, masses of workers marched through the snow to Trade Union House carrying banners with such slogans as 'Death to the Agents of Imperialism!' 'Kill the Wreckers!' and 'No Mercy to these Class Enemies!' One piece of stage business repeated from the Shakhty trial was the demand by the son of one of the defendants, whose name was Xenophon Sitnin, that his father should be shot immediately. 'My father is to me a class enemy, nothing more,' proclaimed young Sitnin in words splashed across the press as an example to Soviet youth.[13]

The British Ambassador, Sir Esmond Ovey, who had deputed a member of his staff to attend the trial, passed some revealing comments on the proceedings to Mr Arthur Henderson, the Foreign Secretary in the then Labour Government in Britain.

It is difficult to report with any degree of impartiality on the trial. It is not a trial at all in the Anglo-Saxon sense of the word.

It is definitely a demonstration. The accused, who have theoretically nothing to look forward to but the certainty of being executed, appear on terms of pleasant and entirely courteous intimacy with the judges, and even with the Public Prosecutor. They evidently take the greatest pains to omit no detail in their self-accusatory statements, and, in rare cases of forgetfulness, their attention is called to their lapse by the prosecuting counsel in a manner reminiscent of a schoolmaster showing off the skill of a favourite pupil. By this attitude they lose any sympathy that might accrue to a fanatic stoutly and loyally defending a lost cause.

Krylenko [the Public Prosecutor] smokes cigarettes, as do the accused. No specially distinguishing costume is worn by the judges, or by anybody else in court. Space in the hall is set aside for various organisations, including the press and the Diplomatic Corps, as if for a gala performance. Gentlemen from the Protocol Department attend the sessions to show the diplomats to their seats, tend to their wants and explain any obscure point of procedure as might be done in the case of an official bullfight.

One asks oneself what is the probable effect of this procedure on the accuracy of the statements made. Probably it is immaterial. The suggestion that the accused have been tortured is presumably quite untrue. They appear well-fed, calm, and self-possessed. The idea of torture, of course, easily suggests itself, as the very name of the Lubyanka prison, from which they are daily brought, is fraught with horror. In this connection, a statement by [the defendant] Feodotov indignantly denying any maltreatment produced the only 'laugh' of the proceedings, the emphasis with which he made his assertion being such that the implied suggestion that the GPU prison was a positive health resort was too much even for the most fanatic adherent of the communist dictatorship. The house is said to have laughed for nearly two minutes.

If torture has not been applied, what method of coercion or persuasion has been used to produce the desired result? Personally, I adhere to the theory of economy of effort on the part of the GPU. The GPU well know that no Russian – with the exception perhaps of the fanatics on the Communist side – will fail to betray his colleagues when interrogated separately, and, as each of the arrested is fully aware of this inherent weakness among the others, the evidence flows like a stream and frequently takes the form of reporting rather what others said than what the accused said himself.[14]

All the defendants made abject confessions of guilt and begged for mercy. This time there were no retractions, a tribute to the increased efficiency of the GPU 'investigators'. The men in the dock behaved just as Stalin wished. 'This is my last public lecture in fifteen years,' said Professor Ramzin. 'Two paths were open to us after the Revolution – one that led to the Kremlin, the other to Paris. We chose Paris and this is where it led us...We came to court not to defend ourselves but to capitulate. I am happy I confessed. My soul is quieter.'

Nevertheless, the evidence given by Ramzin and the others, in which they did everything that was required of them, did not bear critical examination, although the Soviet public had no means of knowing this. For instance, at the time the Professor was supposed to have talked to Lawrence of Arabia in London, Lawrence was not even in England. Again, the two Russian emigré capitalists, Riabushinsky and Vishnegradsky, from whom Ramzin was supposed to have received 'wrecking' instructions, could not possibly have acted as alleged by the Public Prosecutor, since they had both been dead for some years. Incidentally, Vishnegradsky, who had been Minister of Finance in Tsarist times, was supposed to have been earmarked for the same office in the new government envisaged by the Industrial Party, in the event of an economic crash 'raising the question of a successor to Stalin'.

Five of the defendants including Ramzin and Feodotov were condemned to death, but two days later the sentences were commuted to ten years imprisonment. Before long Ramzin and the others were released and back at work, lecturing to technical classes. Their 'last words' in the Hall of Columns had not been their last lectures after all.

Among the prosecution witnesses were various members of the 'Labouring Peasants Party', consisting mainly of agricutural economists and led by Professor Kondratiev, a leading statistician. They were accused of having illegally resurrected the old Social-Revolutionary Party and to have plotted to have put the *kulaks* in power. It was expected that they would be the next to be publicly tried. But something went wrong, exactly what is unclear. For some reason it was not considered that they would make satisfactory defendants in public. They simply disappeared, no doubt 'liquidated administratively', to use the Soviet euphemism, as indeed were forty-eight senior Gosplan official who were similarly dealt with instead of being brought to trials with their colleagues in the 'Industrial Party'. One of those involved in the Labouring Peasants case, an engineer named Palchinsky, is said to have died during the preliminary investigation, and it may have been the inability to produce this key witness in court which determined the authorities to dispose of the others in secret.[15]

The third trial, which took place in March 1931, was that of a group of prominent Menshevik economists and other specialists, including the historian Sukhanov, whose memoirs of the Revolution had been much praised by Lenin. They were charged with conspiring to overthrow the Government, in other words to unseat Stalin. The alleged Menshevik plot turned on a secret visit to Russia supposed to have been made in 1928 by the Menshevik emigré Rafael Abramovich, one of the leaders of the Second International, and all the defendants dutifully 'confessed' to meetings and discussions in detail, some doing so in consideration of a promise made to them by the GPU that they would be secretly released and rewarded for their 'co-operation'. Here again the evidence was patently unconvincing, since at the time of Abramovich's alleged visit to Russia he was attending the International Socialist Congress in Brussels. Needless to add, the promises of favoured treatment were not kept. Sukhanov is said to have revealed the duplicity practised on him to his fellow prisoners when serving his sentence and to have gone on a series of protest hunger strikes. Nothing more was heard of this distinguished revolutionary writer after 1934, and it is safe to assume that he died in prison, probably 'liquidated'. At all events, he paid with his life for having described Stalin during the October Revolution as a 'grey blur'.

Another charge widely exploited against the technical specialists in the Mensheviks' trial was that, if they were not conscious saboteurs, they had underrated the limited potential of the Soviet industrial and party workers in their forecasts of the actual fulfilment of the Five Year Plan. Here again the charge was disproved by the facts, although the defendants confessed in court that 'much higher figures could and should have been fixed'. In fact the defendants were subsequently shown to have been remarkably accurate in their forecasts. In steel, for example, they were accused of having mischievously estimated the production for 1932 at only 5.8 million tons. The actual production was 5.9 millions. Similarly with pig iron. The Plan demanded 17 million tons, but the specialists had estimated a mere 7 millions. In fact their estimate was slightly on the optimistic side, the actual production being 6.1 millions.[16]

When he came to study the details of the Mensheviks' trial, Stalin did not feel altogether comfortable. The most he could say for it, as he told a conference of business executives shortly afterwards, was that 'the conduct of the active wreckers at the famous trial in Moscow was bound to discredit, and actually did discredit, the idea of wrecking'. He now affected to recognise that many of the old technical intelligentsia who had formerly sympathised with the wreckers had come over to the side of the Soviet regime. 'This, of course, does not mean that there are no longer any wreckers in the country,' he added. 'Wreckers exist and will continue to exist as long as we have classes and as long as capitalist encirclement exists.' But he thought the 'active' wreckers were now few in number and isolated and would have to go 'deeply underground for the time being'. Consequently he felt there should be a change in attitude towards the 'old technical intelligentsia'.

> It would be stupid and unwise to regard practically every expert and engineer of the old school as an undetected criminal and wrecker. We have always regarded and still regard 'expert baiting' as a harmful and disgraceful phenomenon.
>
> Hence the task is to change our attitude towards the engineers and technicians of the old school, to show them greater attention and solicitude, to enlist their co-operation more boldly.[17]

Although trials of alleged saboteurs and wreckers continued to be held in secret during the next two years, often followed by executions of those adjudged guilty, it was not until the spring of 1933 that Stalin agreed to the staging of another public show trial. While the charges were equally fantastic, this exhibition attracted more attention outside Russia than any of the other public trials at this period principally because six of the defendants were British engineers employed by the internationally known Metropolitan-Vickers Electrical Company on construction projects in the USSR. The idea that carefully selected and trained employees of a concern, which possessed such a great reputation for engineering skill and craftsmanship as Metro-Vickers and in addition had long-time business connections with Russia, should have conspired to wreck the machinery which they had been engaged to install in various Soviet electric power stations appeared generally ludicrous to the outside world. And so indeed it was in spite of the usual confessions induced by the already familiar GPU methods. The main pretext of the trial seems to have been the desire to find a scapegoat for the shortcomings in the fulfilment of the First Five Year Plan which was due for completion at the end of 1932. In reviewing the record of the Plan before the Central Committee in January 1933, Stalin gave warning that the 'have beens' in the persons of members of the old nobility, priests, *kulaks*, former Tsarist gendarmes, White guardists and the like had reared their heads again and were doing as much mischief as they could on the sly.

They set fire to warehouses and wreck machinery. They organise sabotage. They organise wrecking activities in the collective farms and state farms, and some of them including certain professors, go to such lengths in their passion for wrecking as to inject plague and anthrax germs into the cattle on the collective farms and state farms, help to spread meningitis among horses, etc.[18]

Stalin's concluding admonition that 'revolutionary vigilance is the quality that Bolsheviks especially need at the present time' was regarded as a challenge by the GPU. Hence the discovery of a new capitalist plot, this time inspired by the British.

But Stalin had misjudged the British mood in their own country. When it was learned that six British engineers, including Alan Monkhouse, the Metro-Vickers company's chief engineer in the Soviet Union, and Leslie Thornton, the head of the company's erection and maintenance staff, had been arrested on the night of 11 March 1933, together with five Russians, the British government's reaction was swift. The Anglo-Soviet commercial agreement was due to expire shortly and it was immediately conveyed to the Soviet authorities that, unless a satisfactory explanation for the arrests of the six British subjects was forthcoming, not only would the agreement not be renewed, but diplomatic relations would be broken off and a trade embargo imposed. Stalin immediately backtracked. Five of the six Metro-Vickers engineers were released on bail, an unheard of concession to any Soviet citizens accused of such a political crime, and orders were given to speed up the public hearing of the case. The preliminary investigation did not proceed as smoothly as the Russian authorities wished. Thornton, for instance, signed a confession under great pressure of lengthy interrogation, and he was subsequently to repudiate this confession in court. Even so, the pre-trial pressures were not so great as were usually exerted upon Soviet accused, whose families could be held as hostages and whom the GPU with Stalin's assent thought nothing of shooting out of hand without bringing them to trial at all should they appear unable or unwilling to come up to the mark in the court room.[19]

When the trial opened in the Hall of Columns at noon on 12 April 1933, it was seen that there was a change in the official cast of actors. Krylenko, whose star had been waning in the Soviet hierarchy, no longer appeared in the role of Public Prosecutor. His place was taken by Andrey Vyshinsky, who had been the presiding judge at the earlier trials and who was now replaced on the bench by Vasily Ulrich, a former GPU man and a bloated and sadistic bully, whose uncouth manners were shared by the Assistant Prosecutor A. A. Roginsky. The proceedings lasted for a week; and, since it was watched by a large gathering of foreign press correspondents and reported on a world-wide scale, the trial attracted universal attention. As at the Shakhty trial, several 'confessions' previously made under interrogation were withdrawn in open court, notably by Monkhouse, Thornton, and another of the company's employees named W. L. MacDonald. Monkhouse, who had been questioned for more than thirteen hours at a stretch, never admitted to wrecking, but he did think he had gone too far in admitting to the collection of technical data for the company, which in the eyes of the prosecution amounted to economic espionage. Much play was made by Vyshinsky with the fact that a Russian engineer named Dolgov had been given three thousand roubles by Thornton, but this turned out, far from being a bribe for wrecking activities, to be a simple loan to enable Dolgov to furnish a new flat, a transaction which had been approved by Monkhouse.

Vyshinsky was so enraged by Thornton's withdrawal of his confession to wrecking acts attested by various Russian witnesses, including Monkhouse's Russian secretary Anna Kutuzova, with whom Thornton seems to have been having a love affair, that the Public Prosecutor told Thornton, in language omitted from the official Soviet transcript of the proceedings, that 'in the Soviet Union he could only be of use as manure for the Socialist fields'. In his confession, subsequently withdrawn, Thornton had incriminated twenty-seven members of the Metro-Vickers staff, including A. W. Gregory, a dedicated engineer, who was clearly puzzled as to why he had ever been arrested; he kept protesting that his professional honour had been impugned, and it was clear to everyone that his only desire was to get back to his machines at the Dnieprostroi dam, which he felt were being endangered by his enforced absence.

The most striking incident in court occurred on the second day when MacDonald withdrew his plea of guilty and the court adjourned at Vyshinsky's request. On the resumption of the session after the interval, MacDonald appeared a changed man, his cheeks ashen grey, his demeanour shaky. He thereupon reverted to his original plea, answering Vyshinsky's questions in a low toneless voice. It was obvious to the observers in court that the change was due to the treatment the prisoner had received behind the scenes. One theory at the time was that he had been drugged. However, it seems that he had been subjected to great psychological pressure through his Russian housekeeper whose name was Ryabova. He was deeply attached to her and her two children, since she had nursed him through a serious illness with remarkable devotion. Ryabova had been taken into custody at the time of his own arrest, and apparently he was told that she would be shot unless he went back on his previous recantation. Hence his compliance with his captors' threats.[20]

The verdict of the court, announced on the seventh day, convicted all the British defendants except Gregory on various charges of wrecking and spying. Thornton and MacDonald got three and two years respectively, while Monkhouse and the two other British defendants Cushny and Nordwall were ordered to be deported. With one exception, all the Russians were convicted and received sentences varying from eighteen months to ten years. The sentences were generally considered lenient by standards of Soviet criminal justice.

The British government immediately clamped a trade embargo on Soviet imports. Two months later the embargo was lifted when Thornton and MacDonald were released and repatriated. It was commonly said at the time by foreign observers in Moscow that the British Embassy might have done more for the engineers but that their hands were tied by the fact that the defendants were intelligence agents of the British Secret Service, a belief widely shared inside Russia and fostered by Stalin. There was no truth whatever in this allegation, since neither the engineers nor the Metro-Vickers company ever had any connection with British intelligence. In the case of at least one of the defendants, this was obvious on the face of it since according to the *chargé d'affaires* in the embassy he was incapable of keeping a secret for more than ten minutes. Most thinking people agreed with Monkhouse when he proclaimed in open court that it was 'perfectly clear to me that this case is a frame-up against Metro-Vickers, based on the evidence of terrorised prisoners'.[21]

Among the large corps of journalists covering the trial was a brilliant twenty-five-year-old man named Ian Fleming, who represented the British news agency Reuters. He stayed on in Moscow for a few days after the verdict, when he conceived the idea of getting an exclusive interview with Stalin. With this in mind he teamed up with S. P. Richardson, his American opposite number in Associated Press, and together they wrote to the Kremlin. A few days later they received a courteous note signed by the Soviet dictator regretting that he was too busily engaged at the moment to see them. On the night before he left Moscow, Fleming won the document from Richardson in a crap game. Some years later Stalin's autograph was to remind Fleming that among the more sinister departments of the Soviet government for which the dictator bore some responsibility was the counter-espionage organisation known as SMERSH ('Death to Spies'). To the fictional outwitting of this department Fleming then devised his mythical character James Bond, who was to make his debut while Stalin was still alive.[22]

3

For some months after his wife's suicide, Stalin appeared almost a broken man. He restricted his public appearances to a bare minimum such as reporting to the Central Committee on the qualified success of the first Five Year Plan and attending a memorial meeing in the Bolshoi Theatre on the anniversary of Lenin's death. He could not bear to live any more in the apartment in the Poteshny Palace where Nadya had died and he moved to another set of rooms in the Senate Building. These were converted offices and were located on the floor below his own and Molotov's private offices adjacent to the rooms in which the Council of Commissars and the Politburo held their meetings. In fact Stalin spent little time in his new apartment except to take an evening meal with his two younger children. Nor could he stand the sight of the *dacha* at Zubalovo, which served as an uncomfortable reminder of his dead wife. In its place he had a modest villa built at Kuntsevo, surrounded by fir trees. This was a few miles nearer Moscow than Zubalovo and a short distance from the Mozhaisk Highway. It was to remain his principal home for the rest of his life. He would usually leave it for his office in the Kremlin or the Central Committee building in the early afternoon, returning there about eleven at night after dining in his Kremlin apartment; he would then do several more hours' work before going to bed where he slept until about noon.

Except for his annual summer holiday at Sochi, this was to be his unbroken routine until Hitler's attack in 1941 brought the Soviet Union into World War II, and his private headquarters were temporarily transferred back to the Kremlin. After the war he reverted to Kuntsevo, where he virtually cut himself off from the outside world except for the company of a few favoured intimates. He lived on the ground floor in one room, and in his daughter Svetlana's words made it do for everything. 'He slept on the sofa, made up at night as a bed, and had telephones on the table beside it. The large dining table was piled high with documents, newspapers and books. He used one end for eating when he was alone.' The journey to and from the *dacha* was made in a motorcade consisting of three Packards driven at breakneck speed, Stalin as a rule sitting beside the driver and the position of his car in the profession being frequently changed as a security precaution.[23]

288

Disappointed by the qualified results of the First Five Year Plan, worried by reports of party intrigues to oust him from the leadership, and still suffering from the traumatic shock of his wife's death, Stalin in an unusual outburst of humility actually proposed in the Politburo that he should resign his office of General Secretary, as he had done eight years previously after the disclosure of Lenin's statement. 'Maybe I have become an obstacle to the Party's unity,' he told his colleagues. 'If so, comrades, I am ready to efface myself.' According to Victor Serge, the Soviet poet and novelist, who is the authority for this story, the others looked at each other in embarrassment, since nobody felt inclined to risk his neck by saying, 'Yes, old man, you ought to go, there's nothing better you can do.' Eventually, after a long silence, Molotov, who appears to have been in the chair, brought the others back to a sense of reality. 'Stop it! Stop it!' he told Stalin, showing unaccustomed emotion. 'You've got the Party's confidence.' And so the incident was closed.[24]

Stalin is said to have found consolation in the charms of Lazar Kaganovich's sister Rosa, who is believed to have become his mistress while his wife was still alive and whom he was now reported to have married. Whether in fact he did marry Rosa is unclear, but she certainly behaved as his nominal spouse and ran his household for some years until he seems to have tired of her and she eventually disappeared from sight. 'I am a loyal wife,' she used to say, and this admission, coupled with the common talk of their 'divorce' later on, suggests that they had in fact been husband and wife under Soviet law. She is known to have disliked Voroshilov whom she described as 'a terrible bore', always talking about his heroic achievements in the Civil War, and she resented his going to Stalin with what she considered untrue tales about her brothers.

Unlike Nadya, Rosa Kaganovich certainly encouraged her husband's dictatorial aspirations, as also did her friend the writer Alexei Tolstoy, whose view she shared that Stalin 'was one of the "chosen", that he should lead those around him and not submit to the majority'. Rosa was an accomplished pianist and presided over a kind of salon in a large ground floor apartment opposite the Kremlin which she had occupied before her liaison with the dictator and which somewhat surprisingly he allowed her to retain. Here she had regular musical evenings attended by the intellectuals of the day including among others the writer Boris Pasternak. There would also be displays of folk dancing, which Stalin occasionally condescended to witness and even to join in.[25]

During the winter of 1932–1933, when Nadya Stalina was so disillusioned by her husband's conduct, public as well as private, that she took her own life, there had been a steady rise in discontent both inside and outside the Soviet Communist Party. This feeling was inflamed by Trotsky's conduct in exile. In the hopes of effectively isolating his old rival, Stalin had prevailed upon the Turkish authorities to deport Trotsky to Prinkipo, a tiny island in the Sea of Marmora. But he had reckoned without Trotsky's fiery pen, which found what was for the General Secretary a most irritating vehicle in the *Bulletin of the Opposition*, a Russian language broadsheet edited by Trotsky from his island home and published in Paris. Unlike Lenin's *Iskra* and other clandestine Bolshevik propaganda sheets, the *Bulletin* probably did not reach many Soviet workers, but it did circulate among the more influential party and government officials inside Russia and copies regularly appeared on Stalin's desk.

No. 31 of the *Bulletin*, which came out in the same month that Nadya died, contained a powerful anonymous criticism of Stalin's economic policy supported by a wealth of statistical detail, which could only have emanated from government sources. 'In view of the incapacity of the present leadership to get out of the present economic and political deadlock,' the article concluded, 'the conviction about the need to change the leadership of the party is growing.' Stalin discovered that the anonymous author of this devastating article was Ivan Smirnov, an Old Bolshevik with an outstanding revolutionary record and a brilliant reputation as a Red commander in the Civil War when he decisively defeated Kolchak. Smirnov, who had previously been expelled from the Party for his opposition activities and been reinstated in 1929, was now arrested and thrown into prison. With Blumkin, another opposition supporter, who had actually visited Trotsky at Prinkipo, Stalin went further and had him shot as soon as he returned from abroad. Blumkin is believed to have been the first Trotskyite to have suffered the extreme penalty on purely political grounds.[26]

Another disastrous harvest, following on the famine, and Stalin knew that his leadership, due to be reconfirmed at the next Party Congress, would be doomed to extinction. Hence he exerted the utmost efforts with the spring sowing in 1933. Thousands of party workers were drafted into the countryside to help on the farms, the unwilling were ruthlessly dragooned into working in the fields, and the recalcitrant were summarily dealt with by the GPU. It was a nerve-wracking operation, but the effort succeeded, thanks in part to the fine summer. The harvest was a bumper one, and its results were soon apparent. Food rationing was relaxed with the improvement in the economy, and the General Secretary's critics within the Party became less vociferous.*

The need for party unity was indicated by political developments in Germany where, far from there being a revolution of the Left as had been hoped in the Politburo, the reverse had happened with the rise to power of Hitler and the National Socialist Party pledged to exterminate Communism, maybe to wage war to this end against the Soviet Union. Towards the end of 1933, Stalin and the Politburo became thoroughly alarmed by the discovery of a Nazi plot aimed not only at the collection of military intelligence in the Soviet Union but also the spreading of disaffection in government and party circles. The insidious propaganda was particularly marked in the Ukraine. What was the more remarkable was that it was in substance a homosexual conspiracy. The details of the conspiracy and its immediate outcome were subsequently disclosed in a document known as *The Letter of an Old Bolshevik*, which though written by the Menshevik Nicolaevsky was inspired partly by Bukharin, who had been taken back into the Party fold along with other penitents including Zinoviev, Kamenev, Rykov, Piatakov and Radek. Bukharin later met Nicolaevsky in Paris when he was leading a Soviet delegation with the object of acquiring the archives of the German Social Democratic Party of which Nicolaevsky was the custodian, and the interview between the

* The present writer on his first visit to the USSR, wrote to Lady Londonderry, wife of the British Air Minister, on 15 August 1933, from Moscow:

Industrially and scientifically there is no doubt that the country is making tremendous progress, but the masses suffer great privation and hardship owing to the difficulty of adjusting the new development in the region of vast public undertakings to local conditions and the lethargic national temperament. While Intourist (the official travel bureau) is careful to show the visitor the brighter side of life under the Soviets, no restrictions that I have been able to discover are imposed upon the foreign tourist who cares to go about on his own. I have consequently managed to wander round quite freely, talking to all sorts and conditions of people and gathering information from various sources. Stalin is universally detested on account of his rough and brutal manners, and his behaviour in private life apparently leaves much to be desired! Families live in Moscow at the rate of 5 or 6 to a room and thousands are literally starving. Foreigners on a visit are however well fed and looked after and the hotels generally speaking are very comfortable.

I have been particularly impressed by the numbers of soldiers I have seen everywhere. Every schoolboy, student and worker receives military instruction, and I am convinced that the Red Army will shortly be a force to be reckoned with in world politics. In spite of what I have said however I think the USSR has great advantages to offer us in the way of trade, particularly as regards the import of machinery from England, and that we should remain on as friendly terms as possible.

two men formed the substance of the *Letter* with its interesting revelations.

An assistant of the German military attaché, a friend and follower of the notorious Captain Roehm, managed to enter the homosexual circles in Moscow, and, under cover of a homosexual 'organisation' (homosexuality was still legal in Russia at that time), started a whole network of National Socialist propaganda. Its threads extended into the provinces, to Leningrad, Kharkov, Kiev, etc. A number of persons in literary and artistic circles were involved: the private secretary of a very prominent actor, known for his homosexual inclinations, an important scientific collaborator of the Lenin Institute, etc. These connections were utilised by the Germans not only to procure military information, but also to sow dissent in government and Party circles.

The aims of those directing the conspiracy were so far-reaching that the leaders of Soviet policy were compelled to intervene. Thus, there gradually ensued the change in foreign policy that soon led to Russia's entry into the League of Nations, and to the creation of the 'Popular Front' in France. Naturally this change did not take place without a great deal of discussion. It was not easy to overcome the old, deeply rooted orientation for an alliance with Germany, even with a reactionary Germany, for the purpose of bringing about an explosion in the victorious countries [in World War I]. This was all the more difficult because it was clear that a new orientation in the direction of the democratic parties of Western Europe would inevitably lead to considerable changes in the *internal policy* of the Soviet Union.[27]

It was at this time, as Bukharin went on to point out, that Kirov began to gain great influence. His energy and inflexibility endeared him to Stalin – he had shown great ruthlessness in 'liquidating' the *kulaks*, constructing the Baltic–White Sea Canal with forced labour at the cost of many lives and in the pursuit of other aspects of the Five Year Plan. But there was an independent side to his character as manifested in his opposition to the idea of Ryutin's execution. This annoyed Stalin, who was said to have prevented Kirov for a time from attending the meetings of the Politburo on the pretext that his presence in Leningrad as Party boss there was indispensable. Stalin also noted with uneasiness Kirov's increasing popularity and his view that terror should be discarded as an instrument of government so as to enlist the support of a united party and country in preparing for the war with Nazi Germany

292

which he felt was only a matter of time. Stalin did not know how far he should go along with Kirov and he hesitated as to whether he should come down on the side of liberal concessions or continue his policy of repression.

4

In the foreign field, Stalin's immediate worry in 1933 was occasioned by Japan rather than Hitler's Germany. The Japanese seizure of Manchuria and the installation of a puppet regime in that former Chinese province constituted a direct threat to Soviet security in the Far East. Hence the urgency in establishing diplomatic relations with the United States, whose government and people were traditionally pro-Chinese and opposed to any form of Japanese expansion on the Chinese mainland. On the other hand, successive Republican administrations in Washington had persistently showed themselves disinclined to accord full diplomatic recognition to the Soviet Union despite a high volume of trading which had grown up between the two countries. The Republican Herbert Hoover's defeat by his Democratic opponent Franklin D. Roosevelt in the 1932 campaign for President put a new man with more liberal ideas in the White House. After feeling out the ground, Roosevelt invited Litvinov to visit Washington, and the Foreign Commissar's visit eventually led to an accord, which among other things provided for an exchange of ambassadors. For the Moscow post the President chose Mr William C. Bullitt, whose abortive peace mission in 1919, designed to end the Civil War and the allied intervention, has been described earlier.

Since his previous visit Bullitt had formed a strong emotional attachment to the Soviet Union, and it had been cemented by his marriage to the widow of John Reed, the American Communist author of *Ten Days that Shook the World*, who is buried beneath the Kremlin wall. This involvement was to prove disastrous for Bullitt's second mission, although it began auspiciously enough with a dinner given in his honour by Voroshilov at which Stalin was present along with the rest of the Politburo and other high officials including Litivinov and General Yegorov, the Chief of Staff of the Red Army. Bullitt noted that Stalin went out of his way to be friendly, and that he proposed the first toast: 'To President Roosevelt, who in spite of the mute growls of the Fishes dared to recognise the Soviet Union.' This reference to Hamilton Fish, the right-wing Republican congressman who had strongly opposed recognition, went down particularly well. He also appeared to Bullitt to be quite apprehensive of Japanese intentions. 'This is the man who will lead our army victoriously when Japan attacks,' said Stalin as he introduced the Chief of Staff. Stalin went on to tell the new ambassador that 250,000 tons of steel rails were urgently needed to complete the Trans-Siberian Railway to Vladivostock. 'Your railways are re-equipping themselves and will have many old rails to to dispose of. Can't you arrange for us to purchase the old rails? Without those rails we shall beat the Japanese, but if we have the rails it will be easier.' Bullitt said he would be glad to do what he could.

As the party was breaking up, Stalin said to Bullitt: 'I want you to understand that if you want to see me at any time, day or night, you have only to let me know and I will see you at once.' Then, as he accompanied the ambassador to the door, Stalin asked: 'Is there anything in the Soviet Union that you want?' Bullitt, who had been having difficulty in finding suitable accommodation for his embassy, asked for a piece of land on the Lenin Hills overlooking the city, on which the American embassy could be built. 'You shall have it,' said Stalin. Bullitt could hardly believe his ears. 'This was an extraordinary gesture on his part,' he reported to Washington, 'as he has hitherto refused to see any ambassador at any time.'[28]

As his fellow American Eugene Lyons had predicted, Bullitt's enthusiasm for Russia could not survive a long residence – it was based on romantic assumptions that no longer held good. Socially the ambassador created quite a splash with his lavish parties; he also taught the Red Army to play polo and tried to make the Russians take up baseball, importing the necessary equipment at his own expense. But politically his mission was to prove a failure. He repeatedly clashed with Litvinov, whom he heartily disliked. 'The Soviet foreign office does not understand the meaning of honour or fair dealing,' he once protested to Roosevelt.

As the Japanese menace diminished and a Soviet-American military understanding became less important, Stalin and his colleagues were inclined to pay Bullitt no more than the bare minimum of attention which protocol demanded. A suggestion by Bullitt that he might 'make an airplane tour of the Caucasus and drop in casually on the boss' at one of his villas met with no response from the Kremlin. Furthermore, Stalin conveniently forgot the promise about the land on the Lenin Hills: at all events the Americans never got it for their embassy.

After eighteen months in Moscow, Bullitt's former friendship turned to something near hatred. He would summon the American press correspondents in his office and urge them in their dispatches to 'fan the flames of anti-Sovietism in America'. Eventually the day was to come when Bullitt, completely discredited as a diplomat, was to be denounced by *Pravda* on Stalin's instructions as 'a bankrupt spy' and his public utterances discounted as 'the ravings of an old grey mare'.[29]

5

Stalin now decided to summon another Party Congress, the Seventeenth, in order to mark the victory of the First Five Year Plan and the encouraging start of its successor in the spheres of heavy industry and collectivised agriculture. Appropriately dubbed the 'Congress of the Victors' by Kirov, through whose celebrated allocution it has gone down to Soviet history, it opened in the Grand Palace of the Kremlin on 26 January 1934.

In a lengthy review of the international scene, the General Secretary drew a chilling picture of 'the continuing crisis of world capitalism' as exemplified by 'the victory of fascism in Germany and the triumph of the idea of revenge, which have strained relations in Europe', as well as by 'the withdrawal of Japan and Germany from the League of Nations, which has given a new impetus to the growth of armaments and the preparations for an imperialist war'. By contrast, the situation on the Soviet home front was one of 'ever increasing progress', both in the field of the national economy and in the field of culture, which had 'radically changed the face of the country'.

> During this period, the USSR has become radically transformed and has cast off the aspect of backwardness and medievalism. From an agragrian country, it has become an industrial country. From a country of small individual agriculture it has become a country of collective, large-scale mechanised agriculture. From an ignorant, illiterate and uncultured country it has become – or rather it is becoming – a literate and cultured country covered by a vast network of higher, secondary and elemetary schools functioning in the languages of the nationalities of the USSR.
>
> New industries have been created: the production of machine tools, automobiles, tractors, chemicals, motors, aircraft, combine harvesters, powerful turbines and generators, high-grade steel, ferro-alloys, synthetic rubber, nitrates, artificial fibre, etc., etc.

The speech included a humorous account of a conversation which Stalin had recently had with a farmer who was 'a very respected comrade, but an incorrigible windbag', the type of person who was 'honest and loyal to the Soviet power, but was incapable of leadership, incapable of organising anything'. Judging by the official report, the exchange brought the house down.

Stalin: How are you getting on with the sowing?

Farmer: With the sowing, Comrade Stalin? We have mobilised ourselves. (*Laughter*)

Stalin: Well, and what then?

Farmer: We have put the question squarely. (*Laughter*)

Stalin: And what next?

Farmer: There is a turn, Comrade Stalin; soon there will be a turn. (*Laughter*)

Stalin: But still?

Farmer: We can see an indication of some improvement. (*Laughter*)

Stalin: But still, how are you getting on with the sowing?

Farmer: So far, Comrade Stalin, we have not made any headway with the sowing. (*General laughter*)[30]

According to *Pravda*, Stalin's speech was greeted on its conclusion with 'stormy and prolonged applause from the whole hall', and the Congress gave the General Secretary a standing ovation to the accompaniment of shouts of 'Hurrah for Stalin!' and 'Long Live Stalin!' and the singing of the *Internationale,* after which the ovation was 'resumed with renewed vigour'.

Nor did a single one of the subsequent speakers fail to pay tribute to the General Secretary, 'our genius leader', as he was described by the forty-year-old second secretary of the Moscow party organisation, Nikita Khrushchev. Other typical references were 'the great Stalin', 'the wise Stalin', 'the great theoretician', 'the great master', 'our beloved leader' and 'our own dear Stalin'. Most fulsome of all was Kirov who greeted his chief as 'the greatest leader of all times and all peoples'. At the same time, Kirov likewise received a standing ovation, and there was some discussion in the corridors afterwards whether he had not in fact been more tumultuously applauded than Stalin. The constant refrain of the Leningrad delegates throughout the congress was 'Long live our Mironich!'

Kirov's arguments in his speech to the congress could be summarised in the following terms:

The period of destruction, which was necessary to extirpate the small proprietor elements in the villages, was now at an end; the economic position of the collectives was consolidated and made secure for the future. This constituted a firm basis for future development, and as the economic situation continued to improve, the broad masses of the population would become more and more reconciled to the government; the number of 'internal foes' would diminish. It was now the task of the Party to rally these forces which would support it in the new phase of economic development, and thus to broaden the foundation upon which Soviet power was based. Kirov, therefore, strongly advocated reconciliation with those Party elements who, during the period of the First Five Year Plan, had gone over to the Opposition, but who might be induced to co-operate on the new basis, now that the 'destructive phase' was over.[31]

This went down so well with the delegates that not only was Kirov re-elected to the Politburo but he was also chosen to be one of the four joint secretaries of the Central Committee. In addition, he was elected to the Orgburo, thus becoming the only Party member besides Stalin to belong both to the Politburo and the Orgburo, as well as the Party secretariat. All this would consequently necessitate his removal from Leningrad to Moscow in order to take over the direction of a whole group of departments.

On the other hand, Stalin's position, although he had recovered much of the popularity he had lost, was not quite as strong as the adulatory references to him by the other speakers at the Congress and the applause accorded his own speech suggested. At the plenary meeting of the Central Committee, which immediately followed the conclusion of the Congress, he was significantly not re-elected General Secretary but merely the first of four joint secretaries, so that in theory at least he shared his jurisdiction over the party *apparat* with three others – Kirov, Kaganovich and Andrei Zhdanov.[32] The latter, a newcomer to the inner party counsels, was a young ideological fanatic and Stalinist, who had distinguished himself as party secretary in Nizhni-Novgorod (now Gorki) and was soon to replace Kirov as party boss of Leningrad. Another of Stalin's men, who first came into public prominence at the Seventeenth Congress, was the dwarf-sadist Nikolai Yezhov, now promoted to full membership of the Central Committee, as well as being a member of the Orgburo and becoming Kaganovich's deputy in charge of the disciplinary organ, the Party Control Commission, as the reorganised Central Control Commission was now called. Incidentally the latter body was stripped of its powers so far as matters of state security which involved the Party were concerned. Henceforward these were to be dealt with in secret by the Special Section of Stalin's personal secretariat under the direction of Alexander Poskrebyshev and George Malenkov in co-operation with Yezhov.

The ten full members of the outgoing Politburo (Stalin, Molotov, Kaganovich, Voroshilov, Kalinin, Ordzhonikidze, Kuibyshev, Kirov, Andreyev and Kossior) were re-elected. Rudzutak, whose job as chairman of the Central Control Commission had come to an end with the streamlining of that body, returned to the Politburo but with reduced status as a candidate member, having apparently been forgiven for the open scandals with young girls which had been a conspicuous feature of his private life.[33] Also re-elected as candidates were Stalin's Armenian friend Anastas Mikoyan, the commissar responsible for foreign and domestic trade as well as food industries; the Old Bolshevik Gregory Petrovsky, President of the Ukrainian Soviet Republic; and Vlas Chubar, a peasant's son who had risen to become Chairman of the Council of People's Commissars in Kiev but had recently been removed by Stalin for refusing to collect grain from the Ukrainian peasants in fulfilment of the norms set by Stalin, since he rightly felt that the result would be famine. The only newcomer to candidate membership of the Politburo was Paul Postyshev, a former Central Committee secretary who had also lost his job for opposing Stalin's repressive policies and as a result had been demoted to run the Party secretariat in the Ukraine; he was something of a rough diamond, tall and thin as a lath with a grating bass voice, habitually got up like a Don Cossack in leather boots and riding breeches.[34]

From Stalin's point of view, therefore, the new Politburo was even less satisfactory than the old one which had prevented him from executing the opposition leader Ryutin. What was more, other oppositionists were voted on to the Central Committee either as full or candidate members; they included Pyatakov, Bukharin, Rykov, Tomsky and Sokolnikov. Ivan Tovstukha, the head of Stalin's personal secretariat, was also elected a candidate member of the Central Committee at this time.

'At the Fifteenth Party Congress it was still necessary to prove that the Party line was correct and to wage a struggle against certain anti-Leninist groups; and at the Sixteenth Party Congress we had to deal a final blow to the last adherents of these groups,' so Stalin reminded the 1,966 'victor' delegates who filled the hall of the Kremlin Grand Palace. He went on: 'At this congress, however, there is nothing to prove and, it seems, no one to fight. Everyone sees that the Party line has triumphed.' The policy of industrialising the country had triumphed, the policy of 'eliminating the *kulaks* and of complete collectivisation had triumphed, thus confirming the victory of the policy of socialism in one country'.

298

It is evident that all these successes, and primarily the victory of the Five Year Plan, have utterly demoralised and smashed all the various anti-Leninist groups.

It must be admitted that the Party today is united as it has never been before. (*Stormy and prolonged applause.*)[35]

The sense of euphoria which these remarks engendered among the Party comrades was not to last for long. Out of nearly two thousand delegates, who applauded them so enthusiastically, only fifty-nine were to take part in the next congress. The majority of the rest was to vanish into jails and labour camps and the execution cellars of the Lubyanka and provincial prisons of the GPU. Similarly, of the 139 members and candidate members of the Central Committee, no less than ninety-eight, according to Khrushchev, were subsequently to be arrested and shot on Stalin's orders, most of them in what came to be known as the *Yezhovchina* from the name of the principal instrument of this colossal 'liquidation'.[36]

How Stalin's 'wilfulness *vis-à-vis* the Party and its Central Committee', as Khrushchev described his conduct, became 'fully evident' after the Seventeenth Party Congress, was soon to be revealed through the fate of the comrade who had vied with Stalin for pride of place at this Congress – Sergei Mironovich Kirov.

CHAPTER VIII

The Kirov Affair

I

In the months following the Seventeenth Party Congress, during the spring and summer of 1934, Kirov's 'policy of reconciliation', which had been so warmly endorsed by the delegates, was the main preoccupation of the Politburo. Opinions expressed at the meetings were divided. Stalin, who advocated the use of a strong hand, disliked Kirov's line, and in this he had the unswerving support of Molotov and Kaganovich. The remainder of the Politburo inclined towards Kirov in varying degrees, his most active adherents at first being Ordzhonikidze and Kuibyshev followed by Voroshilov, Kalinin and Rudzutak. Voroshilov as War Commissar was responsible for the defence of the frontier with China, and when General Blyukher, the local commander, informed him that he could not guarantee the frontier's security unless the peasants in these borderlands were exempted from collectivisation, this was agreed to. In addition, there was a limited amnesty for rebellious *kulaks*, while numerous oppositionists and 'wreckers' who had been likewise arrested during the operation of the First Five Year Plan were released from prison and exile. The olive branch was also held out to the literary intelligentsia as well as the 'technicals', and at a Writer's Congress Bukharin and Gorky came forward as the champions of 'proletarian humanism'. A commission was appointed to draft a new constitution, designed to put the peasants' representatives on an equal footing with the workers' on Soviet bodies and to be, said Stalin with an apparent liberal gesture, 'the most

300

democratic in the world'. (Naturally it was to be called the Stalin Constitution.) Finally, the GPU was abolished or rather incorporated in the People's Commissariat of Internal Affairs (*Narodnyi Kommisariat Vnutrennykh Del*); henceforth it was to be known by the initials NKVD, although in fact it now only formed a branch of this commissariat, which also controlled the militia, internal and border guards, and the forced labour camps.

In one respect, however, state security was tightened, following the defection of two Red Air Force pilots with their plane in June 1934, when Stalin signed a decree which made the whole family collectively responsible for the treasonable act of one of its members as well as all other individuals who might have had advance knowledge of the act but had failed to denounce the traitor.[1]

The Government's new look was reflected in the sphere of foreign policy, when after first ignoring Hitler Stalin and the rest of the Politburo executed a *volte-face* and adopted what appeared to be a policy of alliance with the west against him. In September 1934, the Soviet Union joined the League of Nations, which only a short time before Stalin had denounced as the main imperialist weapon of the 'capitalist democracies'. Now it was hoped, as Stalin put it, that 'despite its weakness the League might nevertheless serve as a place where aggressors could be exposed, and as a definite instrument of peace, however feeble, that might prevent the outbreak of war'. Accordingly, the Foreign Affairs Commissar Maxim Litvinov became on Stalin's instructions the strongest protagonist at Geneva of the policy of collective resistance within the framework of the League to the increasingly evident aggressive designs of Nazi Germany.[2]

Meanwhile Kirov's personal relations with other members of the Politburo became strained. He fell out with Mikoyan, whom he blamed as Food Commissar for what he claimed was the haphazard way in which Leningrad received its food supplies. Kirov caused further offence by requisitioning food earmarked as reserves for the Leningrad Military District and turned it over to the factory workers. The matter was raised at the next meeting of the Politburo when Kirov explained that he had only 'borrowed' the food with the intention of restoring its equivalent to the Military District from new shipments. Voroshilov, egged on by Stalin, thereupon remarked with some malice that Kirov's method of transferring food from military stores to factory depots was 'a cheap way of seeking personal popularity among the workers'.

'If the Politburo wants the workers to produce, it is necessary to feed them,' Kirov exclaimed. 'Every *moujik* knows that he must feed his

301

horse if he wants the horse to pull the cartload for him.'

Nor did he deny Mikoyan's charge that the Leningrad workers received supplementary rations above those to which they were strictly entitled. Kirov justified this by citing figures to show that productivity in the Leningrad factories and the value of the increased output far exceeded the cost of the additional rations.

'But why should the Leningrad workers eat better than the other workers?' Stalin broke in.

It was an interjection which made Kirov momentarily lose his usual self control. He retorted angrily: 'I think it is high time to abolish rationing and begin to feed our workers properly!'

Kirov's relations became increasingly strained not only with Stalin, who considered that his outburst in the Politburo was a personal act of disloyalty towards himself, but also with the other members who had come to resent his behaviour. He was consequently subjected to irritating pinpricks, to which his characteristic reactions did not improve his standing in the eyes of his colleagues. For instance, when a delegation of top leaders of Leningrad industry headed by the chairman of the Executive Committee of the Leningrad Soviet was summoned to Mocow by Orzhonikidze, the Commissar of Heavy Industry, for a high level conference, Kirov ordered them to return to Leningrad after they had been kept hanging round the Commissar's offices for three days. Ordzhonikidze brought up the incident at the next meeting of the Politburo, with the result that Kirov's order was censured as 'educating the Leningrad officials in the spirit of partisanship and insubordination to the central authorities'.

'I will always act like that,' said Kirov when taxed with his conduct. 'I need my men to do work in Leningrad and not to lounge about in Ordzhonikidze's reception rooms.'[3]

As the months passed, Kirov's attendances at Politburo meetings became less and less frequent. To every request from Stalin as to when he was coming to Moscow to take up his new duties with the Central Committee, Kirov returned procrastinating answers and pleaded pressure of work in Leningrad. However, he accepted an invitation to spend his summer holiday as he usually did with Stalin and his children at Stalin's villa at Sochi, and he was reported as being there with Zhdanov, one of the other Central Committee Secretaries, in August. The timing of the transfer was discussed during this visit when Kirov made it clear that he was unwilling to give up his work in Leningrad and move to Moscow permanently until the Second Five Year Plan had been completed, a period of at least three years. This intimation was most unsatisfactory to Stalin, whose reason for the transfer was that he could more easily keep an eye on the man he now considered to be his most dangerous political rival.[4]

It was at this point that Stalin finally made up his mind that Kirov must be got rid of. His 'diabolical plan' was succinctly described by the NKVD officer Alexander Orlov after the latter's defection.

> He decided to arrange for the assassination of Kirov and to lay that crime at the door of the former leaders of the opposition and thus with one blow do away with Lenin's former comrades, who despite Stalin's vicious calumnies continued to be the symbol of Bolshevism in the eyes of the rank and file of the party. Stalin came to the conclusion that, if he could prove that Zinoviev and Kamenev and other leaders of the opposition had shed the blood of Kirov, 'the beloved son of the party', a member of the Politburo, he then would be justified in demanding *blood for blood*...[5]

The 'arrangements' were entrusted, apparently with the reluctant assent of Yagoda, to the secret Special Section of Stalin's personal secretariat, which by employing an *agent provocateur* soon found a suitable instrument for the purpose. This instrument was a disgruntled ex-party member in Leningrad named Leonid Nikolayev, who had been expelled by the Control Commission for refusing to accept an assignment in a rural area for health reasons (apparently he suffered from epileptic fits). The Party in turn refused to give him any other work and though his Party card was later restored to him he continued to be unemployed and could not find a job.

Nikolayev incautiously let it be known that he would like to assassinate the member of the Control Commission whom he considered had been responsible for his unemployment. A diary which he kept at this time, and which was shown by the *agent provocateur* to the Deputy Chief of the Leningrad NKVD Vania Zaporozhets, indicated that Nikolayev was quite serious in his intentions. A meeting thereupon took place at which the *agent provocateur* introduced Zaporozhets to Nikolayev under an assumed name, pretending that the NKVD man was a fellow worker in his factory. After this Zaporozhets, who had been let into the secret and was in touch with Stalin, instructed the *agent provocateur* to persuade Nikolayev to direct his attempt against Kirov, an action which it was suggested to Nikolayev would have a much more resounding effect than if it were made against a relatively unknown member of the Control Commission. Nikolayev, who had no idea that the NKVD were indirectly guiding his actions, jumped at the idea and was supplied with a pistol, while a convenient pretext was found for him to obtain a pass to the Smolny where Kirov had his offices.

Unfortunately for Nikolayev, the plan initially misfired, since he was stopped on entering the Smolny building by one of the guards who demanded to see the contents of the brief-case he was carrying. This revealed a loaded pistol and a diary, whereupon the would-be assassin was taken to the commandant's office and detained for questioning by the NKVD. On telephoning the local NKVD headquarters, the commandant was put through to Zaporozhets who on learning what had happened ordered the commandant to release Nilolayev and return his brief-case to him. This was accordingly done.

Nikolayev was reluctant to try a second time. He was eventually prodded out of his apathetic mood by the *agent provocateur*, who succeeded in persuading him to make another attempt some weeks later when Kirov would have returned from an important meeting of the plenum of the Central Committee due to be held in the Kremlin in the last week of November. This time he was advised to go to the Smolny in the late afternoon or evening.

Meanwhile in Moscow Kirov had the satisfaction of seeing the implementation of the liberal policies which he had put forward at the Seventeenth Congress approved in principle. They included the abolition of food rationing, as well as substantial improvements in the position of the collective farmers. Kirov's own future was also discussed and a resolution was tabled providing for his move from Leningrad to take immediate effect. Surprisingly enough, Kirov did not object and undertook to come back for good in a week's time after he had wound up his affairs in Leningrad. He did come back – but in his coffin.

It was shortly after four o'clock in the afternoon of 1 December 1934, as the lights were being switched on throughout Leningrad, that Nikolayev was passed through the guards at the entrance to the Smolny. For five or ten minutes he wandered round the corridors of the historic building until he finally reached the third floor where Kirov's offices and secretariat were situated. No guards appeared to be on duty. Indeed the only person immediately visible to Nikolayev was Kirov's personal assistant Borisov, who was preparing a tray with tea and sandwiches and took no notice of Nikolayev. Borisov then disappeared with the tray into a nearby conference room where Kirov was at a meeting with the Bureau of the Leningrad Party Committee. Nikolayev waited patiently in the corridor.

About 4.30 Borisov, who had in the meantime retired to the ante-room, returned to the conference room with a message that Kirov was wanted on the direct wire from Moscow. A minute or two later Kirov got up from his chair and left the room, closing the door behind him. As he turned in the direction of the teleprinter room, Nikolayev stepped forward and shot him in the back of the neck. When the others opened the door they found their beloved Mironich lying dead in a pool of blood. Nikolayev, who had fainted, was prostrate beside him with his pistol and brief-case nearby. There were no guards anywhere in sight.

As soon as Nikolayev had recovered consciousness, he was arrested and handed over to the local NKVD. At the same time messages were sent to Stalin and Yagoda in Moscow informing them of what had occurred.[6]

2

As soon as Stalin heard the news from the Smolny, he immediately ordered a special train to take him and others he ordered to accompany him to Leningrad to 'conduct the inquiry' into the circumstances of Kirov's murder. His party included Voroshilov and Molotov from the Politburo of the Central Committee, Zhdanov from the Secretariat, Yagoda and two other senior officials from the NKVD, Y. D. Agranov and L. G. Mironov, in addition to Stalin's indispensable chief aide Poskrebyshev.

Before leaving the Kremlin, Stalin gave instructions for the issue of a legislative decree to provide for the immediate execution of death sentences passed by the courts, thus depriving the accused of his traditional right of appeal for clemency. The decree, which was dated 1 December and was probably drafted by Kaganovich who was left in charge in Moscow, was approved by Stalin over the telephone or direct wire from Leningrad and appeared in the press above the signatures of President Kalinin and Abel Yenukidze, the secretary of the Praesidium of the Central Executive Committee of the Supreme Soviet. Known as the 'Kirov Decree', it was to become during the immediately following years what Khrushchev was later to call 'the basis for mass acts of abuse against socialist legality'. According to Khrushchev, it was only confirmed 'casually' by the Politburo two days after its publication.

1 Investigative agencies are directed to speed up the cases of those accused of the preparation of acts of terror.

2 Judicial organs are directed not to hold up the execution of death sentences pertaining to crimes of this category in order to consider the possibility of pardon, because the Praesidium of the

Central Executive Committee of the USSR does not consider as possible the receiving of petitions of this sort.

3 The organs of the Commissariat of Internal Affairs [NKVD] are directed to execute death sentences against criminals of the above mentioned category immediately after passing of the sentences.[7]

While Stalin and his party were on their way to Leningrad by overnight train, the idea occurred to Zaporozhets that he would ingratiate himself with Stalin if he could secure a confession from Nikolayev to the effect that he had killed Kirov on the direct instructions of Kamenev and Zinoviev. Unfortunately for Zaporozhets, he overlooked the fact that Nikolayev might recognise him from their previous meeting at which Zaporozhets had appeared incognito in civilian clothes. Although Zaporozhets wore his NKVD uniform when Nikolayev was brought before him, Nikolayev immediately remembered him and refused to cooperate. Far from appearing a weak neurasthentic type, the assassin gave the impression of a convinced and fearless fanatic when he bluntly told Zaporozhets that 'although he had nothing against Kirov personally, he was glad that he had been able to carry out the terroristic act and, in this way, open an era of struggle against the privileged caste of bureaucracy'.

Nikolayev behaved with similar bravado when he was sent for by Stalin on the latter's arrival at the Leningrad headquarters of the NKVD. When the unfortunate prisoner appeared in the doorway with his head in bandages, the result apparently of the effects of an earlier interrogation, he stopped short. Stalin beckoned him to come nearer his desk. After studying Nikolayev closely for some moments, Stalin then asked him in an almost affectionate tone of voice, which surprised Yagoda and the other NKVD men who were present: 'Why did you kill such a nice man?'

'I did not fire at him, I fired at the Party!' answered the prisoner.

'And where did you get the revolver?' asked Stalin.

'Why do you ask me?' Nikolayev replied in an insolent tone. 'Ask Comrade Zaporozhets about that!'

Stalin's face darkened with anger. 'Take him away,' he told the guards.

As soon as the door closed, Stalin leaped to his feet, and seizing the file on Nikolayev, which lay on the desk before him, hurled it at Yagoda. 'Bungler!' he shouted at the NKVD chief.[8]

Stalin next sent for Zaporozhets and told him that he had been relieved of his duties, as also was Philip Medved, who headed the Leningrad NKVD, although unlike his deputy Medved apparently knew nothing of Stalin's plot to do away with Kirov. Both Medved and Zaporozhets were thereupon placed under arrest, the Leningrad NKVD was taken off the case, and the investigation was turned over to Agranov and Mironov.

Meanwhile Kirov's aide Borisov, whose title was given as chief bodyguard, although his duties seem to have been more those of a personal assistant, had likewise been arrested on suspicion of complicity in the murder. (He was later alleged to have been an accomplice.) What happened to him on the way to being interrogated was briefly alluded to by Khrushchev in his 'secret speech' at the Twentieth Party Congress in 1956 and amplified by him at the Twenty-Second Congress five years later.

When the chief of Kirov's bodyguard was being driven to the interrogation – and he was to have been questioned by Stalin, Molotov and Voroshilov – on the way, as the driver of the vehicle later stated, an accident was deliberately staged by those who were to bring the chief of the bodyguard to the interrogation. They reported that the chief of the bodyguard had died as the result of the accident, although in actual fact it turned out that he had been killed by the persons escorting him...

It has turned out that the driver of the vehicle that was carrying the chief of the S. M. Kirov's bodyguard to the interrogation is alive. He has said that as they were riding to the interrogation an NKVD man was sitting with him in the cab. The vehicle was a truck. (It is strange, of course, that this man Borisov was being driven to the interrogation in a truck, as if in this case no other vehicle could be found for the purpose. It seems that everything had been thought out in advance, down to the smallest detail.) Two other NKVD men were in the back of the truck with the chief of Kirov's bodyguard.

The driver went on to say that as they were driving down the street the man sitting next to him suddenly grabbed the wheel out of his hands and steered the truck straight at a building. The driver grabbed back the steering wheel and straightened out the truck, and they merely 'sideswiped' the wall of the building. He was later told that the chief of Kirov's bodyguard had been killed in this accident.[9]

There had already been rumours of a coolness between Stalin and Yagoda, who was known by Stalin to have expressed sympathy with the 'Rightist' opposition at the time of the secret talk between Bukharin and Kamenev in the summer of 1928. Yagoda's visit to Leningrad with Stalin marked the beginning of an open break between the two men. Although Yagoda was to continue as chief of the NKVD for the next eighteen months, he had already lost Stalin's confidence which so far as secret police operations were concerned now passed to Yakov Agranov, who had proved himself to be a particularly brutal and unscrupulous investigator. Indeed there are grounds for believing that Stalin tried to get rid of Yagoda during the Leningrad visit in the same way as had happened with Borisov. At all events, one night while Yagoda was being driven to a suburb where he expected to interrogate some suspects, his vehicle came into violent collision with a truck, which it appeared had deliberately crashed into it. Yagoda narrowly escaped with his life, much shaken and bruised, while the car in which he was travelling was completely wrecked. Afterwards there was considerable talk in NKVD circles in Moscow about the 'accident'. Some years later, when Yagoda himself was put on trial, he admitted under cross-examination that he had been directed by Stalin's friend Yenukidze 'to assist in the murder of Kirov' and that he had consequently been 'compelled to instruct Zaporozhets, who occupied the post of Assistant Chief of the Regional Administration of the NKVD not to place any obstacles in the way of the terrorist act against Kirov'.[10]

Another individual, who might have proved an inconvenient witness had he been allowed to survive, was the *agent provocateur* who had introduced Nikolayev to Zaporozhets and egged him on to commit the murder. Stalin did not even trouble to see him but had him immediately shot out of hand. This was likewise the fate of most of those whose names appeared in Nikolayev's diary. A lucky exception was Elizabeth Lermolo, an attractive and intelligent young woman, who had met Nikolayev in Pudozh, a small town in north Russia to which she had been exiled for no other reason than that her father had been a Tsarist army officer. Stalin, who interrogated her personally, tried to get her to admit that like many others she was indirectly to blame for Kirov's death.[11]

'According to your viewpoint, the guilt lies only with Nikolayev,' Stalin told her. 'But according to my way of thinking, Nikolayev is not the sole culprit. Those who failed to take measures to prevent the assassination share his guilt. You, too, are guilty in part, because you didn't even try to foresee Nikolayev's crime, or attempt to dissuade him from it. Do you understand?'

'Now, please, wait a moment,' replied Lermolo. 'What right did I, an exile, have to counsel him, a Communist? He had others to turn to

—his own wife, for instance, who is a party member.'

Although Stalin tried hard, he could get little out of her. Asked by Stalin which of the two she sympathised with more, Zinoviev or Trotsky, she exclaimed with some heat that she had no use for either. 'They don't interest me at all. I am much more concerned to know how soon I will regain my freedom. I have committed no crime.'

Turning to Poskrebyshev, who was busy taking notes, Stalin remarked with more than a hint of sarcasm in his voice: 'Did you notice the new type of political exiles we have these days? They don't appear to be the least interested in current political problems. Not like those in our day...'

Poskrebyshev nodded and went on writing, while Stalin continued to question the young woman before him. Suddenly his manner became hostile. 'You're masquerading,' he told her. 'But it's all in vain, I assure you. We can see right through you. No one can pose these days as a non-political exile. Do you understand? Such tactics will never convince us that you have ceased to be a hardened enemy of the revolution.' He shook his finger at her. 'On the contrary, your evasive answers to the simple questions we put to you only strengthen our conviction that you are now, as you have always been, a confirmed foe of the working class.'

Then in a somewhat calmer tone Stalin went on to ask her opinion of banishment as a method of dealing with political criminals. She replied that it did no good that she could see, with its accompanying personal indignities and enforced idleness. 'The wisest thing would be to return exiles to their families for the resumption of useful work.'

'I'm afraid that Agranov would disagree with you,' said Stalin with an unexpected chuckle. Agranov stirred but did not say anything, as Stalin continued. 'To be sure, he also believes that banishment as a measure of social defence should be abolished. But not for the reasons you've given. He thinks that banishment could never transform political exiles into useful citizens of our motherland. Even young people like yourself resist re-education.' Turning towards Poskrebyshev, he added in an aside, 'Write that down!'

Summoning up her dwindling courage, Lermolo again spoke out. 'I can't understand what lack you see in me that makes you think I could never again be a socially useful person.'

At this remark Stalin, according to Lermolo, looked her over appreciatively and said, winking at Agranov, 'Can't say you lack anything!' He then resumed his former serious expression, as he proceeded to admonish her. 'The fact is that you have never ceased to be an alien element to us. You have not become devoted to our cause, the cause of the revolution.'

To the young woman's suggestion that a place of exile was not the ideal environment for cultivating devotion, Stalin retorted: 'Well, what did you expect us to do? Put you in some fashionable finishing school? No, it's your own fault. If you were firmly devoted to the welfare of the Soviet people and wanted to help them build a happier life for themselves, then nothing would have stopped you from doing so. Even under the most adverse conditions one can perform noble deeds. And there is the crux of the matter...you do not love your people, you do not wish them well, you do not love your country!'

'I beg your pardon,' said Lermolo, needled beyond endurance. 'My people and my country I love and have always loved, though for seventeen years it has been drilled into my head that I am an enemy of the people...' Then, unable to control herself any longer, she burst into tears.

'Agranov, take her away!' Stalin ordered. Whereupon Agranov, who had hitherto appeared obsequious, suddenly became stern. 'Stand up! Follow me!' he commanded. Lermolo was then escorted back to her cell, though not until Agranov had told her in the corridor outside to pull herself together. 'What are you trying to do, drench the head-quarters of the NKVD?'

Although subsequently interrogated by relays of questioners and subjected to torture – she was once kept standing for sixteen hours on end and had her fingers deliberately broken in a door – she obstinately refused to sign a confession implicating her in any conspiratorial way with Nikolayev. To this she probably owed the fact that she survived to write a harrowing account of her experiences, while so many others perished in the execution cellars of the secret police.

It is to her story, for example, that we owe such macabre details as prisoners standing in line before the elevator which took them down one at a time to the cellar – 'No pushing! No crowding!' they were told. 'Wait your turn!' – the sounds of shots and shrieks as they were butchered, and heaps of frozen corpses lying in the snow covered courtyard outside the main cellar waiting for disposal by the over-worked NKVD personnel. The shootings were carried out during the night at two- or three-minute intervals. Space was set aside for a kind of rest room and refreshment buffet for the shock brigade of executioners, so that they could be supplied with food and liquor 'to fortify them and maintain their fighting spirit'. Many of the victims were already in custody at the time of Kirov's murder with which they had no connection whatever; they were simply liquidated on the pretext of alleged complicity in the case in order to make room for new batches of suspected 'enemies of the people' and counter-revolutionaries.[12]

Ordering Agranov to follow up the line of laying the murder at the door of Zinoviev and other former oppositionists, Stalin left Leningrad in the same train that carried Kirov's remains to Moscow for the official lying-in-state. This latter ceremony took place in the Hall of Columns in Trade Union House, traditional venue of the obsequies of Soviet leaders as well as of important state trials. According to the Soviet press, Stalin appeared at the side of the bier, where he was so overcome with emotion that he leaned forward and kissed the corpse on the cheek. The NKVD defector Alexander Orlov, who noted the gesture, wondered afterwards whether Stalin might perhaps have re-called the Bible story, which he must have read as a student at the theological seminary in Tiflis, of how Judas Iscariot betrayed Christ with a similar salutation.[13]

Because of Nikolayev's realisation that he had been the dupe of the NKVD, there could be no question of putting the murderer of Kirov on trial publicly. Whether there was a trial behind closed doors and if so exactly what Nikolayev and his fellow defendants testified has not been established for certain. On 30 December 1934 a brief official statement appeared in *Pravda* to the effect that the members of the 'Nikolayev group' had been tried and executed, having admitted that their motive for conspiring together to kill Kirov was part of a plan to replace the Soviet leadership with that of Zinoviev and Kamenev by killing Stalin, Molotov and Kaganovich in addition to Kirov. After Nilolayev the most prominent among the conspirators was alleged to be a former member of the Central Committee of the Komsomol (Young Communists) in Leningrad named Ivan Kotolynov. However, some of them may have been executed earlier, particularly Nikolayev who is said to have been shot shortly after Stalin saw him.

In the meantime Zinoviev and Kamenev had been arrested and brought to trial along with seventeen others forming the alleged 'Mos-cow Centre' of the conspiracy. The trial, briefly reported in the news-papers, was presided over by Judge Ulrich, with Vyshinsky prosecut-ing, but the general public were not admitted. Since all the accused pleaded not guilty, it seems unlikely that torture was applied during the pre-trial investigations. However, during the court proceedings, both Zinoviev and Kamenev admitted 'political and moral responsibility' for the crime, while denying actual complicity in it. 'I must be blind,' said Kamenev when the court announced that he was accused of being the leader of a terrorist centre. 'I have reached the age of fifty but have never seen this centre, of which it appears I am a member.' Zinoviev declared that he did not even know most of the other defendants who stood in the dock with him; he added that he only learned of Kotolynov's role in the Nikolayev group in Leningrad through reading the indictment in that case.[14]

Nevertheless, in this patent judicial frame-up Zinoviev was sentenced to ten years imprisonment and Kamenev to five, the other accused receiving sentences ranging between these figures. (Kamenev was re-tried six months later and sentenced to a further term of ten years.) The actual length of the sentences was in fact merely a formality, since so far as is known none of the nineteen defendants was ever released. The trial was followed by a fresh wave of arrests throughout the country, running into tens of thousands.

A week after the Zinoviev–Kamenev trial, Zaporozhets, Medved and the other senior officers of the Leningrad NKVD, ten in all, were tried on charges that, 'having received information about the preparations for the attempt on S. M. Kirov, they failed to take the necessary measures to prevent the assassination, although they had every possible means of stopping it'. The lenience of their sentences – two to three years – caused general surprise in a case where Stalin might well have ordered the exemplary execution of all the accused for failure to forestall an assassination attempt which could concievably have included himself. More eyebrows were raised in the Soviet hierarchy when it was learned that Medved and Zaporozhets were being treated as highly privileged prisoners in the detention camp to which they were sent, receiving such unheard of luxuries to while away the time as radio sets and gramophone records from the notorious Pauker, the Kremlin black marketeer, who was a ranking officer in the Moscow NKVD as well as Stalin's principal bodyguard. Both Medved and Zaporozhets were released without having to serve the full term of their sentences. It was the remarkably lenient treatment they received that more than any other factor convinced Soviet officials that the man who must have been responsible for Kirov's murder was Stalin.[15]*

No sooner had the Kirov case been disposed of than the sudden death of another prominent member of the Politburo was announced

* In his 'secret speech' at the Twentieth Party Congress in 1956 on the subject of Stalin's crimes, Khrushchev did not go so far as openly to name Stalin as the principal culprit, but he plainly implied it. ('It must be asserted that to this day the circumstances surrounding Kirov's murder hide many things which are inexplicable and mysterious and demand the most careful examination.') Stalin's daughter Svetlana refuses to believe that her father was involved 'in this particular death' and puts the blame on Beria: *Twenty Letters to a Friend*, p. 139. But Beria was in Georgia at the time and it is extremely unlikely that he had anything to do with it.

This was Valerian Kuibyshev, who had been the strongest supporter of Kirov's 'policy of reconciliation' in that body. It was later alleged that Kuibyshev had been the victim of wrong treatment by the Kremlin doctors working under Yagoda's orders. However that may be, his death removed another thorn from Stalin's side, and on the face of it it seems extremely unlikely that this was due to 'natural causes'. Another mysterious death among those close to Stalin at this time was that of Ivan Tovstukha, the relatively mild leader of Stalin's personal secretariat.

Yagoda, who had s badly bungled the Nikolayev affair, was given another chance to prove his worth as the NKVD chief by obtaining an impressive string of 'confessions' from arrested Party members. The instructions he received from Stalin were simple, namely, as Khrushchev was later to put it, 'Beat them, beat them and beat them again!' And Khrushchev was in a position to know since as a devoted Stalinist and a protége of Kaganovich he was appointed First Secretary of the Moscow Party organisation at this time. Other significant appointments included Yezhov, who took Kirov's place as joint secretary of the Central Committee; Malenkov, who became Yezhov's deputy in charge of personnel; and Vyshinsky as Attorney-General responsible for all public prosecutions. Poskrebyshev took over the running of Stalin's personal secretariat from Tovstukha, including the dreaded Special Section, while Beria operated the secret police machine in the Transcaucasus.

Thus by the middle of 1935, Stalin had established a base of key men whom he could rely upon to help him launch the Great Purge of the Party he had in mind. The Kirov murder gave him the opportunity he wished for to introduce the death penalty for Old Bolsheviks and other Party members. 'He could now begin on the systematic extermination of all who, sharing with him the mantle of Lenin and the traditions of the October Revolution, provided a standard around which the discontented and rebellious masses could rally.'[16]

3
If Stalin's security was threatened from within by the Old Bolsheviks, he felt that his security from outside was increasingly endangered by the aggressive tendencies of Hitler in Europe. Stalin had been impressed by the blood bath with which the Fuehrer had eliminated the political opposition led by Captain Roehm on 30 June 1934, and he did not share the view of some of his colleagues in the Politburo that this action of Hitler's had fatally weakened his hold on the country. 'The events in Germany do not at all indicate the collapse of the Nazi

régime,' he had told the Politburo at the time. 'On the contrary, they are bound to lead to the consolidation of that régime and to the strengthening of Hitler himself.'[17]

Stalin's foreign policy was thus dictated by the need to contain Hitler, who talked rashly about the Ukraine and even Siberia as possible outlets for German territorial expansion. Hence Stalin's new found enthusiasm for the League of Nations and his endeavours through the peripatetic Litvinov to bring about an eastern Locarno or multilateral non-aggression pact to which he stated that he was ready to subscribe. When this came to nothing through the opposition of Germany and Poland, Stalin began to court the western Allies with a view to effecting a series of defensive alliances. The first of these was concluded with France, the protocol being signed at Geneva on 5 December 1934, in such a form that left it open for other powers to adhere to it. At the same time, Stalin was determined to leave the door open for an understanding with Germany and he felt he had gone some way in this direction when the Reichsbank offered the Soviet Government a long-term loan of 200 million gold marks in return for Soviet purchases of German goods, particularly industrial machinery. 'Well, now,' said Stalin when the arrangements had been completed 'how can Hitler make war on us when he had granted us such a loan? It's impossible. The business circles in Germany are too powerful, and they are in the saddle.'[18]

Germany had already begun to rearm in defiance of the Versailles peace treaty, and a joint Anglo-French communiqué, issued after conversations between British and French ministers in London in February 1935, warned Hitler that he had no right to take such unilateral action. This resulted in an invitation to the British Foreign Secretary, Sir John Simon, to talk the matter over in Berlin. When he learned of the projected trip, Stalin suggested that the British Minister should come on to Moscow, since he was afraid that the British might do a deal with Hitler to the Soviet Union's disadvantage. This second invitation was conveyed through the able and ingenious Soviet ambassador in London Ivan Maisky. No British Minister had visited Russia since the Revolution, and the British Cabinet welcomed Stalin's gesture as heralding a better phase in Anglo-Soviet relations and as seeming to show that any lingering ill-feeling over the Metro-Vickers affair was at an end. However, Simon was not at all keen to go further afield than Berlin, and so it was agreed that Anthony Eden, the youthful and debonair Lord Privy Seal, soon to become Minister in charge of League of Nations affairs in the British Government, should stand in for the Foreign Secretary in Moscow, after accompanying him to Berlin, and

314

that he should also visit Warsaw and Prague. No objections were advanced on the Soviet side to this arrangement.[19]

Although Eden was only a junior minister and not in the Cabinet, it was made clear by Litvinov that his presence in Moscow would be welcome and furthermore that Stalin would be glad to receive him. This was indeed striking evidence of the dictator's desire to effect an understanding with Great Britain, since with the exception of the American ambassador William Bullitt, no foreign politician or diplomat even when accredited to the Soviet Union had previously been received by Stalin. To all such requests from heads of foreign missions for interviews of this kind, Litvinov would laughingly reply, 'I am very sorry indeed. But Mr Stalin, he is just a private gentleman, and he does not like to see foreigners. He leaves that to me!'[20]

When it was learned in the British Embassy in Moscow that Mr Eden would be arriving shortly and would probably be calling at the Kremlin, the ambassador Lord Chilston wrote an assessment of what he called 'the autocrat's present position' and the possibilities of his 'removal'.* This he did in the form of a confidential and hitherto unpublished dispatch to the Foreign Office, primarily for Eden's information. It was the first assessment of its kind to have been made, and in the light of subsequent events is worth quotation, particularly since the writer like most other heads of missions in Moscow had never met 'the autocrat'.

Moscow, 22 February 1935
...M. Stalin, of course, owes his position in large part to his own remarkable personality, but it is not easy for one who has never met him to form an estimate of this. Seen at a public function he appears to be more human, sociable, friendly with people, than would be expected. One is impressed by an air of calm assurance and strength in the Georgian and somewhat oriental face. Few foreigners have seen him at close quarters. Mr Bullitt...secured an interview. Neither, I believe, was much impressed by the other, Mr H. G. Wells's account of his interview with him last summer, and the subsequent newspaper controversy beweeen Mr Wells, Mr Bernard Shaw and others, shed some interesting but occasionally deceptive light on this question.

It used to be generally assumed, when M. Stalin first came into

* Aretas Akers-Douglas, 2nd Viscount Chilston (1876–1947) had been appointed ambassador in 1933 after his predecessor had been obliged to ask to be recalled following the Metro-Vickers trial. He worked hard to re-establish friendly relations and was held in high regard by Litvinov. He retired in 1938.

prominence, that he was merely a clever political intriguer with a thirst for power. He certainly loves power, and he is certainly a capable intriguer; but it must now be admitted that he is more than that. The 'mere intriguer' generally does not know what to do with power when he achieves it; but M. Stalin has always known that, though he has sometimes changed his mind, and is prepared to change his policy at any time, even in disregard of cherished Communist principles. Moreover, he has not used his power exclusively for his own gratification. Though, no doubt, he has all he wants for his personal use, he employs his virtual omnipotence in this country for the furtherance of a policy which, however mistaken, has undoubtedly a certain 'ideological' basis. Mr Wells represents him as a kindly man who 'owes his position to the fact that no one is afraid of him and everyone trusts him'. Kindliness is not a quality which is easy to reconcile either with M. Stalin's actions or with his published statements; on the contrary, he has always preached, and practised, a high degree of ruthlessness, and, in consequence, it is equally absurd to say that no one in the Soviet Union is afraid of him; there are millions who both fear and loathe him. It is generally believed that Lenin did not favour the idea of his being his successor, describing him as of too brutal and coarse a nature as well as disloyal. But if by trusting him it is meant that everybody knows he will carry out a policy once undertaken, then perhaps there is some truth in the second half of Mr Wells's dictum...His strong points are clearly administrative ability, driving power, and the capacity to evolve and control a large-scale plan.

Mr Bernard Shaw has told us that M. Stalin is a mere party official who can at any time be given a week's notice. This absurd opinion is not one which would be endorsed by anyone with even the most superficial knowledge of this country. There are, as I see it, three possible methods, other than natural death, by which M. Stalin might be removed: assassination, a military *coup d'état*, or a 'palace plot'. No conspiracy in which persons in control of some part at least of the machinery of government do not take part has the least chance of success. The would-be assassin would find his way beset by almost insuperable difficulties: M. Stalin is extremely well guarded, he rarely appears in public, his movements are never announced beforehand in the press, and no one knows where he lives. Nominally he is not the head of the State, and he has no office but that of secretary-general of the Central Committee of the Communist party. MM.

316

Molotov and Kalanin are his tools and his mouthpiece. M. Litvinov is used for dealing with the capitalist powers.

As for a military *coup d'état*, M. Voroshilov could perhaps, if he were so minded, attempt one after due preparation with some chance of success; but the issue would always be doubtful, particularly if the Ogpu troops, which are not under the Commissariat of Defence, remained faithful. The army would be divided in its allegiance, and, in any case, M. Voroshilov is generally believed to be absolutely loyal to M. Stalin. The method most likely to be successful is the 'palace plot'. M. Stalin's immediate associates, or the instruments through which he exercises his control of the State machinery (such as the Ogpu) might conceivably turn against him and be able to defeat him. But neither M. Yagoda, the head of what was, and for all practical purposes, still is, the Ogpu, or any other of M. Stalin's associates, with the doubtful exception of M. Kaganovich, appears to be of the calibre to carry through an intrigue of this kind; moreover, they are all too jealous of each other.

There is the final difficulty presented by M. Stalin's artificially created prestige in the country. Unlike most dictators, his public appearances are very rare, and his speeches still rarer (he has not made one since January 1934). A delegate to the recent Congress of Collective Farmers expressed the hope that the congress might be privileged to hear a few words from the great leader's lips; but this privilege was not granted. But an intensive propaganda campaign has made his name synonymous with the régime dominating Lenin's and eclipsing Marx and Engels entirely. Every speech, every leading article, must allude to him. Since the beginning of this year practically every issue of every daily paper has contained his photograph, and his portrait is everywhere. No achievement of Soviet production, science, exploration or art can be announced without attributing its inspiration to him. As an instance of this propaganda, almost for the deification of M. Stalin, as well as of the intimidation which undoubtedly is exercised over the population, I may mention two incidents of which I was personally a witness. At the opening of the All-Union Congress of Soviets, a function which proved to be little else than a glorification of the Leader, the two thousand delegates rose to their feet whenever the name of M. Stalin was mentioned, cheering and clapping and singing the *Internationale*, sometimes even for ten minutes. It was observable that no person dared to cease clapping, for fear that his neighbour should notice, until the speaker had resumed his seat as a signal for the ovation to end. On another occasion – the opening of an exhibition of theatrical art – a speaker realising when he had finished his speech that the due reference to M. Stalin as the father of the arts and drama of the new Russia had been forgotten, rushed pallid to the platform again and produced a panegyric...[21]

A briefer and less subtle analysis was made by the United States ambassador Joseph E. Davies, who succeeded William Bullitt in 1936. 'Stalin is a simple man, everyone says, but a man of tremendous singleness of purpose and capacity for work,' Mr Davies wrote to his government shortly after his arrival. 'He holds the situation in his hand. He is decent and clean-living and is apparently devoted to the purpose of the projection of the socialist state and ultimate communism, with sufficient resilience in his make-up to stamp him as a politican as well as a great leader.'[22]

4

The meeting with Eden nearly foundered on an unexpected obstacle. Before leaving London, Eden had been assured, and so had the Cabinet, that Stalin would see him and this was confirmed on his arrival in Moscow with Maisky, who had been ordered to escort him on the final lap of his journey from Berlin. At the same time Eden was informed that Stalin would receive him alone with Litvinov, who would act as interpreter. In this event Eden would not be able to bring Lord Chilston with him, as he was anxious to do, since the ambassador spoke Russian and Eden did not. Litvinov repeated his customary argument that Stalin was not a member of the Soviet government and therefore, as Eden put it, there was something more than protocol in his refusal to see an ambassador. Also, if Chilston accompanied Eden, that meant that Maisky must be there too, and Stalin apparently disliked 'discussing international affairs in a crowd'. However, Eden stood firm, since he felt it essential to have another interpreter present who could check Litvinov's translation. 'I had no doubt of Litvinov's good faith,' Eden later remarked. 'Anyone with experience of international conferences will know what risks there are in amateur translations, however brilliantly executed.'

For some days the argument continued, until Eden began to fear that the interview for which he had travelled so many thousands of miles might not take place. Eventually Stalin agreed to a compromise by which the meeting was held in Molotov's private office in the Kremlin, with the Chairman of the Council of Commissars being

318

present in addition to Litvinov, Maisky, Chilston and the two principals. Chilston was also allowed to bring the Embassy Counsellor William Strang as an additional interpreter.

Eden's initial impression was favourable and was to be confirmed in subsequent war-time meetings.

> As we entered I saw standing there a short, thick-set man with hair *en brosse*. He was in a grey tunic, with rather baggy dark trousers and calf-length black boots. I never saw Stalin in anything but a variant of this uniform. He always appeared well laundered and neatly dressed.
>
> Stalin impressed me from the first and my opinion of his abilities has not wavered. His personality made itself felt without effort or exaggeration. He had natural good manners, perhaps a Georgian inheritance. Though I knew the man to be without mercy, I respected the quality of his mind and even felt a sympathy which I have never been able entirely to analyse. Perhaps this was because of Stalin's pragmatic approach. It was easy to forget that I was talking to a Party man, certainly no one could have been less doctrinaire. I cannot believe that Stalin ever had any affinity with Marx, he never spoke of him as if he did. During our several meetings in the war, sometimes with Churchill but as often alone, I always found the encounter stimulating, grey and stern though the agenda often had to be. I have never known a man handle himself better in conference. Well-informed at all points that were of concern to him, Stalin was prudent but not slow. Seldom raising his voice, a good listener, prone to doodling, he was the quietest dictator I have ever known, with the exception of Dr Salazar. Yet the strength was there, unmistakably.[23]

After a preliminary exchange of courtesies, Eden began the discussion by telling Stalin that British ministers believed that the Soviet Government intended to conduct their relations with the United Kingdom 'in the spirit of collaboration and non-interference which was inherent in our common membership of the League of Nations'. He went on to express the British Government's confidence that the Soviet Union 'recognised that the continued integrity, tranquillity and prosperity of British territories were an advantage to peace'. Here Molotov broke in to say that Eden had accurately defined the Soviet attitude. 'The Soviet Government has no desire to interfere in any way in the internal affairs of the British Empire,' Molotov added. Stalin briefly confirmed this.[24]

There was some more somewhat desultory talk to the same effect, and Eden began to wonder whether he should not take his leave, when Stalin suddenly launched into an exposition of the world and particularly the European scene as he saw it, prefacing his remarks with a direct question to Eden.

'Do you consider the present European situation as alarming as, or more alarming than, the situation in 1913?'

'I would use the word "anxious" rather than "alarming",' Eden replied, cautiously feeling his way. 'The existence of the League of Nations, of which every European power but Germany is a member, is an advantage of importance which we lacked before the war.'

'I agree on the value of the League,' retorted Stalin, 'but I think the international situation is fundamentally worse. In 1913, there was only one potential aggressor, Germany. Today there are two, Germany and Japan.'

Future events, as Eden later appreciated, were to justify these words. For the moment, Stalin said he was sure that Japan would not stop with the conquest of Manchuria and that China would be the next victim of Japan's aggressive intentions. So far as Germany was concerned, Stalin went on, he realised that the Germans were 'a great and capable people with exceptional powers of organisation and great industrial strength'. Moreover, they were smarting under a sense of injury inflicted upon them by the terms of the Treaty of Versailles. 'We must expect that they would be actuated by motives of revenge,' he added.

To an interjection from Eden that Germany was losing the sympathy of world opinion by her own acts, Stalin replied that German diplomacy was 'generally clumsy', and maintained that the only way to meet the situation created by Germany was by some scheme of pacts. 'Germany must be made to realise that if she attacked any other nation she would have Europe against her.' To emphasise his point he gave an illustration. 'We are six of us in this room,' he said. 'If Maisky chooses to go for any one of us, then we must all fall on Maisky.'[25]

Stalin chuckled at this idea, while Maisky grinned somewhat nervously. 'Only by this means will peace be preserved,' Stalin went on. 'The League as it is today is not strong enough for the purpose. It has suffered too many humiliations. Even Paraguay has been able to flout it with impunity.'

At this point Stalin got up from his chair and walked across to a map of the world which was hanging on the wall. Indicating with a broad sweep of his hand the extent of British possessions, he remarked in what Eden took to be 'friendly tones' upon the power and influence of so small an island as Great Britain. 'That little island if she chooses can stop Germany by refusing her raw materials without which she cannot pursue agressive designs'.[26] Much must depend upon the part the British Government was willing to play in a collective system in present conditions, he went on, looking at Eden.

It would be fatal to let events drift. If a check is to be placed upon a potential aggressor, there is no time to lose. That should be in our power now, when actual war is probably some little time distant. At the last moment a check might fail.

Complaining of what he called the duplicity of German policy, Stalin somewhat to Eden's surprise revealed details of the long-term credit recently obtained from Germany to cover Soviet purchases from that country. In order to test Germany, said Stalin, the Soviet Government deliberately included in their list of orders some important contracts for the supply of war material. To their astonishment the German Government accepted these orders, 'and now,' added Stalin, 'Herr Hitler says he is frightened of us!' The Germans were also pretending that the Soviet Government had asked them for these credits, according to Stalin, whereas in fact it was Germany who had made the first approaches. All this made Eden wonder whether the Russians were really so astonished as Stalin claimed and whether he himself was not being taken in. There had been many similar orders placed by the USSR before with the Germans, and Eden was soon to note an example of this when he was shown a Junkers aircraft factory near Moscow.

Eden also noted that Stalin referred to a curious story which he stated was being spread about by the Germans to the effect that General Tukachevsky, the Vice-Commissar of Defence, soon to be promoted Marshal, had recently been in contact with General Goering, then Reich Air Minister, and had tried to involve him in some anti-French scheme. Eden found this report even stranger than the one about the Soviet orders for military equipment, since Tukachevsky had recently published an article which was so anti-German in tone that it had drawn a diplomatic protest from Berlin. However, it did seem to indicate that Stalin no longer trusted the country's most brilliant and outstanding military figure. Eden was to have occasion to recall Stalin's story two years later when Tukachevsky was shot for alleged treasonable conspiracy with the Nazis. To the British minister's mind the 'mazes of the Kremlin' were 'impenetrable'.

Finally, Stalin asked Eden why Hitler would not take part in any pacts of mutual assistance. Eden replied that the German Fuehrer had

321

expressed reluctance to enter into any pact which would compel Germany to fight in a quarrel between two other parties, in which she was not directly concerned. In the event of his having a difference with a neighbour, added Eden, Hitler was 'prepared to deal with that himself and did not wish to be helped'.

'Rather than help to keep the peace,' remarked Stalin dryly, 'Hitler may prefer to make a profit out of the differences of others.'

After the meeting was over, Eden returned to the British Embassy, where he sent a telegram to London summarising his impressions of the Soviet leader.

> Stalin showed in the course of this conversation a remarkable knowledge and understanding of international affairs. In the latter respect his sympathies seemed broader than those of Litvinov though his conclusions were no less firm.
>
> Stalin spoke throughout in measured tones so quiet that at times Litvinov himself could not catch what he said. He displayed no emotion whatever except for an occasional chuckle or flash of wit.
>
> The impression left upon us was of a man of strong oriental traits of character with unshakeable assurance and control, whose courtesy in no way hid from us an implacable ruthlessness.

Stalin had given orders that no trouble was to be spared in entertaining Eden and his party. A gala performance of the Tchaikovsky ballet *Swan Lake* was put on in his honour at the Bolshoi Theatre, and against all tradition the orchestra struck up 'God Save the King', the first occasion on which the British national anthem had been played in Russia since the Revolution. On Eden's last night, he was taken to see another ballet, this time a modern one, entitled *The Three Fat Men*.

'Who are those fat men shovelling in the food and fussed over by flunkeys?' Eden asked Litvinov as they sat together in the former Imperial box. 'They look like Michelin tyre advertisements.'

'They represent three capitalists,' replied the Foreign Commissar after an embarrassed pause. Then, as if to excuse the performance he added, 'Personally I dislike politics mixed up with my ballet. I love the ballet for the relaxation it gives me.'

Unfortunately the distinguished English visitor was not able to stay long enough to see the final overthrow of capitalists by the proletariat, as he had to leave to catch his train to Warsaw. Litvinov also left to see him off at the station. 'I wish you success,' he said in tones loud enough to be overheard, as he waved Eden goodbye at the door of the late Tsar's coach, which had been put at Eden's disposal. 'Your success will be our success – now!'[27]

Eden's much trumpeted visit did not achieve any remarkable results; not was it intended to, at least on the British side. Unlike France and Czechoslavakia, whose Foreign Ministers appeared on the Moscow scene shortly afterwards, Britain did not conclude anything in the nature of a non-aggression or mutual assistance pact with the USSR as Stalin and the Politburo may have hoped. But the Eden visit and its accompanying publicity in the Russian press did at least do something to improve Anglo-Soviet relations. Also, the fact that Eden was formally received by Stalin established a precedent which was immediately followed in the case of Pierre Laval and Edward Benes and in some degree with other visiting politicians and diplomats, while Stalin now began to put in an appearance at official receptions for the diplomatic corps at which Litvinov had hitherto been the principal host. However, he did not as a rule attend receptions given by foreign missions, leaving this to Kalinin, Molotov, Voroshilov and Litvinov – not even the party given at the Czech legation for Benes. What he missed on this occasion was described by the British *chargé d'affaires*.

The reception was a great success, largely owing to the provision of kegs of Pilsener beer and platefuls of 'hot dogs', before which guests of all nationalities shamelessly formed queues determined to make the most of a unique opportunity. M. Karl Radek was overhead to remark that on the foundation of such beer any kind of treaty could be negotiated.[28]

Laval's visit coincided with the May Day celebrations. After the principal display was over, the American ambassador William Bullitt wrote to President Roosevelt:

I have just come back from the May Day parade in the Red Square. It had been a great show with tanks galloping across at sixty miles an hour and new pursuit planes at four hundred kilometres per hour. Stalin came late and left early due, I am told, to a last minute hitch in negotiations with the French. It was also noticeable that when he walked the short space from the Kremlin wall to Lenin's tomb he held a handkerchief to his face. He may really, after all, be a bit frightened...

The red carpet treatment accorded to the French Foreign Minister included a performance of Rimsky-Korsakov's opera *Sadko* at the

323

Bolshoi Theatre, 'elaborately staged but indifferently performed', as an observer from the British embassy staff put it. 'M. Stalin also attended the performance; but he remained hidden at the back of his own box and held no communication with M. Laval.'

Incidentally Stalin's interference in matters of culture and the arts caused some amusement among the diplomatic corps. Bullitt commented on an example of this during this period:

> Stalin's latest imitation of *Le Roi Soleil* is to dictate in the field of music and drama. Recently he went to see a modern Soviet opera and a modern ballet which had been praised by the critics as the supreme achievement of the human race. In the ballet the Georgians were shown to be comic, in the opera the Russians were shown to be drunk. Stalin at once caused *ukases* to be issued damning all the musicians and producers who have been heralded in the past few years by the Soviet press as demi-gods. The result is that half the artists and musicians in Moscow are engaged in having nervous prostration and the others are trying to imagine how to write and compose in a manner to please Stalin.[29]

A fragment of the Stalin–Laval discussions was subsequently revealed by Winston Churchill who had his own particular sources of intelligence.

> Stalin and Molotov were of course anxious to know above all else what was to be the strength of the French Army on the Western Front: How many divisions? what period of service? After this field had been explored, Laval said: 'Can't you do something to encourage religion and the Catholics in Russia? It would help me so much with the Pope.' 'Oho!' said Stalin. 'The Pope! How many divisions has *he* got?' Laval's answer was not reported to me; but he might certainly have mentioned a number of legions not always on parade.[30]

Laval posed another question. 'Can you guarantee that the French Communist Party will adopt a patriotic attitude in the case of a military conflict with the Third Reich?'

'Apply to the Secretary-General of the French Communist Party, Jacques Doriot,' replied Stalin. 'He will answer your question. I am not qualified to speak for him. But I do know that Jacques Doriot is as determined as we are to fight the Nazis wherever they find them.'[31]

At the same time, Stalin gave Laval an assurance, which he authorised the French Foreign Minister to announce publicly, that the Soviet

Government approved the policy of national defence being carried out by France in order to maintain her armed forces at security level. This assurance was duly repeated by Laval on his return to Paris, and it did eventually achieve its purpose of gaining the French Communist Party's support for the introduction of conscription and increased military expenditure, although its members continued to be suspicious of Laval whom they rightly regarded as a political renegade. Neither for that matter did Stalin place much faith in Laval, and what he did have progressively decreased as Laval showed himself in no hurry to get the new Franco-Soviet pact ratified by the French Parliament. It was also reported to Stalin through German sources that Laval had met General Goering at Cracow, where they both attended the funeral of the late Polish Head of State Marshal Pilsudski, and in the course of their cordial talks together Laval had made no secret of his distrust and dislike of the Soviets.

Stalin's assurance to Laval had one important consequence. It signalled a complete reversal of the policy of the Comintern which had hitherto aimed at promoting revolution in all foreign countries. Now all members of foreign Communist parties were instructed to join hands with middle-class liberal, radical, and even conservative elements in the formation of 'Popular Fronts' to fight Fascism. To this end a new director of the Comintern was appointed in the person of George Dimitrov, hero of the German Reichstag fire trial, and Stalin made a point of being seen publicly wherever he could with this leading Bulgarian Communist.[32]

Although the Popular Front as an anti-Fascist movement had some effect in the democratic countries of Europe, it failed to stay the course of the dictators. Nor, in spite of Litvinov's efforts at Geneva, was it possible to galvanise the member states of the League of Nations into any real collective resistance to aggression. When Mussolini launched his attack upon Ethiopia, followed a few months later by Germany's reoccuption of the Rhineland in defiance of her treaty obligations, both dictators remained unchecked. Hitler gave as an excuse for his action the Franco-Soviet Pact which had just been ratified at long last by the French Senate, although the pact due to delays and repeated amendments was now virtually meaningless. At the same time, Hitler declared that this action constituted his last territorial demand against the west. Henceforward, he implied, his objectives would lie to the east. The message was not lost upon Stalin.[33]

It was at this period that the Soviet leader came to realise that sooner or later he must fight Hitler in the field. True, Stalin might still be able to reach some sort of accommodation with the Fuehrer, but this would only be buying time if Hitler persisted in his plans for a drive to the east. But first, Stalin had to set his own political house in order, which meant making absolutely sure that every possible domestic opposition to his future policies would be eliminated once and for all time.

5

Within a few days of Hitler's jackbooted battalions marching into the Rhineland, Stalin issued secret orders to the NKVD for putting into operation a plan which he had worked out with Yezhov in his personal secretariat. The details, for the carrying out of which the NKVD chief Yagoda was made responsible, were explained by a senior member of the department, G. A. Molchanov, to a top level conference of some forty key officers at the Lubyanka headquarters. Molchanov informed them that a vast conspiracy had been uncovered, led by Trotsky, Zinoviev, Kamenev and other former leaders of the Opposition. This conspiratorial organisation had apparently been active for several years through terrorist groups in the principal cities of the Soviet Union; and it aimed at assassinating Stalin and the rest of the Politburo and then seizing power. The forty NKVD men, Molchanov told them, would be released from their ordinary duties in order to investigate the conspiracy, and their work, which 'would constitute for them a test not only as Chekists, but party members as well', would be supervised by Yezhov and Stalin himself. Molchanov added unequivocally that 'Stalin and the Politburo considered the information against the leaders of the conspiracy as absolutely trustworthy and, therefore, the task of every investigator must be to get from the accused full confessions and not to pay any attention to their hypothetical attempts to establish alibis for themselves, because it was known that some of the accused had even managed to direct the activity of the terrorists groups from their prison cells'. What Molchanov failed to explain was how such a vast conspiracy could have been in existence for so long seeing that the NKVD had been receiving reports from a whole network of secret informers on the activities of the oppositionists for several years past.[34]

However, it does appear that an attempt on Stalin's life had been made some months previously, although it seems highly unlikely that any of the imprisoned oppositionists let alone the exiled Trotsky could have had anything to do with it. Apparently the unwitting instrument in facilitating the attempt was Stalin's old crony Abel Yenukidze, who introduced a young woman of striking physical beauty named Zoya Nikitina into the Kremlin, having already aroused Stalin's interest by describing her charms and suggesting that she would prove a most suitable mistress under cover of rearranging the Kremlin library. Stalin asked Yenukidze to bring her to the library, and while she was there, looking over the books and making notes, Stalin took the opportunity of observing her through a secret peephole from an adjoining room. While she definitely appealed to him there was one thing about her which aroused his suspicions. She was dressed in a cape, an unusual article of apparel for women in those days. He gave orders for her to be searched, and a pistol loaded with poisoned bullets was discovered concealed underneath her cape. That this had not been done by the guards at the Kremlin entrance was due to her having been with Yenukidze in his car. It appeared that she had strong White sympathies and connections. Certainly her unsuccessful mission besides resulting in her own execution cost the lives of several hundred others, chiefly members of the Komosmol, who were alleged to have known her. According to one account, Zoya Nikitina was in reality the aristocratic Countess Orlova-Davydova and was shot on Stalin's personal order immediately after her arrest without being brought to trial. This may have been the origin of the story of 'the princess in the Kremlin', for whose insinuation into the fortress Yenukidze was blamed. At all events, Yenukidze's fall from favour dated from this time.[35]

Yenukidze was convinced that his main crime in Stalin's eyes was that he tried to dissuade him from his purpose when Stalin told him that he wished to 'stage a trial and shoot Kamenev and Zinoviev'.

'Soso,' Yenukidze pleaded with Stalin, 'there is no denying that they have wronged you, but they have already suffrd nough for that: you expelled them from the party, you keep them in prison, their children hav nothing to eat...They are Old Bolsheviks, like you and me. Surely you are not going to shed the blood of Old Bolsheviks! Think what the world will say about us.'

According to Yenukidze, Stalin gave him a look as if he had murdered his father. 'Remember, Abel,' he said, quoting the Bible, 'who is not with me is against me!'[36]

An additional failing on Yenukidze's part was that he allowed his personal role in the direction of the Bolshevik underground in Baku before the Revolution to be 'exaggerated' in the *Large Soviet Encyclopedia* to the detriment of 'the great Stalin'. Yenukidze admitted his 'error' when the latest Stalin record was promulgated as part of a monumental falsification of history by Lavrenti Beria. This took the form of a series of four lectures which Beria delivered to the party workers in Tiflis in July 1935. Entitled *On the History of the Bolshevik Organisations in Transcaucasia*, the lectures which had Stalin's

327

warm approval were printed in *Pravda* and subsequently published in book form, running into numerous editions and millions of copies during the remainder of the dictator's lifetime.[37]

Some months before the investigation began, a remarkable innovation in the Soviet criminal law took place in the form of a decree, which was to form a most powerful and cruel weapon in the hands of the investigators when dealing with arrested suspects. By Yezhov's order every interrogator was required to have a copy of this diabolical decree on his desk so that he could show it to any prisoner who doubted its authenticity. It made children and young people over the age of twelve liable to the death penalty as accomplices in the treasonable activities of their parents. The publication of the decree created a bad impression abroad, but that Stalin should have publicised it in this way shows that considerable importance must have been attached to it by the Politburo. On the other hand, it is clear that Stalin had no compunction on the score of 'liquidating' children when he thought it necessary. The Tsarevich Alexis who had perished with the rest of the imperial family at Ekaterinburg was only thirteen at the time of his death, and during the famine in 1932, when thousands of stray children jammed the railway stations, Stalin issued secret orders that any children caught stealing food from railways cars in transit should be summarily disposed of. The purpose of the latest decree was to play upon the Old Bolshevik's love of their children and grandchildren, and to a great extent it succeeded.[38]

The plan worked out by Stalin and Yezhov between them provided for bringing about three hundred exiled or imprisoned oppositionists to the Lubyanka for interrogation. It was hoped in this way to break down about one out of every five prisoners and thus to obtain a group of fifty or so who would be prepared to testify in court that they had taken part in the alleged conspiracy under the direction of Trotsky, Zinoviev and Kamenev. The two latter would then be confronted with a series of signed confessions, with the object of making them admit that they had plotted to do away with Stalin and the other party leaders. Although the plan did not meet with the success that was anticipated, important 'confessions' were obtained from three Bolsheviks. These were Valentine Oldberg, a secret NKVD agent who worked in the Foreign Department; Isaac Reingold, a senior official in the Commissariat of Finance, who was acquainted with Kamenev; and Richard Pickel, who had at one time been in charge of Zinoviev's secretariat and latterly managed a Moscow theatre. Reingold proved the most stubborn, but after he had been continuously interrogated for several periods of forty-eight hours, kept without sleep and food, and

328

heard orders given for the arrest of his family, he finally gave in on being told by Yezhov in the name of the Central Committee that he would best prove his innocence and devotion to the Party by helping the NKVD against Zinoviev and Kamenev. Reingold accordingly put his name to a deposition in which it was stated that the assassination of Kirov had been organised by Zinoviev and Kamenev, and further that under the latter's direction he had been similarly plotting to get rid of Stalin, Molotov, Voroshilov, Kaganovich and other Party leaders.[39]

Then a curious thing happened. Reingold's written testimony, carefully revised by Agranov and Mironov, was taken by Yagoda to Stalin. Next day Stalin returned it with the name of Molotov crossed out in Stalin's own hand. This caused a considerable sensation in the Lubyanka, where it was taken to mean that Molotov had fallen out of favour with Stalin and that his arrest could be expected shortly. This impression was confirmed when Molotov left for his annual vacation in the south, and Stalin did not come to the station to see him off as he had previously been in the habit of doing. There is indeed little doubt that Molotov was under a cloud at this time and that Stalin seriously thought of arresting him and putting him in the dock along with Zinoviev, Kamenev and the others. That he did not do so and eventually restored him to favour may well have been due to the value he set upon his abilities, particularly his capacity for hard work, compared with his colleagues in the Politburo. Nevertheless, there was considerable surprise in official circles in Moscow when Molotov returned to his job as Chairman of the Council of Commissars instead of being taken under guard to the Lubyanka. It may be added that his rehabilitation was only gradual. When the trial of the oppositionists finally took place and Vyshinsky for the prosecution recited 'the names of the wonderful companions in arms of Stalin' and 'the tireless and gifted builders of our state', against whom the foul machinations of the defendants had been directed, Molotov's name was noticeably absent from the list. It is scarcely necessary to add that the omission was deliberate and could not have happened on the sole initiative of Vyshinsky.[40]

Impatient at what he considered the slow rate of progress in preparing for the trial, Stalin would often call up the NKVD on the telephone and ask how things were going during a particular interrogation. He would also send for Yagoda and his assistants to hear what they had to say. On one occasion, Mironov reported that Kamenev was displaying determined resistance and he did not think there was much chance of breaking him down.

'You think that Kamenev may not confess?' asked Stalin, giving the NKVD man a sly look.

'I don't know,' answered Mironov. 'He doesn't yield to persuasion.'

'You don't know?' said Stalin, affecting considerable surprise and staring hard at Mironov. 'Do you know how much our state weighs, with all the factories, machines, the army, with all the armaments, and the navy?'

Mironov and the others with him regarded Stalin with astonishment.

'Think it over and tell me,' Stalin persisted.

Mironov smiled, thinking Stalin was about to crack a joke. But Stalin was not in a jesting mood. He looked at Mironov in deadly earnest. 'I am asking you, how much does all that weigh?' he repeated.

Mironov became confused, as Stalin kept him fixed with a stony stare. 'Nobody can know that, Joseph Vissarionovich,' he blurted out at last. 'It is in the realm of astronomical figures.'

'Well, and can one man withstand the pressure of that astronomical weight?'

'No,' answered Mironov.

'Now then,' rejoined Stalin, 'don't tell me any more that Kamenev, or this or that prisoner, is able to withstand that pressure.' Then, pointing to Mironov's brief-case which was lying on the table in front of him, he went on: 'Don't come and report to me again until you have Kamenev's confession in this brief-case.'

After one of the other NKVD men had submitted an equally unsatisfactory report about another Old Bolshevik Ivan Smirov, Stalin returned to the question of Kamenev. 'Tell him,' he said to Mironov, 'that if he refuses to go for trial, we'll find a suitable substitute for him – his own son – who will testify at the trial that on instructions from his father he was preparing acts of terrorism against the Party leaders ...Tell him that you have information that his son and Reingold together were seen trailing Voroshilov's and Stalin's cars on the Mozhaisk Highway. That will bring him to his senses at once!'[41]

The two principal prisoners were both in poor health – Kamenev had heart trouble and Zinoviev suffered from a liver complaint in addition to asthma – but they continued to hold out. Further pressure was therefore applied. Although the weather had now become warm, Yagoda had the steam in the hot pipes in their cells increased to near boiling point, so that the prisoners could only breathe with the greatest difficulty. Finally Zinoviev asked to be allowed to see Kamenev in private. This was after he had been interrogated throughout one sweltering hot night in July by Yezhov, Agranov, Mironov and Molchanov, and been told by Yezhov in Stalin's name that if he agreed to go to public trial voluntarily and testify there himself, his life would be spared, as would Kamenev's if he also confessed – but that, if he refused to do so, he would be tried by a military court behind closed doors, in which case he and all the members of his opposition would be 'annihilated'.

Zinoviev's request was granted, and both men were taken to a cell with a concealed microphone so that their conversation could be overheard by the NKVD. Zinoviev expressed the opinion that it was necessary to go to trial provided that Stalin confirmed the promises given through Yezhov that their lives would be spared. After some argument and hesitation, Kamenev agreed, but added the stipulation that Stalin's confirmation must be made in the presence of all the members of the Politburo. Zinoviev and Kamenev were then taken to Yagoda's office, where they informed the NKVD chief of their understanding.

When he heard this, Yagoda asked for an appointment with Stalin, and he went over to the Kremlin for this purpose accompanied by Mironov and Molchanov. Stalin was highly pleased at their news. 'Bravo boys! Well done!' he said, getting up from his chair and rubbing his hands with excitement. He then ordered that the two prisoners should be brought to his room the following evening.

What happened on that occasion was subsequently related by Mironov to the NKVD defector Alexander Orlov.[42]

On receipt of a telephone call that Stalin was ready for them, Mironov and Molchanov took the prisoners under guard to the Kremlin. Yagoda was waiting for them in the reception room and conducted them to Stalin's office. On entering, they noticed that only one other member of the Politburo was present besides Stalin, namely Voroshilov, and he was sitting on Stalin's right, while Yezhov sat on his left. The prisoners stopped short in the middle of the room, and without a word of greeting Stalin pointed to a row of vacant chairs, on which they seated themselves with their escort. Both men looked pale and drawn, especially Zinoviev.

'Well, what have you got to say?' asked Stalin fixing them with his customary stare.

'We have been told that our case would be examined at the meeting of the Politburo,' said Kamenev.

'Well, you are now at the commission of the Politburo which has been authorised to hear what you have got to say,' Stalin replied.

After exchanging glances with his companion, Zinoviev struggled to his feet and made a brief speech in which, ill as he appeared, there was more than a trace of his old eloquence. He began by reminding Stalin that during the past several years he and Kamenev had been given many promises and not a single one had been kept. How could they, after that, rely on any new promises? He went on to recall that, when they had been forced to take upon themselves 'the moral responsibility for the murder of Kirov' at their previous trial, they had been told by Yagoda as coming from Stalin that 'this would be the last sacrifice demanded of them'. But in spite of that a new and most infamous trial was being prepared, which would cover them with mud and also the whole Bolshevik Party, besides causing 'enormous' harm to the whole Soviet Union. He begged Stalin to call it off.

'Just think of it,' said Zinoviev, near to tears, 'you want to portray members of Lenin's Politburo and his personal friends as unscrupulous bandits and our Bolshevik Party, the party of the proletarian revolution, as a snake pit of intrigue, treachery and murder...If Vladimir Ilyich were alive, if he saw all this!...'

Zinoviev then broke down completely and wept. He was revived with a glass of water.

'It's already late for tears,' Stalin told him sternly. 'What were you thinking of before when you entered on the path of struggle against the Central Committee? The Central Committee repeatedly warned you that your factional struggle would end lamentably. You didn't listen – and it indeed ended lamentably. You are being told even now : submit to the will of the Party and your life and the lives of those you led into the swamp will be spared. But again you don't listen. Well, you will have only yourself to thank for it, if your case ends even more lamentably, so lamentably that nothing could be worse.'

'And where is the guarantee that you will not shoot us?' asked Kamenev.

'A guarantee?' Stalin repeated scornfully. 'What guarantee can there possibly be? It's simply ridiculous! Maybe you want an official treaty certified by the League of Nations?' He gave a characteristic chuckle. Then, turning towards the others present, he said : 'If assurances given by the Politburo are not enough for them, comrades, I don't know whether there is any point in talking further with them.'

'Kamenev and Zinoviev are behaving as if they were in a position to make conditions with the Politburo,' Voroshilov broke in at this point. 'This is outrageous! If they had a drop of common sense left in them, they ought to fall on their knees before Comrade Stalin and thank him for the life belt he is throwing to them. If they don't want to be saved, let them drown. The devil take them!'

Stalin rose and began to pace up and down with his hands clasped behind his back. 'There was a time when Kamenev and Zinoviev were distinguished by clarity of mind and ability to approach problems dia-

332

letically,' he remarked after a few moments' thought. 'Now they reason like philistines. They have got it into their heads that we are organising the trial with the special purpose of executing them. This is quite stupid! As if we could not shoot them without any trial, if we considered it necessary.'

There were three things which Zinoviev and Kamenev forgot, Stalin went on:

First: that the trial is not directed against them, but against Trotsky, the principal enemy of our Party.

Second: if we did not shoot them when they fought actively against the Central Committee, then why should we shoot them after they have helped the Central Committee in its struggle against Trotsky?

Third: the comrades forget also that we are Bolsheviks, disciples and followers of Lenin, and that we don't want to shed the blood of Old Bolsheviks, no matter how grave their past sins have been against the Party.

The two prisoners looked at each other meaningfully. Then Kamenev rose and announced on their joint behalf that 'they would consent to go to trial, if it were promised that none of the Old Bolsheviks would be executed, that their families would not be persecuted, and that in the future the death sentence would not be applied to any of the former members of the opposition'.

'That goes without saying,' replied Stalin, bringing this dramatic confrontation to an end.

On their return to the Lubyanka, the two prisoners were immediately transferred to large and cool cells, given the use of the shower, and supplied with clean linen and books (though not newspapers), and put on a wholesome and tasty diet while physicians were specially assigned to give them the best medical treatment they needed. But when Yagoda tried to make them write ante-dated letters as evidence of their part in the imaginary conspiracy with Trotsky, they refused and told Yagoda that they would limit themselves to the fulfilment of those obligations which they had undertaken when they met Stalin.

Although Yagoda and the other top NKVD officials were disappointed that the conspiracy charges could not be bolstered up in this way, they put no further pressure on the prisoners. At the same time the NKVD men were relieved by the assurance that the lives of such former close comrades of Lenin as Zinoviev, Kamenev and

Smirnov, whom the NKVD still held in considerable respect, would be spared. But, as the day of the trial grew nearer and they listened to Stalin railing against these prisoners with obvious hatred, Yagoda and the rest began to wonder whether Stalin really meant to keep his word.[43]

CHAPTER IX

The Great Purge

I

The trial of Gregory Yevseyevich Radomylsky alias Zinoviev, Lev Borisovich Rosenfeld alias Kamenev and fourteen other alleged members of the 'Trotskyite–Zinovievite centre' charged with plotting the death of Stalin and other Soviet leaders, including Kirov, opened in the Trade Union House in Moscow on 19 August 1936. The scene was not the large Hall of Columns, where the previous show trials had been staged, but the smaller October Hall, formerly a ballroom in what had been the Nobles' Club in Tsarist times. Apparently this venue was chosen as being easier for Yagoda and his men to control the behaviour of the defendants, particularly if they should show inconvenient signs of departing from the script of their testimony in which they had been carefully drilled and rehearsed during their pre-trial interrogation in the Lubyanka. As usual, the bloated looking Ulrich was the presiding judge, having as his colleagues on the bench the veteran I. O. Matulevich, who had sentenced over a hundred 'White Guardists' to be shot after Kirov's murder, and a thin-faced military jurist named I. I. Nikitchenko, who was to become a familiar figure ten years later as the principal Soviet judge at the War Crimes Tribunal at Nuremberg. As usual, too, Vyshinsky sat at the prosecutor's table. Opposite him were the defendants who occupied two rows of seats in the railed off dock on the far side of the hall. The small handpicked audience consisted mostly of NKVD officials and clerks, together with a sprinkling of Soviet and foreign journalists, whose coverage of the proceedings was

335

considered most important. Microphones and loudspeakers had been set up so that not a word of the indictment and the ensuing court drama should be missed.[1]

All the accused formally pleaded guilty and, as previously arranged with Yagoda, declined the assistance of defence counsel. They had clearly been fattened up for the trial and looked much better than they had during the preliminary investigation. But Zinoviev still showed signs of his illness, with his puffy eyes and asthmatic cough – he removed his collar on entering the dock and his shirt remained open at the neck throughout the trial.

In the circumstances there was little for Vyshinsky to do apart from taking the prisoners through their improbable tales and demanding the infliction of the supreme penalty by the judicial bench. ('I demand that these mad dogs should be shot, every one of them.') To their astonishment Zinoviev and Kamenev were called upon to confess not merely to conspiring to murder Kirov and the others but to killing the actual murderers afterwards. But this was too much for them, brainwashed as they were. 'Too horrible,' said Zinoviev, 'something out of Jules Verne...fantastic, like tales from the *Arabian Nights*.' This additional accusation had nothing to do with the original charges and only appeared to have been introduced by Vyshinsky to show 'how deep was their moral and political degradation', as he put it. 'But surely,' he added, 'history can afford many examples of conspirators being murdered by the organisers of the conspiracy.' Vyshinsky might have gone on to say – but an understandable discretion prevented him from doing so – that history was about to repeat itself with three of the defendants (Oldberg, Reingold and Pickel) who had previously agreed to denounce the principal prisoners by testifying against them as well as themselves.

Indeed Kamenev, Zinoviev and Reingold went further, and besides denouncing their co-defendants, proceeded to incriminate a number of other Old Bolsheviks who were not on trial, particularly Tomsky, Rykov, Bukharin, Radek and Pyatakov. This caused Vyshinsky to issue a statement to the effect that he had given orders for these individuals to be investigated. However, the first to be named by Vyshinsky, the trade union leader and former Politburo member Mikhail Tomsky, had no wish to be arrested. As soon as he heard the news of Vyshinsky's statement, he committed suicide by shooting himself with a pistol in his *dacha* outside Moscow. Stalin is said to have been extremely annoyed by the event and to have blamed Yagoda for allowing it to happen.

For three days the defendants, stimulated by Vyshinsky's prompting,

336

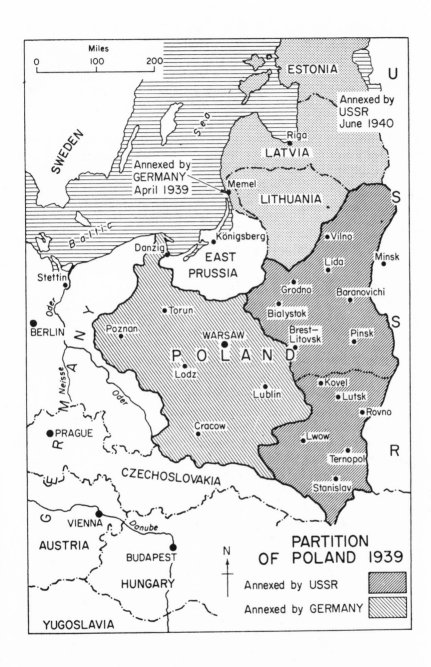

Miles

0   100   200

SWEDEN

Baltic Sea

ESTONIA

U

Annexed by
USSR
June 1940

Riga

LATVIA

Annexed by
GERMANY
April 1939

Memel

LITHUANIA

S

Königsberg

Vilna

Danzig

EAST
PRUSSIA

Lida

Minsk

Stettin

Grodno

Baranovichi

Oder

Torun

Bialystok

BERLIN

Poznan

WARSAW

Brest–
Litovsk

Pinsk

S

P O L A N D

Neisse

Lodz

Oder

Lublin

Kovel

Lutsk

Rovno

PRAGUE

Cracow

Lwow

Ternopol

R

G E R M A N Y

CZECHOSLOVAKIA

Stanislav

VIENNA

Donube

AUSTRIA

BUDAPEST

N

PARTITION
OF POLAND 1939

HUNGARY

Annexed by USSR

YUGOSLAVIA

Annexed by GERMANY

337

recited the astonishing catalogue of their crimes. Only Smirnov, who had been in custody for the past three years, gave his testimony in such an ironical manner as plainly to suggest that the charges against him were deliberately trumped up.[2] To the question, 'When did you resign from the Centre?' he replied with a cynical smile, 'There was nothing to resign from.' Kamenev, although he spoke with some of his old dignity, made an almost complete confession, and in addition he incriminated a number of other Old Bolsheviks who were not in the dock, but of whom the majority were eventually to follow him there. 'Knowing that we might be discovered,' he declared, 'we designated a small group to continue our terroristic activities.' According to Kamenev, this group, separate from the main 'Centre', was led by Sokolnikov and included Serebryakov, Radek and Shlyapnikov from the Left Opposition and Bukharin, Rykov and Tomsky from the Rightists. Zinoviev was equally self-accusatory. He agreed with Smirnov's denunciation of him as a frequent liar. 'Yes, I often tell untruths,' he said. 'I started doing that from the moment I began fighting the Bolshevik Party. In so far as Smirnov took the road of fighting the Party, he too is telling untruths. But it seems the difference between him and myself is that I have decided firmly and irrevocably to tell the truth at this last minute, whereas he, it seems, has followed a different decision.'

Although the wretched defendants all harped upon the terroristic plans they had or were supposed to have concerted for a number of years, neither they nor Vyshinsky were able to cite any concrete results of their conspiracy, with the sole exception of the assassination of Kirov which, as has already been seen, was planned by Stalin himself with the aid of Yagoda and Zaporozhets. Furthermore, on the third day of the trial, one of the last of the defendants to give evidence, E. S. Holtzman, unwittingly demonstrated to the world that his testimony must have been deliberately fabricated by the NKVD.

Holtzman was a genuine Trotskyite, although he said he 'did not share' Trotsky's opinion of the necessity of terror, thus to some extent contradicting his earlier confession in the Lubyanka. He stated that he had met Trotsky's son, Lev Sedov, while on an official mission to Berlin in November 1932; that he had followed Sedov to Copenhagen for the purpose of a secret meeting with Trotsky who was staying there at the time; and that he met Sedov by arrangement in the Hotel Bristol in Copenhagen. 'I went to the hotel straight from the station and met Sedov in the lounge,' said Holtzman. 'At 10 a.m. we went to Trotsky's apartment.' The witness added that Trotsky told him that 'it was necessary to remove Stalin' and for this purpose they must 'choose

338

cadres of responsible people fit for the task'. Holtzman also said he had 'put up' in the Bristol.

As soon as this was reported in the foreign press, Trotsky declared that the whole story was false and demanded that Vyshinsky should ask Holtzman on what kind of passport and under what name he had travelled to Copenhagen. But the prosecutor declined to do this, knowing that if he disclosed these particulars the foreign press would check with the Danish immigration authorities and expose the story as a myth. Shortly afterwards the Danish authorities announced through the Danish Social Democratic Party journal that there was no Hotel Bristol in Copenhagen; it had been pulled down in 1917. Nor, as it was subsequently established, could Sedov possibly have been in Copenhagen on the alleged dates, since he was sitting for his examinations at the *Technische Hochschule* in Berlin at the time.

Stalin was furious when he read the news about the Hotel Bristol. 'What the devil did you need a hotel for?' he shouted at Yagoda and his aides. 'You ought to have said that they met at the railway station. The railway station is always there!'

Apparently the mistake arose in this way. When Yagoda decided on a Copenhagen hotel as the most suitable meeting-place for Holtzman and Trotsky's son, he told Molchanov to obtain the name of a hotel from the Travel Section of the Foreign Affairs Commissariat. Molchanov, anticipating that the name of the hotel might figure conspicuously in the trial proceedings, and bearing in mind the need for caution, asked through his secretary to be supplied with a list of hotels both in Copenhagen and in Oslo, giving as a reason that a group of prominent party comrades was about to leave on a trip to Scandinavia. Molchanov's secretary did as he was instructed, but in typing out the list of hotels for his chief he made an unfortunate slip. The Copenhagen hotels were mistakenly listed under Oslo, where there was a Hotel Bristol, and the Oslo hotels under Copenhagen, where there was not. A feeble attempt was made by Soviet propaganda to explain the error by saying that the meeting took place in the Café Bristol, which was near a hotel of a different name where Holtzman had stayed. It is unlikely that very many of the foreign observers were convinced by this subterfuge.[3]

The fourth morning of the trial was taken up with the closing speech for the prosecution, in which Vyshinsky again traversed the details of the alleged conspiracy. A single example of his oratory must suffice.

These mad dogs of capitalism tried to tear limb from limb the best of the best of our Soviet land. They killed one of the men of the Revolution who was most dear to us, that admirable and wonderful man, bright and joyous as the smile on his lips was always bright and joyous, as our new life is bright and joyous. They killed our Kirov. They wounded us close to our very heart. They thought they could sow confusion and consternation in our ranks.

Vyshinsky's fulmination was followed by the pathetic final pleas of the accused; these occupied the afternoon and most of the following day. One defendant, Sergei Mrachovsky, demanded hysterically that he should be shot as a traitor, although he must have hoped that Stalin would keep his promise and that he would be reprieved. (He was an Old Bolshevik who had been born in a Tsarist prison where his mother was serving a sentence for revolutionary activities.) 'We didn't listen to him at the proper time – and he taught us a lesson', Mrachovsky exclaimed in a strangely masochistic outburst. 'What a whipping he gave us!'[4]

The rest similarly vied with each other in their self-abasement. After Kamenev had repeated his earlier confession, he declared that he deserved no mercy and sat down. But he rose again immediately to say he wished to say a few words to his children, since he had no other way of addressing them. He had two sons, one a pilot in the Red Air Force and the other a boy in the Pioneers, the Bolshevik youth movement. 'Standing, may be, with one foot in the grave, I want to tell them this – no matter what my sentence may be, I consider it will be just. Don't look back! Look forward! Together with the Soviet people follow Stalin!'

Kamenev thereupon resumed his seat in the dock and with one hand he covered his eyes which were filled with tears. It was a painful moment for those in court, perhaps the most painful in the whole farcical trial. According to one Soviet observer, even the expressions on the faces of Ulrich and his fellow judges on the bench momentarily lost their usual stony indifference.

Zinoviev, by now completely cowed, showed none of his old fiery qualities as he likewise grovelled to the court. 'My defective Bolshevism became transformed into anti-Bolshevism, and through Trotskyism I arrived at Fascism,' he declared. 'Trotskyism is a variety of Fascism and Zinovievism is a variety of Trotskyism.' The humiliation of the once powerful head of the Leningrad Soviet could not have been more abject.

At 7.30 in the evening of 23 August the court adjourned to consider

340

its verdict. Although this had been determined in advance, Soviet legal procedure required that the judgment should be written out by the President for subsequent delivery in open court. The drafting of the document could not have taken more than an hour or two at the most. Thus, the fact that the judges were out of the court room for seven hours suggests that some difficulties must have arisen, not on the question of conviction, which was manifestly clear since all the defendants had pleaded guilty, but on the question of the sentences. Possibly the Politburo was consulted, although most of its members including Stalin had already left Moscow for their summer holidays. It is quite likely that a telephone call was put through to Stalin's villa at Sochi. At all events, it was about 2.30 a.m. when the three judges followed by Vyshinsky and his assistant prosecutor filed back into court and the sixteen accused were also brought in by the guards.

Everyone was called upon to stand up while the President declaimed the judgment in a monotonous tone. After droning on for about a quarter of an hour, Ulrich at last came to what everyone had been waiting for. There was an air of tense expectancy punctuated by an outburst of nervous coughing on the part of some of the spectators. After the noise had subsided, Ulrich slowly read out the full names of the sixteen defendants, and then, after a long pause, announced that all of them were sentenced to the supreme penalty – death by shooting. Most of those present, including the NKVD personnel, expected that the President would go on to state that, in consideration of the defendants' past revolutionary services, the supreme penalty would be commuted to imprisonment or at the worst confinement in an 'isolator'. But the expected words never came. Instead the President put the document into the file in front of him, turned and left the court room followed by his two colleagues. As he did so, there was a sudden shout from one of the men in the dock, a small dishevelled looking creature named Lurye. 'Long live the cause of Marx, Engels, Lenin and Stalin!'[5]

Under the existing law, defendants sentenced to death were allowed seventy-two hours in which to file an appeal for clemency to the Head of State, and the sentences were not usually carried out until the expiration of this period, even if the petitions had been rejected earlier. In this instance the rule was disregarded on Stalin's order. On 25 August, barely twenty-four hours later, the Moscow morning papers carried an announcement that all sixteen defendants in the trial had been executed.

Various accounts of the executions leaked out afterwards, largely through secret police gossip. The principal authority for the horrifying details is Victor Serge, the old-time revolutionary writer and Trotskyite who got them from NKVD officers who witnessed the shootings.

According to Serge, Kamenev was the first to die. He left his cell in silence and descended to the execution cellar as if in a dream. Suddenly, as he was walking along, a revolver shot was fired apparently from behind. As he fell, he let out a cry of 'Ah!' He was seen to be still alive. The NKVD lieutenant, who was in charge of the execution, shouted in a hysterical voice, 'Finish him off!' and gave the dying man a kick with his boot. A second bullet in the head finally killed him.[6]

The 'liquidation' of Zinoviev proved more difficult. After signing his petition for clemency during the evening of 24 August, he lay down and went to sleep. He had a high fever, and when he was awakened at one o'clock in the morning he sat up with the sweat pouring down his face. 'Zinoviev, get up!' he was told. 'We have orders to transfer you to another place.' He was also told to get dressed and collect his 'things'. A jailer helped him to pull on his boots. As he made no attempt to move, another jailer threw water on his face. This had the effect of reviving him, and he began slowly to put his few belongings together. When the cell door was opened and he saw the guards waiting for him outside, he suddenly realised why they were there. His legs trembled violently and he would have fallen had he not been held up.

As the execution party passed along the corridor towards the staircase leading to the cellar, the wretched Zinoviev moaned and cried as he struggled with the guards who dragged him along. At one moment he is said to have fallen on his knees, imploring the officer in charge, 'Please, for God's sake, comrade, call up Joseph Vissarionovich!'

Unwilling that this disturbing scene should be prolonged all the way to the execution cellar, Lieutenant Evangulov decided on immediate action. He ordered the guards to open the door of the nearest cell which happened to be empty and the prisoner was pushed inside. Then, seizing him by the hair with his left hand, the NKVD lieutenant jerked his head downward, drew a revolver from its holster with the other hand and immediately put a bullet in Zinoviev's brain. Lieutenant Evangulov subsequently received an award for the presence of mind he showed on this occasion.

Pauker, Stalin's coarse and unscrupulous bodyguard, who was also in charge of the Operations Division of the NKVD, appears to have been among those present at the executions. At all events he reported to his master that they had been carried out. Some months later at a party given by the NKVD to celebrate the anniversary of the founding of the Soviet secret police and attended by Stalin, Pauker gave an obscene imitation of Zinoviev's craven behaviour during his last minutes.

342

'Hear Israel, our God is the only God!' So this Jewish victim of Stalin's vengeance is said to have screamed, raising his hand to heaven. Stalin was reported to have been so convulsed with laughter by Pauker's revolting antics that he bent down and held his belly with his hands and, unable to stand it any longer, made signs to Pauker to stop the performance.[7]

The most calm and self-possessed of all the condemned men in their final moments was the veteran Bolshevik Ivan Smirnov. As they came to fetch him, he exclaimed, 'We deserve this for our unworthy attitude at the trial.'[8]

2

Although the veracity of some of the witnesses was doubted, and there were reservations about the methods employed to obtain the confessions, the latest trial had not gone badly from Stalin's point of view; foreign journalists and even some British lawyers expressed their belief in the existence of a Trotskyite conspiracy.* Nevertheless, Stalin was far from pleased with the way in which Yagoda had prepared the case against Zinoviev and the other defendants, blaming him in particular for the mistake over the Copenhagen hotel. Stalin also formed the view on reading the transcript of the trial proceedings, which was sent to him at Sochi, that Yagoda as head of the NKVD had not been nearly vigilant enough. Accordingly within a week of the conclusion of the trial, he ordered Yagoda with Yezhov's help to select five thousand of the more active members of the former opposition, who were being held in labour camps or isolators or were living under police surveillance in exile in the provinces of Siberia, and have them executed in secret. This was the first but by no means the last time that a mass execution of Bolsheviks and former party members took place without even the formality of a trial – they were simply 'liquidated administratively'.[9]

Three weeks later – on 25 September 1936 to be exact – Stalin, who was still at Sochi, dispatched the following telegram to Molotov and Kaganovich in Moscow. The telegram also bore the signature of Andrei Zhdanov, Stalin's creature who had replaced Kirov as joint secretary of the Central Committee.

* One of these was the left-wing Labour lawyer D. N. Pritt, who attended the trial and subsequently wrote in his autobiography: 'I probably had more knowledge of Soviet procedure than any other non-Soviet present. I thought that their rules of procedure, which – like the Western European ones – are in some respects more favourable to the accused than the English rules, were being properly observed, that the trial was in general fairly conducted, and that the accused were guilty.' D. N. Pritt, *From Right to Left* (1965), p. 110.

We deem it absolutely necessary and urgent that **Comrade** Yezhov be nominated to the post of People's Commissar for Internal Affairs (NKVD). Yagoda has definitely proved himself to be incapable of unmasking the Trotskyite–Zinovievite bloc. The OGPU is four years behind in this matter. This is noted by all Party workers and by the majority of the representatives of the NKVD.

The text of this telegram, first revealed by Khrushchev in his 'secret' speech, is most significant, particularly the reference to the police being four years behind with their investigative work under Yagoda's direction. It was almost exactly four years since the Ryutin affair when Stalin's demand in the Politburo that Ryutin should be shot was thwarted largely through the opposition of Kirov and Ordzhonikidze, and the struggle had been carried on before the whole Central Committee when Stalin had again been defeated. Now 'our beloved Mironich' was no longer alive to make trouble and the time was ripe for Stalin to take a terrible revenge on the Old Bolsheviks and many thousands of other alleged Trotskyites.[10]

Immediate action was taken by the Politburo on the telegram, which was also used as a pretext to get rid of Rykov, who since his recantation had been Commissar of Communications. On 17 September the Moscow papers carried an announcement of Rykov's 'release' from his duties, his replacement by Yagoda, and the appointment of Nikolai Ivanovich Yezhov as the new head of the NKVD. This was the signal for the launching of the Great Purge, the *Yezhovchina*, which was to terrorise the Soviet people for the next two years and cause countless deaths of innocent citizens, between half a million and a million 'legal' executions and about seven million arrests usually followed by long terms of up to twenty-five years in a labour camp. 'You are charged with the task of exterminating ten thousand enemies of the people – report results by signal', Yezhov would cable a provincial NKVD chief. Back would come the reply every few days, 'The following enemies of the people have been shot', followed by a numbered list.[11]

Meanwhile preparations were made on Stalin's instructions for the staging of another big show trial, this time of alleged members of the so-called 'Reserve Centre' which was supposed to have taken over the terrorist activities of the Zinoviev–Kamenev group when the latter was broken up. The principal defendants were Pyatakov, Sokolnikov, Serebriakov and Radek, all respected and distinguished Old Bolsheviks, though not of the prominence of Zinoviev and Kamenev. Gregory ('Yuri') Pyatakov had been one of the six party members

344

specially mentioned by Lenin in his 'testament', all of whom, apart from Stalin himself, were destined to perish at Stalin's orders. Although he had for a time sided with Trotsky after Lenin's death, Pyatakov had later served Stalin loyally in the post of Deputy Commissar for Heavy Industry. Because of his ability and immense technical knowledge, he should by rights have been made head of this commissariat, but on account of his temporary deviation from the Party line, the post was given to Ordzhonikidze, who leaned on him heavily and never took any important departmental decision without consulting his brilliant deputy. Of the others, Gregory Sokolnikov had been a member of the first nominal Politburo in 1917; he had signed the treaty of Brest-Litovsk as leader of the Soviet peace delegation and later on had been the commissar in charge of the Russian oil industry and Assistant Commissar for Foreign Affairs under Litvinov, as well as serving for four years as Soviet ambassador to Britain. The third defendant, Leonid Serebriakov, had been one of the secretaries of the Central Committee before Stalin took over as General Secretary.

Finally, Karl Radek whose real name was Sobelsohn, was an outstanding journalist, who had recanted after being expelled from the Party and banished to the Urals for his support of Trotsky; he had returned to Moscow to become director of *Izvestia* and the official foreign affairs commentator in the Moscow daily press in the early 1930s, in particular lauding the League of Nations at Stalin's behest besides penning a remarkably flattering image of the dictator in a book entitled *The Architect of a Socialist Society*. Radek had a permanent pass to the Kremlin and was frequently seen in Stalin's office as well as at his *dacha* at Zubalovo. Too late the fallen favourite realised his mistake. 'I stood in too close a proximity to the leadership,' he regretfully told the prosecutor at his trial. When he was arrested, Radek was almost beside himself with indignation. 'After all I did for Stalin,' he said, 'I didn't expect such an injustice from him!'[12]

Because most of the other defendants were engineers like Pyatakov, it was decided to revert to the pattern of the Shakhty and Metro-Vickers trials and include charges of sabotage and wrecking in the indictment as part of a general conspiracy with Trotsky and the German and Japanese intelligence services to restore capitalism. This objective was also alleged to have been part of Zinoviev's and Kamenev's 'political platform', although at their trials they had denied that they had any such platform. That Pyatakov, a most dedicated technician who was accustomed to work seventeen hours a day, should have countenanced any form of economic espionage let alone 'wrecking' was in the highest degree unlikely. However, his wife, son and secretary, to all of whom he was greatly attached, were arrested at the same time, and this upset him considerably. His wife, a sloppy woman with a marked taste for vodka, was to terrified by the interrogators in the Lubyanka that she agreed to testify against him in order to save their child. Meanwhile Pyatakov, though much shaken, refused to co-operate until he received a visit in prison from Ordzhonikidze, who appears to have given him an assurance from Stalin that if he pleaded guilty in general terms neither his wife nor his secretary would be called as witnesses and that his own life would be spared. The upshot was that Pyatakov signed a false deposition to the effect that when he was in Berlin on official Soviet trade business in December 1935, he wrote to Trotsky in Norway, asking for instructions. Trotsky allegedly replied to the effect that the Germans were prepared to go to war with the Soviet Union to help Trotsky and his friends to seize power, in return for which Trotsky promised to cede the Ukraine to Germany and make certain economic concessions as well. Consequently Pyata-kov and his fellow conspirators in the alleged 'Anti-Soviet Trotskyite Centre' were urged to step up wrecking activities inside Soviet factories, plants and other installations.[13]

When Stalin was shown Pyatakov's deposition, he ordered Abram Slutsky, the head of the Foreign Department of the NKVD, to look up the times of the trains between Berlin and Oslo so that Pyatakov's trip to see Trotsky fitted in with the schedules. In due course Slutsky re-ported that the journey required a minimum of two days and that it would be dangerous for Pyatakov to assert in open court that he had absented himself from Berlin for so long, since it was known in the Soviet Trade Agency in the German capital that Pyatakov was in daily conference with various German firms and that scarcely a day passed on which he did not sign contracts with them.

'What you say about the train schedules may be true,' Stalin told Slutsky at their next meeting. 'But why couldn't Pyatakov go to Oslo by air? Such a flight there and back could probably be done in one night.'

To this Slutsky objected that the flights carried relatively few pas-sengers and that their names all appeared in the aircraft's manifest which could be produced with as embarrassing results as the mistake about the hotel in the previous trial.

But Stalin, who had already made up his mind, brushed aside Slutsky's objection. 'Pyatakov must state that he flew in a special plane,' said Stalin. 'For such a job as this the German authorities would gladly provide an aircraft.'

Pyatakov's original deposition was accordingly rewritten and the revised legend was put about that, after first meeting an agent of Trotsky's in the Berlin Zoo to make the arrangements, Pyatakov had flown from Tempelhof aerodrome in the morning on a forged German passport, landed at Oslo at 3.0 p.m., driven to Trotsky's home at Veksal and, after a long conference at which Trotsky told him that he had fixed up everything with the Nazi leader Rudolf Hess, flown back to Berlin the same night.

The trial of Pyatakov and sixteen other defendants, including Sokolnikov, Sebriakov and Radek, opened in the October Hall of Trade Union House on 23 January 1937, with Ulrich once more presiding on the bench and Vyshinsky leading the prosecution. The weather was bitterly cold and as the heating in the court room was inadequate most of those present were muffled up in heavy overcoats. Apart from the four leaders the defendants consisted of engineers, miners, railwaymen, industrial chemists, and the like. One of the more bizarre charges concerned an attempt to kill Molotov, who at the time of the trial had been fully restored to Stalin's favour, by his chauffeur deliberately running the car into a ditch or gully. The attempt was not successful, since according to one witness the chauffeur whose name was Arnold 'funked it' and, although the vehicle overturned, none of the occupants was hurt.[14]

Again the defendants recited their well rehearsed stories with a minimum of prompting. Comment is superfluous except in the case of Pyatakov's flight to Norway which was immediately exposed in the Norwegian press as a myth. One local newspaper *Aftensposten*, after checking with Oslo airport, published the information that no civil aircraft had landed there during the whole of December 1935, while *Arbeiderbladet*, the organ of the Norwegian Social Democrats, established after further investigation that no aircraft of any kind had used the Kjeller airfield between September 1935 and May 1936.

The utmost that Vyshinsky could do was at the end of the trial when he quoted a Soviet embassy report in Oslo to the effect that in accordance with international regulations the Kjeller airfield was open all the year round and that it was possible for aircraft to land and take off there 'in winter months'. Of course, this did not establish the fact of Pyatakov's alleged flight but merely its technical possibility. Instead Vyshinsky preferred to divert attention by dwelling on the general charges which he did with characteristic invective. 'Comrade Stalin's forecast has fully come true,' he declared in his closing speech. 'Trotskyism has indeed become the central rallying point of all the forces

347

hostile to socialism, the gang of mere bandits, spies and murderers who placed themselves entirely at the disposal of foreign secret services, and became finally and irrevocably transformed into lackeys of capitalism, into restorers of capitalism in our country.'

Pyatakov's final plea to the court was typical of the others.

Any punishment which you may adjudge will be lighter than the very fact of confession...In a few hours you will pass your sentence. And here I stand before you in filth, crushed by my own crimes, bereft of everything through my own fault, a man who has lost his Party, who has no friends, who has lost his family, who has lost his very self.[15]

The sentences were pronounced at 3.0 a.m. on 30 January – death for Pyatakov and twelve other defendants including Serebriakov; ten years for Sokolnikov, Radek and Molotov's chauffeur Arnold, and eight years for Stroilov, the remaining defendant, who was an *agent provocateur* of the NKVD. There were no reprieves. Surprising for its leniency was the sentence on Arnold, who for his attempt on Molotov's life might normally have expected to be shot. Stalin is said to have shown clemency in his case because the dictator was so amused by the humorous way in which he gave his evidence. Arnold survived his sentence and was last heard of managing a garage in Novosibirsk. Sokolnikov and Radek were not so fortunate. Radek, who was sent to a labour camp inside the Arctic Circle, was eventually murdered by another inmate, an ordinary criminal, his fate being not an uncommon one among political prisoners. Sokolnikov also died in custody. As usually happened, the defendants' families were made to suffer. Serebriakov's widow Galina, a distinguished writer, who had previously been married to Sokolnikov, was to spend most of the next twenty years in Siberian prison and labour camps; she survived this terrible experience, was ultimately rehabilitated and is on record as having appeared at a writers' conference in Moscow in 1962 where she discussed Stalin's 'crimes' with Poskrebyshev.[16]

Later the same day as the trial ended a huge workers' mass meeting was held in the Red Square outside the Kremlin. It was addressed by the First Secretary of the Moscow Party organisation, Nikita Khrushchev, who declared that the purpose of the gathering was 'to raise our proletarian voice in complete support of the sentences passed by the Military Collegium of the Supreme Court against the enemies of the people, the traitors of the motherland, the betrayers of the workers' cause, the spies, diversionists, agents of fascism, the vile despicable

348

Trotskyites'.* In view of Khrushchev's famous 'secret' speech to the Twentieth Party Congress on the evils of Stalin's 'cult of personality' nearly twenty years away, it is interesting to recall his references to the Party leader on the earlier occasion.

These assassins aimed at the heart and brain of our party. They raised their evil hand against Comrade Stalin. Raising their hand against Stalin, they raised it against all of us, against the labouring class, against the workers! Raising their hand against Comrade Stalin, they raised it against the teaching of Marx–Engels–Lenin! Raising their hand against Comrade Stalin, they raised it against all that is best, all that is human, because Stalin is hope, aspiration, the beacon of all advanced and progressive humanity. Stalin is our banner! Stalin is our will! Stalin is our victory![17]

The aftermath of the trial was marked by two noteworthy incidents. The first was the sudden death of Stalin's old Georgian comrade, the Commissar for Heavy Industry, Gregory ('Sergo') Ordzhonikidze, ostensibly from 'paralysis of the heart'. It is known that Ordzhonikidze was much upset by the latest arrests, including that of his deputy Pyatakov, which came as a complete surprise to him, and that he had a row with Stalin about it over the telephone. 'Koba, why do you let the NKVD arrest my men?' he was overheard shouting into the receiver. 'I am still a member of the Politburo, and I am going to raise hell, Koba, if it's the last thing I do before I die!'

According to Khrushchev, 'Stalin permitted the liquidation of Ordzhonikidze's brother and brought Ordzhonikidze himself to such a state that he was forced to shoot himself'. But Khrushchev did not tell the whole story, which was later revealed by a Caucasian party official who was in Moscow at the time. What happened apparently was that Stalin sent several NKVD men to Ordzhonikidze with a revolver, giving him the alternative of committing suicide in his own flat or dying in the cellars of the Lubyanka. Ordzhonikidze chose the former

* Even such a reputable historian of Russia as Sir Bernard Pares stated it as his opinion, after having read the verbatim report of the Pyatakov–Radek trial, that wrecking activities were 'proved up to the hilt' and that 'convincing evidence' had been adduced, although he had written four years previously after the Metro-Vickers trial that the 'confessions of the accused Russians are not worth the paper they are written on' and that the determination of the Soviet authorities to 'reduce human beings to pulp, and implant everywhere fear, suspicion and servility, produce moral casualties which far more than outweigh the possible realisation of any theory'. Cited by Malcolm Muggeridge, *The Thirties 1930–1940 in Great Britain* (1940), p. 246.

and, after saying farewell to his wife, shot himself in the presence of the secret police, while one of the Kremlin doctors was waiting in the next room to certify the death was due to heart failure. The dead man was buried with the highest honours reserved for members of the Politburo. The Caucasian comrade who is the authority for the foregoing account was present at the funeral ceremony in the Red Square and was close enough 'to see the sorrow, the suffering, the unbearable pain depicted on the face of that great actor, Comrade Stalin'.[18]

The other direct result of the Pyatakov–Radek trial was the arrest of two former members of the Politburo, Bukharin and Rykov, who had been incriminated by various witnesses during the proceedings. Apart from Trotsky and Stalin himself, they were the two principal remaining figures among those who had been nearest to Lenin, and they ranked with him as founders of the Bolshevik Party. They were seized during a plenary meeting of the Central Committee in the Kremlin and dragged off to the Lubyanka, protesting their innocence of any part in an anti-Stalin conspiracy. On the contrary, pleaded Bukharin, the real conspiracy was headed by Stalin and Yezhov, who were plotting to install an NKVD regime giving Stalin unlimited personal power.

'That is not the way revolutionists defend themselves,' Stalin broke in. 'If you are innocent, you can prove it in a prison cell!'

Stalin also took this opportunity to attack Yagoda for his lack of vigilance as the recent head of the NKVD. This line was taken up by delegates all over the hall who wished to be seen as agreeing with Stalin and so kept asking Yagoda why he had coddled Trotskyite reptiles and harboured traitors on his staff. At last Yagoda turned on his accusers and remarked in a quiet voice: 'What a pity I didn't arrest all of you before, when I had the power!'[19]

In his political report to the plenum on 5 March 1937, Stalin spoke for two hours on the congenial theme of 'defects in Party work and measures for liquidating Trotskyites and other double dealers'. He analysed the earlier trials, drawing a distinction between the Shakhty wreckers, 'old bourgeois specialists' who 'did not conceal their dislike for the Soviet system', and 'the present-day wreckers and diversionists, the Trotskyites', as depicted in the Pyatakov trial. The latter's strength lay in the possession of a Party card. 'Their strength lies in the fact that the Party card enables them to be politically trusted and gives them access to all our institutions and organisations. Their advantage lies in that, holding a Party card and pretending to be friends of the Soviet power, they deceived our people politically, abused their confidence, did their wrecking work furtively and disclosed our state secrets to the enemies of the Soviet Union.' These enemies were specified as 'the fascist forces of Germany and Japan', who aimed among other objectives at the acquisition of the Ukraine and the maritime region of eastern Siberia. 'We do not fear their sorties from within or without,' Stalin boldly proclaimed amid the delegates' dutiful applause, 'for we shall smash them in the future as we are smashing them now and as we have smashed them in the past.'[20]

This speech, which received the widest publicity both at home and abroad, plainly heralded further purges within the Communist Party. From its delivery and Stalin's reply to the debate which followed it in the first days of March 1937, may be said to date his complete and absolute despotism over the Party and the whole Soviet people. Henceforward he had only to sign his name or pick up one of the telephones on his desk and call Yezhov or Poskrebyshev in order to extinguish any one of his 170 million subjects from the face of the earth.

3

Hitherto the purge trials had been specially staged affairs and in the main confined to the oppositionists or at least those who at one time or another were connected with the opposition. Furthermore, the arrests were announced well in advance, and public opinion was thoroughly coached by Stalin's propaganda organs for weeks and even months before the accused took their places in the dock. But in the middle of 1937 there was a novel departure. Not only was the announcement of the arrests and forthcoming trial followed twenty-four hours later by the news that all the accused had been executed, but the victims were without exception widely regarded as good Party men and sincere Stalinists.[21]

When Muscovites opened their morning newspapers on 11 June 1937 they were amazed to read that Marshal Mikhail Tukachevsky, Vice-Commissar of Defence and Commander-in-Chief of the Red Army, together with seven of his top generals, had been charged with spying for 'a foreign state' and preparing for the army's defeat in the war which was being plotted against the Soviet Union. The general officers were Yon E. Yakir, who commanded Kiev District; I. R. Uborevich, who commanded Byelorussian District; R. P. Eideman, head of the civil defence organisation *Osoaviakhim*; A. I. Kork, head of the Frunze Military Academy; Vitort K. Putna, Military Attaché in London; B. M. Feldman, head of army administration; and V. M. Primakov, Deputy Commander of Leningrad District. It was also disclosed that General Yan Gamarnik, First Deputy Commissar of Defence, whose suicide had been announced ten days previously, was implicated in the conspiracy. Since the 'foreign state' was obviously intended to mean

351

Germany, and in addition to Gamarnik three of the generals were Jews (Yakir, Eideman and Feldman), it seemed all the more incredible that they should be guilty of spying for Hitler.

The official announcement as given over the Moscow radio was as follows:

> The evidence of the preliminary investigation has established the participation of the accused, and also of Y. B. Gamarnik who ended his life by suicide, in anti-State connections with military circles of a foreign state pursuing a policy of hostility to the USSR. Being in the service of the military intelligence of that state, the accused systematically supplied military circles of that state with espionage information on the condition of the Red Army, carried on sabotage aimed at weakening the strength of the Red Army, endeavoured to prepare the defeat of the Red Army in the event of a military attack on the USSR and aimed at bringing about the re-establishment in the USSR of the regime of the landlords and capitalists.
>
> All the accused have admitted their guilt on all counts...[22]

Although the news of the latest trial and executions came as a complete surprise to most people, signs had been noted by discerning observers that Stalin intended to strike at the Red Army as the next mass victim of the purge. At the Pyatakov–Radek trial, two of the military leaders had been mentioned by name – Putna and Tukachevsky himself. Although the Commander-in-Chief was exonerated by Radek on the witness stand – 'I never had and could not have had any dealings with Tukachevsky connected with counter-revolutionary activities, because I knew Tukachevsky's attitude to the Party and Government to be that of an absolutely devoted man,' – Vyshinsky would not have dared to introduce Tukachevsky's name into the proceedings without orders from above. Nor did a man of Tukachevsky's standing have any need to be defended by a prisoner like Radek whose apology for him turned out in the event to be tantamount to the kiss of death. Then, at the Central Committee plenum, at which the activities of the 'Trotskyite double-dealers' were discussed at length, Stalin openly hinted at the existence of spies on the army staff and the harm they could do.

About the same time a proposal came before the Central Committee on Stalin's initiative to provide for the reintroduction of political commissars into army formations of divisional size and over. Tukachevsky is said to have annoyed Stalin by voting with the minority against the proposal which was agreed to and put into effect. At first, Tukachevsky apparently did not worry about his difference with

352

Stalin, since senior officers were immune from arrest by the civil authorities except on the direct orders of Voroshilov, the Defence Commissar, with whom Tukachevsky was on friendly terms. It was only when Voroshilov was confronted by Stalin with what appeared to be convincing proofs of his Vice-Commissar's treachery in the shape of photocopies of documents compromising him with the Germans that Voroshilov reluctantly agreed to the arrest of Tukachevsky and the others under the threat of being branded as a conspirator himself.

The matter seems to have been settled about the end of April when there was talk in government circles that the military leaders were being closely watched by the NKVD and that there was a plan afoot to stage a military coup. Security arrangements inside and outside the Kremlin were increased, all the Kremlin passes were suddenly called in and new passes issued, and unprecedented precautions were taken for the May Day parade in the Red Square. General Krivitsky, a high ranking intelligence officer in the NKVD who later defected, had his ticket and papers inspected no less than ten times on his way to the square.[23]

At these celebrations Tukachevsky was noticeably cold-shouldered both by the Politburo and his army colleagues. When as usual he went to mount the reviewing platform on the top of the Lenin Mausoleum, hoping perhaps to have a word with Stalin, two GPU guards barred his way. He was thus obliged to remain among the small fry at ground level. He did not wait for the civilian march past and was seen to walk away alone.[24] His impending disgrace was further foreshadowed a few days later by the cancellation of his appointment to represent the Soviet Government at the coronation of King George VI in London, followed by the official announcement of his relegation to the relatively minor command of the Volga District. In fact he barely reached his new headquarters at Samara (Kuibyshev) since he was arrested on arrival and taken back to Moscow where he was apparently tried before a secret military court.

Whether Tukachevsky and the seven generals were put on trial at all poses as difficult and controversial a question as whether there really was any kind of conspiracy. For many years the official Soviet statement that there was a trial was generally disbelieved abroad where it was assumed that all the alleged military conspirators had been shot without trial. However, in an autobiographical article covering the purge period, which originally appeared in *Novy Mir*, the monthly periodical of the Soviet Writers' Union, Ilya Ehrenburg recalled how he met General I. P. Belov, who was a member of the court, and how Belov described the scene. 'They were sitting like that – facing us.

Uborevich looked me in the eyes...' Belov also said: 'And tomorrow I shall be put in the same place.'[25] And he was right. Indeed only two of the seven so-called judges survived the purge – Marshal Budenny and General Shaposhnikov. Besides Belov, those who perished included Marshal Blukyer, who commanded the Soviet forces in the Far East, and General Dybenko, who had been one of the defence commissars in the first Bolshevik government and is supposed to have warned Stalin of the impending plot, although this action did not save him.

There is a similar difference of expert opinion on the question of the hypothetical conspiracy. Isaac Deutscher, the leading non-Soviet authority on Stalin's 'political' life, has written as follows:

> The exact circumstances of Tukachevsky's plot and of its collapse are not known. Some deny the existence of any plot, and maintain that Hitler's Secret Services forged evidence of a plot and planted it on President Benes of Czechoslovakia, who transmitted it to Stalin. It is suggested that the real source of the forgery was in the GPU in Moscow and that the forgers calculated the whole plant, probably with Stalin's connivance. But quite a few non-Stalinist sources maintain that the generals did indeed plan a *coup d'état* and did this from their own motives and on their own initiative, not in contact with any foreign power. The main part of the coup was to be a palace revolt in the Kremlin, culminating in the assassination of Stalin. A decisive military operation outside the Kremlin, an assault on the headquarters of the GPU was also prepared. Tukachevsky was the moving spirit of the conspiracy. A man of military genius, the real moderniser of the Red Army, he was surrounded by the glory of his victories in the civil war and was the favourite of the army. He was indeed the only man among all the military and civilian leaders of that time who showed in many respects a resemblance to the original Bonaparte and could have played the Russian First Consul.[26]

On the other hand, English Kremlinologists such as Robert Conquest, Leonard Schapiro and John Erickson are unanimous in the view that there was no plot. Certainly the Nazi secret archives, which were used at the war crimes trial in Nuremberg and are now open to historians, do not contain the slightest evidence of any Nazi penetration of the Soviet government and army. It must also be remembered that Tukachevsky and the generals were all subsequently 'rehabilitated' after they had been cleared by Khrushchev and other speakers at the Party Congresses in 1956 and 1961 of complicity in any plot which Khrushchev declared to be non-existent.

At the Twenty-Second Congress, Alexander Shelepin, then head of the KGB (successor to the NKVD), quoted two letters in the KGB archives which General Yakir had written on the eve of his execution. In the first, which was addressed to Voroshilov, Yakir asked that 'in memory of my many years of honest service in the Red Army in the past' his family, 'helpless and quite innocent', should be 'looked after and given assistance'. Voroshilov minuted the letter: 'In general I doubt the honesty of a dishonest person.' Yakir's efforts were unsuccessful. His wife, brother, sister-in-law, nephew and other relatives were all liquidated. Only his fourteen-year-old son Peter survived, although he was to spend many years in prisons and Arctic camps.

Yakir's other letter was addressed to Stalin. 'My entire conscious life has been spent working selflessly and honestly in full view of the Party and its leaders,' he wrote. 'Every word I say is honest, and I shall die with words of love for you, the Party, and the country, with boundless faith in the victory of Communism.'

The letter was minuted by Stalin and passed by him to three of his colleagues in the Politburo, who also added their opinions.

Stalin: Scoundrel and prostitute.
Voroshilov: A perfectly accurate description.
Molotov: Entire agreement with Stalin.
Kaganovich: For the traitor scum and [here follows an obscene word]: One punishment — the death sentence.[27]

According to Khrushchev, when Yakir was in front of the firing squad, he exclaimed: 'Long live the Party, long live Stalin!'

He had so much faith in the Party, so much faith in Stalin that he never permitted himself the thought that a deliberate injustice was being committed. He believed that certain enemies had wormed their way into the organs of the NKVD.

When Stalin was told how Yakir behaved before his death, he cursed Yakir.[28]

Khrushchev accepted the story, which he described as 'a rather curious report' originally appearing in the foreign press, 'to the effect that Hitler, in preparing the attack on our country, planted through his intelligence service a faked document indicating that Comrades Yakir and Tukachevsky and others were agents of the German General Staff'. He also accepted that the file containing the document, 'allegedly secret, fell into the hands of President Benes of Czechoslovakia who, apparently guided by good intentions, forwarded it to Stalin'. As a result, 'Yakir, Tukachevsky and other comrades were arrested and then killed'.[29]

Khrushchev did not go so far as to suggest that the incriminating data in the file were supplied by NKVD agents abroad in conjunction with émigre White Russian organisations, notably the Russian Armed Forces Union (ROVS) a para-military group of White army veterans with headquarters in Paris at one time headed by Baron Wrangel and currently directed by General E. K. Miller. However, there are some grounds for believing this to be so, particularly since it is now known that a fellow member of ROVS General N. V. Skoblin, a double agent who was working for the NKVD at this time as well as the Whites, was responsible later in the same year for the kidnapping and subsequent death of General Miller at the hands of Soviet secret agents. (This action was quite in keeping with Stalin's practice, since a previous head of the ROVS, General P. A. Kutyepov, had been kidnapped in 1930 and was never seen again.)[30]

To return to the alleged military plot. At the next and last big show trial – that of Bukharin, Krestinsky, Rosengoltz, Yagoda and others – the old charge was repeated from the previous trials that the conspirators were in league with Trotsky. This was publicly denied by Trotsky and it may be dismissed as without foundation. Indeed Trotsky did not believe that there had been any plot at all, preferring to describe Tukachevsky's fall as 'a symptom of a conflict between Stalin and the officer corps which might place a military coup "on the order of the day" '. The prosecution at the Bukharin trial sought to establish a link between Trotsky and the army plotters through Krestinsky and Rosengoltz, who were stated to have discussed with Tukachevsky his plans for 'an armed insurrection'. It is extremely unlikely, to say the least, that Tukachevsky would have worked with civilians like Krestinsky and Rosengoltz – 'these babblers', as Yagoda contemptuously described them at the trial. On the other hand, they may conceivably have got wind of what Tukachevsky was up to, and one cannot altogether discount Rosengoltz's testimony on this point when questioned by Vyshinsky in open court.

Tukachevsky had a number of alternative plans. One of them, the one on which he counted most, was the possibility of a group of military men, his adherents, gathering in his apartment on some pretext or other, making their way into the Kremlin, seizing the Kremlin telephone exchange, and killing the leaders of the Party and the government.[31]

This was confirmed by Yagoda, who was supposed to have gone over to the conspirators after being demoted as head of the NKVD if not before. 'There was one plan, namely to seize the Kremlin,' he said. But he stoutly denied that it was to be timed to coincide with 'a military onslaught' on the Soviet Union by foreign powers. ('The time was of no importance.') Additional confirmation was supplied by Bukharin who described the conspiracy in his evidence as follows:

> The forces of the conspiracy were: the forces of Yenukidze plus Yagoda, their organisations in the Kremlin and in the NKVD. Yenukidze also succeeded about that time in enlisting, as far as I can remember, the former commandant of the Kremlin, Peterson, who à propos was in his time the commandant of Trotsky's train.
>
> Then there was the military organisation of the conspirators: Tukachevsky, Kork and others.[32]

Further details have been given by the NKVD defector Alexander Orlov.[33] According to this source, generally considered to be reliable (though not invariably so), Tukachevsky thought he could persuade Voroshilov 'on some plausible pretext' to ask Stalin to summon a top-level conference in the Kremlin to discuss military questions concerning Moscow District, the Ukraine and other areas whose commanders were privy to the conspiracy. Briefly the plan was that Tukachevsky and the other principal conspirators should come with their trusted aides, and at a given hour or signal two élite regiments of the Red Army would block the main avenues to the Kremlin in order to prevent the approach of NKVD troops. Meanwhile the coup inside the Kremlin, Tukachevsky was convinced, could be carried out quite easily.

According to Orlov, Tukachevsky and the generals were for killing Stalin outright, subsequently justifying their action to the Party Central Committee by producing proof of Stalin's former connection with the Okhrana which had unexpectedly come into their possession. On the other hand, a number of prominent civilians in the Ukraine, who had been let into the secret, favoured first arresting Stalin and then bringing him before a plenary session of the Central Committee where the police evidence of his treachery to the Bolshevik cause would be produced. These civilians included Stanislav Kossior, Ukraine party boss and member of the Politburo, Victor A. Balitsky, head of the NKVD in Kiev, and his acting deputy Zinovy B. Katsnelson, who happened to be Orlov's cousin. (Katsnelson is the authority for the story and how this evidence came to the knowledge of the conspirators.)

Orlov, whose real name was Nikolsky, was a high ranking NKVD officer and had been attached to the Republican forces in Spain shortly after the outbreak of the Civil War. While recovering from a motor accident in a Paris hospital, to which he had been sent for treatment in January 1937, he received an unexpected visit from his cousin Katsnelson. From him Orlov learned that while preparing for the first of the public purge trials Yagoda apparently at Stalin's suggestion had tried to trace some former Okhrana officers who might be persuaded to give evidence allegedly implicating some of the defendants as Tsarist police agents. For this purpose Yagoda had detailed a NKVD officer named Stein to go through the existing Okhrana files in Leningrad which had survived the destruction of many of the police records in 1917, having been rescued by Yagoda's predecessor Menzhinsky and stored in one of his offices.

In the course of his search Stein is supposed to have come across a secret file kept by Vissarionov, the Vice-Director of the St Petersburg Okhrana who was later executed by the Bolsheviks. The file contained letters and reports in Stalin's handwriting addressed to Vissarionov which clearly established Stalin's role before 1912 as a police *agent provocateur*. Stein, so the story goes, was afraid to show such explosive material to Yagoda. Instead he flew with it to Kiev, where he immediately handed it over to Balitsky, who was his closest personal friend in the service. Balitsky then called in his deputy Katsnelson, and after they had examined the file together and had satisfied themselves of the genuineness of the documents, they confided in Yakir and Kossior, the two leading public figures in the Ukraine at this time.

Afterwards Orlov wrote:

> The circle of horrified initiates widened. General Yakir flew to Moscow and conferred with his friend Tukachevsky, supreme commander of the Red Army, whose personal dislike of Stalin was well known. Tukachevsky took into his confidence the deputy commissar of defence, Gamarnik, a man revered by his intimates for his moral integrity. General Kork was also briefed. These were the men Zinovy [Katsnelson] named to me. Other army men were apparently told later.
>
> Out of this there developed a conspiracy headed by Marshal Tukachevsky to end the reign of Stalin. The nightmare of the blood purges then in progress created a climate of distress, moral disgust and soul-searching conducive to conspiracy against Stalin. The sudden realisation that the tyrant and murderer responsible

for the piled-up horror was not even a genuine revolutionary but an imposter, a creature of the hated Okhrana, galvanised the conspirators into plans for action. Together they decided to stake their lives to save their country by ridding it of the enthroned *agent provocateur*.

At their meeting in Paris, which took place in mid-February 1937, Katsnelson told Orlov that Tukachevsky and the generals were still in the process of 'gathering forces', as he put it.* It must be said, however, that it is hardly likely that the conspiracy was the result of the discovery of Stalin's connection with the Okhrana. Tukachevsky and the others were much more concerned with Stalin's present crimes than with his past, although it is just conceivable that they might have used the discovery to justify their action in liquidating Stalin had they succeeded in their plan to capture the Kremlin – if indeed there ever was such a plan. Nor does the alleged involvement of Yakir accord with his last letter to Stalin and his dying words already quoted. Of course, it may well be that the alleged plot amounted to no more than rather vague talk at which the possibility of a coup was mooted. Certainly for a conspirator for whom speed of action was all important Tukachevsky appeared extraordinarily dilatory. He made no known move at any time before his arrest and is reported as having even gone on leave during the most critical period.

On the assumption that there was a conspiracy – even if it never got beyond the embryonic stage – it follows that someone must have given the conspirators away. One theory is that General Putna, who was in custody at the time of the Pyatakov–Radek trial, broke down under prolonged torture by Yezhov's interrogators. According to another version, General Dybenko, who commanded at Kuibyshev, immediately flew to Moscow after being contacted by the plotters and told Stalin everything he knew. Arrests are supposed to have started that same night.[34] Whether or not there really was a military plot, Stalin took fright and acted as if there was one, and furthermore one that was quite different from the fictitious charge of conspiring with the German General Staff on which Tukachevsky was 'framed'. Several senior NKVD officers are quite definite on this point. One of them was Shpigelglas, the deputy head of the Foreign Department. He called it 'a real conspiracy', far from resembling the alleged plots of which men like Zinoviev, Kamenev and Pyatakov had been convicted. 'That could be seen from the panic which spread there on the top,' he

* Katsnelson and Balitsky were subsequently executed. Stein is stated by Orlov to have shot himself.

359

said at the time, instancing the cancellation of all Kremlin passes and the putting of the NKVD troops in a state of alert. Yezhov's deputy Frinovsky was equally specific. 'The whole Soviet Government hung by a thread,' he admitted to Shpigelglas. 'It was impossible to act as in normal times – first the trial and then the shooting. In this case we had to shoot first and try later.'[35]

Stalin's red sickle did not spare the flower of the Soviet navy and air force, but it was the army which suffered most. The result was the virtual elimination of the remaining ex-Tsarist officers and Civil War veterans, who made up about twenty per cent of the officer cadres. Something like thirty thousand senior and middle-grade officers were either executed, imprisoned or sent to labour camps, while ninety per cent of the general officers disappeared.[36] Among the latter was Army Commander Vatsetis, the first Commander-in-Chief of the Red Army, who, it will be remembered, had clashed with Stalin and Voroshilov on the Tsaritsyn front in 1918. He was giving a lecture at the Frunze Military Academy and after an hour there was a short break. When the lecturer was due to resume, the class commissar suddenly got up and announced: 'Comrades! The lecture will not continue. Lecturer Vatsetis has been arrested as an enemy of the people!' As one of the cadets present later recalled, 'we sat there stunned, without even a whisper. It was incredible that a man who had fought all through the Civil War for Soviet power was – an enemy of the people.'[37] Seventy-five out of eighty-odd members of the Supreme Military Council suffered a similar fate, together with all eleven Vice-Commissars of Defence. The latter included Marshal Yegorov, who had commanded the South-Western Front in the Polish campaign when Stalin was political commissar and was later Chief of the Red Army Staff. He had also been a boon companion of Stalin's.

Shortly after the execution of his fellow marshal Tukachevsky, Yegorov was asked by Stalin if he would like to take over Tukachevsky's luxurious country villa. 'No thanks,' said Yegorov, shaking his head. 'I am a superstitious man.' But this action failed to save him when the time came.[38]

The final word on the army purge may be left with Khrushchev when he spoke at the Twenty-Second Party Congress in October 1961.

I knew Comrade Yakir well. I knew Tukachevsky too, but not as well as Yakir. In 1961, during a conference in Alama-Ata, his son [Peter Yakir], who works in Kazakhstan, came to see me. He asked me about his father. What could I tell him? When we investigated these cases in the Presidium of the Central Committee and received a report that neither Tukachevsky nor Yakir nor Uborevich had been guilty of any crime against the party and the state, we asked Molotov, Kaganovich and Voroshilov: 'Are you for rehabilitating them?'

'Yes, we are for it,' they answered.

'But it was you who executed these people,' we told them indignantly. 'When were you acting according to your conscience, then or now?'

But they did not answer this question. And they will not answer it. You have heard the comments they wrote on letters received by Stalin. What can they say?[39]

4

During the years 1937 and 1938, when Yezhov was in charge of the NKVD, no less than 383 lists of people, whose conduct was under consideration by the Military Collegium of the Supreme Court, were submitted by Yezhov to Stalin with the request that they might all be convicted in the first degree, for which the punishment was death by shooting. The lists with these pre-determined sentences – 'a vicious practice', as Khrushchev called it – were usually prepared by Malenkov and Poskrebyshev. They would then be approved by Stalin and countersigned by Molotov, after which they would be returned to Yezhov for immediate action. They usually fell into four categories: (1) general, (2) former military personnel, (3) former NKVD personnel, and (4) wives of 'enemies of the people'. According to Khrushchev, the lists contained 'many thousands of party, soviet, Komsomol, army and economic workers', and judging by the fact that in the two years immediately preceding Khrushchev's first public denunciation of Stalin's crimes in 1956, over 7,600 persons had been 'rehabilitated', many of them posthumously, there must have been few days during the period of the *Yezhovchina* when Stalin did not sign what amounted to forty or fifty death warrants as part of his office routine. Said Khrushchev:

We justly accuse Yezhov for the degenerate practices of 1937. But we have to answer these questions? Could Yezhov have arrested Kossior, for instance, without the knowledge of Stalin? Was there an exchange of opinions or a Politburo decision concerning this? No, there was not, just as there was none regarding other cases of this type. Could Yezhov have decided such important matters as the fate of eminent party figures? No, it would be a display of naïveté to consider this the work of Yezhov alone. It

361

is clear that these matters were decided by Stalin, and without his orders and his sanction Yezhov could not have done these things.[40]

Khrushchev's choice of Stanislav Kossior as an illustration of Stalin's arbitrary arrests was deliberate. Kossior, besides being a member of the Politburo, was First Secretary of the Ukrainian Communist Party, a post in which he was succeeded on his downfall by none other than Khrushchev himself. From the point of view of his own personal record Khrushchev was naturally anxious to show that he had no part in Kossior's removal and Stalin's other purge measures for the Ukraine, which included the elimination of another Politburo member and leading government figure Vlas Chubar, who was a Vice-Chairman of the Council of Commissars and a former Premier of the Ukraine. According to Khrushchev, both Kossior and Chubar were subjected to prolonged torture, allegedly at Stalin's instructions, before they were tried in secret and shot. The investigating judge in charge of their case was one of Yezhov's most detestable subordinates named Rodos, 'a vile person, with the brain of a bird, and morally completely degenerate', as Khrushchev described him. Called before the Presidium of the Central Committee on the eve of Khrushchev's 'secret' speech, Rodos unblushingly summarised the whole technique behind Stalin's purge trials: 'I was told that Kossior and Chubar were enemies of the people and for this reason I, as investigating judge, had to make them confess that they were enemies.'[41]

For all this Khrushchev wished it to be known that he took no responsibility, and of course he could say with truth that he was not a member of the Politburo at the time. On the other hand, it was a different story when it came to carrying out Stalin's instructions. The Moscow party organisation was thoroughly purged during the time Khrushchev was its secretary, and when he took over the unfortunate Kossior's job in Kiev he did his best to wipe out the local Communist intelligentsia and suppress all tendencies towards Ukrainian nationalism. Stalin awarded him a year later with promotion to full membership of the Politburo; he had become a candidate member when he went to the Ukraine.

Nikita Khrushchev was not even a member of the Central Committee when the Seventeenth Party Congress met at the beginning of 1934, and his rapid advancement in the Party hierarchy was unprecedented among Stalin's entourage. In this he was ahead of his most formidable rival Malenkov by seven years. By way of contrast, Mikoyan, who cultivated Khrushchev for reasons of personal gain, had to serve nine years as a candidate member of the Politburo and he was only admitted to full membership because Stalin needed his vote in favour of the purge policy. Khrushchev, on the other hand, got his seat in the Politburo after barely twelve months as a candidate member, not because he voted for the purge but because he proved a most effective instrument in carrying it out. In fact, this was the only distinction between the two in their common responsibility for the Great Purge.[42]

At the May Day celebrations in 1937, when the security precautions were particularly strict, Khrushchev was photographed somewhat ostentatiously wearing a worker's plain cloth cap, standing on top of the Lenin Mausoleum beside Stalin, Kaganovich and the Bulgarian Dmitrov, whom Stalin had made head of the Comintern organisation after Zinoviev's removal.

Among the members of the diplomatic corps present on this occasion was a young Second Secretary in the British Embassy named Fitzroy Maclean, who was later to describe in graphic language the occasion and others like it which he witnessed.

...at least twice a year Stalin would appear in public, on 1 May and 7 November, when, standing on Lenin's tomb, he would take the salute at ceremonial parades of the Red Army. And then there was no doubt about the position he occupied, however unofficial it might be. Unobtrusively, he would emerge from a little side door in the Kremlin wall, followed by the other members of the Supreme Politburo of the Party, and, clambering up to the top of the Mausoleum, would take up his position a little in front of the others, looking out over the great expanse of the Red Square, a squat Asiatic figure in a peaked cap and drab semi-military greatcoat: narrow eyes close set under heavy brows, the downward sweep of his moustache ponderous beneath a hawk-like nose, his expression alternating between benignity and bored inscrutability. Infantry, cavalry, tanks would sweep past, while fighters and bombers roared overhead. Every now and again he would raise his hand, palm outstretched, with a little gesture that was at once a friendly wave, a benediction and a salute. But most of the time he would chat affably to those around him, while they, for their part, grinned nervously and moved uneasily from one foot to the other, forgetting the parade and the high office they held and everything else in their mingled joy and terror at being spoken to by him.[43]

This is not the place to recount the grim details of the *Yezhovchina*. It has been done by a number of outstanding writers, notably Arthur Koestler in *Darkness at Noon* and Robert Conquest in *The Great Terror*, neither of which is likely to be superseded as the authoritative non-Russian work on the subject, at least for a considerable time to come. There is also the question of why so many people should have confessed to crimes which they did not commit. In his novel Koestler put forward one plausible explanation, although he does not claim it to be the sole one. That is that a Communist under interrogation and ultimately on trial would confess to any crime against the Soviet state because he would realise that his confession, even though substantially false, was the only way left to him in which he could advance the cause of Communism. In other words, to abandon belief in Communism after a lifetime as a revolutionary was psychologically impossible for them. Thus with the broken men of the Opposition, particularly Old Bolsheviks, recantation became a kind of ritual habit and accepted routine. For example, Koestler's hero Rubashov, who is largely based on Bukharin, eventually admits to the interrogator that his political demands as a leading oppositionist were objectively harmful to the Party and therefore counter-revolutionary in character. This accords with the reply given by Bukharin in 1935 when asked why the oppositionists had given in to Stalin, a man whose 'insane ambition' he had been denouncing. 'It is not *him* we trust,' said Bukharin, 'but the man in whom the Party has reposed its confidence. It just so happened that he has become a sort of symbol of the Party.'[44] To oppose the will of Stalin, therefore, was to oppose the will of the Party and to defile the ark of the sacred covenant of Bolshevism.

No doubt this explanation was valid in the case of numbers of Old Bolsheviks. But it can hardly apply to non-Party members, thousands of whom confessed to being 'enemies of the people' at this period and even to Party members who confessed not so much out of a desire to render a final service to the Party but because their resistance had been broken down. Confined in a cell under constant surveillance of a guard, under the harsh glare of strong electric light, the prisoner was the prey of ceaseless anxieties and fears. In these surroundings, after nights of repeated questioning, often to the accompaniment of torture, his sense of values became blurred and he gradually became inclined to accept the idea put into his head by his interrogators. This was that his paramount duty was to recover his freedom. The price did not seem unduly high – just his signature on a deposition acknowledging his traitorous acts against the Soviet. In course of weeks and even months – it depended upon how long he could hold out – his reasoning powers would become corrupted. He confused true facts with those suggested to him by the interrogators. Finally, in his determination to confess everything he began to talk about things that had never happened. He would try to remember something he never did, some action he never committed, just to prove conclusively that he did not intend to conceal anything. After the fortieth interrogation or so, the prisoner's deposition would start, 'Yes, I didn't state the truth till now. Now I will tell everything openly...'

By this time he had usually become a nervous wreck. If he was of sufficient importance to be tried publicly, he would be put on a better diet and deliberately fattened up for the trial, as we have seen happened to Zinoviev and Kamenev. Otherwise he would be tried summarily and in private by a three-man tribunal known as a *troika* and sentenced either to be shot or sent to a labour camp, which could be and often was for twenty-five years. Any attempt on his part to deviate from his story in court, particularly if the trial were in public, would be countered by a sharp reminder from the prosecutor of the details of his confession.

A plausible explanation of why the prisoners 'confessed' in the Moscow trials was given by the Estonian Commander-in-Chief General Laidoner. Questioned on the subject by Mr W. H. Gallienne, the British consul in Tallin at this time, the general replied that it was 'perfectly obvious to anyone who knew the Russian mentality: the prisoners were given the choice of confessing and then being shot, or refusing to confess and dying by torture. All the prisoners knew what torture was like; most of them had seen it, and many had ordered other people to undergo it. For instance, Pyatakov was a sadistic monster who had executed hundreds in the most revolting way'.[45]

A story with a grimly humourous twist was current in Moscow during the purges, and even as high ranking a party official as Zhdanov liked to repeat it with a chuckle. According to the story, which has several variants, Stalin lost his pipe. He thereupon telephoned the NKVD and demanded it be found immediately. Two hours later, he found the pipe himself – it had merely fallen into one of his boots behind the sofa in his apartment. He telephoned the NKVD again and asked what progress had been made.

'We have arrested ten men already,' the Minister reported, 'and the investigation is continuing.'

'As it happens,' said Stalin, 'I have found my pipe. So free them instantly.'

'But, Comrade Stalin, seven of them have already confessed!'

In his secret speech to the Twentieth Party Congress, Khrushchev quoted a pathetic plea which an imprisoned Old Bolshevik, Mikhail S.

Kedrov, had addressed to the Central Committee from jail and was no doubt seen by Stalin.

> I am calling to you for help from a gloomy cell of the Lefortovo prison. Let my cry of horror reach your ears...Please help remove the nightmare of interrogations and show that this is all a mistake.
> I suffer innocently. Please believe me. Time will testify to the truth. I am not an *agent provocateur* of the Tsarist Okhrana. I am not a spy. I am not a member of an anti-Soviet organisation of which I am being accused on the basis of denunciations. I am also not guilty of any other crimes against the Party and the Government. I am an old Bolshevik, free of any stain. I have honestly fought for almost forty years in the ranks of the Party for the good and the prosperity of the nation...
> Today I, a sixty-two-year-old man, am being threatened by the investigating judges with more severe, cruel and degrading methods of physical pressure...I am firmly certain that given a quiet, objective examination, without any foul rantings, without any anger, without the fearful tortures, it would be easy to prove the baselessness of the charges. I believe deeply that truth and justice will triumph. I believe. I believe.

Sympathy with Kedrov, who was eventually shot, must be tempered with the knowledge that he had himself been a former member of the Cheka, when his methods of dealing with the Whites during the Civil War on the Archangel front had been distinguished for their brutality, so that he knew what to expect when he faced the interrogators of the NKVD. Of course, comparatively few could resist what Khrushchev called these 'methods of repression'. One who did and survived to tell the tale of his interrogation and torture, also in the Lefortovo, was General A. V. Gorbatov, who was arrested in the wake of the Tukachevsky affair and subsequently reinstated in his command after four terrible years spent largely in labour camps. In his book *Years Off My Life*, which appeared in the Soviet Union during the Khrushchev era, Gorbatov wrote of his experiences in Lefortovo, which had a particularly bad reputation in this respect:

> I accidentally found that my fiend of an interrogator's name was Stolbunsky. I don't know where he is now. If he is still alive I hope he will read these lines and feel my contempt for him, not only now but when I was in his hands. But I think he knew this

well enough. Apart from him, two brawny torturers took part in the interrogation. Even now my ears ring with the sound of Stolbunsky's evil voice hissing 'You'll sign, you'll sign!' as I was carried out, weak and covered in blood. I withstood the torture during the second bout of interrogation, but when the third started, how I longed to be able to die![46]

A Russian civilian, who wrote of the purge in his autobiography, also published in Russia by leave of Khrushchev, was the journalist Ilya Ehrenburg, although he did so somewhat briefly since he was engaged in reporting the Spanish Civil War for most of the time. Once on Ehrenburg's return from Spain, Isaac Babel, the great Russian short story writer, said to him: 'Today a man talks frankly only with his wife – at night, with the blanket pulled over his head!' There was no one in Ehrenburg's considerable circle of acquaintances who could be sure about the morrow; many of them kept a small suitcase with two changes of warm underwear permanently in readiness. The tenants of the apartment house where he was staying asked for the noisy lift to stop working at night, as it kept them awake, listening and wondering where it would stop. Babel, later to be purged and to die in a concentration camp, described for Ehrenburg's benefit how certain people newly appointed to various posts behaved. 'They perch on the very edge of their chairs.' In the *Izvestia* newspaper offices, boards used to hang on the glass doors with the names of heads of departments, but this practice soon ceased. It was not worth having them made, the messenger girl explained to Ehrenburg when he called, 'Here today and gone tomorrow!'

One night during the winter of 1937–1938, while taking his wife's dog for a run, Ehrenburg encountered another fellow writer, Boris Pasternak, in the street outside the apartment house. Pasternak waved his arms about, gesticulating as he stood between the snow drifts. 'If only someone would tell Stalin about it!' he exclaimed. Like Ehrenburg, Pasternak at first believed that the person responsible for the terrible course taken by the purge, particularly in liquidating so many members of the Soviet intelligentsia, was the NKVD chief Yezhov, who indeed has given his name to the period. So too did Babel. He had known Yezhov's wife before her marriage and continued to see her from time to time. Although he realised that this was unwise, Babel wished, so he told Ehrenburg, 'to find a key to the puzzle'. One day, he said, shaking his head: 'It's not a matter of Yezhov. Of course Yezhov plays his part, but he's not at the bottom of it.' The inference was obvious. Nevertheless, Babel was afraid to mention Stalin by name, even to such an old friend and colleague as Ehrenburg.[47]

'How was it that you survived?' Ehrenburg was asked many years later by a young writer who was five years old in 1938.

'I shall never know,' was all the journalist could reply.

Alexander Yakovlev, the well-known Soviet aircraft designer, whose memoirs appeared under Khrushchev's dispensation, makes it quite clear that Stalin must have been aware of what was going on. Yakovlev, who saw a good deal of Stalin and himself escaped the purge, writes that 'Stalin's greyish brown eyes could radiate charm when he wished, but when he became angry they looked daggers, and tiny red spots appeared among the pock marks on his face'. Yakovlev also recalls how Stalin, after dressing down a senior executive, would say: 'I see you like the quiet life. In that case you would be best off in the cemetery. That's the only place you can find tranquillity. The corpses will not argue with you or make any demands upon you.'[48]

Certainly no one was safe from the tyrant's caprices, no matter how exalted he or she might be in the Party hierarchy. 'Why are your eyes so shifty today?' Stalin would suddenly say at random to a party worker he had known for years. 'Why do you turn away? Why don't you look me straight in the face?' As often as not the unfortunate individual was arrested later the same day, sometimes in unexpected public places. Yan Rudzutak, a former full member of the Politburo who had filled many government posts, including that of Vice-Premier, was seized at a supper party after the theatre. At the same time, the NKVD took everyone else present, including four women. The latter were reported to be in the Butyrska prison three months later still in bedraggled evening dress. Nikolai Krestinsky, one of the members of Lenin's original Politburo and successively Secretary of the Central Committee, Soviet Ambassador to Germany and Deputy Commissar for Foreign Affairs, was also pulled in at this time. So too was Arcady Rosengoltz, the Commissar for Foreign Trade. Krestinsky and Rosengoltz had made up a good team under the direction of Litvinov, who was somewhat surprisingly spared, though his wife was English and he had many other connections with the west. No doubt it suited Stalin to keep Litvinov in his important commissariat, notwithstanding that many members of his staff were purged, including eleven ambassadors. Bukharin and Rykov were already in custody, as also was Yagoda, and throughout most of 1937 Yezhov on Stalin's orders worked hard to obtain their 'confessions' before producing them at the last big show trial along with Krestinsky, Rosengoltz and seventeen others.

At the same time, the purge in the Caucasus was in the hands of Lavrenti Beria, who had so spectacularly rewritten local Bolshevik history for Stalin's personal glorification. Among those to suffer in Tiflis was Budu Mdivani, the former Premier of Georgia, whose part Lenin had taken against Stalin. He was accused of having planned terrorist acts against both Beria and Yezhov at the instigation of the British secret intelligence service. He was promised that his life would be spared if he would agree to testify incriminating himself and other local Party leaders.

'You are telling me that Stalin has promised to spare the lives of Old Bolsheviks!' Mdivani replied. 'I have known Stalin for thirty years. Stalin won't rest until he has butchered all of us, beginning with the unweaned baby and ending with the blind great-grandmother!'[49]

Fortunately for themselves, the leading Mensheviks like Zhordania, Uratadze and Arsenidze had managed to escape. But Mdivani and most of the other Old Bolsheviks, comrades of Stalin's youth, were shot. Philip Makharadze was an unaccountable exception.

Georgian victims included the popular Abel Yenukidze, generally regarded as Stalin's closest personal friend – he had been his 'best man' at his marriage to Nadhezda Alliluyeva. After he had fallen into disfavour for intervening on behalf of Zinoviev and Kamenev and also for introducing Zoya Nikitina into the Kremlin, the young woman who had planned to poison Stalin, Yenukidze was eventually arrested at the same time as Bukharin and Rykov. However, there was no question of putting him on trial publicly, since he steadfastly refused to 'confess' and remained unbroken to the end. According to the official announcement, he was shot after being tried by a secret military court with six others on vague charges of espionage and terroristic activities.

'Cain, what hast thou done with thy brother Abel?' Trotsky asked the Soviet dictator in the *Bulletin of the Opposition* which Trotsky edited in exile. 'Cain Djugashvili shall be thy name in Russian history after this hateful murder!'

Trotsky's biblical illusion struck home. Stalin immediately reacted by showing that he had not forgotten his New Testament studies at the Tiflis seminary. He ordered that Trotsky should henceforth be referred to in the Soviet press as Judas in addition to his surname.[50]

In the NKVD, after Yagoda had been superseded by Yezhov, the purge was as severe as in other branches of the armed services. During the year 1937 alone, according to Orlov, three thousand of Yagoda's officers were executed.[51] They included Agranov, Molchanov and Mironov, as well as the detestable Pauker who was accused somewhat improbably of being a German spy. Others committed suicide, such as Chertok, the brutal interrogator who had broken Kamenev – he jumped out of his twelfth-storey apartment. Another victim was

Stanislav Redens, who was married to Stalin's sister-in-law Anna Alliluyeva. He is said to have come into Yezhov's office one day and spat in his face, whereupon Yezhov drew his revolver and killed him on the spot.[52] V. I. Mezhlauk. who succeeded Ordzhonikidze as Commissar of Heavy Industry and joined the Politburo, disappeared probably after a secret trial. Other prominent Old Bolsheviks to perish at this time were Andrei Bubnov and Nikolai Krylenko, who held the portfolios of education and justice respectively. Another was Mosei Rukhimovich, Commissar for the Defence Industry, who had always been a staunch Stalinist and who, it will be remembered, had been conspicuously associated with Stalin and Voroshilov in the intrigues on the Tsaritsyn front during the Civil War. Likewise G. I. Lomov, who was denounced by an official in the Control Commission, where he worked, for having been on friendly terms with Bukharin and Rykov. 'What to do?' Stalin minuted the denunciation, which he passed to Molotov. 'I'm for arresting this scum Lomov immediately,' replied Molotov. Lomov was accordingly taken into custody, charged with being a member of Bukharin's Rightist organisation, summarily convicted and shot.[53]

Yezhov had now been given his head completely. 'In affairs of this sort it is better to strike hard rather than leave intact any nests of dangerous enemies,' said Stalin at this time. 'Remember the Wars of Religion, and the inquisitor who said that God would recognise the innocent later on and separate them from the guilty. Nikolai Ivanovich is our inquisitor. He will submit his accounts to the Party later on.'[54]

5

The trial of Bukharin, Rykov, Krestinsky, Rosengoltz, Yagoda and seventeen others, including the former commissars for agriculture, finance and the timber industry (M. A. Chernov, G. F. Grinko and V. I. Ivanov) and a vice-commissar for foreign affairs and ex-ambassador (Christian Rakovsky) opened in the Hall of Columns in Trade Union House on 2 March 1938. They were all accused of belonging to an anti-Soviet bloc of Rights and Trotskyites. As usual Ulrich presided and Vyshinsky was in charge of the prosecution.[55] This time quite a lot of things went wrong with the prepared script, and from Stalin's point of view it was perhaps the least satisfactory of all the public purge trials. To begin with, Krestinsky, who like the others had previously 'confessed' at the preliminary investigation, astonished everyone by pleading not guilty when he appeared in court. 'I am not a Trotskyite,' he said. 'I was never a member of the bloc of Rights and Trotskyites, of whose existence I was not aware. Nor have I committed any of the crimes with which I personally am charged. In particular I plead not guilty to the charge of having had connections with the German intelligence service.'

This unexpected turn of events caused Vyshinsky to call another defendant S. A. Bessonov, formerly Counsellor at the Soviet Embassy in Berlin, to contradict Krestinsky. This Bessonov obligingly did, declaring that he had acted as Krestinsky's intermediary with Trotsky. Throughout the first day of the trial Krestinsky stuck to his plea, much to the prosecutor's annoyance. But after a session with Yezhov's men that night he changed his tune. Next day he informed the court that he had acted 'under a momentary feeling of false shame, evoked by the atmosphere of the dock and the painful impression caused by the public reading of the indictment, which was aggravated by my poor health', and that he now wished to change his plea to guilty. 'I fully and completely admit that I am guilty of all the gravest charges brought against me personally,' he told the court, 'and that I admit my complete responsibility for the treason and treachery I have committed.'

Krestinsky's *volte-face* was not unprecedented. Skoriutto had behaved in a similar manner at the Shakhty trial as had Macdonald at the Metro-Vickers trial, both possibly for the same reason as Krestinsky. In Krestinsky's case, however, there is no doubt that he was tortured. According to one account, his left shoulder was deliberately dislocated, so that it should not appear in court that he had been physically maltreated. He is also said to have been faced throughout most of the night in the Lubyanka with a battery of bright lights which damaged his already injured eyes. Fitzroy Maclean, who was present in court, records that on his second appearance the unfortunate Krestinsky looked more than ever like 'a small bedraggled sparrow'. At all events the night had not been wasted.

The trial is also noteworthy for the fact that evidence was given by a former Okhrana officer named Vasilyev to the effect that one of the defendants Prokopy T. Zubarev had been recruited as an *agent provocateur* at his home in Kotelnich, a village in Vyatka, in 1908 after a police raid in which a considerable quantity of illegal literature was seized in his father's house, and that he continued to work for the Okhrana for the next seven years in other parts of Russia. This was confirmed by Zubarev himself who stated that for the information he supplied to Vasilyev he was paid sixty silver roubles. 'Twice as much as Judas received?' Vyshinsky mockingly inquired. To the accompaniment of obsequious laughter on the part of the hand-picked spectators, Zubarev agreed that this was so.

371

Of course, the fact that Zubarev may once have been a police spy had nothing to do with the main charge of economic espionage in the Urals for the benefit of Germany in the early 1930s as part of the general Rightist conspiracy of Rykov and A. P. Smirnov. Vyshinsky's purpose in establishing the defendant's earlier connection with the Okhrana seems to have been to show that if Zubarev was capable of working for the Okhrana he was capable of any treasonable enormity. Indeed the chief prosecutor appeared to be particularly pleased with himself for having been able to produce this elderly link with the Tsarist police, as well he might, bearing in mind how difficult it was to trace ex-Okhrana officers let alone persuade one to come forward and testify to this hated occupation. On the face of it, however, the evidence of Vasilyev, who gave his age as sixty-eight, would not seem to be otherwise than genuine.

It might be interesting to speculate upon Stalin's reaction to this story, since in addition to receiving a daily report from Vyshinsky, it is known that he was actually an observer of at least part of the proceedings. We have it on the authority of Fitzroy Maclean who was present throughout that 'at one stage of the trial a clumsily directed arc-light dramatically revealed to attentive members of the audience the familiar features and heavy drooping moustache peering out from behind the black glass of a small window, high up under the ceiling of the courtroom'.

Bukharin, who was billed as the star performer, turned out to be the prosecution's greatest disappointment. True, he readily admitted his connections with the Trotskyite opposition, in particular the so-called Ryutin platform, but he did so in such a way as to convey the impression that he had opposed Stalin's policies because he had come to the conclusion as the leading Bolshevik theoretician in the Soviet Union that they were wrong for the country and the people. In particular, he admitted having established contact with Boris Nicolaevsky, 'who is very close to the leading circles of the Menshevik Party', and whom he had met on his last trip abroad in 1936, having gone to Paris with Stalin's express permission in the hope of purchasing some Marx manuscripts which formed part of the German and Russian Social Democratic archive of which Nicolaevsky was curator. But murder was another thing, and this he stoutly denied.

Vyshinsky: In 1918 were you not in favour of killing the leaders of our Party and government?
Bukharin: No, I was not.

Vyshinsky: What about the murder of Comrades Lenin, Stalin and Sverdlov?

Bukharin: Under no circumstances.

When Vyshinsky moved on to the espionage charges and suggested that Bukharin had been recruited by the Austrian police, the defendant gave a similar denial. 'My only contact with the Austrian police was when they imprisoned me in a fortress as a revolutionary', he declared proudly, adding that the sole evidence connecting him with espionage had been given by two of the other defendants, V. F. Sharangovich and V. I. Ivanov, who were NKVD *agents provocateurs* and undoubted liars in this instance.

'I am asking you again on the basis of the testimony here given against you,' said Vyshinsky in a last despairing effort at cross-examination of this unique witness, 'do you choose to admit before the Soviet Court by what intelligence service you were recruited – the British, German or Japanese?'

'None,' replied Bukharin.

'I have no more questions to put to Bukharin,' said Vyshinsky, for once defeated.

Even more bizarre were the charges of 'medical assassination' brought against Yagoda, who it will be remembered had started life as a pharmacist, and three of the leading doctors, Professor D. D. Pletnev, the best known heart specialist in the country, Dr D. D. Levin, the senior consultant of the Kremlin Medical Department, and Dr I. N. Kazakov, another specialist. Levin had even treated Stalin and his daughter Svetlana, but this did not save him from becoming the victim of an absurd charge that along with the others he had planned and caused the deaths of Kuibyshev, Maxim Gorky, Gorky's son Maxim Peshkov and Menzhinsky, Yagoda's predecessor as head of the NKVD. Yagoda was also accused of attempting to murder Yezhov by spraying the walls of his office with a poison gas. Although the doctors were undoubtedly guiltless of murdering their patients at Yagoda's instigation, Yagoda himself would appear to have been personally involved in some of the crimes. It is now known, for instance, that Gorky died through eating sweetmeats impregnated with cyanide poisoning, incidentally one of the methods used by Prince Youssoupoff to kill Rasputin, and that the NKVD under Yagoda were responsible for the killing, presumably with Stalin's connivance.

Of all the twenty-one defendants at this the last and biggest of the public purge trials, possibly Yagoda had most cause to feel resentful at the treatment he had received for his devoted service to Stalin. He made this clear one evening in the course of a conversation he had with Slutsky, the head of the Foreign Department of the NKVD, who had been sent by Yezhov to talk to Yagoda in his cell.

'You may put down in your report to Yezhov that I have said that there must be a God after all,' said Yagoda as Slutsky was preparing to leave.

'What?' exclaimed Slutsky in surprise.

'Quite simple,' Yagoda is said to have replied, half seriously, half jokingly. 'From Stalin I deserved nothing but gratitude for my faithful service. From God I deserved the most severe punishment for having broken his commandments thousands of times. Now look where I am and judge for yourself whether there is a God or not!'[56]

Vyshinsky concluded his closing speech for the prosecution with a characteristic tirade which he had rehearsed beforehand and in which he demanded the supreme penalty for all the accused.

> Our whole country, from young to old, is awaiting and demanding one thing. The traitors and spies who were selling our country must be shot like dirty dogs! Our people are demanding one thing. Crush the accursed reptile.
>
> Time will pass. The graves of the hateful traitors will grow over with weeds and thistles, they will be covered with the eternal contempt of honest Soviet citizens, of the entire Soviet people. But over us, over our happy country, our sun will shine with its luminous rays as bright and joyous as before. Over the road cleared of the last scum and filth of the past, we, our people, with our beloved leader and teacher the great Stalin at our head, will march as before onwards and onwards towards Communism!

The court responded to this appeal by sentencing eighteen of the defendants to death, and they were duly executed. The remaining three were sentenced to long prison terms. They were Trotsky's friend Christian Rakovsky, former Vice-Commissar for Foreign Affairs and Soviet ambassador in London and Paris, who got twenty years; Sergei Bessonov, who got fifteen years; and Professor Pletnev who got twenty-five years. Pletnev died in a labour camp. Krestinsky and some of the others were later posthumously 'rehabilitated', though not as yet Bukharin and Rykov, in spite of the fact that the charges against them were for the most part equally insubstantial. Unlike Krestinsky, Bukharin and Rykov were essentially political 'deviationists', and not even the Russia of Khrushchev and his successors could countenance such behaviour however opposed to Stalin they might have been.

The remaining trials during the *Yezhovchina* were held behind closed doors. It is possible that another big public trial was slated for the summer of 1938 and that the arrangements were somehow bungled by Yezhov. At least Yezhov's gradual fall from favour may be dated from this time when a number of prominent Stalinists were liquidated 'administratively' instead of first making their bow in the Hall of Columns. They included Yan Rudzutak, V. I. Mezhlauk, Admiral Orlov and Generals Belov, Dybenko and Vatsetis. It also marks the turning point in the Great Purge, although there were still some heads to roll. Among them were five members of the Politburo, namely Kossior, Chubar, Postyshev and Eikhe, as well as Yezhov himself; also A. V. Kosarev, a member of the Orgburo and General Secretary of the Young Communists (*Komsomol*). With the exception of the loathsome sadist Yezhov, who is supposed to have committed suicide in an insane asylum, all these were brave men who either refused to confess or else retracted their confessions after breaking down under prolonged torture. On the other hand, there were some Old Bolsheviks of both sexes who somehow managed to get through the Great Purge unscathed, while so many of their colleagues and staff perished. Among the more remarkable survivors were Maxim Litvinov and Alexandra Kollontai on the civilian side and a few high ranking military officers like Shaposhnikov, Timoshenko and Koniev. Their survival seems to have been a matter of luck as much as any other factor, since Litvinov, for example, after he had served Stalin's purpose and been removed as Foreign Commissar, managed to escape liquidation. Two women particularly associated with Lenin were also spared. They were Lenin's principal private secretary Lydia Fotieva and his widow Krupskaya, whom not even Stalin dared to touch, profoundly irritating as he frequently found her to be.

Robert I. Eikhe, who was aged forty-eight at the time of his arrest, afforded a typical example of an Old Bolshevik's courage. He had held senior government and party posts in Siberia before being elected a candidate member of the Politburo in 1935. He was arrested a few weeks after the Bukharin trial. He held out for more than a year in the face of questioning by two of the most brutal NKVD interrogators, Ushakov and Nikolaev, in the course of which several of his ribs were fractured. As he put it in a letter which he wrote to Stalin from prison, the interrogators, especially Ushakov, 'utilised the knowledge that my broken ribs had not properly mended and were causing me great pain', as a result of which ('not being able to suffer the tortures to which I was submitted by Ushakov and Nikolaev') he was forced to accuse himself and others, notably Rukhimovich and Mezhlauk, whose

375

names were deliberately inserted by the NKVD in the documents he was compelled to sign.

It was when he was eventually informed that the pre-trial investigation was complete and he was shown a copy of the indictment that Eikhe addressed his letter to Stalin. So far as is known it was not acknowledged, but it was kept on the file, so that Khrushchev was able to quote from it in his 'secret' speech. Here is one passage:

> Had I been guilty of only one hundredth of the crimes with which I am charged, I would not have dared to send you this pre-execution declaration. However, I have not been guilty of even one of the things with which I am charged and my heart is clean of even the shadow of baseness. I have never in my life told you a word of falsehood and now, finding my two feet in the grave, I am also not lying. My whole case is a typical example of provocation, slander and violation of the elementary basis of revolutionary legality...
>
> I have never betrayed you or the Party. I know that I perish because of vile and mean work of the enemies of the Party and the people, who fabricated the provocation against me.

When he was at last brought to trial after nearly two years in custody, Eikhe frankly informed the court of how he had been tortured and how the confession had been forced from him which he now withdrew. 'The most important thing for me is to tell the court, the Party and Stalin that I am not guilty,' he concluded. 'I have never been guilty of any conspiracy. I will die believing in the truth of Party policy as I have believed in it during my whole life.'[57]

Eikhe was duly sentenced to death and shot. Needless to add, his case was one of a considerable number of high Party and government officials which was examined by the special commission appointed for the purpose by Khrushchev, and declared to have been 'fabricated'. Eikhe was thus posthumously rehabilitated.

The approaching end of the *Yezhovchina* was foreshadowed by Stalin's appointment of the Georgian police chief Lavrenti Beria as Yezhov's deputy in July 1938. Before the end of the year Beria had taken over completely as head of the NKVD after Yezhov had gone to Stalin with a report in which he proposed to purge Beria besides most of the remaining members of the Politburo, including Voroshilov, Kaganovich, Mikoyan and even Molotov.

According to one story, Beria discovered a document in the Okhrana files at Rostov-on-Don which showed that Yezhov had once been a secret police informer and had worked for Colonel Vasilyev, the same ex-Okhrana officer who had been produced by Yezhov to testify at the Bukharin trial.[58] Possibly the obliging Vasilyev may even have forged it. At all events, it is said to have sealed Yezhov's fate when Beria laid it before the Politburo. From then on, according to Stalin's daughter Svetlana, Beria saw Stalin every day. ('His influence on my father grew and never ceased until the day of my father's death.') Yezhov lingered on for a few weeks as Commissar for Inland Water Transport, after which he vanished behind the walls, so it was reported, of a criminal lunatic asylum. There he is supposed either to have been shot or to have hanged himself from a tree in the grounds. Afterwards a placard was said to have been found pinned to his clothes with the inscription, 'I am filth!' This legend, so said the local wits, was Yezhov's 'spontaneous confession'.[59]

The story of Yezhov's madness, whether true or invented, was at all events a convenient means for Stalin to explain the excesses of the *Yezhovchina*. Stalin once said to the Soviet aircraft designer Alexander Yakovlev, who had remarked on the acute shortage of qualified staff as the result of so many arrests: 'That scoundrel Yezhov! He finished off some of our finest people. He was utterly rotten...That's why we shot him!'[60] Stalin repeated himself in more formal language when the Eighteenth Party Congress met in March 1939, a cowed and docile assembly very different both in character and composition from the 'Congress of Victors' which had preceded it by five years. 'It cannot be said that the purge was not accompanied by grave mistakes,' remarked Stalin in presenting his report to the Congress. 'There were unfortunately more mistakes than were expected. Undoubtedly we shall have no need to resort to the methods of mass purges any more.' Nevertheless, he felt that on the whole the results were beneficial. The number of Party members had decreased by 270,000 since the Seventeeth Congress. 'But there is nothing bad in that. Our Party is now somewhat smaller in membership, but on the other hand it is better in quality. That is a big achievement.'[61] At the same time, although Stalin did not specifically mention them, there were still some old individual scores left for him to settle.

The Great Purge, and in particular the three big show trials which formed its most conspicuous feature, had served Stalin well, and now it was time to call a halt. By exposing Trotsky and his allies – the Germans and Japanese abroad and the Zinovievites and Bukharinites at home – Stalin had succeeded in diverting the Soviet people's attention from the country's continuing economic difficulties. By eliminating the opposition real and potential to himself which stemmed from the remnants of Lenin's Old Guard, Stalin had effectively and successfully established the thesis that such opposition was tantamount to treason to himself and thus deserving of exemplary punishment. The argument advanced in the foreign press that the purge had gravely weakened the Soviet Union's defences and economy, a self-evident proposition to any observant outsider, he dismissed with contempt, pointing to the massive public support for his policies which he claimed before the Eighteenth Congress shown by the elections to the legislative bodies which had taken place under the new constitution.

Certain foreign pressmen have been talking drivel to the effect that the purging of Soviet organizations of spies, assassins and wreckers like Trotsky, Zinoviev, Kamenev, Yakir, Tukachevsky, Rosengoltz, Bukharin and other fiends has 'shaken' the Soviet system and caused its 'demoralisation'. All this cheap drivel deserves is laughter and scorn. How can the purging of Soviet organisations of noxious and hostile elements shake and demoralise the Soviet system?

...In 1937 Tukachevsky, Yakir, Uborevich and other fiends were sentenced to be shot. After that, the elections to the Supreme Soviet of the USSR were held. In these elections, 98·6 per cent of the total vote was cast for the Soviet government.

At the beginning of 1938 Rosengoltz, Rykov, Bukharin and other fiends were sentenced to be shot. After that, the elections to the Supreme Union of the Soviet Republics were held. In these elections 99·4 per cent of the total vote was cast for the Soviet government. Where are the symptoms of 'demoralisation', we should like to know, and why was this 'demoralisation' not reflected in the results of the elections?[62]

Why indeed? The answer was simple, but Stalin did not give it. In the circumstances he could hardly be expected to. There was only one candidate for each of the electoral divisions, the one with the Party ticket, which had been endorsed by Stalin himself. And in practice only votes for and not against the candidate were accepted at the ballot box. There, in his own district of Moscow, a benign looking Stalin led the way by being ostentatiously photographed in the exercise of this foolproof and convenient form of franchise designed to perpetuate his political omnipotence.

CHAPTER X

The Deadly Pact

I

In his report to the Eighteenth Party Congress, which he presented on 10 March 1939, Stalin devoted a significant part of his speech to a survey of the international scene. In this he castigated Japan, Italy and Germany for their aggressive actions in Asia, Africa and Europe; at the same time he attacked Britain, France and the United States for their policy of 'non-intervention' against the aggressors. 'A new imperialist war is already in its second year,' he said, 'a war waged over a huge territory, stretching from Shanghai to Gibraltar and involving over 500 million people...The war is being waged by aggressor states, who in every way infringe the interests of the non-aggressor states, primarily England, France and the USA, while the latter draw back and retreat, making concession after concession to the aggressors.' The appeasers, he argued, hoped among other things to let Germany and Russia exhaust one another; and then, when they had become weak enough, to appear on the scene with fresh strength and to dictate conditions to the enfeebled belligerents. 'That would be cheap and easy,' commented Stalin. But the appeasers had better look out, he warned, particularly if they became warmongers themselves. He then proceeded to formulate a novel aim in Soviet foreign policy, in addition to the perennial aims of striving for international peace and the strengthening of the bonds of working-class friendship among nations.

To be cautious and not to allow our country to be drawn into

379

conflicts by warmongers who are accustomed to have others pull the chestnuts out of the fire for them.[1]

This sentence, subsequently to be much quoted, caught the attention of the new British ambassador in Moscow, Sir William Seeds, a shrewd and humorous Irishman, who had succeeded Lord Chilston, and he underlined it in a dispatch to the Foreign Office. 'Those innocents at home who believe that Soviet Russia is only awaiting an invitation to join the Western democracies,' the ambassador added, 'should be advised to ponder M. Stalin's advice to his party.'[2] In other words, the Soviet Union was not going to fight Britain's or France's battles, but would take whatever steps she considered necessary to protect herself in her own way. The message to Germany implicit in this statement was unmistakable. Stalin was ready to consider doing a deal with Hitler. Nor were the Germans slow in responding to the message.

An additional stimulus was provided later in the same month when Hitler's Panzer troops occupied most of what was left of Czechoslovakia after the Munich settlement of the previous autumn. (The remaining eastern district of Ruthenia was given to Hungary.) Hitler's Reich now bordered Poland's southern as well as her western frontier, while his divisions seemed poised to converge on Warsaw or at any rate the strip of Polish territory known as the 'Corridor' which linked Warsaw with the free port of Danzig and the Baltic and which divided East Prussia from the rest of Germany. Britain's Prime Minister, the Conservative Neville Chamberlain, who had personally negotiated the Munich settlement, reacted with a guarantee of Polish territorial integrity. The guarantee, which was to have fateful consequences for Britain, was a hastily improvised gesture in reply to a Parliamentary question at the end of March, suggesting that a German attack on Poland was imminent and inquiring what action the British Government would take in such an eventuality.[3]

No doubt the declaration of the guarantee was aimed at allaying public anxiety in Britain lest Poland should go the way of Czechoslovakia, but it was a purely ministerial decision apparently taken without consulting the General Staff and the Government's official military and civil advisers and without overmuch concern for how it could be implemented. Similar guarantees were forthcoming shortly afterwards in respect of Roumania and Greece, the latter following on Mussolini's seizure of Albania and the flight of 'the Comic-opera King [Zog] with his suitcases, his sisters, his parrots and his country's gold'.[4]

Realising that the guarantees to Poland and Roumania would be

3rd BELOR'N
(Vassilevsky)

Hamburg

Swinemünde

Waren

Stettin

TOWARDS
VICTORY

2nd BELOR'N
(Rokossovsky)

BRITISH
(Montgomery)

APRIL–MAY
1945

Kustrin

1st BELO-
RUSSIAN
(Zhukov)

BERLIN

Miles

0   50   100   150

Wittenberg

Frankfurt

Oder

TORGAU

Cottbus

JUNCTION
MADE BY
RUSSIANS
AND
AMERICANS
26th MAY

Leipzig

1st UKRAINE
(Konev)

N

Elbe

Breslau

Görlitz

Dresden

20th APRIL

Neisse

Karlsbad

PRAGUE

4th UKRAINE
(Yeremenko)

Nuremberg

C Z E C H O S L O V A K I A

Pilsen

20th APRIL

Regensburg

Danube

2nd UKRAINE
(Malinovsky)

AMERICANS

Passau

Krems

Munich

VIENNA

BUDAPEST

A U S T R I A

3rd UKRAINE
(Tolbukhin)

Klagenfurt

H U N G A R Y

ITALY

Danube

BRITISH
(Alexander)

JUGO-

20th APRIL

Trieste

SLAVIA

Last German
movements

practically ineffective unless underwritten by the Soviet Union, Britain made haste to open negotiations with Moscow in the hopes of securing an anti-Nazi alliance on the basis of offering joint resistance to any action which constituted a threat to the political independence of any European state. This suggestion was accepted on behalf of the Soviet Union by Litvinov, acting on Stalin's instructions, provided that both France and Poland joined in. France agreed to do so; but Poland refused, professing to believe that such an association as was envisaged with the Soviet Union would encourage or impel Hitler to attack her. There was also the question from Poland's point of view as to whether Soviet forces, if they once crossed the Polish border, even in Poland's defence, would ever leave the country, since it was thought they might well prefer to regain the considerable tracts of Polish territory which Russia had received from the three partitions of Poland in the eighteenth century.

The Russians now came up with a new and comprehensive scheme for a joint British–French–Soviet defence treaty under which the contracting parties would bind themselves to come to each other's help if attacked in Europe and also to undertake 'to render all manner of assistance, including that of a military nature, to eastern European states situated getween the Baltic and Black seas and bordering on the Soviet Union in case of aggression against these states'. The parties were also to discuss and settle 'within the shortest period of time' the extent and forms of military assistance to be given by each in fulfilment of these obligations. This proposal was to form the basis of the future negotiations and the Soviet Government held firm to it throughout. However, on the same day as it was put forward, the Soviet ambassador in Berlin, in the course of a routine visit to the German Foreign Ministry in the Wilhelmstrasse, acted on instructions from Moscow in stressing the desirability of a much closer Soviet–German understanding than had existed hitherto. The point was taken by Joachim von Ribbentrop, Hitler's arrogant Foreign Minister and former champagne salesman, who conveyed it to his master. Stalin did not have long to wait for the first fruits of the ambassador's overtures. Hitler suddenly stopped attacking the Russian Communist bugbear in his public speeches and instructed the German press to refrain from anti-Soviet propaganda in future.

Stalin now began to play his cards in the diplomatic game with consummate skill. To put it colloquially, until the deal with Hitler was in the bag – and the chances of getting it there were now looking increasingly hopeful – it would be necessary for Britain and France to be strung along in the parallel negotiations which were already under way as a hedging measure in case the projected deal with Hitler went off. It would also be necessary to have a new head of the Soviet Foreign Office, since the Nazis could hardly be expected to negotiate harmoniously with a Jew like Litvinov. Besides this Litvinov was so strongly identified in the public mind with the League of Nations and the policy of collective security that he was hardly the most suitable instrument to carry through such a novel departure in *Realpolitik*.

The morning newspapers on 4 May 1939 carried a brief announcement that Maxim Litvinov had been relieved of his duties as Commissar for Foreign Affairs 'at his own request' and that his office had been taken over by Vyacheslav Molotov 'in addition to his other duties'. The news came as a complete surprise to the Moscow diplomatic corps, since Litvinov had been prominently and intimately concerned with his country's foreign relations for more than twenty years and was greatly liked and respected, particularly by the statesmen and diplomats of the west. Litvinov had been present with the other members of the Government and Politburo at the May Day parade in Red Square and Stalin had been seen to nod affably to him. He had received Sir William Seeds in his office on the morning of 3 May, having explained that it would not be possible to see him in the afternoon, but he gave the British ambassador no inkling of his impending retirement. 'I assume that he saw M. Stalin in the afternoon,' wrote the ambassador afterwards, 'and that his resignation or, as it would seem more accurate to describe it, his dismissal, followed.'[5] The ambassador's assumption was correct. 'It's all over,' noted Litvinov the same evening. 'I have been sacked like a maid caught stealing...without so much as a day's notice...And what will the foreign diplomats say?'[6]

In fact Litvinov had suspected for the past two months what was in store for him. At the end of January he had been informed that in future all instructions to Merekalov, the Soviet ambassador in Berlin, and his assistant Astakhov, would be sent from Stalin's office. ('It would appear they have already decided to remove me.') He was not asked to report on any aspect of the international situation at the Party Congress, and instead the relevant reports were made by his principal assistants Potemkin, Dekanozov and Lozovsky. Next he was told that he would have to give up his country villa and move to another further from Moscow, 'an honourable banishment', he called it. Finally, when Voroshilov who had apparently been considered as his successor but had been turned down by Stalin, told him that the appointment of Molotov was possible Litvinov was astonished. ('It would be a catastrophe...He is completely lacking in suppleness, has little intelligence and is conceited.')

Litvinov's astonishment was to some extent shared by the British ambassador.

It does not seem to me possible that M. Molotov can adequately discharge both his manifold existing duties in the Government and party, as M. Stalin's right-hand man, and his new duties in the Commissariat for Foreign Affairs. He knows, or rather speaks, no foreign language, has, so far as I am aware, never been outside Russia, and has no practical experience in the conduct of foreign affairs or knowledge of the psychology of foreign countries. I fear, therefore, that access to him will be rare and that foreign representatives in Moscow will, in effect, be compelled to transact business to a large extent with M. Potemkin, who, as I reported...is clearly being maintained in his position as first assistant to the People's Commissar, but who is not of M. Litvinov's calibre.[7]

The ambassador had not as yet come to know the new commissar, nor was he aware of Molotov's immense capacity for sustained industry and application. Writing some years later with the advantage of hindsight, Sir Winston Churchill, who regarded Molotov as a man of outstanding ability and cold-blooded ruthlessness, remarked that he had never seen a human being who more perfectly represented the modern conception of a robot. 'And yet with all this there was an apparently reasonable and keenly-polished diplomatist...One delicate searching, awkward interview after another was conducted with perfect poise, impenetrable purpose, and bland, official correctitude. Never a chink was opened. Never a jar was made. His smile of Siberian winter, his carefully-measured and often wise words, his affable demeanour, combined to make him the perfect agent of Soviet policy in a deadly world.'[8]

Above all his lack of resilience and a sense of humour added to the difficulties of negotiating with Molotov. If a delicate point arose between Seeds and Litvinov, the ambassador could by an expressive cocking of his eye sometimes bring an answering grin to Litvinov's face and a common, if tacit, understanding. With Molotov none of this finessing was possible. 'One had to say exactly what one meant, neither more nor less, and to say it over and over again in the same words.' Later on, when Molotov went to Berlin for talks with Hitler, he stuck so stubbornly to his demands that the Fuehrer lost his temper and what was intended to be a simple exchange of views immediately developed into a sharp conflict. Dekanozov, one of the assistant foreign

The Politburo in 1929. *Left to right* Ordzhonikidze, Voroshilov, Kuibyshev, Stalin, Kalinin, Kaganovich, Kirov. Bust of Lenin in the background.

Top left The Soviet government building in the Kremlin where Lenin, Stalin and the other leading commissars had their offices.

Top right Stalin and his wife Nadezhda on holiday at Sochi in 1929.

Bottom left The Poteshny Palace in the Kremlin. Stalin lived here during World War II and previously with his second wife Nadezhda Alliluyeva.

Bottom right The last photograph taken of Nadezhda Alliluyeva as she was leaving the Industrial Academy in Moscow in 1932. 'Comrade, you shouldn't have done that!' she told the photographer.

Left The marble memorial in the Novodevichy cemetery in Moscow erected by Stalin on the grave of his second wife Nadezhda Alliluyeva who committed suicide in 1932. *From a photograph taken by the author.*

Right Rosa Kaganovich, whom Stalin is supposed to have married as his third wife.

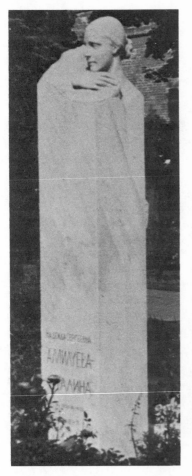

The Lubyanka prison in Moscow, headquarters
of the Soviet secret police. The building was
formerly an insurance company office.

)da   Yezhov   Beria

fs of the secret police
r Stalin. All three were
 Yagoda and Yezhov by
1, and Beria by Stalin's
:ssors.

Top left 'Death to the
Traitors!' Stalin signs a
death warrant.

Top right Cruising on the
Black Sea with his daughter
Svetlana and Kirov in 1934.

Bottom left Trade Union
House in Moscow. Scene of
the purge trials. *Radio Times
Hulton Picture Library*.

Bottom right With two women
admirers at a collective farm
in Tadjikstan, 1935.

Five Marshals of the Soviet Union.
Standing: Budenny, Blyukher.
Seated: Tukachevsky, Voroshilov, Yegorov.
Blyukher, Tukachevsky and Yegorov were shot
during the purge of the Red Army in 1937 and 1938.

Opposite top Stalin's meeting with Eden in Molotov's office, March 1935. Left to right: Eden, Stalin, Molotov, Maisky, Lord Chilston, Litvinov.

Left Molotov about to initial the German–Soviet pact in the Kremlin, 23 August 1939. Ribbentrop and Stalin look on jubilantly, attended by A. A. Shkvartsev, Soviet ambassador to Germany, with a portrait of Lenin in the background.

Stalin watches the initialling of the German–Soviet pact, with the German ambassador Count von der Schulenburg (right) and the German embassy economic counsellor Gustav Hilger.
Both photographs by courtesy of the Hoover Institution, Stanford University.

The official map accompanying the German–
Soviet Boundary and Friendship Treaty and
confirming the partition of Poland. It is signed
by Ribbentrop and Stalin, 28 September 1939.
'Is my signature clear enough for you?' Stalin asked
the Germans. He then autographed the map
again in smaller letters on the actual boundary.
Reproduced from the Political Treaties
file of the German Foreign Ministry (644/244451–56).

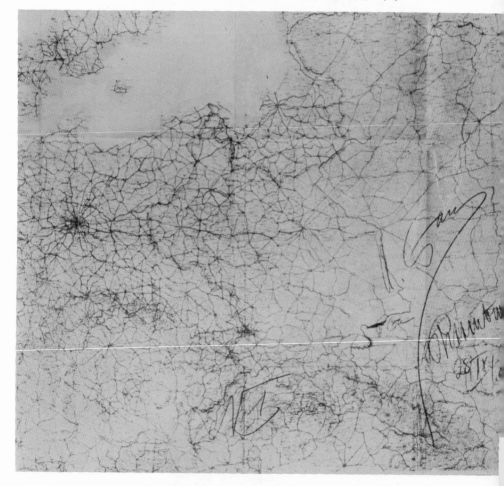

Left Stalin at the front near Moscow, 1941. A widely distributed propaganda picture.

Below The Supreme Commander with members of his civil and military staff. Left to right: Molotov, Voroshilov, Scherbakov, Stalin, Vassilevsky, Rokossovsky.

Chief of Staff Marshal Shaposhnikov gets his orders. An unusual picture taken in the Kremlin since Stalin rarely allowed himself to be photographed smoking a cigarette. In the public image he was a pipe smoker. *By courtesy of the Hoover Institution, Stanford University.*

Zhukov

Eremenko

Rokossovsky

Chuikov

Four of Stalin's Commanders in the 'Great Patriotic War'.

Stalin at Yalta. With
Churchill and his interpreter
Major Birse (top), Roosevelt
(middle), and Molotov,
Vyshinsky, Gromyko
(lower). *US Army photographs.*

Potsdam.
Top The conference
room in the
Cecilienhof.
Lower Leahy, Bevin,
Byrnes, Molotov
(standing). Attlee,
Truman, Stalin
(sitting). *US Army
photographs.*

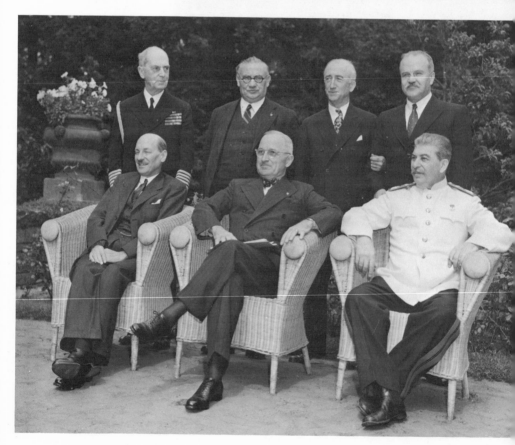

Below Stalin lying in state in Trade Union House. Left to right: Khrushchev, Beria, Malenkov, Bulganin, Voroshilov, Kaganovich.
Left The new grave beside the Kremlin wall. *United Press International.*

The forged Eremin letter
dated 12 July 1913 (*top right*),
with a genuine autograph
signature (*below*) and a
genuine letter of the same
date showing the differences
in style of printed heading
and numbering. *Photographs
by courtesy of* Life *magazine
and the Hoover Institution,
Stanford University.*

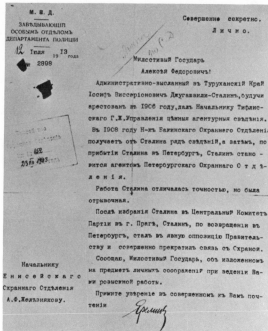

commissars who was present, expressed surprise in relating this incident to Stalin that so 'brainy' a man as Molotov could make such a grave mistake. Stalin pursed his lips and remarked, 'Of course, Molotov is a man with brains, but his brains are stupid!' This struck Litvinov, when he heard it, as 'an excellent definition'.[9]

The absence of anything approaching a sense of humour in Molotov's make-up was illustrated by another incident, which occurred some years previously when Yagoda was head of the NKVD. Someone wrote on the wall of a house in Kitai-Gorod, the old trading quarter of Moscow near the Red Square, the following words: 'Comrade Molotov spent three days in this house in 1912 on his way to the capital. Anyone committing a nuisance here will be prosecuted. By order, Yagoda.' Litvinov was mildly amused when he heard about it, but Molotov reacted very differently. He angrily demanded that Yagoda should find the culprit, 'on your personal responsibility', as he put it. In the result a hundred people were arrested on suspicion of being responsible for the offensive inscription.[10]

The fact that Litvinov was seen at the theatre shortly after his departure from the Foreign Affairs Commissariat prompted the British ambassador to speculate upon his prospects and those of his English born wife of being left in peace. 'Past precedents in the case of Soviet officials who have at their own request asked to be relieved of their duties,' wrote Seeds, 'do not bode happily for M. Litvinov, who must be the repository of many unwelcome and awkward secrets and who, I imagine, has not many friends in high places to speak well for him.' Fortunately for him, Litvinov still enjoyed a measure of Stalin's goodwill, and to this he was to owe not only his survival when so many of his official subordinates had been shot, but also a later modest comeback to the diplomatic scene. 'Whatever may happen, Papasha,' Stalin once told him, 'I shall not let you down.' With Litvinov he kept his word.[11]

2

Contrary to the view expressed by Sir William Seeds on Molotov's appointment, the new Foreign Affairs Commissar personally conducted all the interviews with the British and French ambassadors. Potemkin was also present but only in the role of interpreter. The Anglo-French side was reinforced in the middle of June by the arrival of William Strang from London. Strang had previously served in the embassy as counsellor and was familiar with the Moscow scene, having accompanied Eden to the Kremlin on the occasion of his meeting with Stalin in 1935. He was a career diplomat and by now had reached the position of Assistant Under-Secretary of State at the Foreign Office. Chamberlain, the British Prime Minister, was criticised, by Churchill among others, for not sending someone of ministerial standing to take charge of such a momentous mission instead of 'so subordinate a figure' as Strang which 'gave actual offence'. No doubt Molotov would have preferred a senior minister or ex-minister and Chamberlain should have sent one – Molotov admitted as much to the Germans afterwards – but Strang was certainly not *persona non grata* in Moscow and he got on with Molotov as well as any westerner could be expected to in the circumstances, in spite of finding it so difficult to get to grips with him. ('He seems to be bored with detailed discussion.') As a matter of fact, Eden had suggested himself for the mission, but Chamberlain, who had not forgiven him for resigning as Foreign Secretary as a protest against the Prime Minister's appeasement policy, turned down the suggestion. This was a pity, since Eden would have been an excellent choice and might conceivably have saved the situation for the British and French, since it was not until July that Hitler finally made up his mind to invade Poland.[12]

The truth was that the British Prime Minister had always been suspicious of Soviet Russia and he made no attempt to conceal his feelings. In June 1938, after Chamberlain had been in office for a little over a year and Eden had resigned, Stalin told Joseph Davies, the United States ambassador in Moscow, that 'the reactionary elements in England, represented by the Chamberlain government, were determined upon a policy of making Germany strong, and thus place France in a position of continually increasing dependence upon England; also with the purpose of ultimately making Germany strong as against Russia'. He added that in his opinion 'Chamberlain did not represent the English people and that he would probably fail because the Fascist dictators would drive too hard a bargain'.[13] It was scarcely surprising that Chamberlain should have loathed the idea of negotiating with the Russians and that, when the idea of a four-power anti-Nazi alliance was broached in March, he should have written in a private letter:

I must confess to the most profound distrust of Russia. I have no belief whatever in her ability to maintain an effective offensive, even if she wanted to. And I distrust her motives, which seem to me to have little connection with our ideas of liberty, and to be concerned only with getting everyone else by the ears. Moreover, she is both hated and suspected by many of the smaller states, notably by Poland, Roumania and Finland.[14]

386

The British reply to the Soviet scheme of a three-power treaty of mutual assistance, after Poland had refused to join in the original scheme, was not delivered until 9 May, by which date Litvinov had been replaced by Molotov. It was to the effect, acquiesced in with some reluctance by the French, that the time was not ripe for such a comprehensive scheme as the Soviet Union had proposed. In its place, the Russians were asked to undertake that, 'in the event of Great Britain and France being involved in hostilities in fulfilment of their new obligations towards certain Eastern European countries, the assistance of the Soviet Union would be immediately available, if desired, and would be afforded in such a manner and on such terms as might be agreed'. This was wholly unsatisfactory to Molotov who regarded this latest Anglo-French proposal as 'derisory', since it did not provide for assistance to the Soviet Union in the event of a direct attack upon her, thus lacking reciprocity, nor did it provide any protection to the Baltic states against aggression ultimately aimed at the Soviet Union. The only realistic basis for a resistance front against further aggression in Europe, said Molotov, must be a three-power mutual assistance treaty on the lines he had already put forward.[15]

Churchill, who was not in the Chamberlain government, took the view that 'Britain and France should have accepted the Russian offer, proclaimed the Triple Alliance, and left the method by which it could be made effective in case of war to be adjusted between Allies engaged against a common foe'. As things were, the Soviet attitude at the time was to be expressed by Stalin to Churchill when they met face to face in Moscow for the first time three years later. 'We formed the impression that the British and French Governments were not resolved to go to war if Poland were attacked, but that they hoped the diplomatic line-up of Britain, France and Russia would deter Hitler. We were sure it would not.'[16] In other words, Stalin felt that when it came to the crunch Britain and France would abandon Poland just as they had abandoned Czechoslovakia. Then Germany and Russia would directly confront each other.

The conversations continued during the warm Moscow days of June and July. 'On the whole the negotiations have been a humiliating experience,' wrote Strang on 20 July. 'Time after time we have taken up a position and a week later we have abandoned it; and we have had the feeling that Molotov was convinced from the beginning that we should be forced to abandon it.' All the details had to be referred to Stalin, just as were those of the parleys which had already begun between the Russians and the Germans; indeed Molotov and Mikoyan admitted as much to the Germans when they told them that the ultimate decisions were Stalin's. That Stalin must have known almost immediately of what transpired at each interview with Molotov may be gathered from Strang's recollection of the physical conditions in which the talks were conducted. Molotov sat at his desk which rested on a dais, while the others sat below him in a semicircle, nursing their papers on their knees and making their notes as best they could. There was always a door open, as if someone was listening outside, which disturbed Seeds and Strang – not altogether surprisingly since Stalin's Kremlin office was next door to Molotov's. Neither Molotov nor Potemkin took any record of the proceedings, but Molotov would fiddle from time to time with a switch under the desk-top at his left hand, which Strang assumed, no doubt correctly, was for the purpose of recording those parts of the talks which Molotov considered that his master would wish to have played over to him afterwards.[17]

It was not until the end of July that the two ambassadors were in a position to inform Molotov that their respective governments agreed to the immediate opening of military conversations in Moscow. There was a further delay in the dispatch of the joint Anglo-French mission, which travelled by slow boat instead of by air, eventually reaching Moscow on 10 August. Talks began two days later after a friendly welcome from Voroshilov; but the atmosphere quickly changed on 14 August when Voroshilov was instructed to press the issue of the right of Russian troops to a passage through certain areas of Poland. This produced deadlock, since the movement of Russian troops through any part of Polish territory was one which the Polish Government refused point blank to countenance. 'We have no military agreement with the USSR,' said Poland's Foreign Minister Colonel Beck. 'We do not wish to have one.'[18]

Meanwhile Stalin, who remained in the neighbourhood of Moscow throughout the summer, continued to keep his options open. ('I don't plan to come south this year,' he wrote to his daughter Svetlana on 8 August. 'I'm busy. I can't get away.') Much as he preferred doing a deal with Hitler, he was still prepared to reach an accommodation with the British and French on his own terms if these had been accepted by all concerned before the middle of August. Indeed, as late as 4 August, Count Von der Schulenburg, the able German ambassador in Moscow, reported to his government that, while it was evident that there was a desire on Molotov's part for the improvement of Soviet–German relations, 'the old mistrust of Germany' persisted.

My overall impression is that the Soviet Government is at present determined to sign with England and France if they fulfil all Soviet wishes. Negotiations, to be sure, might still last a long time, especially since the mistrust of England is also great...It will take a considerable effort on our part to cause the Soviet Government to swing about.[19]

At this critical period, President Roosevelt sent Stalin a personal message through Constantin Oumansky, the Soviet ambassador in Washington, as the latter was about to return to Moscow on leave. 'Tell Stalin,' said the American President, 'that if his government joins up with Hitler, it is as certain as that the night follows the day that as soon as Hitler has conquered France, he will turn on Russia, and it will be the Soviet's turn next.' Roosevelt gave a similar message to Joseph Davies, then ambassador in Brussels, and begged him to get it to Stalin and Molotov if he could.[20]

It is not known whether Stalin ever received these messages. If he did so, he lost little time in making up his mind to disregard them.

Having completed his preparations, Hitler could not delay his armed attack on Poland much longer. It was now a matter of paramount urgency for him to reach an understanding with Stalin if he was to be able to launch his planned *blitzkrieg* at the same time and avoid the risk of suddenly being involved in a war with Russia in addition to the western Allies, as Imperial Germany had been in 1914. On 14 August Ribbentrop, after talking to Hitler, telegraphed Schulenburg, instructing him to seek an immediate interview with Molotov with the object of securing a 'speedy clarification of German–Russian relations', for which purpose Ribbentrop stated that he would be 'prepared to make a short visit to Moscow in order, in the name of the Fuehrer, to set forth the Fuehrer's views to M. Stalin'. In Ribbentrop's view, which was Hitler's, 'only through such a direct discussion can a change be brought about, and it should not be impossible thereby to lay the foundations for a final settlement of German–Russian relations'.[21]

Molotov received Schulenburg next day and warmly welcomed the prospect of improved relations. This was the first time that the idea of a non-aggression pact between the two countries was discussed on a high level. On the question of Ribbentrop's proposed visit, however, Molotov stressed that it needed adequate preparation. He repeated this at their next meeting on the evening of the 17th when pressed by Schulenburg to expedite the visit. Stalin was following the conversations with great interest, Schulenburg reported to Berlin on 18 August, he was informed of all the details, and he was in complete agreement with Molotov. Schulenburg and Molotov met for the third time in four days at two o'clock in the afternoon of the 19th, and Schulenburg stressed the urgency of Ribbentrop's visit only to be stalled by Molotov once more.

This last meeting ended at about three o'clock, after which Schulenburg went back to his embassy. Half an hour later an urgent message arrived from Molotov asking the ambassador to call upon him again at the Kremlin at 4.30 p.m. When Schulenburg presented himself for the second time that day in Molotov's room, the Foreign Affairs Commissar told him that he had 'reported to the Soviet Government' and had been instructed to hand him the draft of a non-aggression pact. A trade agreement between the two countries was due to be signed the following day, and Schulenburg was told that Ribbentrop's visit would be agreeable a week later, that is on the 26th or 27th. 'Molotov did not give reasons for his sudden change of mind,' the ambassador reported to Berlin the same evening. 'I assume that Stalin intervened.' The assumption was correct. In fact Stalin had arrived earlier in the day from Kuntsevo in response to Molotov's entreaty on the telephone that a full meeting of the Politburo was imperative to consider the German request.[22]

Hitler now had no time to lose since war with Poland was imminent. He immediately addressed a long-winded and slightly hysterical telegram to Stalin through the German embassy asking him to receive 'my Foreign Minister' on 22 August, or at the latest the 23rd, in order 'to clarify the questions connected with' the draft of the non-aggression pact which 'I accept'. Schulenburg was instructed to hand Molotov the text of the telegram in writing, 'on a sheet of paper without letterhead'. This was done, together with a Russian translation, at 3 p.m. on the 21st. Two hours later, Molotov gave Schulenburg Stalin's reply, which the ambassador immediately transmitted to Berlin with the comment that it was 'couched in very conciliatory form', although it was in fact so cool and detached as to be almost impersonal.

21 August 1939

To the Chancellor of the German Reich, Herr A. Hitler.

I thank you for your letter. I hope that the German–Soviet non-aggression pact will bring about a decided turn for the better in the political relations between our countries.

The peoples of our countries need peaceful relations with each other. The assent of the German Government to the conclusion of a non-aggression pact provides the foundation for eliminating the political tension and the establishment of peace and collaboration between our countries.

The Soviet Government have instructed me to inform you that they agree to Herr von Ribbentrop's arriving in Moscow on 23 August.

J. STALIN[23]

The news published in the form of a brief press communiqué next day that a visit from Ribbentrop was 'imminent' for the purpose of negotiating the conclusion of a non-aggression pact dumbfounded the Moscow diplomatic corps not to mention the members of the Anglo-French military mission. 'We had indeed of late rather been working only with the hope that conversations could be carried on for a period long enough to tide over a critical period in European history,' noted the British ambassador. 'We were, in short, prepared for an eventual decision of Soviet neutrality; but I must frankly confess that I did not contemplate that the Soviet Government, having reached the stage of military conversations which contemplated an attack by Soviet troops on Germany through Poland and Roumania, could have the duplicity to reach out the hand of friendship to the prime mover in the anti-Comintern and, what might be called, aggression front.'[24]

Writing when he heard the news at his final place of exile in a suburb of Mexico City, Leon Trotsky put the matter more bluntly:

> Stalin's union with Hitler satisfied his sense of revenge. Above all, he wanted to insult the governments of England and France, to avenge the insults to which the Kremlin had been subjected before Chamberlain gave up courting Hitler. He took personal delight in negotiating secretly with the Nazis while appearing to negotiate openly with the friendly missions of England and France, in deceiving London and Paris, in springing his pact with Hitler as a sudden surprise.[25]

This passage had been jotted down with other notes by Trotsky for use in the biography of Stalin on which he had been working for some time and which he had brought down to the period of Lenin's death. Trotsky did not live to finish his book. Not long afterwards one of Stalin's secret agents penetrated his closely guarded home under false pretences and killed him as he sat at his desk by smashing his skull with an ice-pick. Trotsky's blood spattered the pages of his manuscript.

The last words shaped by his pen were to prove singularly prophetic. 'A historical explanation is not a justification,' he had written. 'Nero, too, was a product of his epoch. Yet after he perished his statues were smashed and his name was scraped off everything. The vengeance of history is more terrible than the vengeance of the most powerful General Secretary. I venture to think that this is consoling.'[26]

3

About midday on 23 August 1939, Hitler's personal Condor plane, the *Grenzmark*, which the Fuehrer had put at the disposal of Ribbentrop and his senior advisers, touched down at the historic Khodynka Field, an area on the north-western outskirts of Moscow which had some-what grim associations.* The plane had left very early in the morning from Koenigsberg in East Prussia, where the Reich Foreign Minister had broken his journey overnight from Berlin, since German time was two hours ahead of the clocks in Moscow. A second aircraft, a Junkers 52, with the rest of the Minister's retinue numbering thirty in all, had already arrived – 'quite a swig from the bottle', as Schulenburg de-scribed the party. It was the first time that Nazi swastika flags were seen fluttering side by side in the wind with the Soviet red.

After being welcomed by Potemkin, whom Molotov had sent to the airport to represent him, and briefly inspecting a guard of honour from the Soviet Air Force, Ribbentrop drove with Schulenburg to the old Austrian Embassy building at No. 13 Sadovaya Kudrinskaya, a few doors from the house where Chekhov had lived. The former embassy had been taken over by the Nazis after the *Anschluss* to become an official German guest house. It now served as the Moscow head-quarters of Ribbentrop and his large staff. During lunch there was a discussion about the terms of the proposed non-aggression pact in the context of an alternative draft which had been made during the flight from Koenigsberg by Friedrich Gaus, the Director of the Legal Department in the German Foreign Ministry. At the same time Ribbentrop learned from the ambassador that they were expected in the Kremlin at 3.30 p.m.[27]

Escorted by a Russian colonel, apparently Nikolai Vlasik, a brutal character who had succeeded the disreputable Pauker after the latter's 'liquidation' as head of Stalin's personal bodyguard, they drove to the Kremlin in advance of the appointed time in order to give Ribbentrop a chance of seeing a little of the capital since it was his first visit to the

---

* In 1896, the Khodynka, which was also used as a camp for the Moscow military garrison and was intersected by a number of trenches and ditches, was the scene of a terrible tragedy when a huge crowd assembled for the traditional distribution of gifts following Tsar Nicholas II's coronation. Panic ensued and about 1,400 people died as a result of being trampled underfoot, falling into the trenches and being suffocated. The Khodynka contained another mass grave where Zinoviev, Kamenev, Bukharin and other victims of the Great Purge who were executed in Moscow are believed to be buried.

Soviet Union. Eventually they arrived at the entrance to the Narkomindel where they were greeted by Poskrebyshev, also in colonel's uniform, and immediately conducted to the Prime Minister's office on the first floor. When they found Stalin and Molotov waiting for them there, Count Schulenburg could not stifle a cry of surprise, since he had been in Moscow for years and had never yet spoken to Stalin. The only others present at the ensuing discussion were Gustav Hilger, the economic counsellor at the German embassy, who interpreted for Ribbentrop, and a fair haired young Russian named Vladimir Pavlov, who did the same for Stalin and Molotov and who seemed to Ribbentrop 'to enjoy Stalin's special trust'.

After a preliminary exchange of courtesies, Ribbentrop, speaking with full authority, began by expressing the desire to see German–Soviet relations based on a new footing and to achieve an all-round settlement, 'valid for the longest possible time'. He referred to Stalin's speech at the Eighteenth Party Congress, 'into which we had read similar ideas'. He went on to say that he had not come to Moscow, 'as the British and French delegates had come in their time, to ask the Soviet Union for armed assistance in case a war should be forced upon the German Government by England'. The German Government was not in need of assistance for this contingency, but would in this event have sufficient military strength to take up the struggle alone against Poland and the western foes and to carry it to a victorious conclusion.

Stalin then asked Molotov whether he wished to reply first. 'No, Joseph Vissarionovich,' said Molotov. 'I'm sure you'll do a better job than I.'

'Germany is taking up a proud attitude by rejecting at the outset any armed assistance from the Soviets,' Stalin began. 'The Soviet Union, however, is interested in having a strong Germany as a neighbour, and in the case of an armed showdown between Germany and the western democracies the interests of the Soviet Union and of Germany would certainly run parallel to each other. The Soviet Union would never stand for Germany getting into a difficult position.'[28]

Stalin went on to observe that, although they had 'poured buckets of filth' over each other for years, there was no reason why they should not make up their quarrel. He also admitted that when he had made his speech in March he had indeed 'intended to convey the desire to come to an understanding with Germany'. They then got down to what was to form the secret part of the non-aggression pact, namely the delimitation of the two countries' respective 'spheres of interest'. On the Russian side, it was agreed that these should include Finland and two

393

of the Baltic states, Estonia and Latvia, together with Bessarabia which at that time formed a province of Roumania. Ribbentrop then brought up the question of Poland. The Poles, he said, were becoming more and more aggressive, and if they were allowed to break out it would be a good thing for an agreed line to be drawn which would exclude any German and Russian interests coming into conflict with each other. For this purpose the line of the rivers Narew, Vistula and San was agreed between them. However, when Stalin specifically claimed the Latvian ports of Libau (Liepaja) and Windau (Ventspils) for the Russian sphere, Ribbentrop replied that, although he had full powers to conclude an agreement, he felt that he should refer this matter to Hitler for his prior approval. To enable Ribbentrop to do this it was agreed that they should break off the discussion, which had already lasted for three hours, and resume at 10 p.m.

On his return to the former Austrian embassy, Ribbentrop put a call through to Berlin with a request to relay the message to Hitler who was at the Berghof, his Bavarian mountain retreat above Berchtesgaden. When the Fuehrer was told about Stalin's wishes over the two Baltic ports, he sent for an atlas and after looking at a map of Latvia answered 'Yes, certainly.' Indeed, Hitler was so pleased with the way things were going in the Kremlin – 'proceeding in a direction favourable to us' Ribbentrop had told him – he would have been just as accommodating had Stalin asked for the moon. Apparently Hitler also informed his Foreign Minister that he had received the British ambassador to Germany earlier in the day and that the ambassador had given him a personal letter from Mr Chamberlain on the subject of Britain's guarantee to Poland.

While these exchanges were taking place, Molotov received the British ambassador to the Soviet Union in what proved to be a stormy interview. Sir William Seeds bluntly accused the Soviet Prime Minister to his face of 'an act of bad faith', a charge which, as Seeds remarked at the time, an accuser cannot usually make and survive. 'That the accusation had to be made through a subservient and very frightened M. Potemkin as interpreter and witness,' the ambassador went on to note with some satisfaction, 'was particularly galling to the recipient, who savagely asked whether those words figured textually in my instructions.' (They did.) Molotov retorted by accusing the British and French of a lack of sincerity. The height of their insincerity had been reached, he said, when the joint military mission arrived in Moscow 'empty-handed and quite unprepared to deal with the fundamental points on which the whole question of reciprocal assistance depended', namely the passage of Soviet troops through Polish and Roumanian territory. Finally the Soviet Government had made up their mind that they were being 'played with' and had 'accepted the proposal made to them by the German Government'.[29]

Later the same night, and in the same room, the draft Nazi–Soviet non-aggression pact was initialled and signed by Molotov and Ribbentrop together with the secret supplementary protocol defining the parties' respective spheres of influence. The actual treaty was signed well after midnight, although it was dated 23 August. It was expressly designed to last for ten years with an option for a further five. But it went beyond the usual treaty of this kind in that it contained an article to the effect that should either of the contracting parties 'become the object of belligerent action by a third Power', the other party should 'in no manner lend its support to this third Power'. In other words, Stalin bound himself to withhold help from any country that was attacked by Germany. In the secret protocol, Finland, Estonia and Latvia were designated wholly Russian spheres of influence with Lithuania falling to Germany, while Poland was roughly divided between them. In south-eastern Europe the Soviet side emphasised 'its interest in Bessarabia', the German side declaring 'complete political disinterestedness in these territories'.

For sheer political cynicism this agreement would be difficult to beat. In affixing their signatures to it, both sides were aware that it sealed the fate of Poland, since the secret protocol expressly contemplated 'a territorial and political transformation of the territories belonging to the Polish State'.[30] In addition to Stalin, the signing was witnessed on the Soviet side by General Boris Shaposhnikov, the Chief of the General Staff, Alexander Shvartsev, the ambassador in Berlin and Vladimir Pavlov, who, besides acting as official interpreter, was head of the German section of Molotov's commissariat. The Germans were represented by Schulenburg and Hilger.

The signing ceremony was preceded by supper, also served in Molotov's office, at which speeches were made and many toasts proposed and drunk. 'I know how much the German nation loves its Fuehrer,' said Stalin, rising with uplifted glass. 'I should therefore like to drink his health.' Molotov thereupon drank the healths of Ribbentrop and Schulenburg, after which he raised his glass again, this time to Stalin, remarking as he did so that it was Stalin through his speech at the Party Congress in March, 'which had been well understood in Germany', who had 'introduced the reversal in political relations'. Throughout the meal Stalin and Molotov repeatedly drank to the non-aggression pact, to the new era of German–Russian relations, and 'to the honour of the German nation which has given the world illustrious scientists and brilliant writers and musicians', while for his part Ribbentrop with corresponding frequency toasted Stalin, the Soviet Government and 'the favourable development of relations between Germany and the Soviet Union'. So much vodka and champagne were consumed that it was surprising that anyone could stand up when the necessary documents in their final form were produced for Molotov and Ribbentrop to sign.

As befitted recent enemies who had suddenly and unexpectedly become reconciled in a common cause, the principals and their assistants were wary of each other; but the atmosphere warmed as the night went on. Stalin certainly showed himself the more astute politician and he gave nothing away. Fortunately a record of the talk was made at the time for the German side by Gaus, the German Foreign Minister's principal lawyer, and it subsequently came to light with other captured documents in World War II when it was put in evidence at the war crimes trials in Nuremberg. The fact that it passed without contradiction by the Russians at the time may be taken as pointing to its substantial accuracy.[31]

The conversation ranged over a wide geopolitical field. Speaking of Japan, who had been giving the Soviets some trouble on the Manchurian border, Ribbentrop patronisingly undertook to use his good offices 'to contribute to an adjustment of the differences between the Soviet Union and Japan'. That was, of course, if Stalin desired it. 'There are limits to our patience with regard to Japanese provocations,' replied Stalin. 'If Japan wants war she can have it. We are not afraid of it and are prepared for it. If Japan wants peace – so much the better!' He added that, while he considered the assistance of Germany in bringing about an improvement in Soviet-Japanese relations as 'useful', he did not want the Japanese to get the impression that 'the initiative in this direction had been taken by the Soviet Union'.

Undeterred by this slight rebuff, Ribbentrop went on to talk about Italy. Stalin asked him whether he did not think Italy had aspirations beyond the annexation of Albania, a small, mountainous, thinly populated country of no particular value to Italy – perhaps for Greek territory? 'Albania is important to Italy for strategic reasons,' said Ribbentrop. Moreover, Mussolini was 'a strong man who could not be intimidated'. This he had demonstrated in the Abyssinian conflict, in which 'Italy had attained her aims by her own strength against a hostile coalition'.

'Come, come!' said Stalin with apparent incredulity. 'I thought the Ethiopians were only armed with spears and clubs, and that Hoare and

Laval were trying to calm down Mussolini rather than intimidate him.'*

Ribbentrop contented himself with remarking that Mussolini 'warmly welcomed the restoration of friendly relations between Germany and the Soviet Union' and had 'expressed himself as very gratified with the conclusion of the Non-Aggression Pact'.

They were nearer common ground on the subjects of Turkey and England. In this connection Ribbentrop mentioned that England had spent £5 millions in Turkey 'in order to encourage propaganda against Germany'. On the contrary, said Stalin; according to his information, the British had spent considerably more than this sum in 'buying Turkish politicians'. Supported by Molotov, Stalin went on to 'comment adversely' on the British Military Mission, which, he said, 'had never told the Soviet Government what it really wanted'.

'England has always been trying and is still trying to disrupt the development of good relations between Germany and the Soviet Union,' Ribbentrop declared at this point. 'England is weak and wants to let others fight for her presumptuous claim to world domination.'

'I agree,' Stalin rejoined with apparent eagerness. 'The English army is weak. Nor is the British navy as important as it once was. England's air arm is being increased, to be sure, but there is a shortage of pilots. If England dominates the world in spite of this, that is due to the stupidity of the other countries who always let themselves be bluffed. It is ridiculous, for example, that a few hundred Englishmen should dominate India.'

Ribbentrop agreed with this assessment. He then imparted a piece of information to Stalin which he stressed was confidential. It was to the effect that England had 'recently put out a new feeler' to Germany, in which the situation was compared with that which had existed in 1914. It was 'a typically English, stupid manoeuvre', said Ribbentrop. He added that he had 'proposed to the Fuehrer to inform the British that every hostile British act, in case of a German–Polish conflict, would be answered by a bombing attack on London'.

At this Stalin remarked that the 'feeler' was evidently Chamberlain's latest letter to Hitler which had been written from Downing Street on 22 August and which he understood had been handed personally to Hitler at Berchtesgaden by the British ambassador Sir Nevile Henderson in the early afternoon of the 23rd, that is only a few hours before Ribbentrop's arrival at the Kremlin. The text of this document was not

* The premature disclosure of the Hoare–Laval plan to partition Abyssinia between Mussolini and Haile Selassie in December 1935, caused Sir Samuel Hoare's resignation as British Foreign Secretary. He was succeeded by Eden.

published at the time – indeed it was only to emerge at the Nuremberg trials seven years later. Stalin's foreknowledge of it, which no doubt came as a considerable surprise to Ribbentrop, was probably derived from an intercepted telegram or telephone message from Berlin.*

Having thus shown that he was equally in command of the situation, Stalin stated it as his opinion that 'England, despite her weakness, would wage war craftily and stubbornly'. He went on to say by way of contrast that France in his view had an army worthy of consideration. From this Ribbentrop dissented, observing that Germany was twice as strong as France with an annual intake of 300,000 recruits as against France's 150,000. Also the Siegfried Line was twice as strong as the Maginot Line. 'If France attempts to wage war with Germany,' he declared confidently, 'she will certainly be beaten.'

Another topic of discussion was the Anti-Comintern Pact, which had been negotiated between Germany and Japan in November 1936, allegedly for the exchange of information about the activities of the Communist International (which was run from Moscow) and concerting measures against it. Mussolini did not adhere to the pact, which was never taken very seriously in the west and indeed was a target for the wits, who pointed out that the Germans, who had always disliked the Japanese as yellow people, were now ready to dub them 'honorary Aryans'. Remembering that at the time of its negotiation the pact had been denounced in the Soviet press as a smokescreen for a secret military alliance directed against Russia, Ribbentrop now asserted that this was not so and that it was basically aimed at the western democracies. At this point Stalin intervened to say that it had in fact 'mainly frightened the City of London and the English shopkeepers'.

Again Ribbentrop agreed, adding in lighter vein that Stalin was 'surely less frightened' by the pact than the representatives of English society he had mentioned. What the German people thought about it,

* 'Apparently the announcement of a German–Soviet Agreement is taken in some quarters in Berlin to indicate that intervention by Great Britain on behalf of Poland is no longer a contingency that need be reckoned with,' Chamberlain had written. 'No greater mistake could be made. Whatever may prove to be the nature of the German–Soviet Agreement, it cannot alter Great Britain's obligation to Poland, which His Majesty's Government have stated in public repeatedly and plainly.

'It is alleged that if His Majesty's Government had made their position more clear in 1914, the great catastrophe would have been avoided. Whether or no there is any force in that allegation, His Majesty's Government are resolved that on this occasion there shall be no such tragic misunderstanding.' E. L. Woodward and Rohan Butler (eds.). *Documents on British Foreign Policy 1919–1939*, Third Series, Vol. VII (1954), pp. 170–177.

he went on, was evident from a joke which had originated with the Berliners, 'well known for their wit and humour', and which had been going the rounds for several months, namely, 'Stalin will yet join the Anti-Comintern Pact himself'.

'When the bankers of the City of London join the British Communist Party,' Stalin quipped back, 'I will willingly subscribe to the Anti-Comintern Pact – but not before.'[32]

On a more serious note, Stalin said he believed the Germans wanted peace and therefore welcomed friendly relations between the Reich and the Soviet Union. Quite so, Ribbentrop interrupted; but, on the other hand, he continued, indignation against Poland was so great that every single German man was ready to fight. 'The German people will no longer put up with Polish provocation.'

Gustav Hilger, who was present throughout the discussion, afterwards recorded his recollections of Stalin's table talk.

Stalin did not seek to hide his dislike and distrust of England. In his eyes Britain was past her prime and had lost her ability to make great political discussions. However, he spoke with unconcealed respect of the United States and particularly her economic achievements.

Stalin was quite frank in his view of Japan as a dangerous adversary. He boasted of the lesson which Soviet troops had dealt the Japanese during a border incident and mentioned with almost sadistic glee that twenty thousand Japanese had been killed on that occasion. 'That is the only language these Asiatics understand,' he said. 'After all, I am an Asiatic too, so I ought to know.'[33]

Towards the end of the meal, Ribbentrop asked Stalin whether he would allow Hitler's female photographer, who had accompanied the mission and was waiting outside, to take a few pictures. Stalin agreed, probably the first time, noted Ribbentrop, that he had granted such a request to a foreigner in the Kremlin. However, when they were all being taken with glasses in their hands still drinking, Stalin waved the photographer away, as if to say that this was not the kind of publicity he wanted. At Ribbentrop's request the photographer thereupon removed the film from her camera and presented it to Stalin. With a gallant gesture Stalin then returned the spool with the remark that he trusted that the photographs would not be published.*

'The Soviet Government take the new pact very seriously,' Stalin

* Some of them appear for the first time in this book.

told Ribbentrop as they parted in the early hours of the morning. 'I can guarantee on my word of honour that the Soviet Union will not betray its partner.'

'How does our pact square with the Franco-Soviet treaty of 1936?' asked Hitler's Foreign Minister.

Stalin's reply was brief and characteristic. 'Russian interests come before everything.'

4

Ribbentrop and his thirty aides took off from the Khodynka airport on the morning of 24 August, well satisfied with the previous night's business in the Kremlin. The intention was to fly direct to Berchtesgaden to report to Hitler there, but during the flight a message was received over the radio that Hitler had left for Berlin and this caused the *Grenzmark* abruptly to change course and make for Tempelhof. Not wishing to overfly Poland 'for reasons of safety', they had to make a wide detour over the Baltic and did not reach Berlin until late in the afternoon. Consequently Ribbentrop did not see Hitler until the following morning. According to his own account which he wrote at Nuremberg during his trial for war crimes, he 'thought of proposing to him a European conference for the settlement of the Polish question'.[34] If such an idea entered Ribbentrop's head, it was wishful thinking after the event. Hitler had already ordered general mobilisation of the German armed forces. Although the military preparations were temporarily halted later the same day when Ribbentrop told the Fuehrer that the British had now formally ratified their agreement with Poland, the die had already been cast for war. The object of the postponement was simply to give the British a chance to escape from their guarantee to the Poles. Less than a week later, following a steadily increasing series of frontier 'incidents', German troops crossed the Polish border. Three days after that France and Britain declared war on Germany and the second world conflict within a quarter of a century had begun.

During these early September days, while Hitler's Panzer units were pressing rapidly towards Warsaw and the *Luftwaffe* was laying waste the towns and villages of western Poland, Stalin made the same miscalculation as the western Allies. The strength of the Polish army to resist the invader was considerably overestimated by both, while the rate at which the *Wehrmacht's* campaign against the Poles proceeded was correspondingly underestimated. The British War Cabinet and Chiefs of Staff, for example, thought the Poles could hold out for three to four months.

On 8 September the Germans entered Warsaw and Molotov telegraphed his congratulations to Ribbentrop. At the same time the Soviet Premier told Count Schulenburg that the Soviet Government was 'taken completely by surprise by the unexpectedly rapid German military successes'. Although some three million Soviet troops had been mobilised, preparations on the Soviet side to fulfil their obligations under the pact were far from ready and would not, he thought, be completely possible for two to three weeks. There was also difficulty on the political side. Obviously the provisions of the secret protocol could not be disclosed to the world. Consequently after talking over the matter with Stalin, Molotov informed the German ambassador that the pretext for the Soviet occupation of its agreed sphere of influence would be to come to the aid of the Ukrainians and Byelorussians 'threatened' by the German advance. This hypocritical argument, as Schulenburg reported to Ribbentrop, 'was to make the intervention of the Soviet Union plausible to the masses and at the same time avoid giving the Soviet Union the appearance of an aggressor'.[35] It caused Hitler considerable annoyance.

Meanwhile Soviet military preparations were speeded up, a move for which Ribbentrop had been pressing. This, he said, would relieve the Germans of 'the necessity of annihilating the remainder of the Polish army and pursuing it as far as the Russian boundary'. Finally, Schulenburg received a summons to the Kremlin at two o'clock in the morning of 18 September, to which he went along with Hilger and General Ernst Kostring, the military attaché. When they arrived, they were received by Stalin, who had Molotov and Voroshilov in attendance. 'At six a.m., four hours from now,' Stalin announced, 'the Red Army will cross into Poland all along the border, and the Red Air Force will begin bombing the area east of Lvov.' He then asked Schulenburg to notify the German armed forces immediately. General Kostring protested that the notice was much too short. However, Voroshilov brushed aside his objections, remarking 'with unmistakable admiration for German military achievements', as Hilger afterwards put it, 'that the organisational genius of the German Army would surely find time, even on such short notice, to relay the message'. In the event no untoward incidents did take place when the respective forces made contact, although Schulenburg and the embassy staff in Moscow were annoyed by the Russian 'lack of consideration'.[36]

Thus was the joint Nazi–Soviet occupation of Poland accomplished. Each side committed the most frightful cruelties on the unfortunate Poles, the Germans exterminating or deporting thousands because they were Jews and the Soviets doing likewise because they were 'enemies of

401

the people' or 'anti-Soviet elements'. The latter included former Polish soldiers, civil servants, clergy, nobility, landowners, business men and industrialists 'who profited from the work of hired labour'.[37]

Stalin's excuse for the Soviet invasion of Poland, which on its face contravened the existing non-aggression treaty between the two countries, was that Poland had lost all her industrial areas and cultural centres, Warsaw was no longer the capital, the Polish Government had disintegrated and consequently the Polish State had ceased to exist. At first Stalin contemplated a small 'residual' Poland similar to Napoleon's Grand Duchy of Warsaw, but he reverted to the original idea of partition on learning that the German forces had penetrated further east than the line of rivers agreed as the approximate division between the respective spheres. Indeed, in talking to Schulenburg, he expressed doubt that in fact the Germans would withdraw west of the line. His concern, he said, was 'based on the well-known fact that all military men are loath to give up occupied territories'.[38] Schulenburg assured him that the German forces would most certainly withdraw, thus making more troops available for the Western Front. They both agreed that the exact line of demarcation should be settled as soon as possible and Ribbentrop hoped that Molotov would come to Berlin for this purpose. However, he was informed that the Soviet Government wished to conduct the negotiations in Moscow, 'since such negotiations', said Molotov, 'must be conducted on the Soviet side by persons in the highest positions of authority who cannot leave the Soviet Union'.[39] At first Ribbentrop thought that the German side could be handled by Schulenburg, but on second thoughts, probably after taking Hitler's instructions, he decided to fly to Moscow himself.

Accompanied by the Soviet ambassador Shvartsev in addition to his usually large entourage, Ribbentrop left Berlin about nine in the morning of 27 September, and after a brief stop for lunch at Koenigsberg, where they were joined by the Gauleiter of Danzig and heard the news that Warsaw had formally capitulated, the party flew on to Moscow.[40] They landed at the Khodynka field shortly before six o'clock in the evening to an even more spectacular welcome than before, this time all the hangars being lavishly decorated with the bunting and flags of the two countries. As on the previous occasion, Ribbentrop's headquarters were established in the former Austrian embassy. After dinner the German Foreign Minister, accompanied by Schulenburg, Hilger and several other aides, set out to keep the first appointment with Stalin and Molotov which had been set for 10 p.m. in the Soviet Premier's office in the Kremlin. 'There is a unique and mysterious attraction in entering the stronghold of Soviet power, with all its bizarre towers and

402

walls, no matter how often,' wrote one of the German aides afterwards. 'In the dark of the evening and in the expectant mood in which we found ourselves, this had an extraordinarily powerful effect. At the gates of the Kremlin a very strict check was made. No car was admitted whose number had not previously been reported to the Kremlin commandant. Our cars, to be sure, were speedily cleared, but even so they had to stop a moment, so that the officer of the guard could assure himself that all was in order.'[41]

On the occasion of this meeting, Stalin and Molotov gave Ribbentrop what he described as 'a decidedly friendly, almost cordial welcome'. At the same time the Russians showed themselves to be extremely tough bargainers. Stalin began by making it clear that he wished to add Lithuania to the agreed Soviet sphere of influence, in return for which he proposed that Germany should be compensated with an area east of the Vistula, including Lvov province, with the result that the entire ethnic population of Poland would be incorporated in the German sphere. 'History has proved that the Polish people continually struggle for unification,' Stalin argued. 'To partition the Polish population [as distinct from Polish territory] would therefore easily create sources of unrest from which discord between Germany and the Soviet Union might possibly arise.' Ribbentrop's attempts to improve upon the proposed compensation for giving up Lithuania encountered what the minister called 'Stalin's obstinacy'. When Ribbentrop suggested that an oil district to the south-east should be included in the German sphere, 'since Russia already had rich oil resources, while Germany lacked them', Stalin would not accept this on the ground that 'the Ukrainian people' had strongly pressed their claim to this area. However, he promised deliveries of oil equivalent to the whole annual production amounting to 300,000 tons, which it was hoped to increase to half a million, in return for German coal and steel piping.[42]

After some three hours of arguing, Ribbentrop told Stalin that he would like to think the matter over. Consequently the talks were adjourned until the following afternoon. The minister then returned to Sadovaya Kudrinskaya, where he drafted a long telegram to Hitler setting out the pros and cons of Stalin's latest proposal and asking for instructions. Since Hitler was away from Berlin, it took some time for the message to reach him. Indeed it was not until well after the negotiations had been resumed in the Kremlin next day that Hitler came through on the telephone. Ribbentrop took the call from Molotov's desk with Stalin looking on. Although he did not understand German, Stalin probably sensed Hitler's misgivings, as Ribbentrop certainly did,

403

on the question of Lithuania being included in the Soviet sphere. However, the Fuehrer agreed. 'I want to establish quite firm and close relations,' he told Ribbentrop. When the latter repeated this to Stalin through his interpreter, Stalin remarked laconically: 'Hitler knows his business.'[43]

The respective German and Soviet technical experts now got down to work. For this purpose two rooms were set aside for the Germans adjacent to Molotov's office, which was the main conference room, the two other rooms being used by the German cartographers and secretaries. 'Between these offices and the conference room there was much coming and going,' Ribbentrop's aide Andor Hencke later recalled. 'I personally had to supervise entering the new boundary on the maps and frequently had to fetch new instructions from the Foreign Minister or Privy Councillor Gaus or to aid in interpreting. Molotov's aides always watched us with slightly dubious glances whenever we went through the ante-chamber into the office of their lofty chief. Obviously this did not conform to the strict rules prevailing otherwise in the Kremlin, especially when it was a matter of access to Stalin or Molotov. In this case, however, in the interest of expeditious performance of our work an exception was made.'

The boundary, 'at first sketched in great sweeps', according to Hencke, 'was made more and more precise by the use of maps, etc., until finally it was settled. During this time, many changes and consultations were of course necessary. The draftsmen had no easy time keeping their entries current. The greatest care had to be taken here, for later in actually marking the boundary on the ground the slightest error – or even too heavy a line – might be important.' When at last agreement was reached, Hencke presented the draft map to Stalin and Ribbentrop for initialling. Stalin signed his name in large letters and asked jocularly: 'Is my signature clear enough for you?' He then autographed the map a second time in smaller letters on the actual boundary. Ribbentrop signed once, adding the date '28.IX.39'.[44]

Work was interruped at 7 p.m. for a state banquet which Molotov gave in the German Foreign Minister's honour in the Kremlin Grand Palace. This was attended by all the members of the Politburo and the chiefs of the armed services and other leading government officials. As Ribbentrop ascended the great staircase of the palace, he was surprised to see a large portrait of the Tsar Alexander II among his peasants after the abolition of serfdom. ('This, like much else, seemed to indicate an evolution in the course of which world revolutionary principles were giving way to a more conservative tendency.')

Hencke later described the scene:

Here, quite unlike Molotov's sober office building where the conferences took place, there were splendid and majestic halls where once the Tsars resided and held their receptions when they were in Moscow. At the palace entrance the Russian Chief of Protocol received the Foreign Minister and conducted him through the Congress Salon into a reception room decorated in red and gold. Here Stalin, wearing his well known *litevka*, and Molotov, surrounded by Marshal Voroshilov, Commissar for Internal Affairs Beria, and the other highest dignitaries of Soviet officialdom, awaited the Fuehrer's envoy and the other German guests.

After the greeting the door was opened to an oval room where the table was set. Richly decorated with flowers, set with costly porcelain and gilded cutlery, in the bright light of electric candles it presented a thoroughly festive appearance. The Foreign Minister took his place next to Stalin and across from Molotov. An army of waiters dressed in white served a repast that did full honour to the reputation of Russian hospitality. Those of our comrades who were in Moscow for the first time also learned on this occasion what a real Russian *zakuskie* is. Among the many *hors d'oeuvres* they had of course not forgotten the famous Russian caviar. After his official remarks Molotov addressed a special toast to each German and Soviet guest, in accordance with Russian custom. Each time, Stalin himself stood at the chair of the person addressed, to drink his health.

By all accounts, Stalin was in a thoroughly relaxed mood. When Molotov toasted him so often that it became embarrassing, Stalin exclaimed: 'If Molotov really wants to drink, no one objects, but he really shouldn't use me as an excuse!'[45]

An especially strong brown peppery vodka was served, which almost took Ribbentrop's breath away. But the German Foreign Minister noticed that it seemed to have no effect on Stalin. When Ribbentrop expressed his admiration for Russian throats 'compared with those of us Germans', Stalin laughed and confided in the principal guest with a wink that he was only having Crimean wine which was the same colour as the powerful vodka.[46] Gustav Hilger, the German embassy counsellor, found himself seated beside Beria, who kept plying him with the vodka, indeed much more than Hilger wished. This led Stalin to observe teasingly that Hilger and Beria were plainly at odds with each other and asked the reason. Hilger told him. Later, as Hilger got up to take his leave, Stalin said to him amiably, 'Well if you don't want to drink, no one can force you.'

'Not even the chief of the NKVD?' replied Hilger in jest.

'Here at this table,' Stalin promptly rejoined, 'even the chief of the NKVD has no more to say any more than anyone else.'[47]

When the banquet ended, Stalin and Molotov excused themselves as they had to meet a delegation from Latvia, which like the other Baltic states was being asked to allow Soviet troops to be stationed on its territory. Meanwhile, Ribbentrop went off to the Bolshoi Theatre for a performance of *Swan Lake* which he watched from the old imperial box, as Anthony Eden had done four years before, afterwards sending the prima ballerina a bouquet of flowers. Apparently Ribbentrop wanted to express his pleasure in more extravagant form, but Schulenburg who was also in the box dissuaded him with the remark that 'this sort of thing was frowned upon' in the Soviet Union.

After the performance Ribbentrop and Schulenburg returned to Molotov's office where the work with the experts continued throughout most of the night. The Latvians were leaving the Kremlin as Ribbentrop arrived, and he noticed how ashen they looked, for they had just been told by Stalin that they must allow Soviet garrisons in their country.

The ceremonial signing of the agreements by Ribbentrop and Molotov took place about 5 a.m. First there was the 'German–Soviet Boundary and Friendship Treaty', which formally carved up Poland and Lithuania. The exchange of Lithuania as a previously agreed German sphere of influence for parts of Poland east of the Vistula was confirmed in a secret protocol. An additional secret protocol provided that no 'Polish agitation' would be tolerated in the territory of either of the parties, who undertook to 'suppress in their territories all beginnings of such agitation and inform each other concerning suitable measures for this purpose'. Next to be signed after the Boundary and Friendship Treaty was a joint 'Peace Appeal of the German and Soviet Governments' designed to bring the hostilities with Britain and France to an end. Finally, a trade and economic agreement was concluded so as to supplement the existing commercial treaty.[48] The Germans noted that Stalin observed the signing ceremony 'with obvious satisfaction'.

'Now Germans and Russians must never be allowed to fight each other,' said Ribbentrop after the first of the treaties had been signed.

Stalin pondered over this remark for several moments before finally replying: 'This ought to be the case.'

What Stalin said struck Ribbentrop as so unusual that he asked Hilger, who was interpreting, to repeat it.

A few hours later Ribbentrop flew back to Berlin. During the flight he kept turning over Stalin's remark in his mind. In spite of all the lavish entertainment he had received, the German Foreign Minister could not escape the conclusion that the Russian leader was cooler than he was on the question of German–Soviet friendship. Was Stalin perhaps not thinking of one day carrying the Bolshevik revolution into Germany and the rest of Europe, which must mean that the Germans and the Soviets would eventually be fighting each other? Thus Ribbentrop put the matter to his Fuehrer.

After some reflection Hitler construed Stalin's words as meaning that 'the chasm between the two philosophies was too wide to be bridged, so that a dispute was bound to arise sooner or later'.[49] Time was to prove him right.

5

As a security precaution, the Soviet Government now took steps to block all lines of entry from the west. To this end the three Baltic states and Finland were invited to conclude 'Pacts of Mutual Assistance' with the Soviet Union, which would give the latter the right to occupy bases and garrison troops in their territories. The governments of the Baltic states felt they had no alternative but to bow to *force majeure* and they agreed to the Soviet request. However, the Finnish Government refused. This was a serious blow to Stalin, who had not forgotten how near Leningrad had been to falling into the hands of the Whites and their interventionist allies during the Civil War. The Soviet frontier with Finland came within twenty miles of Leningrad, while Finnish territory extended along the whole northern coast of the Gulf of Finland to the Karelian Isthmus. What Stalin and his military advisers wanted was the cession of certain Finnish islands in the gulf and the leasing of other Finnish territory including Petsamo, Finland's only ice-free port in the Arctic Sea; also the Hango peninsula at the entrance to the gulf, great stress being laid upon the importance of the latter as a potential Soviet naval and air base. Accordingly the Finns were asked to send a delegation to Moscow to negotiate the issue.[50]

The Finns responded by dispatching a strong team led by Juho Paasikivi, one of their elder statesmen, who had signed the peace of 1921 with the Bolsheviks and now was the Finnish Minister in Stockholm. The negotiations, conducted on the Soviet side by Stalin, Molotov and Potemkin, extended over the next seven weeks due to the necessity for the Finns to report each Soviet proposal and counter-proposal to the Diet in Helsinki.

Paasikivi began by arguing that no peril threatened the Soviets from the Gulf of Finland. However, he was prepared to yield certain of the islands off the Karelian Isthmus for an agreed compensation, but not Koivisto and adjacent territory amounting to about 1,700 square miles on the Karelian Isthmus, which the Soviets particularly wanted. To this Stalin replied that the Soviet government would be satisfied with nothing less than the boundary existing at the time of the Tsar Peter the Great. On the other hand, in return for the Isthmus territory he was prepared to compensate Finland to the extent of 3,500 square miles by a frontier adjustment further north.

'The line your military command has in mind would be quite impossible on economic grounds alone,' said Paasikivi.

'Soldiers never think in economic terms,' Stalin replied. He went on to point out that passage into the Gulf of Finland could be blocked by the cross-fire of batteries on both shores as far out as the entrance to the gulf.

It is not the fault of either of us that geographical circumstances are as they are. We must be able to bar entrance to the Gulf of Finland. If the channel to Leningrad did not run along your coast, we would not have the slightest occasion to bring the matter up...

You ask what power might attack us – England or Germany. We are on good terms with Germany now, but everything in this world may change. Yudenich attacked through the Gulf of Finland and later the British did the same. This can happen again. If you are afraid to give us bases on the mainland, we can dig a canal across the Hango peninsula, and then our base won't be on Finnish mainland territory. As things stand now, both England and Germany can send large naval units into the Gulf of Finland. I doubt whether you would be able to avoid an incident in that case. England is pressuring Sweden for bases right now. Germany is doing likewise. When the war between these two is over, the victor's fleet will come into the Gulf.

You ask, why do we want Koivisto? I'll tell you why. I asked Ribbentrop why Germany went to war with Poland. He replied, 'We had to move the Polish border farther from Berlin.' Before the war the distance from Poznan to Berlin was about 220 kilometres. We ask that the distance from Leningrad to the line should be seventy kilometres. That is our minimum demand, and you must not think we are prepared to reduce it bit by bit. We can't move Leningrad, so the line has to move. Regarding Koivisto, you must bear in mind that if 16-inch guns were placed

408

there they could entirely prevent movements of our fleet in the innermost extremity of the Gulf. We ask for 2,700 square kilometres and offer more than 5,500 in exchange. Does any other great power do that? No. We are the only ones that simple.

Paasikivi was reassured by Stalin's technical experts that there were precedents for the territorial deal which had been proposed. The Russians had sold Alaska to the United States, and Spain had ceded Gibraltar to Britain. But the Finnish leader seemed doubtful. He remarked that, as this was a question affecting his country's constitituon, a five-sixths majority in the Diet would be needed to get it through.

'You are sure to get ninety-nine per cent support,' said Stalin.

Paasikivi still looked dubious. 'The Hango peninsula concession and the cession of the area on the Isthmus are exceptionally difficult matters.'

'It's nothing really,' Stalin remarked, brushing aside the Finn's doubts. 'Look at Hitler. The Poznan frontier was too close to Berlin for him and he took an extra three hundred kilometres.'

Paasikivi was unmoved by the scarcely veiled threat behind this remark. 'We want to continue in peace,' he said, 'and remain apart from all incidents.'

'That's impossible,' exclaimed Stalin, who was growing annoyed by the Finnish leader's obstinacy.

At this point Paasikivi's military assistant Colonel Paasonen broke in with a question to Stalin. 'How do these proposals of yours fit in with your famous slogan, "We don't want a crumb of foreign territory, but neither do we want to cede an inch of our own territory to anyone."?'

'I'll tell you,' said Stalin. 'In Poland we took no foreign territory. But this is a case of exchange.' Then, turning to Paasikivi, he went on, 'So we will expect you back on the 20th or 21st.'

'We'll sign the agreement on the 20th,' Molotov added, 'and give you a dinner next day.'[51]

'When we come back will depend on our government,' the Finnish leader answered gravely.

The Finns did return on the 21st. But little progress was made and they refused to sign any agreement.

'Is it your intention to provoke a conflict?' Molotov asked them as they were preparing to leave again.

'We want no such thing,' replied Paasikivi, 'but you seem to.'

On this occasion Stalin said nothing but merely smiled, as the Finnish Minister Vaino Tanner who was present noted, 'in his usual enigmatic fashion'.[52]

A final attempt was made to reach a compromise during the first week of November, when the Finns again came to Moscow. Their visit coincided with the annual meeting of the Supreme Soviet, the country's rubber-stamp Parliament, and also with the anniversary celebrations of the Bolshevik Revolution, both of which functions the Finns were invited to attend. Both chambers of the Supreme Soviet – the All-Union Soviet and the Soviet of Nationalities – consisting in all of about 1,200 representatives, met jointly in the great hall of the Kremlin Grand Palace. Tanner, who was much interested in the proceedings, noted that Stalin withdrew into a corner and did not seem to be much concerned with the meeting. Later he came over to sit beside Zhdanov in the row of seats reserved for the top Party officials. For a while they chatted and laughed together, and appeared to Tanner to be 'enjoying themselves very much'. Both smoked one cigarette after another, although smoking was clearly forbidden. Litvinov, who had emerged from obscurity for the occasion, sat in the body of the hall, reading newspapers, of which there was a large pile in front of him, without paying the least attention to what was going on. The papers he had finished with he threw on the floor. So far as Tanner could judge from where he was sitting, few of those present appeared to be manual workers, judging by their well-cared-for hands, and he concluded that the majority was made up of party secretaries and the like.

At the customary march past of the Soviet forces in Red Square, where Stalin took the salute from the top of the Lenin tomb, Tanner found himself beside the American ambassador Laurence Steinhardt. Tanner was quite impresssed by the parade, but not so his neighbour. At every turn the ambassador criticised both the troops and their weapons. The tanks were old and clumsy, he told Tanner; the infantry arms were out of date; there was only a submachine gun to every twenty men, and so on and so forth. Finally Tanner asked him whether he was a military expert, and Steinhardt replied that he had once been a serving officer. As it was cold he took a swig of cognac now and again from his pocket flask. He offered Tanner some. But the Finnish Minister said no thanks, he wasn't cold.

At the official reception and dinner given by Molotov the same evening, to which he was also bidden, Tanner encountered the German ambassador, and told him bluntly that it was not in Germany's interest to let Russia bully Finland like she was doing and probably attack her. 'But what can we do?' exclaimed Schulenburg. 'We're bound. At the moment we can't do anything. Now the Russians have the opportunity they've long been waiting for.'

Tanner also noted that the ambassador spoke of the Russians in most derogatory terms, in particular criticising their behaviour at the evening's entertainment at which there was evidently a good deal of guzzling and swilling. *'Und mit diesen Menchen mussen wir zusammenarbeiten!'* ('And we have to work with these fellows!') Schulenburg remarked with a contemptuous gesture of his hand in their direction.

Later in the evening Tanner also had a word with Mikoyan, the Soviet Commissar of Foreign Trade, to whom he likewise complained about the 'unreasonableness' of his government's demands. Mikoyan affected to be greatly astonished, saying the Soviet government's requirements were 'minimal', an expression which seemed to Tanner to be general in Soviet government circles, so constantly was it repeated. Apparently the matter had been discussed in the Politburo, and it had been 'generally thought that Finland should be offered easy conditions'. They all had great respect for Finland, Mikoyan went on, and quoted the saying, 'The Finns are a tough people,' so they had to be treated with circumspection. 'Consider, if there were just Russians in our government, things would be quite different,' said Mikoyan. 'But Stalin is a Georgian, I'm an Armenian, and many of the rest are minority nationals. We understand the position of a small country very well.'

Mikoyan was loud in his praise of Stalin. Lenin was a very gifted man, he thought, but Stalin was a genius – 'which presumably meant a lot more,' reflected Tanner. Anyway, he also noted, Mikoyan had had a lot to drink, and his conversation tended to reflect it.

Next day the negotiations reached deadlock once more and were finally broken off. Tanner for the Finns made it clear that, if the Soviets dropped their demands for Hango, he would recommend the government in Helsinki to satisfy 'all reasonable Soviet aspirations' on the Isthmus and elsewhere. But Stalin and Molotov stood firm for the Hango peninsula. 'Well then,' said Tanner, 'the best we can do is to agree to disagree.' And with that he and his colleagues took their departure.

The leavetaking was not unfriendly on either side. 'Best of luck!' said Stalin. 'Till we meet again,' echoed Molotov, as the Finns filed out of his office.[53]

The mobilisation of Finland's forces was now complete, and the Finns could do no more than wait for the Soviet blow to fall. This was heralded by Molotov's denunciation of the existing non-aggression pact between the two countries, on 28 November. Two days later the Russians attacked without warning or any formal declaration of war at eight points along Finland's thousand-mile frontier with the Soviet Union. On the same morning Helsinki was bombed by the Red Air

Force. However, the brunt of the Soviet attack fell at first on the Finnish frontier defences in the Karelian Isthmus. This was a strongly fortified zone of about twenty miles in depth in densely wooded and snow-bound country, known as 'The Mannerheim Line' after Field-Marshal Mannerheim, the Finnish commander-in-chief and saviour of his country from the Bolsheviks in 1917. This proved impregnable to the troops of the Leningrad garrison.

Although they had little difficulty in taking Petsamo, elsewhere along the extended front in what was generally known at the time as the 'winter war' the Soviet forces had little success. Though numerically much stronger – the Finns only numbered about 200,000 fighting men – the Soviets were neither so adequately equipped nor so appropriately trained for campaigning in Finland's pine forests, lacking both skis and warm winter clothing. Finnish tactics were the same all along the frontier from the Arctic Sea to Lake Ladoga. The Finnish frontier posts would withdraw to a distance of thirty miles or so followed by the slow moving Red Army columns, who would then be set upon by the mobile Finns on their skis, their flanks constantly harried, their lines of communication cut, and their personnel as often as not being cut to pieces. During the first weeks of the campaign, Soviet losses were enormous. Stalin and Voroshilov, who was in overall charge of the military operations on the Soviet side, had expected a walk-over. Instead, such was the determined and skilful resistance encountered that, by the end of December 1939, the Russians had to drop their plan of penetrating the wide front and concentrate on piercing the Mannerheim Line. By this time thousands upon thousands of corpses of their soldiers lay beneath the Finnish lakes and snows either slain or frozen to death. Other incidents in the fighting were less grim and were even bizarre. A Russian army officer has recalled how a group of Finnish soldiers disguised in Red Army uniforms quietly directed a large Soviet supply column towards their own lines, being subsequently thanked by the Soviets for relieving the traffic jam in that particular sector. Of course, most of the Finns could speak Russian. This enabled a Finnish officer's batman on one occasion to get hot meals and provisions for his officer from a Red Army field kitchen. These facilities continued for fourteen days, when the Finn was accidentally recognised and taken prisoner.[54]

Meanwhile, in anticipation of the rapid collapse of the Finnish forces, Stalin and Molotov proposed to liquidate the 'focus of war infection which the plutocratic government in Finland had created on the frontiers of the Soviet Union for the benefit of the imperialist powers'. The method by which this was to be achieved was by setting up a puppet government headed by a Finnish Communist Otto Kuusinen, who had fled from the country in 1918 and had managed to hold himself in readiness until the Comintern required his services. This moment seemed to have arrived at the beginning of December 1939, when Kuusinen established the so-called 'Finnish Democratic Government' at Terijoki, just over the Finnish side of the border in the Karelian Isthmus, and signed a treaty with the Soviet Government ceding all those parts of his country which Stalin had demanded. At the same time an announcement was made over the Moscow radio that it was hoped soon to ratify the treaty in Helsinki.

Since 1937 there had been a separate Commissariat of the Navy in the Soviet Union. During the 'winter war' the Navy Commissar Admiral N. G. Kuznetsov complained that there was no proper coordination of naval and military operations. For this he blamed the old system when his commissariat formed part of the Defence Commissariat under Voroshilov. Major decisions were taken in Stalin's office, when Voroshilov and Shaposhnikov, the Chief of the General Staff, were usually present; but the top navy men were only summoned on occasion and did not attend regularly, as a result of which important naval decisions were sometimes reached without prior consultation with them. Kuznetsov in his memoirs cites a typical example of this when he heard that Stalin had decided to send submarines to the Finnish port of Abo at the southern end of the Gulf of Bothnia. The Admiral thereupon went to see Stalin and pointed out that such an operation would be extremely difficult on account of the reefs.

'We can send submarines into the Gulf of Bothnia as a calculated risk,' he told Stalin, 'but to go up to the very mouth of Abo through the narrow reef-strewn channel without being seen is almost impossible.'

Stalin interrupted Kuznetsov to send for Admiral Galler, the head of the Supreme Naval Staff. When Geller arrived, he was asked about the feasibility of the operation. At first Galler hesitated and seemed reluctant to give a precise answer. But he eventually came out in support of Kuznetsov's view. 'Getting through to Abo directly is very difficult,' he said.

The result was that the instructions which had been sent to the submarines were changed. This and similar experiences convinced Kuznetsov that Stalin did take the opinions of experts into account. On the other hand, as Kuznetsov wrote afterwards, the men who habitually refrained from opposing Stalin and even lavished praise on any proposal he made had a bad influence on him. 'It was easier to resolve problems with him when he was alone in his office. Unfortunately, that seldom happened.'

For the initial reverses in the 'winter war' Stalin blamed Voroshilov, who in turn put the blame on faulty intelligence. A violent row resulted between Stalin and the Defence Commissar, and this eventually led to Voroshilov being superseded in his office by Marshal Timoshenko. Khrushchev has recalled the scene when they were all at dinner at Stalin's *dacha* near Moscow, and 'Stalin jumped up in a white-hot rage and started to berate Voroshilov'.

Voroshilov was also boiling mad. He leaped up, turned red, hurled Stalin's accusations back in his face. 'You have only yourself to blame for all this!' shouted Voroshilov. 'You're the one who annihilated the Old Guard of the army; you had our best generals killed!' Stalin rebuffed him, and at that Voroshilov picked up a platter with a roast suckling pig on it and smashed it on the table. It was the only time in my life I ever witnessed such an outburst. Voroshilov ended up by being relieved of his duties as People's Commissar of Defence. For a long time afterward he was kept around as a whipping boy.[55]

Meanwhile Finland had appealed to the League of Nations, and this move had been followed almost immediately by the Soviet Union's expulsion from that body. At the same time the Finns aroused a considerable wave of sympathy in the west for their gallant resistance to the predatory Russian bear, and the British and French discussed the possibility of sending an expeditionary force through northern Norway and Sweden to their aid, which would have the additional advantage of cutting off supplies of Swedish iron ore to Germany. Neither did the Germans like their new ally's war with the Finns, on whom they depended for the vital supply of timber and nickel, since Germany was not consulted before hostilities were launched. Nevertheless, Hitler continued to observe the Non-Aggression Pact and Friendship Treaty, and even sent a telegram of congratulation to Stalin on his sixtieth birthday, which cannot have been a particularly happy occasion for the Soviet leader. However, Stalin loyally telegraphed back to Hitler: 'The friendship of the peoples of Germany and the Soviet Union, cemented by blood, has every reason to be lasting and firm.' It was an expression of sentiment that Stalin was soon to regret he had ever uttered.

The western Allies' preparations for the dispatch of an expeditionary force to Finland were retarded by the reluctance of Norway and Sweden to allow troops to pass through their territories, and in the event all that reached the Finns were fifty British bombers and a handful of volunteers disguised as civilians. In the meantime the Russians opened their new offensive against the Mannerheim Line on 1 February 1940, and such was the concentration of their artillery that they were able to breach the line a fortnight later. This achievement, aided by the late break up of the ice in the Gulf of Finland, enabled them to attack Viipuri (Vyborg), which suffered greatly. By the end of the month it was evident that the Finns could not hold out much longer and Marshal Mannerheim advised the Finnish cabinet to sue for terms. Negotiations were begun through Madame Kollontai, then Soviet Ambassador in Stockholm, and these were followed by Paasikivi going to Moscow on 7 March. Five days later the Finns accepted the Soviet peace terms and hostilities ceased.

The actual terms were in effect dictated by Stalin, although he did not participate in the negotiations, preferring to leave them in the hands of Molotov, Zhdanov and General Alexander Vasilevsky, once an officer in the Tsarist army and now a coming man in the Soviet military hierarchy, who was eventually to succeed Shaposhnikov as Chief of the General Staff. The Finns signed under duress and they regarded the terms as onerous. Certainly they had to satisfy all the original Russian demands, as well as to surrender additional territory including Pet-samo, the whole of the Karelian Isthmus and the city and bay of Viipuri. Nevertheless the terms could have been much harsher. Thenceforth Finland was to be left in peace by her powerful neigh-bour, and she was not to be absorbed in the Soviet Union as the three neighbouring Baltic states were a few months later. Also, greatly to the relief of Tanner and his colleagues in Helsinki, there was no demand on the part of Stalin and Molotov that Kuusinen should be taken into the Finnish Cabinet. In fact, he had been kept in the background dur-ing the peace negotiations, and he and his 'Finnish Democratic Government' were thereupon thrown over when they no longer served Stalin's purpose. Maybe Stalin recalled that one of his first acts as Commissar of Nationalities in 1917 had been publicly to proclaim 'com-plete freedom for the Finnish people' with no tutelage, no supervision from above, and for that reason he was prepared to let off the Finns comparatively lightly.

6

Towards the end of March 1940, Ribbentrop, in an attempt to shore up the cracks in the Nazi–Soviet Pact disclosed by the 'winter war' as well as a number of irritating frontier incidents between German and Soviet troops in Poland, invited Stalin and Molotov in Hitler's name to visit Berlin. In fact he had communicated such an invitation orally when he was in Moscow the previous September and it had been accepted 'in principle'. Now, said Ribbentrop, 'the Fuehrer would not only be particularly happy to welcome Stalin in Berlin, but he would also see to it that he would get a reception commensurate with his position and importance, and he would extend to him all the honours that the occasion demanded'. But the Russians showed that they were in no hurry to come to Berlin. Such a demonstration of German–Soviet friendship, as Schulenburg reported, might 'involve the risk of severance of diplomatic relations or even of warlike developments with the Western Powers'. Furthermore, it was a known fact that Molotov, who had never been abroad, had 'strong inhibitions against appearing in strange surroundings', and this applied 'as much if not more to Stalin'. Also, 'Molotov, who never flies, will need at least a week for the trip, and there is really no suitable substitute for him here'. Nevertheless Schulenburg felt that the Soviet Premier, 'conscious of his obligation', would eventually make the visit 'as soon as the time and circumstances appear propitious to the Soviet Government'.[56]

The visit was temporarily shelved as Hitler was about to invade Norway and Denmark. His successful occupation of these countries relieved Stalin's mind, since it put an end to the possibility of any further British operations in Scandinavia. Nazi–Soviet relations again became cordial. Stalin was even more pleased by the ending of the 'phoney war' in the west through Hitler's breakthrough into the Low Countries and France a few weeks later. This Stalin felt should keep the combatants busy fighting for some time.

Gradually his feelings of satisfaction gave place to alarm with the rapid fall of France and the evacuation of the British expeditionary force from the beaches at Dunkirk. His immediate reaction was to seal off Estonia, Latvia and Lithuania by incorporating them in the Soviet Union after their inhabitants had expressed the desire to come under Communist rule through plebiscites organised by Stalin's trusted special representatives on the spot – Zhdanov in Tallin, Vyshinsky in Riga and Dekanozov in Kaunas. At the same time, as Molotov informed Schulenburg, 'the solution of the Bessarabian question brooked no further delay'. Consequently Bessarabia was also annexed to the Soviet Union, as well as the Roumanian province of Bukovina on the ground that the latter had a Ukrainian population, although there had been no mention of this in the original German–Soviet agreement.[57]

Churchill, who had by this time succeeded Chamberlain as Britain's Prime Minister and war leader, now began to play on Stalin's fears of Germany's power seeing that Hitler was in possession of much of western Europe. Anglo-Soviet relations had been noticeably cool since Ribbentrop's diplomatic coup and the humiliating failure of the joint

Anglo-French military mission the previous summer. Sir William Seeds had gone home on leave at the end of the year and did not return, leaving embassy business in the hands of a *chargé d'affaires*. It was not until June 1940 that Seeds's replacement arrived in Moscow in the person of a well-known English political figure outside the ranks of the professional foreign service. This was the fifty-one-year-old left-wing Labour lawyer Sir Stafford Cripps, an austere vegetarian, who had called on Molotov while passing through Moscow the previous February from the Far East; and from what he gathered during his talk on that occasion he thought there was a good chance of improving relations through the conclusion of a new Anglo-Soviet trade treaty. Churchill's War Cabinet considered that Cripps would make an appropriate ambassador at this time and the Soviet government agreed to accept him. At the same time, the British Prime Minister seized the opportunity provided by his accreditation to send a letter to Stalin through the new ambassador which he charged Cripps to deliver personally, since Churchill felt that in the circumstances Stalin could hardly refuse to receive him.

The letter, directly occasioned by the fall of France, was an appeal to the Soviet leader to consider carefully the new factor which had arisen in Europe and which Churchill considered made it desirable that 'both our countries should re-establish our previous contact, so that if necessary we may be able to consult together as regards those affairs in Europe which must necessarily interest us both'.

Churchill continued:

At the present moment the problem before all Europe – our two countries included – is how the states and peoples of Europe are going to react towards the prospect of Germany establishing a hegemony over the continent.

The fact that both our countries lie not in Europe but on her extremities puts them in a special position. We are better enabled than others less fortunately placed to resist Germany's hegemony, and, as you know, the British Government certainly intend to use their geographical position and their great resources to this end.

In fact, Great Britain's policy is concentrated on two objects – one, to save herself from German domination, which the Nazi Government wishes to impose, and the other, to free the rest of Europe from the domination which Germany is now in process of imposing on it.

The Soviet Union is alone in a position to judge whether Germany's present bid for the hegemony of Europe threatens the interests of the Soviet Union, and if so how best these interests may be safeguarded. But I have felt that the crisis through which Europe, and indeed the world, is passing is so grave as to warrant my laying before you frankly the position as it presents itself to the British Government.[58]

Although neither the British Prime Minister nor the Foreign Office expected any reply to this communication – and in the event did not receive one – the gesture was considered worth while making in Whitehall. Molotov with Stalin's concurrence had recently expressed to Schulenburg the Soviet Government's 'warmest congratulations on the splendid success of the German Armed Forces', while the official Soviet news agency Tass had just issued a statement to the world press, believed to have been written by Stalin himself, denying that there had been any deterioration in Soviet-German relations consequent upon the entry of Soviet troops into the Baltic states, as had been represented in certain foreign newspapers, and reasserting the 'fundamental interests of the USSR and Germany' based on these relations rather than on 'motives of opportunism'.[59] Hence the desirability from Churchill's point of view of a British emissary of the status of Stafford Cripps sounding out the Soviet leader.

Stalin received the new ambassador in the Kremlin in the evening of 1 July, having already been supplied with a Russian translation of Churchill's letter so that he could study it. Although Cripps thought that the general tenor of their talk was 'friendly and severely frank', Churchill's impression that it was 'formal and frigid' more nearly approached the mark. Stalin first commented on the letter. Germany could not dominate Europe without command of the seas, he said. ('Whoever dominates Europe will dominate the world.') In any case, Germany was not strong enough to dominate the whole of Europe, nor did Stalin believe that she intended to do so. Neither was he of the opinion, he went on, that the recent German military successes menaced the Soviet Union and her friendly relations with Germany. As for the non-aggression pact with Germany, this was not directed against Great Britain. Its basis had been a common desire to get rid of the old 'balance of power' in Europe, which before the war Great Britain and France had tried to preserve. 'If the British Prime Minister wishes to restore the old balance of power,' Stalin added, 'we cannot agree with him.' On the subject of an Anglo-Soviet trade agreement, Stalin thought this was a possibility, but he could not guarantee that nothing taken from Britain such as non-ferrous metals would not be re-exported to Germany, since the Soviet Government would not break its trade agreement with Germany. 'If this was an impediment to an agreement with us,' Cripps reported to the Foreign Office, 'Stalin was sorry, but it could not be helped.'

The one positive result of the interview was Stalin's acceptance of Britain's offer to assist in improving the Soviet Union's relations with Turkey even to the extent of securing some modification of the international convention which gave Turkey exclusive control of the Straits (the Bosphorus and Dardanelles). On the future of Nazi–Soviet relations Cripps left the Kremlin with the impression that Russia was not ready for war with Germany and that Stalin could 'stall' the Germans until it was too late for an attack before the winter.[60]

A few days after this interview had taken place, Molotov, acting on Stalin's instructions, handed a summary of it to Schulenburg for transmission to Berlin, an action personally acknowledged by Ribbentrop who stated that he had taken a note of the contents and 'greatly appreciated this information'.[61] Cripps was later to complain of the leak without knowing who was responsible. Incidentally, in Molotov's version of the interview Stalin's remarks were made to appear much harsher and less friendly than they really were.

About this time Molotov told Signor Rosso, the Italian ambassador in Moscow, in the knowledge that what he said would be sure to get back to Hitler, that he (Molotov) thought the war would be over by the following winter, and that in the meantime the Soviet Union intended to consolidate its influence in the Balkans, where it was possible that 'Roumanian intransigence' would result in resort to force. This remark, coupled with a reference to the need for the Soviet Union to 'protect itself towards the south and south-east' as the result of being 'hemmed in by a Turkish threat to Batum', suggested that Stalin might have to use Roumania's oil on which Hitler was largely dependent for his conduct of the war.[62]

With the *Luftwaffe* beaten back in the Battle of Britain, Hitler was obliged to call off, at least for the time being, his plan to invade England. Consequently the role he was gradually coming to envisage for Stalin was that of a satellite rather than a partner, a transformation which he felt might have to be achieved through arms. As an alleged precaution against the 'English menace', Hitler now sent troops into both Roumania and Finland, in breach of his agreements with Russia. Ribbentrop still hoped that a meeting might be arranged between the two dictators at which their increasing differences might be amicably settled; but this proved impracticable since neither Stalin nor Hitler felt they could leave their own countries at this time. However, Hitler told his Foriegn Minister that he should write to Stalin and invite

Molotov to pay his promised and much delayed visit to Berlin.[63]

Ribbentrop accordingly addressed a long and somewhat rambling letter to the Soviet leader in which he analysed their relations and reviewed the course of the war in detail, referred to the recent action of Japan in joining the Berlin–Rome Axis, repeated the invitation to Molotov and ended by proposing that he should afterwards pay a return visit to Moscow 'in order to resume the exchange of ideas with you, my dear M. Stalin, and to discuss – possibly with representatives of Japan and Italy – the bases of a policy which could only be of *practical* advantage to all of us'.[64]

Stalin replied briefly a week later in a letter whose form and style in Russian left no doubt in the mind of Schulenburg, to whom it was handed by Molotov for onward transmission to the Wilhelmstrasse, that it had been 'composed by Stalin personally'.

Moscow, 21 October 1940

My dear Herr von Ribbentrop,

I have received your letter. I thank you sincerely for your confidence, as well as for the instructive analysis of recent events which is contained in your letter.

I agree with you that a further improvement in the relations between our countries is entirely possible on the permanent basis of a long-range delimitation of mutual interests.

M. Molotov acknowledges that he is under an obligation to pay you a return visit in Berlin. He hereby accepts your invitation.

It remains for us to agree on the date of his arrival in Berlin. The time from 10–12 of November is most convenient for M. Molotov. If it is also agreeable to the German Government, the question may be considered as settled.

I welcome the desire expressed by you to come to Moscow again in order to resume the exchange of ideas begun last year on questions of interest to both our countries, and I hope that this visit will be realised after M. Molotov's trip to Berlin.

As to joint deliberation on some issues with Japanese and Italian participation, I am of the opinion (without being opposed to this idea in principle) that this question would have to be submitted to prior examination.

Yours etc.,
J. STALIN[65]

Molotov's visit took place, but not – as Ribbentrop ruefully admitted afterwards – under as lucky a star as he had hoped for. Prior to his departure from Moscow, Molotov was well briefed by Stalin to listen to everything the Germans had to say and to be very tough over the Balkans. The expedition was not without its humorous side, so Molotov reported on his return. The Soviet Premier, who was accompanied by a retinue of sixty, including his personal cook, travelled by train. A change to German coaches was necessary at the frontier owing to the difference in the width of the guage, and although the German train was equipped with an excellent *wagon-restaurant*, Molotov insisted upon eating only what his cook had prepared for him much to the dismay and chagrin of his hosts. There was also a hitch at the Berlin railway station when Molotov emerged from the train to be greeted ceremoniously by Ribbentrop. It was the original intention that the national anthems of both countries should be played. However, the Soviet anthem was the *Internationale*, the old European revolutionary song, and fears were expressed in the German Foreign Ministry that if this tune were played the Berliners would join in with embarrassing enthusiasm. The result was that it was decided that neither anthem should be played. This somewhat detracted from the planned effect of the welcome.[66]

Hitler received Molotov and his party in his huge room in the Chancellery, seated at his desk and wearing his customary mouse-green field jacket. He then rose, gave the Nazi salute, turning the palm of his hand out in a rather unnatural way, as was noted by Berezkhov, a Russian official in the Commissariat of Foreign Trade. Without so far having uttered a word, Hitler walked over and shook hands with everyone. His clammy palm reminded Berezkhov of the touch of a frog, while his gaze 'pierced each of us with feverishly burning gimlet eyes'. He then resumed his seat and began a monologue which lasted for about an hour, devoted to outlining a grandiose scheme for dividing Europe and Asia between the three Axis allies and the Soviet Union.[67]

When the Fuehrer had finished, Molotov brought him back to earth by observing that there were 'more concrete, practical questions' to be discussed. Would the Reich Chancellor explain, for instance, what a German military mission was doing in Roumania and why it had been sent there without consultation with the Soviet Government? Furthermore, why had German forces been sent to Finland without similar prior consultation?

Twisting uneasily in his chair, Hitler replied that the mission in Roumania had gone to train the Roumanian troops at the request of the Roumanian authorities, while the German troops in Finland were really in transit to Norway. But these replies did not satisfy Molotov, and it was in an atmosphere of mutual recriminations and suspicions that the talks continued for the next two days. They were brought to an end after supper the following evening when the sounding of the air raid alarm obliged Molotov to repair with Ribbentrop to the latter's luxuriously furnished private air raid shelter. The British had got wind of the conference beforehand and, as Winston Churchill was to put it, though not invited to join in the discussion, they did not wish to be entirely left out of the proceedings.

When they were inside the shelter and Ribbentrop had shut the door, the raid had already begun and the hollow boom of British bombs could be heard as they fell nearby. What happened then was subsequently reported by Molotov to Stalin, who was later to retail it to Churchill when they met for the first time in Moscow in 1942.[68]

When they had settled down in their chairs, Ribbentrop began to expatiate upon the need to partition the spheres of world influence which Hitler had already outlined at some length. 'Now here we are alone together,' said Ribbentrop. 'Why should we not divide?'

'What will England say?' countered Molotov.

Ribbentrop uttered a contemptuous snort. 'England is finished,' he said. 'She is no more use as a Power'.

'If this is so,' Molotov answered drily, 'why are we in this shelter? And whose are these bombs which are dropping so close that we can hear their explosions right here?'

An embarrassing silence followed, broken by Ribbentrop who called the waiter in attendance to bring coffee. When this had been served, Molotov reverted to the question of the German troops in Roumania and Finland. At this Ribbentrop made no attempt to hide his irritation, remarking that if the Soviet Government continued to be interested in these 'non-essential questions', it should discuss them through the usual diplomatic channels.

Ribbentrop spun out the time as the bombs continued to fall by calling for dry white wine. As they drank it he questioned Molotov about the brands grown in the Soviet Union, wine being a subject of which he had more professional knowledge than diplomacy. It was midnight before the all-clear sounded and the Soviet Premier and his aides were free to take their departure. A few hours later Molotov began his return journey to Moscow. Of the high Nazi dignitaries only Ribbentrop was at the railway station to see him off.

7

Stalin's demands, which had been made orally by Molotov in his talks with Hitler and Ribbentrop, were reaffirmed in an official diplomatic note handed by Molotov to Schulenburg in the Kremlin on the evening of 25 November 1940, and immediately transmitted to Berlin.[69] Professor George Kennan, an expert on Soviet affairs and a former United States ambassador in Moscow, regards this note as one of the most interesting documents in the history of Soviet foreign policy, 'showing clearly that Stalin still thought that he was in a position to exact a high price for lining up with the Axis in a four-power pact, and that all this palaver was only a form of preliminary bargaining'.[70] Briefly, Stalin expressed willingness to adhere to the Tripartite Pact provided that German troops were immediately withdrawn from Finland, and Soviet interests in the Balkans and the Straits were recognised through virtual Soviet control of Bulgaria and the establishment of bases in the Bosphorus and Dardanelles.

This was unacceptable to Hitler, since the Fuehrer had not given up the idea that he might attack the Soviet Union nor that Stalin might attack him.[71] In fact, only a few weeks later, on 18 December 1940, Hitler issued 'top secret' orders to the senior military, naval and air commanders to get ready for 'Operation Barbarossa'.[72]

The German Wehrmacht must be prepared to crush Soviet Russia in a quick campaign (Operation Barbarossa) even before the conclusion of the war against England...

I shall order the concentration against Soviet Russia possibly eight weeks before the intended beginning of operations.

Preparations requiring more time to get under way are to be started now – if this has not yet been done – and are to be completed by 15 May 1941.

It is of decisive importance, however, that the intention to attack does not become discernible...

On the same day Hitler also indicated this objective in a speech which he delivered to a closed meeting of several thousand junior officers and cadets in the *Sportspalast* in Berlin. The text of his speech was not released to the press, but it was the subject of news agency reports and a garbled version of it appeared in the *New York Times* on the following day. This prompted Stalin to try to obtain a copy of the speech through a NKVD agent employed in the Soviet embassy in Berlin. The agent was also working for the Germans, to whom he reported that Stalin was 'very much interested' in Hitler's remarks which the Soviet leader understood had 'an anti-Soviet tendency'. A fortnight later it was reported in the Wilhelmstrasse that the Soviet Counsellor of Embassy Kobulov, presumably in charge of the NKVD agent, was

423

'still insisting vehemently that the text of the Fuehrer's speech to the young officers be obtained'. Kobulov was also stated to have given the agent instructions to find out 'whether and which military men were opposed to Ribbentrop's policy and which German personages were opposed to collaboration with Russia'.[73]

Each year, usually in November or December, the Red Army would carry out exercises in combat training. These 'war games' would be followed by a top level conference in the Commissariat of Defence and afterwards the Chief of the General Staff with the divisional, corps and army commanders, and the commanders of the various military districts would be summoned by Stalin to the Kremlin to make their final reports to the Politburo. In 1940 the exercises took place in the last week of December. The Kremlin summons was advanced by twenty-four hours to 13 January 1941, a change which caught some of the participants unprepared, particularly the new Chief of the General Staff Marshal K. A. Meretskov, who had succeeded Shaposhnikov on the latter's temporary retirement through ill health. Meretskov's analysis of the 'war games' made an unfavourable impression upon Stalin and the rest of the Politburo, and later the same day he was replaced by the commander of Kiev district Marshal G. A. Zhukov, forty-four-year-old son of a village shoemaker who had risen from the ranks and who was destined to become the most decorated 'Hero of the Soviet Union' apart from Stalin himself. Also demoted along with Meretskov was Marshal G. I. Kulik, Deputy Defence Commissar and Chief of the Main Artillery Directorate of the Red Army. Kulik, who was later deprived of his marshal's baton, was sharply criticised by Stalin for his advocacy of the continued use of horse artillery in preference to its replacement by mechanised units.

Kulik supports the concept of a large rifle division of 18,000 troops supported by horse traction and speaks out against the mechanisation of the army. The government carries out a programme of mechanising the armed forces, introduces the [internal combustion] engine into the army, and Kulik comes out against the engine. It is as if he had come out against the tractor and the combine and supported a wooden plough and economic backwardness in the countryside. If the government had taken Kulik's point of view, say, at the time of collectivisation, we would still find ourselves with individual peasant farms and wooden ploughs.

Stalin's tongue did not spare old comrades, even if they occupied

424

exalted positions like Voroshilov who had been removed as Defence Commissar after the fiasco in Finland. However, some observers asked themselves why Stalin himself had not taken steps to correct the errors in army equipment once he had seen them, and they recalled that Stalin had participated in the decision, which had been taken in November 1939, to downgrade the independent role of armour and disperse the existing tank force among large infantry units. 'And, of course,' as General Kazakov, one of the district commanders present, later wrote in his memoirs, 'it was with Stalin's knowledge that people like Kulik reached high positions in the army.'

On the other hand, Stalin summarised the position towards the end of the Kremlin session in a manner which could hardly be faulted.

> Modern warfare will be a war of engines. Engines on land, engines in the air, engines on water and under water. Under these conditions, the winning side will be the one with the greater number and the more powerful engines.[74]

According to another observer, Marshal A. I. Eremenko, perhaps the most outspoken of all the Soviet military memoirists, 'Stalin spoke of the impending war and of the possibility of a war on two fronts: in the West with fascist Germany and in the East with imperialist Japan. Therefore he proposed that our military cadres be distributed accordingly. He did not predict the probable date when war was likely to break out but talked in general about the coming war as a war of manoeuvre...He spoke at length of the future war as a war of mass armies and of the necessity of achieving a numerical superiority of two to three times over the probable enemy. Stalin emphasised that a modern motorised army, abundantly equipped with automatic weapons and other technical means of warfare, required that exceptional attention be paid to the organisation of uninterrupted supply. The rear of the military units and the rear in the broad sense of the term was all the more important since foodstuffs, ammunition, armaments, and equipment had to reach the front in an unbroken flow from all parts of the country.'

In this connection Stalin also stressed the necessity of stockpiling foodstuffs and praised the decision of the former Tsarist government to do so particularly in respect of hard-tack, the old-fashioned sea-biscuit which he described as 'a very good product', light in weight and capable of being stored for a long time. 'Tea and hard-tack made a meal,' he said.[75]

During the early months of 1941, Hitler moved increasing numbers of troops into the Balkans. By the middle of February there were 680,000 German troops in Roumania, and Schulenburg received instructions from the Wilhelmstrasse to disseminate this information in Soviet government circles and also among the foreign missions in Moscow.[76] On 1 March, Bulgaria joined the Axis tripartite Pact and German troops immediately began to occupy that country and move towards the Greek border. Bulgaria's example was followed three weeks later by Yugoslavia, but immediately afterwards the Regent Prince Paul's pro-German government in Belgrade was overthrown by a group of Serbian nationalist officers led by General Simovic. This development and the reaction which it produced on Hitler's part were the subject of a telegram from Winston Churchill to Stalin sent in the first instance to Stafford Cripps for personal delivery.

> London, 3 April 1941
> I have sure information from a trusted agent that when the Germans thought they had Yugoslavia in the net – that is to say, after 20 March – they began to move three out of the five Panzer divisions from Roumania to southern Poland. The moment they heard of the Serbian revolution this movement was countermanded. Your Excellency will readily appreciate the significance of these facts.

Cripps was told to convey, if possible in conversation with Stalin, that this change in German military dispositions surely implied that Hitler had been forced by the coup in Belgrade to postpone his plans for attacking the Soviet Union. (In fact, the date had been changed from 15 May to 22 June.) If so, Churchill went on, it should be possible for Stalin to strengthen his own position, such as by furnishing material help to Turkey and Greece, and through the latter to Yugoslavia. 'This help might so increase German difficulties in the Balkans as still further to delay the German attack on the Soviet Union, of which there are so many signs.' What Churchill wanted Stalin and the Soviet Government above all to realise was that 'Hitler intends to attack them sooner or later if he can'.

Cripps replied that it was out of the question for him to try and deliver a message personally to Stalin, adding that in any event he felt the message inopportune as he was sure the Soviet Government was already aware of its implications. He was then told to give it to Molotov. But Molotov, with whom the British ambassador had had no direct contact for the past two months, refused to see him; in the end,

426

as a result of Churchill's insistence, he handed it to Vyshinsky, who had exchanged his office of Public Prosecutor for that of Molotov's deputy in the Foreign Affairs Commissariat. Vyshinsky promised to convey it to Stalin, which he did, although three weeks had already passed since it had arrived in Moscow from Downing Street.

A year later when he talked to Stalin in the Kremlin at the first of their wartime meetings, Churchill was to produce a copy of the telegram which he had sent him through Cripps. It was duly read and translated to him. 'I remember it,' said Stalin, shrugging his shoulders. 'I did not need any warnings. I knew war would come, but I thought I might gain another six months or so.'[77]

Although he appeared to disregard them, there were also repeated warnings from Soviet intelligence sources. One of these was the secret agent Richard Sorge, a German journalist, who headed a spy ring in the Far East and was later arrested and executed by the Japanese. Another was a Czech agent named Shkvor operating in Berlin. In April he reported confirmation of German troop concentrations and the fact that the Skoda works had been ordered by the German authorities to halve deliveries of military equipment to the Soviet Union. Shkvor's report eventually reached the Politburo where Stalin minuted it in red ink to the effect that it was merely 'an English provocation', and ordered that the perpetrator of this 'provocation' should be sought out and punished. (This was duly done.)[78] It is clear, too, that the head of Soviet military intelligence, Marshal F. I. Golikov, was inclined to place emphasis on reports 'in such a way as to please Stalin, at the expense of truth'. The reports were marked either 'From reliable sources' or 'From doubtful sources', the former including everything tending to indicate that Hitler was going to invade Britain and the latter reports of his plans for the invasion of the Soviet Union. Significantly it was only the former that were given any prominence in the Soviet press.[79]

The popular impression that Stalin ignored the warnings he received and was more or less paralysed into inaction is not correct. He seems to have accepted the evidence as valid and his policies were certainly based on rational calculation, even though they proved disastrous.[80] These policies were well summarised at the time by Hilger, the economic counsellor in the German embassy in Moscow and an acute observer, who wrote that everything indicated that Stalin 'thought Hitler was preparing for a game of extortion in which threatening military moves would be followed by sudden demands for economic or even territorial concessions'. Hilger added that Stalin seemed to have believed that he would be able to negotiate with Hitler over such demands when they were presented.[81]*

4

Hess, by this time mentally unbalanced, flew to Scotland, piloting his own plane, on 10 May 1941, on an alleged peace mission to the Duke of Hamilton, whom he had previously met in Germany. He was detained and subsequently handed over for trial to the International War Crimes Tribunal in November. He was sentenced to life imprisonment.

* In this context it is interesting to compare the views of a leading British historian and a leading Soviet historian, reached independently of each other. The British historian John Erickson has written in his work on the Soviet High Command:

> Stalin's attitude was compounded of complacency, confidence and a form of precautionary nervousness which defeated its own objects. The dismissing of warnings emanating from British and American sources would have its roots in disposing of anything which might impede a further Soviet–German compromise. In explaining Stalin's order that no credence should be given to information about a German attack, Khrushchev asserts that this was done 'in order not to provoke the initiation of military operations'. That would presumably refer to the possibility of an 'accidental war' being triggered off by excessive Soviet zeal in dealing with the tense situation; air activity on both sides had steadily increased during the spring.[82]

The Soviet historian Professor A. M. Nekrich wrote in his book *22 June 1941*, which was published in 1965:

> Stalin's actions during this period were extremely contradictory. On the one hand they showed his desire to go on clinging to an obsolete dogma, on the other they gave evidence of his uncertainty and fear of war ...
> His actions, which are difficult to explain, were apparently deeply rooted in his schematic understanding of the outside world, which he could judge only on such information as he received, or rather which he wished to receive ... It is obvious from his statements, speeches and addresses that he considered Britain as the chief enemy of the Soviet state. The feeling must have been even more acute in 1941, since the old enemy of the Soviet regime Winston Churchill, an experienced and wily politician, was at the head of the British Government. There is no doubt that the sudden flight to England of Hitler's deputy in the Nazy Party, Rudolf Hess, increased Stalin's suspicions about the intrigues of 'perfidious Albion' ...
> Hess's flight made a big impression on Stalin. As his subsequent conversations on this subject with Churchill showed he was certain that Britain was inciting Germany to attack the USSR, that secret negotiations were taking place in London based on Hess's proposals. If these circumstances are not taken into account, it is very difficult to understand Stalin's inner hostility to any new reports ... about Germany's preparations for an attack on the Soviet Union. He considered such reports as a British provocation.[83]

Meanwhile, on the night of 5–6 April, Stalin had summoned Gabrilovich, the Yugoslav minister in Moscow, to the Kremlin and concluded a non-aggression pact with him as representing the new government in Belgrade. This was to the effect that if Yugoslavia were attacked the Soviet Union would adopt an attitude of goodwill 'based on friendly relations'. It was at least an amiable gesture, but even as it was made Hitler's bombers were about to strike the Yugoslav capital from the nearby occupied Roumanian airfields. Gabrilovich spent most of the night amicably conversing with Stalin after they had been photographed together.

'And if the Germans, displeased, turn against you?' queried Gabrilovich.

'Let them come!' was Stalin's confident reply.[84]

According to Hilger, 'nothing the Russians did between 1939 and 1941 made Hitler more genuinely angry than the treaty with Yugoslavia; nothing contributed more directly to the final break; and Stalin must have sensed it. Ever since the collapse of Yugoslavia and Greece, he left no stone unturned to appease Germany. The first step was taken as early as April, a week after hostilities had broken out in the Balkans'.[85] Here Hilger was referring to an extraordinary incident which occurred during the visit of Yosuke Matsuoka, the Japanese Foreign Minister, in order to conclude a Neutrality Pact between the two countries.

After the pact had been signed and an appropriate farewell dinner given in the Kremlin on 13 April, the Japanese mission departed for the railway station to return to Tokyo. Stalin, who normally never ventured out in public, suddenly appeared at the station with Molotov, to the astonishment of the diplomatic corps which had assembled to see Matsuoka off. ('We are both Asiatics,' Stalin had already told Matsuoka.) After wishing the Japanese a pleasant journey, Stalin asked for Count Schulenburg, and when he had found him, went up to him, put his arm round the ambassador's shoulders and said: 'We must remain friends and you must now do everything to that end!' He did the same thing to the acting military attaché, General Hans Krebs, whom he had never seen before in his life, having first made sure that he was a German. He then addressed him: 'We will remain friends with you – whatever happens.'[86]

Yet in spite of the warnings Stalin had received both from his own military intelligence and friendly foreign sources, it was remarkable, as Churchill was later to point out in his history of the war, what advantages he sacrificed and what risks he ran to keep on friendly terms with Germany at this time. 'Even more surprising were the miscalculations and the ignorance which he displayed about what was coming to him.' He was indeed 'at once a callous, a crafty, and an ill-informed giant'. For example, he continued to make generous deliveries of grain and raw materials such as oil and manganese to Germany under the trade agreement after the Germans had practically ceased to make counter-deliveries, in particular tank gun turrets, under the plea of 'shortage of labour and priority of the military programmes'.[87]

A fortnight later, at the May Day parade in Red Square, it was generally noticed and commented upon that Stalin gave particular prominence to Dekanozov, the recently appointed Soviet ambassador in Berlin who stood beside him on Lenin's tomb. A few days before this, the naval attaché in the German embassy had reported to Berlin on current rumours of impending war between the two countries which he said were being spread by travellers passing through Moscow from Germany. He also quoted the British ambassador as allegedly predicting – as it was to turn out with astonishing accuracy – the actual date of the outbreak as 22 June. The naval attaché added that he was endeavouring to counteract the rumours, which he characterised as 'manifestly absurd'.[88]

By now Stalin was coming round to the view that war was a probability, although he hoped that it could be postponed until the following year. This became clear from an unpublished speech which he delivered to the graduates of the Military Academy on 5 May. According to the details, which subsequently became known, Stalin warned the officers that war with Germany was approaching, and that the later it came, the better prepared the Soviet Union would be. Therefore it was supremely important to do everything to delay the German attack. If this could be done until late August, it would be too late to start a campaign in the current year on account of the well-known Russian winters. In such case, war was absolutely certain to begin in 1942, as soon as the spring campaigning season arrived. Since that would be infinitely preferable to war beginning in 1941, strict orders had been issued throughout the armed forces to avoid any act or even gesture that could be used by the Germans as the slightest pretext for launching an all-out attack.[89]

Next day, the diplomatic corps in Moscow was shaken by the news that Stalin had taken over the Chairmanship of the Council of People's Commissars from Molotov, thereby becoming in name as well as in fact the head of the Soviet government. Molotov stepped down to become Deputy Chairman, while retaining his portfolio of foreign affairs. The new French ambassador, Gaston Bergery, tried to find out why Stalin had taken this step and put the question squarely to Vyshinsky and two other officials when he called at the foreign affairs commissariat. Schulenburg, who learned of the call, subsequently reported the outcome to the Wilhelmstrasse in a dispatch which showed a certain sense of humour.

The three gentlemen interrogated expressed themselves spontaneously to the effect that the appointment of Stalin to the Chairmanship of the Council of People's Commissars was the greatest historical event in the Soviet Union since its inception. Asked as to the reasons for this appointment, the three gentlemen after brief hesitation declared that the appointment of Stalin had been occasioned by the all too heavy burden carried by Molotov. When the disparity between cause and effect was pointed out to them, the three gentlemen consulted could make no further reply.[90]

For his part Schulenburg attributed the change to the recent mistakes in Soviet foreign policy which had led to a cooling off of the cordiality of German–Soviet relations, 'for the creation and preservation of which Stalin had consciously striven, while Molotov's own initiative often expended itself in an obstinate defence of individual positions'. However, Schulenburg also noted that Molotov kept his Kremlin office and staff, the only difference being a new name plate on the door, where the ambassador found him 'as amiable, self-assured, and well informed as ever'.[91]

To Hilger, the embassy counsellor, Stalin's action appeared as additional proof that the Soviet dictator was determined to keep his country out of a conflict with Germany for as long as he could and to 'use all the authority of his person and his official position to that end, if necessary'.[92]

Schulenburg, who was to die on a Nazi gallows for his part in the abortive anti-Hitler plot in July 1944, had recently returned from a brief visit to Berlin, convinced that Hitler had deliberately lied to him when he told him that he did not intend to attack the Soviet Union. 'The die has been cast,' he told his economic counsellor as soon as he stepped off the plane at Khodynka Field on 30 April. 'War against Russia has been decided!' A few days later, the ambassador told the Russians at considerable risk to himself. He did this at a private luncheon, to which he invited Dekanozov and Pavlov. The only other person present at this confidential meeting was Hilger, who preserved an account of what happened at it.

The two Germans did their best to convince Dekanozov how serious the situation had become and urged that his government should get in touch with Berlin before Hitler decided to strike. They told him at the outset that they were acting on their own responsibility and without the knowledge of their superiors, but Dekanozov kept asking with 'maddening stubbornness' whether they were speaking at the request of the German government, otherwise he could not transmit their statements to higher authority. 'You'll have to speak to Commissar Molotov,' he kept repeating.

Obviously, he could not imagine that we were knowingly and deliberately incurring the greatest danger for the purpose of making a last effort to save the peace. He must have believed that we were acting on Hitler's behalf and that we were trying to make the Kremlin take a step that would damage its prestige and its concrete interests. The more we talked to him, the more it became clear that he had no comprehension of the good will that moved us...

If I am correct in assuming that Stalin believed Hitler was bluffing, we have a plausible explanation as to why he disregarded the many warnings he was given. The very fact that several sources predicted the German invasion for the same date must have confirmed his suspicion that the story had been planted by the Germans. In any event, Dekanozov acted strictly according to Stalin's directives, who, true enough, wanted to appease Germany, but wished to do nothing that might betray his anxieties, because that might make Hitler even more intransigent in his demands. In short, Stalin had to act as if nothing was wrong with the German–Soviet relationship.[93]

During the succeeding weeks, Stalin continued to turn an apparently deaf ear to every piece of admonitory advice he received on Germany's intentions, while Hitler went ahead with his plans, dividing European Russia into regions of military government to be administered by Nazi Gauleiters. In a further attempt to appease the Fuehrer, Stalin expelled the diplomatic representatives of Belgium and Norway, and also closed down the legations of Yugoslavia and Greece. He even expedited the delivery of raw materials to Germany by express trains, such as rubber supplies from the Far East, and these kept on running almost to the moment that Hitler struck.

On 13 June Eden, who had resumed his post as Foreign Secretary in the Churchill Government, gave Maisky, the Soviet ambassador in London, detailed information about the latest German troop concentrations. In the event of an attack against the Soviet Union, Eden offered to send a British mission to Russia representing the three fighting services. Maisky, always in close touch with Moscow, replied that in his opinion the British had exaggerated the German concentrations and that Germany was not intending to attack Russia.

By way of confirmation, the same night the Soviet news agency Tass issued a communiqué, which was broadcast over the Moscow radio to the effect that 'both Germany and the Soviet Union are fulfilling to the letter the terms of the Soviet–German Non-Aggression Pact, so that in the opinion of Soviet circles the rumours of the intention of Germany to break the Pact and to launch an attack against the Soviet Union are completely without foundation, while the recent movements of German troops, which have completed their operations in the Balkans, to the eastern and northern parts of Germany, must be explained by other motives which have no connection with Soviet–German relations'.[94]

Again on 18 June, Maisky cabled Moscow that Cripps, who had been recalled to London for consultation, was 'deeply convinced of the inevitability of armed conflict between Germany and the USSR' and that the Germans had concentrated 147 divisions, including air force and service units along the Soviet borders.* Similar information from United States diplomatic representatives tended to confirm these views, and this was reinforced by a report from Stockholm that Marshal Goering had told a Swedish friend that Germany intended to attack almost at once. All this was passed on to Stalin, who left for his annual vacation in Sochi on 18 June, and it did not produce any apparent reaction. Meanwhile, strict orders were issued to the army to avoid all frontier incidents and 'provocations'.[95]

A day or two previously Admiral Kuznetsov, the Navy Commissar, had warned Molotov of the suspicious behaviour of the Germans in

* Eric Boheman, the permanent head of the Swedish Foreign Office at this time, claims the credit for having given Cripps this information at a dinner at the British Embassy in Stockholm, to which the ambassador Sir Victor Mallet had invited Boheman for the purpose of meeting Cripps when the latter was in transit from Moscow to London. According to Boheman, the Swedes had recently broken the German diplomatic cypher, and were therefore well informed about German intentions. 'I don't believe any negotiations will get under way before the attack is launched,' he told Cripps, without revealing the source of his information. 'It will come suddenly in one vast operation along the whole length of the front, in accordance with German practice.' He added that he was 'absolutely certain' that he was right and that the attack was timed to begin some time between 20 and 25 June. Boheman, who recounts this incident in his autobiography, states that he subsequently received a letter from Cripps in his own handwriting, thanking him warmly for the information he had given him. See Thomas Barman. *Diplomatic Correspondent*, p. 26, for a translation of the relevant passage in Boheman's autobiography (*Pä Vakt*, Stockholm, 1946) which is available only in Swedish.

withdrawing their merchant ships from all Soviet ports. But Molotov was unconvinced. 'Only a fool would attack us,' he said. Pondering on the behaviour of Stalin and his closest aides at this time, with the advantage of hindsight a quarter of a century later, Kuznetsov was inclined to draw the conclusion that 'right up to the last moment they did not believe in the possibility of an attack by Hitler. Stalin was unnerved and irritated by persistent reports (oral and written) about the deterioration of relations with Germany. He brushed facts and arguments aside more and more abruptly'. What finally convinced Stalin that a German attack was imminent was the news that all the German merchant ships had left Soviet waters.

At 2 p.m. on 21 June, General I. V. Tiulenev, the commander of Moscow District, received a telephone call from the Kremlin. 'Comrade Stalin will speak with you.'

The general heard a rather muffled voice at the other end of the line, which suggested that the call was being relayed from Sochi.

'Comrade Tiulenev, how do things stand with the anti-aircraft defence of Moscow?'

Tiulenev reported briefly on the anti-aircraft measures in force for that day.

'Note that the situation is uneasy,' said Stalin. 'You should bring the troops of Moscow's anti-aircraft defence to seventy-five per cent of combat readiness.'

As a result of this conversation, Tiulenev issued orders accordingly, and instructed his deputy not to send any units to camp on a training course which had been planned. He afterwards recalled that he 'got the impression that Stalin had received new information on the German war plans'. Later in the same afternoon Stalin telephoned a warning among others to Khrushchev in Kiev. He also issued orders to Timoshenko and Zhukov for a full combat alert, believing it possible that the attack would be launched that very night. Even so, the order seems to have been carried out in a haphazard manner and it did not reach many units for over twelve hours, by which time the blow had already fallen.[96]

Meanwhile in Berlin Ribbentrop had sent for Dekanozov and delivered a formal declaration of war. This was repeated by Schulenburg to Molotov in the Kremlin shortly before daybreak on 22 June.

'I know it is war,' said Molotov when the unhappy ambassador had finished reading the fatal telegram. 'Your aircraft have just bombarded some ten open villages. Can it really be that we have deserved this?'[97]

CHAPTER XI

Supreme Commander

I

Events quickly showed that the German invasion, launched in the early hours of 22 June 1941, came as a complete tactical surprise to the Soviet High Command. No attempt was made to blow the bridges over the river Bug to the south of Brest-Litovsk, which remained intact and undefended. Soviet troops were caught unprepared in their camps and barracks, and about two thousand Soviet planes were destroyed on the ground in the first lightning attack. 'We are being fired on. What shall we do?' was the desperate signal repeatedly intercepted by the German Army Group Centre, to which the reply would be, 'You must be insane. And why is your signal not in code?' The first order of the Red Army command, issued some three hours after the attack had begun, did not refer to war but merely 'unprecedented aggression', which was to be repelled in those areas where German troops had crossed the frontier, although the Soviet ground forces were forbidden to retaliate by crossing into Germany without special authorisation. For this Khrushchev was to blame Stalin, declaring that 'despite evident facts, he thought that the war had not yet started, that this was only a provocative action on the part of several undisciplined sections of the German army, and that our reaction might serve as a pretext for the Germans to begin the war'.[1]

However, as the morning of the fateful 22 June wore on it became only too clear that war had begun in deadly earnest and on a fifteen hundred mile front extending from Finland to the Black Sea. At

435

noon, Molotov went on the air and broke the news to the Soviet people, denouncing 'the Fascist brigands covered with blood' and the 'Nazi assassins', against whom 'our cause is just' and 'victory will be ours', as it had been in the struggle with Napoleon in 1812. The general public reaction was one of stupefaction, almost disbelief. For the past two years the Soviet press had been singing the praises of 'the great and brilliant Stalin, thanks to whose intelligence our country has not known the horrors of war'. Now the leader's intelligent policy was suddenly shown to be erroneous, a point barely concealed by Molotov when he remarked in his radio speech that Hitler had attacked the Soviet Union without any previous declaration of war or issue of an ultimatum. Stalin's silence also puzzled the public, particularly as no word from him was heard for nearly a fortnight.[2]

According to Khrushchev, Stalin remained completely inert during this period, taking no part in the direction of military operations and 'ceasing to do anything whatever'. ('He only returned to active leadership when some members of the Politburo visited him and told him that it was necessary to take certain steps immediately in order to improve the situation at the front'.) This theme of Stalin's inertia which runs through Khrushchev's famous 'secret' speech to the Twentieth Party Congress, is considerably exaggerated.[3] In fact, Stalin spent much of his time closeted with various advisers, including Beria, who was holidaying at Sukhum, or else on the direct line with Molotov and others in the Kremlin discussing mobilisation measures and strategic plans. An anonymous comrade of Stalin's youth, who called at the Sochi villa late in the afternoon of 23 June, found him sitting at his desk near a large map of the USSR which had not been there three days before. He looked tired and drawn, and his visitor gathered that he had spent most of the previous night talking to Molotov and Timoshenko, the Defence Commissar.

> He said the essential thing was to know what the attitude of the people would be towards German aggression. He expected the German propaganda to exploit the motives of anti-Semitism, and to attempt to obtain support among the older *kulaks* by waging a campaign against the collective farms...Stalin thinks the Red Army inferior in nothing to the *Wehrmacht*, provided the troops fight; he is convinced that they will hurl the Germans across the frontiers.[4]

On the same day a new command GHQ known as the *Stavka* was established, it was soon to be known as the *Stavka* of the Soviet

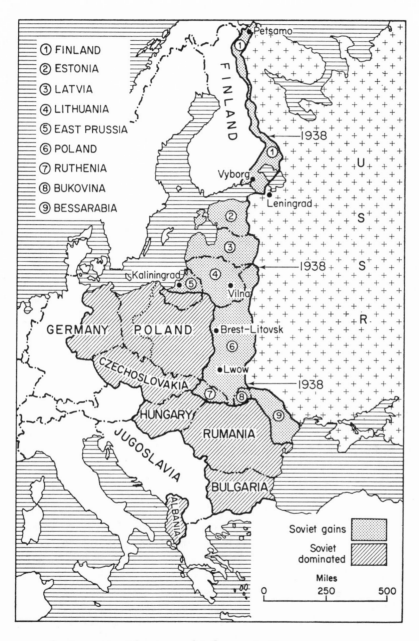

Soviet territorial gains and influence in Europe 1939–1947

437

Supreme Command. Largely organised by Shaposhnikov, it included the latter's brother marshals as well as General Zhukhov, Chief of Army Staff, in addition to Stalin and Molotov, who were *ex-officio* members. The top policy-making body, which largely superseded both the Council of Commissars and the Politburo, came into being on 30 June in the form of the State Defence Committee. Under Stalin's chairmanship it was charged with the overall direction of the war effort. The *Stavka* was theoretically subordinate to the Defence Committee, but since Stalin belonged to both bodies his authority was virtually supreme from the outset in the *Stavka* which met in more or less continuous session in his office, while the Defence Committee only assembled at irregular intervals. Besides Stalin, the Defence Committee consisted of Molotov, Voroshilov, Beria and Malenkov, responsible respectively for foreign relations, liaison between the armed forces and the civil authorities, domestic security and party matters. Beria had a particularly crucial role to play, since his duties included the supervision of the sinister 'rear security detachments', NKVD machine gunners who were to keep the Red Army units up to the mark by preventing unauthorised retreats and executing backsliders. Thus, far from doing nothing as Khrushchev claimed, Stalin was by no means inactive, although it was not until a fortnight or so after the outbreak of war that he took over from Timoshenko as Commissar of Defence, at the same time becoming Supreme Commander-in-Chief and head of the *Stavka*, while Marshal Shaposhnikov remained the military Chief of the General Staff.[5]

On the other hand, there is some evidence that Stalin came near to a nervous breakdown at this time. 'All that Lenin created we have lost for ever,' he is said to have exclaimed in a mood of despair when he learned that the Germans were advancing at the rate of some twenty miles a day all along the front. According to ambassador Maisky, Stalin locked himself in his study for several days and refused to see anyone, while to the embassy staff in London neither he nor Molotov 'showed any signs of life' and Maisky was consequently left without any instructions from Moscow for most of the first week of the war. That Stalin was still labouring under considerable nervous tension was evident, when for the first time since the outbreak of hostilities his voice was heard over the radio early in the morning of 3 July and at repeated intervals throughout the day.[6]

'Comrades, citizens, brothers and sisters, soldiers and sailors,' he began in slow and halting tones, 'it is to you, my dear friends, to all of you, that I am speaking.' It was an unusual style of address, which the leader had never used before and which he was never to use again. It

438

was also a laboured and colourless performance, punctuated by frequent pauses and audible drinking from a conveniently placed glass of liquid, which contrasted strangely with the important content of the message. Indeed it read much better than it sounded. Admittedly there was no attempt to disguise the stark seriousness of the military situation, but it was not a stirring appeal on the Churchillian lines 'blood, sweat and tears'. Nor was it delivered 'live' from the studio, although his vast audience had no means of knowing this. In fact, it had been recorded a day or two previously in Sochi; while it was being broadcast its author was actually in the train bound for Moscow, with frequent stops along the way, apparently to check for possible sabotage attempts on the track.

Stalin prefaced his account with the palpably untrue statement that 'the enemy's finest divisions and finest units of his air force had already been smashed and had met their doom on the field of battle'. Nevertheless, he added, the enemy continued to push forward. German troops had already occupied Lithuania, a great part of Latvia, and the western parts of Byelorussia and the Ukraine. 'Our troops have been obliged to fight a retreating action,' he continued. 'Our country is threatened with a great danger.' He went on to explain that the Germans had obtained an advantage by taking them by surprise and their forces were better prepared for war, and he tried somewhat lamely and disingenuously to justify the Nazi–Soviet non-aggression pact by saying it had enabled the Soviet Union to gain eight months in which to expedite its own preparations. He then called for the implementation of a 'scorched earth' policy, the formation of guerrilla units for sabotage behind the enemy lines. 'In occupied regions conditions must be made unbearable for the enemy and all his accomplices. They must be hounded and annihilated at every step, and all their measures frustrated.'

He made a passing reference 'with gratitude' to the promises of aid which had been immediately forthcoming from Churchill and Roosevelt. Recalling Russia's defeat of Napoleon, he declared that Hitler was no more invincible than Napoleon had been. As in 1812, Russia was fighting 'a national patriotic war', which was also a war for the freedom of all peoples.

Our war for the freedom of our Motherland will merge with the struggle of the peoples of Europe and America for their independence, for the democratic liberties. It will be a united front of the peoples who stand for freedom and against enslavement and threats of enslavement by Hitler's Fascist armies.

He concluded by calling upon the Soviet people to 'rally round the party of Lenin and Stalin', an oddly sounding reference to himself in the third person, and exhorted them 'Forward to victory'.[7]

While there could be no mercy for the enemy, whom he described as 'fiends and cannibals', neither could any mercy be shown in the Soviet ranks to 'whimperers and cowards, panicmongers and deserters', who must be treated with the utmost ruthlessness. On reaching his Kremlin office, Stalin lost no time in showing that he meant what he said. With the rapid crumbling of the Western and North-Western Fronts, a number of generals and their staffs headed by Pavlov, the local Army Group commander, were suspended from duty. Pavlov's successor General Eremenko assumed that 'Stalin's punishing hand' would stop with Pavlov's dismissal. In this he was mistaken, as evidenced by Colonel Starinov, a sapper officer, who was on a visit to Pavlov's headquarters at this time. 'Dmitrii Georgievich [Pavlov] did not suspect that both he and his closest associates would be immediately sacrificed in order to preserve the prestige of the "greatest and wisest sage" who had made a fool of himself,' wrote Starinov afterwards. 'Pavlov was immediately arrested and then shot. He shared his bitter fate with the Chief of Staff of the Army Group, General Klimovsky; the commander of the Army Group's Artillery, Lieutenant General Klich; and several others, without doubt commanders of great merit.' Other commanders were left in no doubt what to expect in the event of failure, even though like Pavlov they were not really responsible for the disasters for which they might be held blameworthy. Needless to add, the effect upon morale was most unhappy. People remembered the bloody events of 1937 in the army only too well. Small wonder was it that, when General I. E. Petrov was appointed to a frontal command in the south, he replied to the congratulations of his friends with the comment: 'So now they are going to shoot me *too*!'[8]*

The observant Colonel Starinov was especially struck by the arrest and execution of General Klich, of whose abilities he had formed a high opinion.

> I was convinced of his honesty and innocence. Wasn't it from Klich that I heard some two weeks before about the complacency of those at the top and about the fact that the country and the army were threatened by mortal danger and that careerists and blind men did not wish to recognise this? Klich was doing every-

* Petrov was more fortunate than Pavlov and his associates. For the alleged bungling of a landing operation in the Crimea, he was merely reduced in rank, being subsequently appointed to another senior command.

440

thing to raise the combat preparedness of the military district's artillery. But his tractors were being taken away from him; his personnel was being employed on defensive construction; his old guns with ammunition were being replaced by new guns without ammunition. What could Klich do about this? Protest? He did protest, but he was snubbed by those who stupidly and repetitiously asserted that 'Comrade Stalin knows all and takes care of everything'.[9]

His almost grudging thanks to Churchill for his spontaneous offer of help showed that Stalin was still suspicious of Britain and in particular of her Prime Minister whose record during the Civil War he had not forgotten and who he seems to have thought might conclude a separate peace with Germany at any moment, thus leaving the Soviet Union to her fate at the hands of the Fascist hordes. He was therefore relieved to learn that Stafford Cripps had just returned from London, bringing with him a British Military Mission and also a personal letter from Churchill. This time there was no delay in receiving the British ambassador. The meeting at which Cripps handed over Churchill's letter took place in the Kremlin on 8 July. 'We are all very glad here,' the British Premier had written from London, 'that the Russian armies are making such strong and spirited resistance to the utterly unprovoked and merciless invasion of the Nazis. There is general admiration of the bravery and tenacity of the soldiers and people. We shall do everything that time, geography and our growing resources allow...We have only got to go on fighting to beat the life out of these villains.'[10]

At the end of an hour's talk an understanding was reached by which Britain undertook to provide the Soviet Union with assistance of all kinds on the basis of 'mutual help without any precision as to quantity or quality', while neither country was to negotiate or conclude a separate peace except with the other's consent. Still inclined to be mistrustful, Stalin insisted on the understanding being embodied in a formal written document to be signed in Moscow. Three days later the 'Agreement for Joint Action between His Majesty's Government in the United Kingdom and the Government of the USSR' was duly signed in the Kremlin by Cripps and Molotov on behalf of their respective countries, in the presence of Stalin and a host of other Russian officials, including Litvinov who had been recalled from the obscurity in which he had been living for the past two years and who was shortly to be appointed Soviet ambassador in Washington. A supplementary protocol provided that the agreement was to come into effect immediately so that no ratification was necessary.[11]

Stalin was unable during these hectic days to reply to Churchill's letter until 18 July, by which date Smolensk had fallen and the German panzer troops were pushing on towards Moscow, less than two hundred miles away. 'I have no doubt that in spite of the difficulties our two States will be strong enough to crush our common enemy,' wrote Stalin. He added that 'perhaps it is not out of place to mention that the position of the Soviet forces at the front remains tense.'[12] This last remark was indeed an understatement, since the front was far from stable and in the course of the enemy's three-pronged drive towards Leningrad in the north, Moscow in the centre, and the Ukraine and the Caucasus in the south, enormous numbers of Soviet troops and equipment had been captured, amounting to 635,000 prisoners, 6,400 tanks and nearly 6,000 guns. The prisoners included Yakov (Yasha) Djugashvili, Stalin's only son by his first wife, who had joined the Red Army as a lieutenant of artillery and had been sent to the front on the outbreak of hostilities. He was captured near Smolensk. He told his interrogators that he had no special privileges as Stalin's son, but said that Stalin had said goodbye to him on the telephone as he was leaving for the front. As a prisoner, he was taken to see Goering, whom he is said to have astonished by predicting that Russia would become the mightiest political, scientific and economic power in the world.

There were also thousands of deserters from the Soviet ranks to the enemy, while many civilians particularly in the Ukraine welcomed the advancing German armies as liberators. It was only when Hitler appeared in his true colours as a brutal and merciless conqueror that the inhabitants of the occupied territories realised that they were merely exchanging one form of domestic tyranny for another, if anything worse.[13]

In his letter to Churchill Stalin made a request which he was to repeat with monotonous frequency during the next two years – that Britain should open a second front against Hitler in northern France. He also asked for an additional front in Norway against the Finns who had come into the war on Hitler's side with the intention of recovering their frontiers as of 1939.

> A frontier in Northern France could not only divert Hitler's forces from the East, but would at the same time make it impossible for Hitler to invade Great Britain. The establishment of the front just mentioned would be popular with the British Army, as well as with the whole population of Southern England.[14]

This demand was completely unrealistic and merely reflected Stalin's ignorance of current British military commitments, not to mention the feelings of the population of southern England, whose contribution to the war effort under Churchill's inspiring leadership was already total. It only remained for Churchill to point out the futility of attempting to mount any such front likely to be 'of the slightest use to you', in view of the fact that the Germans had forty divisions alone in France and had been busily fortifying the coast for more than a year with cannon, wire, pill-boxes and beach-mines. Britain's resources were already strained to the utmost in fighting the Battle of the Atlantic against German submarines and aircraft as well as in the Middle East campaign. Nor was it any more feasible to land troops in German-occupied Norway in the perpetual daylight which prevailed at this time of the year without reasonable fighter air cover, which was simply not available. The most Churchill could promise was to harass German troops and supply transports in northern waters and to furnish Stalin with certain raw materials for which he had asked, such as rubber, tin and woollen cloth, as well as two hundred Tomahawk fighter aircraft and up to two million ankle boots.[15]

On 28 July 1941, Churchill gave Stalin advance notice by cable that President Roosevelt was sending his close friend and personal representative Mr Harry Hopkins to Moscow to negotiate further supplies of war material from American sources. 'I must tell you that there is a flame in this man for democracy and to beat Hitler,' telegraphed Churchill. 'You can trust him absolutely. He is your friend and our friend. He will help you to plan for the future victory and for the long-term supply of Russia. You could talk to him also freely about policy, strategy and Japan.'[16]

2

Having shot those generals who in his opinion had failed in their duty, Stalin turned his attention to the reconstitution of the Red Army command. Three major commands were created, corresponding roughly to the opposing German army groups in the field. The most important of these was the Western under Timoshenko, which was responsible for the defence of Moscow. The others were the North-Western covering the Baltic and Leningrad, and the South-Western which covered the Ukraine; these were respectively entrusted by Stalin to his old Civil War cronies Voroshilov and Budenny. Each commander had a top political commissar attached to his staff with the rank of Lieutenant General, Zhdanov being assigned to Voroshilov, Bulganin to Timoshenko, and Khrushchev to Budenny. This system of political commissars, which had been a conspicuous feature of the Red Army during the Civil War, was duplicated throughout the command in order to ensure each unit's conduct in battle and 'its unflinching readiness to fight to the last drop of blood the enemies of our native land'. The other outstanding figure in the command structure was Zhukov, who relinquished his staff job to Shaposhnikov and was dispatched to the front – or rather to whatever section of it his presence from time to time seemed most necessary as Stalin's principal troubleshooter. When Timoshenko departed to take up his command, Stalin assumed the office of Defence Commissar, which Timoshenko had previously held since Voroshilov's ouster at the time of the débâcle of the Finnish war. Stalin's personal authority was finally established early in August when he was named Supreme Commander of the Soviet Union over the entire field of military operations or, as he later came to be styled, Generalissimo.[17]

The war memoirs which the more senior ranking Soviet officers were permitted and indeed encouraged to publish during the Khrushchev era in the 1960s enable us to form a detailed picture of Stalin in action. Unlike Churchill he seldom if ever visited the troops in the front line to hearten them with stirring words, but remained for the most part immured in the operations room at Supreme Headquarters which had been set up in his suite in the Kremlin and was duplicated in a bomb-proof air raid shelter below the building. Here he kept an extremely tight control over every aspect of the war. At the same time he was quick to assimilate the advice of his military and technical experts, who briefed him well, and for his part he proved himself a rapid learner. The General Staff was required to report to him three times every twenty-four hours, by telephone between ten and eleven in the morning and four and five in the afternoon, and in person at nine or ten in the evening. The latter session often lasted throughout much of the night. Sometimes these late sessions took place at Kuntsevo, but more often than not in the Kremlin. General Sergei Shtemenko, Stalin's forty-year-old Deputy Chief of Operations, has recalled how after a summons by telephone he and his Chief, General Antonov, would set off by car through the deserted streets, entering the Kremlin by the Borovitsky Gate, they would then circle the building of the Supreme Soviet and finally swing into the 'little corner' where Stalin's apartment and private office were located. After passing through the private secretary Poskrebyshev's office and the ante-room of the chief of Stalin's personal guard, they would be admitted to the large main office, which overlooked the river. On one wall hung huge portraits of Suvorov and Kutusov, the two most famous field marshals in Russian history, who were thus elevated to places of honour beside the more familiar likenesses of Marx and Lenin.

On the left-hand side, not far from the wall, stood a long, rect-angular table. Shtemenko and Antonov would roll out their maps on it and use them to report on each army group in detail, starting with the one where major action was taking place at the given moment. No notes were made in advance, as they knew the situation by heart, and it was clearly marked on the maps. At the end of the table, in a corner of the floor, stood a large globe. This was the globe on which, according to a much-quoted passage in Khrushchev's 'secret' speech, Stalin used to plan operations. ('Yes, comrades, he used to take the globe and trace the front line on it.') It is only fair to observe that this contention is not borne out by any of the military witnesses. 'I must say that in the many hundreds of times I visited this office,' Shtemenko has written, 'I never once saw the globe used in a discussion of operational questions.' It is possible, however, that Stalin may have occasionally pointed out places on the globe to visitors if a map was not immediately available.

Other military experts and civilians as well as members of the Polit-buro were often present at these briefings, the civilians sitting opposite the military on the other side of the long table. According to Shte-menko, Stalin used to pace up and down behind the officers as he listened. From time to time, he would go over to his desk, which stood far back on the right, take two cigarettes, tear them open, and stuff the tobacco into his pipe. All orders were signed by Stalin and the Chief of the General Staff Shaposhnikov – later by Vasilevsky after Shaposhni-kov's retirement through ill-health in 1942 – or else by Antonov or Shtemenko when the staff chiefs were absent. Usually Shtemenko wrote out the orders to Stalin's dictation. The text would then be read aloud and corrected by Stalin as the reading proceeded, after which the orders would if urgent be immediately transmitted to the front from the adjacent communications room without being first typed up. So far as incoming documents were concerned, Stalin refused to look at any proposal or draft directive unless it had first been cleared with the de-partment or branch concerned, which could not take even the smallest initiative without Stalin's prior approval. 'He could not tolerate the decision of even secondary matters,' wrote Chief Marshal of Artillery Voronov after the war. 'But people were often afraid to report to him. For that reason many innovations in every possible area were arti-ficially delayed. This caused a great deal of harm.'[18]

It was often three or four o'clock in the morning before Stalin's generals were released and able to return to their officers to implement their latest instructions. According to Shtemenko, Stalin personally regulated the timetable of the General Staff, allowing them only a few hours rest usually in the morning or afternoon.

The rigid work schedule that Stalin had established and no one could change, its excessive volume and urgency, made service on the General Staff extremely exhausting and difficult; it demanded enormous physical and moral resources. It meant work to the point of exhaustion, which not every man could take, the more so because, as a rule, men were dismissed from the General Staff for the slightest mistake, with all the ensuing consequences. It was not by chance, therefore, that a number of officers and generals of the General Staff suffered nervous exhaustion and prolonged heart trouble, and many of them went into the reserve immediately after the war without having served to their retirement age.[19]

For the first year of the fighting Stalin relied largely on the advice of the two Marshals Shaposhnikov and Timoshenko and also on that of George Zhukov, the legendary commander who never lost a battle. While the first two were to be eventually discarded, Shaposhnikov through ill-health and Timoshenko for the failure of the Soviet offensive on the South-Western Front in the same year, Zhukov's influence steadily increased. This was due in large part to the effective steps Zhukov took to defend first Leningrad and then Moscow. For old times' sake Stalin tolerated Voroshilov, but after he had failed to prevent the virtual encirclement of Leningrad in the early months of the war and had consequently been replaced by Zhukov in command of the North-Western Front, Voroshilov received no further military command, although Stalin kept him on as a member of the State Defence Committee and took him along to various allied conferences. Moreover, Voroshilov and his political commissar Zhdanov were called 'specialists in retreat' by Stalin to their faces.

On his arrival at the command headquarters in the Smolny, Zhukov telephoned Supreme Headquarters in Moscow in Voroshilov's presence and asked Vasilevsky who answered to tell Stalin that he had taken over the command and proposed 'to proceed more actively than my predecessor'. Visibly shaken, Voroshilov left the room without a word and flew back to Moscow after bidding his staff a sorrowful farewell. 'They have called me to headquarters,' he said. 'Well, I'm old and it has to be! This isn't the Civil War – it has to be fought in another way.' There is little doubt that he expected to face a firing squad when he got to Moscow. He was indeed lucky to escape the fate of Pavlov and others who had been relieved of their commands at this time.[20]

General Sir Alan Brooke, the British Chief of the Imperial General

Staff, who accompanied Churchill on several of his wartime meetings with Stalin, formed a poor view of Voroshilov's professional ability as compared with Shaposhnikov. He found his military knowledge 'painfully limited, as exemplified by his questions which were entirely childish. There was no difficulty in dealing with the questions, but the reply was never absorbed and the same question was reiterated unendingly'. Brooke could not remember a single instance in which Stalin sought Voroshilov's advice in all their meetings. ('Voroshilov is an attractive personality, but the typical political general who owes his life at present to his wits in the past.') The sixty-year-old Boris Shaposhnikov, on the other hand, had 'a well-trained military brain', though he looked 'terribly ill and worn out'.[21] He suffered from heart trouble. But until his health completely broke down, he was generally regarded as Stalin's 'military mentor', although he seems to have deferred to him in most matters, sometimes with tragic results in the field of battle. He came from a well-to-do family of Moscow merchants and belonged to the old school of professional staff officers, accustomed to give unquestioned obedience to the Commander-in-Chief. 'My dear fellow, there is nothing I can do,' he would answer Zhukov's objections to a strategically erroneous order. 'It is the Chief's personal decision.' Of the same elderly vintage as Shaposhnikov and Voroshilov was Semyon Timoshenko, a former peasant from Bessarabia and later like Budenny a dashing cavalry officer during the Civil War; tall, square-jawed and grim-faced, he was generally credited with having halted the German *blitzkreig* at Smolensk, but before long he too was to give way to the younger generation of commander of the type of Zhukov and Rokossovsky. Incidentally, Timoshenko was one of the very few top Soviet commanders who was to refrain from writing his war memoirs.

Of all Stalin's generals, George Konstaninovich Zhukov, then in his middle forties, was the one most after Stalin's heart. Like Stalin, he came of peasant stock and was the son of a village shoemaker. Heavily set and handsome looking, he was a stern disciplinarian, ruthless with subordinates and never sparing in his use of manpower, regardless of the high cost of human lives. 'If we come to a mine field, our infantry attack exactly as if it were not there,' he was to tell General Eisenhower. 'The losses we get from personnel mines we consider only equal to those we would have gotten from machine guns and artillery if the Germans had chosen to defend the area with strong bodies of troops instead of mine fields.'[22] He enjoyed Stalin's confidence and respect probably more than any other Soviet commander and even achieved some dominance over him, particularly during the battle for Moscow. But, though he was never afraid to argue with Stalin,

Zhukov knew when to drop the argument, even when he knew that Stalin was wrong.

During the Moscow battle, Stalin received news that the town of Dedovsk had fallen to the Germans. This was barely twenty miles from the capital to the north-west, not far from Kuntsevo, so that Stalin was considerably alarmed. He called Zhukov on the field telephone.

'Do you know that they've occupied Dedovsk?'

'No, Comrade Stalin, I didn't know that.'

'A commander should know what's going on at the front!' Stalin retorted angrily. He then ordered Zhukov to proceed immediately to the spot and 'personally organise a counter-attack and retake Dedovsk'. When Zhukov protested that it would be unwise to leave the front headquarters at such a critical moment in the fighting, he was promptly overruled. 'Never mind, we'll get along somehow. Leave Sokolovsky [the Chief of Staff] in charge.'

After Stalin had rung off, Zhukov made inquiries, only to learn that the Germans had not taken Dedovsk at all, but a village called Dedovo considerably further to the west and consisting of a few scattered houses on the side of a steep ravine. Although the village was of no tactical importance whatever, nevertheless Zhukov deemed it prudent to leave his headquarters and dispatch a rifle company and two tanks to drive the Germans out of the houses, a wasteful and wholly unnecessary operation. When this had been accomplished, he duly reported to Stalin, 'who received the information without comment'.[23]

According to Khrushchev, Stalin never visited any sector of the front except once when the situation along the Mozhaisk defence line had been stabilised and he ventured some distance along the Mozhaisk Highway beyond Kuntsevo.[24] No doubt this was the occasion which inspired the painting entitled 'Stalin at the Front near Moscow, 1941' and reproduced at this time in innumerable posters and cards. It showed the Supreme Commander looking much taller than his actual size and standing at the edge of a forest in a heavy fur coat with binoculars trained on Soviet troops who were attacking German positions. However, as will be related in due course, on at least one other occasion he is believed to have come quite close to the front fighting.

Being sent for by Stalin could be a terrifying and unnerving experience. The sapper Colonel Starinov has described the preliminaries, the search for weapons at the Kremlin entrance, and the atmosphere in Stalin's ante-room as it began to fill up. Starinov's immediate neighbour on one of his visits was 'a solid, painstakingly combed and shaved man with a file of papers in his carefully tended hands', who appeared very agitated, as he tried to read the newspapers, opened his file, leafed through its contents, closed it again, and kept looking at his watch.

Time passed. I noticed that those who were acquainted with the waiting room employees, and hence not there for the first time, were considerably more perturbed than those who in all probability were there for the first time. But now a slight noise passed through the room. My neighbour suddenly turned pale. No one said anything, but it was clear to everyone that 'the boss' had arrived. My neighbour wiped drops of sweat from his brow and dried his hands on a handkerchief. In a few minutes, people began to be called in. Soon my neighbour also rose. When the receptionist finally called him by name, he went livid, wiped his trembling hands on his handkerchief, picked up his file of papers, and went with hesitant steps. I remembered my General's parting words to me: 'Don't get excited. Don't think of disagreeing with anything. Comrade Stalin knows everything.'[25]

Although it belongs to a later period in the war, the following incident concerning the army group commander Konstantin Rokossovsky may be conveniently mentioned here. Rokossovsky, a Pole by birth who began his career as a construction worker and was to end up as a Marshal of the Soviet Union and a Marshal of Poland, once dared to argue with Stalin that it was better to breach the enemy's defence line in two sectors rather than in one as Stalin desired. Twice the commander was sent out of Stalin's office into the next room to 'think it over'. On the second occasion his meditations were interrupted by Malenkov and Molotov. 'Don't forget where you are and whom you are talking to, General,' said Malenkov. 'You are disagreeing with Comrade Stalin.' 'You'll have to agree,' added Molotov. 'Agree – that's all there is to it!' But Rokossovsky, who had stood up to three years of pretty rough treatment in prison during the Red Army purge before the war, refused to yield.

'So what is better – two weak blows or one strong blow?' asked Stalin when Rokossovsky went back for the second time.

'Two strong blows are better than one strong blow,' answered Rokossovsky.

'But which of them should be primary in your opinion?'

'They should both be primary.'

There was an ominous silence of the kind which was usually the prelude to an explosion of Stalin's rage. But to the surprise of all present, nothing of the kind happened. Stalin merely remarked, as if musing to himself, 'Can it be that two blows are really better?' The upshot was that Stalin gave in and Rokossovsky had his way. According to the version published on the occasion of Rokossovsky's seventieth birthday in 1966, Stalin smoked his pipe in silence for a minute or two. Then he came up to the commander, put his hand on his shoulder, and said: 'You know, Rokossovsky is right. And generally I like a commander who sticks to his guns. I confirm your decision, Comrade Rokossovsky.'[26]

If Stalin did not spare his generals, he certainly did not spare himself, and his overwork left its mark. General P. A. Belov, a corps commander who had not seen him since 1933, was shocked by his appearance in the latter part of 1941, when they met in the Kremlin air raid shelter. ('Before me stood a short man, with a tired, haggard face. In eight years he seemed to have aged twenty. His eyes had lost their old steadiness; his voice lacked assurance.') By this date, the diplomatic corps and most of the government departments had been evacuated five hundred miles eastwards to Kuibyshev, as Moscow was gravely threatened by the German advance. Stalin was obviously very shaken, which may account for the way in which he deferred to Zhukov, who was also present. According to Belov, Zhukov spoke to Stalin in a sharp, commanding tone. ('It looked as if Zhukov was really the superior officer here. And Stalin accepted this as proper.') At times, according to this witness, a kind of baffled look crossed Stalin's face.[27] Apart from Zhukov none of Stalin's generals dared to stand up to him in this fashion with the exception of Rokossovsky and Antonov, the Chief of Operations, who eventually succeeded Vasilevsky as head of the General Staff.

With foreign visitors whom he considered it politic to receive, Stalin appeared much more self-assured. By the time Harry Hopkins arrived at the end of July 1941, he seems to have completely recovered from his previous nervous malaise. Hopkins was impressed by the way in which he phrased his demands for anti-aircraft and machine guns, rifles and aluminium for aircraft manufacture. 'There was no waste of word, gesture, nor mannerism. It was like talking to a perfectly co-ordinated machine, an intelligent machine. Joseph Stalin knew what he wanted, knew what Russia wanted, and he assumed that you knew.' Apart from a few occasions when Stalin required further information on a particular point raised by Hopkins, when he pressed a button and an alert secretary immediately appeared with the answer, there was only one interruption in the course of their four-hour conversation. That was when the telephone rang and Stalin explained apologetically that he was making arrangements for his supper at 12.30 a.m.

450

This is how he appeared to President Roosevelt's special emissary:

No one could forget the picture of the dictator of Russia as he stood watching me leave – an austere, rugged, determined figure in boots that shone like mirrors, stout baggy trousers, and snug-fitting blouse. He wore no ornament, military or civilian. He's built close to the ground, like a football coach's dream of a tackle...His hands are huge, as hard as his mind. His voice is harsh, but ever under control. What he says is all the accent and inflection his words need...

He offered me one of his cigarettes and took one of mine. He's a chain smoker, probably accounting for the harshness of his carefully controlled voice. He laughs often enough, but it's a short laugh, somewhat sardonic, perhaps. There is no small talk in him. His humour is keen, penetrating. He speaks no English, but as he shot rapid Russian at me he ignored the interpreter, looking straight into my eyes as though I understood every word he uttered.

Incidentally, the interpreter on this occasion was Maxim Litvinov, who had not yet left to take up his new appointment in Washington. To Hopkins he seemed like 'a morning coat which had been laid away in moth-balls when Russia retreated into isolation from the West, but which had now been brought out, dusted off, and aired as a symbol of completely changed conditions'.

Stalin made one extraordinary request when he asked Hopkins 'to tell the President that he would welcome American troops on any part of the Russian front under the complete command of the American Army'.

Hopkins replied that his mission related solely to matters of supply and that the matter of US participation in the war would be decided largely by Hitler himself and 'his encroachment upon our fundamental interests'. He added that he doubted that the US Government in the event of war would want an American army in Russia, but that he would pass Stalin's request on to President Roosevelt.[28]

Nothing more was heard of this request, and Stalin does not seem to have referred to it again. But he continued to harp on the need for a second front in his cables to Churchill. At the beginning of September, when as he told Churchill 'we have lost more than one-half of the Ukraine and the enemy is at the gates of Leningrad', he begged for a diversion 'somewhere in the Balkans'. But a few days later he changed this request to one for the landing of from twenty-five to thirty British

451

divisions in Archangel or else their transport through Persia to the southern regions of the USSR. To Churchill and his hard pressed war cabinet, which had experienced the greatest difficulty in raising and equipping two divisions for dispatch to the Middle East theatre, Stalin's request was completely unrealistic. 'It is almost incredible that the head of the Russian Government with all the advice of their military experts could have committed himself to such absurdities,' Churchill reflected afterwards. 'It seemed hopeless to argue with a man thinking in terms of utter unreality.'[29]

3

After Hopkins had reported to President Roosevelt during the Atlantic Conference with Churchill, which took place in a warship off the coast of Newfoundland in August, there was an immediate agreement that aid to Russia on a big scale was essential.* To this end a high powered Anglo-American supply mission was dispatched to Moscow in the following month. It was headed on the British side by the Minister of Aircraft Production Lord Beaverbrook, a tough and outspoken press lord from Canada, who was described by Churchill in his letter of introduction to Stalin as one of his oldest and most intimate friends. The service members included General Sir Hastings Ismay, Churchill's dedicated personal representative on the British Chiefs of Staff Committee, who was stated by Churchill to be 'thoroughly acquainted with the whole field of our military policy' and was 'authorised to study

---

* William Bullitt, the former ambassador to the Soviet Union, unsuccessfully tried to persuade President Roosevelt at this time that in return for Lend-Lease to Russia he should ask for 'definite, written, public pledges from Stalin that the Soviet Union renounce all claim to any territorial rights or privileges she did not already possess in China and other areas of the Far East; and that the post-war boundaries of the Soviet Union on the European side should be those of August 1939'. According to Bullitt, he warned the President strongly against Soviet imperialism. 'I don't dispute the logic of your reasoning,' replied Roosevelt. 'I just have a hunch that Stalin is not that kind of man. Harry [Hopkins] says he's not ... and I think that if I give him everything I possibly can and ask nothing from him in return, *noblesse oblige*, he won't try to annex anything and will work with me for a world of democracy and peace.'

Bullitt reminded the President that, 'when he talked of *noblesse oblige* he was not speaking of the Duke of Norfolk, but of a Caucasian bandit whose only thought when he got something for nothing was that the other fellow was an ass'. Bullitt's agitated remarks irritated Roosevelt, who showed it as he terminated the interview. 'It's my responsibility not yours,' he said; 'and I'm going to play my hunch.' Events were to prove Roosevelt wrong and his former adviser correct. See Beatrice Farnsworth. *William C. Bullitt and the Soviet Union.* (1967), pp. 3 and 173.

with your commanders any plans for practical co-operation which may suggest themselves'. Since Hopkins was too unwell to make the journey again, the Americans were led by the President's roving ambassador, Mr W. Averell Harriman, who was described by Churchill in the same letter as 'a remarkable American, wholeheartedly devoted to the victory of the common cause'.[30]

Beaverbrook and Harriman had their first meeting with Stalin in the Kremlin during the evening of 28 September and they met again on the two following evenings, each meeting lasting for three hours. On the first occasion they were accompanied by Cripps and Steinhardt, who presented their respective principals to the Supreme Commander. When this had been done, Beaverbook somewhat surprisingly asked the British ambassador to withdraw, which Cripps reluctantly did, barely concealing his annoyance at this departure from diplomatic protocol. In the circumstances his American colleague felt that he had no alternative but to follow suit.* Otherwise the utmost cordiality prevailed at this meeting. As he had done with Hopkins, Stalin gave a candid review of the military situation, stressing that the *Wehrmacht*'s three or four to one preponderance over the Russians in tanks was absolutely essential to the Germans, for without it their infantry was weak compared with the Soviet infantry. He said that of Germany's satellites the best fighters were the Finns, next the Italians (who he estimated had ten divisions in the Eastern theatre), third the Roumanians and last of all the Hungarians. Stalin went into considerable detail as to what he wanted, stressing that his greatest need was for tanks and after that anti-tank guns, medium bombers, anti-aircraft guns, armour plate, and fighter and reconnaissance planes. High on the list was barbed wire, for which Stalin asked the Americans for four hundred tons a month, a request which Harriman was unexpectedly able to satisfy after cabling Washington.

On this occasion, Stalin did not particularly press for the opening of a second front in the west, although he suggested that the British might send an expeditionary force to the Ukraine. When Beaverbrook pointed out that British units were being built up in Persia and these might be moved into the Caucasus, Stalin replied brusquely: 'There is no war in the Caucasus, but there is in the Ukraine.' Beaverbrook's suggestion that Anglo-Soviet staff talks might be initiated in order to

* Steinhardt afterwards told Harriman privately that in his opinion Beaverbrook's request had been prompted by the recognition in London of 'a lack of mutual confidence between the British and the Russians' and the decision to start the negotiations with 'a clean slate'. *Foreign Relations of the United States Diplomatic Papers 1941*. I, p. 837.

plan joint strategy met with an equally negative response. When Harriman offered to deliver American planes by the Alaskan route with American crews, Stalin rejected this as 'too dangerous', considering it a risk likely to provoke Japan.

Stalin then raised the question of enemy reparations when peace came. 'What about getting the Germans to pay for the damage?'

'We must win the war first,' said Beaverbrook realistically.

Finally Harriman mentioned President Roosevelt's concern about the state of American public opinion, particularly on the subject of anti-religious propaganda among the Soviet youth and the restriction of religious worship in Russia. To this Stalin replied that he did not know much about American public opinion on the Soviet Union and he gave Harriman the impression that he did not attach much importance to it. As it was getting late, Harriman did not press the matter but promised to send Stalin a memorandum on it.[31]

The interpreter throughout the meetings was Maxim Litvinov, who had also interpreted at the meetings with Hopkins. On the first occasion, he appeared in a shabby suit and broken shoes, a fact which Stalin was quick to note was not lost on Beaverbrook. Consequently on the next evening Litvinov appeared considerably smartened up. According to Beaverbrook, Litvinov performed his duties as interpreter with competence. But there was always a door open with a dark room beyond it where Beaverbrook was convinced that someone was listening in so as to check Litvinov's translations. On the other hand, Harriman, who in some ways was less perceptive than the British representative, did not consider that the open door had any sinister significance.[32]

Next evening the atmosphere completely changed. Stalin was very restless, pacing up and down the room and smoking continuously; he seemed to his visitors to be under an intense strain. At times he appeared discourteous and uninterested. When Beaverbrook handed him Churchill's letter – presumably this was not done at the first meeting since there was no time to have a translation prepared – Stalin opened it and merely glanced at the contents leaving it on the table unread throughout the meeting. As Beaverbook and Harriman were preparing to leave, Molotov who was present reminded his master of the letter, upon which Stalin thrust it back into the envelope and handed it to a clerk. During the meeting Stalin made three telephone calls, each time dialling the number himself. Neither Beaverbook nor Harriman could account for Stalin's peculiar mood, but they guessed that he had just received some alarming news about the German drive on Moscow. (In fact, Guderian's panzers had broken through in the

Orel sector and in a rapid advance were about to capture the town while the trams were still running.)

'Why is it,' Stalin asked Harriman, 'that the United States can only give me one thousand tons of armour plate steel for tanks – a country with a production of over fifty million tons?' Harriman, who had considerable knowledge of the steel industry, tried to explain the length of time required to increase production capacity, but Stalin brushed this aside with the remark: 'One only has to add alloys!' Only once did he show any enthusiasm. That was when Harriman mentioned the American offer of five thousand jeeps. Stalin asked for more. Harriman countered with an offer of ordinary armoured cars, to which Stalin replied that in his view armoured cars were death traps and he did not want any.[33]

No wonder Harriman described the evening in his report to Roosevelt as 'pretty hard sledding'. Meanwhile Ismay and the other military members of the mission fared no better with their Soviet opposite numbers. Afterwards Ismay wrote:

The discussions were frustrating and achieved nothing. When we tried to elucidate the basis of their astronomical requirements of equipment, we could get no answer out of them. We asked, for example, how many anti-tank guns were allotted to a division, adding that our divisions had seventy-two. The reply was, 'It depends on what sort of division.' When we suggested that an infantry division might be taken as an example, the reply was, 'That depends on where it has to fight.' It became obvious that the Soviet Generals were not authorised to give information of any kind, and that to try to do business with them was a waste of time.[34]

Ismay was surprised to find the Russian soldiery, both officers and other ranks were most punctilious about saluting. This caused Ismay's Royal Marine orderly some embarrassment. In his blue uniform, he was by far the smartest member of the mission, but the red band on his cap was apparently misleading. 'It is very awkward, sir, to be saluted by Russian generals,' he told Ismay. The only advice which the British general could give his servant was to 'acknowledge their compliments handsomely'. Indeed the Royal Marine orderly became quite a legendary figure, and one of Ismay's favourite stories about him was much relished by Churchill, though it must be admitted that it has an apocryphal ring. Even so, it illustrated the strange atmosphere in which these meetings took place.

The Marine was being shown the sights of Moscow by an Intourist guide. 'This,' said the guide, 'is the Eden Hotel, formerly Ribbentrop Hotel. Here is Churchill Street, formerly Hitler Street. Here is the Beaverbrook railway station, formerly the Goering railway station. Will you have a cigarette, comrade?' The Marine took the proferred cigarette, remarking as he did so, 'Thank you, comrade, formerly bastard!'[35]

On the third day of the talks, the German radio by some intuitive guesswork broadcast stories that bitter quarrels had developed and that the British and Americans could never find common ground with the 'Bolshevists'. When Beaverbrook and Harriman went to the Kremlin to resume the discussion in the evening Stalin mentioned the Nazi propaganda with some amusement, remarking that it was for the three of them to prove Goebbels a liar. This time the atmosphere was quite different from the previous evening, once more all cordiality. In Beaverbrook's words, it was sunshine after rain. Beaverbrook now went through a memorandum listing everything Stalin had asked for, indicating those items on which the Soviet demands could not be met immediately, and then a large number which could be satisfied at once with some additional items thrown in. At the end of the recitation, Beaverbrook asked Stalin if he was pleased with the result, on which Stalin replied that he received the list 'with enthusiasm'. Indeed he sent for tea and food, the first time that refreshments had been produced during the talks. 'It was obviously the result of his pleased excitement,' noted Beaverbrook. It also prompted Litvinov, who was interpreting, to bound out of his chair and exclaim 'Now we shall win the war!'

Another incident noted by the observant Beaverbrook was that while Litvinov was translating Stalin would doodle on a pad on the table, 'drawing numberless pictures of wolves on paper and filling in the background with red pencil'. Again Stalin emphasised the need for the greatest possible number of jeeps and also for American three-ton trucks, repeating what he had told his generals more than once that the outcome of the war depended on the petrol engine and that the country with the biggest production of this commodity would be the ultimate victor.

One subject in which Beaverbrook knew Stalin was bound to be interested, although it was not strictly relevant to the business in hand, was the dramatic flight of Hitler's deputy Rudolf Hess. Beaverbrook was well primed with the latest news on this topic. He told Stalin that Hess had reached an advanced stage of paranoia and that he believed that attempts were being made to drug him. Once he had tried to commit suicide by throwing himself over the stairs and in doing so had broken his thigh on a banister. Stalin, who seemed quite amused by this description, said he thought Hess had gone to Scotland not at the request of Hitler but with Hitler's knowledge. Beaverbrook agreed with this interpretation. His view of Hess's extraordinary mission was that the Deputy Fuehrer had come under the impression that 'with a small group of British aristocrats a counter-Churchill government could be set up to make peace with Germany which would be welcomed by the majority of the British. Germany with British aid would then attack Russia'.

This exchange prompted Harriman to express the hope that Stalin would feel free to cable Roosevelt directly on any matters that he considered of importance, and he assured Stalin that the American President would welcome such messages, just as he did those from Churchill. Stalin replied that 'he was glad to hear this, as he had previously felt that he should not presume to address the President directly'. When Beaverbrook suggested that it would be highly desirable for Stalin to have a face-to-face meeting with Churchill, Stalin also agreed, adding that in his view the present Anglo-Soviet agreement should be converted into a formal treaty of alliance, not only for war but for post-war. Beaverbrook answered that he personally favoured this idea and believed it was an opportune time to take it up with Churchill and the British cabinet.

'The meeting broke up in the most friendly fashion possible,' wrote Harriman afterwards. 'Stalin made no effort to conceal his enthusiasm. It was my impression that he was completely satisfied that Great Britain and America meant business.' As they were leaving, Molotov spoke briefly to Stalin in Russian, whereupon Stalin said he hoped that the two visitors would have dinner with him the next evening. The invitation was accepted.[36]

The dinner, which turned out to be a banquet at which nearly a hundred guests sat down in the Kremlin Grand Palace, was preceded by the signing in Molotov's office, with Stalin as usual looking on, of a 'confidential protocol' by Beaverbrook, Harriman and Molotov on behalf of their respective countries. It enumerated over one hundred and fifty items to be furnished by Great Britain and the United States, ranging from tanks, planes and destroyers to army boots, shellac and medical supplies. Stalin, who was in his most affable mood, greeted each guest personally, subsequently drinking more than thirty toasts sometimes accompanied by informal speeches. In one of these he praised the United States for 'giving more assistance as a non-belligerent than some countries in history had given as allies' and expressed the hope that 'before long all three countries would be fighting side by side'. At the same time the imminence of the German threat to Moscow seems to have been generally felt, and the impression was heightened by firing from the Kremlin's anti-aircraft batteries from time to time during the meal.

Beaverbrook, who was seated beside Stalin in the place of honour, noted that the Soviet leader ate his caviar with a knife. He was served with different food from the others, and while the other guests had their glasses filled with wine by the white-coated waiters, Stalin had a bottle of his own over which he kept a glass inverted. Another fact which struck the observant Beaverbrook was that Stalin invariably spoke of Leningrad as Petersburg. 'He is an exacting man, even though he does not look it,' wrote Beaverbrook on his return to London. 'He is a judge of values, and his knowledge of armaments is vast and wide.' The two men evidently got on extremely well together, partly no doubt because Stalin had learned that Beaverbrook was a strong advocate of a second front in Europe. There was, too, a certain earthiness about Beaverbrook's conversation, in which a more conventional British representative would never have dared to indulge but which appealed to Stalin. 'Tell me,' Beaverbrook asked his host, pointing towards President Kalinin, the country's titular head of state, 'does Kalinin have a mistress?' 'No, he's far too old,' retorted Stalin. 'Do you?' (Kalinin was sixty-six, while Beaverbrook was four years younger.)[37]

Beaverbook's opinion of Stalin as 'a kindly man' was not shared by General Ismay who subsequently recorded his initial impression of the Soviet dictator.

> He moved stealthily like a wild animal in search of prey, and his eyes were shrewd and full of cunning. He never looked one in the face. But he had great dignity and his personality was dominating. As he entered the room, every Russian froze into silence, and the hunted look in the eyes of the Generals showed all too plainly the constant fear in which they lived. It was nauseating to see brave men reduced to such abject servility.[38]

After the meal, there was a film show, so that it was nearly one o'clock in the morning when the party broke up. The film, entitled *The War of the Future*, had been made some years previously and foretold the Nazi–Soviet conflict, pointing up Stalin as the victorious war leader. It might have seemed an odd choice to show while the enemy was battling almost at the gates of Moscow. Stalin stayed to the end to bid his guests goodnight, after which he went back to his office to receive the latest reports from the front. These reports indicating a 150-mile advance by Guderian were far from encouraging and were reinforced by Hitler's publicly expressed promise to the German people that Moscow would be captured by Christmas.

A few days later, after the Anglo-American mission had left for home, Stalin suffered a severe attack of influenza. From his sick-bed he decided to summon Zhukov from Leningrad where the front was relatively static. Zhukov arrived at dusk on 7 October and went straight to the Kremlin. Stalin, who was in bed, greeted the general with a nod and, pointing to a map, said: 'Look, we're in serious trouble on the Western Front, yet I can't seem to get a detailed report of what's going on.' He thereupon asked Zkukov to leave at once for the front and report on the situation to him by telephone at any hour of the day or night. 'I'll be waiting for your call,' he said.

Zhukov eventually got through to Stalin at 2.30 in the morning of 8 October to find Stalin still at work in spite of his illness. Zhukov reported that there was no longer a continuous front, that there were large gaps in it and that these could not be closed because the front had run out of reserves. The enemy, which was regrouping its forces, had a superiority in infantry, tanks, guns and mortars, and aircraft. 'The principal danger now is that the road to Moscow is now almost entirely unprotected,' said Zhukov. 'The fortifications along the Mozhaisk line are too weak to halt a breakthrough by German armour. We must concentrate our forces on this defence line as soon as possible from wherever we can.' In reply to a query from Stalin, he added that five Red armies in the command had been encircled in an area to the west of Vyasma.

When Zhukov got through again two days later, Stalin confirmed that he had appointed him to the command of the Western Front in place of Koniev, who had recently taken over from Timoshenko and whom Stalin blamed for the fact that the five armies had been trapped.* Stalin wished to change the whole structure of the command, but Zhukov persuaded him that this policy was wrong and that at least Koniev should be left as deputy commander, to which Stalin agreed. 'But get the Western Front into shape and act as fast as you can,' Stalin added.

* Timoshenko had been transferred to the command of the South-Western Front at the time of the encirclement of Kiev in the middle of September replacing Budenny. The latter was in turn assigned to the Reserve Front (to the rear of the Western Front), but like Voroshilov he never again held an active command of a battle front, being employed for most of the remainder of the war in raising and training troops.

'I will get to work immediately, but I must ask you to start shifting large reserves,' answered Zhukov. 'We must expect the enemy thrust towards Moscow to increase in strength in the near future.'[39]

Zhukov's prediction was speedily fulfilled. By the middle of the month, the situation was regarded as so serious that Stalin agreed to evacuate the government departments, in addition to the diplomatic corps, to Kuibyshev, and also as much of industry in the Moscow region as could be moved to the Urals. He himself was determined to remain in the capital. Three days later, on the night of 19 October, Stalin summoned the members of the State Defence Committee to his office, in addition to General P. A. Artemyev, commander of Moscow military district, A. S. Shcherbakov, head of the city's party organisation, and V. P. Pronin, the mayor of Moscow. Stalin agreed with Artemyev's suggestion that a state of siege should be proclaimed, and he asked Malenkov to draft a decree to this effect in the name of the Defence Committee.

Malenkov's effort turned out to be verbose and was not at all to Stalin's liking. Malenkov had no sooner finished reading his draft when Stalin rushed up to him in a temper and snatched the sheets of paper from his hand; at the same time according to one witness he 'spoke to him sharply'. He then turned to Shcherbakov and told him to take down a fresh draft at his dictation. After the text had been approved by all present, it was given to the secretariat with orders that it should be published in the newspapers, posted in the streets and suburbs and broadcast on the radio. The decree imposed a curfew between midnight and 5 a.m. and put NKVD troops at Artemyev's disposal for the maintenance of order in the capital. It also provided that anyone 'apprehended for inciting disturbances' should be turned over to a military tribunal and 'shot on the spot'.[40]

'Moscow will be defended to the last,' Stalin concluded in an Order of the Day. The order was to be faithfully carried out.

4

Thanks to the combined efforts of Zhukov and Timoshenko on their respective fronts, in addition to the patriotic spirit of the Moscow people who turned out in large numbers to dig trenches, and the arrival earlier than usual of cold weather, the German offensive was halted. At the same time the fronts were reinforced from the Far East, where intelligence of Japanese intentions to strike south instead of north (supplied to Moscow by the double agent Sorge) enabled Stalin to complete the transfer westwards of approximately half the ground strength in that theatre amounting to some 400,000 troops.

On 1 November 1941, Stalin sent for Zhukov and told him that he wished to hold the traditional parade in the Red Square on the anniversary of the Revolution, as well as a public meeting. 'What do you think? Will the situation at the front allow us to hold these festivities in Moscow?'

Zhukov replied that the enemy was in no position to start a major offensive in the next few days. The Germans had suffered heavy losses in the October fighting and were now busy reinforcing and regrouping their troops. But he thought that the *Luftwaffe* was likely to remain active even during this period. Stalin accordingly issued orders to go ahead with the celebrations.[41]

On the eve of the anniversary, Stalin left the Kremlin to address a large meeting of Moscow Party workers in the Mayakovsky Metro Station near the Red Square. 'Ours is a just cause, victory will be ours!' he told his audience. He went on to denounce the Germans, 'these men with the morals of beasts', who had the insolence to call for the extermination of the great Russian nation, the nation of Plekhanov and Lenin, Pushkin and Tolstoy, Glinka and Tchaikovsky, Gorky and Chekhov, Pavlov, Repin, Suvorov and Kutuzov, and other famous names. It was a skilfully calculated appeal to all shades of patriotic sentiment, as evidenced by the linking of the Menshevik Plekhanov with the founder of Bolshevism and the deliberate substitution of 'Russia' for the Soviet Union. Next day, from the top of the Lenin Mausoleum Stalin again invoked 'the heroic images of our great forbears' as an inspiration in the hour of mortal danger for the Russian Motherland. After their march past, the military units went straight off to the front. Stalin took care to see that the occasion received the maximum publicity both in the domestic and the foreign press. As Zhukov afterwards put it, 'that November parade was undoubtedly of tremendous political importance, both internally and abroad'.[42]

But Stalin remained anxious. A fortnight after the parade, he called up Zhukov at the front and asked: 'Are you sure we are going to be able to hold Moscow? I am asking this with an aching heart. Tell me honestly, as a member of the Party.'

'There is no question that we will be able to hold Moscow,' replied the Western Front commander. 'But we shall need at least two more armies and two hundred tanks.'

'I am glad that you're so sure,' Stalin rejoined. 'Call Shaposhnikov and tell him where you want the two reserve armies concentrated. They will be ready by the end of the month – but we have no tanks for the time being.'

This is not the place to trace the course of the ensuing campaign in detail. It is sufficient to state that Zhukov's prediction was fulfilled in the first week of December, when Guderian wrote in his war diary: 'The offensive on Moscow has ended. All the sacrifices and efforts of our brilliant troops have failed. We have suffered a serious defeat.'[43]

5

In addition to his constant military preoccupations at this time, Stalin had to deal with a pressing political problem posed by the Polish Government in exile which had been established under General Sikorski in London. Since Great Britain had gone to war as the direct result of her guarantee to Poland, Churchill felt that he was under a strong obligation to support the Poles. At the same time, he was faced by a dilemma, since it was obviously going to be difficult for Russia to abandon her claim to regions on her frontiers which she had for generations regarded as vital to her security. The Poles had two aims – (1) the recognition by the Soviet Government that the partition of Poland agreed to by Ribbentrop and Molotov in 1939 was now null and void; and (2) the liberation by Russia of all Polish prisoners of war and civilians deported to the Soviet Union after the Russian occupation of the eastern areas of Poland. The first step towards achieving these objectives was the restoration of Polish–Soviet diplomatic relations. After prolonged and difficult negotiations in London between Sikorski and ambassador Maisky, this had been achieved at the end of July 1941, when it was agreed to the formation of a Polish army on Russian soil subordinate to the Soviet Supreme Command.[44] There was no settlement of the frontier question apart from a vague statement from the Russians that the Nazi–Soviet treaties had 'lost their validity'. There remained too the question of the prisoners. This the newly appointed Polish ambassador, Stanislav Kot, took up with Molotov and Stalin on his arrival in Moscow.

'You are the author of an amnesty for Polish citizens in the USSR,' the ambassador told Stalin on being received by him in Molotov's office in the Kremlin on 14 November. 'You made that gesture, and I should be very grateful if you would bring influence to bear to ensure that it could be carried out completely.'

'Are there still Poles not yet released?' asked Stalin, affecting surprise.

'We have not seen one officer from the camp in Starobielsk [in eastern Ukraine] which was disbanded in the spring of 1940,' said Kot. He went on to mention two other camps, of which one was at Kozielsk near Smolensk. There was no trace of the former occupants of any of these camps who were transferred to an unknown destination.

'I shall go into that,' Stalin reassured the ambassador. 'But all sorts of things happen to released people...'

'We have names and lists.'

'Do exact lists exist?'

'All the names are registered with the Russian camp commanders, who summon all the prisoners to a roll call every day. In addition the NKVD interrogated each man separately. Not one officer of the staff of General Anders's army, which he commanded in Poland [in 1939] has been handed over.'

At this point, Stalin, who had been pacing up and down the room smoking a cigarette, went to Molotov's desk and picked up one of the telephones which connected directly with Beria's office. 'NKVD? This is Stalin. Have all the Poles been released from the prisons?' Then, after listening to the reply, he went on, 'Because I have the Polish ambassador with me and he tells me they haven't all been released.' He listened again briefly, replaced the receiver and returned to the conference table.

A few minutes later, the telephone rang and Stalin answered it. Kot could not hear what was being said at the other end of the line. But whatever it was, it seemed to satisfy Stalin, so he rejoined the others muttering almost under his breath, 'They say they've all been released.'[45]

What he did not tell the ambassador was that over four thousand Polish prisoners-of-war, who had been in the Kozielsk camp, had been executed by the NKVD and their bodies had been buried in a mass grave in the nearby Katyn forest.

A fortnight later the matter was raised again when Sikorski and Anders went to the Kremlin with Kot. 'I have to tell you, Mr President, that your declaration of an amnesty is not being put into effect,' said Sikorski to Stalin. 'Many, and those some of our most valuable people, are still in labour camps and prisons.'

'That is impossible, since the amnesty concerned everybody, and all the Poles have been released,' replied Stalin, turning to Molotov for confirmation. Molotov nodded.

Anders, who now commanded the Polish forces in the Soviet Union, went on to complain that only the less physically fit Poles were being released, 'because the commandants of the particular camps, being under obligation to fulfil their production plan, don't wish to lose their best workers, without whom at times it would be impossible to fulfil the plan'. With this Molotov laughingly agreed.

Sikorski: It is not our business to supply the Soviet Government with detailed lists of our people, but the camp commandants have complete lists. I have with me a list of some four thousand officers who were carried off by force and who even now are still in prisons and labour camps. And even this list is not complete, for it contains only the names which it has been possible to set down from memory. I gave instructions to check whether they are not back in Poland, with which we have constant contact. It turned out that not one of them is there, nor are they in the camps of our prisoners-of-war in Germany. Those men. Those men are here. Not one of them has come back.

Stalin: That's impossible. They've fled.

Anders: But where could they flee to?

Stalin: Well, to Manchuria, for instance.

Anders: It isn't possible that they have all fled, especially as from the moment of their transfer from prisoner-of-war camps to labour camps their correspondence with their families ceased completely... The majority of the officers named in this list are known to me personally. Among them are my staff officers and commanders. These people are perishing and dying here in terrible conditions.

Stalin: They must have been released, only they haven't arrived yet.

Sikorski: Russia is a large country, and the difficulties are equally great. Perhaps the local authorities have not acted on their instructions... If any of them have got across the Russian frontiers he would have undoubtedly reported to me.

Stalin: Please understand that the Soviet Government has no reason whatever for detaining a single Pole...

Molotov: We've detained only those who after the war began committed crimes, provoked diversions, set up radio stations, etc. I'm sure you won't be concerned about them.

Kot: Of course not. But I have already asked again and again for us to be given lists of these people, for very often this charge is made against people whom we know to be absolutely innocent and fervent patriots.

Sikorski: Don't let us discuss cases arising in wartime. It would be a good thing now if you, Mr President, were to give public explanations of this question, so as to bring about a fundamental change of attitude in Soviet Russia to the Poles. After all, these people are not tourists, but were carried off from their homes by force. They didn't come here of their own choice, they were deported and endured tremendous suffering.

Stalin: The people of the Soviet Union are well disposed towards the Poles. But officials can make mistakes.

Later in their discussions, when Stalin had implied that the Poles did not want to fight in Russia, Sikorski made it plain in a heated exchange that they were willing and even eager to do so. All he askd for was adequate accommodation and rations as good as the Red Army was getting. 'Our troops are fighting everywhere,' he said. 'In Great Britain we, have a corps which requires reinforcements. We have a navy, which is functioning perfectly. We have in operation seventeen air divisions, which are being given the very latest British machines and are fighting magnificently. Polish pilots have accounted for twenty per cent of the losses of German aircraft over England.'

'I know the Poles are brave,' Stalin admitted.

'When they are well led,' went on Sikorski. 'Thanks to Providence and to you, Mr President, we have here General Anders, my best soldier, whose eight stars for wounds testify to his valour. You shut him up in prison because he wanted to link up with me. He is a loyal commander, not a politician, and he will not allow his subordinates to engage in any politics either.'

'The finest politics is to fight well,' remarked Stalin. Then, turning to Anders, he asked him, 'How long were you in prison?'

'Twenty months,' Anders replied.

'And what sort of treatment did you receive?'

'In Lvov exceptionally bad,' was the answer. 'In Moscow rather better. But you can realise for yourself what "better" means in prison, when you've been there for twenty months.'

'Well, it couldn't be helped,' observed Stalin: 'such were the conditions.'[46]

6

Stalin's views on the political and territorial future of Poland were communicated to Anthony Eden, when the British Foreign Secretary arrived in Moscow for talks shortly afterwards. The United States had now entered the war, following the Japanese attack on Pearl Harbour on 7 December, and Churchill dispatched Eden to discuss the changed situation with Stalin, while he himself flew to Washington to see Roosevelt. So far as Poland was concerned, Stalin wished that the Russian frontier should follow the so-called Curzon line, which had been proposed but not adopted at the Paris Peace Conference in 1919.

To a considerable extent, although not altogether, this corresponded with the Ribbentrop–Molotov line agreed in September 1939. It meant that Poland would lose her former eastern areas, but Stalin proposed that when the war was ended she should be compensated at Germany's expense with territory extending as far west as the river Oder. Stalin went further and demanded the immediate recognition by Great Britain of all Russia's 1941 frontiers as the ultimate frontiers in the eventual peace treaties. Naturally Eden could not agree to this, without referring to London. He added that the Prime Minister had made a statement publicly to the whole world that Great Britain and the British Dominions would not recognise any territorial changes made during the war.

'If you say that,' said Stalin, 'you might well say tomorrow that you do not recognise the Ukraine as forming part of the USSR.'

'That is a complete misunderstanding of the position,' observed Eden. 'It is only changes from the pre-war frontiers that we do not recognise. The only change in the Ukraine is its occupation by Germany, so of course we accept the Ukraine as being part of the USSR.'[47]

Stalin finally agreed to leave open the question of the post-war frontiers for the time being. Of more immediate urgency, while the war was yet to be won by the allies, was the question of supplies. Stalin was particularly worried about the supply of tanks, in which (he said) 'the Germans still have a very great superiority', and he was relieved to learn from Eden that 'they will go on coming just the same', although the Americans might well reduce their deliveries.

Eden's visit ended with the customary banquet in the Catherine Hall of the Kremlin Grand Palace. Early in the evening, he learned that the next day (21 December) was Stalin's sixty-second birthday, so that when midnight struck Eden rose and proposed his health, 'wishing success to him and to Soviet arms'. Innumerable other toasts were drunk and the party did not break up until five o'clock in the morning. Among those who showed signs of having imbibed freely was Marshal Timoshenko, then much of a hero for his recent successes on the South-Western Front.

When Stalin saw that Eden had noticed this, he seemed rather embarrassed and asked, 'Do your generals ever get drunk?'

'They don't often get the chance,' replied Eden diplomatically.

Afterwards Eden wrote:

Stalin asked about our experience of fighting in North Africa and about our commanders on land and sea. I spoke of Wavell and Cunningham and asked about the winter in Russia. We both rehearsed our recollections of our earlier meeting in Moscow six years before and discussed its aftermath, the rise of Nazi power and the failure of France, Soviet Russia and Britain to pursue common policies. Each gave and argued his version.

After dinner we sat in a circle and returned to this theme, when Stalin made a defence of the Ribbentrop–Molotov Pact, for which he brazenly gave Molotov the discredit. He spoke of his lack of confidence in the French armies, his uncertainty about western policies and our failure to send missions of sufficient authority to Moscow soon enough. I countered with complaints of the secrecy and uncertainty of Soviet policies and the activities of the Communist Party in a country like France.[48]

Stalin told Eden that Soviet troops had been able to break through on several fronts and 'now we have the possibility of attacking'. Shortly afterwards, at a meeting in Supreme Headquarters, early in January 1942, plans for future operations were discussed. 'The Germans seem bewildered by their setback before Moscow and are poorly prepared for the winter,' said Stalin. 'Now is the time to go over to a general offensive.'

When asked for his opinion, Zhukov favoured continuing the offensive on the Western Front, provided he had adequate reinforcements of manpower and armour. But he was opposed to offensives in the Leningrad area and the south-west where the lack of artillery support he felt would prevent the Red troops breaking through and would be bound to result in 'heavy and completely unjustified losses'. He was supported by N. A. Voznesensky, the brilliant young Chairman of the State Planning Commission, who had been co-opted on to the Defence Committee. On the other hand, Stalin was supported by Beria and Malenkov, who took the opportunity to attack Vosnesensky who was 'always finding unforeseen difficulties, which could be overcome'.

'I've talked with Timoshenko and he favours the attack,' said Stalin, clinching the matter. 'We must quickly smash the Germans so that they cannot attack when spring comes.'

Shaposhnikov and Zhukov left the headquarters together. 'It was foolish to argue,' said the Chief of the General Staff. 'The boss had already decided. The directives have already gone out to almost all the fronts, and they will launch the offensives very shortly.'

'Then why did Stalin ask for my opinion?'

'I just don't know, old fellow,' answered Shaposhnikov with a sigh. 'I just don't know.'[49]

Except on the Western Front, where the enemy was pushed back up to two hundred miles in places, the offensive was disastrous, particularly in the area of Leningrad where the Russians suffered heavy losses in terrible winter fighting in frozen bogs and marshes. Then, an ill-conceived attempt to retake Kharkov in the spring resulted in three Soviet armies being surrounded, coupled with huge casualties, including the death in action of four generals, and the capture of over a quarter of a million prisoners.

According to Khrushchev, who was Timoshenko's political commissar, Khrushchev put a telephone call through to Supreme Headquarters and spoke to Shaposhnikov's deputy Vasilevsky. 'Alexander Mikhailovich,' he begged. 'Take a map and show Comrade Stalin the situation which has developed...We cannot continue the operation which was planned.' Apparently Vasilevsky replied that Stalin had already studied the matter and he did not propose to see him again on the subject as it would be a waste of time.

What allegedly happened then was described by Khrushchev in his 'secret' speech to the Twentieth Party Congress in 1956.

> After my talk with Vasilevsky I telephoned Stalin at his villa. But Stalin did not answer the telephone and Malenkov was at the receiver. I told Comrade Malenkov that I was calling from the front and that I wanted to speak personally to Stalin. Stalin informed me through Malenkov that I should speak with Malenkov. I stated for the second time that I wished to inform Stalin personally about the grave situation which had arisen for us at the front. But Stalin did not consider it convenient to pick up the telephone and again stated that I should speak to him through Malenkov, although he was only a few steps from the telephone.
>
> After 'listening' in this manner to our plea, Stalin said, 'Let everything remain as it is!'
>
> And what was the result of this? The worst that we had expected. The Germans surrounded our army concentrations and consequently we lost hundreds of thousands of our soldiers. This is Stalin's military 'genius!' This is what it cost us![50]

Zhukov, who claimed to have been present during this conversation, denies Khrushchev's version, blaming both Timoshenko and Khrushchev for not alerting headquarters to the danger earlier. On the other hand, there seems no doubt that Vasilevsky did urge Stalin to halt the Kharkov operation and was rebuffed by Stalin, who cannot escape at least some of the blame for the disaster. 'I was basically in agreement with Stalin's operational and strategic predictions,' Zhukov afterwards wrote in his memoirs, 'but I could not agree with him on the number of proposed separate offensive operations on the grounds that they would absorb our reserves and make it more difficult to prepare for a general offensive...If several reserve armies had been available in the rear of the South-Western Front, we could have avoided the catastrophe of the Kharkov operation in the summer of 1942.'[51]

7

The military reverses suffered by the Red Army in the early part of 1942 made Stalin increase the pressure on his two western Allies for the opening of a second front in Europe. To this end he decided to send Molotov to London and Washington in order to plead the cause personally with Churchill and Roosevelt. In the political field Molotov was also instructed to raise the question of Russia's post-war frontiers.

Molotov arrived in England with a party of fifteen advisers and security guards just as the ill-fated Kharkov operation was at its height. Recalling his air-raid experiences in Berlin in 1940, and fearing the attentions of the *Luftwaffe* during his visit, he asked to be lodged in as safe an area as possible outside London. Churchill thereupon put Chequers, the Prime Minister's official country residence, at his disposal. Molotov and his entourage were accordingly installed in this spacious house, where they surprised Churchill by sleeping with pistols under their pillows and having their own servants remake the beds in such a way that they could jump out quickly in the night if necessary. Russian security guards were posted outside the bedrooms which were kept locked while their occupants were conferring in London, and the furniture and walls of Molotov's room in particular were subjected to meticulous search by the NKVD in attendance. 'It is always right, especially in time of war, to take precautions against danger, but every effort should be made to measure its reality,' commented Churchill. 'For myself, when I visited Moscow I put complete trust in Russian hospitality.'[52]

At first the talks in Downing Street looked like ending in deadlock, since Churchill's war cabinet could not agree to conclude any agreement which guaranteed the permanent inclusion in Soviet territory of the eastern areas of Poland, or of Bessarabia which Stalin had grabbed from Roumania, since these conflicted with British understandings with Poland and the United States. Eden thereupon proposed the conversion of the existing Anglo-Soviet mutual assistance agreement into a

469

formal treaty to last for twenty years, omitting all references to frontiers. After Molotov had referred back to Stalin, Eden's suggestion was agreed to, and the treaty was signed on 26 May in the Foreign Office 'with great cordiality on both sides', as Churchill jubilantly described the occasion to Roosevelt. On the same day the British war leader cabled Stalin:

> Now that we have bound ourselves to be Allies and friends for twenty years, I take occasion to send you my sincere good wishes and to assure you of the confidence which I feel that victory will be ours.[53]

Molotov went on to Washington, where he persuaded the White House to agree to the issue of a communiqué which spoke of a 'full understanding' having been reached 'with regard to the urgent tasks of creating a second front in Europe in 1942'. This caused some consternation in Downing Street as the British Government had not been consulted on its terms, and it was consequently endorsed with some reluctance by the war cabinet since there was no wish to give the enemy the comfort of two conflicting communiqués. At the same time Churchill and Eden took advantage of Molotov's briefly breaking his return journey in London to hand him an *aide-memoire* to take back with him to Stalin, emphasising the limited availability of landing craft and other difficulties of a cross-Channel operation, the main burden of which would fall on British forces. While preparations were going ahead for a landing in August or September, Molotov was told, 'it is impossible to say in advance whether the situation will be such as to make this operation feasible when the time comes. *We can therefore give no promise in the matter...*'[54]

As soon as Molotov got back to Moscow and had reported to Stalin, a meeting of the Supreme Soviet was convened in order to ratify the Anglo-Soviet Treaty. On this occasion no security chances were taken. On reaching the Borovitsky Gate, the delegates were subject to four separate inspections of their identity papers, after which they were obliged to surrender any weapons they might be carrying and were subjected to a final scrutiny to make sure that they had done so. The proceedings in the Grand Palace were brief and to the point. The 'prolonged' ovation which Stalin received on his appearance was abruptly terminated when Beria, at a sign from Stalin, pressed the button on an electric bell and the delegates fell silent. Molotov, wearing a neat blue suit which he had obtained in America, then mounted the rostrum and the treaty was ratified by a unanimous show of hands. The Foreign Commissar went on to speak of the Washington communiqué. 'Comrades,' he said, 'this declaration is of the greatest importance to the people of the Soviet Union, for the establishment of a second front in Europe will create insurmountable difficulties for the Hitlerian armies on our front.' This statement was followed by a further outburst of applause which caused the Japanese embassy representative, who had gone to sleep in the diplomatic box, to wake up and clap loudly, much to Stalin's amusement.[55]

Unfortunately the Anglo-American plans to invade Europe were completely frustrated by Germany's successes in North Africa, culminating in the capture of Tobruk by Rommel's *Afrika Korps*, which thus laid open the road to Egypt. Churchill hurried off to Cairo to reorganise the British Middle East command, having already proposed to Stalin a personal meeting for the purpose of conveying the unpalatable news that there would be no second front in Europe that year, or, as he put it more tactfully in his cable to the Soviet leader, so that they could 'survey the war together and take decisions hand-in-hand'. He suggested Astrakhan, the Caucasus, 'or similar meeting place'. Stalin immediately agreed to a meeting, but indicated that Moscow suited him best, as 'neither I nor the members of the Government and the leading men of the General Staff could leave the capital at the moment of such intense struggle against the Germans'. Stalin also agreed to Churchill's suggestion that he should bring with him Roosevelt's ambassador-at-large Averell Harriman, and also General Sir Alan Brooke, the Chief of the Imperial General Staff, who was to follow in another plane.

Churchill and Harriman landed at Khodynka Field late in the afternoon of 12 August, to be greeted by Molotov, a concourse of Russian generals, the entire diplomatic corps, and a mass of press reporters and photographers. Molotov escorted the British Prime Minister to the state villa which Stalin had arranged for Churchill's accommodation in the woods off the Mozhaisk Highway not far from his own *dacha* at Kuntsevo. On their way Churchill lowered the car window, which he noticed was two inches thick. ('The Minister says it is more prudent that way,' said interpreter Pavlov who sat between them.) From time to time Churchill looked out and gave passers-by his famous V-sign. He was apparently unaware that the initial letter of the Russian word for Victory is not V but P (for *Pobieda*), with the result that his gesture was misunderstood by those to whom it was directed and who thought that it betokened the imminent launching of a second front.[56]

Although advised by his doctor to rest, since he had taken off from

Teheran at six o'clock that morning, Churchill insisted after a bath and a change of clothes in going to the Kremlin for a preliminary talk with Stalin.

He was accompanied by Harriman and the new British ambassador Sir Archibald Clark Kerr, a professional member of the diplomatic service who was more congenial to Stalin than the doctrinaire and ascetic Stafford Cripps. Molotov and Voroshilov were the only others present besides the usual interpreters. The meeting lasted for nearly four hours, of which Churchill afterwards described most of the first two as 'bleak and sombre'.[57]

'I find it difficult to talk about this,' Churchill began.

'There are no people with weak nerves here, Prime Minister,' remarked Stalin.

'The invasion of Europe is impossible this year.'

'That is to say the English and American leaders renounce the solemn promise made to us in the spring...'[58]

As Churchill explained at length with the aid of a map he had brought with him why a second front landing in northern France was simply not practicable in 1942 without inviting a disaster 'which would help nobody' – due to the lack of landing craft and other limiting factors principally of manpower – Stalin grew restless and became glummer and glummer. He brushed aside Churchill's argument that, if the landing of six divisions drew no Germans away from the Russian front and spoiled the prospects of 1943, 'it would be a great error'. His view about war was different, he said. A man who was not prepared to take risks could not win a war. Why were the British so afraid of the Germans? He could not understand it. His experience showed that 'troops must be blooded in battle', he went on. 'If you did not blood your troops, you had no idea what their value was.'

Churchill inquired whether Stalin had ever asked himself 'why Hitler did not come to England in 1940, when he was at the height of his power' and the British had only twenty thousand trained troops, two hundred guns and fifty tanks. 'He did not come. The fact was that Hitler was afraid of the operation. It is not so easy to cross the Channel.'

'That is no analogy,' replied Stalin. 'The landing of Hitler in England would have been resisted by the people, whereas in the case of a British landing in France the people would be on the side of the British.'

An oppressive silence followed after Churchill had pointed out that it was 'all the more important therefore not to expose the people of France by a withdrawal to the vengeance of Hitler and to waste them when they would be needed in the big operation in 1943'. At length Stalin said that if the British could not make the landing in 1942, he was 'not entitled to demand it or to insist upon it', but he was bound to say that he did not agree with Churchill's arguments. To Churchill's assurance that the operation would take place in 1943, Stalin rudely replied asking where was the guarantee that 'this solemn promise, too, will not be broken'.

'The British Prime Minister,' Molotov broke in at this point, 'will once again prove to us that his country is not in a position to sacrifice men.'

The atmosphere showed some improvement when Churchill changed the subject to the effects of the allied bombing, which Stalin agreed were 'having a tremendous effect in Germany', particularly on civilian morale. This seemed to Churchill the psychological moment to acquaint Stalin with the outlines of 'Torch', the joint British and American plan for the autumn invasion of French North Africa, then held by Germany's Vichy French collaborators, which Roosevelt had authorised Churchill to impart to Stalin in strict secrecy. At this Stalin sat up and grinned for the first time, remarking that he hoped nothing about it would appear in the British press. After some reflection, he said he thought the operation was 'militarily right', though he had 'political doubts about its effect on France'.

If the western Allies could end the year in possession of North Africa, having already beaten the Germans in the desert and saved Egypt, Churchill explained, they would be in a position to threaten 'the belly of Hitler's Europe', an important consideration to be taken in conjunction with the 'second front' operation in northern France then planned for 1943. To illustrate his point, Churchill drew a picture of a crocodile, and proceeded to demonstrate to Stalin with the help of the picture how it was the allied intention to attack the soft belly of the crocodile at the same time as they attacked his hard snout. By this time, according to Churchill, Stalin's interest was at the high pitch and he exclaimed, 'May God prosper this undertaking!' ('Oh, he brings in the Deity quite a lot,' Churchill remarked afterwards.)

Stalin reverted to his political doubts about the wisdom of the operation. Would it not be misunderstood in France? And what was being done about General de Gaulle and his Free French? To this Churchill replied that de Gaulle's intervention was not desired at this stage, since the Vichy French were likely to fire on the Gaullists but not on the Americans. This view was strongly backed by Harriman, who referred to the reports of American agents particularly in Algeria which Roosevelt had received and on which he relied.

At this point, to Churchill's satisfaction, Stalin suddenly seemed to grasp the strategic advantages of 'Torch'. Indeed, without any further prompting from Churchill and Harriman, he advanced four reasons for it – 'first, it would hit Rommel in the back; second, it would overawe Spain; third, it would produce fighting between Germans and Frenchmen in France; and fourth, it would expose Italy to the whole brunt of the war'.

Churchill has recorded his reaction to Stalin's words in *The Hinge of Fate*:

> I was deeply impressed with this remarkable statement. It showed the Russian Dictator's swift and complete mastery of a problem hitherto novel to him. Very few people alive could have comprehended in so few minutes the reasons which we had all so long been wrestling with for months. He saw it all in a flash.

Churchill mentioned a fifth reason, namely, the shortening of the sea route through the Mediterranean. Stalin appeared concerned to know whether the allied vessels would be able to pass through the Straits of Gibraltar, but Churchill assured him that this essential preliminary to the North Africa landings would be 'all right'. Finally, they all gathered round the globe in Stalin's office, when Churchill with its aid repeated the immense advantages of clearing the enemy out of the Mediterranean. Stalin agreed to a further meeting the following night. 'He now knew the worst,' noted Churchill, 'and yet we parted in an atmosphere of goodwill.'[59]

Next morning Churchill saw Molotov alone and told him bluntly that he thought he ought to know that Stalin 'would not be wise to be rude' to him and his party when they had 'come all this distance to help him'. Molotov promised to relay this message. 'Stalin is wise,' added Molotov, 'and he will know how you feel, even if he argues.'[60]

For the next meeting, which began at eleven o'clock at night and lasted well into the early hours of the following morning, Churchill had with him his top professional advisers, including Sir Alan Brooke and two other generals as well as Air Marshal Tedder and Sir Alexander Cadogan, the permanent head of the Foreign Office. On this occasion Stalin was very rude to Churchill. Tedder attributed Stalin's behaviour to the fact that Churchill had let himself go at lunch in the official guest villa earlier that day, 'speaking of Stalin as just a peasant, whom he, Winston, knew exactly how to tackle', and that his uncomplimentary remarks had reached Stalin's ears. Tedder, who had been at the lunch, afterwards stated that he warned Churchill of the risk of the room being 'bugged'.* According to one of his secretaries, Churchill was aware of this possibility, but did not care what he said. However, all this is merely conjecture. What is certain is that at the second Kremlin meeting the going was extremely hard.

Most of the ground under previous discussion was covered again, and Stalin seemed to go out of his way to taunt Churchill with such remarks as, 'When are you going to start fighting?' and 'Are you going to let us do all the work whilst you look on?' At last, after he had accused Churchill to his face of a breach of faith in failing to launch the second front in Europe, Churchill could stand it no longer and crashed his fist down on the table. 'I repudiate that statement,' he said, pointing to the *aide-memoire* he had given Molotov. 'Every promise has been kept.' He then burst into a fierce tirade which he prefaced by saying: 'I have come round Europe in the midst of my troubles. Yes, Mr Stalin, I have my troubles as well as you – hoping, hoping, I said, to meet the hand of comradeship' – here he extended his hand towards Stalin – 'and I am bitterly disappointed I have not met that hand.' Eventually he got so worked up that Stalin interrupted him with a broad grin on his face, as he told the interpreter to tell Churchill: 'I do not understand what you are saying, but by God, I like your spirit!' This lowered the temperature somewhat and the atmosphere returned to normal with an apology from Stalin to the effect that he was expressing his sincere and honest opinions, that there was no mistrust between them, but only a difference of view. Sir Alan Brooke, the Chief of the Imperial General Staff, who witnessed the scene, was convinced that Stalin deliberately insulted Churchill with the purpose of finding out what his reactions would be, and of sizing up what kind of man he was. 'He very soon discovered that Winston was made of,' wrote Brooke afterwards, 'and I am certain that this outburst of Winston's had impressed Stalin and started feelings of admiration for what he discovered was a true fighting man.'[61]

8

On the third night of Churchill's visit, Stalin gave the customary banquet, placing the British Premier on his right and Harriman on his left. It was only a qualified success, although previous Kremlin hospitality seems to have been surpassed in lavishness on this occasion. There were nineteen courses and innumerable toasts. However,

* 'Being fairly certain that the whole villa was a network of microphones, I scribbled *'Méfiez-vous'*, and passed it to him [Churchill]. He gave me a glare which I shall never forget, but I am afraid it was too late. The damage was done.' Lord Tedder, *With Prejudice* (1966), p. 330.

Churchill astonished his hosts by appearing in his own peculiar style of battle dress with a zipper and no tie, which he used to call his 'siren suit' as he habitually wore it at home when air raids were threatened. Also he showed that he had not forgotten the harsh things Stalin had said about the British soldiers. By way of getting his own back, he told Stalin that he (Churchill) deserved the highest order and citation of the Red Army because he had taught it to fight so well during the 'intervention' in the Civil War. 'Premier Stalin,' Pavlov interrupted Stalin's comment, 'he says all that is in the past and the past belongs to God.'[62]

One of the many toasts proposed by Stalin was to 'the officers of the Intelligence Service who are doing such important work'. He then made a curious reference to the Dardanelles campaign in 1915, for which Churchill had been largely responsible, saying that the British had really won and the Germans and Turks were retreating, but the British did not know it as their inteiligence was faulty. Churchill thought that this inaccurate reference was intended as a compliment to himself, whereas it was rather two-edged. However, any possible feelings of embarrassment were removed when Captain Jack Duncan, the American naval attaché, rose and said he could reply to the toast as he belonged to the Intelligence Service. 'If we make mistakes,' he added, 'it is because we know only what you tell us and that's not much!'

Stalin burst out laughing when he heard this, and called down the table: 'If there's anything you want to know, ask me. I'll be your intelligence officer!' He then left his seat and went to where the American was sitting, clinked glasses with him and took him familiarly by the arm.

As the evening wore on, at least two members of the Politburo, Voroshilov and Mikoyan, showed distinct signs of wear, Mikoyan eventually staggering from the hall with his arm round a colleague's shoulder. Afterwards Stalin and Churchill were photographed together and also with Harriman, which gave Stalin obvious pleasure. Then something went wrong. Churchill, Harriman and Molotov went over to a table and sat down together. A little later Stalin joined them, taking a chair next to Churchill, who, however went on reading some document and hardly spoke to Stalin. Churchill's physician Charles Wilson (afterwards Lord Moran) saw what was happening and got the impression that Stalin wanted to be friendly but that Churchill would not meet him half way. At last Churchill got up and, turning to Stalin, said 'Goodbye' – not 'Goodnight', as Lord Moran was quick to notice. As they shook hands, Stalin remarked that 'any differences that existed were only of method'. To this Churchill answered that 'we would try to remove even those differences by deeds'. He then moved off and had got about half way through the crowded room when Stalin hurried after him.

What happened then is best described by Lord Moran in his diary:

He [Churchill] walked very quickly, with countenance overcast. His face was set and resolute. Stalin accompanied him through the vast and empty halls which separated the dining-room from the door by which we had come into the Kremlin. I had never seen Stalin move except in a slow and measured fashion. Now to keep up with the Prime Minister he had almost to trot. Watching him I thought of the importunity of the small boy who is asking for a cigarette card and will not take 'No' for an answer. Perhaps Stalin realised that he had gone too far, and that this might be the end; he saw what that would mean.

Sir Alexander Cadogan, who drove back to the guest villa with Churchill, was surprised by the violence and depth of resentment which he had worked up. Later, as he was undressing to go to bed, Churchill told Moran: 'Stalin didn't want to talk to me. I closed the proceedings down. I had had enough. The food was filthy. I ought not to have come.' Then, after a pause, he added: 'I still feel I could work with that man if I could break down the language barrier. That is a terrible difficulty.'[63]

The ambassador Clark Kerr and Cadogan were convinced that Churchill intended to leave Moscow without seeing Stalin again. Next morning, however, the ambassador buttonholed the Prime Minister and argued that this would be disastrous. As a result Churchill's mood became more accommodating and eventually he agreed to see Stalin if it could be arranged, particularly when he heard that, according to Molotov, Stalin's action in coming to the door of the Kremlin Grand Palace to see him off was 'without precedent in the history of the Soviet Union'.

'It was my fault,' he admitted, after some reflection. Then followed a series of frantic telephone calls to the Kremlin only to elicit the information that 'Mr Stalin is out walking'. As the hours passed and Cadogan kept telephoning, the reply was always the same – Stalin was still out walking. At last, after Cadogan had given up hope, a message reached the embassy about six o'clock that Stalin would see the Prime Minister at seven. One circumstance unexpectedly favoured the meeting. The usual embassy interpreter was ill, and at the last moment Major A. H. Birse, a Russian speaking member of the British Military Mission, who had been brought up in St Petersburg and spoke fluent

Russian, was ordered to take his place. In the result Major Birse succeeded in 'getting' Churchill 'across' so well that the Prime Minister insisted on having him as his interpreter at all future meetings with the Soviet leader.

At first the going was decidedly sticky. When they were shown in, Stalin was standing at his desk, looking glum and sulky. They shook hands, but there was no smile of greeting on Stalin's face, and Birse noticed that he looked away as he took Churchill's hand. Then Stalin waved them to the conference table, where they were joined by Pavlov who interpreted for Stalin. No one else was present. The conversation opened with a further discussion on the second front. But gradually and with considerable skill Churchill brought the talk round to more congenial topics, such as 'Torch' and the defence of the Caucasus. Churchill asked particularly whether the Russians would be able to hold the Caucasus mountain passes, and also prevent the Germans reaching the Caspian, taking the Baku oilfields and then driving southwards through Turkey or Persia. 'We shall stop them,' said Stalin confidently, as he spread out a map on the table. 'They will not cross the mountains.' He added that there were rumours that the Turks planned an attack through Turkestan and that if they did he thought he should be able to deal with them too. Churchill observed that there was no danger in this. The Turks meant to keep out, he assured Stalin, and would certainly not quarrel with England.[64]

After about an hour and a half, Churchill got up to go. Stalin asked him when they were to meet again and appeared embarrassed when his visitor said that he was leaving at daybreak. 'Then why should we not go to my house and have some drinks?' Churchill replied that 'in principle' he was 'always in favour of such a policy'. Escorted by NKVD guards, Stalin led the way through several long corridors past doors bearing the names of Beria, Kaganovich and other members of the Politburo, until at last they emerged in a small street, still in the Kremlin. A hundred yards or so then brought them to the entrance to Stalin's old quarters in the Poteshny Palace, to which he had moved back probably because his flat in the Senate building was required for additional offices.

Churchill noted that the rooms which Stalin showed him were of moderate size, simple, dignified and four in number – a dining room, working room, bedroom and a large bathroom. The dining room, where the table was being laid by a rather frightened looking old housekeeper with a white cloth bound round her head, had once been Nadezhda Alliluyeva's bedroom. In the middle of the table there was a variety of bottles which Stalin proceeded to uncork. While he was doing this, his daughter Svetlana appeared and dutifully kissed her father. 'This is my daughter,' said Stalin, introducing her to Churchill. 'She's a redhead.' Churchill smiled and remarked that he too had been red-haired when he was a young man. 'But now look!' And he waved the cigar he had lit up in the direction of his bald head. Svetlana then began to help the housekeeper who by this time had produced several dishes of caviar, smoked salmon, jellied sturgeon and other delicacies, after which the housekeeper withdrew and Svetlana was also dismissed. The others then sat down and Stalin poured wine and vodka into their glasses, touching an even number of glasses with his fork, which made Churchill's interpreter wonder whether Stalin was not superstitious and considered uneven numbers unlucky.

After they had tasted the vodka and the wine, Stalin poured some brown liquid into a small glass which he offered to Churchill. 'You must try my *pertsovka*,' he said, 'It is the best vodka we have. Ordinary vodka is all right, but too weak. This the real thing.'

When he had interpreted this, Major Birse added, lowering his voice so that Pavlov would not hear. 'May I say, sir, that this is vicious stuff, and I cannot recommend it.' The offer was thereupon politely and no doubt wisely declined.[65]

'Why should we not have Molotov?' asked Stalin at this point. 'He is worrying about the communiqué. We could settle it here. There is one thing about Molotov – he can drink.'

So Molotov was sent for, and Churchill realised that he was expected to join them at dinner. As Churchill had invited the Polish General Anders to dine with him at the guest villa, he dispatched Birse to telephone the villa, saying that he would not be back until after midnight. In fact it was 3.30 in the morning when he eventually returned.

As an exercise in public relations, the evening was an immense success. All Churchill's earlier bitter feelings were completely allayed. The talk ranged over a wide variety of topics from northern convoys and army lorries to collective farms and the project of a joint Anglo-Russian landing in Norway. Only once was a slightly discordant note struck, but harmony was quickly restored. It turned on the recent failure of a convoy carrying much needed equipment to get through to Murmansk. 'Mr Stalin asks,' said Pavlov, with some hesitation, 'has the British navy no sense of glory?'

'You must take it from me that what was done was right,' answered Churchill. 'I really do know a lot about the navy and sea-war.'

'Meaning,' said Stalin, 'that I know nothing.'

'Russia is a land animal,' retorted Churchill. 'The British are sea animals.'[66]

There were a few moments of silence, and then Stalin recovered his good humour, particularly as Churchill began to chaff him about Molotov's behaviour in America. Was Stalin aware that when he was in Washington, Molotov said he was determined to pay a visit to New York by himself and that the delay in his return to Moscow was 'not due to any defect in the aeroplane, but because he was off on his own?'

For a moment or two Molotov looked serious. Then Stalin's face lit with merriment as he said: 'It was not to New York he went, he went to Chicago where the other gangsters live!'

Stalin also baited Churchill, who had mentioned his ancestor the Duke of Marlborough and his military genius. 'I think England had a greater general in Wellington, who defeated Napoleon, the greatest menace of all time,' said Stalin, going on to display his knowledge of European history with a reference to the second front which Wellington had opened by invading Portugal and Spain.

Towards midnight Churchill said he would like to go to the lavatory, so Stalin led him through the adjoining bedroom to the bathroom beyond. Birse accompanied them, thus becoming (so he claimed) the first foreigner to see Stalin's bedroom. He noted that it was as simply furnished as the dining room with a marked absence of luxury. A bed and a bedside table, a rug or two on the floor, a few chairs and a large bookcase made up the furniture. Birse had a look at the books. They were a collection of Marxist literature, with a good many historical works, but he could see no Russian classics. He also noticed that a few of the books were in Georgian.[67]

When Churchill reappeared in the dining room he was a little perturbed to find that his interpreter was being plied with questions by Stalin and Molotov. He was reassured that Birse was not divulging any British state secrets but was merely being asked about his upbringing and how he came to acquire such a good knowledge of Russian.

About one o'clock Sir Alexander Cadogan arrived with a draft of the communiqué on the visit which it was intended to release next day. The final version was quickly agreed after Churchill had made a few alterations. ('The discussions, which were carried on in an atmosphere of cordiality and complete sincerity, provided an opportunity of re-affirming the existence of the close friendship and understanding between the Soviet Union, Great Britain and the United States of America, in entire accordance with the Allied relationships existing between them.') Birse afterwards typed up a fair copy on an English typewriter which Pavlov conveniently produced from one of the adjoining rooms.

It was now 1.30 a.m. and, as Churchill noted, around Stalin's usual

480

dinner hour. A sucking-pig was brought in, which Stalin invited Churchill and Cadogan to share. When both declined, he fell on the animal with relish, cleaning out the head and putting it into his mouth with his knife. He then cut pieces of flesh from the cheeks of the pig and ate them with his fingers. Having polished off this victim, Stalin abruptly went into the next room to receive the reports from all sectors of the front which were customarily delivered to him from 2 a.m. onwards. After twenty minutes he came back, by which time the communiqué was ready.

Finally Churchill got up from the table at which he and the others had spent the best' part of six hours, and prepared to take his departure. As he did so, he turned to Molotov and said: 'I will not trouble you to come to the airfield. I will say goodbye to you here.'

'Oh, no,' said Stalin. 'He is a younger man. He will see you off.'

And at 4.30, as dawn was breaking, Molotov obediently arrived at the villa to accompany the Prime Minister to the airfield.[68]

9

While the Stalin-Churchill talks were taking place, the situation on the South-Western Front had become serious. The capture of Kharkov had been followed by the fall of Sebastopol and the evacuation of the Red Army forces by sea. The Germans pushed on along a wide front between Voronezh and the Caucasus, and by the time Churchill left Moscow they were rapidly approaching Stalingrad. To take Stalingrad, 'Stalin's City', now became an obsession with Hitler, and he was determined on its capture for prestige reasons. Stalin and the Defence Committee were equally determined that it should not be captured, particularly after the Germans broke through to the Volga ('an unforgettably tragic day', Vasilevsky called it) and cut off the Sixty-Second Army inside Stalingrad from the rest of the Soviet forces. Three days later on 27 August 1942, Stalin appointed Zhukov Deputy Supreme Commander, a post which Zhukov was to hold for the remainder of the war. At the same time Shaposhnikov was replaced as Chief of the General Staff by Vasilevsky with Antonov as his Deputy.

Roosevelt chose this time to send Wendell Wilkie, his Republican opponent whom he had defeated in the 1940 Presidential Election, on a world goodwill tour as part of a calculated policy to break down the old isolationist feeling in the Republican Party. Wilkie, who was accompanied by two newspaper friends Joseph Barnes and Gardner Cowles, did his best to prove that he was a good fellow, among other antics jumping from his box on to the stage during a performance of *Swan Lake* and presenting the ballerina Tikhomirova with a bouquet, much to Stalin's amusement.[69] But Wilkie, who was an uninhibited advocate of the second front in France, went too far when at a Kremlin banquet he apparently joined with Stalin in accusing the British of stealing Lend-Lease material in the shape of ships diverted from the northern convoys. This caused grave offence in London and also in Washington, where Roosevelt at a press conference had some biting remarks to make about 'typewriter strategists' in an obvious reference to Wilkie and his friends.[70]

The epic battle for Stalingrad which followed can be only briefly summarised here. During September and October the German divisions battered themselves against the city's defences and succeeded in penetrating the suburbs, while the defenders stubbornly fought for each street and even each house. Then, to the surprise of Hitler who considered that a Russian counter-offensive was out of the question, Stalin ordered just that, when the Germans seemed on the point of overcoming the whole city. For over two months he and the General Staff had been building up a massive operational reserve and at the critical moment this was secretly distributed between the three Soviet armies which flanked Stalingrad in the north, the north-west and the south, under the command respectively of Vatutin, Rokossovsky and Eremenko. Beginning on 19 November, the three commanders launched concentric blows at the rear of the German besiegers under Field Marshal von Paulus in order to cut them off from the German armies in the west. The result was that on the fourth day the besiegers found themselves besieged. Hitler then ordered General Manstein to relieve von Paulus from the south.[71]

It was during the intense fighting in and around the city on the Volga that the legend was created that 'Stalin is with us!' Songs were sung by the troops which described Stalin as 'appearing in the trenches, in the streets of the besieged city, in the valleys, on the hills'. So far as is known, Stalin did pay a visit of a few hours to the north-eastern extremity of the Stalingrad front, getting no closer to the centre of the fighting. On the other hand, he had several 'doubles', who appeared at critical points of the front lines to encourage the troops. Meanwhile the real Stalin was in the Kremlin, but the ruse was instrumental in building up an impressive Stalin legend.[72]

A division of opinion developed among the Soviet generals as to which to concentrate on first, von Paulus's army or Manstein's relief, the former objective being favoured by Rokossovsky and the latter by Vasilevsky. The question was referred to Stalin and debated at length throughout the night of 12–13 December. An observer at Supreme

Headquarters later recorded a fragment of Stalin's telephone conversation with the various field commanders.

Stalin (*speaks over the phone*): What is your opinion? Turn against Manstein? Thank you. (*Puts down the receiver and calls again.*) Hullo... There is a proposal from Vasilevsky that we should dispose finally of Manstein. It is proposed that Malinovsky's army be used for that. What is your opinion? To leave it with Rokossovsky? Thank you. (*Puts down the receiver and calls again.*) Vasilevsky proposes to shift Malinovsky's army and to assign it to Eremenko in order to rout Manstein. What is your opinion? (*Listens.*) No, that's no answer. Yes or no? You would like to think it over? All right.[73]

Stalin eventually sided with Vasilevsky, much to Rokossovsky's annoyance, and the crack Second Guards Army commanded by General Rodion Malinovsky was moved from the Don Front.* The operation was completely successful. Manstein's army was halted, thanks in part to the use of the thermal bomb which burned at a temperature of 1,800 degrees, and by the end of December the main German force had been thrown back one hundred and twenty miles from Stalingrad. It only remained to close in on von Paulus, whose army Hitler refused to be withdrawn. In the process 30,000 Germans were killed and von Paulus together with twenty-three other German generals and 90,000 troops surrendered. By 1 February 1943 it was all over. Soon afterwards the Caucasus was cleared of the enemy and the German threat to the Anglo-American supply route which had been opened up through Iran was removed. Most important too was cutting off the Germans from access to the vital oilfields in Transcaucasia.

Stalingrad, where the flower of the German army perished, was to prove the turning point in the war for Stalin since Hitler was never to regain the initiative. Of course, not only were the German generals outmanoeuvred, but Russia was also saved by over-extended German lines of communication, lack of fuel, the winter and the mud, where *Wehrmacht* vehicles which ran on wheels instead of tracks were bogged down. And in the overall process Stalin's stature as Supreme Commander was immensely enhanced in the eyes of his western Allies and indeed of the world. On 6 March 1943, the Praesidium of the Supreme Soviet conferred on the Supreme Commander the rank of Marshal of the Soviet Union and proclaimed him 'the greatest strategist of all times and all peoples'.

* To boost morale divisions that had done well in battle were designated 'Guards Divisions' and their personnel received extra pay.

According to Stalin's daughter Svetlana, who had one of her rare wartime meetings with her father at this time, Stalin spoke of his son Yakov, then in a German prisoner-of-war camp. 'The Germans have proposed that we exchange one of their prisoners for Yasha. They want me to make a deal with them. I won't do it. War is war.' The German prisoner is believed to have been von Paulus. However, nothing further came of the German overture, and shortly afterwards Lieutenant Yakov Djugashvili perished in the camp where he was being held. Stalin never learned the details of how Yakov died, although he later offered a substantial reward for them. They were subsequently revealed in official German documents captured by the Americans and are stated to have been 'kept secret from the Soviet leader to save him pain'.[74]*

Among the first to congratulate Stalin on the surrender of von Paulus and the end of the German Sixth Army was Winston Churchill. 'This is indeed a wonderful achievement,' he cabled the Kremlin. A fortnight or so later Stalin sent Churchill the film of the Stalingrad victory which had been made, portraying most vividly the desperate fighting, the final surrender of von Paulus and the endless lines of German prisoners trudging along wearily through the snow. Churchill responded by sending Stalin *Desert Victory*, the film of the battle of Alamein in which General Montgomery had successfully routed Rommel and saved Egypt.

On 29 March, Stalin cabled Churchill from Moscow:

> Last night, with my colleagues, I saw the film *Desert Victory* you have sent us and was greatly impressed. It shows in a truly splendid way how Britain is fighting, and skilfully exposes those scoundrels – we have them in our country too – who allege that Britain is not fighting but merely looking on. I eagerly look forward to another film of the same kind showing your victory in Tunisia.
>
> *Desert Victory* will be circulated to all our armies at the front and shown as widely as possible to the public.[75]

'These photographs, like the Russian were all taken by the operators under heavy fire and with some loss of life,' wrote Churchill afterwards. 'The sacrifice was not made in vain, for the fruits of their work excited the greatest admiration and enthusiasm throughout the Allied

* Yakov died on 14 April 1943, after having flung himself against the electric fence on the camp's perimeter and been shot by one of the guards apparently at his own request. See reports in *The Washington Star*, 18 February, and *The Times*, 19 February 1968.

world and brought us all closer together in our common task.' Incidentally, unlike Khrushchev, Montgomery greatly admired Stalin's military ability. 'Had it not been for Stalin,' he told the present writer, 'Russia might well have pulled out of the war in 1942 after the first terrible winter and the experience of Hitler's Operation Barbarossa.'[76] Few people today, except Khrushchev and his most fervent disciples in the Soviet Union, would venture to disagree with this opinion.

Useful in Stalin's eyes as were the Anglo-American landings in North Africa and the successful campaign which followed, Stalin really regarded this as a sideshow compared with the fighting in Russia where he felt that the Red Army was still bearing the brunt of the fighting with proportionately high casualties. By the time of Stalingrad, over two million Red soldiers had been killed and three-and-a-half million taken prisoner. On the other hand, the strength of the Red Army had risen to something like nine million, while another sixteen million men of military age were under training and would soon be available for mobilisation when there was the necessary equipment for them, especially aircraft, tanks and other fighting vehicles which were now reaching Russia in increasingly large quantities from the western Allies. Many officers, including such high ranking soldiers as Rokossovsky and Gorbatov, had been released from the prisons and camps where they had been sent in the course of the Tukachevsky purge. Another of Stalin's innovations was the abolition of corps headquarters, divisions being grouped directly into armies, which in turn were under the control of army groups or 'fronts'. There were twelve such 'fronts' at this time. The authority of the political commissars was reduced, and they became merely assistants to the military commanders. New uniforms were introduced with epaulettes similar to those worn in the Tsarist army, and decorations were generously awarded for meritorious conduct on active service.[77]

On the other hand, Stalin saw to it that Beria's security men were not kept idle. When territory was recaptured from the Germans any local inhabitants suspected of collaborating in the slightest degree with the occupying forces was summarily executed. Elsewhere there were arrests for no apparent reason. General A. S. Yakovlev, the top aircraft designer, recalls in his memoirs how he was hampered by the sudden disappearance of V. P. Balandin, the Deputy Commissar in charge of aircraft engine production. After Balandin had been in prison for forty days, Yakovlev took advantage of a business meeting with Stalin to plead for Balandin. 'We don't know what he was arrested for, but we can't conceive that he was an enemy,' said Yakovlev. 'He is needed in the People's Commissariat – the management of engine production has

485

deteriorated significantly. We ask you to examine this case. We have no doubts about him.'

Stalin evidently knew about the case, as he told Yakovlev that Balandin had made no compromising admissions whatever. 'Perhaps he isn't guilty of anything,' he added. 'It is very possible...It can happen that way too...'

Next day, according to Yakovlev, 'Vasily Petrovich Balandin, with hollow cheeks and shaven head, was back at his office in the Commissariat and working as though nothing had happened'.[78]

Not everyone was as fortunate as Balandin, although his was by no means the only case where a friend with access to Stalin and the courage to intervene on the suspect's behalf was able to obtain his release. For instance, according to Khrushchev, Beria succeeded in persuading Stalin that Aloysha Svanidze, Stalin's brother-in-law by his first wife, had been planted near him by the German Intelligence service. Svanidze was arrested by the NKVD and shot. Before his execution he was told that if he asked Stalin's forgiveness his life would be spared. 'What should I ask forgiveness for?' he asked. 'I have committed no crime.' After Stalin was told that the execution had been carried out, he is said to have remarked: 'See how proud he is! He died without asking forgiveness.' (Afterwards Khrushchev commented: 'The thought never occurred to him that Svanidze had been above all an honest man. Thus many completely innocent people perished.')[79]

The carrot was effectively employed as well as the stick, one conspicuous example at this time being the rehabilitation of the Greek Orthodox Church on the grounds that the Church had loyally cooperated in the war effort. Stalin received the Metropolitan Sergius, the head of the Church, and after a cordial interview with him decreed the restoration of the Holy Synod. It was a clever move, coming as it did shortly after the disbandment of the Comintern; while Stalin's action was rightly calculated to create a favourable impression with his western Allies, particularly the Americans, it was also designed to enlist the support of an influential religious body which had been of considerable political advantage to the State in Tsarist times, as Stalin no doubt recalled from his days in the Tiflis theological seminary.[80]

At this time a distinct note of sourness appeared in Stalin's correspondence with Churchill. This was due to a number of factors, such as continued uncertainty about the second front in France, the decision to suspend the northern convoys, and the unqualified acceptance by the Polish government-in-exile of the German accusations charging Stalin with the murder of fifteen thousand Polish officers and other prisoners

486

as evidenced by the discovery of the mass graves in Katyn forest. General Sikorski's action resulted in diplomatic relations between his government and the Soviet Union being broken off. A few months later, when the Russians recaptured Smolensk and the Katyn region, they appointed a committee to inquire into the fate of the Poles and shortly afterwards the committee reported that they had all been slaughtered by the Germans during their rapid advance in July 1941. But few thinking people, at any rate outside the Soviet Union, believed this disclaimer in the face of the proofs to the contrary convincingly produced by Sikorski. 'We have got to beat Hitler and this is no time for quarrels and charges,' Churchill told Sikorski bluntly. But nothing which Churchill could do was able to prevent a rupture between the Polish and Soviet governments, thus resulting in 'many inconveniences' as Churchill put it.[81]

The withdrawal of the Arctic convoys was due partly to the high casualty rate in ships during the long hours of daylight and also to the need of conserving shipping for the invasion of Sicily and southern Italy, an operation which was successfully carried out during the summer. At the same time the Russians were fighting a great counter-offensive in the Orel–Kursk salient which led to the recapture of Kharkov and the pushing back to beyond the river Dnieper of the Germans after immense losses in personnel and equipment (70,000 casualties, 6,000 tanks and 1,400 aircraft). On 21 September, acting on instructions from Stalin, Molotov sent for Clark Kerr, the British ambassador, and 'insisted' that the convoys be resumed, in the expectation that the necessary measures would be taken within the next few days. This peremptory demand erupted into an ugly row between Churchill and Stalin.

On 1 October 1943, Churchill informed Stalin by cable that he had gone into the question with the Admiralty and in spite of the fact that the Battle of the Atlantic had flared up again and U-boats fitted with a new acoustic torpedo were creating renewed havoc both in the Atlantic and the Mediterranean, it was proposed to resume the convoys in November and continue them for the next three months. At the same time, he felt bound to put on record that 'this is no contract or bargain, but rather a declaration of our solemn and earnest resolve'.

After a fortnight's silence, Stalin replied in such offensive language that Churchill refused to receive the communication and returned it to the Soviet ambassador Feodor Gusev, who had recently succeeded Maisky in London. Besides accusing Churchill of breaking his word, Stalin complained that in the last convoys there had been a serious falling off in deliveries compared with the previous year.

Therefore, at the present time, when the forces of the Soviet Union are strained to the utmost to secure the needs of the front in the interests of the success of the struggle against the main forces of our common enemy, it would be inadmissible to have the supplies of the Soviet armies depend on the arbitrary judgment of the British side. It is impossible to consider this posing of the question to be other than a refusal of the British Government to fulfil the obligations it undertook, and as a kind of threat addressed to the USSR.[82]

Another cause of complaint was the behaviour, or rather the alleged misbehaviour, of the British service personnel in Archangel, who according to Stalin had 'attempted, in several cases, to recruit, by bribery, certain Soviet citizens for Intelligence purposes'. There was also an unfortunate incident when two British sailors who had gone ashore in Murmansk had snatched a fur cap off a boy's head in the street and pretended to make off with it. The boy set up a howl, the police appeared and arrested the men for drunkenness, assault and theft, with the result that they were brought before a local court and sentenced to twelve months in a Soviet prison.

Fortunately a conference of allied foreign ministers was about to open in Moscow, and Churchill left it to Eden to try to smooth over the differences. 'The Prime Minister is offended and will not accept my reply,' Stalin glumly told the British Foreign Secretary when they met on 21 October. 'I understand that Mr Churchill does not want to correspond further with me. Well, let it be so.' However, Eden's tact soon relaxed the atmosphere and charmed Stalin into good humour. Eden emphasised that Churchill had at all times been willing to deliver the goods to their ally, but he could not pledge himself to a series of operations which he might not be able to carry out. It was not surprising therefore that the Prime Minister should have been hurt by Stalin's message. Stalin thereupon assured Eden that 'this had not been intended', and went on to acknowledge that the Anglo-American campaign in Italy had helped the Soviet Union. The Germans no longer moved fresh reserves to the Soviet front, he said.

During their talk, the telephone on Stalin's desk rang once, an unusual occurrence during interviews of this kind. Stalin picked up the receiver and spoke a few sentences in Russian. Afterwards Major Birse, who was interpreting for Eden, told him that it was clear from Stalin's end of the conversation that he was giving orders for the bombing of selected targets in the Crimea which was still held by the Germans.

The same night Eden wrote in his private diary:

Joe was friendly enough to me personally, even jovial. But he still had that disconcerting habit of not looking at one as he speaks or shakes hands. A meeting with him would in all respects be a creepy, even sinister experience if it weren't for his readiness to laugh, when his whole face creases and his little eyes open. He looks more and more like bruin.*[83]

A further proof of Stalin's benevolence was afforded by the pardon and release of the two errant British sailors, though Molotov took the opportunity of reading the British delegation a curtain lecture on 'the need to treat Soviet citizens not as natives of British colonies but as equals with the British'.

The most important piece of information which Stalin had to impart was reserved for Cordell Hull, the American Secretary of State, who learned to his delight that 'when the Allies succeeded in defeating Germany, the Soviet Union would then join in defeating Japan'.[84]

Otherwise the main purpose of the foreign ministers' conference was to prepare the ground for a summit meeting of the three allied war leaders. Stalin had never met Roosevelt and for some time the proposal for a tripartite gathering had been under discussion. The main problem was the venue. Roosevelt suggested Fairbanks in Alaska, where the Russians had an air base, while Churchill favoured Iceland or Scapa Flow. But Stalin let it be known that he could not afford to travel so far outside the Soviet Union as he must have absolutely reliable direct telegraph and telephone communication with Moscow. Somewhere in Iraq was then proposed, such as Basra, which Roosevelt favoured, or Habbaniya where the British had a well protected air base. The American President was most reluctant to go any further afield than Basra because he had to deal personally with important matters of state. Stalin eventually settled the matter at his meeting with Cordell Hull when he told him he was 'unable to understand why a delay of two or three days in the delivery of state papers should be so vital a matter, whereas a false step in military operations was not a grammatical error which could be subsequently corrected.' The furthest point outside Soviet frontiers to which Stalin would journey, he said, was Teheran, which was only a few hours flying time from Moscow and which moreover was the capital of a country where Soviet as well as British troops were stationed. Nor would he go to Cairo to meet the Chinese Generalissimo Chiang Kai-shek, as Roosevelt wished. In this as well as the venue he won his point.

On 12 November Stalin sent Churchill a cable, repeated to Roosevelt,

* Bruin, the brown bear in *Reynard the Fox* by John Masefield.

that he and Molotov would come to Teheran at the end of the month. 'It goes without saying that the Teheran meetings should involve only the three heads of the Government as agreed,' he stressed. 'Participation of representatives of any other Powers should be absolutely ruled out.'[85]

Before leaving Moscow, Stalin was the recipient of another honour from the Supreme Soviet. This was the Order of Suvarov, First Class, the highest Soviet military decoration, awarded in his case for 'the successes achieved by his masterly direction of the operations of the Red Army in the Patriotic War against the German invaders'. He accepted it in the knowledge, which he expressed at the time, that the year 1943 had already 'marked the decisive turn' in the war. 'The results and consequences of the Red Army's victories are felt far beyond the Soviet –German front,' he declared proudly and self-confidently. 'They have changed the whole course of the World War and have acquired great international importance.'[86]

CHAPTER XII

The Road to Potsdam

I

'This Conference is over when it has only just begun. Stalin has got the President in his pocket.' The remark was made by Sir Alan Brooke, the British Chief of the Imperial General Staff, before the end of the first day of the Teheran meeting. There was some truth in what Brooke said.[1]

The Big Three, as they had become popularly known, assembled in the Persian capital on 27 November 1943. Unlike Churchill and Roosevelt, who arrived by air, Stalin travelled in great secrecy by ship across the Caspian and thence by road to Teheran, saying that he could not fly since his doctors had expressly forbidden him to do so. Besides his usual retinue of NKVD men and security guards, he was accompanied only by Molotov, Voroshilov and his interpreter Pavlov. The Prime Minister and the President, on the other hand, each brought a strong team of service advisers with them.

It was originally arranged that the principals should stay in their countries' respective legations. So far as Stalin and Churchill were concerned, this presented no security problem, since the Soviet and British legations were situated in large Oriental-style compounds adjoining each other and they were connected by a covered way. But the American legation was a mile or so distant and although he had a number of Secret Service officers in attendance Roosevelt would have to drive to the Soviet legation where the plenary sessions were to be held through crowded streets where there was always the risk of an 'incident' as

Molotov euphemistically called an assassination attempt. After Roosevelt had spent a night at the American legation, he received an invitation from Stalin to transfer to the Soviet legation, since a plot had been discovered whereby German agents planned to abduct the President and also to kill Churchill and Stalin. Neither the Americans nor the British had any evidence from their own intelligence sources of the existence of such a plot, and the British were inclined to regard the invitation as a clever move on Stalin's part to keep a closer watch on the President's movements and even to isolate him from Churchill, or at any rate to exploit any policy differences there might be between them.* It was generally agreed that no chances should be taken with the President's personal safety, and Roosevelt was consequently accommodated in a small house in the grounds of the Soviet legation.[2]

There were three plenary and two private sessions, as well as more intimate talks at luncheons and dinners. The first plenary session was opened with the American President in the chair at 4 p.m. on 28 November. Roosevelt had been installed in the Soviet legation compound about an hour before this and Stalin had already called on him to pay his respects. They were alone except for their interpreters for three quarters of an hour, most of the time being devoted to a survey of the current situation on the battle front as each of them saw it. Contrary to his expectation, Stalin found the President forthcoming and easy to talk to. The military picture having been examined, Roosevelt got on to one of his favourite topics, the education of the peoples of Burma, Indo-China, Malaya and other colonial areas in South-East Asia, in the arts of self-government. He pointed with pride to the American record in helping the people of the Philippines to prepare themselves for independence. This prompted him to warn Stalin against bringing up the problems of India with Churchill, and Stalin agreed that 'this was undoubtedly a sore subject'. Reform in India should begin from the bottom, said Roosevelt, upon which Stalin's comment was that 'reform from the bottom would mean revolution'.[3]

When Stalin took his place at the conference table, it was noticed that he had discarded his familiar workaday clothes, the grey-brown cloth tunic buttoned up to the neck and trousers of the same material

* There does seem to have been a plot which was revealed and frustrated by a Soviet double agent. The details were published in 1968 in Moscow in a book entitled *Plot Against Eureka* by Victor Yegorov, possibly a pseudonym for a member of the Soviet security service whose work was 'authorised'. 'Eureka' was the code name for the Teheran conference. It is suggested in the book that there was a 'leak' in the White House and that as a result by mid-November Hitler was aware of the place and date of the meeting. See the account by Kyril Tidmarsh in *The Times*, 20 December, 1968.

tucked into soft felt knee-boots. Instead he appeared in a mustard coloured uniform, which looked as if it had not been worn before and had been specially designed for the occasion. This was how it struck Lord Moran.

It looks, too, as if the tailor had put a shelf on each shoulder, and on it has dumped a lot of gold lace with white stars. And there is a broad red stripe down the trousers, which are immaculately pressed. All this is crowned by a dreadful hat, smothered with gold braid. His old rig fitted his blunt contempt for appearances; it seemed to scoff at all the uniforms around him, with their five or six rows of meaningless decorations. Has Stalin to make up and play a role like other people? I wish I could follow how his mind works. Why, for instance, did he get into uniform?[4]

In fact, this was the new Soviet marshal's uniform, the epaulettes and other features being part of the recent general scheme of officers' uniforms in the Red Army. Also, Stalin may have wished to vie with Churchill who he anticipated would be wearing some kind of service dress. In this he was correct, as Churchill, who possessed an extensive wardrobe of uniforms acquired in the course of his long service career, appeared throughout the proceedings as an Air Commodore of the Royal Air Force, an honorary rank he held in an auxiliary fighter squadron. This squadron had particularly distinguished itself in the Battle of Britain, and Churchill's insignia included the 'wings' of a qualified pilot. But whether Stalin fully appreciated the gesture is doubtful.

On the other hand, Stalin, who had never held any rank below that of Marshal in the Red Army, impressed the British service chiefs who came to Teheran with his abilities as a strategist, particularly Sir Alan Brooke, himself about to crown a distinguished military career by being promoted Field-Marshal. Brooke knew that Voroshilov could provide Stalin with nothing in the shape of strategic vision, a deficiency which was only too evident to the British Staff Chief when he had discussed the problem of a Second Front during his visit with Churchill to Moscow in the previous year. Brooke's tribute to Stalin's strategic qualities, recorded privately at the time, deserves quotation.

During this meeting and all the subsequent ones we had with Stalin, I rapidly grew to appreciate the fact that he had a military brain of the very highest calibre. Never once in any of his state-

493

ments did he make any strategic error, nor did he ever fail to appreciate all the implications of a situation with a quick and unerring eye. In this respect he stood out compared with his two colleagues. Roosevelt never made any pretence at being a strategist and left either Marshall or Leahy to talk for him.* Winston, on the other hand, was more erratic, brilliant at times, but too impulsive and inclined to favour unsuitable plans without giving them the preliminary deep thought they required.[5]

The opening session quickly developed into something of a wrangle between Stalin and Churchill, who had an extremely bad cold and had almost lost his voice, neither of which disabilities improved his temper. Stalin remained unruffled, speaking in a low voice, smoking and doodling on a writing pad. He remarked that the campaign in Italy had been useful in opening up the Mediterranean to Allied shipping, but he could see no point in the British fighting their way up the leg of Italy, foot by foot. The capture of Rome did not matter to him, he said, and he recalled that Marshal Suvorov in his day had barked his shins against the Alps. He approved of Roosevelt's proposal to close down the operations in Italy and transfer six divisions for the invasion of southern France in the spring of 1944, to be followed by Operation Overlord, the launching of the long awaited second front in the north. On the other hand, he shot down the President's suggestion that American forces should drive into Roumania, and aided by Yugoslav partisans effect a junction with the Red Army there, as he also did Churchill's support for a general Anglo-American campaign in the Balkans. Churchill explained that he was anxious to get Turkey into the war on the allied side. To this Stalin replied quietly, as if he knew, that Turkey had no intention of coming in. It was clear to Brooke who was present that Stalin had no longer any desire, if he ever had, for the opening of the Dardanelles.

> This would bring in the British and Americans on his left flank in an advance westward through the Balkans. He had by then pretty definite ideas as to how he wanted the Balkans run after the war; British and American assistance was therefore no longer desirable in the Eastern Mediterranean.[6]

On Churchill's suggestion that the military staffs should work out the details of the future operations and their timing next morning, Stalin

* General George C. Marshall was Chief of Staff of the US Army. Admiral William D. Leahy was Chief of Staff to President Roosevelt in his capacity of commander-in-chief of the US armed forces.

494

observed that he had not expected that military matters would be discussed at the conference, and consequently he had not brought his military experts with him. Nevertheless, Marshal Voroshilov would do his best, he said, a reflection on his professional competence which the marshal did not appear to resent. ('Nor did his performance the next morning belie Stalin's estimate of his limitations,' noted Brooke's colleague Ismay. 'One of his contributions to the discussion was that the Red Army had experienced little difficulty in crossing wide rivers and that we ought not to make such a fuss about crossing the English Channel.')[7]

The session ended with the announcement by Stalin that when Germany was defeated Russia would join in the war against Japan. It was made so casually and in such a low voice that it was only audible to his interpreter Pavlov who was sitting beside him. Then, as Harry Hopkins put it, he went on doodling as if nothing had happened.

At the dinner given by Roosevelt that evening, the main topic of discussion was the policy to be adopted towards Germany. Although he favoured the application of stringent measures to the point of harshness after Germany's defeat, Stalin could not agree to Roosevelt's demand for nothing short of unconditional surrender.[8] In this the President seems to have been influenced by the precedent in his own country established at the end of the Civil War when the southern states were treated by the successful north as a conquered country. 'To leave the principle of unconditional surrender unclarified would merely serve to unite the German people,' Stalin argued, 'whereas to draw up specific terms, no matter how harsh, and tell the German people that this was what they would have to accept, would, in my opinion, hasten the day of German capitulation.' However, it was Roosevelt's view which eventually prevailed, and it was supported by Churchill. 'It is false to suggest that it prolonged the war,' wrote Churchill afterwards. 'Negotiation with Hitler was impossible. He was a maniac with supreme power to play his hand out to the end, which he did; and so did we.' Stalin, on the other hand, did not share the view that Hitler was mentally unbalanced, emphasising at the dinner that 'only a very able man could accomplish what Hitler had done in solidifying the German people, whatever we thought of his methods'.[9]

After dinner they sat in a circle over their coffee and cigars, talking mostly about the progress of the war. 'I believe that God is on our side,' Churchill remarked at one point. 'At least I have done my best to make Him a faithful ally!'

When this had been translated, Stalin looked up and said with a grin: 'And the devil is on my side. Because, of course, everyone knows

495

that the devil is a Communist, and God, no doubt, is a good Conservative!'[10]

Next day's plenary session was prefaced by an incident which deeply touched Stalin. This was the presentation by Churchill of a four-foot ceremonial sword of honour to Stalin on behalf of the British sovereign. It bore the inscription: 'To the steel-hearted citizens of Stalingrad, the gift of King George VI in token of the homage of the British people.' Stalin took the sword and kissed the scabbard. Roosevelt said afterwards that there were tears in his eyes as he did so. At all events he appears to have been deeply moved, or, as Lord Moran put it, 'this hard-boiled Asiatic thawed and seemed to feel the emotions of ordinary people'. Stalin then handed the sword to Voroshilov, who, surprised by its weight, nearly dropped it out of its scabbard. Eventually by what looked like a clever conjuring trick he managed to retrieve it and clasped it to his breast. As Stalin shook Churchill's hand, Voroshilov in turn passed the sword to the Soviet officer in charge of the guard of honour who marched smartly out of the room bearing the sword shoulder high.[11]

That night Stalin was the host at a small dinner party, to which besides Roosevelt and Churchill he invited Molotov, Hopkins, Harriman, Eden and Clark Kerr. Half way through the meal it was 'gate crashed' by the President's son Elliot Roosevelt who had unexpectedly flown in to see his father and now took his seat at the table. On this occasion Stalin was in the most genial mood and joined Roosevelt in teasing Churchill so much that the British Premier no longer thought it funny. Talking of Germany, Stalin suggested that the whole General Staff should be 'liquidated' at the end of the war, as only by this means could German military strength be extirpated.

'The British Parliament and public will never tolerate mass executions,' said Churchill, who took Stalin's remarks in the utmost seriousness. 'The Soviets must be under no delusion on this point.'

'Fifty thousand must be shot,' insisted Stalin. 'The General Staff must go.'

'I would rather be taken out into the garden here and now,' replied Churchill, 'and be shot myself than sully my own and my country's honour by such infamy.'

'I have a compromise to propose,' Roosevelt broke in. 'Not fifty thousand but only forty-nine thousand should be shot.'

Eden made signs across the table to Churchill that it was all a joke. But Churchill at first refused to believe this, particularly as Elliot Roosevelt rose from the place he had taken at the end of the table and made a speech, saying how cordially he agreed with Marshal Stalin's plan and how sure he was that the United States Army would support it. Showing plainly that he resented what he called 'this intrusion', Churchill then got up and left the table, going off to the next room which was in semi-darkness. A few moments later, he felt a pair of hands clapped on his shoulder, and turned round to see Stalin, with Molotov at his side, 'both grinning broadly and eagerly declaring that they were only playing, and that nothing of a serious character had entered their heads'.

Although he was not fully convinced that it was all chaff and that there was no serious intent lurking behind, Churchill returned to the dining room, where the rest of the evening passed pleasantly. According to Clark Kerr, it ended with a convivial embrace, Stalin and Churchill standing with their hands on each other's shoulders, looking into each other's eyes. Then Stalin put his arm affectionately round Churchill. 'I wish we had a record of what was said,' the British ambassador remarked afterwards, 'that people might know what piffle great men sometimes talk.'[12]

Roosevelt later confessed to Frances Perkins, the Secretary of Labour in his cabinet, that for the first three days at Teheran he was unable to establish any real personal relationship with Stalin. ('He was correct, stiff, solemn, not smiling, nothing human to get hold of.') The President was discouraged and eventually hit upon a means of breaking the ice, first apologising to Churchill for what he was going to do. As soon as he entered the conference room for the next plenary session, Roosevelt went out of his way to appear what he called 'chummy and confidential' with Stalin. Still there was no smile. Then, lifting up his hand to cover a whisper, which of course had to be interpreted, the President said, 'Winston is cranky this morning, he got up on the wrong side of the bed.'

A vague smile passed over Stalin's eyes, and I decided I was on the right track. As soon as I sat down at the conference table, I began to tease Churchill about his Britishness, about John Bull, about his cigars, about his habits. It began to register with Stalin. Winston got red and scowled, and the more he did so, the more Stalin smiled. Finally Stalin broke out into a deep hearty guffaw, and for the first time in three days I saw light. I kept it up until Stalin was laughing with me...

From that time on our relations were personal, and Stalin himself indulged in an occasional witticism...The ice was broken and we talked like men and brothers.[13]

497

The same night, 30 November, which happened to be Churchill's sixty-ninth birthday, the British Premier was host at a large dinner in the British legation. The long dining table was beautifully set with a huge cake in the middle on which sixty-nine candles flickered. Stalin was placed on the host's left with Roosevelt on his right. At first Stalin sat uncomfortably on the edge of his chair, puzzled by the display of different sized knives and forks before him. 'This is a fine collection of cutlery,' he said to Churchill's interpreter Major Birse, who was seated on his left. 'It is a problem which to use. You will have to tell me, and also when I can begin to eat. I am unused to your customs.' The interpreter advised him to eat and drink when he pleased. Then Stalin quickly relaxed after Churchill announced that they would dine in the Russian manner and anyone could propose any toast he liked at any time during the meal. In due course Stalin clinked glasses with nearly everyone, going round the table to each person whose health was being drunk. Towards the end of the dinner he asked Birse whether it would be in order for him to drink the health of the Persian waiter who had been serving them. On Birse replying he was sure the man would be very happy if he did so, Stalin poured out another glass of champagne and handed it to the Persian, wishing him and his comrades the best of luck. The Persian seemed quite overcome and at a loss what to do with his glass, so that Birse came to the rescue by telling him to drink its contents on the spot which the man thereupon did.

For the pudding, the legation cook surpassed himself with an enormous ice-cream dish known as Persian Lantern and perched on a large block of ice in the middle of which burned a candle. The waiter who carried it round was less intent on his job than in looking at Stalin who was making a speech. This was being interpreted by Pavlov who was dressed in the smart new uniform of the Soviet Diplomatic Corps. At the moment the waiter approached, the tower of ice slid off the plate and cascaded over the unfortunate Pavlov. 'Mr Stalin says that the Red Army is worthy of the Soviet people...' The interpreter continued his translation as if nothing had happened, while the ice cream covered him from head to foot. Churchill afterwards made him a Commander of the British Empire, an order which he richly deserved, though not merely for his devotion to duty on this particular occasion. It should be added that Stalin responded by giving Major Birse the Order of the Red Banner of Labour.[14]

After dinner, when the President and most of the guests had left, Stalin lingered for a final drink with Churchill. 'England is becoming a shade pinker,' observed the Prime Minister.

'That is a sign of good health,' replied Stalin. Then, after this remark had been translated, he added: 'I want to call Mr Churchill my friend.'

'Call me Winston,' said the Prime Minister. 'I call you Joe behind your back.'

'No,' said Stalin. 'I want to call you my friend. I'd like to be allowed to call you my good friend.'

The two clinked glasses for the umpteenth time.

'I drink to the proletarian masses,' Churchill proposed.

'I drink to the Conservative Party,' replied Stalin.[15]

Next day the Teheran Conference ended with the issue of a communiqué drafted by the British and American Chiefs of Staff and warmly approved by Stalin. Unlike the usual document full of platitudes and generalities, this one, as Churchill suggested, sounded a note of mystery and a foretaste of impending doom to Germany.

> The Military Staffs of the three Powers concerted their plans for the final destruction of the German forces. They reached complete agreement as to the scope and timing of the operations which will be undertaken from east, west and south, and arrangements were made to ensure intimate and continuous co-operation.[16]

On his way home through Cairo, President Roosevelt addressed a few lines of thanks to Stalin for his hospitality. 'I view those momentous days of our meeting with the greatest satisfaction as being an important milestone in the progress of human affairs,' he wrote.

'I hope the common enemy of our peoples, Hitler's Germany, will soon feel this,' replied Stalin. 'Now there is certainty that our people will co-operate harmoniously both at present and after the war.'[17]

2

Among the matters agreed by the Big Three at Teheran was that the partisans fighting in German-occupied Yugoslavia 'should be supported by supplies and equipment to the greatest possible extent, and also by Commando operations'. The partisans were led by a brilliant fifty-one-year-old Croatian Communist named Josip Broz, better known as Tito, whose National Liberation Committee had recently turned itself into a provisional government of the whole country, thereby assuming the authority of King Peter and the royalist government-in-exile in Cairo, and at the same time had named Tito President and Defence Minister with the military rank of Marshal. The British had had a mission led by Brigadier Fitzroy Maclean attached to Tito's

headquarters for the past six months, and this was now to be reinforced by Churchill's only son Randolph, who made a successful para-
chute landing with Maclean early in the New Year, bringing with
them a warm letter of encouragement to Tito from the Prime Minister,
a copy of which Churchill sent Stalin.[18]

In acknowledging its receipt, Stalin wrote to Churchill on 14
January 1944:

> Our armies have indeed achieved success of late, but we are still
> a long way from Berlin. What is more the Germans are now
> launching rather serious counter-attacks...Hence you should not
> slacken, but intensify the bombing of Berlin as much as possible.
> By the time we all arrive in Berlin the Germans will have had a
> chance to rebuild certain premises you and we here shall need.
>
> Your message to Tito, whom you are encouraging so much with
> your support, will be of great importance.[19]

In telling Stalin about his contacts with Tito, Churchill added that all
the officers of the British mission had been instructed 'to work in the
closest harmony with any mission you may send'. At Teheran Stalin
had given the impression that he did not set much store on the Yugoslav partisans or indeed on guerrilla activities generally. However, he
was persuaded, largely by Eden, to send a mission, and this eventually
arrived towards the end of February led by an alcoholic general named
Korneyev, who had been chief of staff to an army commander on the
Stalingrad front and for some reason was now being given an easier
billet. ('The poor man is not stupid,' said Stalin contemptuously, 'but
he is a drunkard, an incurable drunkard.') The members of the Soviet
mission, which was flown in by gliders of the British air force from a
base in southern Italy, brought with them a welcome supply of vodka
and caviar, but this gesture was immediately offset by complaints of
inadequate lavatory accommodation in their quarters, which as a result
had to be hastily rebuilt to their specifications.[20]

Tito reacted by dispatching a Yugoslav military mission to Moscow.
Headed by Milovan Djilas, a Montenegrin and one of Tito's most
trusted comrades, this mission was a much more highly powered body
than its Soviet counterpart. Its main object was to seek aid, particularly
a loan of $200,000, to meet the expenses of partisan missions to London
and elsewhere in the west, but it also aimed at re-establishing direct
contact with Soviet Communist Party officials which Tito felt had
been lost after the abolition of the Comintern. As a result Djilas saw a
good deal of Stalin and the Politburo, and it is to the record that Djilas

kept of these meetings that we owe some of the most revealing side-lights on Stalin and his Party colleagues at this period.

At the first meeting which took place in the Kremlin, the question of the loan was raised. However, according to Djilas, Stalin described it as a trifle, saying that the Yugoslav partisans could not do much with such an amount, but that the sum would be allocated to them immediately. On Djilas remarking that Yugoslavia would repay this as well as all shipments of arms and equipment 'after the liberation', Stalin became quite angry. 'You insult me,' he said. 'You are shedding your blood, and you expect me to charge you for the weapons! I am not a merchant, we are not merchants. You are fighting for the same cause as we. We are duty bound to share with you whatever we have.'

On the method of getting the arms and equipment to the partisans, it was decided to ask the western Allies to allow the establishment of a Soviet air base in Italy for the use of transport planes. 'Let us try,' said Stalin. 'We shall see what attitude the West takes and how far they are prepared to go to help Tito.'*

There was also the delicate problem of relations with the Yugoslav government-in-exile. 'Couldn't we somehow trick the English into recognising Tito, who alone is fighting the Germans?' he asked, turning to Molotov, who was also present.

'No, that is impossible,' said Molotov. 'They are perfectly aware of developments in Yugoslavia.'

Stalin then inquired where the Yugoslav King Peter II had found a wife. When Djilas replied that he had found a Greek princess, Stalin again turned to Molotov with a roguish laugh. 'How would it be, Vyacheslav Mikhailovich, if you or I married some foreign princess? Maybe some good would come of it!'[21]

At their next meeting, when he invited Djilas to dinner at Kuntsevo on the eve of the allied invasion of France, Stalin impressed upon his guest that Tito and his provisional government should not 'frighten' the English into becoming alarmed that a Communist revolution was taking place in Yugoslavia. 'What do you want with red stars on your caps?' he asked. 'By God, stars aren't necessary!'

'It is impossible to discontinue the red stars,' replied Djilas, 'because they are already a tradition and have acquired a certain meaning among our fighters.'

Stalin let this pass, and he went on to tell his fellow Communist with malicious humour what he really thought of the western Allies and their leaders. 'Perhaps you think that because we are allies of the English that we have forgotten who they are and who Churchill is,' he

* The base was established shortly afterwards at Bari.

remarked. 'They find nothing sweeter than to trick their allies. During the First World War they constantly tricked the Russians and the French. And Churchill? Churchill is the kind who, if you don't watch him, will slip a kopec out of your pocket. Yes, a kopec out of your pocket!' As for Roosevelt, he said, he was if anything worse. 'He dips in his hand only for bigger coins.'

In the course of their talks, Stalin repeatedly warned Djilas to beware of the machinations of the British Intelligence Service, which might well endanger Tito's life. 'They were the ones who killed General Sikorski in a plane and then neatly shot down the plane,' he added. 'No proof, no witnesses!'[22]*

The warnings were duly passed on to Tito, who acted accordingly when he had his first meeting with Churchill in Naples a few weeks later. On this occasion the partisan leader was attended by two ferocious bodyguards with automatic pistols at the ready, 'in case of treachery on our part', noted Churchill afterwards.[23]

King Peter had recently been persuaded by Churchill to dismiss the pro-German General Mihailovic from his councils, and a fresh government had been formed under Dr Ivan Subasic, a moderate politician and former Governor of Croatia, who was anxious to reach an accommodation with Tito. Stalin now advised Djilas on no account to ignore the new royalist premier. 'Do not attack him immediately,' he said. 'Let us see what he wants...You cannot be recognised right away...You ought to talk with Subasic and see if you can't reach a compromise somehow.' This shrewd advice was also passed on to Tito who took it when he reached an agreement with Subasic, by which their respective resources should be pooled in the struggle against the German invader, although it was evident by this time that the monarchy had ceased to be a unifying influence in Yugoslavia.[24]

When they met a few months later in Moscow, Stalin urged Tito to work with royalist politicians, even the King. 'You need not restore him for ever,' said Stalin. 'Take him back temporarily. Then you can slip a knife into his back at a suitable moment.'[25]

During the dinner with Djilas, Stalin received two dispatches which

---

* General Sikorski, Prime Minister of the Polish government-in-exile, lost his life in an aeroplane accident at Gibraltar in July 1943. The allegations that Sir Winston Churchill had acquiesced in the engineering of the accident and that the pilot had deliberately crashed the plane were made by the German writer Rolf Hochuth in his play *The Soldiers*. When the play was produced in London, the pilot sued the theatre licencees and obtained substantial damages with an unqualified apology from the licencees who 'regretted that their theatre should have been used for the publication of a serious and, in their view, wholly unfounded libel'. See *Prchal* v. *Albery and Others*, reported in *The Times*, 1 August 1970.

he handed to his guest to read. One contained a report of what Subasic had been saying to the American State Department. Noticing the look of astonishment on his guest's face, Stalin remarked, 'They steal our dispatches, we steal theirs!'

The second dispatch was from Churchill and confirmed that the landing in northern France would start next day. According to Djilas, Stalin began to make fun of it. 'Yes, there'll be a landing, if there is no fog,' he said. 'Until now there was always something that interfered. I suspect tomorrow it will be something else. Maybe they'll meet up with some Germans! What if they meet up with some Germans? Maybe there won't be a landing then but just promises as usual.'

'No,' Molotov broke in. 'This time it really will be so.'

Nevertheless, Djilas got the impression that this was a piece of malicious banter on Stalin's part and that he did not really doubt that the landing would take place after the many postponements which he described for his guests' benefit.[26]

Very different was the language Stalin employed a few days later when he heard from Churchill that 400,000 British and American troops had been disembarked together with massive tank and artillery support. On 11 June 1944, he cabled Churchill:

> It appears that the landing, planned on a tremendous scale, has been crowned with success. I and my colleagues cannot but recognise that this is an enterprise unprecedented in military history as to scale, breadth of conception and masterly execution. As is known, Napoleon's plan for crossing the Channel failed disgracefully. Hitler the hysteric, who for two years had boasted that he would cross the Channel, did not venture even to make an attempt to carry out his threat. None but our Allies have been able to fulfil with flying colours the grand plan for crossing the Channel. History will record this as a feat of the highest order.[27]

There was always a certain streak of naïveté in Stalin's character, and he gave a remarkable example of it at this time when in the midst of his military preoccupations he received an obscure American Catholic priest named Orlemanski from Springfield, Massachusetts. Father Orlemanski, who as his name suggests was of Polish origin, left his parish without his bishop's permission on a self-imposed mission on which he sought to bring about a 'reconciliation' between the Kremlin and the Vatican and also between Russia and Poland. Much to everyone's surprise, Stalin saw the priest twice, on each occasion spending several hours with him, at the end of which Father Orlemanski emerged with a solemn written statement signed in Stalin's own hand

503

offering to collaborate with the Pope. On his return to Springfield, Father Orlemanski was taken to task for his antics in Moscow, which had received world-wide publicity, and was sent off to a monastery to do penance. Thus his well-meant aspirations came to nothing. The question remains, why did Stalin contemplate making use of an unknown parish priest when he could easily have approached the Pope through the normal diplomatic channels? It may be, as Isaac Deutscher has suggested, that 'he was more eager to advertise his own respectable moderation than to seek peace with the Vatican; but even then he had no need to resort to a stunt which for a few days made him the laughing-stock of the world. The incident was, nevertheless, characteristic of the opportunistically rightist colouring of Stalin's policy in those days.'[28]

At the same time a Polish National Liberation Committee came into being behind the Soviet lines, consisting of reliable.Communists who established their headquarters in Lublin: its members included Boleslav Bierut, a staunch Stalinist, who was soon to take charge as head of a Soviet-sponsored Provisional Government, rivalling the London based government-in-exile which it declared illegal.

By the end of July Soviet troops had reached the Vistula and were within sight of Warsaw; indeed Red Army patrols actually entered Praga, a suburb of the capital on the east bank of the river. However, Rokossovsky's main forces halted on Stalin's orders and for the time being made no move to cross the river and storm the city, where the Polish Underground fighters under General Bor-Komorowski were about to stage an armed rising against the Nazi occupation authorities. General Bor had authority to do this at any moment of his own choosing, and seeing that what he took to be the Red Amy of liberation was so close he gave the signal for revolt which began in the afternoon of 1 August. No doubt his decision was hastened by the cruel manner in which the Warsaw civilian population was being treated by the Nazis; also he was no doubt encouraged by the allied successes in Normandy and by the opposition to Hitler which had developed inside Germany and which culminated in the abortive plot to assassinate him and seize power on 7 July. Alas for the unfortunate Poles, Stalin persistently turned a deaf ear to calls for help, whether from Churchill, Roosevelt, General Bor or Stanislav Mikolajcyk, who had succeeded Sikorski as Prime Minister of the government-in-exile and had flown from London to Moscow at Churchill's suggestion to plead with Stalin.

On 16 August Stalin cabled Churchill:

Now, after probing more deeply into the Warsaw affair, I have come to the conclusion that the Warsaw action is a reckless and fearful gamble, taking a heavy toll of the population. This would not have been the case had Soviet headquarters been informed beforehand about the Warsaw action and had the Poles maintained contact with them.

Things being what they are, Soviet headquarters have decided that they must dissociate themselves from the Warsaw adventure since they cannot assume either direct or indirect responsibility for it.

Churchill and Roosevelt reacted in unison four days later with a joint appeal to Stalin.

We are thinking of world opinion if the anti-Nazis in Warsaw are in effect abandoned. We believe that all three of us should do the utmost to save as many of the patriots there as possible. We hope that you will drop immediate supplies and munitions to the patriot Poles in Warsaw, or you will agree to help our planes in doing it very quickly. We hope you will approve. The time element is of extreme importance.[29]

Stalin remained unmoved. He had nothing but contempt for what he called 'the handful of power-seeking criminals who launched the Warsaw adventure'. He could not prevent the Americans and British from dropping arms and supplies by air, he said, 'since this is an American and British affair', but he refused to allow the allied aircraft to land and take off from Soviet territory. 'I can assure you that the Red Army will spare no effort to crush the Germans at Warsaw,' he told Churchill and Roosevelt. 'That will be the best and most effective help for the anti-Nazi Poles.'[30] Of course, he realised that the majority of the latter were anti-Communist as well, and it was part of his calculated and deliberate policy that this patriotic majority should be destroyed, which indeed they were in the hand-to-hand struggle in the streets and sewers of the city. In the terrible process fifteen thousand men and women of the Polish Underground were killed in addition to about one-fifth of the one million inhabitants, before the gallant General Bor surrendered at the end of sixty-three days of the most bitter fighting with little food and water to sustain their physical needs. 'When the Russians entered the city three months later,' Churchill was to write after the war, 'they found little but shattered streets and the unburied dead. Such was their liberation of Poland where they now rule.'[31]*

* This took place on 17 January 1945. Churchill subsequently told his private secretary John Colville that it was Stalin's behaviour over the Warsaw rising that 'finally revealed to him (though apparently not to President Roosevelt and the

On 9 October 1944, a week after the surrender, Churchill arrived in Moscow to try to settle the problem of Poland's political future with Stalin, in addition to other questions including the Balkans. Roosevelt, who would have liked to have joined them, was prevented from doing so by the Presidential election campaign in which although in failing health he successfully campaigned for a fourth term. Meanwhile he asked Harriman to stand in for him as an observer.

'Let us settle about our affairs in the Balkans,' said Churchill to Stalin at their first meeting. 'So far as Britain and Russia are concerned, how would it do for you to have ninety per cent predominance in Roumania, for us to have ninety per cent of the say in Greece, and go fifty-fifty about Yugoslavia?'

While this was being translated Churchill wrote down the suggested proportions on a piece of paper, to which he added Hungary (fifty-fifty) and Bulgaria (seventy-five per cent Russian), and then pushed the paper across the table to Stalin. After a pause, Stalin produced a blue pencil and made a large tick on the paper, which he passed back to Churchill and Eden.

'Might it not be thought rather cynical if it seemed we had disposed of these issues, so fateful to millions of people, in such an offhand manner?' Churchill asked reflectively. 'Let us burn the paper!'

'No,' said Stalin, 'you keep it.' And this Churchill accordingly did.[32]

The Polish question proved more difficult of solution and resulted in a deadlock, although Churchill did his best with Mikolajcyk who had been summoned from London and whom he tried without success to persuade to accept the Curzon line as the basis for the future Polish–Soviet frontier. It was plain that Stalin intended to transform the Lublin National Liberation Committee into a puppet Communist Government, and that in Bierut and his colleagues he had willing stooges. Throughout the discussions the Lublin Poles behaved like well-oiled automata. 'We are here to demand that Lvov shall belong to Russia,' said Bierut at one point. 'This is the will of the Polish people.' As a Polish friend of Lord Ismay remarked, to cede Lvov with its historic religious associations for Poland was like asking the British to deliver Canterbury into the hands of unbelievers. But Stalin wanted Lvov for the Ukraine and that was that. When Bierut's remarks had been translated into Russian, Churchill happened to catch Stalin's eye,

<hr>

State Department) the chasm which divided the Western from the Soviet code of honour. When Churchill returned to power in 1951 one of his first acts was to make enquiries about General Bor-Komorowski who had escaped the final massacre, and to demand assurances that provision had been made for his comfort and well-being'. *Action This Day* (1968), p. 92.

where he saw an understanding twinkle, as much as to say, 'What about that for our Soviet teaching!'[33]

'Mikolajcyk is a peasant and extremely obstinate,' said Churchill to Stalin after one of the meetings.

'I am a peasant too,' replied Stalin.

'You can be as obstinate as any of them,' was Churchill's candid rejoinder, which Stalin did not contradict.[34]

No doubt because he was getting his own way, Stalin was more agreeable and pleasant than at any of their previous meetings. This was particularly reflected in their social relations. Although he could see from his Kremlin office the Union Jack fluttering from the roof of the British embassy on the other side of the river Moskva, Stalin had never set foot in the ornate and heavily decorated building which had belonged in Tsarist days to a sugar millionaire named Haritonenko. Now he accepted an invitation to dinner and after the embassy building had been thoroughly infiltrated by NKVD guards, he appeared resplendent in his Marshal's elaborate full dress uniform. 'Apparently the Red Army has had another victory,' said Vyshinsky to Major Birse as they walked up the stairs together. 'It has occupied the British embassy.'

Stalin remarked that he liked the English habit of serving cocktails and sherry before dinner, but could not understand why his hosts weakened their whisky by putting water in it. Pausing before a lifesize portrait of King George V in the dining room, he asked, 'Is that our Nicholas II?' He was informed that the two were first cousins and that their striking physical resemblance to each other had often been noted. He also asked Churchill about the next General Election in Britain and expressed the opinion that the Conservatives would win, comparing the Labour Party with the Mensheviks at the time of the Revolution in 1917. 'It is even harder to understand the politics of other countries than those of your own,' reflected Churchill afterwards.[35]

After dinner they discussed the future of Italy and Yugoslavia among other subjects. Churchill, who had recently been in Rome, admitted that for the first time his attitude towards the Italians had changed, due to the welcome the cheering crowds had given him. He was not at all pleased when Stalin remarked that the crowds had supported Mussolini with equal enthusiasm. On the subject of Yugoslavia, Stalin said that in Tito's opinion the Croats and Slovenes would refuse to join in any government under King Peter, adding that he himself considered the exiled monarch to be 'ineffective'. Eden replied that he was sure Peter had courage and he thought he had intelligence as well. On Churchill interjecting that he was very young, Stalin asked what age he was. 'Twenty-one,' said Eden. 'Twenty-one!' echoed Stalin. 'Peter the Great was the ruler of Russia at seventeen.'* To his British hosts at that moment Stalin appeared more nationalist than communist, 'the same mood', as Eden reflected afterwards, 'as had seen the disappearance for the time being of the portraits of Marx and Engels from the Kremlin rooms and their replacement by Kutuzov and Suvorov'.[36]

'Stalin is more friendly these days,' Churchill told Lord Moran. 'The invasion and the number of prisoners taken by us have sent us up in his eyes. He talks freely to me.' On the future of communism, for example, Stalin denied 'with great earnestness' that Russia wished to convert the whole world to this political creed. 'We could not even if we wanted to,' he assured Churchill. 'We Russians are not as clever as you think; we're simple, rather stupid. No one in Europe can be persuaded that England is either simple or stupid!' Other remarks he made to Churchill in the course of casual conversation were equally characteristic:

Fear is a psychological factor. But it has very practical results. It was the fear of invasion that prevented the Germans transferring fifty divisions to the Russian Front in 1942. Those fifty divisions might have made the difference. I do not speak much, but drinking eases the tongue...I am a rough man and not much good at compliments...Only the aggressors can be prepared. Are all of us to be aggressors?[37]

One night there was a command performance of ballet and opera at the Bolshoi Theatre, at which Stalin, Churchill, Eden and Harriman occupied the old imperial box. The first two received a standing ovation from the packed house, Stalin deliberately pushing his guest to the front, while he himself remained for most of the time in the shadows. 'Many of us were astonished,' remarked Ismay who was in the audience below, 'that such a ruthless man of steel as Stalin should be capable of such old-world courtesy.'[38]

* In fact Peter was only eleven when his father King Alexander was assassinated in Marseilles in 1934 and he succeeded to the throne. His uncle Prince Paul acted as Regent until he was deposed in March 1944. Peter then assumed the powers of sovereign, but on the German invasion of his country a month later he flew to England and established a Yugoslav government-in-exile in London, later moving to Cairo. In 1944, he married Princess Alexandra of Greece. He was a great-great-grandson of the English Queen Victoria through the maternal line. He never returned to Yugoslavia after Marshal Tito took control. He died of pneumonia in 1970 at the age of forty-seven.

Towards the end of one of the intervals on this occasion, Churchill and Eden asked where they could wash their hands, and were conducted to the appropriate department. While they were thus engaged, Churchill suddenly became excited by an idea which had come into his head for the solution of the Polish dilemma and he proceeded to expound it eagerly and at some length to Eden. After repeated efforts to stop him, Eden remarked that they should go back to the box as the audience must have been waiting for quite a while. On their return, Stalin made no comment on the delay they had caused, but a few nights later when he entertained them to a late night meal in his flat in the Poteshny Palace, he showed that he had not forgotten the incident and in addition that in Stalin's Russia even the lavatory walls had ears. As they arrived in the hall, Stalin nodded in the direction of a door in the corner, saying: 'That's where you can wash your hands if you want to, the place as I understand it where you English like to conduct your political discussions!'[39]

Next day Churchill described the session to his physician:

> Stalin ate heartily, pork mainly. I picked at things. He dines at
> 1 a.m. as a rule, goes to bed at four and rises between noon and
> one o'clock, a relic of the days when it was safer for him to lie
> low during the day...
> Stalin's sense of humour is his strongest characteristic. He
> talked about my private war with Russia in 1919, all in a friendly
> way. I said: 'I'm glad now that I did not kill you. I hope you are
> glad that you did not kill me?' Stalin agreed readily, quoting a
> Russian proverb: 'A man's eyes should be torn out if he can only
> see the past.' We all made a move at three in the morning, but
> Stalin would not let us go and kept us till four. All the time he got
> more animated and expansive.[40]

3

A few weeks later, in December 1944, the Free French leader General Charles de Gaulle visited Moscow with his Foreign Minister Georges Bidault for a general discussion on the future peace settlement. He did so at Stalin's invitation, since a Provisional Government headed by de Gaulle had been established in Paris following the liberation of the French capital in the previous August. By December the Provisional Government had been recognised by most other governments including that of the Soviet Union, and de Gaulle was now eager to conclude a security and non-aggression pact similar to that which already existed between the Soviet Union and Great Britain. While the details of this treaty were being hammered out by Bidault and Molotov, Stalin talked at length with de Gaulle, devoting some fifteen hours in all from his other preoccupations to the General, to whom he appeared relaxed and even playful.

'It must be very difficult to govern a country like France, where everyone is so restless!' remarked Stalin at their first conversation.

'Yes,' answered de Gaulle. 'And I cannot imitate your example, for you are inimitable!'

When Stalin mentioned Maurice Thorez, the French Communist leader whom the Provisional Government had allowed to return to Paris, de Gaulle remained silent. 'Don't take offence at my indiscretion,' said Stalin. 'Let me only say that I know Thorez and that in my opinion he is a good Frenchman. If I were in your place, I would not put him in prison.' After a moment's pause, he added with a smile, 'At least, not right away!'

'The French Government treats the French according to the services it expects from them,' de Gaulle rejoined stiffly.

The question of Poland's future nearly proved fatal to the new Franco-Soviet pact, since Stalin and Molotov tried hard to make it conditional upon de Gaulle's agreeing to recognise the Lublin Committee of Polish Communists as the government of Poland. De Gaulle was willing to meet Bierut and his colleagues as Churchill and Eden had done, but he flatly refused to go any further than dispatching a French officer to Lublin to deal with such questions as the French prisoners-of-war and deportees whom the retreating Germans had left behind in the parts of Poland they had occupied. A farewell banquet was arranged for the French delegation on 9 December, the day before de Gaulle and his party were due to leave, when Stalin hoped that the French leader would be in a more amenable mood. In the event Stalin was disappointed, in spite of all the warm words and compliments to France and his principal guest which accompanied his toasts.

Asked by Stalin during the meal what impression he had formed of the Lublin Poles, de Gaulle replied cautiously that they seemed to him to be 'a group capable of being turned to account', though in his view they did not represent 'independent Poland'. De Gaulle noted that Stalin ate heavily and served himself copiously from a bottle of Crimean wine which was frequently replaced in front of him. He also noted the watchful and constrained manner of the Russians present, who never took their eyes off the Marshal. ('On their part, manifest submission and apprehensiveness; on his, concentrated and vigilant authority.') Whenever Stalin toasted a Russian, he would shout 'Come here!' to the individual whom he named. The latter would then jump from his place and run over to Stalin with whom he would dutifully clink glasses. Nor was Stalin's rough manner and the threats behind some of the toasts lost on the perceptive de Gaulle. For instance, in toasting Marshal Novikov, the chief of the Soviet Air Force, he remarked, 'You are the one who uses our planes. If you use them badly, you know what's in store for you!' A few minutes later he rubbed in the point, when he indicated another Russian and said: 'There he is! That's the supply director. It is his job to bring men and material to the front. He'd better do his best. Otherwise he'll be hanged for it – that's the custom in our country!'

This calculated display of Soviet might and the domination of the man at its head did not impress de Gaulle at all favourably, any more indeed than the film which Stalin put on later in the evening for the entertainment of his guests. The film, which seems to have been a regular feature on these occasions, was *The War in the Future*; it had been made in 1938 as anti-German propaganda and was the same one that had been shown to Beaverbrook and Harriman in 1941. It forecast the treacherous Nazi invasion of the Soviet Motherland and depicted the eventual defeat of Hitler and the triumph of revolution in Berlin, thanks to the courage of the Red Army and the inspiring leadership of the great Stalin.

'I'm afraid Monsieur de Gaulle was not pleased by the end of the story,' said Stalin, as he laughed and clapped his hands.

'On the contrary,' replied his guest with a touch of annoyance. 'Particularly since at the beginning of the actual war, relations between you and the Germans were not as we saw them in his film.'

Finally, after he had instructed Bidault to break off the negotiations for the projected pact, de Gaulle rose to say goodbye. Stalin and Molotov were flabbergasted, as they had been sure that the French leader would agree in the end to recognise the Lublin Government. However, an hour or two after he had returned to the French embassy where he was staying, de Gaulle received a message from the Kremlin to the effect that Stalin and Molotov had climbed down and that the draft of the treaty was ready for signing and ratification in Molotov's office without any strings attached. Accordingly de Gaulle got dressed again and went back to the Kremlin about four o'clock in the morning. Bidault and Molotov immediately set their signatures to copies in French and Russian, as the official Soviet press cameras clicked and flashed. Stalin shook hands with de Gaulle and exclaimed, 'We must celebrate this!' In a moment tables were brought with food and drink, and everyone present sat down to another meal.

Although he disliked Stalin personally, de Gaulle had to admit to himself that he was a good loser. 'You played your hand well!' Stalin congratulated him in a low voice. 'Well done! I like dealing with someone who knows what he wants, even if he doesn't share my views.' De Gaulle thought that Stalin now spoke in a peculiarly detached and serene way, quite different from the fierce pugnacity he had shown earlier in the evening. He talked about the war and Hitler. 'After all,' he said, 'only death wins.' As for Hitler, he pitied him as 'a poor wretch who won't escape from this one'. To de Gaulle's invitation, 'Will you come and see us in Paris?' he answered, 'How can I? I'm an old man. I'm going to die soon.'

Stalin insisted on drinking a fresh round of toasts, including one to Poland, although no Pole was present. 'The Tsars had a bad policy of trying to dominate the other Slav peoples,' he said. 'We have a new policy. Let Slavs everywhere be independent and free. Then they will be our friends. Long live a strong, independent and democratic Poland! Long live the friendship of France, Poland and Russia!' Then, looking hard at his guest, he asked, 'What does Monsieur de Gaulle think of that?' De Gaulle, whose sobriety contrasted strongly with his host's alcoholic condition, replied that he was in complete agreement with what Stalin had said about Poland. He repeated his words to make sure that Stalin had understood them.

As dawn broke over the Kremlin's golden spires and cupolas, General de Gaulle rose to go. Stalin was most effusive in his protracted farewells. 'You can count on me!' he assured the departing visitor. 'If you or France needs us, we will share what we have with you down to our last crumb!' Suddenly his expression changed from one of benevolence to grimness as he turned to Podzerov, the interpreter who had attended every meeting and translated every exchange between the two leaders, and addressed him harshly. 'You know too much! I'd better send you to Siberia.'

De Gaulle left the room with Bidault and his other ministers. Turning back for a moment at the door, the General saw Stalin sitting, alone, at the table. He had started eating again.[41]

4

While the British Ministers were in Moscow, Stalin and the *Stavka* had already begun to plan a concerted drive on Berlin. In the central sector of the front the Soviet armies had been halted since mid-August on the line of the rivers Vistula and San in central Poland. This was a political rather than a military decision on Stalin's part occasioned by the desire to clear the Balkans of the enemy and thus secure Soviet influence in all the Balkan countries with the exception of Greece, which Stalin had agreed with Churchill to leave to the British. Roumania, Bulgaria, Yugoslavia and Hungary were successively 'liberated', and at the same time the Germans were expelled from all but a few segments of Russian territory.

The usual celebrations on the anniversary of the Revolution in November 1944 were a convenient pretext for summoning the front commanders and other senior officers to Moscow without arousing the enemy's suspicions. It was then agreed that the final big offensive should be launched in the third week of January 1945 and that the operation should be carried out in two stages which would take altogether forty-five days, although there might be a pause between the stages. As the commander of the First Byelorussian Army Group, Rokossovsky, by now promoted Marshal, looked like being the captor of Berlin. But no sooner had he and his fellow officers returned to their commands than Stalin telephoned him with the news that he was to hand over his command to Zhukov and instead to take command of the Second Byelorussian Army Group to the north. Naturally Rokossovsky was extremely disappointed by this decision. 'Why am I being penalised?' he asked Stalin, only to be told curtly that he would be given any further details of his new command he needed from the *Stavka*. Stalin also let it be known that he would personally co-ordinate the operations of the four army groups which had been earmarked for the offensive. Berlin, he made it clear, should be captured by the Deputy Supreme Commander, Marshal Zhukov.

While the final touches were being given to these preparations in Moscow, the western Allies sustained a serious reverse on a lightly held section of the Belgian front in the region of the river Meuse south of Liège. Hitler threw his last reserves into a desperate attempt to entrap as many as thirty allied divisions and capture the strategic port of Antwerp, which he hoped might perhaps lead to a negotiated peace with the west. On 16 December, Runstedt's armies broke through an 88-mile front in the Ardennes, and there followed the so-called Battle of the Bulge, which resulted in the Americans losing 8,000 dead, 48,000 wounded and 21,000 prisoners. The counter-measures taken by General Eisenhower, who commanded the Allied Expeditionary Force, included the dispatch of his deputy commander the British Air Marshal Tedder on a special mission to Moscow with the object of ascertaining when they might expect the opening of a major Russian offensive on the Vistula front or elsewhere, thereby relieving their forces of some of the German pressure. As Tedder was held up by bad weather in Cairo, Churchill cabled Stalin on 6 January 1945, urgently requesting this information. Stalin replied promptly next day to the effect that regardless of weather the Supreme Command (in other words himself) had decided to speed up the preparations and commence large-scale offensive operations against the Germans along the whole Central Front not later than the middle of January. 'You may rest assured,' he added, 'that we shall do everything possible to render assistance to the glorious forces of our Allies.' Churchill gratefully acknowledged 'your most thrilling message', which he passed on to Eisenhower.[42]

In fact, the opening of the offensive was advanced by one week to 12 January, so that it had already begun by the time Tedder reached the Kremlin three days later. As Tedder walked along the corridor leading to Stalin's office carrying Eisenhower's present of two boxes of cigars, he noticed the guards eyeing him suspiciously, apparently fearing a concealed bomb. Eventually he was ushered into the presence and he handed over the boxes. Stalin took his pipe out of his mouth and, pointing to the boxes on the table, asked, 'When do they go off?' Somewhat taken aback, Tedder glanced at his wrist watch and then answered with a perfectly straight face, 'They do not go off until I have gone!' Stalin grinned and seemed to appreciate the joke. They then got straight down to business.[43]

Tedder was accompanied by one British and two American generals as well as a British admiral. Stalin had Antonov, his Chief of Operations, with him. Molotov was not present, since it was a strictly military conference. As usual, Pavlov and Birse acted as interpreters.

'I know why you have come,' said Stalin, opening the conversation. 'You want to know what we are doing and what we are going to do.' Thereupon, to Tedder's surprise, he spread out a map on the table, and clearly and concisely, and as it later appeared accurately, he described both current operations and future plans for the Russian drive to the Oder. He thought that the Germans must be moving some of their forces from the west, otherwise they could not resist on the eastern front. 'In my opinion the war will not end before the summer,' he added. 'There is no will inside Germany around which opposition to the Hitler regime can coalesce. The final break will very probably be produced by famine. We must not forget, however, that the Germans are frugal and enduring. They have more stubbornness than brains. In fact, they should not have undertaken the Ardennes offensive. That was very stupid of them.'

After Tedder had outlined the allied plans for a resumption of the western offensive, Stalin cross-examined Eisenhower's deputy on tactical details. In particular, he showed interest in the air campaign against the German synthetic oil plants and its widespread effects. In this connection Tedder pointed out that the Blechhammer Synthetic Oil Plant was at extreme range for British and American bombers from the west and consequently had so far escaped attack; on the other hand, it was at short range from Soviet bomber bases. Stalin did not wait for Tedder to underline the obvious deduction, but turned to Antonov and, with a flash of anger which inspired Tedder with awe, asked why this key-point had not been attacked. The unfortunate Chief of Operations went pale and rose shakily to his feet to reply. Tedder, as he afterwards admitted, saw no particular advantage in pushing Antonov's head under the hammer, so he intervened to say that he would, of course, give Antonov all the technical and topographical details necessary. (To the best of Tedder's knowledge, this had been done some months previously.) Tedder also noted that this incident gave an impressive glimpse of the fear that ruled the Soviet regime, as indeed it had appeared or was to appear to other British military visitors like Ismay and Montgomery.

'We are comrades,' said Stalin to Tedder at the end of the meeting. 'It is proper, and also sound, selfish policy, that we should help each other in times of difficulty. It would be foolish for me to stand aside and let the Germans annihilate you; they would only turn back on me when you were disposed of. Similarly it is to your interest to do everything possible to keep the Germans from annihilating me.'

'Despite unfavourable weather the offensive is developing according to plan,' Stalin cabled Churchill after he had seen Tedder. 'The troops are in action all along the Central Front, from the Carpathians to the Baltic Sea. Although offering desperate resistance, the Germans have been forced to retreat.' He added that the British Air Marshal had 'made a very good impression' on him, an opinion confirmed by Major Birse. 'That is what I like,' said Stalin, as soon as Tedder had left. 'A clear business-like statement without diplomatic reservations.' A few more days saw the end of the Battle of the Bulge with Hitler conceding defeat. The Fuehrer's last gamble had failed.

Three weeks later, when Stalin met Roosevelt and Churchill at Yalta, he told them that Air Marshal Tedder had asked that the Soviets continue their offensive until the end of March, and that he had given Tedder an assurance that, weather and road conditions permitting, they would do so. He mentioned this, he said, 'only to emphasise the spirit of the Soviet leaders, who not only fulfilled formal obligations but who went further and acted upon what they considered to be their moral duties to their Allies'.[44] Indeed the speed of the Soviet advance across Poland had been almost incredible. General G. I. Chuikov's Eighth Guards Army, which acted as the spearhead of Zhukov's army group, covered two hundred and twenty miles in fourteen days, so that, by the time the Yalta Conference opened, Soviet troops had already reached the river Oder and had actually crossed it at several points, thus coming within shelling distance of Berlin.

The meeting of the Big Three in the neighbourhood of the well-known Crimean watering-place, was largely due to Roosevelt's initiative, since the President had been unable to come to Moscow in the previous autumn. His main purpose was to discuss the proposed creation of a post-war international peace organisation, the future United Nations, the rough details of which had already been sketched out at Dumbarton Oaks in Washington. At the same time the President wished to discuss the current military and political problems posed by the allied advances into Germany and the German satellite countries, as well as the Soviet Union's role in the Far East.

The plenary sessions were held in the Livadia Palace, an imposing building of white granite overlooking the Black Sea and set in a fine park, which had been completed in Italian Renaissance style by the last Tsar shortly before the First World War. Because of his poor health, Roosevelt and his personal staff including Hopkins, who was also a sick man, were accommodated in the palace so as to ease the strain of the business work for them. Fortunately there was no shortage of bedrooms, since fearing attempts on his life the Tsar liked to sleep in a different room every night; indeed he would sometimes change his room during the night. According to Lord Moran, Stalin, in referring to this habit, remarked with a grin that the only place where one could be certain of finding the Tsar was in the bathroom first thing in the morning. ('Probably Stalin felt that the Imperial security technique was rather an amateur business.')[45]

Stalin and his entourage, which included Molotov, Vyshinsky, Maisky and Andrei Gromyko from the Foreign Affairs Commissariat, in addition to General Antonov and other *Stavka* officers, stayed at Koreiz, a large estate with numerous guest houses which had once belonged to Prince Youssoupov. On Stalin's orders Churchill and his advisers were given the Vorontsov Palace at nearby Alupka for the duration of their stay, possibly because its former owner had filled it with English pictures and other works of art, but more likely because it had been the headquarters of Field-Marshal Manstein during the German occupation and was the only large house which had not been stripped of its furnishings by the invaders on their departure. On the sloping terrace facing the sea were two fine lions in white marble, which pleased Churchill immensely and which it is said that he would like to have taken home with him, no doubt because they reminded

516

him of the traditional British symbol. But there were limits even to Soviet hospitality.*

Churchill arrived at Alupka on 4 February, and Stalin called on him there as soon as he had settled in. The British war leader found his host optimistic about the war. Germany was short of bread and coal, he said, and her transport was seriously damaged. Asked by Churchill what the Russians would do if Hitler moved south – to Dresden, for example – Stalin replied: 'We shall follow him!' He went on to say that the Oder was no longer an obstacle as the Red Army now had several bridgeheads across it and the Germans were using untrained, badly led, and ill-equipped *Volksturm* for its defence.

Later Churchill took Stalin into his travelling map-room, where Field-Marshal Alexander explained the progress of the campaign in Italy, which impressed Stalin by its clarity and preciseness as he had been similarly impressed by Tedder's exposition in Moscow. As the Germans seemed largely a spent force, certainly in Italy, Stalin suggested that Alexander should transfer most of his divisions in the direction of Vienna through Yugoslavia and Hungary, where they could join up with the Soviet armies and thus jointly outflank the Germans south of the Alps. 'The Red Army may not give us time to complete the operation,' answered Churchill, who must have realised that the Russians were likely to reach Vienna well ahead of their western Allies. 'It cost him nothing to say this now,' reflected Churchill at the time, 'but I made no reproaches.'[46]

The first of the conference's eight plenary sessions opened in the Grand Ballroom of the Livadia Palace on 5 February. At Stalin's suggestion, President Roosevelt presided as he had done at Teheran. But he was now a tired, ailing man, very different from the buoyant figure of fourteen months before. Churchill's physician, who saw the President the same day, was convinced that he was suffering from hardening of the brain arteries and had only a few months to live at the most.[47] Harry Hopkins, who sat beside him at the round conference table, was in little better physical shape, although mentally as alert as ever, unlike the President. Naturally the Americans were most interested in the proposed peace body and were consequently shocked to hear that Stalin had not read a proposal for voting on the Security Council which had been sent to him from Washington two months

---

* The Vorontsov Palace, a bizarre mixture of Moorish and Gothic styles, was built by Prince Michael Vorontsov, Governor of South Russia in the reign of Nicholas I. He inherited the English works of art including several fine portraits by Lawrence from his father Count Ivan Vorontsov, who was for many years Russian ambassador in London. It is now a state museum.

previously. 'That guy can't be much interested in this peace organisation,' remarked Hopkins privately.[48] Indeed Stalin was quite frank in his indications that he saw no point in vague sentiments and misty aspirations for the freedom of small nations. 'We are interested in decisions and not in discussions,' he said at Yalta. And, it should be noted, the decisions taken during the week which the conference lasted, were almost all favourable to Stalin, who gained much and gave away little, although on the face of it he made several apparent concessions. This was due in great part to the almost blind faith in Stalin's good intentions shown by the American President and his advisers.

There was some talk about Germany being divided after the war into a number of small states, but the idea of large-scale dismemberment was eventually dropped, although she was eventually to lose some of her former territory east of the rivers Oder and Neisse to the Soviet Union and Poland. It was also agreed that following her unconditional surrender she should be subjected to a period of military government, besides paying substantial reparations in kind and yielding up her major war criminals. After some argument Stalin agreed to France being represented in the proposed Allied Control Commission and to her having a separate zone of occupation, provided this was carved out of what had already been allotted to the Americans and the British.

On the question of reparations Stalin felt very strongly. Harry Hopkins afterwards recalled the scene at one of the sessions for Lord Moran's benefit:

> How Stalin rose and gripped the back of his chair with such force that his brown hands went white at the knuckles. How he spat out his words as if they burnt his mouth. Great stretches of his country had been laid waste, he said, and the peasants put to the sword. Reparations should be paid to the countries that had suffered most. While he was speaking no one moved.[49]

Linked with reparations was the question of the extent she should be deprived of territory to compensate her eastern neighbours. For the Soviet Union Stalin demanded most of East Prussia including Koenigsberg. He also felt that the new Polish state, whatever its eventual form of government, should get Silesia with its minerals and that her frontier should extend as far as the river Neisse in the west. To Churchill's objection that 'it would be a pity to stuff the Polish goose so full of German food that he will die of indigestion' and that the proposed operation would involve moving six million Germans,

Stalin replied that the number would be much smaller since, 'when our troops come in, the Germans run away'.

So far as Poland's border with Russia went, Stalin was content to accept the Curzon Line in principle, which gave Lvov to Russia, although he was willing that there should be some minor alterations of the line in Poland's favour. 'For the Russian people the question of Poland is not only a question of honour but also a question of security,' he told the conference. 'Throughout history, Poland has been the corridor through which the enemy has passed into Russia. Twice in the past thirty years our enemies, the Germans, have passed into Russia. It is in Russia's interest that Poland should be strong and powerful, in a position to shut the door of this corridor by her own force.'[50]

Russia's interests in the Far East were also safeguarded. This was done in a secret understanding with Roosevelt, to which Churchill subsequently assented for the sake of unity. In return for the Soviet Union declaring war against Japan within three months of Germany's surrender and the end of the war in Europe, the Kurile Islands were to be 'handed over' to the Russians, besides which the territorial losses sustained by Russia in the war with Japan in 1904 were to be made good: these consisted of the return of the southern part of Sakhalin and the adjacent islands, the internationalisation of Dairen, the lease of Port Arthur as a Russian naval base, and the joint Sino-Soviet operation of the Chinese Eastern and South Manchurian railroads so as to provide an outlet to the port of Dairen. Since this would involve the concurrence of Marshal Chiang Kai-shek, Roosevelt undertook to use American influence to obtain this. Stalin insisted that 'these claims of the Soviet Union shall be unquestionably fulfilled after Japan has been defeated', and an undertaking to this effect was embodied in a secret protocol which was signed by the Big Three before the end of the conference. (Eden bluntly described the documents as 'a discreditable by-product of the Conference'.) If these conditions were not met, Stalin told Roosevelt, it would be very difficult for him to explain to the Russian people why they must go to war with Japan. From the Soviet point of view the contemplated arrangement had one defect which was bound to lead to trouble later on, although this may not have been foreseen by Stalin and the others at the time. Soviet control of the Manchurian railroads would constitute a patent infringement of Chinese sovereignty over an integral part of her territory.[51]

As for the United Nations, Stalin agreed to an early meeting of those nations who declared war or broke off diplomatic relations with Germany, and in doing so was able to obtain separate representation in the new body for Byelorussia and the Ukraine. He also agreed to the holding of 'free elections' as soon as practicable in the 'liberated' countries of eastern Europe.

'Poland will be the first example of operating under this declaration,' said Roosevelt. 'I want the election in Poland to be beyond question, like Caesar's wife. I did not know Caesar's wife, but she was believed to have been pure.'

'It was so said about Caesar's wife,' Stalin smilingly replied, 'but, in fact, she had certain sins.'[52]*

In his private talks with Churchill, Stalin referred to Greece only once, when he asked what was happening there. 'I don't want to criticise anything, nor to interfere,' he told Churchill. 'I'm quite content to leave it to you.'†

> Stalin isn't going to butt in in Greece [said Churchill at Yalta]. In return, he expects a free hand in Bulgaria and Roumania. The fifty-fifty plan arranged at Moscow is working out in his favour. He'll let his people be beaten up in Greece for the sake of his larger plans. I find he does what he says he will do. It isn't easy to get him to say he will do it, but once he says something, he sticks to it.

On the other hand, Stalin was seen to defer to Roosevelt throughout the conference. Even when he had such a strong case that Churchill supported him, Stalin would say: 'We attach importance to this, it means a good deal to us, but if the President feels it will conflict with his plans, I'll withdraw it.' Some observers like Lord Moran affected to see in this behaviour a determination on Stalin's part to drive a wedge between the two great western democracies. Certainly Stalin seemed to derive considerable satisfaction from Churchill's openly expressed differences with Roosevelt, such as when the President said he thought that Britain should give back Hong Kong to the Chinese after the war. On the other hand, Stalin went out of his way to praise Churchill when he proposed his health at one of the dinners, stressing the British

---

* According to well established historical tradition, Julius Caesar's wife Calpurnia was regarded by her contemporaries as 'above suspicion' of complicity in his murder in 44 BC. That she was also 'above suspicion' of marital infidelity is a popular belief belonging to a much later period. However, there is no evidence that she was unfaithful to Caesar in spite of his known homosexual habits. It is unclear to what supposed 'sins' Stalin was referring.

† After the German evacuation, civil war broke out between the Greek army and the Greek Communist guerrillas. The guerrillas received no help from Stalin, nevertheless they were able to continue their struggle until they were finally overwhelmed by the army in 1949.

Premier's 'guts' and saying that he could think of no other instance in history where the future of the world had depended on the courage of one man.

Only once did Stalin seem put out with Roosevelt at Yalta. That was when the President blurted out at dinner: 'We always call you Uncle Joe.' Stalin was not amused and refused to be mollified even when told by one of the Americans that 'Uncle Joe was no worse than Uncle Sam'. He huffily demanded how much longer he must remain at the dinner, which incidentally was being given by the President. On being told half an hour he was only persuaded with some difficulty to stay until the end. Asked on this occasion whether Stalin had a sense of humour, Churchill said at once that he had, but that he was not always amused by American or British jokes as he was meant to be. 'You could not be certain how he would take things.'[53]

The Yalta Conference has been generally considered as the high tide of Big Three unity. But to some observers at the time this unity was more apparent than real. Stalin himself realised the difficulties inherent in prolonging it after the war. 'It is not so difficult to keep unity in time of war, since there is a joint aim to defeat the common enemy, which is clear to everyone,' he observed at Yalta. 'The difficult task will come after the war when diverse interests tend to divide the Allies.'[54]

5

There is evidence that it was during the week that he spent in Yalta that Stalin made up his mind to halt the advance of Zhukov's armies on Berlin. His decision, unlike that which resulted in Rokossovsky's troops remaining so long on the Vistula in the latter part of 1944, seems to have been a military rather than a political one. The distance to Berlin from Chuikov's Oder bridgehead, which had been established in the neighbourhood of Kuestrin on 3 February, was not more than thirty-five miles, and Chuikov was convinced that if Zhukov had been allowed to push on the capital would have been quickly taken. On the following day, according to Chuikov, he was summoned to a conference at the headquarters of General Kolpakchi's Sixty-Ninth Army along with three other army commanders as well as Zhukov. While they were sitting round the table studying their maps and discussing the offensive against Berlin, the telephone rang. It was Supreme Headquarters for Zhukov and in a few moments Stalin was on the line. Chuikov, who was sitting next to Zhukov, heard their conversation quite clearly.

'Where are you?' asked Stalin. 'What are you doing?'

'I am at Kolpakchi's headquarters,' replied Zhukov. 'All the commanders of the group's armies have gathered here. We are planning the operation against Berlin.'

'You are wasting your time,' said the Supreme Commander peremptorily. 'After first consolidating on the Oder, you must turn as many forces as possible to the north, to Pomerania, and in conjunction with Rokossovsky crush the enemy's Army Group Vistula.' Zhukov was then instructed to let Stalin have his views as soon as possible on how this operation would be carried out.

Without any argument Zhukov replaced the receiver, got up from the table, and after bidding the others goodbye, went back to his own headquarters. Thus, as Chuikov afterwards recalled, 'we understood that the offensive against Berlin was being postponed for an indefinite period'. In the same Soviet journal, in which he recounted this episode in 1964, Chuikov also wrote:

> To this day I do not understand why Marshal Zhukov, as First Deputy Supreme Commander-in-Chief and as someone who knew the situation perfectly, did not attempt to convince Stalin of the necessity of waging the offensive against Berlin instead of against Pomerania. All the more so since Zhukov was not alone in his view; he was well aware of the mood of the officers and the troops. Why then did he agree with Stalin without a murmur?[55]

In his own military memoirs, Zhukov strongly contested Chuikov's views about Berlin, although he himself had originally been in favour of a rapid Berlin push as part of the January offensive and indeed had urged it on Stalin and the *Stavka* planners. First of all, he denies that the conference as described by Chuikov ever took place, as he was visiting another army headquarters on 4 February. However, it is extremely unlikely that Chuikov invented the details which he has so vividly described. Quite possibly he made a mistake in the date, which gave Zhukov a convenient pretext for contradicting him. Secondly, Chuikov argued that in war time risks must be taken and that the importance of capturing Berlin in February 1945 justified them, since it would have meant the end of the war in Europe three months before the actual surrender took place. Many Soviet lives would have been saved and the Red Army might have occupied virtually the whole of Germany as far west as the Rhine. 'History shows that risks should be taken, but not blindly,' countered Zhukov. 'A useful lesson in this connection is offered by the Red Army's drive against Warsaw in 1920, when a reckless, unsecured advance turned success into a serious defeat.'[56]

Certainly Stalin had never forgotten the lesson of Tukachevsky's ignominious rout before Warsaw, for which he himself was largely responsible, as has already been related. Thus, when in Shtemenko's words the *Stavka* advised that 'failure at the gates of Berlin threatened to have unpleasant political consequences', he appreciated the implications only too well. Far from the Red Army conquering all Germany east of the Rhine and so making most of the country ripe for Communist rule, the Allies might end up on the west bank of the Oder, leaving the Russians with only East Prussia. Had Warsaw fallen to Tukachevsky in 1920 and the Red Army occupied the whole of Poland, Bolshevism could conceivably have triumphed in Germany. Might not all Germany beyond the Oder be saved for the German capitalist warmongers again by a similar tactical blunder?

There were also strong military reasons in favour of standing on the Oder, while at the same time reinforcing Rokossovsky's Second Byelorussian Army Group which had met with stiff opposition in Pomerania and consequently had not been able to advance fast enough to cover Zhukov's right flank. Nor, in spite of the relatively weak German defences on the Berlin front, did Zhukov have enough men and tanks to press on to Berlin without grave risk, while at the same time helping Rokossovsky to deal effectively with the forty German divisions which constituted Army Group Vistula to the north of Stettin. Indeed, Rokossovsky was to admit that he could not have smashed the German army group without the help of Zhukov's armies after encircling and capturing large numbers of the enemy trapped in Danzig and other strongholds.[57]

Meanwhile, in the south Soviet troops were advancing into Hungary. On 15 February Budapest fell after fierce fighting, which was continued well into March round Lake Balaton. When the German counter-attack, the last to be mounted in the war, yielded to the sheer weight of Soviet artillery, Red Army troops pushed on into Austria and Czechoslovakia, making for Vienna and Prague. Everywhere the *Wehrmacht* was cracking. In the west Montgomery's forces began to cross the Rhine during the night of 23–24 March, an operation personally witnessed by Churchill. 'A beaten army not long ago master of Europe retreats before its pursuers,' Churchill wrote in Montgomery's autograph book at the time. 'The goal is not long to be denied to those who have come so far and fought so well under proud and faithful leadership. Forward on wings of flame to final Victory.' Soon the divisions of Montgomery's Twenty-First Army Group were racing across Germany towards the Baltic. 'My object,' he admitted afterwards, 'was to get there in time to be able to offer a firm front to the Russian endeavours to get up into Denmark, and thus control the entrance to the Baltic.'[58] The intrepid 'Monty' also hoped to be allowed the honour of taking Berlin on the way. However, this was not to be. But he did succeed in beating the Red Army to it on the Baltic, when he reached Lubeck and Wismar with about six hours to spare before the Russians arrived, and so was able to seal off the Danish peninsula from Soviet military occupation.

On 1 April 1945, Stalin summoned Zhukov and Koniev, the commander of the First Ukrainian Army Group, to a meeting in the Kremlin headquarters. Others present were the members of the State Defence Committee in addition to Antonov and Shtemenko. Stalin's first question was, 'Are you aware of the way in which the situation is developing?' Both Zhukov and Koniev replied that the situation was clear to them so far as it was reflected in the information available on their respective fronts.

'Read them the telegram,' said Stalin, turning to the Chief of Operations.

Shtemenko thereupon read from a document in his hand, the gist of which was that the Anglo-American command was preparing an operation designed to capture Berlin and to capture it before the Soviet Army could do so. It appeared that the main thrust by Montgomery's forces was planned to take place north of the Ruhr by the shortest route separating the Twenty-First Army Group and Berlin. After going into details about the precise deployment of forces, Shtemenko concluded by saying that the plan to take Berlin before the Soviet Army was regarded at Allied Headquarters as 'entirely feasible' and that 'preparations for its execution were in full swing'.

'So who's going to take Berlin, we or the Allies?' asked Stalin when Shtemenko had finished.

Koniev replied first, saying that they were going to take Berlin and that they would take it before the Allies did.

'That's just like you,' said Stalin with a slight grin. 'And how will you be able to carry out the necessary regrouping? Your main forces are on your southern flank and you will obviously have to carry out a large-scale regrouping.'

'Comrade Stalin,' replied Koniev, who ardently wished to be allowed to participate in the attack, 'you may rest assured that my army group will take all the necessary steps, and the regrouping for launching an attack in the direction of Berlin will be completed on time.'

Zhukov spoke next, saying that his troops were ready for the capture of Berlin. Furthermore, his army group was closer to the city and he did not have to regroup.

'Very well,' said Stalin. 'Then both of you, while you are still here in Moscow must prepare your plans in the *Stavka* and as soon as they are ready – say, in a couple of days – submit them to Supreme Headquarters so as to return to your army groups with the plans approved.'

The plans were duly drawn up and approved by Stalin at a staff conference two days later. After some discussion it was agreed that the attack should begin on the respective fronts at dawn on 16 April as two distinct operations which would be co-ordinated by Supreme Headquarters.[59]

Whether the document which Shtemenko read out at the first conference really was a telegram is unclear. Possibly it was an appreciation by Soviet military intelligence prepared in Moscow. It is true that Montgomery had telegraphed his immediate tactical plan to Brooke, the British CIGS, on 27 March, but it is hardly likely that this communication was intercepted by the Soviets. Thus Shtemenko appears to have divined Montgomery's plan with remarkable accuracy. 'My intention is to drive hard for the line of the Elbe,' Montgomery had intimated. 'The situation looks good and events should begin to move rapidly in a few days...My tactical HQ moves will be Wesel–Munster–Herford–Hanover – thence via the *autobahn* to Berlin, I hope.'[60]

On the other hand, Eisenhower's plan for co-ordinating his advance with the Russian offensive did not include any attack on Berlin by the forces under his command. On 29 March he telegraphed Stalin direct in this sense. In his telegram which was dispatched without any reference either to Tedder, his deputy, or to the Combined Chiefs of Staff, the allied supreme commander revealed that after isolating the Ruhr he proposed to make his main thrust along the axis Erfurt–Leipzig–Dresden. Thus, by joining hands with the Russians, he would cut in two the remaining German forces. This operation would be under the American General Omar Bradley's command, while on his left flank Montgomery's army group (from which the Ninth US Army had been transferred to Bradley) would clear the northern ports. A secondary advance would be made southwards from Erfurt through Regensburg to Linz, again linking up with the Russians and thus preventing 'the consolidation of German resistance in the redoubt of Southern Germany'. Eisenhower made no reference to Berlin, although he had earlier regarded it as 'the main prize'. As he now told Montgomery, 'that place had become, so far as I am concerned, nothing but a geographical location, and I have never been interested in these. My purpose is to destroy the enemy's forces and his powers to resist'.[61]

Stalin readily agreed with Eisenhower's plan, which, he said, 'entirely coincides with the plan of the Soviet High Command'. As for Berlin, he added, this 'has lost its former strategic importance. The Soviet High Command therefore plans to allot secondary forces in the direction of Berlin'. As will be seen, this statement was not borne out by events.

Churchill and Brooke were both extremely annoyed with Eisenhower for communicating directly with Stalin, since they felt that this was short-circuiting the highest military and political authorities. Churchill also thought Eisenhower was wrong in supposing Berlin to be 'largely devoid of military and political importance', and he told him so clearly.

> The fall of Berlin would have a profound psychological effect on German resistance in every part of the Reich. While Berlin holds out great masses of Germans will feel it their duty to go down fighting. The idea that the capture of Dresden and junction with the Russians there would be a superior gain does not commend itself to me. The parts of the German government departments which have moved south can very quickly move southward again. But while Berlin remains under the German flag it cannot, in my opinion, fail to be the most decisive point in Germany.[62]

Eisenhower defended himself to General Marshall in Washington and the American Chiefs of Staff supported him.

> The message I sent to Stalin [Eisenhower told Marshall on 7 April] was a purely military move taken in accordance with ample authorisations and instructions issued by the Combined Chiefs of Staff. Frankly, it did not cross my mind to confer in advance with the Combined Chiefs of Staff because I have assumed that I am held responsible for the effectiveness of military operations in this theatre and it was a natural question to the head of the Russian forces to inquire as to the direction and timing of their next major thrust, and to outline my own intentions.[63]

The last word may be left with Brooke, who wrote in his diary at this time:

> 3 April 1945. Tedder attended our Chiefs of Staff meeting and tried to explain that Ike was forced to take immediate action with

Stalin, as Monty had issued a Directive that Ike did not agree with! I said that I was astonished that Ike found it necessary to call in Stalin in order to control Monty. Furthermore, I could not accept this excuse as the boundaries of the Twenty-First Army Group and the Ninth US Army still remained the same in Ike's Order as in Monty's, the only difference being the transfer of the Ninth Army from Monty to Bradley. Surely Stalin's help need not be called in for such a transfer![64]

6

A few days later, on the eve of the attack on Berlin, Stalin received the news of President Roosevelt's death. In recent weeks their correspondence had been clouded by a misunderstanding occasioned by peace feelers put out by a German general, Karl Wolff, who commanded the SS in Italy, and two exploratory meetings took place between him and Mr Allen Dulles, the head of the American Intelligence organisation in Switzerland. The second of these meetings was attended by British but not Soviet representatives, although the Soviet Government was informed through Clark Kerr in Moscow of what was afoot. Stalin reacted angrily by accusing the allies in Italy of having, as a result of these 'negotiations', made an agreement with the Germans whereby Marshal Kesselring, the German western front commander, was 'to open the front to the Anglo-American troops and let them move east, while the British and Americans have promised, in exchange, to ease the armistice terms for the Germans'. Needless to state, there was no truth whatever in this charge, and in one of his last messages Roosevelt told Stalin that he could not avoid 'a feeling of bitter resentment towards your informers, whoever they are, for such vile misrepresentations of my actions or those of my trusted subordinates. The matter was smoothed over with an assurance from Stalin that, while he had never doubted the President's 'integrity or trustworthiness', just as he had never doubted Churchill's, a difference of views had arisen between them over 'what an Ally may permit himself with regard to another and what he may not', and he maintained that the Russian view was 'the only correct one'.

In the same cable, dated 7 April, Stalin rubbed in the fact that whereas the Germans were fighting the Russians desperately for an obscure place in Czechoslovakia named Zemlenice 'which they need just as much as a dead man needs a poultice', they were surrendering to Eisenhower's troops without any resistance such important towns in the heart of Germany as Osnabruck, Mannheim and Kassel. 'You will admit that this behaviour on the part of the Germans is more than strange and unaccountable.' There was, of course, nothing either strange or unaccountable about it. The Germans preferred to surrender themselves to the Allies so as to avoid being transported to forced labour in the east, which they knew would be their fate if they gave themselves up to the Russians.

On 12 April Roosevelt replied that no 'minor misunderstandings' of this kind should be allowed to arise in the future. 'I feel sure,' he added, 'that, when our armies make contact in Germany and join in a full co-ordinated offensive, the Nazi armies will disintegrate.' A few hours after he had signed this message, Roosevelt was dead. Stalin's next communication with the White House was addressed to the new President, Harry S. Truman, and was one of condolence in which he described the late President as 'a great statesman of world stature and champion of post-war peace and security'.[65]

By this date the Russians had captured Vienna and were thrusting forward up the Danube towards Linz, which they in due course reached only to find the Americans had got there before them. A few days later Allied and Soviet troops also joined hands on the Elbe, thus cutting Germany in two. Meanwhile the battle for Berlin, which had begun according to plan, was raging fiercely. From his command post near the river Spree, Koniev reported to Stalin, while under fire from a German battery.

'Things are going badly for Khukov,' Stalin interrupted. 'He is still trying to break through the city's defences.' Then, after a pause, he asked, 'Would it not be possible to transfer Zhukov's mobile troops and let them through the gap in your front in the direction of Berlin?'

'Comrade Stalin, that will take a lot of time and will greatly complicate the situation,' replied Koniev. 'There is no need to transfer tank forces from the First Byelorussian Army Group into the breach we have made. Things are going well with us. We have sufficient forces, and we can turn both our tank armies towards Berlin.' Koniev added that they would make for Zossen, a small town about twenty miles south of Berlin.

After another pause, to give Stalin time to find Zossen on his office map, Stalin replied, 'Very good. Do you know that the German General Staff is at Zossen?'

'Yes, I do,' said Koniev.

'Very good, I agree,' said Stalin. 'Turn your tank armies towards Berlin.'[66]

The long-range bombardment of Berlin by Soviet artillery began on 21 April so as to lay the basis for the final assault on the capital. After the most bitter fighting in streets, roof tops and cellars, while much of the city was in flames, Berlin fell to the combined armies of Zhukov, Koniev and Rokossovsky. Negotiations for the surrender of the burning city were opened with Chuikov at his command post on 1 May. By an ironic coincidence, the German representative was General Krebs, whom Stalin had embraced at the Moscow railway station when bidding farewell to the Japanese in the spring of 1941. Now he was the *Wehrmacht* Chief of Staff and the only officer of any importance in Hitler's entourage whom the army still respected.[67]

The garrison eventually surrendered next day, and the Soviet red flag with its emblems of hammer and sickle was hoisted above the Reichstag and the Brandenburg Gate. Hitler was already dead, having shot himself or (as the Russians at first claimed) taken poison in his bunker underneath the Chancellery, along with his mistress Eva Braun whom he married a few hours before the end. The German armies in Italy also surrendered on 2 May, and two days later the German forces in the north-west, including those in Holland and Denmark, surrendered to Field-Marshal Montgomery in his tent on Luneburg Heath. All hostilities ceased on 8 May, the formal ratification of Germany's unconditional surrender taking place under Soviet auspices in Berlin in the early hours of 9 May, the three signatories being Zhukov, Tedder (on behalf of Eisenhower), and Field-Marshal Keitel for Germany.

To mark the occasion Stalin sent appropriate congratulations to Truman and Churchill:

> The joint effort of the Soviet, US and British Armed Forces against the German invaders, which had culminated in the latter's complete rout and defeat, will go down in history as a model military alliance between our peoples.[68]

In accordance with Stalin's orders, the Russians in Berlin officially withheld the details of the circumstances in which Hitler and his wife had died. The first news of the suicide had been given to Chuikov by Krebs, who added that he had seen the bodies and that they had been burned in accordance with Hitler's will. This was confirmed, according to Chuikov, when troops of the Eighth Army Guards broke into the courtyard of the Chancellery on the morning of 2 May and found the remains of Hitler's body wrapped in a rug which was still smouldering. It is now known from Russian sources that an autopsy was carried out on 8 May and that this proved beyond doubt that the body was Hitler's, since an X-ray was made of the jaw and teeth and this exactly matched a similar X-ray which had been previously made by Hitler's dentist.[69] But no public announcement was made to this effect, apparently because the evidence was not accepted by Stalin. In fact, Stalin told Hopkins and Harriman, when he saw them later the same month, that in his opinion Hitler was not dead but was 'hiding somewhere'.

He said the Soviet doctors thought they had identified the body of Goebbels and Hitler's chauffeur, but that he, personally even doubted if Goebbels was dead, and said the whole matter was strange and the various talks of funerals and burials struck him as being very dubious. He said he thought that Bormann, Goebbels, Hitler, and probably Krebs, had escaped and were in hiding.

Hopkins remarked that he knew the Germans had several very large submarines, but that no trace of these had been found. According to the official American account of the conversation,

Marshal Stalin said he also knew of those submarines which had been running back and forth between Germany and Japan, taking gold and negotiable assets from Germany to Japan. He added that this had been done with the connivance of Switzerland. He said he had ordered his intelligence service to look into the matter of those submarines, but so far they had failed to discover any trace, and therefore he thought it was possible that Hitler and company had gone in them to Japan.[70]

It is possible that Zhukov, who received Chuikov's reports, did not pass on everything he heard to Moscow, fearing Stalin's wrath that Hitler had not been captured alive. At first Zhukov was as convinced as Chuikov and the doctors who had carried out the autopsy, and when the allied commanders-in-chief arrived in Berlin shortly afterwards Zhukov and his staff seemed to treat the evidence as conclusive. But the Soviet commander abruptly changed his view at a press conference, at which Vyshinsky sat beside him, having just arrived from Moscow with Stalin's latest instructions. 'The circumstances are very mysterious,' Zhukov told the journalists present. 'We have not identified the body of Hitler. I can say nothing about his fate. He could have flown out of Berlin at the very last moment.' According to the Russian version, it had been established that a small aircraft with three men and a woman on board had taken off from the Tiergarten in the direction of Hamburg at dawn on 30 April, and that a large submarine had left Hamburg before the arrival of Montgomery's troops on 2 May.

'Mysterious persons were on board the submarine, among them a woman.'[71]*

Although he appointed Zhukov head of the Russian element of the Allied Control commission as commander of the Soviet occupation forces, Stalin made it very clear to Hopkins and Harriman that 'Zhukov would have very little power concerning political affairs in Germany'. At a Kremlin reception on 24 May for the various Red Army commanders, Stalin also went out of his way to praise the Russian people in a toast in which he described them as constituting 'the most remarkable of all the nations of the Soviet Union'.

> I drink to the health of the Russian people not only because it is the leading people, but also because it has a clear intelligence, a firm character and great patience. Our government made quite a few errors, we had moments in 1941–1942 when the situation was desperate, when our army was retreating, abandoning our own villages and towns...because there was no other way. A different people could have said to the Government: 'You have failed to justify our expectations – get out! We shall install another Government which shall make peace with Germany and secure for us quiet lives.'

The Russian people, however, did not take this path, Stalin went on, because it trusted the 'correctness' of the Government's policy, and their confidence had proved to be 'the decisive factor which insured our historic victory over the enemy of mankind – Fascism'.[72]

As might be expected, Stalin was the recipient of many honours and presentations at this time. These included Hero of the Soviet Union, Order of Victory and, most exalted of all military ranks, Generalissimo of the Soviet Union. On 24 June 1945, there was a huge Victory Parade in the Red Square led by Marshal Rokossovsky and reviewed by Stalin. The 'supreme and unforgettable moment' was when the Soviet soldiers flung down the enemy's captured flags at the foot of the Lenin Mausoleum, just as Kutusov had done with the flags of Napoleon's Grand Army before Tsar Alexander I.

Afterwards there was an impromptu banquet in a room just inside the Kremlin wall. In replying to the many toasts to his health, Stalin remarked that he was in his sixty-sixth year and rather unexpectedly

---

* It was not until June 1965, a dozen years after Stalin's death, when Zhukov published his account of the battle of Berlin in the *Voenno–istoricheskii Zhurnal* that he publicly admitted for the first time that 'Hitler and Goebbels, seeing no other way out, ended their lives by suicide'.

531

began talking about how much longer he would be able to remain at his post. 'I'll work another two or three years,' he said, 'and then I'll have to retire.'[73]

7

Immediately after the German surrender Churchill suggested to Truman that they should try to get Stalin to a tripartite meeting at some 'agreed unshattered town in Germany', but that they should not rendezvous at any place within the present Russian military zone. ('Twice running we have come to meet him.') Truman replied that he would get Hopkins to convey the proposal personally to Stalin when he went to Moscow later in the month. This Hopkins duly did and as a result Stalin agreed to a meeting in the middle of July. However, he insisted that it should take place 'in the vicinity of Berlin', which was of course in the Russian zone. Truman saw no objection to this, although he would have preferred Stalin to come to America. Churchill reluctantly assented, and the arrangements consequently went ahead for the meeting to take place in Potsdam, which on Churchill's suggestion was given the code-name Terminal.

Although Soviet and Allied forces had joined hands in Europe and had begun to fraternise, less cordial feelings were engendered on the higher political level. One cause of discord was posed by the situation in Austria where the Russians after taking Vienna had pushed south-west across the Semmering pass into Styria. Marshal Koniev, who commanded the Russian occupation forces in Austria, received orders from Moscow to find the man Stalin had designated as head of the provisional government which was about to be established in Vienna. This was Dr Karl Renner, a Social Democrat with Marxist sympathies, who had been Austrian Chancellor and Foreign Minister immediately after the First World War. He was discovered unharmed on the small farm near the Semmering to which he had long since retired, and although at this date he was in his middle-seventies Renner agreed to take on the job he had held a quarter of a century earlier. Accordingly he was installed in the old, familiar building in the Ballhausplatz where Metternich had ruled for so long and where more recently Dolfuss had bled to death at the hands of the Austrian Nazis. This was done without any prior consultation with the Americans or British.

Stalin also refused to allow any allied missions to proceed to Vienna until the European Advisory Commission, on which the Russians were represented in London, had agreed on the precise zones of occupation for Vienna. But this could not be accomplished without an examination on the spot. Churchill and Truman were afraid that the Russians were 'trying their old trick of organising a country to suit themselves'. Both leaders accordingly sent strongly worded telegrams to Stalin, protesting against this violation of 'the spirit of the Yalta declaration on liberated Europe'. And in the end they won their point. 'We had insisted on a particular thing being done, as a right under our agreement, and the Russians gave in,' wrote Truman afterwards. 'I doubt whether we could have gotten anywhere by broad demands. It would have given them too many loopholes.'[74]

Another cause of trouble was provided by the behaviour of President Tito whose troops had occupied Trieste and Fiume and, as Churchill told Stalin, had 'inflicted great cruelties on the Italians in this part of the world'. Tito was suspected by the British of wishing to incorporate the Trieste–Istria region in the new Yugoslavia, and talks to this end between his military staff and the British so annoyed Alexander that he openly likened Tito to the two Axis dictators. Tito protested to Stalin who in turn came back to Churchill on 21 June.

In my desire not to make matters worse, I have hitherto not drawn attention in our correspondence to the behaviour of Field-Marshal Alexander, but now it is time to emphasise that I cannot accept the supercilious tone with regard to the Yugoslavs which Field-Marshal Alexander has occasionally adopted in these conversations. It is absolutely unacceptable that Field-Marshal Alexander in an official and public message allowed himself to compare Marshal Tito with Hitler and Mussolini. Such a comparison is unjustified and offensive to Yugoslavia.

Churchill replied two days later:

The actual wording of Field-Marshal Alexander's telegram has been largely taken from the President's draft. We do not see why we should be pushed about everywhere, especially by people we have helped, and helped before you were able to make any contact with them. Therefore I do not see any reason to make excuses for Field-Marshal Alexander, although I was not aware he was going to draft his telegram exactly in this way.

It seems to me that a Russianised frontier running from Lubeck through Eisenach to Trieste and down to Albania is a matter which requires a very great deal of argument conducted between good friends.

These are just the things we have to talk over together at our meeting, which is not long now.

However, in spite of Stalin's representations on his behalf, Tito had to agree to withdraw his troops from Trieste behind the so-called Morgan Line.* Apart from Stalin's need to preserve good relations with his western Allies, he had to consider possible repercussions from the Italian communists had he backed Tito's claim to Trieste. Tito had already learned of the fifty-fifty agreement which applied to Yugoslavia as a sphere of influence, and the discovery did not improve his temper. He had no intention of being a satellite of either Great Britain or the Soviet Union. 'We do not wish to be used as small change in international bargaining,' he declared.[75]

One suggestion of the British Prime Minister, which rather surprised Stalin, was that King George VI should visit Potsdam during the forthcoming conference and entertain the 'Big Three' to dinner in the British sector. 'My plan did not envisage a meeting with the King,' replied Stalin. 'It had in view the conference of the three of us, on which you, the President and myself had exchanged messages earlier. However, if you think it necessary that I should meet the King, I have no objection to your plan.' This somewhat lukewarm response was reported by Churchill to the sovereign, whose father had always refused after the establishment of diplomatic relations between Great Britain and the Soviet Union to shake hands with the ambassador of a country whose revolutionary leaders had executed his first cousin Tsar Nicholas II and his family. Consequently Churchill informed Stalin that 'the King now finds it impossible for him to make his tour in Germany at the present time, as so many detectives and special service officers will be required for the tripartite conference. He has now informed me of his wish to visit Ulster at this time'.[76]

Just before leaving Moscow for Potsdam, Stalin suffered a slight heart attack, which delayed his departure by one day. He could still have arrived in Potsdam by 15 July, the agreed day for the opening of the conference, if he had travelled by air, but this he refused to do. Accordingly the journey was made in a special train consisting of eleven carriages, which also accommodated Molotov, Vyshinsky, Maisky, Gromyko and the rest of his staff including the three service chiefs. The four most luxurious carriages had once formed part of the imperial train and had later been used by Trotsky as his mobile headquarters during the Civil War and had afterwards been put in a museum from which they were now removed so that the Generalissimo could make his triumphal progress to Berlin as befitted a conquering hero. The normal route would have been through Warsaw,

* After Alexander's Chief of Staff, Lieut.-General Sir F. E. Morgan, who was responsible for carrying out the agreement.

but because of the anti-Soviet feeling in Poland, Beria and his principal assistant in the NKVD, Victor Abakumov, decided that Poland was too great a security risk so that the train was diverted through Lithuania and East Prussia.[77]

Stalin had arranged that all three delegations should be accommodated in Babelsberg, near Potsdam, about twelve miles south-east of the capital. It was a thickly wooded area bordered by lakes and before the war was a popular summer resort much frequented by the Berlin film colony, whose members built themselves a number of fine villas. Most of these had escaped the effects of the allied bombing and were now to be occupied by the Big Three and their staffs, although it was otherwise in Potsdam itself. ('Devastation of Potsdam terrible and all this I am told in one raid of fifty minutes,' noted Eden. 'What an hour of hell it must have been.')[78] The Conference meetings were held in the Cecilienhof, a large neo-Gothic mansion in the town, which had miraculously survived intact; it had been built by the late Kaiser's son the Crown Prince ('Little Willy') for his wife Cecilie and had been aptly described as a 'stockbroker's Paradise'. It contained an enormous salon with a large circular table in the middle where the plenary sessions took place. The mansion consisted of four wings which provided plenty of working discussion rooms for the delegations. In the middle was a courtyard in which the Red Army had planted geraniums in the design of a twenty-four-foot wide Red Star.

On the morning of 16 July, shortly after his arrival in Babelsberg, Stalin paid a courtesy call on Truman, accompanied by Molotov and the interpreter Pavlov. It was their first meeting. Stalin apologised for being late, explaining that the doctors would not let him fly because of 'weakness in the lungs', although it was already an open secret that he was suffering from a cardiac ailment. Truman pressed him to stay for lunch, but he replied that he could not. 'You could if you wanted to,' said the President. The result was that Stalin stayed. At the meal he was much impressed by the wine which was served and asked to see the label on the bottle. It turned out to be Californian. Truman made a note to send several cases to the Kremlin, which he later did.[79]

The twenty-four hours delay in Stalin's arrival had enabled Truman and Churchill to visit the ruins of Berlin, notably the Reich Chancellery, and to see the bunker where, as the Soviet soldier who showed them round pointed out, Hitler had committed suicide. Consequently Truman was greatly surprised when Stalin repeated what he had told Hopkins and Harriman in Moscow, namely that he believed the Fuehrer had escaped and was hiding somewhere, possibly in Spain or else in Argentina. He added that 'careful search by Soviet investigators

535

had not found any trace of Hitler's remains or any other positive evidence of his death'.[80]

With the President was James F. Byrnes, who had replaced Stettinius as Secretary of State. They both gathered from Stalin that the Soviet Government would declare war on Japan about the middle of August. They also sensed that Stalin was far from keen on British participation in the Pacific war and was generally opposed to British Pacific war policy. This seemed to them to confirm the suspicion already conveyed to the President by ex-ambassador Joseph Davies that 'Churchill's hostility towards the Soviet Union was no secret in Moscow'. However, the import of Stalin's intentions with regard to Japan was considerably reduced by the news which had reached Truman the previous evening of the successful explosion of the first atomic bomb at the Almogordo air base in the New Mexico desert. The flash and noise could be seen and heard nearly two hundred miles away and aroused such curiosity in the neighbourhood that the commanding officer of the air base was obliged to issue a press release to the effect that an explosion had occurred in a remotely located ammunition magazine. It was intended to use the atom bomb to hasten the end of the war with Japan as soon as possible after it had been perfected and successfully tested; consequently Russia's entry into the war would make little practical difference now that America planned to use such a terrible weapon of devastation. 'Here then was a speedy end to the Second World War,' noted Churchill after he heard the news, 'and perhaps to much else besides.'[81]

For the moment Truman said nothing about it to Stalin, but after he had consulted Churchill it was agreed that the Generalissimo should be told and that this should be done by the President quite casually after one of their meetings. The occasion arose a week later after Truman had received a detailed account of the experiment from his War Secretary Henry Stimson, who flew to Potsdam with the particulars. Truman simply walked up to Stalin, who was alone with Pavlov, and told him that the Americans had a new bomb far more destructive than any other known bomb, and that they planned to use it very soon unless Japan surrendered. 'That's fine,' said Stalin, apparently unimpressed. 'I hope you make good use of it against the Japanese.'[82]

Truman and Byrnes were surprised by Stalin's evident lack of interest. Afterwards this was put down to the Generalissimo's cunning, when it became known that he had long been kept informed of the American experiments in nuclear fission by the spy Klaus Fuchs. But Stalin's apparent lack of interest may not have been so contrived as was supposed, since there is some evidence that before it actually happened

Fuchs did not believe that the experiment would be successful. Stalin's immediate reaction may have been to think that Truman was bluffing. Byrnes, who concluded that Stalin had not grasped the importance of the discovery, thought that he would be certain to ask for more information about it. But he did not. Nor did he suggest that Soviet officers or technicians should be allowed to examine the bomb or witness its use. 'Later,' wrote Byrnes, 'I concluded that, because the Russians kept secret their military weapons, they thought it improper to ask us about ours.'[83]

Having got pretty well what he wanted at Yalta, Stalin could afford to be generous at Potsdam. This time the new American President tended to support Churchill on most questions, unlike Roosevelt at the previous conference, so that Stalin often found himself in the minority. When the first plenary session opened in the great hall of the Cecilienhof later in the afternoon on 17 July, Stalin proposed that Truman should preside and this was unanimously agreed. It was a wise selection. At sixty-one Harry S. Truman was the youngest of the Big Three; he was also the fittest physically. He gave the impression of a polite but firm company chairman determined to get through the directors' board meeting with the minimum amount of argument. 'I told Stalin and Churchill that we should discuss the next day some of those points on which we could come to a conclusion,' Truman recalled afterwards. 'I said I did not just want to discuss. I wanted to decide. Churchill asked if I wanted something in the bag each day. He was as right as he could be. I was there to get something accomplished, and if we could not do that, I meant to go back home.'[84]

At the same time the new American President showed himself much stronger in dealing with Stalin than his predecessor at Yalta, where Roosevelt had played up to Stalin and had tended to distort Britain's role as an imperialist and colonialist power. Also, while at the previous conference Churchill had largely made the running, now he surrendered this role to Truman to a great extent, holding himself back but coming to Truman's support when necessary. This was no doubt due to his preoccupation with the General Election of the new British Parliament, of which the results were not yet known owing to the time required to count the votes of those serving overseas. 'From this first meeting until he left for London to hear the result of the election,' noted the President's Chief of Staff Admiral Leahy, 'it was evident that Churchill had not prepared himself very thoroughly for Potsdam. Several times matters came up which revealed that he did not seem to know what was happening.' Truman, on the other hand, was 'positive in his manner, clear and direct in his statements. He seemed to know exactly what he wanted to say and do. As for Stalin, nothing had occurred to ruffle the Soviet chieftain and he was his usual courteous self'.[85]

Lord Moran, who attended most of the open meetings as he had done at Yalta, was convinced that Churchill's 'method of jocular bluntness' was 'the right method of tackling Stalin'.

> Stalin's tenacity and obstinacy have no counterpart on our side. He knows exactly what he wants, and he does not mind how he gets it. He is very patient too and never loses his temper. Indeed, the Russians are courteous in conference. It is rather like a game of poker, with Joe trying to bring off a big bluff.
>
> Truman is like a Wesleyan minister who does not know anything about the game and is not very sure whether it is quite nice for him to play at all, but who is determined, if he does play, to make his full weight felt.[86]

8

For Stalin and the Soviet delegation, the most important issue was the acquisition of booty from Germany in the form of punitive reparations. There was also the question of Poland and the other satellites. In his demands Stalin was conscious that he was playing from a position of strength. In the satellite countries the Russians had installed their own puppet governments and in Poland had allowed Bierut and the Lublin Poles to occupy eastern Germany as far as the Oder and the western Neisse. In Vienna, it looked as if Renner might also become a Soviet puppet, since the Red Army was still in exclusive possession of the Austrian capital and the whole surrounding area. On the Anglo-American side there were not many bargaining counters, although there were one or two of some importance. The principal was the fact that the British and American zones of occupation in Germany comprised the larger and richer part of the country. Also, the Anglo-Americans possessed the German and Italian fleets.

'Dined alone with him [Churchill] and again urged him not to give up our few cards without return,' noted Eden at the start of the conference. 'But he is again under Stalin's spell. He kept repeating, "I like that man." I am full of admiration of Stalin's handling of him.'[87]

The conference lasted from 17 July to 1 August with a short break in the middle when Churchill and Eden returned to London for the election results and were replaced by Clement Attlee and Ernest Bevin as soon as the Labour landslide victory was announced. Since Attlee had been present at Churchill's invitation from the beginning as an ob-

538

server, the new British Premier experienced little difficulty in taking over from Churchill at this last of the Big Three meetings.

It is not possible to mention the politics of Potsdam in more than the briefest detail. Although Stalin got his way over the Polish frontier and the satellite countries of eastern Europe, in other respects he gained surprisingly little, contrary to the opinion generally held in the west at that time. It is true that the Soviet zone of Germany eventually became a Communist puppet state (still politically unrecognised by the western Allies). On the other hand, the fact that Allied troops were allowed into Vienna during the period of the conference prevented Austria from being incorporated in the Soviet orbit. Stalin also agreed to the withdrawal of the Red Army from Persia, although he failed to secure the withdrawal of British forces from Syria. Elsewhere in the Middle East and North Africa, the Generalissimo was unable to obtain a foothold. His claim that the Soviet Union should have a naval base in the Bosphorus, which he argued was no less unreasonable than Britain's control of the Suez Canal, was effectively met with the counter-argument that the Canal was an essential means of communication between the different parts of the British Empire and moreover was recognised by a treaty with Egypt, whereas the Black Sea Straits were quite different inasmuch as the Soviet Union possessed no territories beyond them to the west.

Nor was Stalin any more successful in extending Soviet influence in the Mediterranean through the international administration of Tangier, which had been taken over by the Spaniards after the fall of France, and in which the Soviet Union now expressed a desire to participate. 'I have not considered the possibility of the Soviet Union desiring to acquire a large tract of the African shore,' Churchill declared. 'If this is the case, it will have to be considered in relation to many other problems.'[88] Finally, thanks to the stout-hearted stand taken by Britain's Labour Foreign Minister Ernest Bevin, supported in some measure by America's Secretary of State James Byrnes, the reparations which Stalin originally demanded to be paid by Germany were drastically scaled down to one-quarter of the company shareholdings in west Germany, although Stalin insisted on keeping all the shareholdings in east German companies as well as German investments in the satellite countries. Even this turned out to be largely a Pyrrhic victory, since only a few token payments were made from west Germany, and in less than a year they ceased altogether. Stalin also demanded reparations from Austria and Italy, but this was flatly rejected by Truman and Attlee, and the Generalissimo eventually acquiesced. In the case of Austria this was no very great concession, since the Soviets had already taken over much Austrian property in their zone of occupation which had previously been seized by the Germans.

Stalin's principal success at Potsdam was over Poland, where he achieved what he had announced as his objective at Yalta, both in regard to the composition of the future Polish government and the establishment of Poland's frontier with Germany on the Oder–Neisse line. At the same time the Soviet Union was able to retain a considerable slice of East Prussia for herself including Koenigsberg, which was to be renamed Kaliningrad. Furthermore, in spite of the promise to hold free elections, Communist rule was consolidated in Hungary, Roumania and Bulgaria, while President Tito remained unchallenged in Yugoslavia. Indeed what was probably the bitterest debate of the conference developed over the satellites, between Italy and whom Stalin argued that 'an abnormal distinction was being drawn' in an attempt to discredit the Soviet Union. Was the Italian Government, he asked, any more democratic than the governments of other countries? And no 'democratic' elections had been held in Italy.

Truman replied that everybody had free access to Italy, but the Americans had not been able to move about freely in Hungary, Roumania and Bulgaria, and had been unable to get any information concerning them. When this was put right, the United States would recognise their governments, he said, but not before. Truman was warmly supported by Churchill, who stated that the British mission in Bucharest had been 'penned up with a closeness approaching internment'.

At this point Stalin broke in to ask Churchill how he could make such unverified statements. This evoked a reply from Churchill that the Generalissimo would be astonished at the catalogue of difficulties encountered by the British mission. 'An iron fence has come down around them,' he declared.

'All fairy tales!' exclaimed Stalin. British representatives in Roumania, he added, were accorded the same courtesies received by Soviet officials in Italy.

This remark was hotly contested by Churchill. 'Statesmen can call one another's statements fairy tales if they wish,' he said. But so far as the British mission in Bucharest was concerned, he had complete confidence in it, and the manner in which it was being treated there had caused him 'the greatest distress'.

It is quite possible that Stalin was ignorant of the conditions in Bucharest. At all events, Vyshinsky, who had the job of briefing Stalin on the satellites, was observed to be perspiring freely and was 'plainly unhappy'. Major Birse, the British interpreter, told Churchill that he was sure that 'Vyshinsky was in for a real dressing down from Stalin'.[89]

Only in Czechoslovakia was a semblance of political independence restored after its liberation from Nazi domination by American and Soviet forces and the return of President Benes and the Czech government-in-exile to Prague from London. But this independence was not destined to last for long. Incidentally the new Czechoslovakia lost three-quarters of a million inhabitants, largely Ukrainians, and four thousand square miles of territory in Ruthenia which she was obliged to cede to the Soviet Union. Stalin was also able to hold on to Bessarabia. Territorially and in respect of spheres of influence, therefore, his gains were quite substantial, but they were confined to eastern Europe.

If the differences which appeared between Stalin and the western leaders at the conference table were varied and pronounced, they did not in any way impair their social relations which were most cordial throughout. 'Stalin was very amiable, but he is opening his mouth very wide,' Churchill told his doctor after the first plenary session. 'He has started cigars. He says he prefers them to cigarettes. If he is photographed smoking a cigar with me, everyone will say it is my influence! I said so to him.' Next day Churchill gave Stalin a box of his largest cigars and noted with satisfaction that he smoked one for three hours. 'I touched on some delicate matters without any clouds appearing in the sky,' continued Churchill. 'He takes a very sensible line about the monarchy...He sees it binds the Empire together. He seemed surprised that the King had not come to Berlin.' When Churchill remarked that the Germans were like sheep, Stalin agreed and repeated his oft-told story about the party of German Social Democrats on their way to a political meeting in the time of the last Kaiser, who spent two hours on a railway station platform in Berlin and missed the meeting because there was no one to take their tickets.[90]

Owing to the lead given by Truman, the Potsdam conference turned out to be the most musical of all the summit meetings. In addition to daily dinner concerts at his residence, the American President discovered a brilliant young pianist, who was a sergeant in the United States army, and could play the music of Chopin, Truman's favourite composer, which he did at great length at the first of the formal dinners at which Truman was host. On this occasion Stalin insisted on toasting the pianist, much to that virtuoso's embarrassment. (Leahy noted that 'his face was white as a sheet'.) Not to be outdone, when it was Stalin's turn to give a dinner, the Generalissimo imported two pianists from Moscow, as well as two excellent female violinists, who 'made up in musical ability what they lacked in looks', according to

Leahy. (Truman and Leahy calculated that they must have weighed about two hundred pounds each.) Churchill, to whom these lengthy renderings of classical compositions were well-nigh unbearable, managed to get his own back at his dinner, where he arranged that a large band of the Royal Air Force should play long and loudly throughout the evening; indeed they kept it up until past two o'clock in the morning.[91]

Churchill made a point of including a strong service element in his guest list. From the Soviet side among others he asked Zhukov, Antonov and Admiral Kuznetsov, from the Americans there were General Marshall and Admirals Leahy and King, while the British numbered Field-Marshals Alexander, Montgomery, Brooke and Maitland Wilson. Before the guests sat down, Churchill took Stalin round the table and introduced him to each one. When they came to Montgomery, the Generalissimo paused for a moment, looked hard at him and said, 'Oh!' – an exclamation which Montgomery afterwards took to mean that Stalin was 'obviously impressed'. Later in the evening, Montgomery produced his autograph book which he asked Stalin to sign. Stalin obligingly did so, not once but three times on the same page in progressively larger script. When Montgomery asked him why he had signed three times, Stalin replied, 'That is the greatest compliment!'[92]

During the meal, Stalin remarked to Major Birse, the British interpreter who was seated beside him, that he 'liked these English dinners, they were simple and at the same time dignified'. Then, looking over the faces of those on the opposite side of the table, he singled out General Marshall, Chief of the US Army Staff, who was sitting beside Montgomery. 'That is a man I admire,' he told Birse. 'He is a good general. We have good generals in the Soviet Army, but so have you and the Americans. Only ours still lack breeding, and their manners are bad. Our people have a long way to go.'[93]

When Truman proposed the healths of the British and Soviet Chiefs of Staff, Sir Alan Brooke in reply took the opportunity to remind the Generalissimo of a toast which he had proposed at Yalta to 'those men who are always wanted in war and forgotten in peace'. He said that he 'had studied Antonov's face with care to find out whether he was forgotten and was glad to see that he was not'. At the same time he reminded the politicians and diplomats present that 'even in peace there might be a use for soldiers'. He ended by toasting 'the hope, perhaps a pious hope, that soldiers might not be forgotten in peace'.

Brooke noted afterwards that this went down well with Stalin, who replied at once that soldiers would never be forgotten.[94] Nor were they by Stalin, though not in the way that the British Chief of the Imperial

General Staff anticipated. Zhukov and Antonov were to be banished to remote provincial commands, Zhukov to the Crimea and Antonov to Transcaucasia. The absurd pretext for Zhukov's ouster, spread by the NKVD, was that he had looted jewellery in Berlin. ('You know, Comrade Stalin cannot endure immortality!') Antonov, first downgraded to the post of Deputy Chief of the General Staff, was 'exposed' as being of Jewish origin.[95]

But no hint of the fate of these gallant Soviet commanders disturbed the harmony of Churchill's dinner, at which the host repeated the enthusiastic toast he had proposed at Yalta to 'Stalin the Great'. The British Premier was due to fly to London next day. 'I must apologise for having to leave here and interrupt the sessions of the conference,' he said in his farewell speech. 'But, as you know, I am going back to England to take part in what is a very important element in English democratic processes – the counting of the ballot. We will be back here on Monday,' – at this point he paused and looked down the table until his gaze fell on Attlee when he resumed, – 'in such order as the British people may determine!'

'Mr Attlee does not seem very eager,' interjected Stalin, looking at Attlee, whose diminutive figure was sitting hunched up in his chair.[96]

But Churchill did not return after his party's electoral defeat. Nor did Eden. Their places were taken by Attlee and Bevin, although of course the permanent officials remained unchanged, Attlee even taking over Churchill's private secretary. 'Strangely Hanoverian atmosphere at Potsdam, contrasting with the gay regime of the Stuarts,' noted one of the Foreign Office men a few days later. 'They are very business-like and imperturbable, these new people, and give confidence to all around them. Bevin does not fuss in the slightest, takes every problem in his stride, and relaxes comfortably in the evening over whiskies and anecdotes.'

Stalin quite took to the rough mannered and plain spoken Bevin, so different from his elegant and refined predecessor. Indeed he relished Bevin's reply to his request that Hitler's deputy, whom the British had been holding since his dramatic flight in 1941, should be handed over as a war criminal. 'All right,' said Bevin. 'You can have Hess, but we'll charge you with his keep for two years.' The bill, the new English Foreign Secretary added, could be set against Stalin's claim on reparations.

'We want an advance delivery,' insisted Stalin.

'You have Goebbels,' Attlee countered. And so the matter was left until the war crimes trials.[97]

On the other hand, Stalin did not find Attlee nearly as congenial as

Churchill had been. Nor could he and Molotov understand the election results. 'But you said the Election would be a close thing and now you have a big majority,' they remarked. 'Yes,' said Attlee with characteristic modesty, 'we could not tell what would be the result.' This obviously did not satisfy the Russians who appear to have thought that Churchill should have been able to 'fix' the voting figures to his satisfaction.[98]

Stalin was absent from the sessions for two days towards the end of the conference. It was given out that he had a cold; but, as he had suffered so many reverses in argument, the British and Americans thought that his illness was what is commonly called 'diplomatic'. However, in the light of his known medical history, it is much more likely that he had a slight recurrence of his heart ailment at this time.

The Potsdam Conference met for the last time on 1 August 1945. During a break in the session, the Big Three and their advisers posed in the Cecilienhof gardens for American army photographers, who took both motion pictures and stills. It was the occasion of a slightly bizarre incident, which was caught by the movie camera. One of the operators called out in Russian that a chair was in the way and asked a guard to remove it. Stalin, thinking that he was being addressed, quickly hurried forward, and showing unexpected physical vigour, picked up the chair and deposited it some distance away.

> Then he stood back to observe what he had done, and at that moment his crooked left arm jerked and dangled helplessly from the shoulder, as though its mechanism had suddenly become out of control. Then that swinging, dangling arm, which appeared to have no connection with him, like the arm of a marionette, gradually resumed its normal position.[99]

The final act of the Conference was the signing of the communiqué. After the text had been formally approved, the Soviet delegation raised the question of who should sign first. They pointed out that at the previous two conferences this had been done either by the Prime Minister or the President. According to this procedure of rotation, said Stalin, he felt that his signature should come first on the Potsdam document.

Attlee remarked that he was in favour of alphabetical order. 'That way,' he added jokingly, 'I should score over Marshal Zhukov.'

However, Truman sided with Stalin. So Stalin signed first, followed by the President and the Prime Minister in that order.

Truman then stated in his customary, brisk manner, that there was no further business and that the Conference was now ready to adjourn. He expressed the hope that 'our next meeting might be in Washington'.

'God willing,' said Stalin.[100]

CHAPTER XIII

The Curtain Falls

I

On 6 August, Stalin's daughter Svetlana, who had telephoned her father as soon as she heard that he had returned from Potsdam, was invited to come out to Kuntsevo. She was now a student at Moscow University and had recently married a fellow student of Jewish origin named Gregory Morozov. But Stalin had refused to meet his son-in-law, apparently because he had avoided any form of war service, so Svetlana did not bring him with her to the *dacha*. By this time she had a three-month-old son and she was eager to give her father this news. According to her, when she reached Kuntsevo, she found that her father had 'the usual visitors' with him, in other words the Politburo.[1] But no one, not even her father, was particularly interested in her family affairs. Everyone was talking about the dropping of the first atomic bomb by the Americans on Hiroshima, which President Truman had just described as 'the greatest thing in history'. (The bomb killed 78,150 human beings.) Stalin's immediate comment on this momentous news has not been recorded. But his reaction was swift, since his hand had been forced and he realised that he must hurry before it was too late. On 8 August, the Soviet Union formally declared war on Japan, and next day Red Army troops crossed the frontier into Manchuria.[2]

The same evening Stalin saw Averell Harriman, the American ambassador, and emphasised that the Soviet Union had strictly lived up to its promise to enter the Pacific War. Harriman's report of the meeting to Washington contained the following:

> In discussing the Japanese situation he [Stalin] said that he thought the Japanese were looking for a pretext to set up a Government that would surrender and he thought that the atomic bomb might give this pretext. He showed great interest in the atomic bomb and said that it could mean the end of war and aggression but that the secret would have to be well kept. He said that they had found in Berlin laboratories in which the Germans were working but that he did not find that they had come to any results. Soviet scientists had also been working on the problem but had not been able to solve it.[3]

Stalin's prognosis was correct. Even as he talked with Harriman, the Americans were preparing to drop their second atomic bomb, this time upon Nagasaki. The bomb's explosion put the Tokyo government in a panic and peace overtures promptly began. They were followed by Japan's unconditional surrender five days later. However, the news was slow to reach Manchuria, so that the fighting there continued until 19 August. Although the campaign had lasted for only eleven days in all, there had been some sharp skirmishes and Soviet losses had been by no means negligible; they were officially put at 8,219 killed and 22,264 wounded. As against these figures, the Russians claimed to have inflicted some 80,000 casualties on the Japanese and to have taken 594,000 prisoners. Besides removing considerable quantities of war booty, for which they used Japanese forced labour to strip the area of practically anything of value, the Red Army took over the running of the railway in Manchuria. In other respects too Stalin got what had been secretly agreed at Yalta. This gave the Soviet Union commanding strength in the Far East and changed the structure of power politics in the Pacific.[4]

Compared with the casualties in the short war with the Japanese, the cost in human life in the struggle with Germany had been stupendous, not to mention the extensive areas of land laid waste by the opposing armies. The Russian people were never told the truth about the death roll, for the simple reason that Stalin was afraid to do so in the interests of national morale. Officially the numbers of dead were stated to be seven millions; but the real figure was in the region of twenty millions, with perhaps thirty millions wounded or incapacitated. The magnitude of the national loss was not to be revealed until after Stalin's death by the population census taken in 1959, which showed that of the age groups that had fought in the 'Great Patriotic War' there were only thirty-one million men compared with fifty-two million women, while the survivors included millions of cripples and invalids. In other words, a whole male generation had perished. Very different, too, from the homecoming of American and British prisoners-of-war was the fate of the captured Russians. Branded by Stalin as traitors because they had allowed themselves to be taken prisoner, they merely exchanged one prison camp for another, being sent off to Siberia or the Arctic Circle without even seeing their families as soon as they had crossed the frontier and been interrogated. Over a million civilians in the areas occupied by the Germans were accused of collaboration with the enemy and deported in cattle trucks, mostly Crimean Tartars, Kalmyks, Chechens and Inguishi. 'The Ukrainians escaped this fate because there were too many of them,' Khrushchev has claimed. Nevertheless, numerous suspected collaborators in the Ukraine were likewise uprooted and dispatched to prison camps.[5]

Well might Stalin say, as he did at this time, 'Eternal glory to the heroes fallen in battle for the freedom and independence of the fatherland.' Nevertheless, any hopes that the Russian people had nurtured that life would be freer and easier after the war were soon dissipated. To rebuild the ruined Soviet economy, Stalin demanded greatly increased productivity with the emphasis on heavy industry and armaments to meet the challenge posed by America's nuclear monopoly. Meanwhile there would be few consumer goods, food would continue to be scarce, and housing conditions difficult. It was an austere and depressing programme, which he put before the people in a speech delivered on the eve of the elections to the Supreme Soviet in February 1946.

As regards long-term plans, our party intends to organise another powerful upswing of our national economy that will enable us to raise our industry to a level, say, three times as high as that of pre-war industry. We must see to it that our industry shall be able to produce annually up to fifty million tons of pig iron, up to sixty million tons of steel, up to five hundred million tons of coal, and up to sixty million tons of oil. Only when we succeed in doing that can we be sure that our fatherland will be insured against all contingencies. This will need perhaps another three Five Year Plans, if not more. But it can be done, and we must do it.[6]

While trying hard to conceal from the country as a whole the importance of the atomic bomb, Stalin enlisted a team of Russian and captive

German scientists and gave them a directive to catch up with the Americans as quickly as possible. The political direction of the project was entrusted to the secret police chief Beria. This soon led to the imprisonment of the great physicist Peter Kapitsa who had been put in charge of the technical side but refused to work on the military uses of nuclear energy. Kapitsa's place was taken by Sergei Vavilov, the more compliant President of the Academy of Sciences, who had been co-opted on to the State Defence Committee during the war.

Although the State Defence Committee, with its drastic powers of directing labour, was dissolved immediately after the end of hostilities, the Russian people noticed little change, since Stalin did not relinquish the office of Chairman of the Council of People's Commissars (known from 1946 as the Council of Ministers). He also continued as Defence Minister and First Secretary of the Party, thus concentrating supreme political power in his own person. The Politburo, which had in practice been largely superseded by the State Defence Committee during the war, now resumed its normal functions as the highest policy-making body. Besides Stalin, the older members consisted of Molotov, Kaganovich, Voroshilov, Kalinin (who died in 1946), Andreyev and Shvernik. The younger element, which Stalin used to play off against the older as well as against each other, comprised Zhdanov, Khrushchev, Beria, Voznesensky, Malenkov, Bulganin and a newcomer named Alexei Kosygin. The latter, a forty-two-year-old textile engineer by training, was a protégé of Zhdanov and a former chairman of the Leningrad Soviet. He was representative of the new managerial type of Soviet politician like Vosnesensky, the brilliant chairman of the State Planning Commission, also a Zhdanov man and like Kosygin in the early forties. Zhdanov and Malenkov, between whom little love was lost, also continued in their old offices as secretaries of the Central Committee immediately subordinate to Stalin.[7]

Though it was still to some extent Stalin's mouthpiece, the Politburo in Molotov's hands appeared to exercise more power than formerly. This was due to the state of Stalin's health which necessitated long absences in the south, where communications were sometimes difficult. The Kremlin physicians had advised Stalin to take things easy for five or six months each year, to avoid the Moscow winters, and to spend as much time as possible between September and March in each year at health resorts in the Caucasus. A special commission was appointed by the Politburo, consisting of Molotov, Beria and Malenkov, to supervise his medical treatment, including a strict diet, so as 'to make Comrade Stalin a centenarian'.[8] However, from his villa above the Black Sea at Sochi, Stalin did manage to exercise a certain remote control. He continued to correspond with President Truman on topics like the withdrawal of American and Soviet forces from Czechoslovakia, fixed for 1 December 1945, apologising for the delay in mail delivery 'because of the irregular functioning of the airline between Moscow and Sochi due to weather conditions'.[9] Foreign ambassadors would on occasion be invited to the villa. To Averell Harriman, who visited him at Sochi in the autumn of 1945, he said that he had 'decided' to go his own way in foreign relations. 'America was isolationist after the First World War,' he told the ambassador. 'We will be isolationist after the second.'[10] He would also convene sessions of the Politburo or its committees from time to time at Sochi, but in the main he lived in semi-retirement and left the Politburo and the Council of Ministers under Molotov to get on with the day to day running of the country.

The censorship of foreign correspondents' press messages was temporarily lifted at this time, and this gave rise to suggestions that Stalin had in effect been exiled by the Politburo, whose prisoner he had become. 'I was on leave at the time,' Stalin later told the American Harold Stassen during a discussion on press control. 'They started to write stories that Molotov had forced me to leave Moscow, and then wrote that I should return and fire him. These stories depicted the Soviet Government as a sort of zoological garden. Of course, our people got very angry and they had to resume the censorship.'[11]

Stalin returned to Moscow for a few days in December when a conference of allied foreign ministers was held to discuss such questions as peace treaties with the Balkan states and the withdrawal of Soviet troops from Iran, also the situation in the Far East, where North Korea above the 38th Parallel was now recognised as a Soviet sphere of influence. The political discussions Stalin had with Byrnes and Bevin were amicable enough, but the conference ended on a rather sour note. Before he left again for Sochi, Stalin gave the usual banquet in the Kremlin, after which he invited the foreign ministers and their staffs into his private cinema to see a film. This turned out to be about the Soviet war with Japan and gave the impression that the Russians had taken the decisive if not the major part in the whole struggle against Japan, that the American role had been secondary and that the English had done nothing. Byrnes left rather stiffly at midnight, having pointedly refused Stalin's offer to show another film.[12]

President Truman had recently written to Stalin asking him to sit for the portrait painter Douglas Chandor for a portrait, which it was hoped would hang in the Capitol in Washington alongside those of Roosevelt and Churchill 'as a testimony of the historical importance of the meetings at Teheran and Yalta'. Stalin now informed Truman that, in view of his 'numerous duties', occasioned by a long absence from Moscow, he was unable to oblige Mr Chandor. But he offered to send him his photograph and with this the artist had to make do.[13]*

Stalin had agreed to the withdrawal of Soviet troops from Iran by March 1946 at the latest. When at the beginning of that month it appeared that no move was being made in this direction, Winston Churchill, then the leader of the Conservative Opposition in the British Parliament, was prompted to make his famous 'Iron Curtain' speech at an American college (Fulton, Missouri), where he had accepted an invitation to receive an honorary degree.

> Nobody knows what Soviet Russia and its Communist international organisation intends to do in the immediate future, or what are the limits, if any, to their expansive and proselytising tendencies...
> From Stettin, in the Baltic, to Trieste, in the Adriatic, an iron curtain has descended across the Continent. Behind that line lie all the capitals of the States of Central and Eastern Europe – Warsaw, Berlin, Prague, Vienna, Budapest, Belgrade, Bucharest and Sofia. All these famous cities and the populations around them lie in the Soviet sphere, and all are subject in one form or another, not only to Soviet influence, but to a very high and increasing measure of control from Moscow.[14]

Stalin reacted sharply in an interview which he gave *Pravda* a week later. He described Churchill's speech as 'a dangerous act' and its author 'inveterate Tory that he is' as 'the warmonger of the Third World War', comparing him with Hitler. 'I don't know whether Mr Churchill and his friends will succeed in organising a new armed campaign against Eastern Europe after the Second World War,' he added, recalling for good measure Churchill's intervention in the Civil War in 1919, 'but if they do succeed, which is not very probable, because millions of plain people stand over the cause of peace – it may be confidently said that they will be thrashed, just as they were thrashed once before, twenty-six years ago.'[15]

Stalin's subsequent utterances were more conciliatory, due to the

* Douglas Chandor was an Englishman who settled in America in 1926 and painted Presidents Hoover and Roosevelt and some two hundred others prominent in American social and political life. Roosevelt, who discussed the project of the Big Three portraits with Chandor before his death, considered that this artist 'possessed the peculiar kind of gift for doing this particular kind of painting better than anyone else'. *Stalin's Correspondence with Churchill, Attlee, Roosevelt 1941–1945*, II, p. 274.

firm line taken by Britain and America at the United Nations. But he still felt bitter about Churchill as he showed some weeks later when he received the new American ambassador General Bedell Smith. 'Churchill tried to instigate war against Russia and persuaded the United States to join him in an armed occupation against part of our territory in 1919,' he told the ambassador. 'Lately he has been at it again. But Russia, as the events of the past few years have proved, is not stupid. We can recognise our friends from our potential enemies.'

'Is it possible that you really believe that the United States and Great Britain are united in an alliance to thwart Russia?' asked Bedell Smith.

'Yes,' replied Stalin.

'I must affirm in the strongest possible terms that this is not the case,' the ambassador declared. 'In the first place I know Mr Churchill well, having in a sense served under him as an Allied staff officer. He is far-seeing in international affairs, but I could never visualise him as an instigator of war. I hold no brief for his Fulton speech, but I must say that it reflects an apprehension which seems to be common to both the United States and Britain. In the second place, the Soviet Government will understand that while we have many ties with Britain, including a common language and many common interests, our primary concern is world security and justice. This concern and responsibility extend to small nations as well as large, and while recent events have required the United States to vote with Britain in the United Nations Assembly and in the Security Council, this was because we felt that justice required us to do so.'

He too, observed Stalin, believed in the United Nations and subscribed to the Charter. But he commented rather acidly on the fact that the United States had pressed for a debate on Iran's complaint before the UN and had opposed Gromyko's request for a postponement. 'You don't understand our situation as regards oil and Iran,' he went on. 'The Baku oilfields are our major source of supply. They are close to the Iranian border and they are very vulnerable. Beria and others tell me that saboteurs – even a man with a box of matches – might cause us serious damage. We are not going to risk our oil supply.'[16]

Tension was in some degree relaxed by the departure of Soviet troops from Iran in May. Nevertheless, although the world was longing for peace, a new kind of war was on the way – the so-called Cold War.

2

During the summer of 1946, while Stalin was spending most of his time in Sochi, the Soviet and Allied foreign ministers were conferring in Paris on the peace treaties eventually concluded with Italy, Bulgaria, Roumania, Hungary and Finland. So far as Austria was concerned, Stalin would not sanction the opening of peace negotiations until a peace treaty had been concluded with Germany. Thus the discussions in Paris concentrated mainly on Russia's control of the Danube basin, and thanks to the fact that Soviet armies were in occupation of much of this area, Stalin's diplomacy was successful in keeping the greater part of eastern Europe within the Soviet orbit. In achieving his objective, Stalin was also helped by the fact that the western powers were not yet ready to make a concerted response to the implications of Churchill's Fulton speech.

In August 1946, Stalin made a brief trip from Sochi to Moscow in order to receive a delegation of the British Labour Party led by Morgan Phillips, the Party Secretary; also included were Miss Alice Bacon, MP, and the left-wing Professor Harold Laski, who had recently said that in his opinion Ernest Bevin, the British Foreign Secretary, regarded the Soviet Union as 'a breakaway from the Transport and General Workers' Union', and that he was trying to build up an anti-Soviet bloc instead of negotiating a give-and-take settlement of outstanding political questions with the USSR. Miss Bacon, who was particularly impressed with Stalin, described him on her return to London as 'very human, a man with a fine sense of humour and a keen intellect', and proudly exhibited his 'autograph on Kremlin notepaper' which he had given her.[17]

A few weeks later, back in Sochi, Stalin answered a series of written questions which had been submitted to him by Alexander Werth, the correspondent of the London *Times* in Moscow.

Werth: Do you believe that virtual monopoly by the United States of America of the atomic bomb constitutes one of the main threats to peace?

Stalin: I do not believe the atomic bomb to be as serious a force as certain politicians are inclined to regard it. Atomic bombs are intended for intimidating the weak-nerved, but they cannot decide the outcome of war since atomic bombs are by no means sufficient for this purpose. Certain monopolist possession of the secret of the atomic bomb does create a threat, but at least two remedies exist against it—(a) monopolist possession of the atomic bomb cannot last long; (b) use of the atomic bomb will be prohibited.

Werth: Do you believe that with the further progress of the Soviet Union towards Communism the possibilities of peaceful co-operation with the outside world will not decrease as far as the Soviet Union is concerned? Is 'Communism in one country' possible?

Stalin: I do not doubt that the possibilities of peaceful co-operation, far from decreasing, may even grow. 'Communism in one country' is perfectly possible, especially in a country like the Soviet Union.[18]

Stalin's replies were on the whole welcomed by the foreign press, and Ernest Bevin expressed the opinion that 'there has been a little lifting of the clouds'. As for Stalin's predictions about the future of the atomic bomb, these were to be realised in due course. Meanwhile, pending the discovery of the secret of the bomb by Russian scientists under the supervision of the secret police chief Beria, the only answer which Stalin could give to American nuclear supremacy lay in the Soviet Union's superiority in conventional weapons. Consequently Soviet armed forces, which had been reduced to less than four million since the war, were now to be progressively increased, thus imposing a further drain on the country's economy.

In an attempt to minimise the effect of his Fulton speech, in which he had conjured up the spectre of a Red invasion of western Europe, Churchill sent Stalin a greetings telegram on 21 December, – 'All personal good wishes on your birthday, my war-time comrade' – to which Stalin returned his 'warm thanks'. On the same day, Stalin received Elliott Roosevelt, the late American President's son, in the Kremlin, and in their talk he took the opportunity to discount the possibility of fresh international conflict. 'No single great power, even if its Government were anxious to do so, could at present raise a large army to fight another great power,' he told his visitor. 'People are unwilling to fight. They are tired of war. Besides, there are no understandable objectives to justify a new war. In view of all these considerations, I think the danger of a new war is unreal.'[19]

A further relaxation of tension took place in January 1947, when Lord Montgomery, who had now succeeded Alanbrooke as Chief of the Imperial General Staff, spent a week in Moscow as Stalin's guest. Having been told that the British Field-Marshal did not like staying up late, Stalin received him at five o'clock in the afternoon. The interview began with Montgomery presenting his host with copies of his books recounting his campaigns in North Africa and Europe, together with a case of Scotch whisky bearing the legend 'Britain delivers the goods'.

'You bring me these presents,' said Stalin, as they shook hands. 'What do you want of me?'

Montgomery replied that he wanted nothing for himself, but that he would like to see a closer relationship between the British and Soviet armies, continuing and expanding their war-time association. The Field-Marshal told Stalin that he had met all the Soviet Marshals and had invited Vasilevsky and Koniev to come to England. He hoped that this would lead to a regular exchange of officers. Stalin replied that he thought the time had not yet come for such an interchange of military personnel, as he might be 'blackguarded in the world press as a warmonger'. However, although nothing was to come of it, he did favour the idea of a military alliance between Britain and the Soviet Union to replace or reinforce the non-aggression treaty of 1942 which he felt had fallen into abeyance.[20]

The conversation was not entirely devoted to military subjects. At one point Stalin asked, 'Have you seen Lenin?'

'I thought he was dead,' answered Montgomery.

'So he is,' said Stalin. 'But all the same you ought to go and see him in the mausoleum in the Red Square.' Before leaving Moscow, Montgomery did so, afterwards remarking that Lenin looked 'pretty waxen and yellow'.[21]

> We parted with great friendliness. Stalin was in good health; his brain was very clear; he gave me the impression that if you did not know your subject you would quickly get tangled up in argument with him.

The same evening Stalin gave a dinner for his distinguished guest. About thirty others were bidden, including Voroshilov, Bulganin, Vasilevsky and other marshals and generals as well as Molotov and Vyshinsky. Conspicuously absent was Marshal Zhukov, with whom Montgomery had worked closely in Berlin when they commanded their countries' respective occupation forces. In 1946, Stalin who resented Zhukov's popularity recalled him from Berlin and shortly afterwards banished him to Odessa, replacing him by Marshal V. D. Sokolovsky who had been Zhukov's Chief of Staff. ('He was lucky not to be bumped off,' remarked Montgomery). At the same time Bulganin took over Zhukov's duties as Deputy Defence Minister. At dinner Bulganin who had also recently been elected to the Politburo sat opposite Stalin and between Molotov and Vyshinsky, where he seems to have given Montgomery the impression that he was a coming man in the Soviet hierarchy. A red-faced political marshal with a goatee beard, fifty-one-year-old Nikolai Aleksandrovich Bulganin was a heavy drinker, who reminded a visiting American journalist of 'an unsuccessful river boat gambler who has been living it up'. Like Voroshilov, he was something of a lightweight and toadied to Stalin.

While Montgomery was having drinks before dinner in the anteroom, suddenly a hush fell on the party. Montgomery looked round and saw Stalin coming through the door. It was clear to him, as it had been to Alanbrooke and Ismay, that 'the Marshals, Ministers (including Molotov and Vyshinsky), and Generals were all in the greatest awe of Stalin and shut up like an oyster in his presence'. This atmosphere of constraint persisted at dinner and was only broken up when Montgomery, according to his account, began to 'rag' Molotov.

I asked him about his life in New York, and made him describe a typical day. I said it was obvious that he spent the mornings planning how to outflank his opponents in the afternoons; he spent the afternoons in developing his outflanking movements; and he spent the evenings in dancing and drinking. Obviously the politicians did no work.

This promised very badly for the [forthcoming] Moscow Conference in March 1947; nothing would be accomplished, except to decide to have some more conferences; would he give me the programme of conferences for the next two years?

Stalin enjoyed all this hugely. He joined in with great keenness, taking my side; he talked about 'we soldiers' as against 'you politicians', and obviously liked to be considered a soldier. He ragged the politicians with great enjoyment. I urged him on and said some dreadful things about politicians, for which I hope I may be forgiven. Stalin said I ought to join with him; between us we would defeat any combination of civilian politicians. I said I was a soldier only. He said that he welcomed the present world tendency for soldiers to take over the direction of affairs and become Ambassadors, etc., etc. He was delighted that General Marshall had become the American Secretary of State. He said that soldiers of experience made very good soldier-politicians, because they were much more sensible than civilian-politicians.

Earlier in the day, Vasilevsky had presented Montgomery with the full dress overcoat of a Marshal of the Soviet Union. After dinner, Montgomery told Stalin that he would like to put on the uniform and salute the Generalissimo. According to Montgomery, Stalin was delighted, and when Montgomery appeared dressed in his new uniform, the Generalissimo, who was similarly attired, insisted on their being photographed together.

556

Stalin then asked what I would like to do next. Would I like to have some music, or see a film in his private cinema, or go out in the city to a theatre? I replied that I would like to go home to bed. It was 10 p.m. and I had an early start next day for my flight back to London. Stalin said: 'Certainly, let's all go to bed.' And I suppose for the first time in the history of Russia an official banquet in the Kremlin broke up soon after 10 p.m.

Montgomery, who had not seen Stalin since Potsdam, thought he now looked his age; he seemed to have shrunk in size and was thinner and not so firm on his legs. Also he ate and drank sparingly, and gave the impression that he was on a diet, although he chain-smoked cigarettes throughout the meal.[22]

Shortly after Montgomery's departure, Stalin attended a plenary session of the Supreme Soviet when he asked to be relieved of his office of Defence Minister 'in view of the excessive burden of his main work'.[23] The Supreme Soviet granted his request. In his place the obsequious Bulganin was nominated head of the Defence Ministry.

Stalin was again in Moscow for the resumed Foreign Ministers' Conference at the beginning of March, when he received Ernest Bevin, the British Foreign Secretary, and they discussed the future of Germany. However, any hopes Stalin had for an agreed political settlement were dissipated by President Truman's formal declaration of the 'Cold War' while the conference was still in session.

The American President's dramatic pronouncement was the direct result of Britain's decision for economic reasons to withdraw from Greece, whose government she had been helping with arms and subsidies in the struggle against the Communist guerrillas. In a message which he read to both Houses of Congress and a nation-wide radio audience on 12 March 1947, Truman stated that the United States would step into the breach to prevent Greece going Communist, providing 'immediate and resolute action' in the form of money and personnel. He also undertook to finance and arm the Turks as well, since a Communist take-over in Greece was bound in his view to have 'an unsettling effect' upon Turkey, where he knew that Stalin still hankered after a naval base from which to participate in the control of the Straits. Henceforward, Truman added, his Government would support any nation resisting Communism, and in his view it was the duty of 'nearly every nation' to resist. This was the Truman Doctrine, America's answer to Stalin's advocacy of 'Communism in one country'.

I believe that it *must* be the policy of the United States to support free peoples who are resisting attempted subjugation by armed minorities or outside pressures.

I believe that we *must* assist free peoples to work out their own destinies in their own way.

I believe that help should be primarily through economic and financial aid which is essential to economic stability and orderly political processes.[24]

Truman's doctrine found concrete expression in the Marshall Plan put forward by his Secretary of State for the provision of economic aid to any country, including Germany and Japan, that was struggling with poverty and hardship consequent upon the war. The plan made a strong appeal to the Russian satellites, particularly Czechoslovakia, whose immediate reaction was to apply to participate in its benefits. Even Stalin thought there might be something in the Marshall Plan for Russia and he dispatched Molotov and a team of eighty experts to go into it at the next Foreign Ministers' Conference, which was held in Paris in July 1947. He eventually rejected it and recalled Molotov and his team to Moscow when he realised that in order to qualify for aid the Soviet Union would have to submit a balance sheet of her economic resources. No doubt he feared that American economic penetration into eastern Europe might encourage anti-Communist elements and promote counter-revolution.

Poland and the other satellites with exclusively Communist governments might be expected to fall into line obediently, as indeed they did. The position in Czechoslovakia, however, was rather different. Although the Communists secured a majority of votes at the post-war elections, and Klement Gottwald, the Prime Minister, was a Communist, it was a bare majority with Gottwald heading a coalition government in which the Social Democrats and other parties opposed to the Communists were represented. Edward Benes, who headed the Czechoslovakian government-in-exile in London, had returned to Prague as President, while Jan Masaryk, another 'westerner', held the key ministry of Foreign Affairs in the Gottwald administration. Nevertheless, the decision to participate in the Marshall Plan was unanimously approved by the Czechoslovak cabinet. As a result, Masaryk was invited, or perhaps one ought to say, summoned to Moscow. It was agreed by the Czechoslovak cabinet that he should go and in due course he appeared in the Kremlin.

'We consider this a question of principle, on which our friendship with the Czechoslovak Republic depends,' Stalin bluntly told Masaryk when they met. 'If you go to the Paris Conference, you will demonstrate that you mean to collaborate in Western actions to isolate the Soviet Union.' All the other Slavic states had therefore backed out, he continued, and the Soviet Government had been 'surprised to note that you are acting differently'.

Masaryk thereupon produced a personal and confidential memorandum on the subject from President Benes, which had been secretly drawn up a few hours before the Czech Foreign Minister left for Moscow. Its contents were presumably only known to Benes and Masaryk and perhaps the President's secretary. As Masaryk began to read it, Stalin interrupted him brusquely. 'Don't bother,' he said. 'I've already seen it.' He then picked up a copy of the document which lay on his desk and waved it in the direction of his visitor. Masaryk was staggered, as he admitted afterwards, since it showed that Stalin had spies in the Czechoslovak President's private office, probably in the Foreign Ministry as well.

When Masaryk reported back to Prague, it was hardly surprising that Gottwald and his cabinet should have had second thoughts and reversed their previous decision. Jan Masaryk returned home a broken man. 'I went to Moscow the Foreign Minister of a sovereign state,' he said cynically, 'and I came back a stooge of Stalin. *Finis Bohemiae.*'[25]

3

During the winter of 1946–1947 Stalin was seriously ill for some weeks with recurrent heart trouble, aggravated by high blood pressure, but the news was kept from the Russian people. Apart from its physical effects, the illness seems to have caused some change in personality which became apparent to his intimates at this time. He was prone to bouts of irritation and anger and he also appeared increasingly suspicious of those about him. In this he exhibited some symptoms of paranoia. His daughter Svetlana remembers a typical incident which occurred when she was staying with him at Sochi in the summer of 1947. They were having dinner and several other members of the Politburo were present, including Andrei Zhdanov, who was unusually silent on this occasion. Angered by his silence, Stalin suddenly turned on Zhdanov and exclaimed: 'Look at him sitting there, like Christ, as if nothing was of any concern to him! There – looking at me now as if he were Christ!' Zhdanov, who also suffered from heart trouble, grew pale, and beads of perspiration stood out on his forehead. Svetlana thought he was going to have an attack and gave him a glass of water. Everyone else fell silent. It was an embarrassing incident.[26]

Stalin could be just as rude to his daughter, criticising her appearance and clothes. 'Why do you wear that tight-fitting sweater?' he once said to her. 'You are a grown girl now. Wear something loose!' Svetlana was so upset that she immediately left the room. 'Modesty embellishes a Bolshevik,' he often told her. On another occasion, when she sent him a photograph of herself for his birthday, he returned the picture, on which he had scrawled in blue pencil: 'You have an insolent expression on your face. Before, there used to be modesty there and that was attractive.' After she had divorced her first husband and went to live with the Zhdanovs, whose son Yuri she subsequently married, Stalin got angry with her and bawled her out in front of everyone at table, calling her 'a parasite'. No good had come of her yet, he told her. At this time he was having a second floor added to the *dacha* at Kuntsevo and would no doubt have liked her to come and live there. 'What do you want to move to the Zhdanovs' for?' he asked. 'You'll be eaten alive by the women there. There are too many women in that house.'[27]

At the boring dinners at Kuntsevo or Sochi, Stalin would sometimes order his daughter to dance for the entertainment of the company. As often as not she would run off to the kitchen, saying she was going to complain to the cook. 'Spare me!' her father would respond in a mocking tone. 'If you complain to the cook it will be all over with me.' Then, after she had been out of the room for some time and he noticed her absence, he would send one of the others to bring her back. 'Comrade hostess!' he would say when she reluctantly appeared. 'Why have you left us poor unenlightened creatures without giving us some orientation? Now we don't know where to go. Lead us! Show us the way!' This was an allusion to the slogan then in vogue glorifying the leader: 'Comrade Stalin leads us along Lenin's way!' But it did not amuse Svetlana.[28]

Khrushchev, who was frequently invited to these parties, has this to say about Stalin's relations with his daughter, whom Khrushchev called Svetlanka:

No doubt Stalin loved Svetlanka very much. He was very proud and fond of her. Yet look how he showed his fatherly feelings towards his daughter! He behaved so brutishly not because he wanted to cause Svetlanka pain. No, his behaviour towards her really was an expression of affection, but in a perverse, brutish form which was peculiar to him.

Svetlana's visit to Sochi, in August 1947, was the first time that she and her father had been together for any length of time for some years.

She found it difficult to adjust herself to his ways, which meant sleeping half the day, having a meal at three o'clock in the afternoon, dining at ten and sitting up half the night at the dinner table. Sometimes old films would be shown, particularly those starring and directed by Charlie Chaplin such as *Modern Times*, which delighted him by how 'cleverly' it made fun of work on an assembly line under capitalism.

The whole crowd would come for dinner, Beria, Malenkov, Zhdanov, Bulganin and the rest. I found it dull and exhausting to sit three or four hours at the table listening to the same old stories as if there were no news and nothing whatever going on in the world! It made me dead tired and I would go off to bed. They sat up late into the night.

Svetlana and others present at these dinners like Milovan Djilas are agreed that Stalin drank little, but that it gave him pleasure to see others drinking their fill and becoming inebriated. On these occasions there was plenty of rough horseplay and crude practical jokes, of which Mikoyan and Poskrebyshev were the most frequent victims. Stalin would look on and puff away at his pipe, while a tomato was slipped on to someone's chair or vodka and salt surreptitiously mixed with his wine, practical jokes which invariably produced great hilarity. Poskrebyshev, whom Stalin used to call the 'Chief', since he headed his secretariat, was often carried home dead drunk, having previously lain vomiting in the bathroom. At Kuntsevo there was a pond in the grounds, into which, when it was not frozen over, the unfortunate 'Chief' would frequently be thrown in order to sober him up. 'All this reminded one of Peter the Great's imperial pranks with boyars,' remarked Svetlana, who was gravely shocked by these goings-on. 'Needless to say, nothing of the sort had ever happened in my mother's day, when guests arrived with their wives, and the spirit of debauchery was absent.'

Khrushchev has described Stalin's 'interminable dinners' at Kuntsevo as 'agonising' and 'frightful'.

We would get home from them early in the morning, just in time for breakfast, and then we would have to go to work. During the day I usually tried to take a nap in my lunch hour, because there was always a risk that if you did not take a nap and Stalin invited you to dinner, you might get sleepy at the table; and those who got sleepy at Stalin's table could come to a bad end.[29]

'It's good to know you haven't forgotten your father,' Stalin wrote to his daughter on her return to Moscow in October, 1947. 'I'm well. Everything's fine. I'm not lonely.'[30] According to Khrushchev, 'he suffered terribly from loneliness'.

> He needed people around him all the time. When he woke up in the morning, he would immediately summon us, either inviting us to a film show or starting some conversation which could have been finished in two minutes. But he stretched it so that we could stay with him. This was an empty pastime for us. It is true that sometimes state and party questions were decided, but we spent only a portion of our time on those. The main thing was to occupy Stalin's time so he would not suffer loneliness. He was depressed by loneliness and he feared it.

It was usually one or two o'clock in the morning when the film show ended and Stalin would say: 'Well, let's go and get something to eat.'

> It was time to go to bed, and the next day we had to go to work. But everyone would say yes, he was hungry too. This lie about being hungry was like a reflex. We would all get into our cars and drive to the *dacha*.
>
> Beria and Malenkov would usually get into Stalin's car. I usually rode with Bulganin. Our caravan used to make detours into side streets. Apparently Stalin had a street plan of Moscow and worked out a different route every time...
>
> Every time we got to the *dacha* we used to whisper among ourselves about how there were more locks than the time before. All sorts of bolts were attached to the gate, and there was a barricade set up. There were two walls, and between the walls there were watchdogs. An electric alarm system and all sorts of other security devices were installed.

According to Khrushchev, Stalin got the idea that attempts were being made to poison him. Although everything that was served at the table had previously been passed by the Kremlin analysts, Stalin still made the others taste the dishes first. 'Look, here are the giblets, Nikita. Have you tried them yet?' Or, 'Look, here's some herring!' 'Oh, I forgot,' Khrushchev would reply, noting that Stalin wished to try them himself but was afraid to do so before Khrushchev had taken some first.[31]

Allied with these suspicions were common symptoms of senility, such as lapses of memory and an increasing tendency to compare recent happenings with his experiences of long ago, during his childhood in the Caucasus or as an exile in Siberia: 'Yes, I remember, the same thing...'[32]

About this time, Svetlana recalled Poskrebyshev telling her father who would be present at dinner on a particular evening and naming, among others, Alexei Kuznetsov, a member of the Orgburo and former Leningrad Party Secretary, whom Stalin used frequently to telephone during the siege, giving him instructions on the city's internal defences, how barricades should be built and so forth. When Poskrebyshev mentioned Kuznetzov, Stalin made no objection. But when Kuznetsov duly appeared and approached Stalin with a smile, the ageing dictator suddenly drew back his hand, saying coldly, 'I didn't summon you.' According to Svetlana, Kuznetsov turned pale and seemed to shrink. He was, of course, obliged to leave. Not long afterwards he was arrested with other members of the Party organisation in the so-called 'Leningrad affair' and shot in prison, apparently without trial.[33]

Khrushchev has recalled how at dinner Stalin once turned to Bulganin and started to say something but could not remember his name. Stalin looked at him intently and said: 'You there, what's your name?'

'Bulganin.'

'Of course, Bulganin. That's what I was going to say.' According to Khrushchev, 'Stalin became very much unnerved when this kind of thing happened. He did not want others to notice. But these slips of memory occurred more and more frequently, and they used to drive him crazy.'[34]

The Yugoslav Minister Milovan Djilas, who dined at Kuntsevo in January 1948, was astonished at the change in Stalin's demeanour which had taken place in two or three years.

When I had last seen him, in 1945, he was still lively, quick-witted, and had a pointed sense of humour. But that was during the war, and it had been, it would seem, Stalin's last effort and limit. Now he laughed at inanities and shallow jokes. On one occasion he not only failed to get the political point of an anecdote I told him in which he outsmarted Churchill and Roosevelt, but I had the impression that he was offended, in the manner of old men. I perceived an awkward astonishment on the faces of the rest of the party.

In one thing, though, he was still the Stalin of old: stubborn, sharp, suspicious whenever anyone disagreed with him. He even cut Molotov, and one could feel the tension between them. Everyone paid court to him, avoiding any expression of opinion before he expressed his, and then hastening to agree with him.[35]

This was the period of the ascendancy of Andrei Zhdanov in Stalin's counsels, to the detriment of his rival George Malenkov. Zhdanov had been put in charge of the arts after the war and in this role had issued a stream of 'decrees' condemning western cultural influences and extolling 'Socialist realism' in literature and painting. In this context, for example, Djilas asked why the works of Dostoyevsky had been proscribed. 'We are not publishing him because he is a bad influence on the youth,' replied Stalin. 'But a great writer!'

Djilas described Zhdanov as 'rather short, with a brownish clipped moustache, high forehead, pointed nose, and a sickly red face. He was educated and regarded in the Politburo as a great intellectual...Although he had some knowledge of everything, even music, I would not say that there was a single field that he knew thoroughly – a typical intellectual who became acquainted with and picked up knowledge of other fields through Marxist literature'. At this time Zhdanov was preparing a 'decree' on music, taking to task such Russian composers of international repute like Prokofiev and Shostakovich. He mentioned in passing that he liked opera and asked Djilas, 'Do you have opera in Yugoslavia?'

Surprised by this question, Djilas replied, 'In Yugoslavia operas are being presented in nine theatres!' How little they know about Yugoslavia, Djilas reflected to himself. ('Indeed, it is not noticeable that it even interests them except as a given geographic location.')

Earlier in the evening, while waiting for the other guests to foregather in the hall of the *dacha*, Djilas had a comparable object lesson in Soviet topography. A large map hung on the wall, and Stalin looked on it for Koenigsberg, which had just been renamed Kaliningrad in honour of the late titular Head of State. In doing so, his attention was caught by several German places named in the Leningrad region, such as Peterhof and Oranienbaum, which dated from the time of Catherine the Great and earlier.

'Change these names,' he ordered Zhdanov curtly. 'It is senseless that these places still bear German names!' Whereupon Zhdanov obediently took out a small notebook from his pocket and recorded Stalin's order with a little pencil.

564

The dinner began with Stalin proposing that everyone guess how many degrees below zero it was, and that everyone guessing wrong should be made to drink as many glasses of vodka as he was out in his reckoning. Luckily, while Djilas was still in his hotel, he had looked at the thermometer, with the result that his guess was only one degree out. Beria, on the other hand, missed by three, remarking that he had done so on purpose so that he could drink more glasses of vodka. Like Svetlana, Djilas was shocked by the behaviour of Stalin and his associates in their cups. As he afterwards wrote, it 'suddenly brought to my mind the confinement, the inanity and senselessness of the life these Soviet leaders were living about their superannuated chief even as they played a role that was decisive for the human race'. Like Svetlana, too, he was reminded of the precedent of Peter the Great and his courtiers.

Zhdanov was the only one present who was excused from the consequences of the guessing game. He was also the only one who drank orangeade throughout the meal, explaining to Djilas that this display of temperance was due to the fact that he had a bad heart. 'I might die at any moment, and I might live a very long time,' he remarked. In fact, he was to die barely six months later, an event which was to have a marked beneficial effect on Malenkov's political fortunes.

Malenkov was not present on this occasion. Besides Zhdanov, Beria and Molotov, the only other Soviet guest present was Zhdanov's protégé Voznesensky, the economic expert in the Politburo. He was the youngest present and, as Djilas noted, comported himself like a junior among seniors. He only opened his mouth once during the meal, when Stalin asked him a question about the construction of the Volga–Don canal. Like Zhdanov he produced pencil and notebook and took down Stalin's directive.

Djilas has given a graphic picture of how the evening concluded.

Stalin ended the dinner by raising a toast to Lenin's memory: 'Let us drink to the memory of Vladimir Ilyich, our leader, our teacher – our all!'

We all stood in mute solemnity, which, in our drunkenness we soon forgot, but Stalin continued to bear an earnest, grave, and even sombre expression.

We left the table, but before we began to disperse, Stalin turned on a huge automatic record player. He even tried to dance, in the style of his homeland. One could see that he was not without a sense of rhythm. However, he soon stopped, with the resigned explanation, 'Age has crept up on me and I am already an old man!'

But his associates – or, better said, courtiers – began to assure him. 'No, no, nonsense. You look fine. You're holding up marvellously. Yes indeed, for your age...'

Stalin then put on a record in which the coloratura warbling of a singer was accompanied by the yowling and barking of dogs. This seemed to give him considerable amusement, since he laughed immoderately. But when he perceived an expression of mingled incomprehension and displeasure on Djilas's face, he remarked apologetically, 'Well, still it's clever, devilishly clever.'

Eventually Djilas took his leave. 'There was truly nothing more to say after such a long session, at which everything had been discussed except the reason why the dinner had been held.'[36]

4

Now that the countries constituting Soviet spheres of influence in eastern Europe had been forbidden by Stalin to participate in Marshall Aid, the Politburo had to consider ways and means of more closely regulating the relations of these countries both with the Soviet Union and each other. The Comintern would have been a useful instrument for this purpose, but it had been dissolved during the war owing to pressure from the western Allies. The idea of providing a substitute was mooted when the various foreign Communist parties sent delegations to the funeral of President Kalinin in August 1946. On this occasion Stalin told Tito, 'It would be best if you Yugoslavs took the initiative.'[37] The upshot was the founding of the Information Bureau of the Communist Parties in the autumn of 1947. Known for short as the Cominform, the idea was that it should have its headquarters in Belgrade and should include the Communists of all the Balkan states except Greece and Albania, in addition to Poland, Czechoslovakia, Italy and France. Zhdanov was charged with setting up the new organisation. So far as the Italians and French were concerned, Zhdanov made it clear that, unlike the old Comintern, the Cominform was not aimed at promoting international revolution, although they should try to obstruct the Truman Doctrine and the Marshall Plan. So far as the other participants were concerned, the Cominform was designed to facilitate the conversion of their countries into obedient Soviet satellites.

The security services and economies of these countries were already largely under Soviet control. Only Czechoslovakia retained the semblance of a bourgeois western democracy, although the Prime Minister Gottwald and several members of his cabinet were Communists. What added to Moscow's uneasiness was the fact that support for the Com-

566

munists in Czechoslovakia appeared to be waning. The local party comrades were therefore instucted to take appropriate remedial measures. Fortunately for Gottwald, the non-Communist Ministers in the government played into his hands by resigning. Then the Social Democrat Zdanek Fierlinger treacherously split his party by combining with the Communists to form a parliamentary majority. Thus the coup which Gottwald brought off in February 1948 was on the face of it quite constitutional. Vainly hoping he might act as a brake on the new government, Jan Masaryk agreed to stay on as Foreign Minister. A few days later, his dead body was found lying in the courtyard of his ministry, where he also had living quarters. He was dressed in pyjamas and had either deliberately jumped out of his bathroom window to his death or, as seems on the evidence more likely, had been pushed out by one of Stalin's agents. After all there was a precedent for defenestration in Prague.

Events next obliged Stalin to turn his attention to Germany, and here he met with much less success than he had in Czechoslovakia. Under the Potsdam agreement, it will be remembered, the country had been divided into four zones, administered by a four-power Control Council, pending the conclusion of a peace treaty. It had also been decided in Potsdam that for the time being no Central German Government should be established, but that administrative departments acting under the direction of the Control Council should be set up in such fields as finance, transport, trade and industry. In addition, Berlin was also administered by the four powers. However, since the city was in the Soviet zone, there was a striking contrast between conditions in the affluent western sectors of Berlin and the hardship and poverty prevailing in the Soviet sector. By the beginning of 1948, it was clear that the division of Germany into two separate administrations was inevitable, since the economy of the territory comprised in the American, British and French zones of occupation was now being restored on capitalist lines under the Marshall Plan, while the economy of the Soviet zone was mainly harnessed to Moscow's needs. Quadripartite control was now virtually impossible in practice. It came to an end in March 1948, when the Russians on Stalin's instructions withdrew from the Control Council. Thus the way was open for the creation of two idealogically opposing states, the capitalist Federal German Republic as an independent polity in the west and the communist German Democratic Republic as a Soviet satellite in the east.

There remained the capitalist enclave of west Berlin for Stalin to deal with. Here he took an ill calculated risk when he ordered an economic blockade of the three western sectors of the city, hoping thereby to paralyse West Berlin's industry and starve her inhabitants into submission to Soviet rule, when the garrisons of the western powers abandoned the city which he reckoned must follow. Unfortunately for this design, Stalin had overlooked the clause in the Potsdam agreement which provided for the allied use of narrow air corridors between west Germany and Berlin which traversed the Soviet zone. By means of a combined 'air-lift' the western Allies were able to keep the west Berliners supplied with food, fuel and raw materials during the critical months that the blockade lasted. Eventually, after nearly a year, Stalin yielded and called off the operation, at the same time agreeing to the restoration of the city's former status. This status, in spite of subsequent periodic troubles, Berlin still nominally retains, although the puppet German Democratic Republic (unrecognised in the west) has had its headquarters in the east sector of the city since 1949.

Apart from the GDR, which under the stern rule of the Soviet-trained Communist Walther Ulbricht proved thoroughly docile, the satellites gave Stalin varying degrees of trouble. All were eventually brought to heel with the exception of Yugoslavia which was inspired by President Tito to break away completely from the Soviet orbit. Coming so soon after the establishment of the Cominform, the unlooked for defection of Tito was a terrible blow to Stalin's authority and prestige in eastern Europe.

The trouble with Tito can be traced to Yugoslavia entering into relations with her Communist neighbours without first having secured the approval of the Soviet Union. In particular, Albania was a source of discord.

It first arose when Edvard Kardelj, the Yugoslav Vice-Premier, called on Stalin with the Yugoslav ambassador Vladimir Popovic in Moscow. The following dialogue took place:

Stalin: How are things with the Albanians? Enver Hoxha [the Albanian Communist leader] has complained about your political advisers in their army; he says that they are weakening discipline, or something of the sort.
Kardelj: That is news to us. They said nothing to us about it.
Stalin: What is the origin of the Albanians?
Kardelj: They are descendants of the Illyrians.
Stalin: I remember Tito told me they were related to the Basques.
Kardelj: Yes, that's right.
Stalin: They seem to be rather primitive and backward people.
Popovic: But they are very brave and faithful.

Stalin: Yes, they can be as faithful as a dog; that is one of the traits of the primitive. Our Chuvash were the same. The Russian tsars always used them for their bodyguard.[38]

Before Kardelj followed Djilas to Moscow early in 1948, arrangements had been made to send two Yugoslav divisions to Albania at Hoxha's request. 'This could lead to serious international complications,' Stalin shouted at Kardelj when they met. 'Albania is an independent state. What do you think? Justification or no justification the fact remains that you did not consult us about the sending of two divisions into Albania.'

Only a short time before this, Stalin had informed Djilas that 'the Government of the USSR has no pretensions whatever concerning Albania,' and that 'Yugoslavia is free to swallow Albania at any time she wishes to do so'. Stalin suited the word 'swallow' to the action, licking his lips and pointing to his throat.

'But, Comrade Stalin,' replied the astonished Djilas, 'there is no question of swallowing Albania, only of friendly and allied relations between the two countries.'

'Well, that's one and the same thing,' Molotov interjected.

George Dmitrov, the Bulgarian Communist leader and Premier, was taken to task for negotiating with Yugoslavia and other neighbouring countries with a view to establishing a customs union. 'You didn't consult with us,' Stalin also shouted at him. 'We learn about your doings in the newspapers. You chatter like women from the housetops about whatever occurs to you, and then the newspapers grab hold of it!'

Dmitrov, one-time secretary of the Comintern and Stalin's favourite, blushed scarlet and looked utterly dispirited. Djilas could not help feeling sorry for the man who had once bravely defied Goering in the dock at the Reichstag fire trial.

'A customs union, a federation between Roumania and Bulgaria,' said Stalin contemptuously. 'This is nonsense.' Anyhow, he added, such unions were generally unrealistic.

Kardelj observed that some customs unions had shown themselves to be not so bad in practice.

'For example?' Stalin asked.

'Well, for example, Benelux,' said Kardelj. 'Here Belgium, Holland and Luxemburg joined together.'

'No, Holland didn't,' Stalin interrupted him. 'Only Belgium and Luxemburg. That's nothing – insignificant.'

'No, Holland is included too,' Kardelj persisted.

'No, Holland is not,' Stalin repeated stubbornly and, as it happened, incorrectly. 'When I say "no" it means "no"!'

Djilas was tempted to intervene and explain that the letters 'ne' in Benelux stood for the Netherlands, as Holland was officially designated. But, as no one else said anything, Djilas also kept silent, 'and so it remained that Holland was not in Benelux'.[39]

This time there was no dinner at Stalin's country villa. The visit ended with Kardelj being obliged to sign a treaty providing for future consultation with the Soviet Union, but he was so confused and upset that he affixed his signature where Molotov ought to have put his and the documents had to be prepared afresh.

On 27 March 1948, Stalin sent Tito a letter signed by himself and Molotov, upbraiding the Yugoslavs for their unco-operative behaviour and accusing their leaders of slandering the Soviet Union behind its back, adding that it was 'absurd to listen to stories about the Soviet Communist Party from dubious Marxists of the type of Djilas...and others'. The letter concluded with a scarcely veiled threat as to what might happen to Tito. '*We think Trotsky's political career is sufficiently instructive.*'[40]

Khrushchev, who happened to be on a visit from Kiev where he was working at this time, was asked to come to Stalin's office to discuss the situation in the Ukraine. When he entered the room, Stalin pointed to a copy of his letter to Tito. 'Have you read this?' he asked Khrushchev. Without waiting for a reply he went on, 'I will shake my little finger – and there will be no more Tito. He will fall.'[41]

But Tito did not fall in spite of all Stalin's efforts to topple him. He was denounced by Soviet propaganda as a paid British secret service agent, a troubadour of Wall Street, and an insolent dwarf. Yugoslavia was expelled from the Cominform and the headquarters of the organisation were transferred from Belgrade to Bucharest. Stalin ordered a strict economic boycott of the recalcitrant country, hoping to ruin her economy and bring her to her knees. Soviet troops were ready to invade her territory given a suitable pretext. Indeed Stalin thought he could crush Tito as he had crushed Trotsky and Bukharin and he endeavoured to promote conspiracies to assassinate him. But in all this he failed miserably. It was another of his political miscalculations. In this case he underestimated the support not merely of the Yugoslav Communist Party but also the mass of Tito's followers who were not Communists, and who preferred his rule to the more rigid Soviet model. As Khrushchev was later to point out, Tito had behind him a state and a people who had gone through a severe school of fighting for independence. 'Stalin envisaged us as being his satellites after the war,'

Tito afterwards told his biographer Phyllis Auty. 'We did not even think of it as a possibility. Still, in 1948, he was clever enough not to attack us when he saw what the consequences would be and he saw that we were ready to fight. He did everything possible to provoke a fight and he had his forces massed on our frontiers in case the opportunity should arise. But he recognised what the situation was in our country and he came to the right conclusion.'[42]

At the same time all the Soviet satellites denounced their treaties of friendship with Yugoslavia. Local Communists suspected of 'Titoism' were imprisoned, tortured and executed after rigged trials which recalled the worst excesses of the Great Purge. The process began in Hungary, where Matyas Rakosi who had arrived with the 'liberating' Soviet troops towards the end of the year obediently carried out the orders he received from Moscow. The first victim was the Foreign Minister Laszlo Rajk who was tried on fabricated charges of plotting counter-revolution, pleaded guilty after protracted brainwashing and was executed along with several colleagues. Next to be charged with Titoist heresy was the former Bulgarian Vice-Premier Traicho Kostov. Apart from having had the misfortune to entertain Tito when he visited Sofia, Kostov had also fought a long and losing battle to save his country's tobacco stocks and most valuable asset from being appropriated by Russia. It was said at the time that 'Kostov was hanged with a rope of tobacco leaves'.[43]

During the next three years these dismal spectacles were to be re-enacted in every Soviet satellite country, ending with Czechoslovakia, the scene of the greatest slaughter, where fourteen leading Communists, headed by Rudolf Slansky, former Secretary-General of the Czech Communist Party, and Vladimir Clementis, Masaryk's successor as Foreign Minister, appeared together in the dock of the People's Court in Prague.

After the Berlin air-lift had been called off in the summer of 1949, Stalin made a conciliatory gesture by receiving the new American and British ambassadors. With the British envoy, Sir David Kelly, he dwelt on the possibilities of continuing co-existence, in spite of mutual suspicions engendered by the North Atlantic Treaty, a pact which he characterised as 'meaningless'. Asked by Stalin if he could be of any service to him, Sir David replied that he hoped he would help him to have really useful exchange of views with the Foreign Ministry, adding that too much time in the past had been taken up with such personal questions as the relations of the embassy staff with Russian ladies. 'Such problems arise from boredom,' commented Stalin with a laugh.[44]

On the eve of his seventieth birthday, Stalin invited the Chinese

Communist leader Mao Tse-tung to Moscow. Mao had at last emerged the victor in the long struggle with the Kuomintang forces of Chiang Kai-shek. As one Asiatic to another, Stalin treated his guest with every show of outward respect, having learned his lesson with Tito and having no wish to repeat the experience. The visit, dragged out with private talks and state banquets, resulted in a formal alliance, by which Stalin undertook to surrender Port Arthur and relinquish control of the Manchurian railway by the end of 1952, a promise which incidentally was not kept. Mao also got a loan and other technical aid. In return he agreed to the 'independence' of Outer Mongolia, in other words that this province should become a Soviet satellite as North Korea already was, and he also gave Stalin a foothold in Sinkiang as well as Manchuria.

Elsewhere in the Far East, notably Korea, Stalin's judgment was less sound. In encouraging the North Korean Communist leader Kim Il Sung to attack the south now that American troops had left, he thought the conflict could be localised. But it developed into an international conflagration when the United States decided to intervene and called on other members of the United Nations to do likewise, a decision implemented when the Soviet representative unwisely withdrew during the critical session of the Security Council. Stalin also condemned the United Nations for declaring the Chinese People's Republic an aggressor for trying to recover Formosa which had been occupied by Chiang Kai-shek with American help.

The United Nations, which was founded as a bulwark of peace, is turning into an instrument of war, into a means of precipitating another world war. The aggressive core of UNO comprises ten member countries. It is the representatives of these countries that now decide the destiny of war and peace in UNO. It is they that carried through UNO the disgraceful decision declaring the Chinese People's Republic an aggressor.

It is characteristic of the present order of things that the tiny Dominican Republic, for instance, which has scarcely two million inhabitants, now carries as much weight in UNO as India, and far more weight than the Chinese People's Republic, which has been deprived of a voice in UNO.[45]

The utmost Stalin could do to retrieve the situation was to supply the North Koreans with arms and to leave it to Mao Tse-tung and his Chinese 'volunteers' (in reality seasoned regular troops) to sustain the brunt of the Korean campaign. Fortunately the Americans did not extend their attacks to Manchuria, which General MacArthur was anxious to bomb, as this would have brought the Soviet Union into the war by virtue of the recently signed treaty with Mao. Not that Stalin would have minded if the struggle had spread to the Chinese mainland, since this would have weakened the Mao regime and made it more dependent on the Kremlin. In fact, the Soviet threat to Mao's leadership was bound to last as long as Stalin was alive. It was only Stalin's death that was to enable Mao to render his personal position secure and at the same time to end the Korean War which Stalin's action with Kim Il Sung had sparked off.

5

The eighteen months immediately preceding Stalin's seventieth birthday celebrations witnessed a wave of terror originating in what was known as the 'Leningrad Affair'.[46] This affair followed Zhdanov's sudden death in August 1948, apparently from heart failure. (It was subsequently alleged that he had been poisoned by the doctors who were treating him.) As has been seen, Zhdanov suffered from a chronic heart ailment and his death came as no surprise. On the other hand, he had recently fallen into disfavour with Stalin, who blamed him for the failure to handle Tito effectively after the establishment of the Cominform in Belgrade. Even if he had been in perfect health Zhdanov probably would not have lasted much longer in the leadership where he was being rapidly outstripped by Malenkov. For the latter, Zhdanov's departure from the political scene could not have come at a more opportune moment, since it removed his greatest rival for the succession to Stalin. It also enabled Malenkov, with the aid of V. S. Abakumov, the new Minister of State Security, to remove Zhdanov's known associates and protégés in the Leningrad party organisation and install his own nominees.

During the war the secret police had been taken out of the jurisdiction of the Interior Ministry (NKVD) and placed under the specially created Ministry of State Security (NKGB later MGB). Victor Abakumov, appointed Minister in 1946 on the nomination of Beria, had begun his career in Stalin's personal secretariat and later headed the sinister counter-intelligence organisation SMERSH ('Death to Spies'), which among other achievements had been responsible for the murder of Trotsky. He appears as a character, and a most unpleasant one at that, in Alexander Solzhenitsyn's *The First Circle*, a novel founded on fact. When Abakumov and his assistants were brought to trial in Leningrad after Stalin's death and, to quote Khrushchev, 'received what they deserved', the former Minister was convicted of having trumped up cases against certain officials of the Party and Soviet apparatus and against representatives of the Soviet intelligentsia, then arrested those persons and, using criminal methods of investigation forbidden by Soviet law [i.e. torture], together with his accomplices...extracted from those arrested false evidence and a confession of guilt of serious state crimes. In this way Abakumov falsified the so-called 'Leningrad Case', in which a number of Party and Soviet officials were arrested without grounds...[47]

Although Khrushchev made some disclosures about the Leningrad Affair in the course of rehabilitating the principal victims, all the details have yet to be revealed. It is inconceivable that Abakumov should have acted as he did except on Stalin's instructions. Beria, as well as Malenkov, would also seem to have been deeply implicated in the affair, in which as many as two thousand are believed to have been arrested in Leningrad alone. The chief victims included P. S. Popkov, the Mayor of Leningrad, and all the other local Party secretaries; M. I. Rodionov, the Prime Minister of the Russian Federated Republic; General I. V. Shikin, head of the Red Army Political Directorate; Alexei Kuznetsov, Secretary of the Central Committee; A. A. Voznesensky, Rector of the Leningrad University, and his brother Nikolai, the chairman of the State Planning Commission and leader of the Zhdanovite faction in the city.

Nikolai Voznesensky was also a full member of the Politburo and, as has been seen, used to be asked to dine from time to time at Kuntsevo, where Stalin would discuss economic questions with him. He had recently published a book on the economy of the Soviet Union during the war and it was thought that in this work he had taken credit for himself as director of planning instead of giving it to Stalin, where it did not so obviously belong. According to Khrushchev, he fell foul of Beria. 'He had sought to redistribute the country's economic resources more evenly, and this meant taking money away from certain commissariats which enjoyed Beria's patronage. Beria had many commissariats under him, and he always demanded that they receive much more than their share of funds.' No doubt this was an additional reason for his becoming an 'unperson'. Apparently he was kept in prison for some time after it was briefly announced in *Pravda* that he had been 'released' from his various posts.

Khrushchev has also recalled what would happen when Stalin mentioned Voznesensky's name at their meetings.

I remember more than once during this period Stalin asked

Malenkov and Beria, 'Isn't it a waste not letting Voznesensky work while we are deciding what to do with him?'

'Yes,' they would answer, 'let's think it over.'

Some time would pass and Stalin would bring up the subject again: 'Maybe we should put Voznesensky in charge of the State Bank. He's an economist, a real financial wizard.'

No one objected but nothing happened. Voznesensky was still left hanging.

Stalin obviously had what Khrushchev called 'a certain residual respect' for Voznesensky. Khrushchev's uncorroborated and rather implausible view was that Stalin was grooming 'that *troika* of bright young men – Voznesensky, Kuznetsov and Kosygin – as successors to Beria, Malenkov and Molotov in the Kremlin old guard, and indeed had been systematically promoting them in the hierarchy before the Leningrad Affair was 'exposed'. For instance, as a First Deputy Prime Minister Voznesensky had often at Stalin's request presided at meetings of the Council of Ministers. Kuznetsov at one time seemed destined to replace Malenkov as Stalin's understudy in the Central Committee secretariat. 'This Malenkov is a good clerk,' Stalin used to say. 'He can write out a resolution quickly, but he has no capacity at all for independent thought or initiative.'

It is difficult for me to say exactly how the old guard managed to undermine Stalin's confidence in these young men. As I've already mentioned, Beria was the most accomplished at undermining Stalin's confidence in others, and he had Malenkov to use as a battering ram. Malenkov sat on the Central Committee Secretariat and had access to all the information which was given to Stalin. He could manipulate it in such a way as to provoke Stalin's anger and distrust.

Some time later, Khrushchev (according to his own account) accompanied Molotov and Malenkov to see Stalin by appointment in his Kremlin office one day at noon. In the course of their talk Voznesensky's name came up in connection with certain economic measures which he had 'proposed' for the current Five Year Plan and which Khrushchev and the others now told Stalin they had 'seen and approved'.

'Before you go on,' Stalin interrupted, 'you should know that Voznesensky was shot this morning. Are you telling me that you, too, are enemies of the people?'[48]

After Stalin's death, Khrushchev gave a simple explanation for his inaction and that of his colleagues in the Politburo on this and similar occasions. 'What could we do? A man is prepared to be a martyr, but what use is it to die like a dog in the gutter? There was nothing we could do while Stalin lived.' Khrushchev repeated this excuse in his 'secret' speech.

Why did we not do something earlier, during Stalin's life, to prevent the loss of innocent lives? It was because Stalin supervised the 'Leningrad Affair' personally and the majority of the Political Bureau members did not at that time know all the circumstances in these matters, and could not therefore intervene.

When Stalin received certain materials from Beria and Abakumov, without examining these slanderous materials, he ordered an investigation of the 'affair' of Voznesensky and Kuznetsov. With this their fate was sealed.[49]

Of the principal victims of this purge only General Shikin survived to enjoy a living rehabilitation. Voznesensky's closest associate in economic affairs was the Deputy Premier Alexei Kosygin who had recently been elected a full member of the Politburo. For months his life hung by a thread and he lived in the shadow of Stalin's executioners. His survival was little short of miraculous.

As Khrushchev has pointed out, Kosygin was on shaky ground from the beginning because he was related by marriage to Kuznetsov. His position was made worse by 'ridiculous accusations' levelled against him by some of those arrested in the Leningrad Affair. Although he had for a time been very close to Stalin, he was now relegated to the relatively unimportant post of Minister of Light Industry. Khrushchev was at a loss to explain at the time how he was saved from being liquidated along with so many others. 'Kosygin, as they say, must have drawn a lucky lottery ticket.'[50]

Most of the other members of the Council of Ministers at this time lost their posts, but the political purge was less drastic inasmuch as heads did not actually roll. In this process Molotov was replaced at the Foreign Ministry by Vyshinsky and Bulganin at the Defence Ministry by Vasilevsky, while Kaganovich and Mikoyan gave way to relatively minor officials. Malenkov had been under a cloud for a time, when he was relieved of his job in the Central Committee Secretariat in 1946 and sent off to a subordinate party post in Turkestan. According to Khrushchev, Beria used his influence with Stalin to allow Malenkov to return to Moscow and resume his old office, after which the two became 'inseparable'.

Stalin's new terror embraced prominent Russian Jewish intellectuals who were denounced for their 'rootless cosmopolitanism' and 'uncertain allegiance'. Among the victims were S. A. Lozovsky, the popular Deputy Foreign Minister, and Solomon Mikhoels, an outstanding actor and artistic director of the State Yiddish Theatre in Moscow until it was compulsorily closed down by Stalin. Both Lozovsky and Mikhoels were prominent members of the Jewish Anti-Fascist Committee, which was dissolved at the same time on the grounds that it had been trying to obtain 'special privileges for the Jews'. After being held in prison for more than three years, Lozovsky and other Jewish writers were shot on the implausible grounds that they had been plotting to detach the Crimea from the USSR. By chance Stalin's daughter Svetlana overheard her father arranging on the telephone for the liquidation of Mikhoels. 'Well, it's an automobile accident,' he said. Shortly afterwards Stalin told her that Mikhoels had been 'accidentally' killed in a car crash when travelling near Minsk.[51]

Nor did Stalin spare his own relations. His sister-in-law Anna Alliluyeva, whose husband Stanislav Redens was purged in 1938, wrote a slim volume of memoirs which annoyed Stalin on account of its 'impermissible familiarity'. She was sentenced to ten years solitary confinement. At the same time, Eugenia Alliluyeva, the widow of Svetlana's uncle Paul, had married again, her second husband being a Jewish engineer. This also upset Stalin. Both she and her second husband were likewise thrown into prison. 'They knew too much' was how Stalin explained these arrests to Svetlana. 'They blabbed a lot. It played into the hands of our enemies.' Eugenia was also accused of having poisoned her first husband, who really died of a heart attack, harried by Stalin who never forgave him for supplying his sister Nadya with the pistol with which she shot herself.[52]

Another victim of Stalin's anti-Semitic purge was J. G. Morozov, Svetlana's father-in-law by her first husband.

'That first husband of yours was thrown in your way by the Zionists,' Stalin told his daughter.

'Papa,' Svetlana replied, 'the younger ones couldn't care less about Zionism.'

'No, you don't understand,' said Stalin. 'The entire older generation is contaminated with Zionism, and now they're teaching the young people too!'[53]

It was in this atmosphere laden with overtones of terror that Stalin's seventieth birthday was celebrated on 21 December 1949. So many presents poured in from all over the Soviet Union and abroad that neither his apartment nor the *dacha* at Kuntsevo could contain all the ornamental swords, tankards, cups, embroidered cloth, tapestries and carpets that arrived in Moscow. Consequently a museum had to be specially set aside to accommodate them. A Frenchwoman sent Stalin the cap worn by her daughter who had been tortured to death by the Gestapo.[54] Never had the dictator's praises been so fulsomely sung. Molotov extolled his virtues in seven thousand words of the most blatant flattery. 'We once again wish our great and dear Stalin, our leader, teacher and friend, good health and long years of life for the benefit and glory of our people, and for the happiness of all progressive mankind.' Beria, Khrushchev, Malenkov and Voroshilov vied with each other in encomium. Even Kosygin, who had escaped the Lubyanka execution cellar by a hairsbreadth, publicly declared that 'there is no other person in the world who is better known, more loved and esteemed than our Comrade Stalin.' Thousands of large balloons bearing Stalin's familiar likeness were wafted across the sky over Moscow. The height of this deification was reached when the novelist Leonid Leonov prophesied in the pages of *Pravda* that the day would come when Stalin's birthday would be celebrated by all peoples the world over and the new calendar would begin with his birth instead of the birth of Christ.

Svetlana has described the uneasy relations she had with her father at this period, culminating in her leaving the Kremlin with her children and moving into an outside apartment. (She had by now divorced her second husband Yuri Zhdanov.) Stalin seemed to her to be embittered against the entire world. 'You too make anti-Soviet statements,' he said to her at this time, quite seriously. In the end, she had no feeling left for her father except fear and revulsion, and was in a hurry to get away whenever they met. The last occasion on which they spent a holiday together was during the summer of 1951 when Stalin journeyed south, also for the last time. This year, besides the Black Sea coast, he went to Borzhom, the Caucasian mountain spa in his native Georgia frequented by his mother. There he stayed in an old hunting lodge known as the Likani Palace, which had belonged to the Vorontsov family in Tsarist times and was now a museum. Apparently it was far from being a luxurious residence, being poorly constructed and lacking in taste, with very few bedrooms, so that visitors and staff had to double up. On the other hand, it was set in a pleasant park with attractive views across the valley of the river Kura where there was plenty of good fishing. It was warm enough to have meals out of doors under the trees. Svetlana realised that something must have drawn him to Borzhom, possibly memories of bygone days. But all he would tell her was that he had been there with her mother shortly after the birth

of her brother Vasily in 1922. According to Svetlana, Stalin could remember the Georgian names for the various fish which the servants
produced from the river at his bidding and was 'pleased at the
memories they brought to mind. But he never said so in so many
words. He didn't like talking about his feelings and used to remark
that that kind of thing was "for women".'[55]

Khrushchev has recalled that he was on holiday at Sochi and received a summons to Borzhom, as did Beria and Mikoyan. 'It was
awful,' said Khrushchev. 'We depended on Stalin for everything. We
were on an entirely different schedule from his. In the morning we
would have been up and taken a walk, and Stalin would still be sleeping. Then he would get up, and the day would begin officially.'

Stalin's increasing suspicions of individuals was illustrated by the
action of the Hungarian Communist leader Rakosi in deciding to take
a holiday in the neighbourhood that summer. 'How does Rakosi know
whenever I am in the Caucasus?' he asked Khrushchev and the others.
'Apparently some sort of intelligence network is informing him. He
should be discouraged from this.' Of course, there was nothing suspicious about it. Rakosi had simply called up the Central Committee
Secretariat and been told where the General Secretary was. On this
occasion, Rakosi was invited to dinner on two or three nights. After
one session he let fall a comment about the heavy drinking that was
going on. 'All right,' said Stalin, when this was reported to him. 'We'll
see about that!' Accordingly, the next night that Rakosi was there,
Stalin began to pump drinks into him, forcing him to consume two or
three bottles of champagne in addition to quantities of vodka and
Caucasian red wine. Khrushchev thought that Rakosi might collapse
with fatal results. But somehow he survived the ordeal and staggered
off. Next day Stalin was in a jovial mood and joked with the others:
'You see what sort of a state I got him into!'[56]

No doubt one of the subjects discussed in Borzhom was the progress
of the purges in the satellite countries. The show trials were over in
Hungary and Bulgaria, but the pre-trial investigations were still proceeding in Czechoslovakia where Soviet 'specialists' in the extraction of
confessions had been dispatched to help the local security police.
Clementis, the Czech Foreign Minister, who had succeeded the ill-fated
Masaryk, and Otto Sling, the Party secretary in Moravia, were already
in custody, and the interrogators were suggesting that a more exalted
member of the hierarchy must be behind the anti-Party conspiracy.
The name of Rudolf Slansky, the Secretary-General of the Czechoslovak Central Committee, cropped up from time to time and there
was a tendency to implicate him. At first Stalin, who had been follow-

ing the course of the investigation closely, considered that the evidence against Slansky was 'not conclusive' since it had been obtained from 'known criminals'. Meanwhile Slansky was awarded the highest Czech decoration on the occasion of his fiftieth birthday, although no birthday greetings came from Moscow. Eventually Stalin dispatched Mikoyan to the Czech capital with a personal message to President Gottwald to the effect that 'Slansky must be arrested lest he escape to the West'.

What happened on Mikoyan's arrival at the Hradcany Palace in Prague was summarised in an official document from the Czechoslovak Communist Party archives recently smuggled out of the country.

Gottwald hesitated...Mikoyan's reaction was to break off the conversation and contact Stalin from the Soviet embassy. When the talks resumed, Mikoyan confirmed that Stalin insisted on his point of view and reminded Gottwald of his grave responsibility.

Gottwald, without any concrete facts, finally concluded that Stalin as usual had reliable sources of information and that his advice was sound. He sent a message to Stalin through Mikoyan that he agreed with Stalin's insistence on Slansky's arrest.[57]

Mikoyan's meeting with Gottwald took place on 11 November 1951. Slansky was arrested thirteen days later. After a year's concentrated brainwashing he was at last brought to trial along with thirteen other defendants. Slansky, Clementis, Sling and eight others were sentenced to death and hanged; the remainder got life imprisonment but were released after serving nine years and were eventually rehabilitated by the Dubcek regime.

Slansky's arrest coincided with Stalin's decision to remove Abakumov from the post of Minister of State Security. Superficially these two events may seem to have little if anything in common, but in fact they were closely connected and betokened a significant change in Soviet foreign policy. It will be remembered that, in spite of his anti-Semitic drive at home, Stalin had helped the infant state of Israel. This he had done with money and supplies which were channelled through Prague, an operation for which Abakumov seems to have been jointly responsible with Slansky. Now Soviet support was suddenly switched to the Arab side. It is significant that one of the counts in the indictment against Slansky charged him with having pursued an anti-Arab policy – no doubt on Stalin's direct instructions, though naturally this was not revealed in court.

Abakumov's dismissal at the end of November 1951 has been seen as a policy victory of the Politburo majority over Stalin, and within the Politburo as a triumph of Malenkov over Beria. Abakumov was a Beria man. His successor Semyen Ignatiev, who had been employed in Party work in Bashkiria and Central Asia, probably owed his appointment to Khrushchev's influence. 'When you deserve it, we'll shoot you,' Alexander Solzhenitsyn makes Stalin say to Abakumov in *The First Circle*. Stalin may well have actually said this, since it was left to his heirs to carry out the execution after Stalin's death. Similarly, a number of Beria's prominent henchmen in Georgia were dismissed from their posts and arrested, allegedly for fomenting nationalist aspirations in the western part of the country known as Mingrelia. 'Beria assigned himself to go to Georgia and administer the punishment of the imaginary enemies,' noted Khrushchev afterwards. 'Those poor fellows were led to the slaughter like sheep.'[58]*

Meanwhile the weather at Borzhom had turned cool and before returning to Moscow which he did not do until towards the end of the year, Stalin visited another of his Black Sea villas, at Afon, between Sochi and Sukhum. Khrushchev and Mikoyan, who were still holidaying at the latter resorts, were summoned to Afon. Afterwards Khrushchev recalled a striking incident which took place during this visit.

One day Mikoyan and Khrushchev were taking a walk around the grounds and Stalin came out on to the porch of the house. He seemed not to notice the other two. 'I'm finished,' he said to no one in particular. 'I trust no one, not even myself.'[59]

6

The whole of the year 1952 Stalin spent in and near Moscow, mostly immured at Blizhny, as the *dacha* at Kuntsevo was called. He did not go away anywhere for the summer holidays. 'And when Stalin did not go on vacation,' said Khrushchev, 'nobody went.' Blizhny had been rebuilt and enlarged several times and now had a second floor with a spacious reception room. But this was not used after a large party which Stalin gave there for the visiting Chinese delegation led by Mao Tse-tung in the winter of 1949–1950 when the Sino-Soviet treaty of alliance was signed. Incidentally, the Soviet journalist Ilya Ehrenburg, who saw him at another reception given for Mao Tse-tung and his entourage at the Metropole Hotel in Moscow, remarked that Stalin

* 'Stalin published a decree saying that the Mingrels had connections with the Turks, and that some of them were politically oriented towards Turkey. Of course the allegation was utter nonsense.' N. S. Khrushchev. *Khrushchev Remembers* (1970). p. 312.

was not like his portraits. 'An old man, short of stature, with a face that looked pitted by the years, a low forehead, a pair of sharp lively eyes,' was how Ehrenburg described him on this occasion. 'He glanced curiously round the hall in which he had probably never set foot for a quarter of a century. Then there was an ovation and he was piloted to where the Chinese were standing.'[60]

If Stalin's portraits were everywhere, their subject was rarely seen in the flesh by his people. His public appearances, never very frequent during the past two decades, were now restricted to state occasions and funerals of old comrades, when he would walk a short distance with the other mourners. The popular acclaim which he had once relished no longer gave him much thrill. 'They open their mouths and yell like fools,' he said to Svetlana after his last enthusiastic reception in Georgia.[61] Nevertheless, he read the newspapers with particular care every day to see what was being said about him as well as what he himself said. For several weeks he carried on a correspondence in the pages of *Pravda* on the subject of Marxism and linguistics, attacking the philologist Nikolai Marr, who had asserted for many years with Party backing that language had an essentially class basis and that the rulers and oppressed masses of a nation really spoke different languages. Stalin now came out against this absurd theory and reasserted the obvious truth that language is not a class but a national matter, rejecting Marr's theory as 'anti-Marxist and unscientific'. As a result, 'Marrism' became a term of official abuse.[62]* Less happy was Stalin's intervention in the field of genetics where he supported the theory of the biologist Trofim Lysenko, considered by modern geneticists to be as absurd in its way as Marr's, that heritable changes can be brought about in plants by environmental influences, such as subjecting wheat to extremes of temperature, and by grafting. Not surprisingly Khrush-

---

* Stalin's continuing interest in comparative philology was reflected in his conversation with the Indian ambassador K. P. S. Menon shortly before his death. 'Stalin then asked me what was the chief language of India. Was it Urdu or Hindi – or, as he called it, "Hindu"? Were all the languages derived from the same stock? How did they come to have separate individual developments? In particular, what was the language spoken by the Gujeratis? ... Towards the end of our conversation, Stalin reverted to the subject of languages and asked whether it was true that Pakistan had been evolving a language of its own. I said that Urdu had developed as a language of the camp in India but that a number of Persian and Arabic words were now being added to it. "In that case," said Stalin, "it cannot be a real national language." This, I thought to myself, is the man who recently settled the Marr controversy on linguistics with one stroke of the pen!' K. P. S. Menon *The Flying Troika* (1963), pp. 27-28.

chev was to blame Lysenko for the backward state of Soviet agronomy when he later seized power.

According to Svetlana, her father lived in the large dining room on the ground floor at Blizhny, which served all purposes. He slept on a sofa by the wall made up at night as a bed, with several telephones beside him. The large dining room table was usually piled high with papers and books, which would be cleared away for meals. There was a sideboard containing china and a cupboard with various medicines and drugs. 'My father picked out his medicines himself,' noted Svetlana, 'since the only doctor he trusted was Vinogradov, whom he called once or twice a year.'* In winter time there was usually a log fire, one of the few luxuries which Stalin allowed himself. In front of the fireplace there was a large Oriental rug. Besides the hall, there were three other rooms on the ground floor which the architect Miron Merzhanov originally designed as an office, bedroom and dining room, and they were all simply furnished exactly like the main room. From time to time Stalin would move into one of these other rooms and arrange it to his liking. At Yalta he had laughed at the story of the Tsar Nicholas II frequently changing his bedroom for fear of assassination. A similar apprehension may have motivated Stalin's periodic moves.

An indifferent portrait of Lenin hung on one of the walls of the main room. There was also a reproduction of Repin's famous painting, 'The Zaphorezhe Cossacks' Reply to the Sultan.'† This work was a favourite of Stalin's and Svetlana tells us that it gave him great pleasure to recite the obscene words of the letter being penned by the Cossack spokesman in the picture for the benefit of any visitor who happened to notice Repin's work. Latterly it appears that Stalin took to covering the walls with photographs of children cut out of magazines. They included a boy skiing, a girl drinking goat's milk from a horn and children at play under cherry trees. Above the sofa on which he used to sleep was a picture of a little girl feeding a baby lamb with a spoon. When Svetlana called to see her father at this time, she found this display all very 'weird and surprising', since he had never cared much for pictures or photographs.[63]

Throughout 1952, during which Stalin spent so much time at Kuntsevo, Malenkov's star was in the ascendant, while Beria's waned noticeably. 'I don't trust that man,' Stalin told Svetlana. In the order of

* Professor V. N. Vinogradov, a leading Moscow physician and President of the Moscow Medical Society.
† The Sultan was Mohammed IV, during whose reign in the second half of the seventeenth century the Turks fought the Poles and Cossacks for the possession of the Ukraine, which was eventually absorbed in the Russian empire.

portraits of the Soviet leaders displayed at the anniversary of the Revolution, it was remarked that Beria's had dropped from fourth to sixth place, coming after Bulganin. At one time or another, Kaganovich, Molotov, Mikoyan, Voroshilov and Andreyev were also out of favour.[64] Indeed the two latter were deliberately excluded from meetings of the Politburo and no longer had documents circulated to them. Stalin's exclusion of Andreyev was afterwards characterised by Khrushchev as 'one of the most unbridled acts of wilfulness'. Furthermore, said Khrushchev, Stalin 'toyed with the ridiculous and absurd suspicion that Voroshilov was an English agent' and had his apartment 'bugged' with a concealed listening device. Voroshilov would telephone and ask to be allowed to attend the meetings. Sometimes Stalin allowed him, but 'always showed his dissatisfaction'.[65]

During one session Stalin suddenly became indignant and asked: 'How did Voroshilov worm his way into the Bureau?'

'He did not worm his way in,' the others answered. 'You appointed him yourself.' (Voroshilov had been a full member of the Politburo since 1926, having been elected on Stalin's nomination.)

Molotov likewise fell under suspicion of having sold himself to the Americans. According to Khrushchev, Stalin conceived the idea that as he travelled by railroad between Washington and New York, Molotov must have his private car which the Americans had given him. He went so far as to instruct Vyshinsky, who was then attending the United Nations, to find out as much as he could about Molotov's activities in the United States. 'Of course,' Vyshinsky answered immediately 'Molotov did not have, and could not have had a railway car.'[66]

There had been no full Party Congress since 1939 and Stalin would have liked to have postponed its meeting at least until after the new purge which he was secretly planning. But the Central Committee met in plenary session in August, which no doubt accounts for Stalin's not going south for his annual holiday. The Committee decided to convene the Nineteenth Congress within two months. This decision involved Stalin in a considerable amount of planning with Malenkov and Khrushchev, the Party secretaries, and it kept him busy until the Congress opened. He was also occupied in putting the finishing touches to a long essay entitled *The Economic Problems of Socialism in the USSR*, which appeared on the eve of the opening on 5 October 1952, and gave the delegates an opportunity which they were not slow to seize of interspersing their speeches with quotations from the Leader's latest reflections on domestic and foreign affairs. Otherwise Stalin remained very much in the wings throughout the sessions, only coming forward at the end to make a brief closing statement. His remarks, as

Pravda noted, were greeted with 'an alpine avalanche of applause', for then he made a point of assuring the visiting foreign delegates that, just as they had supported the Soviet Union in its struggle for peace, so also 'our Party must in turn extend support to them in their struggle for liberation, in their struggle for the maintenance of peace'. This aggressive expression was widely interpreted as indicating a revival of the Soviet Union's determination to interfere in the internal affairs of other countries outside the Soviet satellite bloc.[67]

The role of chief rapporteur was taken by Malenkov and not by Stalin, as at previous congresses. The other principal speakers were Khrushchev and Poskrebyshev. All dwelt on the dangers of the 'capitalist encirclement' of the Soviet Union by the west, echoing the main theme of Stalin's economic essay. Molotov and Mikoyan, who might have been expected to hold forth on this topic, were conspicuously silent, as also was Kosygin. It was also noted that Stalin assigned a particularly prominent role to the sinister Poskrebyshev who still headed his personal secretariat and usually operated off stage. Now he was elected both to the Central Committee and the Moscow Soviet. In his speech at the Congress Poskrebyshev urged the need for 'the display of political vigilance' against the divulging of Party and State secrets to the agents of 'the brazen US imperialists'.[68]

By this date Stalin had made up his mind to liquidate the majority of the Politburo, whose members had become distasteful to him. In Khrushchev's words, 'he often stated that the Political Bureau members should be replaced by new ones'. Accordingly, at Stalin's prompting, the new Central Committee elected an enlarged body of twenty-five called the Praesidium in place of the old Politburo. The Praesidium was described by Khrushchev as consisting of 'less experienced persons' who might be relied on to 'extol him [Stalin] in all sorts of ways'. As Khrushchev was later to remark in his 'secret' speech, 'we can assume that this was also a design for the future annihilation of the old Political Bureau members and in this way a cover for all of Stalin's shameful acts'. All the members of the old Politburo appeared in the new body except Andreyev, but Kosygin was downgraded to candidate status. Of the others the most important were the deputy prime ministers Mikhail Pervukhin and Maksim Saburov. Both were engineers by profession, managerial types who had been brought forward by Malenkov. Indeed Saburov had succeeded the unfortunate Voznesensky as the country's chief economic planner. In addition to the Praesidium's twenty-five full members, there were eleven alternates or candidate members who included Vyshinsky and Brezhnev, besides Kosygin, who was lucky to have survived with his head on his shoulders.

According to Khrushchev, Stalin never convened a full meeting of the newly elected Praesidium. Instead he proposed that, 'because a group of that size would be cumbersome, we had to select a Bureau from the Praesidium membership'. Although this was contrary to the new Party statutes, Stalin immediately nominated a Bureau of nine. Besides himself, this consisted of Malenkov, Beria, Khrushchev, Voroshilov, Kaganovich, Saburov, Pervukhin and Bulganin. The merit of this arrangement in Stalin's eyes was that individual members could be replaced from the larger body without any difficulty or fuss. It is noteworthy that Molotov and Mikoyan were omitted from the Bureau, while Voroshilov was included. 'Voroshilov's inclusion was strange,' noted Khrushchev, 'because Stalin had started having doubts about him long before Molotov and Mikoyan fell out of favour.' However, in practice the Bureau was restricted by Stalin to an inner circle of five, whom he would summon at his discretion. Apparently Kaganovich and Voroshilov were rarely invited, and Saburov and Pervukhin only when the occasion demanded. Thus the usual five were made up of Malenkov, Beria, Bulganin, Khrushchev and Stalin himself. 'The Bureau decided all questions, and the Bureau usually meant the inner circle of five,' Khrushchev later recalled. 'All decisions were made by the same methods which Stalin had put into practice after 1939...So much for collective leadership.'*

According to Khrushchev, Molotov and Mikoyan were 'put on ice' after the Nineteenth Congress. 'It is not to be excluded,' said Khrushchev in his 'secret' speech at the next Congress, 'that had Stalin remained at the helm for another few months, Comrades Molotov and Mikoyan would not have delivered any speeches at this congress.'[69]

For a while Molotov and Mikoyan continued their old practice of appearing at Stalin's informal meetings with Khrushchev and the others in favour. They did not telephone to ask permission but would simply show up at the Kremlin or Kuntsevo. They were always admitted, but it was obvious that Stalin was never very pleased to see them. Eventually Stalin said: 'I don't want these two coming around any

---

* 'It was considered a great honour to be invited to meet with Stalin. On the other hand it was considered a bad omen if you were invited once but weren't invited back.' *Khrushchev Remembers*, p. 281. Khrushchev's list of names, though not published officially at the time, was corroborated by the order in which the leaders appeared on top of the Lenin Mausoleum on 7 November 1952.

more.' He then gave orders to the staff that they were not to be told where he was in future.

Afterwards the two had a talk with Khrushchev, Malenkov and Beria, who agreed to try to soften Stalin's attitude towards them. Khrushchev and the other two also agreed to tell them when Stalin was going to the *dacha* or the Kremlin cinema. Seeing them on several occasions at the film shows, Stalin checked with his staff and was told that they had never informed Molotov and Mikoyan of their master's whereabouts, just as Stalin had ordered. Stalin immediately rounded on Malenkov and the rest whom he suspected of being to blame. 'You think I don't know how you let Molotov and Mikoyan know when we are going to the films so that they can come along?' he stormed. 'Stop this! Stop telling them where I am. I won't tolerate it!' Consequently Malenkov and Khrushchev abandoned any further attempts to effect a reconciliation. 'We saw it was useless to persist,' Khrushchev later recalled. 'It would not do Molotov and Mikoyan any good, and it might jeopardise our own position in Stalin's eyes.'[70]

By this time Stalin appeared to have completely recovered his health, at any rate physically. As in years past, he stood for several hours taking the salute at the march past in Red Square on 7 November. On the previous evening he had attended a crowded performance in the Bolshoi Theatre, which included a programme of dancing and music and a boring political lecture by Pervukhin. The newly appointed Indian ambassador, Mr K. P. S. Menon, who had just arrived in Moscow, was present, and he noted that Stalin occupied an inconspicuous seat in the second row on the dais.

> Looking at him one would not have thought that this was the man who wielded greater, and more concentrated power, than any mortal had ever done. He was just Comrade Stalin, grown grey in the service of his people and exuding an almost avuncular benevolence. To the audience, of course, he was, as *Pravda* described him, 'the great Stalin, the wise leader and teacher, the organiser and inspirer of the historic victories of the Soviet people, the genius of all progressive mankind'. Whenever his name was mentioned the audience sprang to their feet and cheered vociferously.[71]

Several weeks after the Nineteenth Congress ended, Stalin received a letter from an unknown woman doctor named Lydia Timashuk, who accused Professor Vinogradov and seven other leading physicians of conspiring 'to cut short the lives of active public figures of the Soviet

Union through sabotage medical treatment'. This was the so-called 'Doctors' Plot' in which the accused were alleged to have killed Zhdanov and Scherbakov, two former Politburo members, and also to have 'sought to put out of action' several chiefs of the armed forces including Vasilevsky, Koniev and Shtemenko. The doctors were said to be working for American and British intelligence and it was significant that seven of them were Jews connected with an international Jewish welfare organisation. One doctor 'confessed' that under cover of this organisation he had received orders 'to wipe out the leading cadres of the USSR'.[72] It transpired that Dr Timashuk was an elderly woman, who worked in the Kremlin polyclinic as an electrocardiograph specialist; indeed she was a grandmother and had lost her only son in the Soviet Air Force during the war.

It is highly unlikely that she would have dared to write to Stalin unless she had been 'influenced or ordered by someone', as Khrushchev later suggested. ('After all she was an unofficial collaborator of the organs of state security.') Most probably she received her instructions from M. D. Ryumin, Ignatiev's deputy in the MGB. Ryumin may conceivably have been put up to it by Stalin himself in order to provide material for what he planned as the first of a series of show trials. At all events Stalin ordered the immediate arrest of the doctors and (so Khrushchev tells us) 'personally issued advice on the conduct of the investigation and the method of interrogation of the arrested persons. He said that academician Vinogradov should be put in chains, another one should be beaten'. Stalin also sent for the Minister Ignatiev and told him curtly: 'If you do not obtain confessions from the doctors we will shorten you by a head!'

Khrushchev was later to be instrumental in saving Ignatiev from the executioner's bullet when his deputy Ryumin was tried and shot. He knew the minister quite well and has described him as mild, considerate and well liked. At this time Ignatiev was a sick man and suffered from heart trouble. According to Khrushchev, 'Stalin used to berate him viciously over the phone in our presence. Stalin was crazy with rage, yelling at Ignatiev and threatening him, demanding that he throw the doctors in chains, beat them to pulp and grind them into powder.' It was no surprise to Khrushchev when almost all the doctors 'confessed' to their imaginary crimes. Unfortunately two of them died under interrogation.

In due course, Khrushchev and the other members of the Praesidium inner circle were handed copies of the doctors' statements by Stalin. 'You are blind like young kittens,' he told them. 'What will happen without me? The country will perish because you do not know how to recognise enemies.'

Khrushchev later commented on the affair in his 'secret' speech:

> The case was so presented that no one could verify the facts on which the investigation was based. There was no possibility of trying to verify facts by contacting those who had made the confessions of guilt.
>
> We felt, however, that the case of the arrested doctors was questionable. We knew some of these people personally because they had once treated us. When we examined this 'case' after Stalin's death, we found it to be fabricated from beginning to end.[73]

Although the doctors' arrests took place some time in November 1952, it was not until 15 January 1953, that the details of the 'plot' were released by *Pravda*, which called them 'vile spies and murderers in the guise of professors', who had been 'trying to undermine the health of leading Soviet military figures, to put them out of commission, and thereby weaken the country's defences'. According to *Pravda*, they had done this on the instructions of 'foreign intelligence services'. A week later Dr Timashuk was awarded the Order of Lenin for her help in exposing 'the thrice-accursed murdering doctors' and publicly thanked for 'restoring the honour and purity of the white gown'. *Pravda* printed extracts from her fan-mail which was as copious as any Hollywood star could expect and her local telephone exchange was jammed with congratulatory calls for her. *Pravda* also ran several articles, which were certainly inspired if not actually written by Stalin, urging that all 'hidden enemies supported by the capitalist world' should be 'squashed like disgusting vermin', and for that purpose 'an end be put to lack of vigilance in our ranks'. One such leading article ended with a reference to Stalin's speech before the Central Committee in March 1937, on 'defects in Party work and measures for liquidating Trotskyite and other double dealers', which marked the crescendo of the Great Purge.

For any Party worker at the time of the Doctors' Plot who could read between the lines of *Pravda* editorials – and this was not difficult – it was abundantly clear that a new purge was being prepared on an extensive scale. Indeed arrests of the small fry got under way immediately after the public announcement of the discovery of the Doctors' Plot, but they were mainly confined to Jewish officials in the public health, economic and foreign ministries. Jews were also arrested in Moscow University and the Academy of Sciences. Even the Jewish band-leader Utnesov did not escape. Another victim was Palgunov, the head of the news agency Tass, who for many years had been very close to Molotov. Molotov's Jewish wife Zemchuzhina, former head of the perfume and cosmetics industry, had already been exiled to Siberia on a vague charge of 'Zionist plotting', although Molotov himself was left undisturbed. Diplomatic relations with the state of Israel were broken off. 'If I had my way, I'd expel all Jews from Moscow,' the wife of N. A. Mikhailov, one of the Central Committee secretaries, said to Svetlana at this time. 'Her husband was obviously of the same mind,' noted Svetlana. 'It was the official temper of the times, and its origin, as I could easily guess, stemmed from the very top of the ladder.'[74]

The only other well known public figure to be purged was General L. Z. Mekhlis, a former Chief Political Commissar of the Red Army and old Central Committee member, who had begun his career in Stalin's personal secretariat and had held various senior government posts including that of Deputy Defence Commissar. At one time he was much in Stalin's confidence, but for the past few years he had been in poor health and it is difficult to see why he was made a victim at this time, since he had been one of Stalin's most prominent eulogists in the past, except that he was a Jew. Fearing for his life, Mekhlis left Moscow but, according to the report, he was followed by the secret police to Saratov and brought back to the Lefortovo prison, where he was shot early in February after an interview with Poskrebyshev who is said to have presented him with a lengthy 'confession' and ordered him to sign it.[75]

It is significant that the purge was halted after the execution of Lev Mekhlis, as also was the concurrent press campaign against 'lack of political vigilance'. Kremlinologists like Boris Nicolaevsky have affected to see in these developments the existence of two factions in Kremlin ruling circles, respectively favouring and opposing the purge. For the purge were Stalin, Poskrebyshev, and also Ryumin, and a number of others including the secretary of the Party Organs Department, A. B. Aristov, the Party Secretary Mikhailov, and Svetlana's divorced husband Yuri Zhdanov, head of the science and culture department of the Central Committee. It is known that Beria, who was technically Ignatiev's boss, came out against the purge and for this purpose joined forces with Malenkov, who had again fallen out of favour with Stalin since the recent Party Congress. Beria's action was undoubtedly prompted by the attacks on 'the lack of vigilance in the security forces', which had been appearing for some weeks in the Soviet press. He reckoned that in the next show trial which Stalin was planning he would stand in the dock, as had Yagoda and Yezhov for their 'lack of vigilance' during the Great Purge of the 1930s.[76]

The anti-purgers consisted of virtually the whole of the old Politburo whose members like Beria now all feared for their own skins. The fact that the pro-purge press campaign tailed off at this time would seem to indicate a victory for the members of the old Politburo who were now more or less solidly united against Stalin. Here indeed were the elements of a growing conspiracy against the dictator within the Central Committee itself. Admittedly the conspiracy did not progress very far, but that it existed at this time was later to be clearly indicated after Khrushchev's 'secret' speech to the Twentieth Congress in 1956, when the Central Committee passed a resolution condemning the 'cult of pesonality'. This resolution referred to *a nucleus of Leninist leaders'* within the Central Committee, which had begun to operate against Stalin and the few Committee members like Poskrebyshev and Aristov who remained loyal to him.[77]

That Stalin seems to have been meditating a counter-blow may be inferred from his behaviour during his conversation with K. P. S. Menon, the Indian ambassador, whom he received in his Kremlin office on 17 February. The ambassador noticed that Stalin was doodling with a red pencil and drawing wolves, singly, in pairs and in packs. Observing the ambassador's interest in what he was doing, Stalin looked at him and said with a grim smile: 'The Russian peasant is a very simple man but a very wise one. When the wolf attacks him, he does not attempt to teach it morals but tries to kill it. And the wolf knows this and behaves accordingly.' The ambassador was puzzled by this reference. They had been talking about America and at first Mr Menon thought that Stalin was referring to the capitalist 'wolves' in the United States. But afterwards he wondered whether Stalin also had had in mind some 'wolves' who were nearer home. It was an interesting speculation.[78]

At this meeting the Indian was impressed by Stalin's vigour and energy, as were other foreign visitors whom he saw at this time. These included the Argentinian ambassador, Leopold Bravo, with whom he discussed the possibility of bringing a football team from Buenos Aires to Moscow and other trivialities. Stalin also told the Indian that he considered it was his duty to receive foreign ambassadors. As it turned out, Mr Menon was the last one to enjoy this experience.

During the next fortnight the only news the outside world heard of Stalin was that he had been elected to the Moscow Soviet along with Poskrebyshev and several others. In fact, by the time this announcement was made in the early hours of 4 March 1953, he was near death.

At eight o'clock the same morning the general public were given the news by the voice of the chief Soviet radio announcer Yuri Levitan breathlessly reciting a communiqué which showed distinct signs of hasty composition.

> The Central Committee of the Communist Party of the Soviet Union and the Council of Ministers of the USSR announce the misfortune which has overtaken the Party and the people – the serious illness of Comrade J. V. Stalin.
>
> During the night of 1–2 March, while in his Moscow apartment, Comrade Stalin suffered a cerebral haemorrhage affecting vital areas of the brain. Comrade Stalin lost consciousness and paralysis of the right arm and leg set in. Loss of speech followed. There appeared to be serious disturbances in the functioning of the heart and breathing.
>
> The best medical brains have been summoned to Comrade Stalin's treatment...[79]

7

In announcing Stalin's illness to the Russian people and the world, the official communiqué stated that he had been stricken in his Moscow apartment. This was not so. After his death a story got about, apparently through emigré sources, that he had died in a fit of rage in his Kremlin office following a stormy meeting with Molotov, Mikoyan, Kaganovich and other members of the old Politburo who attacked his proposal to deport all Soviet Jews to Siberia. Kaganovich, the only Jewish member of the Praesidium inner circle, is said to have torn up his Party membership card and flung the pieces in Stalin's face. 'If we do not leave your office freely within half an hour,' Stalin was allegedly warned, 'the Red Army will occupy the Kremlin.' According to this story, Stalin ordered Beria to arrest 'all the scum here', but the security chief refused. 'The Soviet leader then rose from his chair, screamed incoherently and fell unconscious on a sofa.'

Another version has it that in falling he struck his head on the side of a table, after which Molotov rushed to a cabinet where various bottles were kept, poured out a glass of poisoned brandy, which Stalin promptly drank with fatal results.[80]

The only conceivable element of truth in this largely fanciful tale is that some such meeting may have taken place at the end of February and that Kaganovich may have behaved in the manner described. In fact, the evidence is virtually conclusive that Stalin was not poisoned in the Kremlin, but became ill from natural causes in his *dacha* at Kuntsevo where he suffered a stroke during the evening or night of 1 March 1953.

According to Khrushchev, Stalin watched a film in the Kremlin theatre on the evening of 28 February, along with Malenkov, Beria, Bulganin and Khrushchev. After the performance, Stalin invited the others, as was his wont, to come out to Kuntsevo for a meal. Not unexpectedly the dinner lasted until five or six o'clock in the morning. Stalin was in high spirits and 'pretty drunk after dinner', which was unusual for him, as latterly he had been drinking sparingly. Nevertheless, as Khrushchev noted, 'he did not show the slightest sign that anything was wrong with him physically'. When the others eventually got up to leave, Stalin came into the hall to see them off, joking and playfully jabbing Khrushchev in the stomach with his finger, calling him 'Nikita' in a Ukrainian accent as he always did when he was in a good mood. 'We all went home happy because nothing had gone wrong at dinner,' Khrushchev recalled afterwards. 'Dinners at Stalin's did not always end on such a pleasant note.'[81]

Next day, 1 March, was a Sunday and 'supposed to be a day off'. Khrushchev felt sure that Stalin would telephone him and the others during the day for a meeting of some kind. Consequently he delayed dinner at his own *dacha*. Finally he gave up waiting and had something to eat. After dinner there was still no call. Khrushchev thought this strange as he could hardly believe that Stalin would let a whole day go by without summoning him and the others. Meanwhile Svetlana had been trying to call her father without success. Apparently getting through to Stalin on the telephone when he was at Blizhny was a complicated business. First one had to call the guard post. After a delay the duty officer would say, if he was stirring about the house, 'There's movement,' or else, 'There's no movement at present', in which case he would either be asleep or else reading or working in his room when he could not be disturbed. On this occasion 'no movement' was reported, and consequently Svetlana was unable to speak to him.[82]

Tired of waiting any longer, since it was well past midnight, Khrushchev got undressed and went to bed. No sooner had he done so than the telephone rang. It was Malenkov, who had just heard from the security guards at Stalin's *dacha*. 'They think something has happened to him. We'd better get over there.' He said he had already told Beria and Bulganin. 'You'd better leave at once,' Malenkov added.

Khrushchev called for his car and fifteen minutes later was at Kuntsevo. When the rest arrived, Vasily Khrustalyov, the chief security guard, and the other duty officers explained why they were worried. 'Comrade Stalin almost always calls someone and asks for tea at eleven o'clock. Tonight he didn't.' They went on to say that they had sent his old housekeeper Marya Petrovna to find out why. According to Khrushchev, she was not very bright, but she was honest and devoted to Stalin. When she came back about 3 a.m., she told the guards that Stalin was lying asleep on the floor of the large room where he usually slept. The guards thereupon went into the room and lifted him off the floor and laid him on the sofa in the small adjoining dining room. Apparently everyone thought at first that Stalin was merely sleeping off the effects of the drinks he had taken the night before. Hence, as Khrushchev noted, they decided that it would not be appropriate to make their presence known while Stalin was 'in such an unpresentable state'. Accordingly they separated and all went home.[83]

Later that night, Khrushchev had another telephone call from Malenkov. 'The boys have called again from Comrade Stalin's,' he told Khrushchev. 'They say that something is definitely wrong with him. Marya Petrovna said he was sleeping soundly when we sent her to look in on him again, but it's an unusual sort of sleep. We'd better go back.' It was arranged that doctors should be sent for and that Voroshilov and Kaganovich, who had not been at the dinner on the previous night, should also be alerted.

By the time the doctors arrived it was daylight. The leading member of the medical team was Professor P. E. Lukomsky, a prominent heart specialist and member of the Soviet Academy of Medical Science. Stalin was still lying recumbent on the sofa when the professor approached him very cautiously. Shaking all over, Lukomsky nervously touched Stalin's hand as though it was a hot iron. 'You're a doctor, aren't you?' Beria asked him gruffly. 'Go ahead and take hold of his hand properly.'

The specialist did as he was told. A few moments later he said that Stalin could not move his right arm. His leg was also paralysed, and he was unable to speak. They thereupon undressed him and after covering him up moved him back into the large room where there was more air, placing him on the sofa on which he usually slept. By this time he was unconscious. Then, when the doctors were taking a urine sample, he tried to cover himself as if he felt the discomfort of the operation. Once during the day he recovered consciousness for a short time. A nurse from the Kremlin hospital was spoon-feeding him soup and sweet tea. He raised his left hand and pointed to the wall above the sofa. His lips began to move as if he were trying to say something, and he seemed to manage a feeble smile. On the wall near the sofa on which he lay was the picture cut out of a magazine which showed a baby lamb being fed with a spoon by a little girl. Now, as he seemed to indicate by his gestures, he was just as helpless as that baby lamb. Then with his good left hand he shook hands with Khrushchev and the others one by one.

Malenkov and Beria took charge of matters and arranged that they should keep watch by day, and Khrushchev and Bulganin at night. However, the two latter also spent most of the day either in the sick room or within call in the *dacha*. It was then, according to Khrushchev, that Beria came out in his true colours. When Stalin was in a coma, Beria abused him roundly, stirring up hatred against him and mocking him. However, when the sick man showed signs of consciousness which suggested that he might recover, Beria suddenly changed his manner, dropping on his knees, seizing Stalin's hand and kissing it. 'Dear Joseph Vissarionovich, forgive me!' he pleaded. 'Dear Joseph Vissarionovich, you know how faithful I have been to you in the past! Believe me, I will be faithful again! Forgive me!' No wonder Khrushchev remarked, in recalling this craven exhibition, that it was 'simply unbearable to listen to Beria'.[84]

Meanwhile Svetlana had been sent for and when she arrived she joined in the painful bedside vigil. Her brother Vasily also put in a brief appearance. 'But he was drunk, as he often was by then, and he soon left,' Svetlana noted. 'He went on drinking and raising Cain in the servants quarters. He gave the doctors hell and shouted that they had killed or were killing our father. Finally he went home.'[85]

Three bulletins were issued by the doctors, the first immediately after the initial communiqué on 4 March, the second at 2 a.m. on 5 March, and the third during the evening of the same day. They were all in technical language, as if addressed to other medical men rather than the general public; they described in detail the progressive deterioration in the patient's condition and the treatment being applied in an effort to arrest it. The cerebral haemorrhage was complicated by coronary disease, which caused two electro-cardiograms to be done. The patient was being given oxygen to aid respiration, drugs such as camphor, strophanthin and caffeine, to strengthen the heart, and penicillin to reduce his temperature and to prevent infection due to the excess of white corpuscles in the blood. Leeches were also applied to his neck and the back of his head. The use of this old-fashioned but time-honoured remedy may have been resorted to in order to reassure the Soviet people that this treatment, which was still in use particularly among the rural population in Russia, had not been overlooked. The superstitious also regarded leeches as exercising some magical quality in sucking any poison there might be out of the system.[86] Svetlana held her father's hand as she sat beside the sofa. 'A nurse kept giving him injections and a doctor jotted it all down in a notebook. Everything was being done as it should be.'

On the morning of 5 March his condition showed some improvement. There was a decrease in cardiac disturbance and his pulse beats became more regular. But shortly before midday there was a relapse, accompanied by increased difficulty in breathing. Khrushchev, who had gone home for a brief rest, was again summoned from his bed. When he got back to the *dacha*, the doctors told him that the patient's case was hopeless and they doubted if he would survive the night.

'The last hours were nothing but a slow strangulation,' Svetlana recalled afterwards. 'The death agony was horrible. He literally choked to death as we watched.' His final gesture was to glance round the room, taking in the faces of the unfamiliar doctors, and raise his left hand as if he were pointing to something above and bringing down a curse on them all. Suddenly he stopped breathing. One of the medical assistants stepped forward and started the motions of artificial respiration, massaging his chest. 'Stop it please,' said Khrushchev. 'Can't you see he is dead? You won't bring him back to life.' The man gave up trying to resuscitate him.

Voroshilov, Kaganovich, Malenkov, Bulganin and Khrushchev all broke down and wept. Among the dictator's intimates gathered at the final scene only Beria appeared to have dry eyes. Suddenly he too broke the silence, shouting to the chief of Stalin's bodyguard in tones of ill-concealed triumph, 'Khrustalyov! My car!'[87]

A little later, Malenkov and most of the other leaders left to go to the Central Committee building where all the senior party and government officials were waiting for the news which they had been expecting all day. Only Bulganin and Mikoyan stayed behind to comfort Svetlana. The exact time of Stalin's death was 9.50 p.m. But it was not until four o'clock on the following morning, 6 March, that the official announcement came over the Soviet radio, prefaced by a solemn roll of drums, that 'the heart of the comrade-in-arms and inspired continuer of Lenin's cause, the wise leader and teacher of the Communist Party of the Soviet Union, has ceased to beat'.

Towards daybreak a white car drove up to the front door of the *dacha*. The body of the dead leader, which had been washed by the nurse, was placed on a stretcher and carried out to the car. 'It was the first time that I had seen my father naked,' noted Svetlana. 'It was a beautiful body. It didn't look old or as if he'd been sick at all.' The car then drove off to the Kremlin mortuary where an autopsy was performed later that morning. According to the official report of the

596

pathologists who carried out this operation, 'the examination established a large centre of haemorrhage in the left hemisphere of the brain, and this haemorrhage had destroyed vital parts of the brain and affected breathing and blood circulation. The examination confirmed that the doctors' diagnosis was correct and all the measures taken could not have prevented the fatal outcome of Marshal Stalin's illness'. In order to do their job properly, the pathologists had to trepan Stalin's skull so as to remove the brains for dissection. The rest of the remains were then handed over to the embalmers, and the skill with which they discharged their task may be gauged by the fact that no visible trace of the pathologists' work appeared when the body was exposed to public view for the lying-in-state. This ceremony began the same afternoon in the Hall of Columns of Trade Union House, scene of Lenin's lying-in-state and of the later purge trials of the Old Bolsheviks which Stalin had staged.

For the remainder of the day the ceremony was restricted to the Soviet leaders, government ministers, Party secretaries and senior officers of the armed forces. A carefully contrived official photograph was taken for press distribution. It showed the bier and its central figure dressed in his marshal's tunic with five rows of ribbons and resting on a cushion surrounded by a mass of flowers. Beside the coffin stood the individuals composing the new 'collective' leadership ranged in two rows in strict order of precedence. Nearest the bier was Malenkov with Beria beside him, both looking away from Stalin. Facing the bier in the front row were Voroshilov, Bulganin, Kaganovich and Molotov. Standing in the second row were Vasilevsky, Koniev, Sokolovsky, Zhukov, Mikoyan, and Khrushchev in that order. Khrushchev, the farthest away from Stalin, seems to have been added as an afterthought as part of the whole montage, since he appears to be the only one of Stalin's twelve disciples here depicted who was not in the original picture. He may conceivably have replaced Shvernik, who does not appear at all in the touched up version, contrary to what one would have expected of the titular head of state. However, the decision had already been taken to replace Shvernik in this office by the more colourful Voroshilov.

Next day the diplomatic corps and foreign press were admitted, after which the general public were allowed into the hall to pay their last respects to the man they had long regarded as a remote father figure. A military band of some two hundred musicians, mostly trumpeters, played Chopin's Funeral March as the mourners were kept on the move; indeed they were forced into a brisk trot by Beria's security guards in their blue and red caps, who were much in evidence. 'Hurry along there!' they kept saying. In the kitchens below the hall, an aroma was wafted from the pots of steaming *borscht* being prepared for the troops on duty. It was remarkable how quickly Beria's men had taken control of the city, sealing off streets and regulating access to the main thoroughfares and squares. This was particularly marked during the final ceremony two days later in Red Square.[88]

Meanwhile the city had taken on a certain holiday air in spite of the winter winds. Bonfires were lit in the streets, there was singing and playing of balalaikas, as the crowds waited for the funeral cortège to emerge from Trade Union House. *Boris Godunov*, which happened to be Stalin's favourite opera, was being performed at the Bolshoi, and the audience clapped and applauded the death of Boris with unwonted enthusiasm. But tragedy stalked nearby. As the crowds surged forward to the Red Square, several hundreds of people were trampled underfoot and crushed to death between the traffic lights and the trucks of Beria's security guards. It was as if Stalin had claimed his last victims from the grave.

Khrushchev was put in charge of the funeral arrangements thus fulfilling the same duty which Stalin had carried out at Lenin's obsequies twenty-eight years earlier. On the morning of 9 March, the pall bearers led by Malenkov and Beria and including Vasily Stalin, Voroshilov, Molotov, Mikoyan, Bulganin, Kaganovich and Khrushchev, carried the coffin from Trade Union House to the Lenin Mausoleum, where the leadership had decided that Stalin should be laid to rest beside the founder of the Soviet state. When the cortège had reached the mausoleum, it was seen that Stalin's name had already been carved above the entrance underneath Lenin's.

Unlike the earlier occasion when panegyrics were delivered lasting for most of the day, there were only three speeches, all commendably brief. Malenkov, who as Premier seemed destined to assume the mantle of the departed dictator, spoke first. ('Boundless is the greatness and significance of Comrade Stalin's work for the Soviet people and for the working people all over the world.') He was followed by Beria, arrogant in tone and condescending in manner. Predictably Beria warned against the 'enemies of the people' and spoke of the Government's concern to maintain the security of the Soviet state. The final oration was delivered by Molotov, the only one of the trio to appear deeply moved; he paused from time to time to dab his eyes with a handkerchief. Unlike Beria, who had spoken of Malenkov as Stalin's loyal colleague, Molotov paid no passing tribute to the new Premier. Also, he repeatedly used the word 'we' as if to emphasise his own role in Stalin's achievements.[89]

We may be justly proud that during the past thirty years we have lived and worked under the leadership of Comrade Stalin...

Stalin came from the people; he was always conscious of his kinship with the people, with the working class and the labouring peasantry; and to the people he dedicated all his mighty energies and his supreme genius...

Stalin's immortal name will live forever in our hearts, in the hearts of the Soviet people and of all progressive mankind. The glory of his great deeds for the welfare and happiness of our people and the working people of the whole world will live through the ages.

A few minutes before noon, the cortège bore the embalmed figure into the mausoleum and laid it beside that of Lenin. Then by a pre-arranged signal there was a concerted firing of guns, blowing of factory whistles and ships' sirens, very much as had happened at Lenin's last rites.

The final word may be left with Nikita Khrushchev, who did not speak at the funeral. Some time afterwards he found himself talking to Averell Harriman, the former American ambassador in Moscow. After describing how Stalin had died, Khrushchev paid his own tribute, eloquent in its brevity. 'Like Peter the Great, Stalin fought barbarism with barbarism, but he was a great man.'[90]

Postscript

The manner of Stalin's posthumous rehabilitation has been officially determined by the course of power politics in the Kremlin. The three years immediately following his death witnessed the arrest and execution of Beria, the deposition of Malenkov and the emergence of Khrushchev as the leading figure in the new collective leadership. During this period Stalin's policies were continued by his political heirs. Nevertheless, although their author was lying beside Lenin in the great tomb in the Red Square, his name virtually disappeared from the Soviet press, a reaction which can be traced in part to the exoneration of all the accused in the Doctors' Plot. Bulganin, who delivered the main speech at the May Day celebrations in 1953, made no reference to any of Stalin's military or other achievements. Meanwhile *Pravda* stressed the advantage of the collective as opposed to the role of a single leader. 'Decisions taken by individuals are always or almost always one-sided', it declared in a powerful leading article.[1] The first anniversary of Stalin's birthday went similarly unnoticed in the Soviet press. The 1936 Constitution was no longer referred to as the Stalin Constitution but as the New Constitution, while victory in the Great Patriotic War was attributed not to Stalin but to the Party. All this was principally due to the influence of the Premier Malenkov, who despite his funeral tribute had turned against the memory of his old master.

As opposition to Malenkov and his policies within the now stream-lined Praesidium continued to grow, Stalin ceased to be ignored and complimentary allusions to him began to appear from time to time in the press. His second birthday anniversary was marked by *Pravda* with a photograph and a long article.[2] ('It was he who mercilessly exposed the enemies of the people. Under the leadership of its Central Committee and of Stalin the Communist Party destroyed the traitors and defeatists.') After Malenkov's removal from the Soviet Premiership in February 1955, Stalin appeared to be gradually coming into his own again. 'A great revolutionary and profound thinker' and 'great fighter for the peace and security of peoples' was how *Pravda* described him on 21 December 1955. 'The name of Stalin is close and dear to millions of toilers in all corners of the earth...In millions of hearts burns the inextinguishable flame of his word.' At the time of his death, thirteen volumes of Stalin's collected works had been published, extending in date to the beginning of 1934. On 12 January 1956, the Soviet news agency Tass announced the forthcoming publication of the fourteenth volume, which would have covered the period of the Great Purge. But it never appeared, due to Khrushchev's surprising disclosures at the Twentieth Party Congress a few weeks later.[3]

Even when Malenkov was ousted from the Premiership, Khrushchev, whose name was now exclusively linked in the Soviet press with those of Lenin and Stalin, had not yet become convinced of the late dictator's 'criminal acts', or, as he put it in his own words, he had not yet begun 'to challenge the very basis of Stalin's claim to a place of special honour in history'. Everything continued to be blamed on Beria. 'We did everything we could to shield Stalin,' said Khrushchev. Khrushchev first began to sense what he called 'the falsity of our position' when he and Bulganin, who had succeeded Malenkov as Prime Minister, visited Yugoslavia in May 1955, in an attempt to heal the quarrel with Tito.[4] ('When we mentioned Beria as the culprit behind the crimes of the Stalin period, the Yugoslav comrades smiled scornfully and made sarcastic remarks.') The impression of where the guilt really lay was confirmed when Khrushchev went on to visit Roumania. But he still hesitated for several months before making up his mind to come out publicly against his old leader. What finally determined him to do so, according to his own account, was the report of a special commission which had been set up shortly after Beria's execution to inquire into the facts of the purges, the number of arrests, methods of interrogation used, and the possibility of rehabilitating the victims. Voroshilov, Molotov and Kaganovich were far from enthusiastic about the commission, but Khrushchev argued that it could provide the answer to one question which was bound to come up at the next Party Congress. Why were so many people still in prison or labour camps and what was to be done about them?

Peter Pospelov, one of the Central Committee Secretaries and a former editor of *Pravda*, who had begun his career in Stalin's personal secretariat, was appointed to head the commission. Its findings were passed on piecemeal to the Military Collegium of the Soviet Supreme Court, so that by the time the delegates to the Twentieth Congress arrived in Moscow, nearly eight thousand persons had been cleared of the offences of which they had been convicted, many of them being rehabilitated posthumously.[5] The report of the Pospelov commission took about two years to compile and copies appear to have been in the hands of Khrushchev and the other Praesidium members only a little time before the opening of the Congress on 14 February 1956. According to Khrushchev, its contents came as a complete surprise to him and a number of others including Bulganin, Pervukhin and Saburov.[6] On the other hand, the report cannot have been much of a surprise to Molotov, Voroshilov, Kaganovich and Malenkov.

When the Congress assembled, no decision had been taken on whether to publish the commission's findings. Khrushchev did not mention it in his formal report as First Secretary of the Central Committee, although he did inform the delegates that the Leningrad Affair had been 'fabricated by Beria and his henchmen in order to weaken the Leningrad Party Organisation', and that those responsible had been brought to justice, while those falsely condemned had been rehabilitated. It was left to Mikoyan to make the first anti-Stalin speech two days later, attacking 'the cult of the individual' and openly hinting that 'Comrade Kossior' and others had been 'wrongly declared enemies of the people' as the result of Stalin's actions.[7] Finally, during a recess towards the end of the Congress, Khrushchev brought the matter to a head at an informal gathering of Praesidium members.

'Comrades, what are we going to do about Comrade Pospelov's findings?' he asked. 'What are we going to do about all those who were arrested and eliminated? The Congress is coming to a close, and we'll all disperse without having said a single word about the abuses committed under Stalin. We now know that the people who suffered during the repressions were innocent. We can't keep people in exile or the camps any longer.'

'What's the matter with you?' Voroshilov exclaimed. 'How can you talk like that? You think you can bring all this out at the Congress and get away with it? How do you think it will reflect on the prestige of our party and the country? You won't be able to keep what you say secret. Word will get about and the finger will be pointed straight at us. What will we be able to say about our own roles under Stalin?'

Voroshilov was strongly supported by Kaganovich and Molotov, while Khrushchev received backing from Bulganin, Pervukhin and Saburov. Malenkov also seemed to be for Khrushchev. The argument was conducted with considerable heat on either side, but Khrushchev stuck to his guns. 'We are conducting the first congress after Stalin's death,' he argued, 'and therefore we're obliged to make a clean breast to the delegates about the leadership during the years in question.' He finally clinched the matter by reminding the others of the right of every Praesidium member to speak at the Congress and express his own point of view even if it did not coincide with the line set by the First Secretary's formal report. 'If we are going to make a clean breast of the abuses committed by Stalin, then we must do so now, at the Twentieth Party Congress. The Twenty-First Congress will already be too late, even if we get that far without being taken to task.'

Eventually it was agreed, though with considerable reluctance by some of those present, that a speech should be delivered 'on the cult of personality and its consequences'. Khrushchev suggested that Pospelov as the comrade primarily responsible for the commission's report should discharge this task. But this was objected to by others, who argued that people would wonder why Khrushchev had said nothing about it in his earlier speech and that this 'could contribute the impression of dissension in the leadership'. Thus Khrushchev consented to make the speech himself on the basis of the commission's report, and Pospelov was accordingly instructed to redraft it in the form of a speech. At the same time arrangements were made for a special closed session of the Congress.[8]

The fact that the session was postponed from the evening of 24 February to the following morning suggests that discussion was still continuing as to the wording of Khrushchev's speech. In the event internal evidence showed that it was the work of several hands. Its delivery lasted for about three hours and it was listened to in stunned silence by the delegates. The burden of this extraordinary discourse was an amplification of the theme expressed in the opening sentences.

The role of Stalin in the preparation and carrying out of the Socialist Revolution, in the Civil War, and in the fight for the construction of Socialism in our country is universally known. Everyone knows this well. At the present we are concerned with a question which has immense importance for the Party now and for the future. We are concerned with how the cult of the person of Stalin gradually grew, the cult which became at a certain specific stage the course of a whole series of exceedingly serious and grave perversions of party principles, of party democracy, of revolutionary legality.

Because of the fact that not all as yet realise fully the practical consequences resulting from the cult of the individual, the great harm caused by the violation of the principle of collective leadership of the Party and because of the accumulation of immense and limitless power in the hands of one person – the Central Committee of the Party considers it absolutely necessary to make this material available to the Twentieth Congress of the Communist Party of the Soviet Union.[9]

Since Khrushchev's speech, although delivered in secret session, was heard by over fourteen hundred delegates from every part of the Soviet Union as well as representatives of satellite and other foreign Communist Parties, it could hardly be expected to remain a secret for long. It appears that the United States Central Intelligence Agency obtained a copy from Polish sources, and it was from this that the State Department prepared the translation which was later published throughout the world. The Soviet authorities neither confirmed nor denied its authenticity. When foreign journalists tackled Khrushchev, he used to say that he 'knew nothing about it and that they would have to direct their questions to Mr Allen Dulles – that is American intelligence'.[10]

Having thus led the attack against Stalin, Khrushchev had to defend his line when the reaction to the 'secret' speech set in. This led to an abortive attempt by the so-called 'Anti-Party Group' to remove him from office in June 1957 and the expulsion of Molotov, Kaganovich, Malenkov and other diehard Stalinists from the Party. Particular blame was attached to Malenkov for having allegedly been a tool in Beria's hands. 'Occupying a high position in Party and State,' said Khrushchev, 'Comrade Malenkov not only failed to restrain J. V. Stalin, but very adroitly exploited Stalin's weaknesses and habits in the last years of his life. In many cases he egged him on to actions which merit the severest condemnation.'[11] Bulganin at first sided with the opposition, but afterwards made an abject recantation. For this Khrushchev never forgave him and in the following year he was eased out of the Premiership which Khrushchev took over himself in addition to being First Secretary of the Party.

At the same time Khrushchev was faced with an ideological problem in how Stalin should be treated in the new edition of the *Large Soviet Encyclopedia*, of which all the volumes had been published except that containing Stalin's entry. When the relevant volume appeared in

1958, after a delay of eighteen months, it was seen that this entry had been reduced to six pages as compared with forty-four in the previous edition. Little appeared about Stalin's role in the purges, the main responsibility being attributed to Yagoda, Yezhov and Beria. Stalin was given credit for the defence of the country during the late war, but was blamed for the initial unpreparedness and for attaching undue significance to the pact with Hitler. While condemning the personality cult, the article considered that it had no great influence on the development of the Soviet state. As for Stalin, his name in spite of his failings, was declared to be 'inseparable from Marxism–Leninism'.[12]

The defection of Albania from the Soviet orbit instigated by Mao Tse-tung, and the refusal of the Albanian leaders who were staunchly Stalinist to send any representatives to the Twenty-Second Congress in October 1961, obliged Khrushchev to return to the attack. Whereas in 1956 he spoke behind closed doors, he now came into the open in a speech in which he publicly repeated and in some measure amplified his original charges, notably on the subject of Kirov's murder. His remarks were widely reported. 'Stalin is no longer among the living,' Khrushchev proclaimed, 'but we have thought it necessary to denounce the disgraceful methods of leadership that flourished in the circumstances of the Stalin cult. Our Party is doing this to prevent phenomena of this sort from ever being repeated.' He went on to argue that the Albanian Communist leaders opposed his criticisms of Stalin's methods because they were still employing similar methods inside their own country.[13]

Khrushchev arranged that his friend Nikolai Podgorny, the future Head of State, then First Secretary of the Party in the Ukraine, should propose that the continued presence of Stalin's body in the Lenin Mausoleum was 'no longer appropriate' in view of his 'abuse of power, mass repressions against honourable Soviet people, and other activities in the period of the personality cult'. Podgorny's resolution was formally put by Khrushchev to the assembled delegates and carried unanimously.[14]

Two nights later, on 31 October 1961, Stalin's embalmed remains were secretly removed from the mausoleum, which displayed a notice on the outside that it was 'closed for repairs'. Stalin's name was also obliterated from the entrance. His body was then cremated and the ashes were buried below the Kremlin wall near those of four of his former comrades – Kalinin, Sverdlov, Frunze and Dzerzhinsky. For the time being Stalin's new resting-place was marked by a black granite slab with the bare inscription, 'J. V. Stalin 1879–1953'.

During the months that followed, countless statues and portraits of the late dictator were removed throughout the country. There was some reluctance to do this in his native Georgia, where one of the largest statues overlooked the old city of Tiflis. But this too eventually disappeared, on the eve of Khrushchev's visit to Georgia with Fidel Castro.[15] Similarly in hotels and museums not only were pictures of Stalin taken down, but where he had appeared with Lenin his likeness would be rubbed out and someone or something else substituted in its place. For instance, the familiar picture in the foyer of the Metropole Hotel in Moscow showing Lenin seated at a table reading from his works to Stalin was altered to show Lenin reading to a large empty chair draped with a white dust cover.[16] The commonest reminders of Stalin were the towns named or renamed after him. Hence Stalingrad now became Volgagrad, and a score or so of other places, such as Stalino (formerly Yuzovka where Khrushchev had served his apprenticeship as a mechanic), received new appellations or else reverted to their old nomenclature. Streets, parks and squares called after Stalin were also renamed throughout the Soviet Union.

Many thousands of survivors from the purges had now been released and resettled with government help. Their experiences were recorded by Alexander Solzhenitsyn in his short novel *One Day in the Life of Ivan Denisovich,* which Khrushchev allowed to be published in the literary journal *Novy Mir* (November 1962) and which became an international success overnight. About the same time *Pravda* published some bitter verses by the young poet Yevgeni Yevtushenko, written to mark the first anniversary of the removal of Stalin's body from the Lenin Mausoleum. Yevtushenko attacked those of Stalin's heirs who were 'in retirement cutting roses' and thinking secretly that their retirement was only temporary. ('They do not like the time when the camps are empty and halls where people hear poetry readings are crowded.') It seemed to the poet that Stalin had a telephone in his coffin and from there gave instructions to Enver Hoxha, the Albanian party leader, and other Stalinists who were hoping to make a comeback in the Soviet Union. 'I cannot be calm while Stalin's heirs remain on earth,' wrote Yevtushenko. 'And Stalin would seem to me to be still in the mausoleum.'[17]

In the course of a speech which he made in March 1963, on the subject of the class struggle in Russian history, Khrushchev put forward the explanation which in his view accounted for the popular support Stalin had received for his role in the purges. 'When plots against the Revolution were discovered,' he said, 'Stalin as Secretary of the Central Committee carried out the struggle for cleansing the country of conspirators, and he did so under cover of the slogan of the struggle against the enemies of the people. The public believed him and supported him. And this could not have been otherwise, for had there not been in the past history of our Party more than one case of betrayal and treason to the cause of the Revolution, for example the activities of the double-agent Malinovsky, a member of the Bolshevik faction in the State Duma?'[18]

Khrushchev's reference to Malinovsky is interesting. One wonders what other cases of treason to the revolutionary cause he had in mind, and whether he had any inkling of Stalin's record as an alleged agent of the Tsarist secret police. If he had, he kept silent. Certainly there is no hint of any such knowledge in his other public utterances or in his published reminiscences.

By the time Khrushchev was himself toppled from power in the autumn of 1964, Stalin's downgrading was complete and he had virtually become an 'unperson'. Thereafter he was to enjoy a mild measure of rehabilitation, to be developed slowly and cautiously by those responsible, with the emphasis on his wartime leadership. Soviet militarists and historians were officially encouraged to write articles or reminiscences discreetly praising Stalin's role in the war, although they were not inhibited from making reasoned criticisms. Among the first to do so were the three top marshals, Zhukov, Rokossovsky and Budenny. When Leonid Brezhnev, who had succeeded Khrushchev as the party boss, spoke on 8 May 1965 at the twentieth anniversary of the ending of the war in Europe, a passing reference to Stalin as Chairman of the State Defence Committee was received with prolonged applause by the audience, a demonstration which is said to have come as a surprise to some of the leaders present.[18]

This may be seen in particular as a reaction to the work by the Soviet historian A. M. Nekrich entitled *22 June 1941*, which had just been published and was making a considerable stir. In his book the author blamed Stalin entirely for Russian unpreparedness at the time Hitler launched his sudden attack. Later the book was denounced as 'politically harmful' and banned, and at the same time its author was expelled from Party membership.

The new Party line was expressed by another historian Professor G. A. Deborin at a discussion between Old Bolsheviks and Soviet historians on the demerits of Nekrich's work, which took place in the Institute of Marxism–Leninism in Moscow during the winter of 1966–1967.[19]

In estimating Stalin's action it is unnecessary to refer to Khrushchev's declarations which are not objective. For example, it is difficult to accept the statement that Stalin was afraid of war. In so far as he received false information, Stalin reached false conclusions. He placed too much hope in the German–Soviet pact, while the Germans, protected by the pact, were getting ready to attack. But Stalin's estimate of German intentions was endorsed by those around him. So Stalin cannot be considered solely responsible for his mistakes.

In 1962, the outside world had been given a completely novel and unconventional picture of the late dictator by the Yugoslav ex-Minister Milovan Djilas in his *Conversations with Stalin*. As a result the author got five years in a Yugoslav prison for allegedly divulging state secrets. (He was already serving a prison term for his revelations in a previous work.) In his highly indiscreet book, Djilas penned a most revealing picture of the dictator holding court in the Kremlin and in his *dacha* at Kuntsevo, which attracted world-wide interest.

Stalin's name again became world news through his daughter Svetlana's dramatic flight to the west after having sought refuge in the United States Embassy in New Delhi on the evening of 6 March 1967. She had been allowed to pay a short visit to India for the purpose of bringing home to his family the ashes of her common law husband Brijesh Singh, who had recently died in Moscow. Some years previously, in September 1957, she had changed her name from Stalina, to which she had reverted after her divorce from her second husband Yuri Zhdanov, to her mother's maiden name Alliluyeva, since under Soviet law a child could use either its father's or its mother's name. 'I could no longer tolerate the name of Stalin,' she admitted afterwards: 'its sharp metallic sound lacerated my ears, my eyes, my heart...' Voroshilov, by this time Head of State, helped her with the formalities and told her that in his opinion she had done right to make the change.

In her suitcase, with which she eventually reached New York where she was granted political asylum by the United States Government, Svetlana carried the manuscript of an autobiographical work; this was to appear in the following autumn as *Twenty Letters to a Friend*. It had been written in a few weeks during the summer of 1963 in a village outside Moscow, primarily it appears for the information of her two children Joseph and Catherine, and not really intended for publication. It gave some vivid glimpses of her upbringing in the sheltered circle of Kremlin officialdom, of her father as a family man and her mother as a disillusioned and unhappy wife. A series of affectionate notes from her father in which he addressed her as his 'little sparrow' and 'little housekeeper' had previously been on public view in the

608

Stalin Museum in Gori, but had attracted little if any attention. Their publication in Svetlana's tender reminiscences showed an unexpected side of the dictator's character. Readers of *Twenty Letters* also learned that Stalin was 'courteous and unassuming' with his underlings (not always borne out by other witnesses) and that his household staff 'loved and respected him for the most ordinary human qualities'. His misdeeds she blamed on others like Yezhov and Beria, and concluded that he was a victim or captive of the Communist *apparat*. 'All powerful as he was, he was impotent in the face of the frightful system that had grown up round him like a huge honeycomb, and he was helpless either to destroy it or bring it under control.'

After a year's residence in America, during which she tore up her Soviet passport, talked to many informed people like Professor George Kennan and Mr Louis Fischer and read widely such authorities as Isaac Deutscher and Alexander Solzhenitsyn, Svetlana considerably revised her earlier judgment. In *Only One Year*, which came out in 1969, her father was transformed into 'a moral and spiritual monster' and 'a despot', who 'had brought about a bloody terror, destroying millions of innocent people'.

> He gave his name to this bloodbath of absolute dictatorship. He knew what he was doing. He was neither insane nor misled. With cold calculation he had cemented his own power, afraid of losing it more than anything else in the world. And so his first concentrated drive had been the liquidation of his enemies and rivals. The rest followed later.

Svetlana's action in allowing what the Soviet authorities considered to be the exploitation of herself and her writings to discredit her native country – Premier Kosygin publicy described her as 'morally unstable' and 'a sick person' – may well have given a fillip to the slow process of her father's rehabilitation. In the same year as *Only One Year* appeared *They Fought for the Fatherland*, a new novel by Mikhail Shokolov, was published in the Soviet Union. Although *Pravda* printed some extracts, it was widely reported that the author had been in trouble with the censorship and that the more derogatory references to Stalin in his novel had been omitted or toned down. A more vocal anti-Stalinist was the historian Peter Yakir, son of General Yon Yakir, who had been shot in connection with the Tukachevsky affair. Besides penning a devastating indictment of Stalin's abuse of power which he sent to the party journal *Kommunist* – the editor declined to publish it but it was clandestinely circulated – young Yakir took a prominent part in an anti-Stalin demonstration in Red Square on Stalin's ninetieth birthday anniversary (21 December 1969), when several arrests were made.[20] Otherwise the occasion was not marked by the flood of laudatory articles that had been anticipated by Yakir and his friends. Indeed *Pravda* in an unsigned editorial reminded its readers of Stalin's failings as well as his other attributes.

Rather more praise was bestowed upon Stalin at the VE Day celebrations in Moscow in May 1970, when Marshal Bagramian, Deputy Defence Minister, publicly held forth at a press conference on the 'great part played by the General Headquarters and our commander Stalin'. But, the Marshal added, Stalin 'did not always act in accordance with those advisers'.[21] At the same time Stalin received star billing in the film *Liberation*, which had been made in reply to *The Longest Day*, the western production about the Anglo-American landings in Normandy on 6 June 1944. In the Soviet film, Stalin was shown as Commander-in-Chief in frequent consultation with his marshals and generals at Command Headquarters in the Kremlin. Chatting with an officer in the public relations branch of the Red Army after the preview of the film, the Moscow correspondent of the *Christian Science Monitor* suggested that perhaps the character of Stalin was a bit too gentle. 'Oh, not at all,' replied the Lieutenant-Colonel. 'That is just how Stalin was. His softness hid his hardness underneath.'[22]

On 25 June 1970, a quarter of a century almost to the day after the Victory Parade in the Red Square at which the Soviet armed forces marched past Lenin's tomb and threw down the captured German flags before 'the great Commander Stalin', the plain grave at the foot of the Kremlin wall was refashioned on the model of those of the recently dead Voroshilov and other Old Bolsheviks close by. Like theirs too, Stalin's grave was surmounted by a specially sculptured bust of himself on a plinth, looking larger than life. There was no ceremony at the unveiling of the bust. But a young policeman nearby was overheard to comment: 'It doesn't mean anything. It's just a monument.'[23]

In Georgia at least it meant something. Speaking in Tbilisi on 14 May 1971 at a celebration to mark the fiftieth anniversary of Soviet rule in the republic, Brezhnev was astonished at the thunderous applause produced by his passing reference to Stalin among other Georgians who had contributed to the communist cause. As the Moscow correspondent of the London *Times* put it, 'it proved once more, if proof were needed, that to his fellow Georgians, Stalin is still a hero.'[24]

On the other hand, in composing what amounted to his final epitaph on Stalin at this time, Khrushchev declared:

His pretensions to a very special role in our history were well founded, for he really was a man of outstanding skill and intelligence. He truly did tower over everyone around him, and despite my condemnation of his methods, I have always recognised and acknowledged his strengths. In everything about Stalin's personality there was something admirable and correct as well as something savage. Nevertheless, if he were alive today, I would vote that he should be brought to trial and punished for his crimes.[24]

When all is said and done, something like this may well be the ultimate verdict of history on the record of this unique dictator in his country and in his times.

Appendix

A letter, dated 12 July 1913, from the St Petersburg Police Department
(Okhrana) signed on the face of it by Colonel A. M. Eremin, Chief of
the Special Section, and addressed to Captain A. F. Zhelezniakov, the
officer in charge of the Okhrana at Yeniseisk, to which district of
Siberia Stalin had been exiled in the spring of 1913, came to light for
the first time shortly after the end of the Second World War.[1] Typed
in Russian on official Okhrana stationery and marked 'Very Secret'
and 'Personal' it referred to Stalin's work as an agent of the Tsarist
secret police. A translation follows:

Dear Alexei Fedorovich,
  Joseph Vissarionovich Djugashvili-Stalin, who has been exiled
by administrative order to the Turukhansk region, provided the
Chief of the Tiflis Provincial Gendarme Administration with
valuable denunciatory information when he was arrested in 1906.
  In 1908 the Chief of the Baku Okhrana Section received from
Stalin a series of intelligence reports, and afterwards upon
Stalin's arrival in Petersburg Stalin became an agent of the
Petersburg Okhrana Section.
  Stalin's work was distinguished by accuracy, but was frag-
mentary.
  After Stalin's election to the Central Committee of the Party in
Prague, Stalin, upon his return to Petersburg, went over into

open opposition to the Government and completely broke off his connection with the Okhrana.

I am informing you, dear sir, of the above for your personal consideration in the conduct of operational work.

With assurances of my high esteem,

EREMIN

Isaac Don Levine, who had written the first biography of Stalin to appear in English, heard of the letter through Mr Vadim Makarov, son of the Russian admiral Stepan Makarov, whom Mr Levine met at the house of Mrs Claire Booth Luce in Connecticut in 1946. Makarov told him that he and two other Russians, Boris Bakhmetev and Boris Sergievsky, had jointly acquired it from Professor M. P. Golovachev, a well-known Russian emigré living in Shanghai. Bakhmetev had been Russian ambassador in Washington for a short time under the Kerensky regime and Sergievsky was a noted airman and pioneer of Russian aviation. According to Don Levine, 'the three gentlemen were of unimpeachable reputation', as also was Professor Golovachev. The latter had obtained the letter from a certain Colonel Victor Nikolayevich Russianov, who was stated to have brought it with him together with other papers belonging to the Siberian Okhrana when he escaped to China after the Revolution.[2]

Apparently Russianov was responsible for the Okhrana office in Yeniseisk, where Captain Zhelezniakov the recipient of the Eremin letter had been in charge. In March 1917, Russianov was arrested in the Okhrana headquarters in Yeniseisk, the order for his detention being signed at the request of the local mayor Boris Nicolaevsky on behalf of the Kerensky Government. 'When they came to get him,' Nicolaevsky afterwards recalled, 'they found him trying to burn the files in his office.'[3] Russianov was later released and succeeded in making his way to Shanghai where he found employment as a chauffeur with a wealthy American family. There he parted with the letter no doubt for a financial consideration. It should be noted that he also had with him a supply of Okhrana stationery, so that there is a possibility that he fabricated the letter and incorporated in it what he remembered seeing in the files at Yeniseisk which he had tried to burn.

The letter was eventually acquired by the Tolstoy Foundation in New York at a cost of nine thousand dollars. But before this it was turned over to Mr Levine for publication if he was satisfied as to its authenticity. His inquiries, which he pursued with considerable diligence, led him to a modest apartment on the outskirts of Paris inhabited by a former high ranking Okhrana officer, General Alexander

Spiridovich, under whom Colonel Eremin had served in Kiev. Spiridovich remembered Eremin well and spoke highly of his professional abilities. On being shown the letter, Spiridovich expressed the belief that it was genuine, and in support of this opinion he produced a silver decanter which bore an engraved facsimile of Eremin's signature along with the signatures of other officers in the Kiev special section who had presented Spiridovich with the decanter when he left Kiev on promotion to St Petersburg. 'A comparison of the two left no doubt in our minds that it was Eremin's authentic signature', wrote Don Levine after this meeting.[4]

Of course, it would have placed the matter beyond dispute had it been possible to trace Eremin himself, who was last heard of serving in Helsinki. But he had disappeared after the Revolution with his family. His name does not appear in the detailed lists of officers who fought on the side of the Whites during the Civil War and there is no mention of his death either in the Finnish or White Russian emigré press. It must be presumed, therefore, that he perished at the hands of the Bolsheviks in the early days of their rule. The only person whom Spiridovich considered might throw some light on Eremin was another ex-Okhrana officer named Ivan V. Dobrovolsky, who had escaped to Germany and had become sexton in the Greek Orthodox church in the Berlin suburb of Charlottenburg. Don Levine subsequently found the church only to learn that during the war Dobrovolsky, whose nickname in the service was 'Nikolai of the Golden Glasses', had migrated to Wiesbaden as sexton to a chapel erected there by a Russian Grand Duke in memory of his wife. But by the time Mr Levine reached Wiesbaden, Dobrovolsky was already dead and lay buried in the adjoining cemetery.

However, Don Levine considered that what he had learned from his meeting with General Spiridovich justified him in publishing the text of the letter. This he did with accompanying photographs of the document and the silver decanter showing Eremin's authenticated signature in an article which he contributed to *Life* magazine (23 April 1956), subsequently expanded into a short book entitled *Stalin's Great Secret*, and published later in the same year. Both the article and the book aroused considerable controversy and the letter was denounced in pro-Soviet circles as a hoax. There is no doubt that Don Levine published the letter in good faith, convinced of its authenticity. Equally there can be little if any doubt that the letter is a forgery, although this does not vitiate the truth of its contents as a statement of Stalin's connection with the Okhrana.

There are a number of suspicious features about the letter which lend weight to the conclusion of fraudulence. First, the addressee's Christian name was Vladmir and not Alexei, a fact easily ascertainable from the biographical register of Okhrana officers available in Colonel Eremin's office at the time. Secondly, the use of 'Vissarionovich' is curious since in Okhrana inter-departmental correspondence the 'ich' was normally dropped in patronymics. Thirdly, Stalin had only adopted his pseudonym a few months previously and one might have expected Eremin to refer to him as Djugashvili; yet the pseudonym occurs seven times in the letter. Fourthly, the style is unlike Eremin's other letters and reports, of which there are many examples extant both in the Finnish State Archives in Helsinki and the Okhrana collection in the Hoover Institution at Stanford University, California. Fifthly, Eremin was appointed Chief of the Okhrana in Finland on 21 June 1913. It has been suggested that Eremin did not take up his new post immediately, and that there was consequently nothing unusual in his writing to Captain Zhelezniakov from St Petersburg on 12 July.[5] On the other hand, there is evidence in the Finnish Archives in the shape of a document dated 19 July which suggests that by this date Eremin was deeply immersed in his new duties and had been *en poste* for several weeks.

Admittedly all these are circumstantial objections which are capable of explanation, although the explanation in some instances may not carry much conviction. Greater importance may well be attached to expert evidence on the physical composition of the document. Testifying before the Senate Internal Security Committee in 1957, Mr Martin K. Tytell, a handwriting and typewriting expert, stated that the machine on which the Eremin letter was typed was an Adler, manufactured by a German company which first supplied machines with Russian characters in 1912.[6] The Eremin letter, according to this witness, could not possibly have been written in 1913, because the type, instead of being comparatively fresh, which one would expect from a machine of 1912 or 1913 vintage, was worn and battered, which suggests that it was written many years later. Secondly, Mr Tytell paid a visit to the Finnish State Archives in Helsinki, where he found eighty-five examples of Eremin's signature on official correspondence. He showed five of the archivists the letter of 12 July 1913, and their opinion which he corroborated by his own expertise was that the signature to the letter in question was not in Eremin's hand.

However, what conclusively establishes the spuriousness of the letter in the present writer's opinion is the printed heading or letter head. This particular style was not adopted by the Okhrana headquarters until 1914 or 1915, after the existing stocks of stationery had been exhausted. A search conducted by the present writer in the collection of Okhrana papers at the Hoover Institution revealed a genuine letter of identical date, which clearly shows the difference. For one thing in the genuine letter the name of the Ministry of Internal Affairs (*Ministerstvo Vnutrennykh Del*) appears in full instead of being abbreviated as MVD. In the Eremin letter the words 'Police Department' and 'Special Section' are transposed. Finally, in the Eremin letter the number under the date is typed rather than impressed by means of a rubber stamp, the usual practice in all office correspondence of the period.

Don Levine, who published the Eremin letter in the belief that it was genuine, is now convinced of its spuriousness. Thus the document in the vaults of the Tolstoy Foundation may now be relegated to the list of documentary forgeries by White Russians which, as has been noted above, includes a better known name than Eremin in the history of Stalin – Gregory Zinoviev.

Bibliography

The principal source material for Stalin's life, on which I have drawn largely, is his published writings. More than one thousand articles, speeches, interviews, letters and telegrams have been listed by Robert H. McNeal in his comprehensive 'annotated' bibliography, *Stalin's Works*, published by the Hoover Institution on War, Revolution and Peace at Stanford University, California, in 1967. When Stalin died in 1953, thirteen volumes of his *Sochineniia* revised by himself had appeared in Moscow, bringing the story up to January 1934. The fourteenth volume which would have covered the period of the Great Purge was announced for publication early in 1956, but neither it nor the other volumes which had been planned were ever officially published, due to Khrushchev's revelations of Stalin's 'crimes' at the Twentieth Party Congress. The omission was made good by the Hoover Institution, which brought out an unofficial Russian language edition of Vols. XIV–XVI in 1966 under Mr McNeal's editorship.

Without doubt the most important manuscript material on Stalin is the Stalin Collection in the Archives of the Central Committee of the Soviet Communist Party in Moscow. But this is closed to historians native and foreign alike and is likely to remain so for a long time to come, if indeed access to it is ever permitted. Its interest for students of the period may be judged by the tantalising quotations from a few of the documents made by Khrushchev in his 'secret' speech to the Twentieth Congress.*

For Stalin's early career in the Bolshevik underground, the Archive of the Imperial Russian Secret Police (Okhrana), at present preserved in the library of the Hoover Institution at Stanford, is invaluable. This unique collection was formerly housed in the Paris office of the Okhrana, where it formed the central depository of all available intelligence on the revolutionary movement at home and abroad from 1886 to 1917, duplicating the records of the Okhrana headquarters in St Petersburg in addition to its own official files. After the Revolution, Basil Maklakov, the last Imperial Russian ambassador to France, who had been responsible for its custody, had the collection secretly shipped to Stanford subject to the condition that it should not be opened and made publicly available until after his death. Following this event which took place in 1957, examination of the archive revealed over 100,000 documents, index cards, photographs, letter books, newspaper clippings, etc. It is hardly necessary to add that the disclosure came as a complete surprise to the Soviet authorities, who believed that the collection had been destroyed many years previously. The reports on Stalin, together with copies of his letters which had been intercepted by the Tsarist censorship, are of prime importance.

Interesting unpublished recollections of two Okhrana officers, Colonel A. Martynov and Lieutenant N. V. Veselago, are also preserved in the Hoover library, independently of the Okhrana archive. Veselago's recollections, which were recorded on tape and transcribed by Edward Ellis Smith, afford strong proof that Stalin was an Okhrana agent between 1906 and 1912. The Lincoln Hutchinson Papers, also in the Hoover library, are concerned with the experiences of American engineers in Soviet Russia in the 1920s and early 1930s, and throw light on Stalin and the First Five Year Plan.

The Trotsky Papers in the Houghton Library of Harvard University

---

* Khrushchev's speech is now known to have been drafted by P. N. Pospelov, one of the secretaries of the Central Committee, and chairman of the commission appointed after Beria's execution to investigate the arrests in the Great Purge. As Director of the Institute of Marxism–Leninism Pospelov had also been entrusted by Stalin with preparing his *Sochineniia* for publication. The quotations by Khrushchev in his speech included the letter from Lenin to Stalin dated 5 March 1923, in which Lenin rebuked Stalin for his rude behaviour to his wife Krupskaya and threatened to break off relations with him if Stalin did not withdraw his words and apologise: see above p. 200. According to Khrushchev, the letter was found after Stalin's death in a secret compartment. ('I was astonished that this note had been preserved. Stalin had probably forgotten all about it.') *Khrushchev Remembers* (1970), p. 44.

are likewise of considerable importance, particularly for the period of the Civil War, although many of these have been used by Isaac Deutscher in his admirable three-volume biography of Trotsky.

I have derived considerable help from the unpublished reports on Stalin and the Soviet scene compiled by the British embassy staff in Moscow. These are in the Public Record Office in London and are available to the end of 1940.

The Kerensky Papers, now at the University of Texas, are of use in the history of the Provisional Government in 1917 and also for the passages omitted from the published version of Kerensky's memoirs. But, apart from a single telegram from Kerensky to Stalin during the Second World War, they are generally only of background interest.

The published literature on Stalin is enormous, since more books have been written about him than any other character in history, including Napoleon and Jesus Christ. For his underground life before 1912, the most fully documented work is the Soviet police chief Beria's history of the Bolshevist movement in Transcaucasia, in spite of the changes, suppressions and additions which appear in its later editions as part of Stalin's policy of rewriting history. Among other official Soviet works, Yaroslavsky's *Landmarks* and the official 'short biography' by Alexandrov, Pospelov and others, both of which were approved by Stalin, contain much useful information, although they naturally portray the dictator as he liked to see himself rather than as he really was. Another officially approved biography is the work of the French Communist Henri Barbusse; it was written with the assistance of its subject and contains hitherto unpublished material. An equally informative work, although biased and even spiteful, is the unfinished study of Stalin by Trotsky; this contains important documents and recollections of various contemporaries of both men. The fullest and best documented biography by a Russian exile is Boris Souvarine's 'critical survey', which originally appeared in French in 1935 and in an English edition four years later with a postscript on the Great Purge. On Stalin's life before 1917, *Three Who Made a Revolution* by Bertram D. Wolfe and *The Young Stalin* by Edward Ellis Smith also contain significant new material. *Stalin's Russia* by Francis B. Randall is a useful 'historical reconsideration' of the subject in the light of his ideology. Finally, there is Isaac Deutscher's great 'political biography', which I have found of the utmost value in spite of its author's essentially Marxist and Stalinist approach. The more intimate side of Stalin's life has been covered in fascinating detail by Khrushchev in his speeches at the Twentieth and Twenty-Second Congresses and in his putative memoirs, as well as by the Yugoslav writer Milovan Djilas in his *Conversations with Stalin* and by Stalin's daughter Svetlana Alliluyeva in her two books of reminiscences.

The following printed works are confined to those which have been consulted by me in the composition of this book. English language titles are indicated wherever possible. Russian titles are given either where no English translation exists or else where the Russian text is fuller than the English and is essential for reference.

ABRAMOVITCH, Raphael R. *The Soviet Revolution 1917–1939*. London, 1962.

ALEXANDROV, G. F., POSPELOV, P. N., and others. *Joseph Stalin. A short Biography*. Moscow, 1949.

ALEXANDROV, Victor. *The Kremlin*. Translated by Roy Monkcom. London, 1963.

ALEXANDROV, Victor. *The Tukachevsky Affair*. London, 1962.

ALLILUYEV, Sergei. *Proidenniye Put*. Moscow, 1946.

ALLILUYEV, Sergei and ALLILUYEV, Anna. *The Alliluyev Memoirs*. Translated and edited by David Tutaev. London, 1968.

ALLILUYEVA, Anna. *Vospominaniya*. Moscow, 1946.

ALLILUYEVA, Svetlana. *Twenty Letters to a Friend*. Translated by Priscilla Johnson. McMillan. New York and London, 1967.

ALLILUYEVA, Svetlana. *Only One Year*. Translated by Paul Chachavadze. New York and London, 1969.

ARSENIDZE, R. Review of the various editions of L. P. Beria's history of the Bolshevik organisations in Transcaucasia. *Caucasian Review*, Vol. I. Munich, 1955.

ARSENIDZE, R. *Iz Vospominanii o Staline. Novy Zhurnal*, No. 72. New York, June, 1963.

AUTY, Phyllis. *Tito. A Biography*. London, 1970.

AVON, Earl of, *The Eden Memoirs*. Vol. 1 *Full Circle*. Vol. II *Facing the Dictators*. Vol. III *The Reckoning*. London, 1960–1965.

AVTORKHANOV, Abdurakhman. *Stalin and the Soviet Communist Party. A Study in the Technology of Power*. London, 1959.

BAIKALOFF, A. V. *I Knew Stalin*. London, 1940.

BAJANOV (Bazhanov), Boris. *Avec Staline dans le Kremline*. Paris, 1930.

BALABANOFF, Angelica. *My Life as a Rebel*. New York and London, 1938.

BARBUSSE, Henri. *Stalin*. Translated by Vyvyan Holland. London, 1935.

BARMINE, Alexander. *One Who Survived*. New York, 1945.

Batumskaya demonstratsiya goda 1902. Moscow, 1937.

BERIA, L. P. *K Voprusu ob Istorii Bolshevistskikh Organizatsii v Zakavkazje*. Third edition. Moscow, 1935.

BERIA, L. P. *On the History of the Bolshevik Organisations in Trans-caucasia*. Translated from the Seventh Russian edition. Moscow, 1949.

BESSECHES, Nikolaus. *Stalin*. Translated from the German by E. W. Dickes. London, 1951.

BESSEDOVSKY, Gregory. *Revelations of a Soviet Diplomat*. Translated by Mathey Norgate. London, 1931.

BESSEDOVSKY, Gregory, and LAPORTE, Maurice. *Staline 'L'Homme d'Acier'*. Paris, 1932.

BIAGI, Enzo. *Svetlana. The Inside Story*. London, 1967.

BIALER, Seweryn. *Stalin and his Generals: Soviet Military Memoirs of World War II*. New York, 1969. London, 1970.

BIRSE, A. H. *Memoirs of an Interpreter*. London, 1967.

BORISOV, S. M. *V. Frunze*. Moscow, 1940.

BRYANT, Arthur. *The Turn of the Tide 1939-1943. Based on the Diaries of Field Marshal Viscount Alanbrooke*. London, 1957.

BRYANT, Arthur. *Triumph in the West 1943-1946. Based on the Diaries of Field Marshal Lord Alanbrooke*. London, 1959.

BURNS, James MacGregor. *Roosevelt: The Soldier of Freedom 1940-1945*. London, 1971.

BYRNES, James F. *Speaking Frankly*. New York and London, 1947.

CASSIDY, Henry C. *Moscow Dateline*. Boston, 1943.

CHAMBERLIN, W. H. *The Russian Revolution*. 2 vols. London, 1935.

CHURCHILL, Winston S. *The Second World War*. 6 vols. London, 1948-1954.

CIANO, Count G. *Ciano's Diary 1939-1943*. Edited by Malcolm Muggeridge. London, 1947.

CILIGA, Anton. *The Russian Enigma*. London, 1940.

CLEMENS, D. S. *Yalta*. New York, 1971.

COLE, David M. *Josef Stalin Man of Steel*. London, 1942.

CONQUEST, Robert. *The Soviet Deportation of Nationalities*. London, 1960.

CONQUEST, Robert. *Power and Policy in the U.S.S.R.* London, 1961.

CONQUEST, Robert. *The Great Terror*. London, 1968.

CONQUEST, Robert. *The Human Cost of Soviet Communism*. U.S. Senate Committee of the Judiciary. Washington, 1970.

Council on Foreign Relations. *The Soviet Union 1922-1962. A Foreign Affairs Reader*. Edited by Philip E. Mosely. New York, 1963.

CRANKSHAW, Edward. *Khrushchev*. London, 1966.

DALLIN, David J., and NICOLAEVSKY, Boris I. *Forced Labor in Soviet Russia*. London, 1947.

D'ASTIER, Emmanuel. *Sur Staline*. Lausanne, 1967.

DAVIES, Joseph E. *Mission to Moscow*. New York, 1941.

DE GAULLE, Charles. *War Memoirs* Vol. III. *Salvation 1944-1946:* Translated by Richard Howard. London, 1960.

DEAKIN, F. W. and STORRY, G. R. *The Case of Richard Sorge*. London, 1966.

DEANE, John R. *The Strange Alliance. The Story of American Efforts at Wartime Cooperation with Russia*. London, 1947.

DEDIJER, Vladimir. *Tito Speaks. His Self Portrait and Struggle with Stalin*. London, 1953.

DELBARS, Yves. *The Real Stalin*. Translated from the French by Bernard Miall. London, 1953.

DERIABIN, Peter, and GIBNEY, Frank. *The Secret World*. London, 1960.

DEUTSCHER, Isaac. *Stalin. A Political Biography*. London, 1949 and 1966.

DEUTSCHER, Isaac. *The Prophet Armed. Trotsky: 1879-1921*. New York and London, 1954.

DEUTSCHER, Isaac. *The Prophet Unarmed. Trotsky: 1921-1929*. New York and London, 1959.

DEUTSCHER, Isaac. *The Prophet Outcast. Trotsky: 1929-1940*. New York and London, 1963.

DEUTSCHER, Isaac. *Heretics and Renegades*. London, 1955.

DEUTSCHER, Isaac. *Ironies of History. Essays on Contemporary Communism*. London, 1968.

DEUTSCHER, Isaac. *Russia, China, and the West. A Contemporary Chronicle, 1953-1966*. Edited by Fred Halliday. London, 1970.

DIXON, Piers. *Double Diploma. The Life of Sir Pierson Dixon*. London, 1968.

DJILAS, Milovan. *Conversations with Stalin*. New York and London, 1962.

Documents on British Foreign Policy 1919-39. Edited by E. L. Woodward and Rohan Butler. 2nd Series, Vol. VII. 3rd Series, Vols. IV-VII. London, 1951-1958.

Documents on German Foreign Policy 1918-1945. Series D, Vols. VIII-XII. Washington and London, 1954-1962.

DURANTY, Walter. *Stalin & Co: The Politburo – the Men who run Russia*. London, 1949.

EASTMAN, Max. *Since Lenin Died*. London, 1925.

EISENHOWER, Dwight D. *Crusade in Europe*. London, 1948.

EHRENBURG, Ilya. *Men, Years – Life*. Vols. IV, V and VI. London, 1963-1966.

ELLIS, C. H. *The Transcaspian Episode*. London, 1963.

ERICKSON, John. *The Soviet High Command: A Military-Political History 1918–1941.* London, 1962.

ESSAD-BEY (Nisselbaum). *Stalin: The Career of a Fanatic.* Translated from the German by Huntley Paterson. London, 1932.

ESTORICK, Eric. *Stafford Cripps.* London, 1949.

FAINSOD, Merle. *Smolensk under Russian Rule.* London, 1959.

FAINSOD, Merle. *How Russia is Ruled.* Cambridge, Mass., 1953.

FARNSWORTH, Beatrice. *William C. Bullitt and the Soviet Union.* Bloomington, 1967.

FARRER, David. *G — For God Almighty. A Personal Memoir of Lord Beaverbrook.* London, 1969.

FEIS, Herbert. *Churchill Roosevelt Stalin: The War They Waged and the Peace They Sought.* Princeton, 1957.

FEIS, Herbert. *Between War and Peace: The Potsdam Conference.* Princeton, 1960.

FLOYD, David. 'Generalissimo Stalin. New Version.' *Daily Telegraph,* London, 8 July 1965.

FEIS, Herbert. *From Trust to Terror: The Onset of the Cold War 1945–1950.* London, 1970.

FISCHER, George. *Soviet Opposition to Stalin.* Cambridge, Mass., 1952.

FISCHER, Louis. *The Life and Death of Stalin.* London, 1953.

FLEMING, Peter. *The Fate of Admiral Kolchak.* London, 1963.

Foreign Relations of the United States. Diplomatic Papers. The Soviet Union 1933–1939. Washington, 1952.

FOTIEVA, L. A. *Pages from Lenin's Life.* Moscow, 1960.

FUTRELL, Michael. *Northern Underground.* London, 1963.

GLENNY, Michael. 'Leonid Krassin: The Years before 1917. An Outline:' *Soviet Studies.* Vol. XXII, No. 2. Oxford, October 1970.

HARRIMAN, W. Averell. *Peace with Russia?* London, 1960.

HART, B. H. Liddell. *The Red Army.* London, 1956.

HILGER, Gastav, and MEYER, Alfred G. *The Incompatible Allies. A Memoir-History of German-Soviet Relations 1918–1941.* New York, 1953.

HINGLEY, Ronald. *The Russian Secret Police.* London, 1970.

HULL, Cordell. *Memoirs.* 2 vols. London, 1948.

HUTTON, J. Bernard. *Stalin – the Miraculous Georgian.* London, 1961.

Institute of Marxism–Leninism. 'The Personality Cult.' Discussion of the draft third volume of *The History of the CPSU* and of *22 June 1941* by A. M. Nekrich. *Survey.* No. 63. London, April, 1967.

IREMASHVILI, J. *Stalin und die Tragödie Georgiens.* Berlin, 1932.

ISMAY, General Lord. *Memoirs.* London, 1960.

KAMINSKY, V. and VERESHCHAGIN, I. *'Detstvo i iunost Vozhdia: dokumenty, zapisi, rasskazy.' Molodaya gvardiya.* No. 12. Moscow, December, 1939.

KATKOV, George. *Russia 1917: The February Revolution.* London, 1967.

KATKOV, George. *The Trial of Bukharin.* London, 1969.

KELLY, David. *The Ruling Few.* London, 1952.

KENNAN, George F. *Russia and the West under Lenin and Stalin.* London, 1961.

KENNAN, George F. *Memoirs 1925–1950.* Boston, 1967.

KERENSKY, Alexander. *The Kerensky Memoirs: Russia and History's Turning Point.* London, 1966.

KESSEL, Georges. *'La Nuit ou Staline est Mort.' Paris Match.* Paris, 30 March 1963.

KNICKERBOCKER, H. R. *The Soviet Five-Year Plan and its Effect on World Trade.* London, 1931.

KHRUSHCHEV, N. S. *Khrushchev Remembers.* With an Introduction, Commentary and Notes by Edward Crankshaw. Translated and edited by Strobe Talbott. Boston, 1970. London, 1971.

KHRUSHCHEV, N. S. *The Crimes of the Stalin Era. Special Report to the Twentieth Congress of the Communist Party of Soviet Union.* Annotated by Boris I. Nicolaevsky. New York, 1956.

KOT, Stanislaw. *Conversations with the Kremlin and Dispatches from Russia.* Translated and arranged by H. C. Stevens. London, 1963.

KRASSIN, Lubov. *Leonid Krassin. His Life and Work.* London, 1929.

KRAVCHENKO, Victor. *I Chose Freedom.* London, 1947.

KRIVITSKY, W. G. *I Was Stalin's Agent.* London, 1939.

KRUPSKAYA, N. K. *Memories of Lenin,* 2 vols. London, 1930–1933.

KUBY, Erich. *The Russians and Berlin, 1945.* Translated by Arnold J. Pomerans. London, 1968.

KUSNIERZ, Bronislaw. *Stalin and the Poles: An Indictment of the Soviet Leaders.* London, 1949.

LABIN, Suzanne. *Stalin's Russia.* Translated by Edward Fitzgerald. London, 1949.

LAKOBA, N. *Stalin i Khashim 1901–1902.* Sukhum, 1934.

LANG, David Marshall. *A Modern History of Georgia.* London, 1962.

LAUE, Theodore H. Von. *Why Lenin? Why Stalin? A Reappraisal of the Russian Revolution 1900–1930.* London, 1966.

LEAHY, William D. *I Was There.* New York, 1950.

LENIN, V. I. *Collected Works.* 45 vols. Moscow, 1960–70.

LENIN, V. I. *The Letters of Lenin* Translated and edited by Elizabeth Hill and Doris Mudie. London, 1937.

LENIN, V. I. *Leninskii Sbornik.* 20 vols. Moscow, 1924–32.

LERMOLO, Elizabeth. *Face of a Victim*. Translated from the Russian by I. D. W. Talmadge. London, 1956.

LEVINE, Isaac Don. *Stalin*. New York, 1931.

LEVINE, Isaac Don. *Stalin's Great Secret*. New York, 1956.

LEVINE, Isaac Don. *The Mind of an Assassin*. New York and London, 1959.

LEVINE, Isaac Don. *I Rediscover Russia*. New York, 1964.

LEWIN, Moshe. *Lenin's Last Struggle*. Translated from the French by A. M. Sheridan Smith. London, 1959.

LISSANN, Maury. 'Stalin the Appeaser'. *Survey*, No. 76. London, Summer 1970.

LITVINOV, Maxim. *Notes for a Journal*. Edited by E. H. Carr. London, 1955.

LOCKHART, B. H. Bruce. *Memoirs of a British Agent*. London and New York, 1932.

LUDWIG, Emil. *Stalin*. London, 1942.

LUNGHI, Hugh. 'Stalin Face to Face'. *The Observer*, London, 24 February, 1963.

LUNACHARSKY, A. V. *Revolutionary Silhouettes*. Translated from the Russian and edited by Michael Glenny. New York, 1968.

LYONS, Eugene. *Assignment in Utopia*. London, 1938.

LYONS, Eugene. *Stalin. Czar of all the Russias*. London, 1941.

MACLEAN, Fitzroy. *Eastern Approaches*. London, 1949.

MCNEAL, Robert H. *Lenin Stalin Krushchev: Voices of Bolshevism*. New Jersey, 1957.

MCNEAL, Robert H. 'Soviet Historiography on the October Revolution: A Review of Forty Years'. *American Slavic and East European Review*. Vol. XVII. No. 2. New York, October, 1958.

MCNEAL, Robert H. 'Caveat Lector. A Preface to Stalin's *Sochineniia*.' *Survey*, No. 49. London, October 1963.

MCNEAL, Robert H. *Stalin's Works. An Annotated Bibliography*. Stanford, 1967.

MAISKY, Ivan. *Journey into the Past*. Translated from the Russian by Frederick Holt. London, 1962.

MAISKY, Ivan. *Memoirs of a Soviet Ambassador. The War 1939-43*. London, 1967.

MARIE, Jean J. *Staline*. Paris, 1967.

MENON, K. P. S. *The Flying Troika*. London, 1963.

MOLOTOV, V. M. *Stalin and Stalin's Leadership*. Moscow, 1950.

MOLOTOV, V. M. *Speech at the Funeral of Joseph Vissarionovich Stalin*. Moscow, 1953.

'Monitor.' *The Death of Stalin*. London, 1933.

MONKHOUSE, Allan. *Moscow 1911–1933*. London, 1933.

MONTGOMERY OF ALAMEIN, Field-Marshal Viscount. *Memoirs*. London, 1958.

MORAN, Lord. *Winston Churchill: The Struggle for Survival 1940–1965*. London, 1966.

MURPHY, J. T. *Stalin 1879–1944*. Introduction by Sir Stafford Cripps. London, 1945.

Nazi–Soviet Relations 1939–1941. Documents from the Archives of the German Foreign Office. Edited by Raymond J. Sonntag and James S. Beddie. Washington, 1948.

NICOLAEVSKY, Boris I. *Power and the Soviet Elite*. Edited by Janet D. Zagoria. New York, 1965.

O'BALLANCE, Edgar. *The Red Army*. London, 1964.

ORLOV, Alexander. *The Secret History of Stalin's Crimes*. New York, 1953.

ORLOV, Alexander. 'The Sensational Secret Behind Damnation of Stalin.' *Life*, New York, 23 April, 1956.

PAYNE, Robert. *The Rise and Fall of Stalin*. New York, 1965. London, 1966.

PALOCZI-HORVATH, George. *Khrushchev: The Road to Power*. London, 1960.

People's Commissariat of Justice of the U.S.S.R. *Report of Court Proceedings in the Case of the Anti-Soviet 'Bloc of Rights and Trotskyites.'* Moscow, 1938.

PERKINS, Frances. *The Roosevelt I Knew*. London, 1947.

PETROV, Vladimir and Evdokia. *Empire of Fear*. London, 1956.

PIPES, Richard. *The Formation of the Soviet Union. Communism and Nationalism 1917–1923*. Cambridge, Mass., 1964.

POSSONY, Stefan, T. *Lenin: The Compulsive Revolutionary*. Chicago, 1964.

RANDALL, Francis B. *Stalin's Russia. An Historical Reconsideration*. New York, 1965.

RANSOME, Arthur. *Six Weeks in Russia in 1919*. London, 1919.

RANSOME, Arthur. *The Crisis in Russia*. London, 1921.

RAUCH, Georg von. *A History of Soviet Russia*. New York, 1958.

REED, John. *Ten Days that Shook the World*. New York, 1919 and 1967.

RIBBENTROP, J. von. *The Ribbentrop Memoirs*. Translated by Oliver Watson. London, 1954.

RIGBY, T. T. *The Stalin Dictatorship. Khrushchev's 'Secret Speech' and Other Documents*. Sydney, 1968.

ROOSEVELT, F. D. *Franklin D. Roosevelt and Foreign Affairs*. Edited by Edgar B. Nixon. 3 vols. Cambridge, Mass., 1969.

626

RUBIN, J. H. *Moscow Mirage*. London, 1935.

Royal Institute of International Affairs. *The Soviet-Yugoslav Dispute. Text of the Published Correspondence*. London and New York, 1948.

SALISBURY, Harrison E. *Stalin's Russia and After*. London, 1955.

SALISBURY, Harrison E. 'Stalin survivors tell their story.' *The Times*, London, 3 October, 1967.

SALISBURY, Harrison E. *The 900 Days The Siege of Leningrad*. New York, 1969. London, 1970.

SCHAPIRO, Leonard. *The Communist Party of the Soviet Union*. New York, 1960. London, 1970.

SCHELLENBERG, Walter. *The Schellenberg Memoirs*. Edited and translated by Louis Hagen. London, 1956.

SCHUELLER, George K. *The Politburo*. Stanford, 1951.

SEATON, Albert. *The Russo-German War 1941-45*. London, 1971.

SERGE, Victor. *From Lenin to Stalin*, New York, 1937.

SERGE, Victor. *Portrait de Staline*. Paris, 1940.

SERGE, Victor. *Memoirs of a Revolutionary 1901-1941*. London, 1963.

SHEPHERD, Gordon. *Russia's Danubian Empire*. London, 1954.

SHERIDAN, Clare. *Russian Portraits*. London, 1921.

SHERWOOD, Robert E. *The White House Papers of Harry L. Hopkins*. 2 vols. London, 1948-1949.

SHUB, David. *Lenin*. New York, 1948.

SHUKMAN, Harold. *Lenin and the Russian Revolution*. London, 1968.

SILVERLIGHT, John. *The Victors' Dilemma: Allied Intervention in the Russian Civil War*. London, 1970.

SMITH, Edward Ellis. *The Young Stalin. The Early Years of an Elusive Revolutionary*. New York, 1967. London, 1968.

SMITH, Edward Ellis. 'The Okhrana.' *The Russian Department of Police. A Bibliography*. Stanford, 1967.

SMITH, Edward Ellis. 'The Alliluyevs.' *Per-Se*. Vol. 3, No. 1. Stanford, 1968.

SMITH, Walter Bedell. *Moscow Mission 1946-1949*. London, 1950.

SOUVARINE, Boris. *Stalin: A Critical Survey of Bolshevism*. London, 1939.

SOUVARINE, Boris. *'Faux et Faussaires'* in *le Contrat Social*, Vol. XII, No. 4. Paris, December 1968.

STALIN, J. V. *Works*. 13 vols. Moscow, 1952-1955.

STALIN, J. V. *Sochineniia*. Vols XIV-XVI. Stanford, 1966.

STALIN, J. V. *Problems of Leninism*. Moscow, 1953.

STALIN, J. V. *War Speeches*. London, 1946.

STALIN, J. V. *Stalin's Kampf. Joseph Stalin's Credo Written by Himself*. Edited by M. R. Werner. London, 1940.

STALIN, J. V. *Stalin's Correspondence with Churchill, Attlee, Roosevelt and Truman 1941–1945.* 2 Vols. Moscow and London, 1957–1958.

STALIN, J. V. *For Peaceful Coexistence Postwar Interviews.* New York, 1951.

STALIN, J. V. *Josif Vissarionovich Stalin.* Commemorative Volume on his Seventieth Birthday. Moscow, 1949.

STERLING, Claire. *The Masaryk Case.* New York, 1969.

STETTINIUS, Edward R. Jr. *Roosevelt and the Russians. The Yalta Conference.* London, 1950.

STRANG, Lord. *Home and Abroad.* London, 1956.

STRIK-STRIKFELDT, Wilfried. *Against Stalin and Hitler. Memoir of the Russian Liberation Movement 1941–5.* Translated by David Footman. London, 1970.

SUKHANOV, N. N. *The Russian Revolution 1917.* London, 1955.

SVERDLOVA, K. T. *Jacob M. Sverdlov.* Translated by Pauline Rose. Moscow, 1945.

SVERDLOVA, K. T. *Yakov Mikhailovich Sverdlov.* Moscow, 1960.

SZAMUELY, T. 'The Elimination of Opposition between the Sixteenth and Seventeenth Congresses of the CPSU.' *Soviet Studies.* Vol. XVII, No. 3. Oxford, January 1966.

TANNER, Vaino. *The Winter War. Finland Against Russia 1939–1940.* Stanford, 1957.

TEDDER, Air Marshal Lord. *With Prejudice: War Memoirs.* London, 1966.

THOMSON, George Malcolm. *Vote of Censure.* London, 1968.

Tiflis Institut istorii partii. Istoricheskiy Mesta Tbilisi. Tiflis, 1944.

TOKAEV, G. A. *Stalin Means War.* London, 1951.

TOKAEV, G. A. *Betrayal of an Ideal.* London, 1954.

TOKAEV, G. A. *Comrade X.* Translated by Alec Brown. London, 1956.

TOVSTUKHA, I. P. *Josif Vissarionovich Stalin. Kratkya Biografia.* Moscow, 1927.

TROTSKY, Leon. *Stalin. An Appraisal of the Man and his Influence.* Translated from the Russian by Charles Malamuth. London, 1947.

TROTSKY, Leon. *My Life. The Rise and Fall of a Dictator.* London, 1930.

TROTSKY, Leon. *Trotsky's Dairy in Exile 1935.* Translated from the Russian by Elena Zarudnaya. London, 1959.

TROTSKY, Leon. *The Trotsky Papers.* Edited by J. Meijer. Vol. I. The Hague, 1964.

TROTSKY, Leon. *The Stalin School of Falsification.* Translated by John G. Wright. New York, 1962.

TROTSKY, Leon. *The History of the Russian Revolution.* London, 1936.

TRUMAN, Harry S. *Year of Decisions 1945.* London, 1955.

TRUMAN, Harry S. *Years of Trial and Hope 1946–1953.* London, 1956.

ULAM, Adam B. *Lenin and the Bolsheviks.* London, 1966.

United States Senate Committee on the Judiciary. *Hearings before the Subcommittee to investigate the Scope of Soviet Activity in the United States.* Part 66. Washington, 1957.

URATADZE, Gregory. *Reminiscences of a Georgian Social Democrat.* In Russian with an English Preface by Leopold Haimson. Stanford, 1968.

VAKAR, N. 'Stalin po vospinaniyam N. N. Zhordania.' *Posledniya Novosti.* Paris, 16 December, 1936.

VERESHCHAK, Semyen. 'Stalin v Tyurme.' *Dni.* Paris, 22–24 January, 1928.

VOROSHILOV, K. E. *Stalin and the Armed Forces of the USSR.* Moscow, 1951.

WELLES, Sumner. *Seven Major Decisions.* London, 1951.

WERTH, Alexander. *Russia at War 1941–1945.* London, 1964.

WOLFE, Bertram D. *Three who Made a Revolution: A Biographical History.* London, 1956.

WOLFE, Bertram D. *Khrushchev and Stalin's Ghost.* New York and London, 1957.

WOLFE, Bertram D. *Strange Communists I Have Known.* London, 1966.

WOLIN, Simon, and SLUSSER, Robert M. *The Soviet Secret Police.* New York, 1957.

WOODWARD, Sir Llewellyn. *British Foreign Policy in the Second World War.* London, 1962.

WOODWARD, Sir Llewellyn. *British Foreign Policy in the Second World War.* Vol. I. London, 1970.

Wrecking Activities at Power Stations in the Soviet Union. The Case of L. C. Thornton, W. L. MacDonald, J. Cushny, A. Monkhouse, C. Nordwall, A. W. Gregory, A. S. Kutuzova and eleven others. Moscow, 1933.

YAKIR, Peter. 'Stalin: A Plea for a Criminal Investigation.' *Survey.* No. 70/71. London, Winter/Spring 1969.

YAROSLASKY, E. *Landmarks in the Life of Stalin.* London, 1942.

YENUKIDZE, A. 'Leaves from my Reminiscences'. *The Life of Stalin: A Symposium.* London, 1930.

YOUNG, Gordon. *Stalin's Heirs.* London, 1953.

YOUNG, Kenneth. *Churchill and Beaverbrook.* London, 1966.

ZHGENTI, Leontii, *Prichiny revolutsii na Kavkaze i rukovodstvo.* Paris, 1963.

ZHUKOV, Georgi K. *Marshal Zhukov's Greatest Battles.* Edited by Harrison E. Salisbury. London, 1969.

Sources and Notes

Chapter I   The Education of a Revolutionary

1 Leon Trotsky. *Stalin* (1947), p. 1.
2 S. and A. Alliluyev. *The Alliluyev Memoirs* (1968). Edited by David Tutaev, pp. 36–7.
3 Essad-Bey. *Stalin* (1932), p. 7.
4 L. P. Beria. *On the History of the Bolshevik Organisations in Transcaucasia* (1949), pp. 193–4.
5 H. R. Knickerbocker. 'Stalin. Mystery Man even to his Mother', *New York Evening Post*, 1 December 1930. V. Kaminsky and I. Vereshchagin. *'Destvo i iunost Vozhdia: dokumenty, zapisi, rasskazy'*, in *Molodaya gvardia*, No. 12. (Moscow, 1939).
6 J. Iremashvili. *Stalin und die Tragodie Georgiens* (Berlin, 1932), *passim*.
7 E. Yaroslavsky. *Landmarks in the Life of Stalin* (1942), p. 7.
8 Svetlana Alliluyeva. *Twenty Letters to a Friend* (1967), p. 203. Harrison Salisbury. *Stalin's Russia and After* (1955), p. 95. Henry Kamm. 'Stalin's Russia Georgian Hero', *New York Times*, 6 April 1965.
9 G. Uratadze. *Reminiscences of a Georgian Social Democrat* (in Russian) (Stanford, 1968), p. 209. Alliluyeva, *loc. cit.* Knickerbocker, *loc cit.* Alliluyev, pp. 122–3.
10 J. V. Stalin. *Works* (1951–55), I, p. 415. G. F. Alexandrov and

others. *Joseph Stalin* (1949), p. 5. Yaroslovsky, p. 7. Trotsky, p. 6. Yves Delbars. *The Real Stalin* (1953), p. 17.

11 Edward Ellis Smith. *The Young Stalin* (1967), p. 18 and sources there cited.

12 Cited Isaac Deutscher. *Stalin: A Political Biography* (1949), p. 3. Smith, p. 27.

13 Svetlana Alliluyeva. *Only One Year* (1969), p. 360.

14 Knickerbocker, *loc. cit.* Essad-Bey, p. 17.

15 Stalin, I. p. 317.

16 Delbars, p. 21.

17 Yaroslavsky, pp. 8–9.

18 Delbars, p. 22.

19 D. M. Lang. *A Modern History of Georgia* (1962), pp. 122–4. Beria, p. 13ff. Iremashvili, cited Smith, pp. 32–3.

20 Stalin, XIII, pp. 115–16.

21 Yaroslavsky, pp. 111–18. *Finskii Vestnik*, 17 December 1900, cited Francis B. Randall. *Stalin's Russia* (1965) pp. 10–11.

22 Beria, 29.

23 Yaroslavsky, p. 24.

24 Boris Souvarine, *Stalin* (1939), p. 32. *Stalin's Kampf* (1940), p. 17.

25 Cited Smith, pp. 52–53.

26 Yaroslavsky, p. 16.

27 Yaroslavsky, p. 18. Stalin, I, p. 416. Alexandrov, p. 9.

28 Essad-Bey, p. 30. Souvarine, p. 112.

29 Yaroslavsky, p. 18.

30 Yaroslavsky, p. 25.

31 Alliluyev, pp. 28–30.

32 Beria, pp. 31–2.

33 Henri Barbusse. *Stalin* (1955), pp. 18–19.

34 Yaroslavsky, p. 27.

35 Beria, pp. 32–3.

36 Alexandrov, p. 13.

37 Delbars, p. 33.

38 Alliluyev, pp. 49–51.

39 *Iskra* No. 6, July 1901 : cited Beria, p. 34.

40 Delbars, p. 35. Krassin was employed at an electric power station in Baku at this time. In June–July 1901, Lenin wrote from Germany to L. E. Halperin, another agent in Baku who was working with Krassin : 'As for organising *Iskra* in the Caucasus ... it is essential for us to know what the plan is – a legal or illegal printing press, how near it is to realisation, for how much printed material it is

intended (can *Iskra* be a monthly?) how much money they need at once and how much a month. Our cash position at present is very bad ... Do your utmost to get money': *The Letters of Lenin* (1937), pp. 146–7.

41 Cited Smith, p. 84.
42 Yaroslavsky, pp. 26–7.
43 Stalin, I, pp. 24–6.
44 Yaroslavsky, p. 27. Beria, p. 35 and note.
45 Trotsky, p. 30.
46 Cited Smith, p. 89. Yaroslavsky, p. 28.
47 Uratadze, p. 67.

Chapter II   In the Bolshevik Underground

 1 Smith, p. 93.
 2 Yaroslavsky, p. 30. Smith, p. 99.
 3 N. Lakoba. *Stalin i Kashim 1901–1902* (1934), *passim*. After the outbreak of war in 1914 Kashim left Batum and his house was occupied by troops, who found the press which Kashim had buried. Finding it of no interest, they threw the pieces about the garden, where Kashim retrieved them on his return in 1917 and asked his son to keep them in memory of Stalin, since the press 'helped to make the Revolution'.
 4 Barbusse, p. 23.
 5 Souvarine, p. 44.
 6 Souvarine, p. 44. Smith, p. 104.
 7 Trotsky, pp. 33–4.
 8 Trotsky, p. 37.
 9 *Batumskaya demonstratsiya goda 1902* (Moscow 1937), p. 215.
10 Smith, p. 390.
11 Alliluyev, pp. 63–4.
12 Robert Payne. *The Rise and Fall of Stalin* (London 1966), p. 85.
13 Deutscher, pp. 58–59.
14 *Batumskaya demonstratsiya*, p. 111.
15 Stalin, I, p. 420. Alexandrov, p. 16. Yaroslavsky, p. 35. Alliluyev, p. 65. Smith, p. 111.
16 Smith, p. 112.
17 Stalin, VI, p. 54.
18 Trotsky, p. 49. Stalin, I, p. 420. Smith, p. 116.
19 Delbars, p. 42.
20 Barbusse, p. 25. Alliluyev, p. 65.
21 Yaroslavasky, p. 34. Trotsky, pp. 43, 45.

22 Police Circular No. 5500 dated 1 May 1904, on file at the Hoover Institution.
23 Alliluyev, pp. 65–6.
24 Yaroslavsky, pp. 36–7. Alliluyev, p. 59.
25 Trostky, pp. 85–6. Delbars, p. 46. Wolfe, p. 449. Svetlana Alliluyeva. *Only One Year*, p. 367. Iremashvili states that the marriage took place in 1903, which was when he was in prison, and although according to Trotsky cases of prison marriages were 'not rare', the date given by Iremashvili may well be a slip for 1904. The police circular dated 1 May 1904 (see note 22 above) described him as a bachelor as of that date.
26 Iremashvili, pp. 30–9.
27 S. Alliluyev. *Proidennyi Put* (Moscow 1946), pp. 132–4.
28 Yaroslavsky, p. 40. Stalin, I, p. 421, pp. 55–8.
29 Cited Payne. *The Life and Death of Lenin* (London 1964), p. 178.
30 Stalin, I, pp. 31–54.
31 Leontii Zhgenti. *Prichiny revolutsii na Kavkaze i rukovodstvo* (1963), pp. 23–7.
32 Arsenidze, cited Smith, pp. 122, 128, 135.
33 Stephen Gwynn (ed.) *The Letters and Friendships of Sir Cecil Spring Rice* (London 1929), pp. 425–6.
34 Stalin, I, pp. 90–132. Arsenidze, cited Smith, p. 135.
35 Yaroslavsky, p. 51. Stalin, I, p. 423.
36 Essad-Bey, pp. 64–65.
37 Trotsky, p. 67. Stalin, I, pp. 195–7, 405.
38 Trotsky, p. 63. Souvarine, p. 110. Arsenidze, cited Smith, p. 143.
39 Beria, p. 137.
40 Yaroslavsky, p. 52. Stalin, I, p. 424. Smith, p. 147.
41 Stalin, VI, p. 56. Yaroslavsky, p. 53.
42 Yaroslavsky, p. 52. Smith, p. 149.
43 Beria, p. 150.
44 Deutscher, pp. 80–1.
45 Stalin, I, pp. 198–207.
46 Stalin, I, pp. 208–215.
47 Essad-Bey, pp. 71–75. Souvarine, p. 100. Trotsky, p. 101.
48 David Shub, cited Smith, p. 203. Souvarine, pp. 92, 101.
49 Cited Smith, p. 161. Trotsky, p. 447.
50 R. Arsenidze. '*Iz Vospominanii o Staline*' in *Novy Zhurnal* No. 72 (New York, June 1963), p. 222.
51 Isaac Don Levine. *Stalin's Great Secret* (New York, 1956), p. 61.
52 Smith, pp. 170–1. Levine, p. 75.
53 Uratadze, cited Smith, p. 396.

54 Smith, pp. 162, 174-5. Alliluyev, p. 60.
55 Stalin, I, pp. 238-40. Deutscher, pp. 82-3.
56 Stalin, II, pp. 28-32.
57 N. Krupskaya. *Memoirs of Lenin* (1930), I, pp. 75-6. Barbusse, pp. 43-4. Smith, pp. 194, 199.
58 *Daily Express*, London, 10 May 1907.
59 Litvinov, p. 134.
60 Stalin, III, pp. 47-80. Payne, *Lenin*, pp. 212-16. Trotsky, p. 90. Report No. 170 of 15 May NS 1907: Okhrana Collection, Hoover Institution.
61 Stalin, VI, pp. 58-9.
62 Trotsky, p. 92.
63 Wolfe, p. 385. Angelica Balabanoff. *My Life as a Rebel* (London 1938), p. 90. Trotsky, *My Life*, p. 175. Ivan Maisky, *Journey Into the Past* (London, 1962), pp. 137-44.
64 *Justice*, London, 1 June 1907.
65 Essad-Bey, p. 82. Souvarine, p. 97. Frank Owen, *The Three Dictators* (1940), pp. 114-15.
66 Trotsky, pp. 106-7.
67 Emil Ludwig, *Stalin* (1942), pp. 42-3.
68 N. Krupskaya. *Memories of Lenin* (1933), II, p. 12. Trotsky, p. 110.
69 Wolfe, pp. 470-1.
70 Stalin, II, pp. 42-6. Alliluyev, *Proidemnyi Put* (1946), pp. 132-4. *Krasny Arkhiv* (1934), No. 2, p. 3.
71 Stalin, II, pp. 81-3, 398, 425.
72 Stalin, XIII, p. 124. Robert E. Sherwood. *The White House Papers of Harry L. Hopkins* (1949), II, p. 777. Lord Moran. *Winston Churchill* (1966), p. 275.
73 Iremashvili, p. 40. Trotsky, p. 87. According to Delbars (*op. cit.* 52) Ekaterina Djugashvili died on 10 April 1907; but this does not accord with Alliluyev's statement that he visited her and her husband in Baku in July of that year.

Chapter III   Prison and Exile
1 Yaroslavsky, pp. 57-8.
2 Stalin, II, pp. 424-5.
3 Stalin, II, p. 111.
4 S. Vereshchak. '*Stalin v tinorme*'. *Dni*. Paris, 22 January 1928.
5 *id.*, 25 January 1928.
6 Cited Smith, p. 216.
7 Stalin, II, pp. 427-8. Smith, p. 221.
8 Beria, pp. 224-5.

9 Zhgenti, pp. 58–62.
10 Smith, p. 231.
11 Beria, p. 225.
12 Stalin, II, p. 430.
13 Stalin, II, pp. 215–18.
14 Cited Smith, pp. 235–6 from police intercept on file at the Hoover Institution.
15 Cited Smith, p. 240.
16 Stalin, II, p. 461. Smith, p. 243.
17 Alliluyev, pp. 132–5.
18 Stalin, II, p. 431.
19 Smith, p. 247.
20 David Shub. *Lenin* (New York, 1948), p. 117.
21 Stalin, II, p. 432.
22 Stalin, II, pp. 219–24.
23 Stalin, II, p. 225.
24 Stalin, II, p. 434. Souvarine, p. 133. Vereshchak, *Dni*, 24 January 1928.
25 Alliluyev, pp. 139–40.
26 Stalin, II, pp. 257–9, 413.
27 Smith, p. 264, citing A. Shotman.
28 Alliluyev, pp. 142–4. Stanislaw Kot. *Conversations with the Kremlin and Dispatches for Russia* (London, 1963), pp. xxiii–xxv.
29 Trotsky, p. 147. Stalin, II, pp. 278–94.
30 Cited Smith, p. 291. Stalin, II, pp. 417–18.
31 Trotsky Archives, cited Deutscher. *The Prophet Armed* (1954), p. 209. Letter to Malinovsky, cited Smith, p. 276 from police intercept on file at the Hoover Institution.
32 Stalin, II, pp. 300–81, 417.
33 Shub, pp. 121–2. Smith, p. 299, citing A. Shotman.
34 Stalin, II, p. 438.
35 Smith, pp. 300–01, citing police intercepts at the Hoover Institution.
36 'The Department of Police 1911–13. The Recollections of Nikolai Vladiminovich Veselego': TS transcribed from tape-recording by Ellis Tennant (Edward Ellis Smith) in 1962 and preserved in the Hoover Institution.
37 Alexander Orlov, 'The Sensational Secret Behind Damnation of Stalin': *Life*, New York, 23 April 1956. (International edition, 14 May, 1956).
38 Alliluyev, pp. 190, 217–18.
39 Stalin, cited Smith, p. 309.
40 Moran, p. 204.

41 Yaroslavsky, p. 84–5.
42 Trotsky, p. 171. Alliluyev, p. 145.
43 Yaroslavsky, pp. 86–7.
44 Trotsky, p. 175–7.
45 Alliluyev, p. 145.
46 Yaroslavsky, p. 88. Alliluyev, p. 189.
47 Baikaloff, p. 27–9.
48 Smith, p. 324, citing *Leninsky sbornik*, III, p. 271.

Chapter IV   Revolution and Civil War
1 Alliluyev, p. 186 ff.
2 Krupskaya, II, p. 233.
3 Cited Smith, p. 332.
4 Payne, p. 180.
5 Alexandrov, p. 50. Yaroslavsky, p. 94. Stalin, III, p. 440.
6 *Pravda,* June 16, 1936: cited Alexandrov, p. 52.
7 Vereshchak, *Dni*, January 24, 1928. Trotsky, p. 207.
8 F. Raskolnikov, cited Smith, p. 333.
9 Krupskaya, II, pp. 232–5.
10 Alliluyev, pp. 207–11.
11 Alliluyev, p. 212 ff.
12 Payne, p. 193.
13 Trotsky, pp. 220–1.
14 E. H. Wilcox 'The Secret Police of the Old Regime', in *Fortnightly Review*, December, 1917.
15 W. H. Chamberlin. *The Russian Revolution 1917–1921* (1935), I. p. 217. Smith, p. 356.
16 Alliluyev, pp. 213–14, 220–21.
17 Alliluyev, p. 223.
18 N. N. Sukhanov. *The Russian Revolution 1917* (1955), p. 556. Chamberlin, II, p. 292.
19 Trotsky, p. 230.
20 Lubov Krassin. *Leonid Krassin His Life and Work* (1929), pp. 54–5.
21 Trotsky, p. 236.
22 John Reed, *op. cit.* (1967), pp. 186, 345.
23 Sukhanov, pp. 229–30.
24 Alliluyev, pp. 225–6.
25 Chamberlin, I, p. 318. Trotsky. *The History of the Russian Revolution* (1936), p. 1048 ff.
26 Alliluyev, p. 226.
27 Shub, p. 253.
28 Reed, p. 186. Chamberlin, I, p. 327.

29 Shub, p. 255.
30 Trotsky, pp. 243-4.
31 Reed, p. 347.
32 Trotsky, p. 245.
33 Reed, pp. 358-61. Chamberlin, I, p. 352.
34 Trotsky, p. 246.
35 Alexander Kerensky. *The Kerensky Memoirs* (1966), pp. 445-6.
36 Stalin, IV, p. 4.
37 Kerensky, p. 457.
38 Chamberlin, I, p. 363. Sir George Buchanan. *My Mission to Russia and Other Diplomatic Memories* (1923), II, p. 233 ff.
39 Simon Wollin and Robert M. Slusser. *The Soviet Secret Police* (1957), p. 3 ff.
40 Trotsky, pp. 247-8.
41 Krassin, p. 74.
42 Chamberlin, I, pp. 368-70.
43 Svetlana Alliluyeva. *Twenty Letters to a Friend*, p. 90.
44 Trotsky. *My Life*, pp. 311-57.
45 Trotsky, *id.*, pp. 301-2.
46 Trotsky. *Stalin*, p. 255. Victor Alexandrov. *The Kremlin* (1963), pp. 249-50. Delbars, p. 120 ('Stalin himself was greatly interested in poisons').
47 Pestkovsky, cited Trotsky, pp. 256-7. J. Bernard Hutton. *Stalin The Miraculous Georgian* (1961), pp. 61-2.
48 Trotsky, pp. 182-5.
49 Stalin IV, p. 118.
50 Shub, p. 316.
51 Stalin, IV, pp. 120-1.
52 Stalin, IV, pp. 122-3.
53 Trotsky, pp. 289-90.
54 Souvarine, p. 226.
55 Sir Thomas Preston. 'Last Days of the Tsar': *Sunday Telegraph*, 14 July 1968. Preston was British Consul in Ekaterinburg at the time. 'It was Tchoutskaev, the Deputy Head of the Regional Soviet, that I mostly saw in representations on the Royal Family's behalf.' Preston afterwards wrote in the above article: 'Tchoutskaev told me that the Soviet greatly resented my representations on behalf of the Royal Family. He also said that Anglo-American troops had landed at Archangel and he did not recognise me as Consul as I represented a power with which they were at war. In fact, he once said he did not know whether to confer with me or shoot me! . . . I hit back as best I could. As a parting shot I once reminded him

that his Comrade Litvinov was still in our British gaol in Reading. Perhaps the hint went home ... In the end no amount of persuasion or bluff or personal contacts was of any avail. By the middle of July the White Army and the Czech Legion, which was also fighting the Bolsheviks, had advanced so close to Ekaterinburg that we could hear their guns booming on the outskirts of the town. This sealed the Tsar's fate.'

56 Stalin, IV, pp. 130–2.
57 Payne, pp. 230–1.
58 Trotsky, pp. 288–91. *Trotsky Papers* (1964), I, p. 135.
59 *Trotsky Papers*, I, pp. 159–61. Sverdlov's letter is mistakenly attributed to Lenin by Trotsky in his autobiography and also in his *Stalin*.
60 *Trotsky Papers*, I, p. 167.
61 C. H. Ellis. *The Transcaspian Episode* 1918–1919 (1963), pp. 57–65; also Ellis's 'Operations in Transcaspia 1918–1919 and the 26 Commissars Case' in *St Antony's Papers* No. 6 pp. 129–47.
62 Stalin, IV, pp. 261–5.
63 Bertram D. Wolfe. *Strange Communists I Have Known* (1966), pp. 191–5.
64 Trotsky, p. 293. Stalin, IV, p. 190.
65 Trotsky, pp. 295–7.
66 Stalin, IV, p. 222.
67 Deutscher, pp. 230–1. Leonard Schapiro. *The Communist Party and the Soviet Union* (1960), pp. 34–41, 606.
68 Elizabeth Lermolo. *Face of a Victim* (1956), pp. 218–20. Delbars, p. 112.
69 Krassin, p. 105.
70 Peter Fleming. *The Fate of Admiral Kolchak* (1963), p. 133.
71 Edgar O'Ballance. *The Red Army* (1965), p. 59.
72 Trotsky. *My Life*, pp. 369–70.

Chapter V   Struggle for Power
1 Trotsky. *Stalin*, p. 326.
2 Trotsky, p. 329.
3 Alexander Barmine. *One Who Survived* (New York 1945), p. 79.
4 Trotsky, p. 329.
5 Trotsky, p. 354.
6 Trotsky, p. 359. Uratadze, pp. 68–9.
7 Trotsky, p. 267.
8 Lang. *A Modern History of Georgia*, p. 239.
9 Iremashvili, cited Trotsky, p. 360.

10 Yaroslavsky, p. 127.

11 Lang, p. 242.

12 Deutscher, *Stalin*, p. 222.

13 Yaroslavsky, p. 128.

14 Deutscher, p. 233.

15 Barbusse, p. 135.

16 Schapiro, pp. 245–6.

17 Trotsky, *Stalin*, p. 357; *My Life*, p. 398.

18 Yaroslavsky, p. 129.

19 Deutscher, p. 234.

20 Stalin, V, p. 443. Alexandrov, p. 75. Deutscher, p. 232.

21 Trotsky. *My Life*, p. 475. Stalin, IV, pp. 136–9. 'Comrade Lenin on Vacation' appeared in an illustrated Supplement to *Pravda* on 15 September 1922.

22 Moshe Lewin. *Lenin's Last Struggle* (1959), pp. 35–7.

23 Lewin, p. 43 ff.

24 Lenin. *Collected Works*, XLII, p. 421.

25 P. N. Pospelov, cited Lewin, pp. 51–2.

26 Lewin, pp. 33–4.

27 Lenin, XLII, pp. 463–94.

28 Lewin, pp. 55–6. Pipes, p. 281.

29 Cited Lewin, p. 68.

30 Lenin. *Sochineniia*, pp. 327–8.

31 *id*, pp. 674–5. The text of this letter stated to be in the Party Central Archives in the Marx–Lenin Institute was first quoted by Khrushchev in his 'secret' speech in the Twentieth Party Congress, 24 February 1956.

32 Lenin, XXXVI, pp. 593–7.

33 Stalin, V, p. 161.

34 Lenin, pp. 605–11. Pipes, pp. 282–7. Lang, p. 242.

35 Fotieva. *Pages from Lenin's Life*, p. 177.

36 Fotieva, pp. 178–9. Lenin, XLII, pp. 433–40. Schapiro, p. 228..

37 Lenin, XLII, p. 484. Fotieva, p. 181.

38 Fotieva, cited Lewin, p. 95.

39 Trotsky, *Stalin*, pp. 376–8. *Trotsky's Diary in Exile*, p. 44.

40 Fotieva, p. 192.

41 Trotsky, pp. 374–5.

42 Lenin, XLII, p. 493.

43 Trotsky, p. 361.

44 Lenin. *Sochineniia*, LIV, pp. 329–30. The text of this letter was first publicly revealed by Khrushchev in his 'secret' speech to the Twentieth Party Congress, 24 February 1956.

45 Trotsky, pp. 363–4.
46 Trotsky. *My Life*, p. 413. Deutscher. *The Prophet Unarmed*, p. 91.
47 Lenin. *Collected Works*, XLII, pp. 493–4.
48 Fotieva, p. 193.
49 Lewin, p. 103.
50 Souvarine, p. 322.
51 Wolfe. *Khrushchev and Stalin's Ghost* (1957), pp. 277–9.
52 Trotsky, p. 362.
53 Stalin, V, pp. 227–40.
54 *id*, pp. 257–8.
55 Souvarine, p. 485.
56 Stalin, V, p. 308 ff.
57 Trotsky, p. 417. Pipes, pp. 250–2. Schapiro, p. 348.
58 Boris Bajanov. *Avec Staline dans le Kremline* (1930), pp. 26–7.
59 Levine, p. 226. Payne, pp. 322–3.
60 Deutscher. *The Prophet Unarmed*, p. 112.
61 Bajanov, pp. 76–7.
62 Trotsky, cited Deutscher, p. 118. Levine, p. 229.
63 Deutscher, p. 132.
64 Delbars, p. 130. Trotsky, pp. 381–2.
65 Lermolo, pp. 136–7.
66 Trotsky. *Stalin*, p. 381.
67 Delbars, pp. 129–30.
68 Stalin, VI, p. 52.
69 Deutscher. *Stalin*, p. 269.
70 Yaroslavsky, p. 133.
71 Deutscher, pp. 272–3. Delbars, p. 133.
72 Schapiro, p. 284. Robert Conquest. *The Great Terror* (1968), p. 15.
73 Stalin, VI, pp. 338–73.
74 *id.*, VII, pp. 6–10.
75 *id.*, VII, p. 390. Trotsky. *My Life*, p. 442.
76 Delbars, pp. 134–5. Trotsky. *My Life*, p. 126.
77 Trotsky. *My Life*, p. 445.
78 Delbars, pp. 144–5.
79 Trotsky. *Stalin*, p. 418.
80 S. Borisov. *Frunze* (Moscow 1940), p. 301.
81 Deutscher. *Stalin*, p. 306. Stalin, VII, p. 256.
82 Deutscher, p. 307. Trotsky. *Stalin*, p. 417.
83 Delbars, p. 150. Deutscher, pp. 309–10.
84 Stalin, X, pp. 177–82.
85 Delbars, p. 152. Deutscher. *The Prophet Unarmed*, pp. 380–4.
86 Stalin, X, p. 367.

87 Wollin and Slusser, p. 13. Delbars, pp. 152-4.
88 Souvarine, p. 476.
89 *id.*, pp. 482-5. Deutscher. *Stalin*, p. 313.
90 Delbars, p. 159.
91 Stalin, XI, pp. 289, 297.
92 *id.*, XI, p. 229.
93 Deutscher, pp. 316-17. Schapiro, p. 376.
94 Souvarine, p. 509.
95 A. Yenukidze. 'Leaves from my Reminiscences in *The Life of Stalin: A Symposium* (London, 1930), p. 96.
96 Stalin, XII, p. 146.
97 A. Avtorkhanov. *Stalin and the Communist Party*, p. 157.

Chapter VI   A Domestic Tragedy
1 British Foreign Office Archives. Russia. N247/247/38. Chilston to Eden, 1 January 1937.
2 Barmine. *One Who Survived*, pp. 209-15. Khrushchev describes a similar incident where a young Soviet diplomat in Latin America was summoned home to appear before the Politburo for having giving an indiscreet press interview: *Krushchev Remembers*, p. 50.
3 Nicolaevsky. *Power and the Soviet Elite*, pp. 28-30, 93 ff.
4 Avtorkhanov. *Stalin and the Soviet Communist Party*, p. 102 ff.
5 Lermolo. *Face of a Victim*, pp. 280-1.
6 Levine. *Stalin*, p. 337.
7 Bajanov. *Avec Staline dans le Kremline*, p. 24.
8 Nicolaevsky, p. 109.
9 Avtorkhanov, p. 105.
10 Orlov. *The Secret History of Stalin's Crimes*, pp. 338-42.
11 H. G. Wells. *Experiment in Autobiography* (London 1934), II, p. 804.
12 *Stalin-Wells Talk. The Verbatim Record* (London 1934), p. 17.
13 St John Ervine. *Bernard Shaw* (London 1956), p. 518.
14 Hesketh Pearson. *G. B. S. A Full Length Portrait* (New York 1942), pp. 329-31. Moran, p. 58.
15 Eugene Lyons, *Assignment in Utopia* (London 1938), pp. 387-8. Louis Fischer. *The Life and Death of Stalin* (London 1953), p. 106.
16 Stalin. *Works*, XIII, p. 109.
17 Walter Duranty. *Stalin & Co.* (London 1949), 39.
18 Stalin. XIII, p. 122.
19 *Finskii Vestnik*, cited Francis B. Randall. *Stalin's Russia*, pp. 75-7.
20 John Gunther. *Inside Europe*, p. 532. This story may well be apocryphal

21 Stalin, XIII pp. 107–25.
22 Lyons, p. 388.
23 Levine, p. 325. S. Alliluyeva. *Twenty Letters to a Friend*, p. 101.
24 Essad-Bey. *Stalin*, p. 369.
25 S. Alliluyeva, pp. 95–8, 19 ff.
26 Bajanov, p. 120.
27 Alliluyeva, pp. 103–4.
28 Orlov, pp. 316–18.
29 Litvinov. *Notes for a Journal*, pp. 63, 95, 149, 188–90. Lermolo, pp. 228–9.
30 S. Alliluyeva, pp. 108–10.
31 Lermolo, pp. 229–32.
32 S. Alliluyeva, pp. 112–14. Svetlana's statement that her father 'didn't even go to the funeral' is untrue. The fact of the letter to Stalin from his wife was mentioned in an article in the Russian emigré journal *Posledniye Novosti*, 8 August 1934.
33 Litvinov, pp. 191–2. Lermolo, p. 289.
34 Orlov, pp. 319–20.
35 *Izvestia*, 12 November 1932.
36 Stalin, XIII, p. 147.
37 S. Alliluyeva, pp. 113–14.

Chapter VII First Five Year Plan
1 Stalin, XIII, p. 41. *Problems of Leninism*, p. 356.
2 Lyons, pp. 458–64.
3 Winston Churchill. *'The Second World War*, IV, pp. 447–8.
4 *Pravda*, 2 March 1930: Stalin, XII, pp. 197–205. Souvarine, p. 524.
5 Stalin, XII, p. 214.
6 Deutscher. *Stalin*, p. 331
7 Lincoln Hutchinson MS 'American Engineers in Russia': Hoover Institution, HD 70, R9, H97.
8 Souvarine, p. 531. Orlov, p. 153.
9 Avtorkhanov, pp. 28–9. Conquest, p. 549.
10 Stalin, XI, pp. 57, 67–8.
11 Lyons, p. 114 ff.
12 Stalin, XIII, p. 17. T. Szamuely. 'The Elimination of Opposition between the Sixteenth and Seventeenth Congresses of the CPSU.' Soviet Studies, XVII, pp. 318–38. (Oxford, January 1966).
13 Lyons, p. 370 ff.
14 *Documents on British Foreign Policy 1919–1939*. Edited by E. C. Woodward and Rohan Butler. 2nd Series. Vol. VII, p. 186. (London 1958).

15 Souvarine, pp. 529–30. Conquest, p. 552.
16 Szamuely. *Soviet Studies*, XVII, p. 333.
17 Stalin, XIII, pp. 74–5.
18 *id.*, XIII, p. 212.
19 Lord Strang. *Home and Abroad* (London 1956), p. 78 ff. Alan Monkhouse. *Moscow 1911–1933* (London 1933), *passim. Wrecking Activities at Power Stations in the Soviet Union. Verbatim Report of the Moscow Trial* (Moscow 1933), *passim.* A. J. Cummings. *The Moscow Trial* (London 1933), *passim,* Lyons, pp. 561–71.
20 *Documents on British Foreign Policy*, 2nd Series, Vol. VII, p. 456.
21 Conquest, p. 555.
22 John Pearson. *The Life of Ian Fleming* (London 1966), pp. 69–70.
23 S. Alliluyeva, p. 20. Gunther, p. 532.
24 Victor Serge. *Portrait de Staline* (Paris 1940), p. 95.
25 Nicolaevsky, p. 73. Jack Fishman and Bernard Hutton. *The Private Life of Josif Stalin* (London 1962), p. 115.
26 Deutscher, pp. 348–50.
27 Nicolaevsky, p. 31.
28 *Foreign Relations of the United States. Diplomatic Papers. The Soviet Union 1933–1939* (Washington 1952), pp. 59–60.
29 Farnsworth, p. 110 ff, p. 177.
30 Stalin, XIII, pp. 288–9, 313–14, 379.
31 Nicolaevsky, p. 33.
32 Schapiro, pp. 397–8. Nicolaevsky, p. 92.
33 *Pravda*, 18 February 1934.
34 G. A. Tokaev. *Betrayal of an Ideal* (London 1934), p. 166.
35 Stalin, XIII, p. 354–5.
36 Rigby, p. 37.

Chapter VIII   The Kirov Affair
1 Conquest, p. 39. Nicolaevsky, p. 90.
2 Stalin. *Problems of Leninism* (1953), p. 757. Kennan. *Russia and the West under Lenin and Stalin,* p. 292 ff.
3 Orlov, pp. 24–7.
4 Conquest, pp. 41–2.
5 Orlov, pp. 27–8.
6 Conquest, p. 43 ff. Nicolaevsky, p. 69 ff. Orlov, p. 28 ff.
7 T. H. Rigby. *The Stalin Dictatorship* (1959), pp. 38–9.
8 Orlov, p. 35.
9 Rigby, pp. 97–8.

10 W. G. Krivitsky. *I Was Stalin's Agent* (1939), p. 206. *Bukharin Trial. The Case of the 'Anti-Soviet Bloc of Rights and Trotskyites'* (Moscow 1938), pp. 522, 376.

11 Lermolo. *Face of a Victim*, pp. 13–31.

12 *id.*, pp. 50–1, 163–4.

13 Orlov, p. 37.

14 Conquest, p. 58. Orlov, p. 38.

15 Conquest, p. 59.

16 Krivitsky, p. 208.

17 *id.*, p. 18.

18 *id.*, pp. 30–1.

19 Earl of Avon. *The Eden Memoirs. Facing the Dictators* (1962), p. 124 ff.

20 Fitzroy Maclean. *Eastern Approaches* (1949), p. 18.

21 Foreign Office Records. Viscount Chilston to Sir John Simon, 22 February 1935: N 1017/6/38.

22 Joseph E. Davies. *Misson to Moscow* (1941), pp. 67–8.

23 Avon, p. 155.

24 Eden to Foreign Office (telegram) 30 March, 1935. F.O. 371/19468.

25 Avon, p. 155.

26 Chilston to Eden 31 January 1936: F.O.371/20352.

27 Avon, pp. 157–62.

28 Charles to Simon, 13 June 1935: N3140/160/38.

29 Edgar B. Nixon (ed). *Franklin D. Roosevelt and Foreign Affairs* 1969), II, p. 493, III, p. 207. British Foreign Office Archives, Russia. N2647/53/30.

30 Churchill, I, p. 105.

31 Delbars, p. 206.

32 Deutscher. *Stalin*, p. 420.

33 Kennan, p. 304.

34 Orlov, pp. 72–3.

35 Lermolo, pp. 205 ff, 225–6. Orlov, p. 311.

36 Orlov, pp. 312–13.

37 For a critical analysis of the various editions of Beria's works and how they changed over the years, see the review article by R. Arsenidze in the *Caucasian Review* (Munich 1955), Vol. I, pp. 163–5.

38 Orlov, pp. 52–3.

39 *id.*, p. 73 ff.

40 *id.*, pp. 81–2, 163–5.

41 *id.*, 129–30.

42 *id.*, pp. 136 ff.

43 *id.*, p. 141.

Chapter IX The Great Purge

1 Conquest. *The Great Terror*, p. 104 ff.
2 Orlov, pp. 164, 171.
3 *id.*, pp. 66–71.
4 *id.*, p. 175.
5 *id.*, p. 177.
6 Victor Serge. *From Lenin to Stalin* (1937), pp. 146–7.
7 Orlov, p. 350.
8 Serge, p. 145.
9 Orlov, p. 179.
10 Rigby, pp. 39–40.
11 V. and E. Petrov. *Empire of Fear* (1956), pp. 73–4.
12 Orlov, p. 105.
13 *id.*, p. 184 ff.
14 Conquest, p. 164 ff.
15 Orlov, p. 193.
16 Conquest, p. 183.
17 R. H. McNeal. *Lenin Stalin Krushchev: Voices of Bolshevism,* pp. 141–2.
18 Orlov, p. 198. Avtorkhanov, p. 229.
19 Krivitsky, p. 228.
20 Stalin. *Defects in Party Work and Measures for Liquidating Trotskyite and Other Double-Dealers* (Moscow 1937), *passim.*
21 The literature on the military purge is considerable. See particularly John Erickson. *The Soviet High Command* (1952), p. 449 ff; Leonard Schapiro. 'The Great Purge' in *The Soviet Army* edited by B. H. Liddell Hart (1956), pp. 65–72; Geoffrey Bailey. *The Conspirators* (1961), p. 133 ff; Victor Alexandrov. *The Tukachevsky Affair* (1962), *passim;* W. G. Krivitsky. *I Was Stalin's Agent* (1939), pp. 233–66; Alexander Orlov. *The Secret History of Stalin's Crimes* (1954), p. 239 ff; article in *Life* magazine, international edition, 14 May, 1956; and R. Conquest. *The Great Terror* (1969), p. 200 ff.
22 G. A. Tokaev. *Comrade X*, pp. 77–8.
23 Krivitsky, p. 250.
24 Delbars, p. 186.
25 Ehrenburg. *Men, Years, Life,* III, p. 197. *New York Times,* 19 May 1962.
26 Deutscher. *Stalin* (revised edition 1966), pp. 375–6.
27 Conquest, p. 222.
28 Rigby, p. 101.

29 *id.*, pp. 99–100.
30 Bailey, pp. 89, 227.
31 *Bukharin Trial*, p. 253.
32 *id.*, pp. 419, 575.
33 Orlov, *Life* (international edition), 14 May 1956.
34 Bailey, p. 214.
35 Orlov. *The Secret History of Stalin's Crimes*, p. 242.
36 O'Ballance, p. 131.
37 Seweryn Bialer. *Stalin and his Generals* (1969), p. 80.
38 Orlov, p. 246.
39 Rigby, p. 100.
40 *id.*, p. 49. *Pravda*, 31 October 1961, cited Conquest, p. 260.
41 Rigby, pp. 51–2.
42 Avtorkhanov, p. 314.
43 Maclean, p. 28.
44 Cited Conquest, p. 126.
45 British Foreign Office Archives Russia. Sir E. Monson to Eden, 8 February 1937. N917/250/38.
46 Rigby, pp. 69–70. A. V. Gorbatov. *Years Off My Life* (1964), p. 113.
47 Ehrenburg, III, p. 197.
48 A. S. Yakovlev. *Tel' Zhini (Aim in Life)*, cited by Edmund Stevens in *The Times*, 4 February 1949.
49 E. S. Ginsburg. *Into the Whirlwind* (1954), p. 115. Orlov, p. 249.
50 Delbars, p. 185.
51 Orlov, p. 225.
52 Maxim Litvinov. *Notes for a Journal*, p. 228.
53 Cited Conquest, p. 262.
54 Delbars, p. 183.
55 *Bukharin Trial, passim*. Maclean, pp. 83–121.
56 Orlov, p. 264.
57 Rigby, pp. 44–5.
58 Litvinov, p. 248.
59 S. Alliluyeva. *Twenty Letters to a Friend*, p. 136. Delbars, p. 188.
60 Yakovlev, *loc. cit.*
61 Stalin. *Problems of Leninism*, pp. 782–3.
62 *id.*, pp. 778–9.

Chapter X   The Deadly Pact
 1 Stalin. *Problems of Leninism*, pp. 746 ff., 759.
 2 *Documents on British Foreign Policy 1919–1939*. 3rd series, IV, p. 419.

3 Strang. *Home and Abroad*, pp. 160–1.
4 Litvinov. *Notes for a Journal*, p. 262.
5 *D.B.F.P.* 3rd Series, V, p. 542.
6 Litvinov, p. 263.
7 *D.B.F.P.* 3rd Series, V, p. 544.
8 Churchill. *The Second World War*, I, p. 288.
9 Litvinov, p. 271.
10 *id.*, p. 204.
11 *D.B.F.P.* 3rd Series, V, p. 545. Litvinov, p. 134.
12 Churchill, I, pp. 303–4. Strang, p. 181. Avon. *The Reckoning*, p. 55.
13 Davies. *Mission to Moscow*, p. 345.
14 Keith Feiling. *Life of Neville Chamberlain* (1946), p. 403.
15 Strang, pp. 163–6.
16 Churchill, I, pp. 284, 305.
17 Strang, pp. 175, 181.
18 *id.*, p. 189.
19 *Nazi–Soviet Relations 1939–1941. Documents from the Archives of the German Foreign Office.* Edited by Raymond J. Sonntag and James S. Beddie (Washington 1948), p. 41.
20 Davies, p. 450.
21 *Documents on German Foreign Policy 1918–1945.* Series D. VII, pp. 62–4.
22 *D.G.F.P.*, pp. 149–50.
23 *id.*, pp. 157, 168.
24 *D.B.F.P.* 3rd Series, VII, p. 384.
25 Trotsky. *Stalin*, p. 415.
26 *id.*, p. 383.
27 J. von Ribbentrop. *The Ribbentrop Memoirs* (1954), pp. 110 ff. Gustav Hilger and Alfred G. Meyer. *The Incompatible Allies* (New York 1953), p. 300.
28 *D.G.F.P.* VIII, pp. 309–320.
29 *D.B.F.P.* VII, p. 385.
30 *D.G.F.P. id.*, pp. 245–7.
31 *id.*, pp. 225–9.
32 Delbars. *The Real Stalin*, p. 249.
33 Hilger and Meyer, p. 304.
34 Ribbentrop, p. 115.
35 *D.G.F.P.* VIII, pp. 34, 44.
36 Hilger and Meyer, pp. 312–3.
37 Bronislaw Kusnierz. *Stalin and the Poles* (1949), *passim*.
38 *D.G.F.P.* VIII, p. 92.

39 *id.*, p. 105.
40 Ribbentrop, p. 129 ff.
41 *D.G.F.P.* VIII, p. 941.
42 *id.*, pp. 159–61.
43 Ribbentrop, p. 129.
44 *D.G.F.P.* VIII, Appendix VI (A).
45 *id.*, p. 942.
46 Ribbentrop, p. 132.
47 Hilger and Meyer, p. 314.
48 *D.G.F.P.* VIII, pp. 164–9.
49 Ribbentrop, pp. 130–31.
50 The fullest account of the negotiations and their political aftermath is by the Finnish Foreign Minister Vaino Tanner, *The Winter War: Finland against Russia 1939–1940* (Stanford 1950).
51 Tanner, pp. 16–30.
52 *id.*, p. 42.
53 *id.*, pp. 63–4, 69–72, 75–6.
54 B. H. Liddell Hart. *The Soviet Army* (London 1956), p. 90.
55 Bialer, p. 135, citing Admiral N. G. Kuznetsov. Khrushchev. *Khrushchev Remembers*, p. 154.
56 *D.G.F.P.* IX, pp. 40, 53.
57 *id.*, pp. 662, X, 3.
58 Sir Llewellyn Woodward. *British Foreign Policy in the Second World War* (London 1970), I, p. 461 ff. Churchill, II, p. 119. Eric Estorick. *Stafford Cripps* (London 1949), p. 250 ff.
59 *D.G.F.P.* X, pp. 10–11.
60 Woodward, pp. 468–71.
61 *D.G.F.P.* X, p. 207.
62 *id.*, p. 22.
63 Ribbentrop, p. 148.
64 *D.G.F.P.* XI, p. 291.
65 *id.*, p. 353.
66 Ribbentrop, p. 148. Kennan, p. 342.
67 D.G.F.P. XI, pp. 533–70. Bialer, p. 122, citing V. M. Berezhkov.
68 Churchill, II, pp. 517–18.
69 *D.G.F.P.* XI, p. 714.
70 Kennan, p. 344.
71 Ribbentrop, p. 150.
72 *D.G.F.P.* XI, p. 899.
73 *id.*, p. 980.
74 Bialer, p. 145, citing General M. T. Kazakov.
75 *id.*, citing Marshal A. I. Eremenko.

76 *D.G.F.P.* XII, p. 126.
77 Churchill, III, pp. 320–1; IV, p. 443.
78 Erickson, p. 577.
79 G. A. Deborin, cited in *Survey*, April 1967, p. 173.
80 Maury Lissann. 'Stalin the Appeaser' in *Survey*, Summer 1970, p. 54.
81 Hilger. *The Incompatible Allies*, p. 330.
82 Erickson, p. 579.
83 Cited in *Survey*, April 1967, p. 172.
84 G. Gafencu. *Prelude to the Russian Campaign* (London 1945), p. 192.
85 Hilger, pp. 326–7.
86 Churchill, II, p. 511. *D.G.F.P.* XII, p. 537.
87 Churchill, II, p. 511. *D.G.F.P.* XII, p. 475.
88 *D.G.F.P.* XII, p. 632.
89 Lissan. *Survey*, p. 59. *D.G.F.P.* XII, p. 964. Hilger, p. 330.
90 *D.G.F.P.* XII, pp. 730, 790.
91 *id.*, p. 870.
92 Hilger and Meyer, p. 329.
93 *id.*, 331–2.
94 *Nazi-Soviet Relations*, p. 345. Maisky states that he first heard of the German troop concentrations from Sir Alexander Cadogan, Permanent Under-Secretary for Foreign Affairs, on 10 June; and that he immediately telegraphed the details to Moscow in the belief that, although they might be somewhat overdrawn, nevertheless 'they should give Stalin some food for thought.' He was amazed by the Tass communiqué, but reassured himself with the reflection, 'Perhaps Stalin is right after all?' Maisky. *Memoirs of a Soviet Ambassador. The War 1939–1943*, pp. 148–50.
95 Woodward, I, p. 621; Rigby. *The Stalin Dictatorship*, p. 54. Delbars, p. 291.
96 Bailer, pp. 191, 194, 202, citing Kuznetsov and Tiulenev.
97 Hilger and Meyer, p. 336. Kennan, 345.

Chapter XI Supreme Commander
1 Erickson, p. 587.
2 Deutscher, p. 461.
3 Rigby, p. 57.
4 Delbars, p. 194.
5 Erickson, p. 598.
6 Rigby, p. 57. Harrison E. Salisbury. *The Siege of Leningrad* (1969), p. 80.

7 Stalin. *On the Great Patriotic War*, pp. 13–16; *War Speeches*, pp. 7–12. There is a good description of the speech and its effect on the inmates of a field hospital in Konstantin Simonov's novel *The Living and the Dead* (1958).

8 Bialer, p. 234. Erickson, p. 626.

9 Bialer, p. 236.

10 Churchill, III, p. 340.

11 Woodward, pp. 152–3.

12 Churchill, III, p. 342.

13 O'Ballance, p. 159. Payne. *Stalin*, p. 100.

14 Churchill, III, p. 343.

15 *id.*, p. 346.

16 *Stalin's Correspondence with Churchill, Attlee, Roosevelt, and Truman 1941–45*, p. 16.

17 Erickson, p. 603. Alexandrov, p. 160.

18 Bialer, p. 351 ff, p. 367.

19 *id.*, p. 354.

20 Salisbury, pp. 218, 321.

21 Arthur Bryant. *The Turn of the Tide*, p. 467.

22 G. K. Zhukov. *Marshal Zhukov's Greatest Battles*. Edited by Harrison E. Salisbury (1969), p. 8.

23 *id.*, p. 86.

24 Rigby, p. 57.

25 Bialer, p. 456.

26 *id.*, pp. 459–61, 611–13.

27 *id.*, p. 296.

28 Sherwood, I, pp. 343–5.

29 Churchill, III, pp. 405, 411.

30 *id.*, p. 414.

31 Sherwood, I, p. 388 ff.

32 G. M. Thomson, *Vote of Censure*, p. 83.

33 Sherwood, I, p. 390.

34 Lord Ismay, *Memoirs*, p. 230.

35 Churchill, III, p. 416.

36 Sherwood, I, p. 392.

37 David Farrer. *G—— For God Almighty*, p. 76.

38 Ismay, p. 233.

39 Zhukov, p. 35 ff.

40 Bialer, p. 304. Alexander, p. 161. Churchill, III, p. 419.

41 Zhukov, p. 63.

42 Stalin. *War Speeches*, p. 12 ff. Zhukov, p. 63.

43 Zhukov, pp. 70, 72 note.

44 Churchill, III, p. 348.
45 Kot. *Conversations with the Kremlin*, p. 106 ff.
46 *id.*, p. 140 ff.
47 Avon. *The Reckoning*, p. 296.
48 *id.*, p. 302.
49 Zhukov, pp. 90–92.
50 Rigby, p. 58.
51 Zhukov, pp. 117–22.
52 Churchill, IV, p. 301.
53 *id.*, p. 302.
54 *id.*, p. 305.
55 Delbars, p. 319.
56 Churchill, III, pp. 490–10, 429–9. Delbars, p. 324.
57 Churchill, III, p. 430 ff. Bryant, p. 460 ff.
58 Deutscher, p. 478.
59 Churchill, IV, p. 434.
60 Moran, p. 56.
61 Bryant, p. 461.
62 Payne, p. 582. Henry C. Cassidy. *Moscow Dateline* (Boston, 1943), p. 249.
63 Moran, pp. 59–60.
64 Churchill, IV, p. 445.
65 Alliluyeva. *Twenty Letters*, p. 171. A. H. Birse. *Memoirs of an Interpreter* (1967), p. 102.
66 Churchill, IV, p. 447.
67 Birse, p. 103.
68 Moran, p. 64.
69 Delbars, p. 325.
70 Sherwood, I, pp. 632–3.
71 Zhukov, p. 107 ff.
72 Delbars, p. 327.
73 Cited Deutscher, p. 478.
74 Alliluyeva. *Twenty Letters*, p. 161.
75 Churchill, IV, p. 675. *Stalin's Correspondence*, p. 110.
76 Communicated by Lord Montgomery.
77 O'Ballance, p. 179.
78 Bialer, p. 301.
79 Rigby, p. 101.
80 Deutscher, p. 490.
81 Churchill, IV, pp. 679–81.
82 *id.*, V, p. 231 ff.
83 Avon. *The Reckoning*, p. 413.

84 Hull. *Memoirs*, II, p. 1309.
85 *Stalin's Correspondence*, p. 176.
86 Alexandrov, p. 177.

Chapter XII   The Road to Potsdam
1 Moran, p. 133.
2 Churchill, V, p. 303. Moran, p. 195. Ismay, p. 337. Leahy, p. 203. *Foreign Relations of the United States. Diplomatic Papers. The Conferences at Cairo and Teheran* (Washington 1965), p. 476.
3 Sherwood, II, p. 771–2. A complete transcript of the proceedings at the Teheran Conference has been published by the Soviet Government in *International Affairs,* Nos. 7 and 8. (Moscow, July and August 1961).
4 Moran, p. 136.
5 Bryant. *Triumph in the West,* p. 90.
6 Moran, p. 135. Bryant, p. 91.
7 Churchill, V, p. 315. Ismay, p. 338.
8 Moran, p. 135.
9 Sherwood, II, p. 777. Churchill, V, p. 317 ff.
10 Avon. *The Reckoning*, p. 427.
11 Churchill, V, p. 321. Bryant, p. 92. Birse, p. 158.
12 Moran, pp. 141–2.
13 Perkins. *The Roosevelt I Knew*, pp. 70–1.
14 Birse, pp. 160–1. Churchill, V, p. 339 ff. Bryant, pp. 97–101.
15 Moran, p. 143.
16 Ismay, p. 340.
17 *Stalin's Correspondence.* II, pp. 111–2.
18 *id.,* I, p. 181. Churchill, V, p. 408 ff.
19 *Stalin's Correspondence*, I, p. 184.
20 Maclean. *Eastern Approaches*, p. 434. Auty. *Tito*, p. 121.
21 Djilas. *Conversations with Stalin*, p. 62 ff.
22 *id.,* p. 73.
23 Churchill, VI, pp. 78–84.
24 Churchill, V, p. 422. Djilas, p. 74.
25 Auty, p. 243.
26 Djilas, p. 81.
27 *Stalin's Correspondence*, I, p. 227.
28 Deutscher. *Stalin*, pp. 519–20.
29 Churchill, VI, pp. 118–20.
30 *Stalin's Correspondence*, I, p. 255.
31 Churchill, VI, p. 128.
32 *id.,* VI, p. 198.

33 *id.*, VI, p. 105.
34 Moran, p. 202.
35 Birse, p. 174. Churchill, VI, p. 200.
36 Avon. *The Reckoning*, p. 485.
37 Moran, p. 195.
38 Ismay, p. 377.
39 Avon, p. 487.
40 Moran, p. 104.
41 De Gaulle. *Salvation 1944–1946*, pp. 61–82.
42 Zhukov, p. 261 ff. Churchill, VI, pp. 141–4.
43 Tedder. *With Prejudice*, p. 646 ff. Birse, pp. 176–7. *Stalin's Correspondence*, I, p. 298.
44 On the Yalta conference see generally Stettinius *Roosevelt and
   the Russians* (1950) and *International Affairs,* Nos. 6, 7, 8, and 9
   (Moscow 1965); also D. S. Clemens. *Yalta* (New York, 1971).
45 Sherwood, II, p. 842 ff. Moran, p. 222.
46 Churchill, VI, pp. 303–4.
47 Moran, pp. 223, 226.
48 *id.*, p. 225.
49 *id.*, p. 229.
50 Byrnes. *Speaking Frankly*, pp. 30–32.
51 Avon. *The Reckoning*, p. 513.
52 Byrnes, p. 33.
53 Moran, p. 232.
54 Byrnes, p. 44.
55 Bialer, p. 504–5.
56 Zhukov, p. 277.
57 Reuben Ainsztein. 'The Russian Road to Berlin 1944–45.' *International Affairs,* Vol. 46, No. 1 (London, January 1970).
58 Montgomery. *Memoirs*, p. 332.
59 Bialer, p. 516 ff.
60 Bryant, p. 442.
61 Montgomery, p. 331. Cp. Stalin's comments on Eisenhower's action.
   'Stalin said that if it hadn't been for Eisenhower, we wouldn't
   have succeeded in capturing Berlin. The Americans could have
   been there first . . . Stalin appealed to Eisenhower in a letter to hold
   back his armies; Stalin told Eisenhower that according to his agreement with Roosevelt and in view of the amount of blood our
   people had shed, our troops deserved to enter Berlin before the
   Western Allies. Eisenhower then held his troops back and halted
   their offensive, thus allowing our troops to take Berlin.'
   Krushchev Remembers, p. 221.

62 Churchill, VI, p. 405.

63 Eisenhower. *Crusade in Europe*, p. 440.

64 Bryant, p. 446.

65 Churchill, VI, p. 386 ff. *Stalin's Correspondence*, II, p. 214.

66 Bialer, pp. 516–27. David Floyd. 'Generalissimo Stalin. New Version.' *Daily Telegraph*, London, 9 July 1965.

67 Bialer, p. 533 ff.

68 *Stalin's Correspondence*, II, p. 231.

69 Kuby. *The Russians and Berlin 1945*, p. 175 ff.

70 Sherwood, II, p. 880.

71 *id.*, II, p. 903.

72 Stalin. *War Speeches*, p. 138. Bialer, p. 563.

73 Churchill, VI, p. 496 ff. *Stalin's Correspondence*, I, p. 360.

74 Truman. *Year of Decisions*, 1945, p. 136.

75 Churchill, VI, pp. 487–9. Auty, p. 245. Truman, p. 164 ff.

76 *Stalin's Correspondence*, I, pp. 365–71.

77 Delbars, p. 390.

78 Avon, p. 545.

79 Truman, p. 267. Leahy, p. 396.

80 Byrnes, p. 68.

81 Churchill, VI, p. 552.

82 Byrnes, p. 263.

83 *id.* p. 263.

84 Truman, p. 275, Birse, p. 207. The Soviet Government later published a full transcript of the proceedings at the Potsdam Conference in *International Affairs*, Nos. 10 and 12 (Moscow 1965), and No. 1 (Moscow 1966).

85 Leahy, pp. 398–9.

86 Moran, p. 279.

87 Avon, p. 545.

88 Byrnes, p. 76.

89 *id.*, p. 74. Moran, p. 284.

90 Moran, p. 274.

91 Leahy, pp. 411–12.

92 Communicated by Lord Montgomery.

93 Birse, p. 209.

94 Bryant, p. 479.

95 Djilas, p. 170.

96 Moran, p. 282.

97 Piers Dixon. *Double Diploma* (1968), pp. 173–5.

98 C. R. Attlee. *As It Happened* (1954), p. 149.

99 Payne. *Stalin*, p. 624.

100 Truman, pp. 340–1. Byrnes, p. 86.

Chapter XIII   The Curtain Falls
1 S. Alliluyeva. *Twenty Letters*, p. 188.
2 Leahy. *I Was There*, p. 430.
3 Truman. *Year of Decisions*, p. 357.
4 Werth. *Russia at War*, p. 1040.
5 Deutscher. *Stalin* (ed. 1966), p. 560.
6 *id.*, p. 558.
7 Schapiro, p. 505 ff.
8 Delbars, p. 398.
9 *Stalin's Correspondence*, II, p. 277.
10 Delbars, p. 399.
11 Interview with Harold Stassen: *The Times*, London, 10 April 1947. Stalin. *For Peaceful Coexistence*, pp. 32–6.
12 Dixon. *Double Diploma*, p. 202.
13 *Stalin's Correspondence*, II, pp. 273–4, 281.
14 *The Times*, 6 March 1946.
15 *Pravda*, 13 March 1946.
16 Bedell Smith. *Moscow Mission*, p. 37 ff.
17 *Daily Herald*, London, 16 August 1946.
18 *The Times*, 25 September 1946.
19 *id.*, 30 December 1946; 23 January 1947.
20 Montgomery. *Memoirs*, p. 446 ff.
21 Communicated by Lord Montgomery.
22 Montgomery. *Memoirs*, p. 445.
23 *The Times*, 4 March 1947.
24 Truman. *Years of Trial and Hope*, p. 111.
25 Sterling. *The Masaryk Case*, p. 8.
26 S. Alliluyeva. *Only One Year*, p. 384.
27 *id.*, p. 369. *Twenty Letters*, p. 192.
28 *id.*, *Only One Year*, p. 384.
29 *id.*, *Twenty Letters*, p. 191. *Only One Year*, p. 386. *Khrushchev Remembers*, p. 300.
30 Alliluyeva. *Twenty Letters*, p. 192.
31 Khrushchev, pp. 298–9.
32 Djilas, p. 152.
33 Alliluyeva. *Only One Year*, p. 385.
34 Khrushchev, p. 308.
35 Djilas, p. 152.
36 *id.*, pp. 157–61.
37 Dedijer. *Tito Speaks*, p. 300.

38 *id.*, p. 312.

39 Djilas, pp. 176–81.

40. Royal Institute of International Affairs. *The Soviet–Yugoslav Dispute*, pp. 12–17. Dedijer, p. 343.

41 Rigby, p. 65.

42 Auty, p. 254.

43 Gordon Shepherd. *Russia's Danubian Empire*, p. 50.

44 Kelly. *The Ruling Few*, p. 430.

45 *Pravda*, 17 February 1951.

46 Conquest. *Power and Policy in the U.S.S.R.*, 95 ff. Khrushchev, 245 ff.

47 *Pravda*, 24 December 1954. Rigby, p. 63.

48 Khrushchev, *loc. cit.* Richard Lowenthal. *The New Leader*, (New York, February 1959), cited Payne, p. 642.

49 Rigby, p. 64.

50 Khrushchev, pp. 253, 257.

51 S. Alliluyeva. *Only One Year*, p. 154. Khrushchev, pp. 261–2.

52 Alliluyeva, p. 374.

53 Alliluyeva. *Twenty Letters*, p. 196.

54 Ehrenburg, VI, p. 304. (*Post-War Years*). Payne, p. 645.

55 Alliluyeva. *Twenty Letters*, p. 200.

56 Khrushchev, pp. 304–5.

57 'Scenario for Stalin's Last Purge.' *Sunday Times*, London, 1 March 1970.

58 Khrushchev, p. 312.

59 *id.*, p. 307.

60 Ehrenburg, p. 302.

61 Alliluyeva. *Twenty Letters*, p. 201.

62 Deutscher. *Stalin* (ed. 1966), p. 600.

63 Alliluyeva. *Twenty Letters*, pp. 20–22.

64 Salisbury. *Stalin's Russia and After*, p. 150.

65 Rigby, p. 81. Khrushchev, p. 308.

66 Khrushchev, p. 309.

67 Conquest, p. 154 ff. Schapiro, pp. 517–21.

68 Conquest, p. 156.

69 Khrushchev, pp. 280–2. Rigby, p. 81.

70 Khrushchev, p. 310.

71 Menon. *The Flying Troika*, p. 7.

72 Conquest, p. 163.

73 Rigby, pp. 66–7.

74 Alliluyeva. *Only One Year*, p. 155.

75 Payne, p. 668.

76 Conquest, p. 178 ff. Nicolaevsky, p. 105 ff.

77 Avtorkhanov, p. 259. Khrushchev, pp. 274–5. According to Khrushchev, Poskrebyshev was removed from his post for having 'leaked' secret documents. But, if this is so, it must have been within a few weeks at the most of Stalin's death.

78 Communicated by Mr K. P. S. Menon. See also Menon. *The Flying Troika*, pp. 26–32.

79 'Monitor', *The Death of Stalin*, p. 4.

80 These details are said to be in a secret report now in the State Department's archives: *The Detroit News*, 19 July 1967. Cp. J. Bernard Hutton. *Stalin the Miraculous Georgian*, p. 350.

81 Khrushchev, p. 316.

82 Alliluyeva. *Twenty Letters*, p. 211.

83 Khrushchev, p. 317.

84 *id.*, p. 318.

85 Alliluyeva, p. 212.

86 'Monitor', pp. 56–7.

87 Khrushchev, p. 320. Alliluyeva, pp. 8, 10.

88 Salisbury. *Stalin's Russia and After*, p. 170 ff.

89 Molotov. *Speech at Stalin's Funeral*, Moscow, 1953.

90 Harriman, p. 103.

Postscript

1 *Pravda*, 13 July, 1953.

2 Cited Conquest. *Power and Policy in the U.S.S.R.*, p. 276.

3 *id.*, p. 277.

4 Khrushchev. *Khrushchev Remembers*, p. 343.

5 Rigby. *The Stalinist Dictatorship*, p. 49.

6 Khrushchev, p. 345.

7 Conquest, pp. 280–81.

8 Khrushchev, pp. 347–50.

9 Rigby, p. 23.

10 Khrushchev, p. 351.

11 *Pravda*, 28 August 1957, cited Conquest, p. 323.

12 Conquest, pp. 354–5.

13 Rigby, p. 95.

14 *The Times*, London, 30, 31 October 1961.

15 Isaac Don Levine. *I Rediscover Russia*, p. 132.

16 *The Times*, 7 November 1961.

17 *id.*, 22 October, 1962.

18 *Pravda*, 10 March 1963. *Survey*, April 1967, pp. 170–80.

19 *Sunday Telegraph*, London, 16 May 1965.

20 *Survey*, Winter/Spring 1969, pp. 261–9. *Daily Telegraph*, London, 22 December 1969.
21 *Daily Telegraph*, 29 April 1970.
22 *Christian Science Monitor*, 6 April 1970.
23 *Daily Telegraph*, 26 June 1970.
24 *The Times*, London, 15 May 1971.
25 *Khrushchev Remembers*, pp. 5–6.

Appendix
1 First published by Don Levine in *Life*, 23 April 1956.
2 Levine. *Stalin's Great Secret*, p. 78 ff.
3 Communicated by Don Levine.
4 Levine, p. 105.
5 Smith. *The Young Stalin*, p. 307.
6 U.S. Senate Committee on the Judiciary. *Hearings before the Subcommittee to investigate the Scope of Soviet Activity in the United States, 1957*. Part 66, pp. 4183–6.

Index

Note: Italics refer to newspapers, periodicals, book or film titles

*and † refer to footnotes on page cited

Figures in parenthesis refer to matter in the appendix, bibliography or notes, and references to these are given immediately after the reference to the page of text concerned

Illustrations are not included in the index

SDP stands for Social Democratic Party; SU for Soviet Union; WWI and WWII for World War I and World War II.

659

126–7, 136–7; 142; married, 169, 258, 270; memoirs of, 133, 141, 577; imprisoned, 577

Alliluyeva, Eugenia (wife of Paul), 577

Alliluyeva, Nadezdha ('Nadya') (Stalin's second wife), 18; girlhood, 126–7, 136–9, 142; letters from, 151; in Lenin's secretariat, 152, 153, 168, 188–90, 192; Stalin courts, 168–9; married life, 254, 255, 256–7, 258–64; at Industrial Academy, 259; suicide of, 264–7, 270–1; funeral of, 267–71; last letter to Stalin, 267–8

Alliluyeva, Olga (mother of Nadya), 106, 133, 134, 137; Stalin's letter to, 122–3

Alliluyeva, Svetlana (daughter of Stalin): childhood, 17, 254, 255–6, 267; later career, 479, 484, 546, 559–61, 562, 577, 578–9, 583, 593, 595–6; relations with Stalin, 559–62, 578, 608–9; changes name, 608; goes to West, 608–9; memoirs published, 608–9; *cited*, 16, 17, 22, 59, 258, 264–5, 267–8, 271, 288, 312*, 582, 590

All-Russian Congress of Soviets of Workers' & Soldiers' Deputies: I (May (*1917*), 130–1; II (Oct *1917*), 140, 142–3, 150–1; X (*1922*), 194; Chairmanship of Executive of, 146; praesidium of, 131 and †

All-Union Congress of Soviets, *1935*, 317–18

Alma-Ata (Kazhakstan), 226, 229

Amilakhavari, Prince Simeon, 13

Anders, Gen., 463–5, 479

Andreyev, Andrei, 223, 227, 298, 549, 584, 585

Andreyevna, Yolka, 260

Antonov, Gen. A. I., 444–5, 450, 481, 514–15, 516, 524, 542–3

Antonov-Ovseenko, Vladimir, 140 and *, 144, 210, 226

Archangel, 171, (637); British in, 488

Ardennes, the, Battle of the Bulge in, 513, 514, 515

Aristov, A. B., 590, 591

Arkomed, S. T., 44

Armenia: sends delegation to Congress IV, 76; declares independence, 163; and RSFSR, 186, 206

Army, *see* Red Army *and* Russian Army

Arnold, chauffeur, 347, 348

Arsenidze, Razden, 63, 73, 369

Artemyev, Gen. P. A., 460

arts, the, dictates re, 324, 564

Ashkhabad govt., 163

Asia, S.E., self-govt. in, 492

Astor, Lord, meets Stalin, 246, 248

Astor, Nancy Lady, 246–9

Astrakhan, 163

Atlantic: conference, *1941*, 452; battle of the, 443, 487; NATO, 571

atomic bomb, the, 536–7, 584–9, 553–4; dropped, 546–7

Attlee, Clement, 538–9, 543–4

Aurora, cruiser, 142

Austria: *see also* Vienna; in WWI, 120, 147, 155; WWII, 523; post-war govt. of, 532–3, 539, 539–40, 553

Avlabar (suburb of Tiflis): workers meet in, 43; secret press in, 58, 72; police trace, 72–4, 75, 77

Axelrod, Pavel, 65, 66*

Azerbaijan: declares independence, 163; and RSFSR, 186, 206

Azev, Yevno, 35

Babel, Isaac, 367

Babelsberg (nr Potsdam), 535

Bacon, Alice, 553

Bagramian, Marshal, 610

Baikaloff, Anatole, 124

Bailov prison, Stalin in, 93–6, 97; SD committee, 95

Bakinsky Proletary, 88

Baku (Georgia): *described*, 88; secret press in, 41, 58; Stalin in, 59, 60, 88–91, 92, 96–7; SDP committee of, 92; strikes at oil fields of, 88–90, 93, 163; Bolsheviks and Mensheviks of, 92, 96–7; Police dept., 97; falls to Turks, *1918*, 163; oil supplies from, 552

Balabanoff, Angelica, 80, 83, 84–5

Balandin, Vasily P., 485–6

Balagansk (Siberia), 55

Balitsky, Victor A., 357, 358, 359*

Balkans, the; *see also names of countries;* in WWII, 419, 421, 426, 494, 512–13; post-war control of, 506, 520, 566

ballet; Stalin dictates re, 324; *see also under* Bolshoi Theatre

Baltic States, the; *see also names of;* 'Pact of Mutual Assistance' with SU, 407; in WWII, 407, 415, 439; annexed to SU, 416;

Baltic–White Sea canal, construction of, 292

Barbusse, Henri, 37–8, 56, 79, (619)

Barmine, Alexander, 176, 235–7

Basmichis, the, 207

Batum (Georgia); *described,* 46; Stalin goes to, 44–5; Marxist activities in, 46–50, 63; press concealed in, 47, 48–9; jail, 48; demonstration re, 48; Stalin in, 50–2, 53, 88; Stalin returns to, 56

Bazhanov, Boris, 208–9, 212, 214, 240

Beaverbrook, Lord, 452–4, 456–8

Bedny, Damyan, verse by, 270

Beletsky Col. S. P., 116–17, 117*, 164

Belo-Ostrov railway station, 130

Belov, Gen. I. P., 353–4, 375

Belov, Gen. P. A., 450

Benelux, 569–70

Benes, Edward, 323, 354, 541, 558–9

Berdzenishvili, Vaso, 35–6, 38

Bergery, Gaston, 430

Beria, Lavrenti Pavlovich; publications re Stalin, 30, 34–35, 43, 51, 69*, 96, 327–8, (644), 368–9, (619); in Caucasus, 313,

364; *Letter to an Old Bolshevik*, 291–2; heard by Central committee, 230; demoted, 231; incriminated, 336, 338; arrested, 350; trial of, 356–7, 370–4; death, 135*, 374; not rehabilitated, 374

Bulganin, Nikolai Aleksandrovich; *described*, 555–6; rise of, 555, 557; in Politburo, 235, 549; Minister, 576, 584; in war *v.* Germans, 443; and Stalin in private life, 561, 562, 563; in Bureau, 586; at death of Stalin, 593, 595, 596, 597, 598; subsequently, 600, 601, 602–3, 604

Bulgaria; *see also* Balkans *and* satellites; 426, 540, 569

Bulletin of the Opposition, 290, 369

Bullitt, William Christian; *1919* visit to Moscow, 170–1; *1933*, 293–5, 315 452*; *quoted*, 323, 324

bureaucratisation, 210, 237

Butyrska prison, 368

Byelorussia; and RSFSR, 186; and UN, 519

Byrnes, James F., 536–7, 539, 550

Cadogan, Sir Alexander, 474, 477, 480–1

calendar, the Russian, 20, 144

capitalism, rural, 77

Catholic religion, the, 324, 503–4

Caucasian Union of the SDP, 67, 72*

Causasian Workers' Newsheet, 66

Caucasus; *see also* Georgia; nationalities of, 13, 61; Russification of, 13, 25; *1937* purge in, 368–9; in WWII, 453, 478, 483

censorship, of foreign correspondents, 550

Central committee, *see under* Russian Social Democratic Labour Party

Central Control Commission, SDP, 182, 183 and *, 238; in *1934*, 241; becomes Party Control Commission, 297; expels member, 303

Chaikin, Vadim, 163–4

Chamberlain, Austen, 217

Chamberlain, Neville, 380, 386, 391; *1931* note to Hitler, 394, 397–8, 398*

Chandor, Douglas, portraits by, 550–1

Chartist movement, the, 245

Chavchavadze, Ilya, poems of, 24

Cheka (secret police organisation); *see also* GPU, NKVD *and* Lubyanka prison; 149–50, 156, 186, 210, 240; in Civil war, 158–9, 160; in Georgia, 180; denunciation to, 210

Chequers (Bucks), Molotov stays at, 469

Chertok, of NKVD, 369

Cheveni Tskhovreba, 78

Chicherin, Yury, 154, 171

children, treatment of Russian, 246-7; liable to death penalty, 328

Chilston, 2nd Viscount, 234, 315*, 318–19; assessment of Stalin, 315–18

China, 293, 519, 520; frontier with, 300

Chinese People's Republic, 572–3

Chkeidze, Nikolai, 46, 47

Chubar, Vlas, 298, 362, 375

Chuikov, Gen. G. I., 515, 521–2, 529, 530

Church, the Christian; in Georgia, 12; Russian attitude to, 324, 454; Catholic, reconciliation sought, 503–4; Greek, rehabilitated in SU, 486

Churchill, Randolph, 500

Churchill, Sir Winston, 91, 119, 170, 274, 324, 386, 387, 422; as Prime Minister, WWII, 416–18, 426–7, 439, 441–3, 451–3, 457, 462, 465, 471, 489, 503, 504–5, 513–14, 523, 526, 529; *1940* letter to Stalin, 417–18; Molotov visits, 469–70; and Stalin, 248, 484, 486–8, 554; Stalin speaks of, 501–2, 551–2; in Moscow, 471–81, 506–9; at Teheran, 491–9; at Yalta, 515–21; in postwar disputes, 532–4; at Potsdam, 535–43; speech at Fulton, 551; meets Tito, 502; *quoted*, 384, 429–30

Civil war, Russian, *1918–20*, 154–64, 165–6, 170–2, 174

Clementis, Vladimir, 571, 579, 580

Cold war, the, 552, 557–8

Collective Farmers, Congress of, 317

collectivisation, farm, 223, 227–8, 259, 272, 274–5; resistance to, 274; right to leave, 237–8; exemption from, 300; *see also* Five-Year Plans

Cominform (Information Bureau of the Communist Party), set up, 566

Comintern (Communist International), 209, 231, 325, 413; Anti-pact, 398–9; disbanded, 486, 566

Commissars, Council (*Soviet*) of People's (*Sovnarkom*); (Workers' & Peasants' Government); formed, 143; first meeting, 144; first government by, 145–52; moves to Moscow, 152–4; under Molotov, 234, 235; purged, *1949*, 576

Communism, after WWII, 553–4

Communist Party; Bolshevik wing of SDP renamed, 129; organisation of, Soviet, 249–50; and confessions, 364; in Britain, 217; France, 324–5, 566; Germany, 209; Italy, 566; Russia, *see* Russian Social Democratic party *and* Soviet Communist Party

confessions, Communist, 281–2, 364–5

Congresses, of Russian SDP, *see under* Russian Social Democratic Labour Party *and* Soviet Communist Party

Conquest, Robert, 354, 364

Constituent Assembly, *1918*, 150–1

constitution, Russian; granted, *1905*, 66; *1917*, of Power, 143, 147; *1922*, of USSR, 194–5; *1934*, Stalin –, 300–1; renamed, 600

Copenhagen (Denmark); refuses SDP Congress, 78–9, 80; alleged meeting in, 338–9

Council of People's Commissars, *see* Commissars, Council of People's

Cracow (Poland); SDP Central committee meets in, 107–8, 110, 113; Stalin travels to, 107, 108–10; Lenin expelled from, 120

667

Labour Party, British, sends delegation to Moscow, 553
Labouring Peasants' Party, 282
Laidoner, Gen., 365
Lansbury, George, 80
Lashevich, Mikhail, 105, 165, 209; dismissed, 222-3
Laski, Prof. Harold, 553
Latvia; see also Baltic states; in German-SU pact, 394, 395; SU troops in, WWII, 406; incorporated in SU, 416
Laval, Pierre, 323-5
Lawrence, T. E., 280, 282
League of Nations, 295, 314, 320, 345; Russia joins, 292, 301; pre WWII, 325; SU expelled from, 414
Leahy, Adm. William D., 494*, 537, 541-2
Lefortovo prison, 365, 590
Lelashvili, Gigi, 58
Lenin (Vladimir Ilyich Ulyanov): Revolutionary activities outside Russia, 36, 40-1, (631), 81, 87, 98, 101, 106, 112-13, 114, 115, 120-1, 125, 128; at II Congress, 53; founds Bolshevik party and Vpered, 61; Stalin first reads, 32; and Stalin, before meeting, 54-5, 65, 121; first meets Stalin, 68; at III Congress, 67-9; V, 79, 82-5; secret meetings with Stalin, 79, 90; reads letters of Stalin, 100-1; at VI Congress, 103-4; calls meeting in Cracow, 107-8, 110; manifesto at WWI, 120; comes to Russia after Feb. revolution, 128-9, 130; 'April Thesis', 129; and Stalin, 129-30, 150, 166, 172, 174-5, 177, 180, 181, 184-8; Stalin's letters to, 156-8; opinion of Stalin, 194, written, 195-6; final quarrel with, 199-203; and Stalin's name, 19; work after Feb. revolution, 130-2; leaves for Finland, 132-3, 136; returns, 137-8; and Oct. revolution, 138-40, 142-4; in government, 144-7, 149-61, 164-8, 172; attempted assassination of, 160; offers deal with Allies, 1919, 170-1; and nationalities, 179-81; New Economic Policy, 181-2; 1921-2 govt., 182-4; first stroke, 184; work during illness, 184-204; office diary, 188-90; restrictions imposed, 193, 196; political testament, composed, 190, 193-4, 195-6; considers successor, 194, 196; memo on Nationalities, 195; final works dictated, 196, 197; final letter to Stalin, 200-2, (618*); asks for poison, 198-9; third stroke, 203; death, 211-13; burial, 213; mausoleum, 213-14, 555, 598-9, 605; fate of political testament, 203, 214, 222, 224; Collected Works, 240; Leninism, cult of, 213-14
Leningrad (formerly Petrograd, q.v.); named, 213, 458; Soviet of, 223, 297; food supplies for, 1934, 301-2; delegates from, 296, 302; Kirov murdered in, 304-5; NKVD of, 303-5, 306-7; officers tried, 312; Okhrana files of, 358; close-ness to border, 407, 408; in war v. Germans, 446, 451, 467-8, 563
'Leningrad affair', the, 563, 573-6, 602
Leonov, Leonid, 578
Lermolo, Elizabeth, 266, 308-10
Levin, Dr D. D., 373
Levine, Issac Don, 73, 74, (612-14, 616)
Levitan, Yuri, 592
Liberal party: British, 79; Georgian, 26*; Russian, 53
Liberation (film), 610
Life, 74, (614)
linguistics, 582 and *
Lithuania: see also Baltic states; in German-Soviet pact, 395, 403-4, 406; incorporated in SU, 416
Litvinov, Maxim Maximovich ('Papasha', M. M. Wallach): early career, 81; at London Congress, 81, 83; shares flat with Stalin in London, 81; revolutionary activities, 87; in govt., 171; interpreter, 247, 248, 318-19, 450, 451, 454; Commissar for Foreign Affairs, 260-2, 293, 294, 301, 314, 315, 317, 322-3, 325, 382; in USA, 293; staff purged, 368; survives, 375, 385; demoted, 383-4; recalled, 410, 441, 451; appearance, 451, 454
Lloyd George, David, 171, 181, 247-8
Lobov, Aleksei, 112, 113
Lobova, Valentina, 107, and *, 112-13
Lomdzhariya, Silibistro, 47, 48
Lominadze, 169
Lomov, George I., 135, 138, 143, 148; death of, 135*, 370
Lomtatidze, Chola, 62
London; SDP II Congress in, 53; V, 75, 79, 80-5; reception in Holborn, 85; raid on Soviet premises, 223; Molotov in, 469-70
Longest Day, The, (film), 610
Longjumeau, school for revolutionaries, 101
Lothian, Lord (Philip Kerr), 171; meets Stalin, 246-8
Lozovsky, S. A., 383, 577
Lublin, 504, 506, 510, 538
Lubyanka prison, 208, 225, 273, 281; 1935 interrogations in, 328-31, 333, 335; execution cellars, 310; confessions obtained in, 364-5
Luch, 105
Ludwig, Emil, interviews Stalin, 14, 27, 86-7, 91, 249-51, 252-4
Lukomsky, Prof. P. E., 594
Lunacharsky, A. V., 143
Lutovinov, 206, 269
Luxemburg, Rosa, 80, 81
Lvov, Prince George, 125, 128, 133
Lvov (Poland), 176, 403, 519; ceded to SU, 506, 519; prison, 465
Lyons, Eugene, 249, 254, 273, 294
Lysenko, Trofim, 582-3

MacArthur, Gen., 573
MacDonald, Ramsay, 217

668

gress, 80–1; Stalin works for, 67, 72–5, (612–16), 80–1, 96, 97–8, 101, 115–17; evidence re, 358–9, 371–2; discovered, and Yezhov, 376–7; St Petersburg HQ broken into, 135; Kamenev investigated re, 135; Malinovsky and, see under Malinovsky, Roman; Paris HQ, 35, (618); Archive of, (618)

Okulov, 166

Oldberg, Valentine, 328, 336

Omsk, 170, 172

opposition groups banned, 181

Ordzhonikidze, Gregory ('Sergo'), 186, 346; in Baku, 93, 94; in Paris with Lenin, 101; on Bolshevik Centre committee, 103, 104; in Cheka, 150; in Civil war, 155, 158; Commissar in Tiflis, 179, 180, 181, 191; censured by Lenin, 195, 201, 202; supports Stalin, 101, 104, 209; and Stalin in private life, 184, 256, 259, 267; in Politburo, 238, 298, 300; Commissar for Heavy Industry, 302, 345; opposes Stalin, 238, 344; death of, 349–50

Orel, 170

Orgburo, the, 167, 183, 206–7, 297

Orlemanski, Father, 503–4

Orlov, Adm., 375

Orlov, Alexander (Nikolsky), 117, 358; cited, 243, 303, 311, 331, 357–9

Oslo (Norway): SDP attempt Congress in, 79; alleged flight to airport of, 346–7

Ossetes, the, of N. Caucasus, 11–12

Ossinsky, V. V. (Prince Obolensky), 205

Oumansky, Constantin, 245, 389

Outer Mongolia, 572

Ovey, Sir Esmond, 280–1

Paasikivi, Juho, in Moscow, 407–9, 415

Paasonen, Col., 409

Palchinsky, death of, 282–3

Palgunov, 590

Pares, Sir Bernard, 349*

'parilka', 273

Paris (France); Lenin in, 98, 101; Nicolaevsky in, 291–2; White emigré organisations in, 356; 1937 conspiracy in, 358, 359; 1946 conference in, 552–3; 1947 conference, 558

Pasternak, Boris, 289, 367

Pauker, K. V.; career and relation to Stalin, 242–3; and Nadya, 259, 260; in NKVD, 312, 342–3; purged, 369, 392

Paulus, Field Marshal von, 482–3, 484

Pavlov, Dmitrii G., Army commander, 440

Pavlov, Vladimir, interpreter, 395, 431, 471, 476, 478, 479, 480, 514, 535; Stalin and, 393; at Teheran, 491, 495, 498

Pearson, Hesketh, 248

peasants; see also collectivisation and kulaks; Labouring Peasants' Party, 282; serfdom, 12–15; workers and, 181

People's Commissariat of Internal Affairs, 301

'People's Courts', established, 144

People's Will group, 36

Perm (Urals); in Civil war, 165; Nadya Stalin in, 262

Persia; (Iran); in WWII, 452, 453; after, 539, 550, 551, 552

'personality, cult of', attacked, 591, 603–5

Pervukhin, Mikhail, 585–6, 587, 602–3

Pestkovsky, Stanislav, 145–6, 150, 153–4

Peter the Great, Tsar, 252, 508, 561

Peter II, King of Yugoslavia, 499, 501, 507–8, 508*

Peter and Paul Fortress, 129, 132, 142

Peters, Jacob, 150

Peterson, Commandant of Kremlin, 357

Petrograd (also St Petersburg and Leningrad, q.v.): so named, 125; Feb. revolution in, 125; Alliluyevs' flat in, 127, 132–3; in 1917, 139–40; at Oct. revolution, 142–3, 216; after revolution, 1918, 151; Bolshevik govt. leaves, 152; in Civil war, 170, 172; renamed Leningrad, 213; see also Smolny Institute

Petrograd Soviet; originates, 127, 132; under Trotsky, 138, 139; Military Revolutionary Committee of, see Military Revolutionary Committee

Petrov, Gen. I. E., 440 and *

Petrovna, Marya, 594

Petrovsky, Gregory, 240, 298

Phillips, Morgan, 553

Pickel, Richard, 328, 336

Pilsudki, Marshal, 175; funeral of, 325

Pirveli Dasy, 26*

Plehve, V. K., 35

Plekhanov, George; Bolshevik, 53; Menshevik leader, 79, 82, 85; alliance with Lenin, 98–9; mentioned by Stalin, 121, 461

Pletnev, Prof. D. D., 262, 373, 374

Podgorny, Nikolai V., 605

Podvoisky, Nikolai, 140 and *

Podzerov, 512

Poincaré; President of France, 280

Pokrovsky, Mikhail, 83

Poland; see also Lvov and Warsaw; Stalin crosses frontier of, 1912, 108–10; 1920 war re frontiers, 175–6; 1939, German-Russian partition, 394, 395, 403–4, 406; German threat and British guarantee to, 380–2, 386, 387, 388, 389, 398*; invaded, 400; Nazi–Soviet occupation, 401–2; government in exile, 462; prisoners of Russians, 462–5, 486–7; Polish–Soviet diplomatic relations restored, 462; frontiers after war v. SU, 462, 465–6, 469; liberation of, 1944, 504–6; frontiers and government of after WWII, 506, 510, 512, 518–19, 520, 535, 538, 539, 540

Poletayev, N. G., 105

police, secret, see Cheka, GPU, NKVD and Okhrana

Polish Intelligence Service, 276

countries; territorial gains in WWII, map, 437; frontiers, 465–6, 469–70, *see also under* Poland; influence in Europe after WWII, 547–8, 551; *see also* satellite countries; with other countries, 585

Soviets, Congresses of: *see* All-Russian–*and* All-Union Congress of Soviets; *also* Supreme Soviet, the

Sovnarkom, see Commissars, Council of People's

Spandaryan Suren, 92, 103; in exile, 119, 122; death of, 123

Special Secret Political Section of State Security, 239, 241–2, 297, 313; and Kirov affair, 303

Spiridovich, Gen. Alexander, (613–14)

Spring-Rice, Cecil, *quoted*, 64

Stalin (Joseph Vissarionovich Djugashvili), ('Soso', 'Koba'): appearance, 52, 124, 363, 451, 582; physical defects, 21; clothes, 134, 319, 492–3; character, 91, 94–5, 179, 207; birth, 11, 16, 20; family history, 14–16; childhood, 13, 14, 16, 20–3, 24–5; education, 22, 24–5, 25–33; religion, 25, 29; denounces students, 34; joins revolutionary movement, 27, 30–2; leads *1900 mayevka*, 36–7; pseudonym, 19, 110; acts as tutor, 34–5; at Tiflis Observatory, 33, 35–6; official police report on, 50; early revolutionary activities, 34–45, 46–50, 56–8, 60–91; in prison and exile, 50–2, 53–6, 93–6, 97–102, 103, 104, 105–6, 114–25; first marriage, 59–60; death of first wife, 91; second marriage, 168–9; death of second wife, 266–8; first meets Lenin, 68; at early SDP and Bolshevik conferences, 68–9, 75–85, 106–10; co-opted on SDP Central Committee, 104; first voted on, 131; during *1917* revolution, 125–42; investigates Kamenev re Okhrana, 135; Commissar of Nationalities, 143–55, 178–9, 186–7; in Civil war, 155–62, 165–6, 172; decorated, 172–3; and Malinovsky, 164–5; Commissar for State Control, 166–71, 174; in Polish war, 175–7; illness, 177, 180; and invasion of Georgia, 177–81; appointed General Secretary of Central committee, 183; during Lenin's illness, 184–203; Krupskaya, 192–3; increasing power, 203–33, 234–7; defied over shooting of Ryutin, 237–8; homes, *see* Kuntsevo, Poteshny Palace *and* Zubalovo; forms 'troika' *v.* Trotsky, 205; *50th* birthday, 231–3; personal secretariat, 239–43; offices, 243–4; personal opinions, 250–3; family life, 254–7; third marriage, 289; domestic routine, 288, 561–2; offers resignation, 289; *1935–6* assessments of, 315–18, 319, 322; absolute despotism, 351; public appearances, *1937*, 363; *60th* birthday, 410; attends Supreme Soviet, 410; Chairman of Commissars, 430–1; on

German invasion, *1941*, 436–8; broadcasts, 438–40 (650); Defence Commissar and Supreme Commander, 444–5; directs military operations, WWII, 444–50, 459, 467–9; at the front, 448; summons to office of, 448–9; *described*, *1941*, 450, 451; addresses Moscow meeting, *1941*, 461; *62nd* birthday, 466; Marshal of SU, 483; awarded Order of Suvorov, 490; presented by British with sword, 496; strategic qualities of, 493–4; *1945*; honours, 531–2; at Potsdam, Teheran and Yalta, and relations with Churchill and Roosevelt, *see those entries;* travels to Teheran, 491; to Potsdam, 534–5; filmed, 544; ill health, 549, 559; senility, 562–3; *70th* birthday, 577–8; last illness, 592–7; death, 596, lying-in-state, 597–8, funeral, 598–9; cremated, 605; grave, 610; posthumous reputation, 600–11; statues, pictures of and towns named after, 605–6; museum, 16

LETTERS FROM: to Olga Alliluyeva, 122–3; to Lenin, 121, 156–7, 174; to Malinovsky, 111–12; to Ribbentrop, 420; to Isaak Shvarts, 98–100; to party comrade, *1904*, 60–1; to Moscow Bolsheviks from exile, 100–1

WORKS OF: (*in chronological order*): Georgian newspaper article, 23–4; poem 'To the Moon', 29–30; article on street demonstrations, 42–3; memorial pamphlet re Batum demonstration, 48; pamphlet re Mensheviks, 65; of *1905*, 66–7; *1906*, 78; 'Two Clashes' pamphlet, 69–70; article on Duma, 70; Duma II, 88–9; on *For the Party* leaflet, 104–5; *1913* leaflet, 106–7; article re elections, 110; thesis on nationalities, 110–11, 112, 113; *1926* speech at Tiflis, 31, 130; *1917* speech at Helsinki, 148; appeal to Moslems, 149; speech re NEP, 182; speech re SU, 194–5; *On the Road to October*, 216; 'Dizzy with success', 274–5; speech re Shakhty affair, 277; *The Economic Problems of Socialism in USSR*, 584; *Sochineniia*, (618*); fourteenth vol. proposed, 601, (617)

Stalingrad (previously Tsaritsyn, *q.v.*), and German army, 481, 482–3; film of, 484

Stalino (previously Yuzovka) 606

Stanko-Import, 235–6

Starinov, Col., 440, 48–9

Stassen, Harold, 550

State Control Ministry, *see* Workers' and Peasants' Inspectorate

State Defence committee, 438, 446, 549

State Planning Commission (Gosplan), and trials, 280, 282

State Security: Ministry of (NKGB, then MGB), 573–4; *see also* Special Secret Political Section of, *and* police, secret

State Yiddish Theatre (Moscow), 577

DATE DUE			
MAR 3 1980			
DEC 19 1980			
JAN 19 1981			
APR 0 9 1998			